ORACLE 10*g* DATABASE ADMINISTRATOR II:

BACKUP/RECOVERY & NETWORK ADMINISTRATION

ORACLE 10*g* DATABASE ADMINISTRATOR II:

BACKUP/RECOVERY & NETWORK ADMINISTRATION

Claire Rajan

Australia • Canada • Mexico • Singapore • Spain • United Kingdom • United States

Oracle 10*g* Database Administrator II: Backup/Recovery & Network Administration

by Claire Rajan

Senior Acquisitions Editor:
Maureen Martin

Senior Product Manager:
Alyssa Pratt

Production Editor:
GEX Publishing Services

Compositor:
GEX Publishing Services

Cover Designer:
Laura Rickenbach

Senior Manufacturing Coordinator:
Justin Palmeiro

Printed in Canada

1 2 3 4 5 6 7 8 9 WC 10 09 08 07 06

For more information, contact Thomson Course Technology, 25 Thomson Place, Boston, Massachusetts, 02210.

Or find us on the World Wide Web at: www.course.com

ISBN-13: 978-1-4188-3664-1
ISBN-10: 1-4188-3664-8

TABLE OF CONTENTS

PREFACE

Though it may not be readily apparent, the large volumes of data that businesses and individuals store have made the database one of the most important building blocks of modern IT infrastructure. Oracle database administration is a very desirable skill thanks to the growth and popularity of Oracle Corporation's database products. Oracle's current database product, Oracle Database 10*g*, is an object-oriented database that allows enormous quantities of data to be stored and managed with ease. It is the first database that supports Enterprise Grid Computing and has self-managing capabilities. Grid Computing provides the most flexible and cost-effective way to manage data storage. Many new features, automated management capabilities, and performance enhancements in Oracle 10*g* help to reduce IT management costs and enhance user productivity.

The focus of this text is to present the reader with useful and important features of the Oracle 10*g* database. The book covers a number of administrative, tuning, and networking topics. The book approaches the subject using a hands-on approach giving the reader an opportunity to understand the material and master concepts by implementing them on the computer. As database administrators must be familiar with the graphical administrative tools and command-line syntax, this book tries to present almost all topics using both interfaces.

In addition, the text has been organized to correspond to the published certification objectives for the Exam 1Z0-043: Oracle Database 10*g*: Administrator II. You may find these objectives at *http://education.oracle.com*.

Intended Audience

This textbook is designed to support individuals and technical students studying database courses who need to learn how to administer, backup, recover and tune the Oracle Database 10*g*.

Students must have a basic knowledge of the Oracle 10*g* database architecture, backup, recovery and networking concepts. In addition, the reader must have a basic knowledge of Structured Query Language (SQL). It is preferable that the reader also have a basic understanding of PL/SQL.

Oracle Certification Program

The Oracle 10*g* Certification (DBA Track) requires a student to successfully complete two exams:

- The 1Z0-042 Oracle Database 10*g*: Administrator 1 exam tests an individual on basic Oracle 10*g* administration, backup, recovery, and networking. Upon passing the exam the individual will obtain the Oracle Certified Associate (OCA) credential.
- The 1Z0-043 Oracle Database 10*g*: Administration II exam tests an individual on advanced Oracle 10*g* administration, backup, recovery, tuning and networking. Successful completion of this exam results in an individual obtaining the Oracle Certified Professional (OCP) credential.

This textbook prepares you for the 1Z0-043 Oracle Database 10*g*: Administrator II exam. Each chapter in the book begins with a section detailing the exam objectives covered in the chapter. Additional exam information may be found at *http://education.oracle.com*.

The Approach

The concepts introduced in this textbook are presented in the context of a hypothetical "real world" business—Keller Medical Center. The medical center runs an Oracle 10*g* database called DB101. The two main characters in the scenario are Anita, a senior DBA, and Ryan, a junior DBA, as well as a new hire at Keller Medical Center. Ryan brings with him expertise in administering an Oracle9*i* database and tends to approach most problems based on solutions and features available in Oracle versions 9*i* and earlier. Joining Keller Medical Center gives him an opportunity to exploit his current knowledge about databases, but it also presents a learning curve.

Each chapter presents a challenge faced at Keller Medical Center. The challenge gives Ryan and you, the reader, the opportunity to experiment and learn many of the new and exciting features present in Oracle 10*g*. The chapter presents various concepts and methods that may be implemented to find a suitable solution to the problem. Each chapter contains plenty of practice examples that give the reader the opportunity to simulate the challenge or problem and learn the subject using a hands-on approach.

The chapter concludes with a summary, a syntax guide, review questions, hands-on assignments, and case studies to help reinforce concepts. The contents of Appendix A and Appendix B are particularly important and need to be reviewed before you move on to the chapters in the book. They present certain fundamental concepts related to the Oracle architecture and Enterprise Manager.

The book integrates content and theory with practice exercises to help you put into practice what you are reading. This textbook distinguishes itself from other Oracle books because it is designed specifically for users and instructors in educational environments.

Overview of the Book

The content, examples, assignments, and case studies in this book will help the student master the following objectives:

- Perform backups using Recovery Manager
- Perform recoveries using Recovery Manager
- Understand the Flashback Technologies in Oracle 10*g*
- Tune the Oracle 10*g* database
- Deal with block corruption
- Understand the advisors available in Oracle 10*g*
- Monitor and manage storage
- Monitor and manage memory
- Understand the ASM feature in Oracle 10*g*
- Understand the functions of the Scheduler
- Understand globalization support
- Understand the functions of the listener and its vulnerabilities

The book is made up of two main parts with a total of 14 chapters. The two parts identify two distinct functions of the database administrator, namely backup/recovery and Administration.

Part I — The first part of the book deals with backup and recovery in the Oracle Database 10*g*. The student is introduced to the methods available for performing backups. Different types of failures are presented and methods to resolve them are covered in the topics associated with recovery. This section consists of six chapters: **Chapter 1** is an introduction to the Recovery Manager (RMAN). It is an extremely powerful and versatile tool that can be used for performing backup and recovery operations. **Chapter 2** deals with performing backups using the RMAN utility. **Chapter 3** deals with the different kinds of failures that can occur in the database and procedures that can be used for recovery. The lesson lays emphasis on incomplete recovery and recovery from non-critical failures. **Chapter 4** describes a new functionality available in Oracle 10*g* known as Flashback Database. It discusses the flash recovery area and the methods available for performing flashback database. **Chapter 5** presents a number of new features available in Oracle 10*g* that are used to recover from user errors. **Chapter 6** deals with block corruption and the different methods available for detecting and resolving it.

Part II — In the second part of the book we discuss important topics associated with administering and tuning the Oracle 10*g* Database. **Chapter 7** describes the Common Manageability infrastructure available in Oracle 10*g*. The topics include the Automatic Workload Repository, Server-Generated Alerts, and the Advisory Framework. **Chapter 8** deals with the Database Resource Manager utility, its purpose, and its configuration. The utility provides the ability to manage resources within the Oracle database more efficiently. **Chapter 9** discusses the Scheduler that is available in Oracle 10*g*. The utility helps to simplify the administration of repetitive tasks within the Oracle database. **Chapter 10** describes space management in tablespaces and segments. Various advisors that can provide useful recommendations to manage space more efficiently in the database are also discussed. **Chapter 11** discusses Automatic Memory Management in Oracle 10*g*. **Chapter 12** discusses the Automatic Storage Management feature that is new in Oracle 10*g*. The topics include an introduction to the ASM, its architecture, components, configuration, and management. **Chapter 13** discusses the need for globalization support. It also discusses the features available within the Oracle database that make it possible. **Chapter 14** discusses diagnostic tools available in Oracle 10*g* and certain aspects of the Listener process and external procedures. The book concludes with two appendices: because this book discusses advanced topics, a quick guide to the Oracle architecture is presented in **Appendix A** for the student to review certain basic and important concepts associated with the Oracle 10*g* architecture. **Appendix B** is a comprehensive guide to the Oracle Enterprise Manager. This appendix has been provided since the interface is becoming increasing popular and a student should be familiar with it.

Glossary includes key terms along with definitions for easy reference.

Features

To enhance the student's learning experience, each chapter includes the following elements:

Chapter Objectives: Each chapter begins with a list of objectives to be mastered. The list provides a quick overview of the chapter contents.

Step-By-Step Methodology: Each chapter introduces new concepts, explains the concepts, and provides practice exercises to demonstrate the concepts. Detailed step-by-step instructions lead you through each step and numerous illustrations and figures have been included to direct your attention to outputs and specific details. When appropriate, both command-line and graphical interfaces have been presented.

Exam Objectives: Each chapter also begins with a list of exam objectives that will be covered in the chapter. These exam objectives are based on the objectives of the 1Z0-043 exam.

Running Case: The production databases managed and maintained at Keller Medical Center serve as the basis for demonstrating the procedures in each chapter.

Notes: These explanations, designated by the Note icon provide important or additional information about a concept.

Chapter Summaries: Each chapter concludes with a summary to reiterate chapter concepts.

Syntax Guides: A syntax guide table is supplied after the chapter summary. It reviews the commands and parameters discussed in the chapter.

Review Questions: The end-of-chapter assessment consists of a set of 20 reviews questions and is presented to challenge a student's understanding of the lesson. The questions are in true/false, fill-in-the-blank, or multiple choice formats.

Hands-On Assignments: Each chapter presents hands-on assignments based on the chapter's content. The assignments provide students the opportunity to master commands and procedures discussed in the chapter.

Case Projects: One or more case studies are provided at the end of each chapter. The cases are designed to help students summarize major procedures performed in the chapter or apply what has been learned to real-world situations.

The Oracle Database 10*g* (10.2.0) CD, which is in the envelope adhered to this book, enables users to install this software on their own computers at home. Users can then connect to either an Oracle 10*g* Enterprise Edition, Standard Edition, or Personal Edition database. You can use the Database 10*g* software with Microsoft Windows NT, Windows 2000 Professional or Server, Windows 2003 Server, and Windows XP Professional operating systems. The installation and configuration instructions for Database 10*g* are available at *www.course.com/cdkit*. Look for this book's title and front cover, and click the link to access the information specific to this text.

Before proceeding to use the software, **you must** register the software and agree to the Oracle Technology Network Developer License Terms in order to receive the key code to unlock the software. Please go to *http://otn.oracle.com/books/*. Upon registering the software, you agree that Oracle may contact you for marketing purposes. You also agree that any information you provide to Oracle may be used for marketing purposes.

Supplemental Materials

The following supplemental materials are available when this book is used in a classroom setting. All teaching tools available with this book are provided to the instructor on a single CD-ROM.

Electronic Instructor's Manual: The Instructor's Manual that accompanies this textbook includes instructional material to assist in class preparation, including suggestions, chapter outlines, technical notes, quick quizzes, discussion topics, and key terms.

Sample Syllabi and Course Outline: The sample syllabi and course outline is provided as a foundation to begin planning and organizing your course.

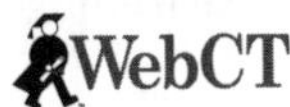

ExamView® Test Bank. ExamView® allows instructors to create and administer printed, computer (LAN-based), and Internet exams. The Test Bank includes hundreds of questions that correspond to the topics covered in this text, enabling students to generate detailed study guides that include page references for further review. The computer-based and Internet testing components allow students to take exams at their computers, and also save the instructor time by grading each exam automatically. The Test Bank is also available in Blackboard and WebCT versions posted online at *www.course.com*.

PowerPoint Presentations: Microsoft PowerPoint slides are included for each chapter. Instructors may use the slides as a teaching aid within the classroom, distribute it to students as a handout or use it as a network-accessible resource for chapter review. Instructors are free to add their own slides.

Figure Files: Figures and table files from each chapter are provided for your use in the classroom.

Student Data Files: The script files referenced within the chapters are available through the Course Technology website at *www.course.com* and are also available on the Instructor Resources CD-ROM.

Solution Files: Solutions to the end-of-chapter review questions and hands-on assignments are provided on the Teaching Tools CD-ROM. Solutions may also be found on the Thomson Course Technology Web site at *www.course.com*. The solutions are password-protected.

ACKNOWLEDGEMENTS

First and foremost, I would like to thank God for the countless blessings he showers on me and my family.

I would like to dedicate this book to my dearest husband Mario for all his love, encouragement, and support, and my adorable son, Siddarth, who is always my greatest joy. I would also like to thank my parents, family, and friends for all their encouragement and prayers.

I am particularly grateful to the Thomson Course Technology development team and all those who were directly or indirectly involved in the completion of my book. Thanks to Maureen Martin for giving me the opportunity to pursue a dream. I would like to extend my earnest appreciation and thanks to my Product Manager, Alyssa Pratt, for her patience, guidance, support, and professionalism. Thanks to Lori Cavanaugh, who read and corrected the document. A special thanks to Chris Scriver and Peter Stefanis for validating and testing each and every practice example and hands-on assignment. Thanks to Jennifer Muroff who guided me during the creation of the supplemental materials. I also wish to extend my thanks to the technical reviewers—Reni Abraham, Houston Community College–Southwest; Gerry Waldrop, Strayer University; Randy Winchester, Johnson County Community College; and Bill Wright, Humber Institute of Technology and Advanced Learning—for their invaluable comments and suggestions. Thanks also to the GEX Publishing team, especially Sandra Mitchell for all her help and assistance.

READ THIS BEFORE YOU BEGIN

Student Data Files

Many chapters in this book contain practice examples and hands-on exercises that require the execution of scripts. These scripts are available in the Student Datafiles. Your instructor will provide you with these datafiles or your may obtain them electronically from the Thomson Course Technology Web site by accessing *www.course.com* and then searching for this book title.

A chapter may contain a section "Setup for the Chapter" describing the script(s) to be executed *before* you begin the practices. Scripts may be also referenced in individual practice examples and assignments. You will be clearly instructed about the specific script to execute and where it can be found.

The script files for Chapter 1 through Chapter 14 are found in the Data folder with folder names such as Chapter01, Chapter03, Chapter11, and so on. Scripts of a particular chapter folder are found in their respective folder.

Installation Instructions

A comprehensive guide to Installing Oracle 10g on the Windows platform along with instructions to create the databases referenced in the textbook is available at the *www.course.com/cdkit* Web site. Look for this book title and front cover and click the link to access the installation instructions specific to this book.

Set Up your Computer for the Book

To use your own computer to work through the chapter examples and to complete the hands-on assignments, you will need the following:

- **Hardware:** A computer capable of using Microsoft Windows 2003 or XP Professional (with Service Pack 2) operating system. You should have at least a minimum of 512 megabytes of RAM and between 2.5G to 4G of hard disk space before installing the software. You are strongly advised to make a complete backup of all the data on the machine that you will install Oracle on, prior to the installation of the Oracle 10g Database software.
- **Software:** Oracle Database 10g Release 2 (10.2.0). Although the examples in this textbook use the Enterprise edition, you can use the Standard edition and Personal edition. The Course Technology Kit for Oracle 10g Software contains the database software necessary to perform all the tasks shown in this textbook.
- **Installation Instructions:** Detailed installation, configuration, and logon information for the software in this kit is provided at *www.course.com/cdkit*. Look for this book title and front cover, and click on the link to access the information specific to this book.
- **Databases:** The database that is referenced in this book is called DB101 and may be created during the installation of the Oracle Database 10g software.

This database may be created as a general purpose database using the Database Configuration Assistant tool. During the installation of the Oracle Database, you will be prompted to set the passwords of certain administrative accounts. Make sure you record the names and passwords of these accounts. Make a note of the URLs mentioned after database creation that may be used to access the Enterprise Manager and *i*SQL*Plus. In addition to the DB101 database, two other databases are created in the book—RCDB and ASMIG. These databases may also be created using Database Configuration Assistant. The instructions for the creation of these databases are available at the *www.course.com/cdkit*. Search for this book title and select the link to access the information specific to this book.

- **Data Files:** You will require the Student Datafiles to successfully complete the practice examples and hands-on assignments presented in the chapters of this textbook. You can get the data files from your instructor, or you can obtain the data files electronically by accessing the Course Technology Web site at *www.course.com* and then searching for this book title.
- **Additional Users:** After the creation of the DB101 database, using SQL*Plus, log in as the SYS user and execute the script called ***prech01.sql*** script found in the Chapter01 folder of the Student Datafiles. This script creates two users called DB_ADMIN whose password is DB_ADMIN and the user MEDUSER whose password is MEDUSER. The DB_ADMIN user is granted the SYSDBA role and this user account name may be used in all practice examples and hands-on assignments whenever you need to log in with administrative privileges. You may use the convention CONNECT DB_ADMIN/DB_ADMIN AS SYSDBA (much in the same way as you would to log in as the SYS user). The user MEDUSER is a regular user of the database and is referenced in many practice examples and hands-on assignments.
- **Setting the Host Credentials for Enterprise Manager:** Within Enterprise Manager you may be prompted to specify a valid username and password of a Host User. For example, you would need to specify a host username and password when you select the Maintenance tab and try to schedule backups or perform recoveries. In order to successfully specify a username and password of a host user on a Windows Platform (XP or 2000) please make sure you perform the following steps.
  - Create an operating system user.
  - Click **Start** on the Windows taskbar.
  - Select **Administrative Tools**.
  - Select **Local Security Policy**.
  - Under Security Settings select **Local Policies** and then **User Rights Assignment**.
  - Double-click the entry for **Log on as batch job**.
  - Click **Add User or Group**.
  - Under **Enter the object names to select**, add the **Windows Username.**
  - Click **OK** to close both dialog boxes and close local security settings.
  - Log out and back into Windows for the changes to take effect.

To the Instructor

It is advisable to review the contents of Appendix A and Appendix B before you begin the chapters of the book. The appendices review the basic architectural and concepts that students reading this book must be familiar with.

To complete the assignments and practice examples presented in this book, the students must have access to the Student Datafiles that are included in the Instructor Resources Kit. They may also be obtained electronically by accessing the Course Technology Web site at *www.course.com* and then searching for this book title. The Student Datafiles consists of scripts that are executed either at the beginning of the chapter, within the chapter or during the hands-on assignments. After the Student Datafiles is copied you should instruct your students on how to copy the files to their computers or workstations.

The practice examples and hands-on assignments in this book have been tested and presented using Microsoft Windows XP Professional and Windows 2003 Server with Oracle 10*g* Release 2 Enterprise Edition.

You will need to provide you students with the following:

- **Installation Instructions** — for installing Oracle 10*g* Release 2 and the creation procedures for the databases mentioned in the textbook namely DB101, RCDB and ASMIG. This is available at the *www.course.com/cdkit* Web site. You may look for this book title to find the installation instructions applicable to this text.
- **User Account Information** — The students should be requested to pay special attention to the passwords of the SYS and SYSTEM users. Inform students that the users DB_ADMIN and MEDUSER, referenced in the book, are created by executing the script *prech01.sql* found in the Chapter01 folder of the Student Datafiles. (See Section on *Additional Users*). The DB_ADMIN user is a privileged account possessing SYSDBA privileges and the user MEDUSER is a regular user of the database.
- **Environment Variables** — Inform students of the ORACLE_HOME directory on their workstations. ORACLE_HOME is the directory where the Oracle 10*g* executable files are stored. On Windows, the ORACLE_HOME is typically C:\ORACLE\PRODUCT\10.2.0\DB_1. Because the ORACLE_HOME directory is referenced in the textbook, students must know the path they need to substitute.
- **URLs** — The addresses or URLs that may be used to access the Enterprise Manager and *i*SQL*Plus.
- **Computer Name** — The computer name of the workstation.
- **Host Credentials** — Inform students on how to configure host credentials for the Enterprise Manage. (See section on *Setting the Host Credentials for Enterprise Manager.*)

Visit Our Web site

Additional resources designed especially for this book are available at *www.course.com.* Visit this Web site periodically for more details.

CHAPTER 1

RECOVERY MANAGER

LEARNING OBJECTIVES

After completing this lesson you should be able to understand:

- The different backup options available to the database administrator
- The Recovery Manager Architecture
- How to launch RMAN and connect to the databases
- Channels and Automatic Channel Allocation
- Configuration of persistent parameters of the RMAN

ORACLE CERTIFICATION EXAM OBJECTIVES COVERED IN THIS CHAPTER INCLUDE:

Configuring Recovery Manager

- Configure database parameters that affect RMAN operations
- Change RMAN default settings with CONFIGURE
- Manage RMAN's persistent settings
- Start the RMAN utility and allocate channels

INTRODUCTION

Database administrators are faced with many challenges on a daily basis. One of the most challenging tasks is recovering the database in the event of failure. Successful recovery largely depends on the backups that are taken in the database. Sometimes backups are inconsistent, incomplete, or invalid and cannot be used for recovery. In the event of recovery, it is also necessary that the correct backup be used from among all the backups that are available. Oracle has been introducing new utilities with every new release of its database software to help administrators do their job more efficiently and simplify day-to-day tasks. The Recovery Manager is one such tool that was introduced in Oracle 8*i*.

The Recovery Manager is a specialized utility that may be used for backing up the database and performing recovery procedures in the event of failures. New and robust enhancements have been made to the Recovery Manager since Oracle 8*i*, making it a "must-use" utility. In this chapter you will be introduced to the Recovery Manager and its components, and learn how to configure parameters that determine the behavior of the Recovery Manager environment.

THE CURRENT CHALLENGE AT KELLER MEDICAL CENTER

KELLER MEDICAL CENTER is a hospital located in Maryland. The hospital has approximately 200 employees. The medical center has many databases. One of the databases maintained by the Information Technology (IT) department is called DB101. The database contains a number of tables where details about the physicians, patients, medical procedures, nurses, emergency assistants, and billing information is stored. The DB101 database is accessed by all employees constantly and should be available at all times.

Ryan is the new database administrator at Keller Medical Center. He and his team members are responsible for ensuring that the DB101 database is always available and running optimally as the data maintained in the database is vital to the smooth functioning of the hospital. During his interview for the position of "junior DBA" he was questioned extensively regarding the Recovery Manager utility. At his previous job, Ryan was used to performing backups using manual procedures and executing custom scripts. Though he had read about RMAN he wasn't familiar with the utility and failed to answer many of the questions with clarity.

Prior to Ryan's joining the team, a decision had been made by the IT department that all backup and recovery procedures would hereafter be handled using the Recovery Manager. After much reading on the subject, Ryan soon realized that the Recovery Manager was extremely versatile and greatly simplifies the process of performing backups and makes recovering the database quite easy.

As you work through this chapter you will be introduced to the Recovery Manager utility and its architectural features. In subsequent chapters you will explore the Recovery Manager in greater detail and see for yourself how adopting this tool can make your day-to-day administrative tasks easier.

SET UP YOUR COMPUTER FOR THE CHAPTER

Please read and complete the procedures listed in **Read this Before You Begin** as part of the **Setup Your Computer for the Book** section.

IMPORTANT TERMS

Before you proceed to explore the Recovery Manager, it is essential that you familiarize yourself with some basic terms frequently used in this chapter.

Failures There are two main categories of failures that can occur in the Oracle database: non-media failure and media failure. Non-media failures can occur as a result of a logical error in a program unit or may be user errors that occur when users try to enter invalid data into a table. These kinds of errors are resolved by the Oracle server automatically or by the user without the intervention of the database administrator. Media failures arise when a physical file of the database is accidentally deleted or a hard disk or disk controller fails. Media failures are much more crucial and can render the database unusable until the failure has been resolved. A database administrator must be prepared for media failures by taking backups regularly and testing them on a regular basis to ensure that they can be used to recover the database successfully in case a failure occurs.

Backup Data is one of the most valuable assets maintained by an Enterprise. It is vital to the day-to-day functioning of the organization and hence should be protected from failure or loss. Unavailability of the database can result in loss of thousands or even millions of dollars in revenue. Unavailability of the database at Keller Medical Center would result not only in losses of revenue, but delays in medical procedures and schedules which could result in the loss of life. Backing up your data ensures that when a failure arises the chances of recovery are possible. Backing up a database involves storing redundant copies of the data in secondary storage devices such as disks or tapes.

Archiving The redo log files contain a record of all the changes that occur in the database. These can be CREATE, ALTER, DROP, TRUNCATE, INSERT, UPDATE, DELETE, MERGE, GRANT, REVOKE, COMMIT, or ROLLBACK statements. The changes are written to the redo log files by the Log Writer (LGWR) background process. Let us assume there are two redo log groups in the DB101 database. The LGWR initially begins writing to the first redo log file. When this redo log file becomes full, Oracle performs a **log switch** and the LGWR starts writing to the second redo log group. When the second redo log file becomes full, it once again performs a log switch and returns to the first redo log group. At this point LGWR will overwrite the previous contents of the log file based on the archiving mode of the database.

A database may operate in **archivelog** mode or **noarchivelog** mode. The default archiving mode in a database is noarchivelog. In noarchivelog mode the LGWR process can overwrite the contents of the first redo log file without first saving its contents.

When a database is operating in archivelog mode, the LGWR will overwrite the contents of the first redo log file, only after the contents of the redo log file have been stored to an offline file called an **archive file**. An archive file is a copy of the redo log file, before it can be overwritten. Archive files are used for recovering a database in the event of media failure. It is highly recommended that archive files be stored in an offline site in a fireproof storage facility.

Archive files are created automatically by the ARCH background process whenever a log switch occurs. This is known as automatic archiving. In Oracle 10g enabling archiving in a database, by default, enables automatic archiving. Figure 1-1 describes automatic archiving in the database.

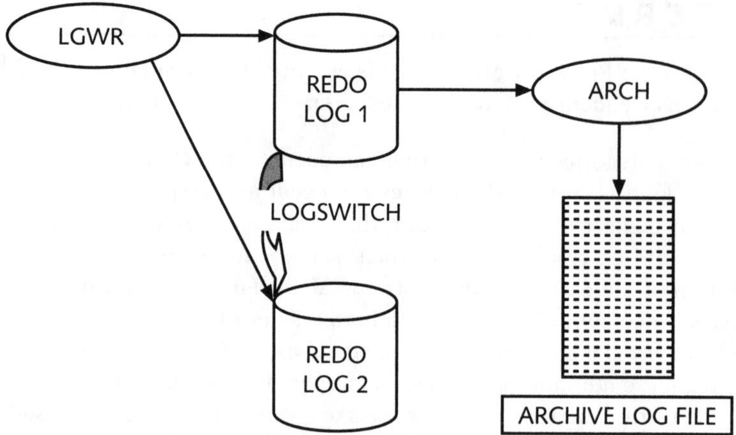

FIGURE 1-1 Archiving in an Oracle Database

The backup and recovery strategies available to a database administrator vary depending on the archiving mode of the database.

NOTE

Most production environments should operate in ARCHIVELOG mode.

Practice 1

The following steps can be used to put a database in archivelog mode.

1. Launch SQL*Plus, and logon as a user with SYSDBA privileges.
   ```
   SQL>CONNECT DB_ADMIN/DB_ADMIN AS SYSDBA
   ```
2. Shut down the database properly.
   ```
   SQL> SHUTDOWN IMMEDIATE;
   ```
3. Mount the database.
   ```
   SQL> STARTUP MOUNT;
   ```
4. Put the database in archivelog mode.
   ```
   SQL> ALTER DATABASE ARCHIVELOG;
   ```
5. Open the database.
   ```
   SQL> ALTER DATABASE OPEN;
   ```
6. Exit SQL*Plus
   ```
   SQL> EXIT
   ```

Archiving may also be enabled using Enterprise Manager (EM).

Practice 2

The following steps describe how to enable archiving using Enterprise Manager.

- Launch a browser and enter the URL to access the Enterprise Manager. Appendix B describes how the Enterprise Manager may be launched.
- When you are prompted to login, specify the username and password of a user with SYSDBA privileges.
- The **Database Control Home** page will appear.
- Select the **Maintenance** tab. From the **Backup/Recovery Settings** section select **Recovery Settings**.
- The **Recovery Settings** page will be displayed.
- On this page, in the **Media Recovery** section, is a checkbox for Archiving Mode. Check the box to indicate that you wish to enable archiving. Figure 1-2 displays how archiving may be enabled from the Recovery Settings page.

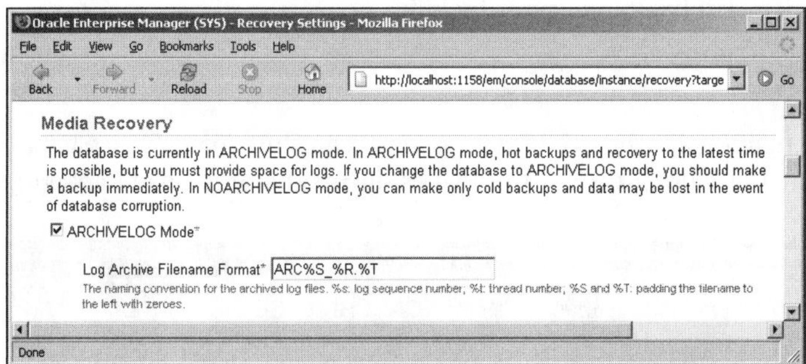

FIGURE 1-2 Enabling Archiving from Oracle Enterprise Manager

- Select the **Apply** Button at the bottom of the page.
- From the **Confirmation** page, select **Yes** so that the database is restarted for the change to take effect.
- The next page displayed will require you to enter your host credentials and database username and password. Select the OK button.

TIP

If you are unsure about the host credentials on Windows machines, you may read the last section of Appendix B that describes how to correctly specify the OS username and password for actions that require host credentials in EM.

- The **Restart Database: Confirmation** page will be displayed. Select the **Yes** button. The **Restart Database: Activity Information** page will be displayed. Wait for a few minutes and **Refresh** the page. At this point you have successfully enabled archiving.
- Log out of Enterprise Manager and close the browser.

BACKUP METHODS

Database administrators should perform regular backups. These backups may be used when failures such as the loss of a file occurs in the database. Administrators should also check the validity of backups on a regular basis. Oracle offers two methods for performing backup. They are:

- User Managed Backups
- Recovery Manager

User-managed Backups

The user-managed method of backup has been around for a while. In this method the database administrator performs backups manually by using operating system commands. The COPY command may be used in Windows and the cp command in UNIX. The user-managed method allows the administrator to perform backups when the database is either offline or online. The user-managed backup options include:

- Cold backups
- Hot backups

Cold backups should be taken only when the database has been shut down. These backups are consistent because changes do not occur to the files during the process of backup.

NOTE

Cold backups may be taken when running the database in either NOARCHIVELOG or ARCHIVELOG mode.

The following is a quick review of the steps involved in performing a cold backup:

- Start SQL*Plus and connect to the database as a privileged user.
- Make sure you have an accurate compilation of all the physical files recognized by the database. You may query the `V$DATAFILE`, `V$CONTROLFILE`, `V$LOGFILE` and `V$TEMPFILE` performance views to compile this list.
- Shutdown the database properly. Do not use the ABORT option.
- Copy the Datafiles, Control Files, Redo Log Files, Password File, and Parameter File of the database to your backup device using the operating system "copy" command.
- Start up the database.

A hot backup is taken when the database is open and is useful in non-stop business environments. Hot backups are performed at a tablespace level.

NOTE

A hot backup can be performed only when operating the database in ARCHIVELOG mode.

The following is a quick review of the steps involved in performing a hot backup:

- Start SQL*Plus and connect as a privileged user of the database.
- Issue the command to put a certain tablespace in backup mode. For example, to put a tablespace called USERS in backup mode you would issue:

```
SQL>ALTER TABLESPACE USERS BEGIN backup;
```

- Using an operating system command, copy the datafiles belonging to the USERS tablespace to the backup destination.
- Issue the command to end the backup and take the tablespace off backup mode. To take the USERS tablespace off backup mode issue:

```
SQL>ALTER TABLESPACE USERS END BACKUP;
```

The above steps may be repeated for each tablespace of the database. This form of backup is often referred to as an inconsistent backup because users may continue to make changes to the datafiles during the backup procedure.

Backups using Recovery Manager

Performing backups using manual steps can be a huge administrative burden on the database administrator. Maintaining, cataloging, and tracking the backups can be a difficult task. Sometimes an error in the database such as the accidental drop of a table may not be identified for several days and recovering from such an error would require the restoration of the correct backup, which need not necessarily be the latest backup taken. For these and many other reasons Oracle recommends the use of the Recovery Manager.

In the following sections you'll be introduced to Recovery Manager. You will learn its architecture, how to launch it using both the command-line and the Enterprise Manager, and how to set various configuration parameters.

RECOVERY MANAGER

Recovery Manager (commonly referred to as RMAN) is Oracle's preferred and revolutionary tool for backup and recovery. It may be invoked using a command-line interface as well as Enterprise Manager.

In addition to providing backup and recovery functions, RMAN seamlessly integrates with leading tape and storage media products using its Media Management Layer (MML) API. RMAN provides a number of reporting commands that display backup files that are no longer required from recovery purposes—files that have not been backed up and information about backups created and maintained by it. It supports incremental or block-level backups that are smaller than regular backups and take less time.

RMAN also allows the administrator to test the backup to ensure it is usable in the event of an error. This ensures the validity of the backup. It also provides the ability to create scripts that may be used for repetitive backup tasks.

In Oracle 10g the Recovery Manager utility provides a host of new features that allow the database administrator to better organize and manage backups. Some of these features include automatic detection of block corruption in files, space-saving techniques such as compression and file multiplexing during backup and optimizing incremental backup performance using block change tracking. These and many more useful features of RMAN are discussed in this and subsequent chapters.

RMAN Architecture

The RMAN environment is made up of a number of components. They include:

- **The Target Database:** This is the database that RMAN would need to backup, restore, or recover.
- **The RMAN Client or Executable:** The RMAN client may be invoked using a command-line or using Enterprise Manager. The RMAN client receives commands, interprets them, and directs server sessions to execute the commands. It has its own command syntax. A user of RMAN would need to learn this syntax to be able to interact and issue commands to the RMAN executable. It also records the backup and recovery activity in the control file of the target database.
- **The RMAN Repository:** The RMAN repository is a collection of tables maintained by RMAN that stores metadata about the target database along with information about backup and recovery operations that may have been performed against it. It also holds a record of the configuration settings for RMAN. The RMAN repository is always maintained in the control file of the target database. A database administrator may alternatively choose to store the RMAN repository in a separate database schema known as the Recovery Catalog.

Optional components of the RMAN environment include:

- **The Flash Recovery Area:** It refers to a centralized location where files related to backup and recovery may be stored and managed. The flash recovery area is configured using initialization parameters. Using a flash recovery area greatly simplifies maintenance of backup files and the increases the speed of restorations.
- **The Media Management Library (MML) Interface:** This interface allows RMAN to access sequential storage devices such as tape drives. The MML interface is used to communicate between the Oracle Server and the media management software. Media management software is provided by the vendor to control the devices during backup and recovery by managing the loading, labeling, and unloading of media.

NOTE

Oracle Secure Backup (OSB) is a new feature in Oracle 10*g* Release 2. The Oracle database provides an integrated media management solution for accessing tapes. Using this feature, the third-party Media Management Library is no longer required.

- **The Recovery Catalog:** The Recovery Catalog is a separate database schema that may be created to hold the RMAN repository. Oracle recommends the use of a recovery catalog for medium-to-large databases. It can prove useful for recovery in the event of the loss of the control file itself. If the control file of the database becomes unavailable the RMAN repository will still be available in the recovery catalog database. In addition to holding the RMAN repository, it allows the DBA to create and store scripts. The recovery catalog makes working with RMAN more flexible and allows you to use the complete functionality of the RMAN tool. Figure 1-3 displays the various RMAN components and their interactions with each other.

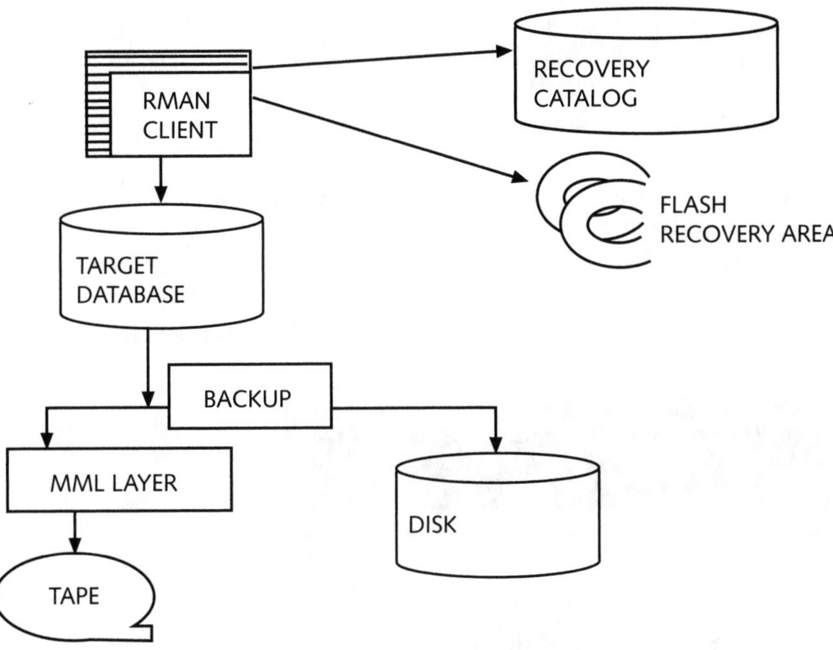

FIGURE 1-3 The Architectural Components of RMAN

Connecting to RMAN

Recovery Manager is started by launching the RMAN executable. The RMAN executable is invoked from either an operating system command prompt or using the RUN option on the Windows operating system.

Practice 3: Connecting to RMAN

This practice example demonstrates the different methods available to connect to RMAN.

1. Click the **Start** button on the Windows task bar. Select the **Run** option from the Start Menu.
2. Type **rman**, at the Run prompt. Click **OK**. The Figure 1-4 describes how RMAN is launched using the RUN dialog window.

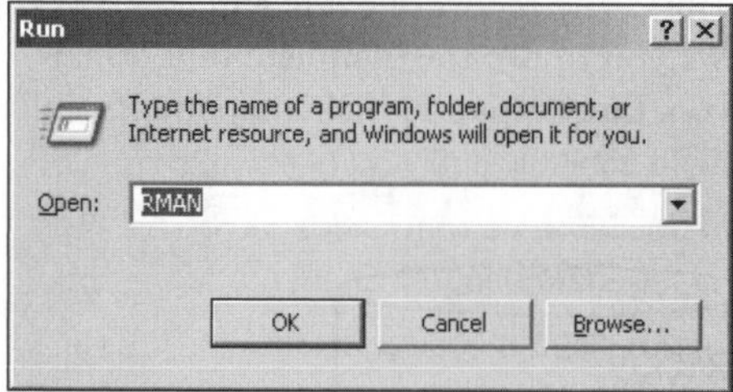

FIGURE 1-4 Launching RMAN in Windows

Alternatively, you can launch an operating system command prompt, and type RMAN at the prompt.

```
Start -> All Programs -> Accessories -> Command Prompt
C:\>RMAN
```

3. The **RMAN prompt** is then displayed. Figure 1-5 displays the RMAN prompt.

FIGURE 1-5 The RMAN Prompt

4. To exit RMAN, type **`EXIT`** at the RMAN Prompt.

```
RMAN>EXIT
```

After launching RMAN the next step is to connect to the target database. This is the database that RMAN will backup or recover. The command used to connect to the target database is CONNECT TARGET.

Practice 4: Connecting to the target database

The following steps demonstrate how to launch RMAN and connect to the target database, DB101. RMAN information will be stored only in the control file of the target database. This is the method to use if you have not created a recovery catalog database (see Figure 1-6).

NOTE

The ORACLE_SID is an environment variable that holds the name of the default database. On a machine with multiple databases, it may be necessary to clearly identify the database that you wish to access. You can do so by issuing the SET ORACLE_SID=<instance_name> command from the operating system command prompt.

1. Launch a Command Prompt, and set the Oracle System Identifier (ORACLE_SID) to the target database DB101.

```
C:\> SET ORACLE_SID=DB101
```

2. Launch the RMAN executable, from the command prompt.

```
C:\> RMAN
RMAN>
```

3. Connect to the target database, using the CONNECT TARGET command. Notice that the target database has a unique ID specified by DBID.

```
RMAN> CONNECT TARGET
Connected to target database: DB101 (DBID=1045344061)
```

```
Command Prompt - RMAN
C:\>SET ORACLE_SID=DB101

C:\>RMAN

Recovery Manager: Release 10.2.0.1.0 - Production on Thu Dec 1 12:28:47 2005

Copyright (c) 1982, 2005, Oracle.  All rights reserved.

RMAN> CONNECT TARGET

connected to target database: DB101 (DBID=1045344061)

RMAN>
```

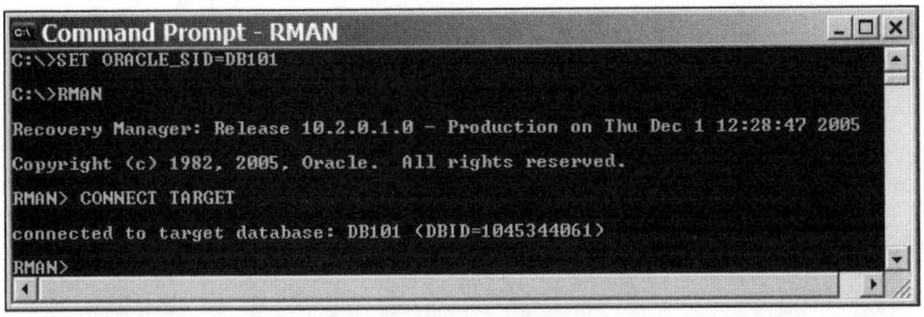

FIGURE 1-6 Connecting to the target database from RMAN

NOTE

You may also explicitly use the NOCATALOG keyword to indicate that you do not wish to connect to the recovery catalog database. This alternate method (shown below) may be used to connect to the target database when launching RMAN:

```
C :\> RMAN TARGET / NOCATALOG
connected to target database: DB101 (DBID=1045344061 )
using target database control file instead of recovery catalog
```

4. Log out of RMAN.

```
RMAN> EXIT
```

The RMAN Repository

The RMAN repository is a collection of tables that store information or metadata about the target database along with details of backup and recovery operations that have been performed. The RMAN repository is always stored in the control file of the target database. It is stored in the reusable section of the control file known as *circular reuse records*. Because RMAN data is constantly generated, the control file may become quite large. The size of the control file can be controlled to some extent by the `CONTROL_FILE_RECORD_KEEP_TIME` initialization parameter. This parameter determines, in terms of days, how long RMAN data should be retained in the control file. The default value is 7 days. Once the time period indicated by the parameter has elapsed, the RMAN metadata in the control file is considered obsolete and may be overwritten.

The RMAN repository may be optionally stored in a recovery catalog database. A recovery catalog gives you the ability to store the backup and recovery information of multiple databases. In this way you can centrally maintain RMAN data rather than have the information dispersed in the control files of different databases. The recovery catalog also enables the RMAN metadata to be stored for longer periods of time. You can also create and store scripts that may be used for repetitive backup tasks such as weekly or daily backups. A script is a sequence of RMAN commands that are grouped together. A script is assigned a name and may be executed when required. The recovery catalog also stores the physical and logical structure of the target databases. Finally, the recovery catalog database should be backed up like all other databases.

Creating the Recovery Catalog Database

It is recommended that the recovery catalog be stored in a database different from the target database. The CONNECT CATALOG command is used to connect to the Recovery Catalog database. The CREATE CATALOG command is used to create the repository of tables in the schema of the recovery catalog owner.

Practice 5: Creating the Repository in the Recovery Catalog Database

This practice example demonstrates the creation of the RMAN repository in a separate database called RCDB that has been created solely for this purpose.

1. To perform the steps described in this practice you must create a general-purpose database called RCDB using the Database Configuration Assistant or a method specified by your instructor. Refer to the Read this Before You Begin—Setup Your Computer for the Book—Databases section.
2. Using the Network Configuration Assistant you should create a network service name called RCDB for this database.
3. Make sure the target database (DB101) is in ARCHIVELOG mode.
4. Start SQL*Plus, connect to the RCDB database using an account with SYS DBA privileges such as the SYS user. The nolog option shown below takes you directly to the SQL prompt without prompting you for a username and password.

   ```
   C:\>SQLPLUS /NOLOG
   SQL> CONNECT SYS/<password>@RCDB AS SYSDBA
   ```

5. Create a user called RMANUSER whose password is RMANUSER. The code shown below assigns this user a default tablespace called USERS and a temporary tablespace called TEMP. If these tablespaces do not exist on your machine, please use appropriate alternate tablespace names.

   ```
   SQL>CREATE USER RMANUSER
       IDENTIFIED BY RMANUSER
       DEFAULT TABLESPACE USERS
       TEMPORARY TABLESPACE TEMP;
   ```

6. Grant the RMANUSER the privileges required to connect to the database, the privilege to create objects, and the RECOVERY_CATALOG_OWNER role. Granting this role makes the RMANUSER the owner of the RMAN repository.

   ```
   SQL> GRANT CONNECT, RESOURCE,
        RECOVERY_CATALOG_OWNER TO RMANUSER;
   ```

7. Exit SQL*Plus.

```
SQL> EXIT
```

8. Next, invoke the RMAN executable. The steps are displayed in Practice 3.
9. At the RMAN prompt connect to the catalog database as the user RMANUSER. The RCDB network service name is specified to indicate that you wish to connect to the RCDB database.

```
RMAN> CONNECT CATALOG RMANUSER/RMANUSER@RCDB
```

10. Finally, create the recovery catalog using the CREATE CATALOG command in the RMANUSER schema.

```
RMAN> CREATE CATALOG;
recovery catalog created
```

11. Exit RMAN.

```
RMAN> EXIT
```

After creating the repository in the recovery catalog database you should connect to both the target and recovery catalog database when using RMAN for backup or recovery operations. If you connect in this manner, RMAN metadata will be stored in the control file of the target database as well as the recovery catalog database.

Practice 6: Connecting to the Target and Recovery Catalog Database

This practice example demonstrates how to launch RMAN and then connect to the target database and recovery catalog database. The steps to be performed are described in the following section and in Figure 1-7:

1. Launch a command prompt, and set the Oracle System Identifier (ORACLE_SID) to the target database DB101.

```
C:\> SET ORACLE_SID=DB101
```

2. Launch the RMAN executable.

```
C:\> RMAN
RMAN>
```

3. Connect to the target database.

```
RMAN>CONNECT TARGET
connected to target database: DB101 (DBID=1045344061)
```

4. Connect to the recovery catalog database as RMANUSER.

```
RMAN> CONNECT CATALOG RMANUSER/RMANUSER@RCDB
connected to recovery catalog database
```

5. Exit RMAN.

```
RMAN> EXIT;
```

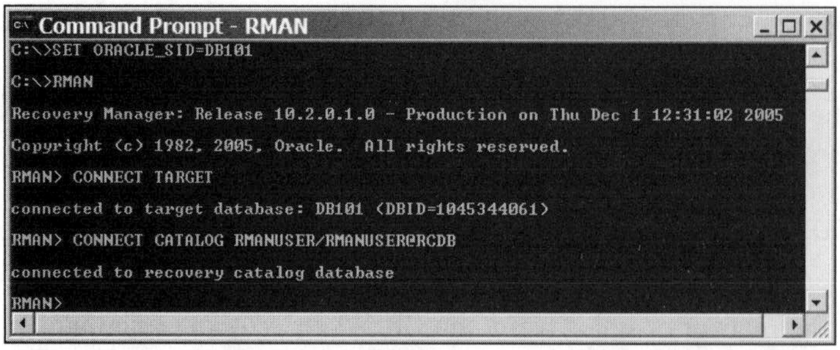

```
Command Prompt - RMAN
C:\>SET ORACLE_SID=DB101

C:\>RMAN

Recovery Manager: Release 10.2.0.1.0 - Production on Thu Dec 1 12:31:02 2005

Copyright (c) 1982, 2005, Oracle.  All rights reserved.

RMAN> CONNECT TARGET

connected to target database: DB101 (DBID=1045344061)

RMAN> CONNECT CATALOG RMANUSER/RMANUSER@RCDB

connected to recovery catalog database

RMAN>
```

FIGURE 1-7 Connecting to the recovery catalog database

NOTE

An alternate method to connect to the target database and the recovery catalog when launching RMAN is:

```
C :\> RMAN TARGET / CATALOG RMANUSER/RMANUSER@RCDB
connected to target database: DB101 (DBID=1045344061)
connected to recovery catalog database
```

Registering the target database

Every target database whose backup and recovery information needs to be stored in the recovery catalog database must be registered with the recovery catalog. The REGISTER DATABASE command is used for this purpose. In Oracle 10g the UNREGISTER DATA BASE command can be used to "unregister" a target database.

Practice 7: Registering the target database

In this practice example the steps involved in registering a target database will be demonstrated. Please complete Practice 5 before attempting this practice.

1. Make sure the ORACLE_SID has been set correctly so that RMAN references the correct target database. In our case it is the DB101 database. Open a Command Prompt window and type:

   ```
   C:\>SET ORACLE_SID=DB101
   ```

2. Launch the RMAN executable and connect to the target database in the following manner. A message is displayed indicating that you are connected to the target database.

   ```
   C:\>RMAN
   RMAN>CONNECT TARGET
   connected to target database: DB101 (DBID:1045344061)
   ```

3. Next connect to the recovery catalog database as the RMANUSER user.

   ```
   RMAN>CONNECT CATALOG RMANUSER/RMANUSER@RCDB
   connected to recovery catalog database
   ```

4. Issue the REGISTER DATABASE command to register the target database.

```
RMAN>REGISTER DATABASE;
database registered in recovery catalog
starting full resync of recovery catalog
full resync complete
```

5. Log out of RMAN.

```
RMAN>EXIT
```

Configuring Channel Allocation

When a backup or restore operation is performed using RMAN it configures channels which in turn initiate one or more server processes on the instance of the target database. A channel represents a single stream of data to a backup device. Multiple channels may be configured to speed up backup and recovery procedures. The server processes perform the actual backup, restore, and recovery operations.

Channels may be allocated manually using the ALLOCATE CHANNEL command. A channel may be configured to interact with a tape device (SBT) or a disk (DISK). For example, a channel called C1 that would access a disk is created using the command:

```
RMAN>ALLOCATE CHANNEL C1 TYPE DISK;
```

Since Oracle 9*i*, manual channel allocation is optional. RMAN can automatically allocate channels when a BACKUP, RESTORE, or RECOVER command is issued. This process is referred to as **Automatic Channel Allocation**. Figure 1-8 shows how channels interact with server sessions, which in turn interact with the backup media.

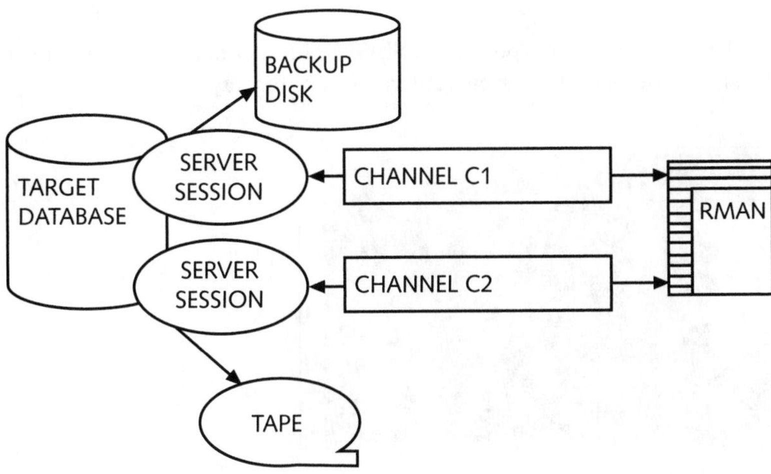

FIGURE 1-8 Channel Allocation

Parallel channels may be started to speed the process of backup and restore operations. This may be done using the `CONFIGURE DEVICE TYPE DISK PARALLELISM 'n'` command. A value for '*n*' greater than 1 would indicate '*n*' parallel channels. For example, if you specify a value of 2, then RMAN will automatically configure two parallel channels during backup or recovery tasks. Two parallel channels would perform the operation faster than if a single channel were to perform the same task.

Persistent Parameters of RMAN

A database administrator may optionally configure various parameters that would affect the behavior, backup, restore, and maintenance tasks performed by RMAN. The configuration parameters are referred to as the persistent parameters of RMAN. The configurations are in effect for any RMAN session until they are either cleared or modified. Configuration parameters are stored in the RMAN repository. Persistent parameters may be set using the command-line or Enterprise Manager.

Setting RMAN parameters using the Command-Line

You may configure the RMAN parameters from the RMAN prompt. The current RMAN configuration can be viewed using the SHOW ALL command.

Practice 8: The SHOW ALL command

This practice example displays the output of the SHOW ALL command.

1. Launch RMAN and connect to the target database. You may optionally connect to the recovery catalog database if you have created one.

   ```
   C:\> RMAN TARGET /
   ```

2. Issue the SHOW ALL command to view the current values of the RMAN parameters.

   ```
   RMAN>SHOW ALL;
   ```

   Figure 1-9 displays the output of the SHOW ALL command in which a list of configurable options and their current values are displayed.

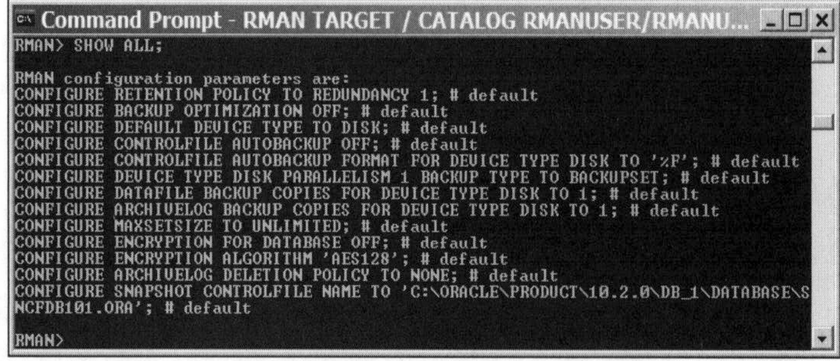

FIGURE 1-9 The SHOW ALL Command

3. Log out of RMAN.

   ```
   RMAN> EXIT
   ```

In the following section, you will be introduced to some of the important configurations from the list displayed in Figure 1-9.

Configuring Retention Policy The retention policy is defined to establish how long a backup must be retained by RMAN before it can be considered obsolete. The retention policy may be specified in terms of a REDUNDANCY or a RECOVERY WINDOW. When using the REDUNDANCY option you establish the number of redundant backup copies that RMAN should retain as current and required for recovery. You can set RETENTION POLICY TO REDUNDANCY *n*, where *n* is a number establishing the number of backup copies of a file that RMAN should retain as valid. If the value *n* is set to 1 it would indicate that the latest backup is the only one that must be retained, all previous backups may be considered obsolete.

Setting a retention policy in terms of a recovery window establishes the number of days backups must be retained. You can set RETENTION POLICY TO RECOVERY WINDOW OF n DAYS, where *n* is a number establishing the number of days the backup should be retained as valid and required for recovery.

The redundancy and the recovery window policies are mutually exclusive and either of them may be defined at a time. A backup is considered obsolete if it does not satisfy the configured retention policy. RMAN does not automatically delete obsolete backups. The DELETE OBSOLETE command is used to manually remove obsolete files.

Practice 9: Setting the Retention Policy

To change the retention policy to a value other than the default of 1, perform the following steps:

1. Launch RMAN and connect to the target database. You may optionally connect to the recovery catalog database if you have created one.

   ```
   C:\> RMAN TARGET /
   ```

2. To set the retention policy to a redundancy of 2, issue:

   ```
   RMAN> CONFIGURE RETENTION POLICY TO REDUNDANCY 2;
   ```

3. To view the current retention policy you can use the SHOW command.

   ```
   RMAN> SHOW RETENTION POLICY;
   ```

4. To set the retention policy to a recovery window of 10 days, you may issue:

   ```
   RMAN> CONFIGURE RETENTION POLICY TO RECOVERY WINDOW OF 10 DAYS;
   ```

5. To clear the modified retention policy and return it to the default value, the CLEAR keyword is used in the CONFIGURE command.

   ```
   RMAN> CONFIGURE RETENTION POLICY CLEAR;
   ```

6. Exit RMAN.

   ```
   RMAN> EXIT;
   ```

Configuring Default Device Type The parameter DEFAULT DEVICE TYPE specifies the default device type for automatic channels. The default device type may be set to SBT (System Backup to Tape) or DISK (Disk). If you set it to disk, then automatic channels are by default configured to interact with disks. If you set it to SBT, then automatic channels are by default configured to interact with tapes.

Practice 10: Configuring the Default Device Type

The following practice demonstrates how to configure a default device type for automatic channels.

1. Launch RMAN, and connect to the target database. You may optionally connect to the recovery catalog database.

```
C:\> RMAN TARGET /
```

2. Configure the default device type for automatic channels to tape.

```
RMAN> CONFIGURE DEFAULT DEVICE TYPE TO SBT;
```

3. Set the default device type for automatic channels to disk.

```
RMAN> CONFIGURE DEFAULT DEVICE TYPE TO DISK;
```

4. To view the current default device type, you could issue:

```
RMAN> SHOW DEFAULT DEVICE TYPE;
```

5. Clear the current value and reset it to the default device type.

```
RMAN> CONFIGURE DEFAULT DEVICE TYPE CLEAR;
```

6. Exit RMAN.

```
RMAN> EXIT;
```

Configuring Control File Autobackup The control file is one of the most important files of the database. The database cannot operate without a control file. The control file should be backed up as often as possible. Using RMAN you may configure the control file to be automatically backed up whenever a BACKUP or COPY command is issued at the RMAN prompt or within a RUN block. A control file is also backed up when structural changes such as the addition or deletion of a physical file occurs within the database. The command to automatically back up control files is CONTROLFILE AUTOBACKUP ON. Alternatively you may disable this option using the OFF keyword. Control file autobackups are only done to disk.

Practice 11: Configuring Controlfile Autobackup

This practice example demonstrates how to configure control file autobackups.

1. Launch RMAN, and connect to the target database. You may optionally connect to the recovery catalog database.

```
C:\> RMAN TARGET /
```

2. From the RMAN prompt, type the following command to turn on the control file autobackup feature.

```
RMAN>CONFIGURE CONTROLFILE AUTOBACKUP ON;
```

3. The FORMAT option may be used to explicitly specify the location of the controlfile autobackup. In the example shown below the control file will be automatically created in the C:\ drive.

```
RMAN>CONFIGURE CONTROLFILE AUTOBACKUP FORMAT
     FOR DEVICE TYPE DISK TO 'C:\%F';
```

4. The SHOW command is used to view the current control file autobackup setting.

```
RMAN>SHOW CONTROLFILE AUTOBACKUP;
```

5. To view the current format and location of control file autobackups you would issue:

```
RMAN>SHOW CONTROLFILE AUTOBACKUP FORMAT;
```

6. To clear the current configuration and reset it to the default:

```
RMAN>CONFIGURE CONTROLFILE AUTOBACKUP CLEAR;
```

7. To clear the location of the control file autobackup and reset it to the default, you may execute:

```
RMAN>CONFIGURE CONTROLFILE AUTOBACKUP FORMAT FOR
      DEVICE TYPE DISK CLEAR;
```

8. Exit RMAN.

```
RMAN> EXIT;
```

Configuring Default Backup Type The BACKUP TYPE option allows you to configure the default backup type. You may set it to be an image copy (COPY) or a backup set (BACKUPSET). Backupset is the default. These types of backups are explained in Chapter 2 of this book.

Practice 12: Configuring the Default Backup Type

This practice example demonstrates how to configure the default backup type.

1. Launch RMAN, and connect to the target database. You may optionally connect to the recovery catalog database.

```
C:\> RMAN TARGET /
```

2. At the RMAN prompt, execute the command shown to configure the backup type to be "backupset" when automatic channels perform backups to disk.

```
RMAN> CONFIGURE DEVICE TYPE DISK BACKUP TYPE TO BACKUPSET;
```

3. To configure the backup type to be an image copy, when automatic channels perform backups to disk, issue:

```
RMAN> CONFIGURE DEVICE TYPE DISK BACKUP TYPE TO COPY;
```

   In Oracle 10*g* backupsets may be compressed during their creation to save space and reduce the size of the backup file that is created. You would include the keyword COMPRESSED in the command.

4. To configure the backup type to be a compressed backupset, when automatic channels perform backups to disk, issue:

```
RMAN>CONFIGURE DEVICE TYPE DISK BACKUP TYPE
      TO COMPRESSED BACKUPSET;
```

5. To view the current setting for device type, use the SHOW command.

```
RMAN> SHOW DEVICE TYPE;
```

6. To clear the current configuration and reset the backup type to the default value, use the CLEAR option.

   ```
   RMAN> CONFIGURE DEVICE TYPE DISK CLEAR;
   ```

7. Exit RMAN.

   ```
   RMAN> EXIT;
   ```

Configuring the Default Location and Naming Format The CHANNEL DEVICE TYPE ... FORMAT option is available if you wish to specify the location and naming convention for backups created by automatic channels. Format elements may be used when establishing the file name. Table 1-1 displays some commonly used format elements. A combination of these format elements may be created to generate a unique name for the backup file that is created.

TABLE 1-1 Format elements that may be used for specifying a naming format

Format	Description
%d	Name of the database
%T	Specifies backup set timestamp
%s	Specifies backup set number
%p	Specifies backup piece number
%U	System-generated unique filename (This is the default)

Practice 13: Configuring the Default Location and Naming Format

This practice example demonstrates how you can configure the default location and naming format for backups.

1. Launch RMAN, and connect to the target database. You may optionally connect to the recovery catalog database.

   ```
   C:\> RMAN TARGET /
   ```

2. From the RMAN prompt, issue the command shown to ensure that backups created by automatic channels will be created in the C:\ drive with a file name format of bks_%d_%s_%p_%T.

   ```
   RMAN> CONFIGURE CHANNEL DEVICE TYPE DISK
         FORMAT 'C:\bks_%d_%s_%p_%T';
   ```

   A backup set created would have a name like bks_DB101_12_1_20050602, where DB101 is the name of the database, 12 is the backupset number, 1 is the backup piece number, and 20050602 is the timestamp (2nd June, 2005).

3. Exit RMAN.

   ```
   RMAN>EXIT
   ```

Setting RMAN parameters using EM

The persistent parameters of Recovery Manager may also be set using the Enterprise Manager (EM). We will set some of the configurations described earlier using EM.

Practice 14: Accessing Recovery Manager from Enterprise Manager

1. Launch a browser and specify the correct URL to start Enterprise Manager. Log in as a user with SYSDBA privileges.
2. In the **Database Control Home** page, select the **Maintenance** tab.
3. In the **Backup/Recovery Settings** section, select the link **Backup Settings**.
4. The **Backup Settings** page is displayed. You can configure RMAN options from this page. For example, you can configure the degree of parallelism to **3** for automatic channels and the default backup type to **Compressed Backup Set** from the DEVICE tab as shown in Figure 1-10.

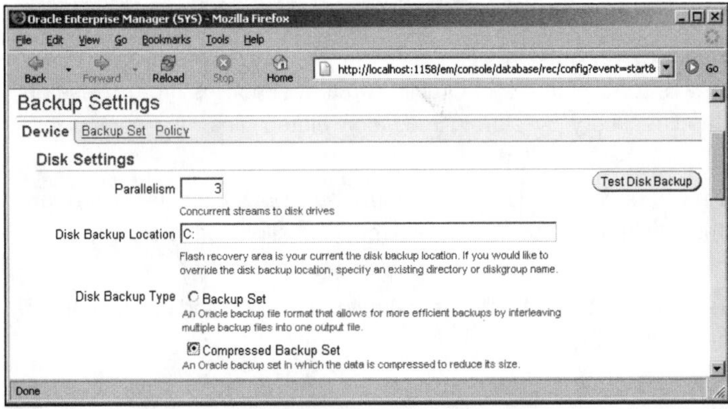

FIGURE 1-10 Configure RMAN parameters from EM.

5. You can choose to test the setting by selecting the button **Test Disk Backup**. Before selecting the button, make sure you enter valid **Host Credentials** at the bottom of the page.
6. You can set other options such as the MAXPIECESIZE and RETENTION POLICY by selecting the BACKUPSET tab and POLICY tab respectively.
7. Exit Enterprise Manager.

This chapter introduced you to the Recovery Manager. You learned some simple tasks such as launching RMAN and configuring parameters that govern its behavior. The chapter also reviewed the RMAN architecture and the Recovery Catalog database. In Chapter 2 you will learn how easy it is to perform backups using Recovery Manager.

Chapter Summary

- The RMAN utility simplifies the process of taking backups and performing restorations and recoveries.
- The options available for backing up the database depend on the archivelog mode of the database.
- The options for recovering the database in the event of failure depend on the backups available.
- The default archiving mode is noarchivelog.
- Production databases should operate in archivelog mode. This provides the ability to recover the database completely in the event of failure.
- The RMAN executable may be invoked using the command-line or using the Enterprise Manager.
- The RMAN repository is always stored in the control file of the target database; however, using a recovery catalog gives you the ability to use the complete functionality of RMAN.
- The flash recovery area is a new feature in Oracle 10*g* that simplifies the process of backup, restoration, and recovery by storing recovery-related files in a centralized location.
- Channels provide a means of communication between the RMAN executable, the target database, and the backup device. Channels may be allocated manually or automatically.
- Persistent parameters allow you to configure the behavior of RMAN and its components. They are stored in the RMAN repository.

Syntax Guide

SYNTAX GUIDE		
Element	Description	Example
RMAN	Command to launch the RMAN utility. It is to be invoked from the Operating system prompt.	`C:\>RMAN`
CONNECT	Command to connect to either the target database or recovery catalog database from within the RMAN utility.	`RMAN> CONNECT TARGET` `RMAN> CONNECT CATALOG "username/password@servicename"`
REGISTER	Command to register the target database within RMAN.	`RMAN> REGISTER DATABASE;`
CONFIGURE	Command to set or clear the value of a persistent parameter from within RMAN. The CLEAR keyword may be used to reset the persistent parameter back to its default value.	`RMAN> CONFIGURE CONTROLFILE AUTOBACKUP ON;` `RMAN> CONFIGURE CONTROLFILE AUTOBACKUP CLEAR;`

SYNTAX GUIDE		
Element	**Description**	**Example**
SHOW ALL	Command to display the current values held by all the persistent parameters of RMAN.	`RMAN> SHOW ALL;`
SHOW	Command to display the current value of a specific parameter.	`RMAN>SHOW RETENTION POLICY;`

Review Questions

1. A failure, such as the loss of a datafile, is known as a ________________ failure.
2. Name the optional file that is created using the contents of the redo log files.
3. Manual backups are done using the operating system ________________ command.
4. The database being backed up or recovered using RMAN is known as the ________________ database.
5. The RMAN repository is always stored in the ________________ of the target database.
6. The ________________ is a centralized area for storing backups.
7. The target database must be ________________ with the recovery catalog database.
8. Before performing a backup or a restore, a ________________ needs to be allocated.
9. The ________________ keyword when specified in the CONFIGURE command resets the parameter to its default value.
10. The ________________ command is used to set the configuration parameters for RMAN.
11. Identify the optional components of the RMAN. [Choose 2]
    a. RMAN Repository
    b. Flash Recovery Area
    c. Recovery Catalog
    d. Target database
12. The amount of RMAN information stored in the control file depends on the value of the ________________ initialization parameter.
    a. CONTROL_FILE_KEEP_TIME
    b. CONTROL_FILE_RECORD_KEEP_TIME
    c. CONTROL_FILE_KEEP_FOR_DAYS
13. The recovery catalog provides support for which of the following functions of RMAN? [Choose all that apply]
    a. Script creation and maintenance
    b. Short-term storage of RMAN data
    c. Long-term storage of RMAN data
    d. RMAN data for multiple databases
    e. Automatic backup of the control file

14. It is mandatory for the recovery catalog to be on a separate database on a separate server. True or False?
    a. TRUE
    b. FALSE
15. Which of the following roles, when assigned to a user, makes the user the owner of the recovery catalog?
    a. RECOVERY_CATALOG_USER
    b. RECOVERY_CATALOG_ROLE
    c. RECOVERY_CATALOG_OWNER
    d. None of the above
16. A backup command has been issued with a file naming format of " bk_%p_%s". Identify the correct filename using the format.
    a. bk_1_4 (where 1 is the backup piece number and 4 is the backupset number)
    b. bk_1_4 (where 1 is the backupset number and 4 is the backuppiece number)
    c. bk_db01_3 (where db01 is the database name and 3 is the backupset number)
    d. A name cannot be created successfully using this format
17. What is the name of the API that interfaces RMAN with sequential storage devices such as tapes?
    a. Media Management Interface
    b. Media API Layer
    c. Media Management Layer
    d. Management Media Interface
18. Which of the following commands may be used to display the configuration settings of RMAN?
    a. SHOW
    b. DISPLAY
    c. CONFIGURE
    d. PRESENT
19. Which process created on the target database is responsible for interacting with the backup media, when using RMAN?
    a. User Process
    b. Target Process
    c. Server Process
    d. Channel Process
20. What is the keyword used to reset the value of an RMAN parameter to its default value?
    a. REMOVE
    b. UNDO
    c. DEFAULT
    d. CLEAR

Hands-On Assignments

Assignment 1-1 Checking the archiving mode of the target database

1. Open SQL*Plus and log on as the SYSTEM user or the DB_ADMIN user.
2. Issue the ARCHIVE LOG LIST command to verify the archiving mode of the database.
3. If it is in ARCHIVELOG MODE with automatic archiving enabled you can go to Assignment 1-3. If you are in NOARCHIVELOG mode, perform Assignment 1-2.

Assignment 1-2 Changing the database to Archivelog mode with automatic archiving enabled

1. Open SQL*Plus and logon as the SYSTEM user or the DB_ADMIN user.
2. Shutdown the database using any option other than abort.
3. Mount the database.
4. Issue the command to put the database in archivelog mode.
5. Open the database.

Assignment 1-3 Launching RMAN and connecting to the target database

1. Open a command prompt, and set the ORACLE_SID to the target database (DB101).
2. At the prompt type the command to launch Recovery Manager.
3. At the RMAN prompt, issue the command to connect to the target database.
4. Exit RMAN.

Assignment 1-4 Connecting to the Recovery catalog database if one has been created

To perform this hands-on assignment successfully you must complete the steps mentioned in Practice 5 and Practice 7 of Chapter 1.

1. Open a command prompt, and set the ORACLE_SID to the target database.
2. Launch Recovery Manager.
3. At the RMAN prompt, issue the command to connect to the target database.
4. Issue the command to connect to the recovery catalog database. Make sure you specify the schema name of the recovery catalog owner during the connection.
5. Exit RMAN.

Assignment 1-5 Viewing the configuration parameters of RMAN

1. Launch RMAN and connect only to the target database. The RMAN repository should only be the control file.
2. Issue the command to display all the current configuration settings of RMAN.
3. Exit RMAN.

Assignment 1-6 Setting the persistent parameters of RMAN

1. Launch RMAN and connect to both the target database and the recovery catalog database.
2. Configure RMAN to automatically back up the control file whenever a BACKUP command is issued or a structural change to the database is made. Verify your change.

3. Configure RMAN to ensure that three valid backups are always maintained by RMAN, that is, set the RETENTION POLICY. Verify your change.
4. Configure the automatic channels to create backupsets during backup jobs to disk. Verify your change.
5. Configure the automatic channels that by default back up to disk to create compressed backupsets during backup jobs. Verify your change.
6. Configure the file naming format for automatic channels to be the database name_ backupset_backupiece_unique string. Verify the change.
7. Clear the change you made in the above step so that the default location and file-naming format is used. Verify your change.
8. Clear the retention policy to its default of REDUNDANCY 1. Verify your change.
9. Clear the control file autobackup configuration to its default value, OFF. Verify your change.
10. Exit RMAN.

Case Study

Ryan has now become quite comfortable launching RMAN and setting various configuration parameters. However, the senior DBA at Keller Medical Center has also been thinking of using Ryan's skills at user-managed backups to create custom scripts that create cold and hot backups. She has assigned Ryan the task of writing two scripts called **coldbackup.sql** and **hotbackup.sql**. These scripts, when executed from either SQL*Plus or iSQL*Plus, must back up the database using operating system commands. The following are the guidelines used by Ryan to create the script. As a case, write down the actual commands you would issue to perform the actions mentioned by Ryan.

Case 1: Script to take a cold backup of the database

1. Log on as the SYSTEM user or the DB_ADMIN user and create a list of the physical files of the database. You may query the V$DATAFILE, V$TEMPFILE, V$LOGFILE, and V$CONTROLFILE performance views.
2. Open SQL*Plus and issue **ed coldbackup.sql** to open the default editor. On Windows the editor is Notepad. The file called **coldbackup.sql** should contain the sequence of steps to create a cold consistent backup of the database.
3. Write appropriate commands within the **coldbackup.sql** file to perform the following sequence of steps.
   a. Connect as a user who has the SYSDBA role. You can use the SYS user or the DB_ADMIN user.
   b. Shut down the database using any option other than abort.
   c. Issue a series of host commands as in the sample shown. The host commands should copy all the physical files of the database to a backup device.

      For example, if all the datafiles of the database have an extension of .dbf, you can type;
      host copy <original location of files>.dbf e:\coldbackup*
      where <original location> refers to the directory containing the datafiles of the database and E:\coldbackup is the destination for the backup files.

d. Start up the database.

e. Save the script.

To verify that the script works, issue the `START <PATH>\coldbackup.sql` at the SQL prompt.

This script can be used whenever a cold backup of the database needs to be taken.

Case 2: Script to create a hot backup of the Database

1. Log on as the SYSTEM user or the DB_ADMIN user and create a list of all the tablespaces and their corresponding datafiles. You may query the DBA_DATA_FILES data dictionary view to obtain the information.
2. Open SQL*Plus and issue **ed hotbackup.sql** to open the default editor. The file **hotbackup.sql** should contain the sequence of steps to create a hot backup of the database.
3. Write the appropriate commands within the **hotbackup.sql** file to perform the following sequence of steps.
   a. For each of the tablespaces identified in step 1 you will repeat the following sequence of steps.
      i. Put the tablespace in backup mode.
      ii. Issue the operating system copy command and copy the datafiles of the tablespace to the backup location.
      iii. Take the tablespace off backup mode.

For example, if the USERS tablespace was being backed up and the datafiles belonging to the USERS tablespace were users01.dbf and users02.dbf, the steps you would write are:

```
ALTER TABLESPACE USERS BEGIN BACKUP;
Host copy <path>\users01.dbf  E:\hotbackup
Host copy <path>\users02.dbf E:\hotbackup
ALTER TABLESPACE USERS END BACKUP;
```

Note: The E:\hotbackup folder must exist to store the backups that are generated.

4. Save the hotbackup.sql file.
5. To verify if the script works issue `START <PATH>\hotbackup.sql` at the SQL prompt.

This script may be used whenever a hot backup of the database needs to be created.

CHAPTER 2

BACKUPS USING RMAN

LEARNING OBJECTIVES

After completing this lesson you should be able to understand:

- Flash Recovery Area
- Types of Backups
- Block Level Incremental Backups
- Commands for performing backups at various levels
- The RUN command
- Setting Duration and Throttling
- The Block Tracking Feature
- RMAN commands that displays information about backups

ORACLE CERTIFICATION EXAM OBJECTIVES COVERED IN THIS CHAPTER INCLUDE:

- Use the RMAN BACKUP command to create backup sets and image copies
- Enable block change tracking
- Manage the backups and image copies taken with RMAN with the LIST and REPORT commands

INTRODUCTION

Backing up the database is one of the primary functions of a database administrator. Data is vital to almost all enterprises and must be protected from failure and loss. A huge administrative burden lies on the DBA to ensure that backups are done in a timely and organized manner. Further, backups should also be tested periodically to ensure their validity.

In Chapter 2, you learned the architecture of Recovery Manager and the different methods available to launch RMAN. You also learned about the Recovery Catalog database that holds the RMAN repository.

In this chapter you will learn about the different options available to a database administrator to perform backups using RMAN. A number of examples and sample outputs are displayed in this chapter to help you understand how backups are performed. You will also learn how to group RMAN commands and run them as a single block and save them to a script for repetitive use. A number of new features included in Oracle 10*g* such as setting duration and throttling during backups, block change tracking , the Flash Recovery Area are also reviewed. In this chapter you will also learn how to perform RMAN backups using the Enterprise Manager. Finally, some commonly used commands to display information about the backups and the files that are in need of backup will be discussed.

THE CURRENT CHALLENGE AT KELLER MEDICAL CENTER

Backups at Keller Medical Center were being taken manually by the database administrators. This arrangement was working until the junior administrator who was performing the backups left suddenly. His temporary replacement was unable to locate the correct backup to perform an incomplete recovery when erroneous data had been accidentally committed into the PATIENT table. He finally succeeded with the recovery operation after a great deal of effort. The whole incident left the administrators frazzled, causing them to rethink their backup strategy. A decision was finally reached to use Oracle's much talked about backup tool called Recovery Manager.

Ryan, the new junior DBA has been trying to keep abreast of the new features in Oracle 10g as well as older features that he isn't quite comfortable with. He has already familiarized himself with the Recovery Manager tool and is eager to learn how to create backups using RMAN.

BACKING UP THE DATABASE USING RMAN

At this point you must be comfortable launching RMAN and setting various parameters. The target database, which needs to be backed up at Keller Medical Center, is the Oracle 10g database, called DB101. Backups of this database need to be taken using Recovery Manager. A recovery catalog database called RCDB has also been configured.

A new feature of Oracle 10g known as **Flash Recovery Area** can help database administrators manage backup, restoration, and recovery procedures. We begin this chapter by taking a closer look at the Flash Recovery Area and its configuration before we learn how to take backups using RMAN.

The Flash Recovery Area

The flash recovery area is a centralized location for the management of backup and recovery related files. Configuring a flash recovery area makes administering backup and recovery related files faster and simpler. Oracle can maintain backups of datafiles, control files, archive logs, and flashback logs within this area.

If the flash recovery area is configured, the archive destination indicated by the LOG_ARCHIVE_DEST_10 initialization parameter is automatically set to use it. Backupsets and Images copies (discussed later in this lesson) are also created in this area. Once you have configured a flash recovery area, it becomes the default location for storing backups and the location that RMAN looks at for files required when performing restorations and recoveries.

The flash recovery area may be a directory on the filesystem or an ASM disk. The flash recovery area may be created during database creation, if the database is created using the Database Configuration Assistant. It may be configured manually after database creation by specifying the DB_RECOVERY_FILE_DEST and DB_RECOVERY_FILE_DEST_SIZE initialization parameters.

The DB_RECOVERY_FILE_DEST initialization parameter is a mandatory parameter. It indicates the location of the flash recovery area. Its value is a location on disk (i.e., a directory or folder name) or an ASM disk. A null value for this parameter disables the flash recovery area.

The DB_RECOVERY_FILE_DEST_SIZE initialization parameter is also mandatory to enable the flash recovery area. It indicates the amount of space allotted to the flash recovery area. The value you assign for this parameter should consider the total database size, the size of all backups that need to be stored, and the total size of archive log files that have not yet been transferred to tape.

Practice 1

In this practice example you will view the parameters that are used to configure the Flash Recovery Area from within Enterprise Manager.

1. Launch OEM, and log in as a user with SYSDBA privileges.
2. The **Database Control Home** page will be displayed.
3. Select the **Administration** tab.
4. Under the section **Database Configuration** select the **All Initialization Parameters** link. Figure 2-1 displays the All Initialization Parameters link.
5. The **Initialization Parameters** page will be displayed. Scroll along the page until you reach DB_RECOVERY_FILE_DEST and DB_RECOVERY_FILE_DEST_SIZE parameters. Figure 2-2 displays the two parameters as viewed from Enterprise Manager.
6. Log out of Enterprise Manager.

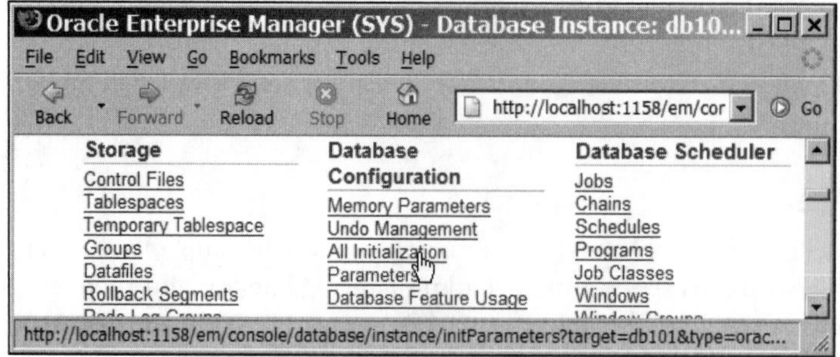

FIGURE 2-1 The All Initialization Parameters Link

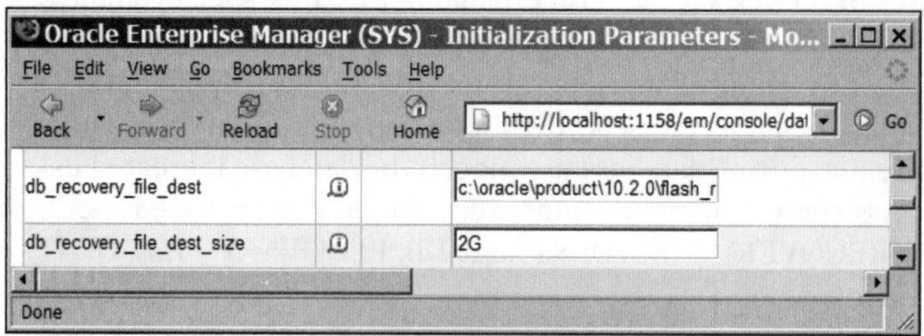

FIGURE 2-2 The parameters that configure the flash recovery area

Practice 2 Disabling the Flash Recovery Area

This practice demonstrates the configuration of the flash recovery area using SQL commands. The ALTER SYSTEM command is used to modify the values of initialization parameters. The SCOPE option may be set to indicate whether the change should affect just the current instance (MEMORY), future instances (SPFILE), or both current and future instances (BOTH).

1. Open SQL*Plus and connect as a user with SYSDBA privileges.

```
SQL> CONNECT DB_ADMIN/DB_ADMIN@DB101 AS SYSDBA
```

2. View the current values of the flash recovery parameters namely DB_RECOVERY_FILE_DEST and DB_RECOVERY_FILE_DEST_SIZE using the SHOW PARAMETER command.

```
SQL> SHOW PARAMETER DB_RECOVERY
```

3. Issue the ALTER SYSTEM command to disable the flash recovery area. Setting the DB_RECOVERY_FILE_DEST parameter to a null string will disable the flash recovery area.

```
SQL> ALTER SYSTEM SET DB_RECOVERY_FILE_DEST='' SCOPE=BOTH;
```

4. Next, issue the ARCHIVE LOG LIST command. The Archive Destination indicates the location of the archive files. This is the default location when the flash recovery area is disabled. Figure 2-3 displays the destination of the archive files as C:\ORACLE\PRODUCT\10.2.0\DB_1\RDBMS.

```
SQL> ARCHIVE LOG LIST;
```

```
Oracle SQL*Plus
File Edit Search Options Help
SQL> ARCHIVE LOG LIST;
Database log mode              Archive Mode
Automatic archival             Enabled
Archive destination            c:\oracle\product\10.2.0\db_1\RDBMS
Oldest online log sequence     5
Next log sequence to archive   7
Current log sequence           7
SQL>
```

FIGURE 2-3 The output of the Archive Log List command

5. Issue the ALTER SYSTEM command to dynamically change the value of the DB_RECOVERY_FILE_DEST initialization parameter. Create a directory called FRA in the C:\ drive and set the flash recovery area to C:\FRA. Oracle will automatically create a directory called DB101 (the same as the database name), under this directory.

```
SQL> ALTER SYSTEM SET DB_RECOVERY_FILE_DEST='C:\FRA' SCOPE=BOTH;
```

6. Re-issue the ARCHIVE LOG LIST command. The archive destination now displays as USE_DB_RECOVERY_FILE_DEST.

```
SQL> ARCHIVE LOG LIST;
Database log mode      Archive Mode
Automatic archival     Enabled
Archive destination    USE_DB_RECOVERY_FILE_DEST
Oldest online log sequence     31
Next log sequence to archive 33
Current log sequence           33
```

7. Next, issue the ALTER SYSTEM command to set the value of the DB_RECOVERY_FILE_DEST_SIZE initialization parameter. Set it to a value based on the amount of space you have on your machine. In the example it has been set to 20 G.

```
SQL> ALTER SYSTEM SET
      DB_RECOVERY_FILE_DEST_SIZE=20G SCOPE=BOTH;
```

8. Issue the SHOW PARAMETER command to view the parameters you set as part of this practice. Figure 2-4 displays the values of the parameters that configure the flash recovery area.

```
SQL> SHOW PARAMETER DB_RECOVERY
```

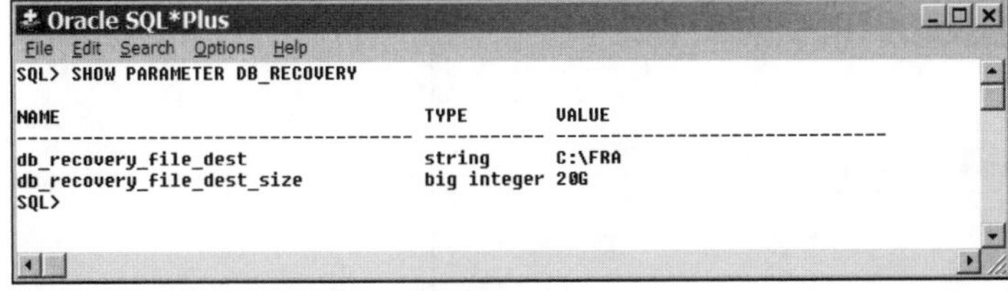

FIGURE 2-4 The parameters associated with the Flash Recovery Area

9. Exit SQL *Plus.

From this point on, the flash recovery area is C:\FRA and it becomes the default location for all backup files.

NOTE

To explicitly change the location of a backup you may use the FORMAT option of the RMAN BACKUP command.

As backups are stored in the flash recovery area, the space allocated to it is exhausted. The Enterprise Manager displays warnings when the flash recovery area becomes 85% (warning) and 97% (critical warning) full.

NOTE

Threshold warnings for the flash recovery area are automatically displayed by Oracle without any manual configuration.

When these warnings are issued, the administrator must take corrective action by adding more space or deleting obsolete files that are not required for recovery. If no action is taken and 100% of the space is used up, RMAN will automatically start deleting obsolete files and write a message to the Alert Log file. When space usage reaches 100%, the DBA may query the DBA_OUTSTANDING_ALERTS data dictionary view to view the recommended action for adding additional space to the flash recovery area.

A query similar to the one displayed below may be executed to see if Oracle has made any suggestions regarding the flash recovery area. Since the flash recovery area has just been created it is unlikely that any suggestions would be displayed.

```
SQL>SELECT SEQUENCE_ID, OBJECT_NAME, REASON, SUGGESTED_ACTION
     FROM DBA_OUTSTANDING_ALERTS;
```

The V$RECOVERY_FILE_DEST data dictionary view can be queried to determine the current location, disk quota, space in use and total number of files in the flash recovery area. The view can help you detect whether sufficient space has been allocated to the flash recovery area. Figure 2-5 displays the contents of the V$RECOVERY_FILE_DEST view.

```
SQL> SELECT * FROM V$RECOVERY_FILE_DEST;
```

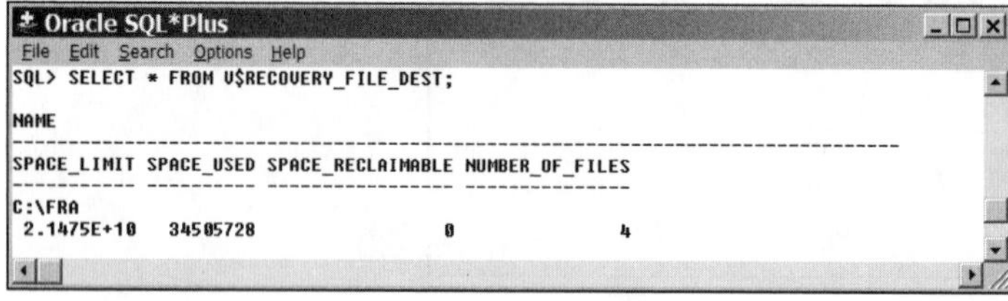

FIGURE 2-5 The contents of the V$RECOVERY_FILE_DEST view

Oracle recommends the configuration and use of the flash recovery area for managing backup and recovery related files.

BACKUP USING RMAN

In Chapter 1, you were introduced to Recovery Manager. You learned how to launch RMAN, configure the Recovery Catalog database, and set some of its persistent parameters. In this chapter you will learn how to use RMAN to backup the Oracle database.

Backing up the database is one of the primary functions of a database administrator. It ensures recovery in the event of failure or loss. To this end, it is important that you understand all the backup options available in Recovery Manager. You can then choose and decide on an appropriate backup strategy. It is also important to test and validate backups on a regular basis to ensure they can be utilized as expected if a failure occurs.

Types of Backup

You can backup datafiles, control files, and archivelog files using Recovery Manager. Redo log files are not backed up. To perform a backup using RMAN, the database must either be mounted or opened.

When operating the database in noarchivelog mode, RMAN can take a backup only when the database is mounted. When operating the database in archivelog mode the database may be mounted or opened during the backup.

Using Recovery Manager, two types of backups may be created. They are known as **backupsets** and **image copies**. The Figure 2-6 describes the different types of backup options available using RMAN.

Backupsets

A backupset is the output of a backup, done using Recovery Manager. A backupset is a logical object that stores the data that has been backed up in an RMAN-specific format. Backupsets require additional tasks to be performed during restoration; but are more space efficient. Backupsets are made up of backup pieces.

Backup pieces are the actual backup files that are created on the operating system. By default, backupsets always contain only a single backup piece, unless the DBA specifies an option to create multiple smaller backup pieces. A single backup piece can store data blocks from different datafiles in such a way that blocks of one datafile may be interspersed with the blocks of another datafile. As a result, RMAN performs additional steps during restoration to make the backup usable. This feature is known as **multiplexing**. In Figure 2-7 three datafiles are being backed up. Oracle creates a single backupset containing a single backup piece. Within the backup piece, Oracle writes a few blocks of datafile SYSAUX01.DBF, followed by a few blocks from USERS01.DBF, followed by blocks from INDX01.DBF, this is followed by blocks from SYSAUX01.DBF and this process continues for all the blocks from all 3 files. Multiplexing is achieved by using the FILESPERSET keyword when taking backups. Multiplexing reduces continuous I/O against the input datafiles during the backup process, especially when the backup is being done during a period of high activity.

Backupsets may be created on tape or on disk. A backupset may hold blocks from datafiles or archivelog files but never both. Archivelog files do not support the multiplexing

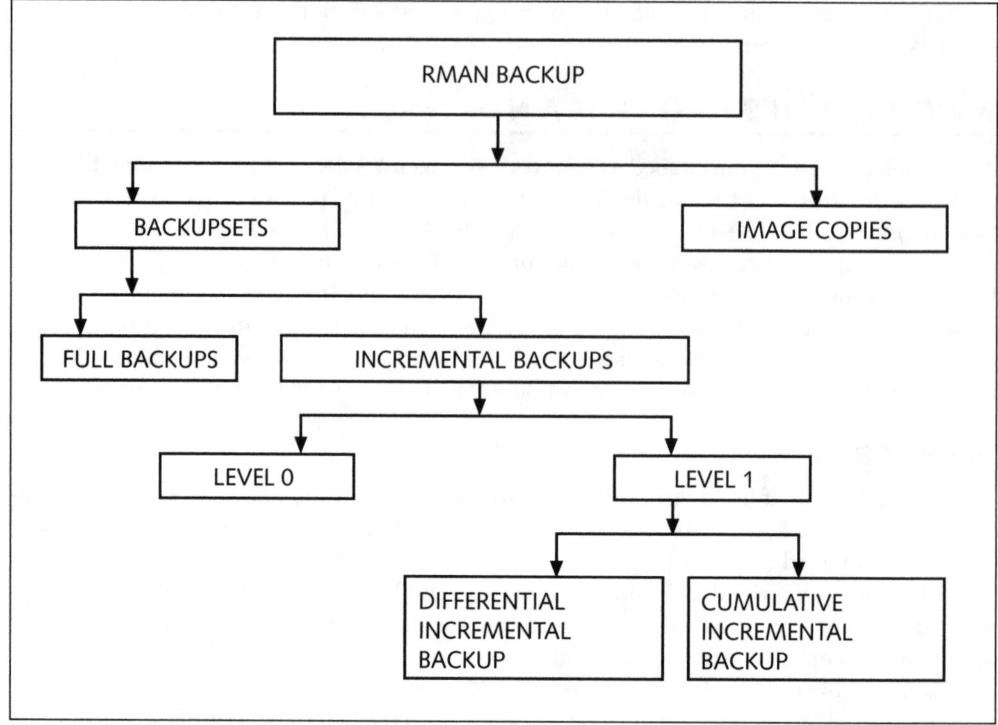

FIGURE 2-6 The backup options available using RMAN

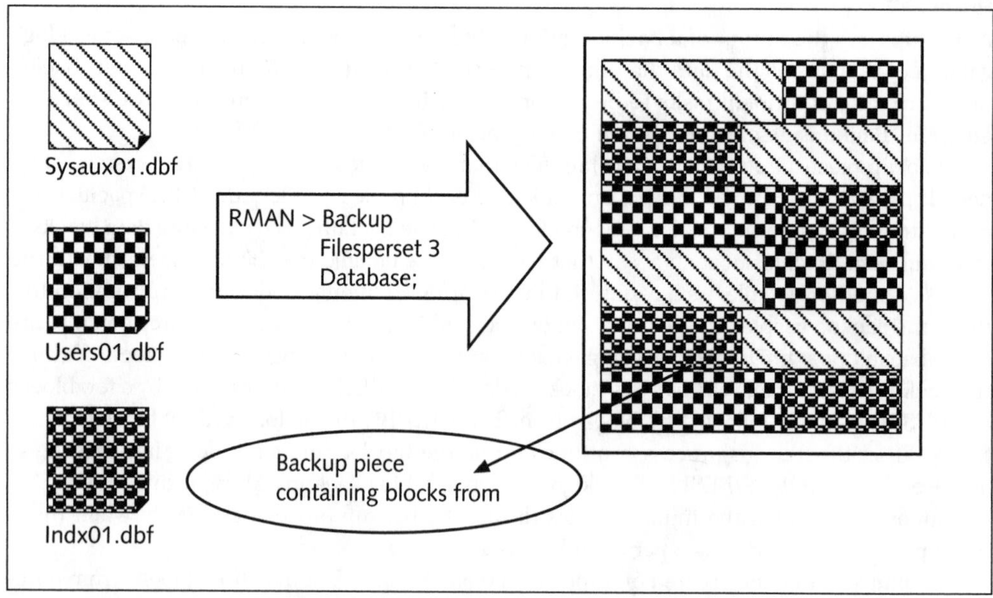

FIGURE 2-7 Multiplexing in a backup set

feature. When a BACKUP command is issued and both datafiles and archivelogs need to be backed up during the backup run, separate backupsets will be created, one for the datafiles and another for the archivelog files.

Backupsets never contain unused blocks in datafiles, which saves storage space. As a result, you may notice that the total size of the backup is smaller than the total size of the input files.

If the entire database or the datafiles of the SYSTEM tablespace are backed up, Oracle automatically includes the control file as part of the backup even if CONTROLFILE AUTOBACKUP has been disabled.

In Oracle 10g, backupsets may be compressed to further save storage space. The size of the compressed backup is considerably smaller than an uncompressed backupset. Compression is done using the COMPRESSED option of the CONFIGURE DEVICE TYPE or BACKUP command.

Backupsets are created using the BACKUP command of RMAN.

Full and Incremental Backups Using Recovery Manager, a DBA can create full or incremental backups. These options are only available with backupsets.

A full backup is a backup of all the used blocks of the datafiles. Blocks that have never been used are not copied.

An incremental backup is one that contains all the blocks that were modified since the previous incremental backup. The size of incremental backups is considerably smaller than a full backup. If you wish to use the incremental backup strategy, a base backup or a level 0 backup must be created first. It is against this level 0 backup that other incremental backups may be applied.

Using RMAN you can create incremental backups of the database, tablespaces, or individual datafiles. When performing incremental backups, Oracle reads the entire datafile even if very few changes were made to it. This can take a considerable amount of time. In Oracle 10g, a new feature called **Block Change Tracking** has been introduced to minimize the amount of time spent reading the datafile for modified blocks.

Incremental Backups may be taken at two levels, level 0 and level 1. A level 0 backup is similar to a full backup in that all the used blocks of the datafile are backed up. A level 1 backup is taken against a level 0. In an incremental backup strategy the base backup cannot be a full backup. It should always be a level 0 backup. A level 1 backup can be either differential or cumulative.

Differential Incremental Backup is a level 1 backup that backups up all blocks that have been modified since the most recent incremental level 0 or level 1 backup.

The following example describes a differential incremental backup strategy developed by Ryan.

"A level 0 backup of the entire database will be taken on Sunday. This will backup all used blocks in all the datafiles. On Monday, and all other days of the week—Monday through Saturday—a level 1 backup will be taken. The level 1 backup on Monday will backup all blocks modified since the level 0 backup taken on Sunday. The level 1 backup on Tuesday will backup all blocks modified since Monday's level 1 backup. The level 1 backup on Wednesday will backup all blocks modified since Tuesday's level 1 backup. This continues until Saturday. The level 0 backup taken on the following Sunday will backup all used blocks. This backup will render the first level 0 backup obsolete." Figure 2-8 illustrates his differential incremental backup strategy.

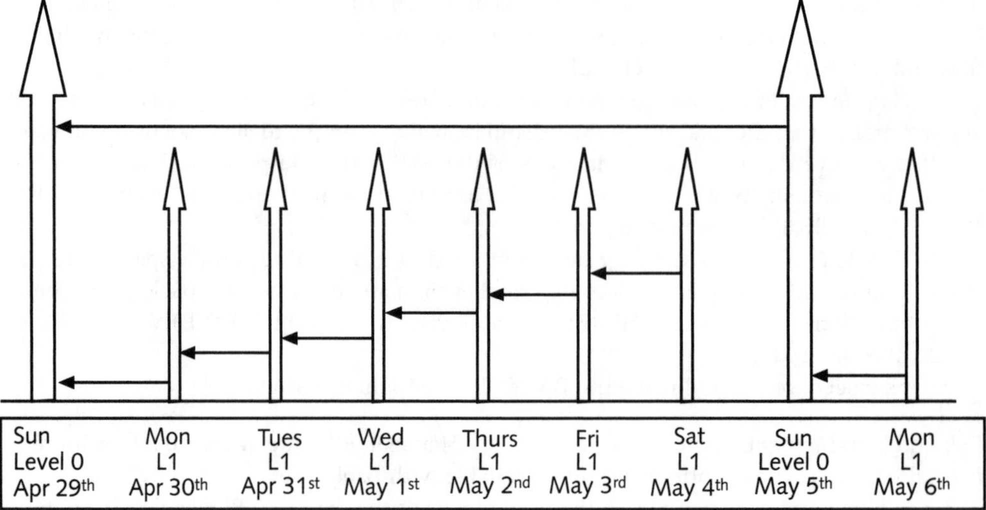

FIGURE 2-8 Differential Incremental Backups

Cumulative Incremental Backup is a level 1 backup that backs up all blocks that have been modified since the most recent incremental level 0 backup.

This next example describes a cumulative backup strategy developed by Ryan.

"A level 0 backup of the entire database will be taken on Sunday. This will backup all used blocks in all the datafiles. A level 1 backup will be taken on all other days of the week Monday through Saturday. The level 1 backup taken on Monday will copy all blocks modified since the most recent level 0 backup taken on Sunday. Tuesday's level 1 backup will also contain all blocks modified since Sunday's backup. Therefore Tuesday's backup includes the changes in Monday's backup. Wednesday's backup will contain all blocks modified since Sunday, and therefore will include both Monday's and Tuesday's backup. The cumulative backup on all subsequent days will include the incremental backup taken on the previous day(s). The level 0 backup taken the following Sunday will contain all used blocks. This will render the first level 0 backup obsolete." Figure 2-9 illustrates his cumulative incremental backup strategy.

Cumulative backups are larger in size than incremental backups and take longer to complete. However, the advantage of using the cumulative incremental strategy over differential can be seen during the process of recovery. If a failure occurs, fewer files need to be restored when using the cumulative method, though the changes to be applied would be the same for both. For example, if a failure occurred on Thursday May 2nd, after the backup was taken, restoration will involve restoring the level 0 backup taken on Sunday, and only Thursday's level 1 backup. If you were using the differential backup strategy and a similar failure occurred, you will restore the level 0 backup taken on Sunday and all level 1 backups taken Monday through Thursday.

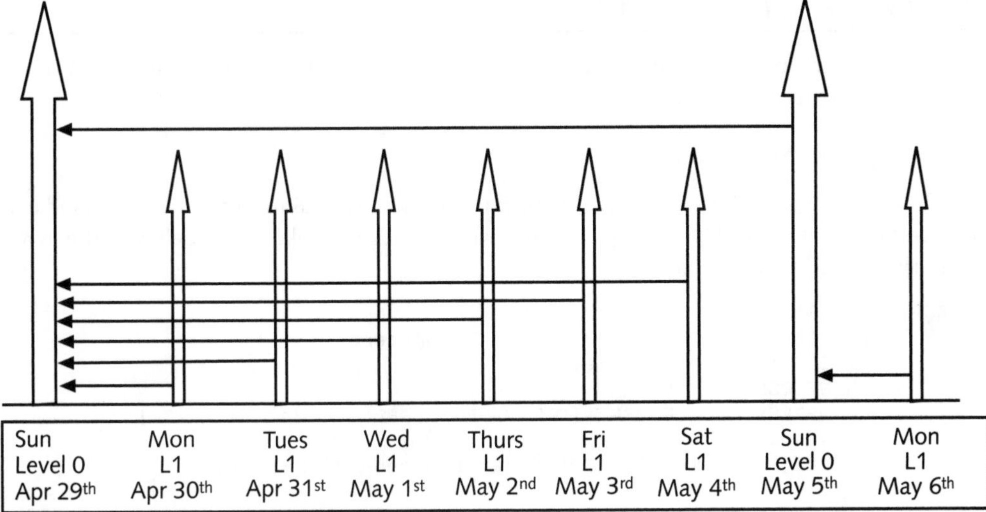

FIGURE 2-9 Cumulative Incremental Backups

Image Copies

Another type of backup that may be created using RMAN is an image copy. Image copies are identical to the actual physical file being backed up. Image copies are easier to work with because they can be used directly during the restoration process. For example, an image copy of a file USERS01.DBF with a size 2.5 GB will be an identical file with a size 2.5 GB. All the blocks of the input datafile, used or unused will be copied. Since this file is exactly like the original file, RMAN can use this file directly during the process of restoration.

An image copy is created using the COPY or the BACKUP AS COPY command of RMAN.

Parallelizing Backups

RMAN can perform backups in parallel to optimally use hardware resources and speed up the process of taking backups. To parallelize backups, multiple channels need to be allocated. This can be done using the CONFIGURE DEVICE TYPE PARALLELISM *n* command, where *n* is a numeric value greater than or equal to 1. The default value is 1.

If you have configured PARALLELISM to be greater than 1 and issue a backup command where more than one datafile is being backup up in a single command, parallel channels will be allocated to perform the backup. Each parallel channel will create a separate backupset.

If Ryan was to perform backups with a parallelism of 2 he would first configure multiple channels using:

```
RMAN> CONFIGURE DEVICE TYPE DISK PARALLELISM 2;
```

If he then issued a command to backup the datafiles 2 and 3 as shown in the example code below, two channels will be started simultaneously. The first channel will begin the backup of datafile 2 and the second channel will backup datafile 3. Two backupsets will be created.

```
RMAN> BACKUP DATAFILE 2, 3;
```

PERFORMING BACKUPS

In this part of the chapter, you will learn the RMAN commands and the options that may be issued to create backups.

The BACKUP Command

The BACKUP command is used to create backups in Recovery Manager. This command can be specified from the RMAN prompt or from within a RUN block. Given below is the syntax of the BACKUP command.

```
BACKUP DATABASE
       TABLESPACE {tablespacename [, tablespacename...]}
       DATAFILE {n|name[,n|name,...]}
       CURRENT CONTROLFILE
       AS COMPRESSED BACKUPSET [DATABASE | TABLESPACE | DATAFILE]
       ARCHIVELOG ALL
       AS COPY [DATABASE|TABLESPACE tablespacename| DATAFILE]
where:
```

`tablespacename`*:* is the name of the tablespace being backed up. More than a single tablespace name may be mentioned separated by commas.

`n:` stands for datafile number. More than one datafile name or number may be mentioned separated by commas.

As displayed by the syntax of the BACKUP command, it is possible to back up an entire database, one or more tablespaces or individual datafiles.

The last option displayed BACKUP AS COPY is used to create image copies.

Backup Command Options

When issuing the BACKUP command, you may also specify options to help you better manage the backups. Some available backup options are:

TAG: Is a user-defined string that can identify a backup. For example, a level 0 backup taken every Sunday may be tagged as `weekly_backup` and the level 1, taken daily, tagged as `daily_backup`. If you do not specify a tag, RMAN generates a default tag for backups using the format `TAGYYYYMMDDHHMMSS`, where `YYYY` is the year, `MM` is the month, `DD` is the day, `HH` is the hour (in 24-hour format), `MM` is the minutes, and `SS` is the seconds.

MAXSETSIZE: This keyword influences the number of backupsets created during a single backup run. Normally, when a BACKUP command is issued, RMAN puts all datafiles into a single backupset. Separate backupsets are created for the control file and archivelog files. You can have RMAN create multiple backupsets by specifying the MAXSETSIZE to a value larger than the largest datafile being backed up and less than the overall size of all files put together. For example, if the size of the largest file is 2 GB and the overall size of the backup was 6 GB, setting MAXSETSIZE to 3 GB, would result in 2 backupsets being created, each approximately 3 GB in size.

MAXPIECESIZE: This clause specifies the maximum size of a backup piece. The backup piece is the physical file that is created during a backup. If the backup media imposes restrictions on file size, specifying MAXPIECESIZE helps you to stay within the limits. Specifying the MAXPIECESIZE clause may result in multiple backup pieces being created in a backupset.

FORMAT: This option indicates the location and naming convention for the backup piece. If you do not specify it, then the location will be either the flash recovery area if one has been created, or the location specified in CONFIGURE CHANNEL DEVICE TYPE DISK FORMAT command. If neither have been configured or specified, a default location is used. Format elements may be used in the FORMAT option to define the name of the backup piece. Table 2-1 displays a list of the commonly used format elements. A complete list may be obtained from the Oracle Official Documentation.

TABLE 2-1 Format elements for the FORMAT command

Format Element	Description
%d	Database name
%N	Tablespace name
%p	Backup piece number
%s	Backup set number
%t	Specifies backup set timestamp
%T	Specifies the year, month and day in Gregorian calendar
%u	A system-generated unique filename

For example, a format "`db_%N_%T_%s_%p`" would create a backup piece with a name like `db_USERS_20051202_20_1`, where `db` is a prefix, `USERS` is the name of the tablespace, `20051202 is` the year (2005), month(12), and date(02), 20 the backupset number and 1 the backup piece number.

RATE: The default behavior of RMAN is to use all the available I/O bandwidth during reads and writes to disk. The database administrator may limit the I/O resources consumed by a backup job using the RATE option. For example, setting it to 500 K, limits RMAN to reading and writing 500 K of data per second on a channel. This option will not be available in future versions of Oracle.

Examples of Backing Up the Database

In this part of the chapter, a number of practice examples will be presented to help you understand how backups may be taken using RMAN.

Practice 3: Backing Up the Entire Database

This practice example demonstrates a backup of the entire database using the BACKUP DATABASE command. When the entire database is backed up, RMAN creates a number of backupsets. By default, the first backupset will contain all the datafiles of the database. The second backupset will contain the control file and the spfile of the database.

1. From the command prompt, set the ORACLE_SID to DB101. Connect to RMAN; connect to the target database and to the recovery catalog database if you have created one.

```
C:\>SET ORACLE_SID=DB101
C:\> RMAN
RMAN> CONNECT TARGET
RMAN> CONNECT CATALOG RMANUSER/RMANUSER@RCDB
```

2. Issue the following command to clear any modifications to the device type parameter.

```
RMAN> CONFIGURE DEVICE TYPE DISK CLEAR;
```

3. Issue the BACKUP DATABASE command to backup the entire database. Observe the output generated by RMAN. (The output may vary on your machine.)

```
RMAN> BACKUP DATABASE;
Starting backup at 01-DEC-05
using channel ORA_DISK_1
channel ORA_DISK_1: starting full datafile backupset
channel ORA_DISK_1: specifying datafile(s) in backupset
input datafile fno=00001 name=C:\ORACLE\PRODUCT\10.2.
0\ORADATA\DB101\SYSTEM01.DBF
input datafile fno=00003 name=C:\ORACLE\PRODUCT\10.2.
0\ORADATA\DB101\SYSAUX01.DBF
input datafile fno=00002 name=C:\ORACLE\PRODUCT\10.2.
0\ORADATA\DB101\UNDOTBS01.DBF
input datafile fno=00004 name=C:\ORACLE\PRODUCT\10.2.
0\ORADATA\DB101\USERS01.DBF
channel ORA_DISK_1: starting piece 1 at 01-DEC-05
channel ORA_DISK_1: finished piece 1 at 01-DEC-05
piece handle=C:\FRA\DB101\BACKUPSET\2005_12_01\O1_MF_NNNDF_
TAG20051201T151013_1RYP56C7_.
BKP tag=TAG20051201T151013 comment=NONE
channel ORA_DISK_1: backup set complete, elapsed time: 00:00:45
channel ORA_DISK_1: starting full datafile backupset
channel ORA_DISK_1: specifying datafile(s) in backupset
including current control file in backupset
including current SPFILE in backupset
channel ORA_DISK_1: starting piece 1 at 01-DEC-05
channel ORA_DISK_1: finished piece 1 at 01-DEC-05
piece handle=C:\FRA\DB101\BACKUPSET\2005_12_01\O1_MF_NCSNF_
TAG20051201T151013_1RYP6OGN_.
BKP tag=TAG20051201T151013 comment=NONE
channel ORA_DISK_1: backup set complete, elapsed time: 00:00:03
Finished backup at 01-DEC-05
```

Observe the following in the output displayed:

- The automatic channel allocated for the backup job is called ORA_DISK_1.
- Two backupsets are created for this backup. The first backupset consists of a single backup piece called O1_MF_NNNDF_TAG20051201T151013_1RYP56C7_.BKP. This backup piece contains all the datafiles of the database. The backup piece was created in 45 seconds indicated by elapsed time.

- The second backupset contains a backup piece consisting of the control file and spfile and is called O1_MF_NCSNF_TAG20051201T151013_1RYP6OGN_.BKP.
- The backup was done serially.
- The backup was done to the flash recovery area (C:\FRA).

The backup pieces are created in the flash recovery as shown in Figure 2-10. Also observe the DB101, BACKUPSET and 2005_12_01 (current timestamp) directories created in the flash recovery area.

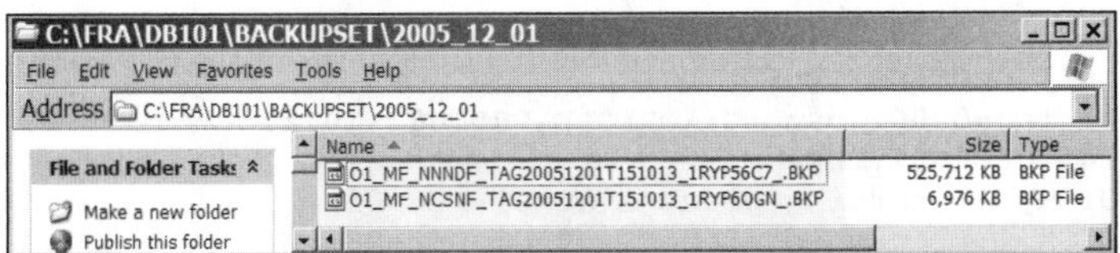

FIGURE 2-10 The resultant backup pieces of a complete backup of the database

4. If you wanted to explicitly specify the location and naming convention of the backupset, you could have used the FORMAT option in the BACKUP command. In this example, the entire database is being backed up to C:\RMAN\BACKUPS\. Please create the C:\RMAN\BACKUPS directory path before executing the command. A file naming format of db_%u_%d_%s_%p has been used.

```
RMAN> BACKUP DATABASE FORMAT 'C:\RMAN\BACKUPS\db_%u_%d_%s_%p';
Starting backup at 01-DEC-05
...
input datafile fno=00001 name=C:\ORACLE\PRODUCT\10.2.
0\ORADATA\DB101\SYSTEM01.DBF
...
channel ORA_DISK_1: finished piece 1 at 01-DEC-05
piece handle=C:\RMAN\BACKUPS\DB_09H57D6A_DB101_9_
1 tag=TAG20051201T151834 comment=NONE
...
channel ORA_DISK_1: backup set complete, elapsed time: 00:00:03
Finished backup at 01-DEC-05
```

   Observe the output; the backup piece is created in C:\RMAN\BACKUPS. The filename generated is DB_09H57D6A_DB101_9_1, where DB is a prefix, 09H57D6A is a unique eight-character string, DB101 is the name of the target database, 9 is the backupset number, and 1 the backup piece number.

5. By default, two backupsets are created after a backup of an entire database. In Figure 2-10, observe that the backupset that contains the input datafiles is approximately 525 MB. The size of the largest datafile in the database is 480 MB (not displayed in the figure). In the next backup command you will set MAXSETSIZE to 500 MB. This value is larger than the largest datafile, and less than the overall size of the backup.

```
RMAN> BACKUP DATABASE MAXSETSIZE=500M;
Starting backup at 01-DEC-05
using channel ORA_DISK_1
channel ORA_DISK_1: starting full datafile backupset
channel ORA_DISK_1: specifying datafile(s) in backupset
```

```
input datafile fno=00001 name=C:\ORACLE\PRODUCT\10.2.
0\ORADATA\DB101\SYSTEM01.DBF
channel ORA_DISK_1: starting piece 1 at 01-DEC-05
channel ORA_DISK_1: finished piece 1 at 01-DEC-05
piece handle=C:\FRA\DB101\BACKUPSET\2005_12_01\O1_MF_NNNDF_
TAG20051201T152314_1RYPXLNZ_.
BKP tag=TAG20051201T152314 comment=NONE
channel ORA_DISK_1: backup set complete, elapsed time: 00:00:35
channel ORA_DISK_1: starting full datafile backupset
channel ORA_DISK_1: specifying datafile(s) in backupset
input datafile fno=00003 name=C:\ORACLE\PRODUCT\10.2.
0\ORADATA\DB101\SYSAUX01.DBF
input datafile fno=00002 name=C:\ORACLE\PRODUCT\10.2.
0\ORADATA\DB101\UNDOTBS01.DBF
input datafile fno=00004 name=C:\ORACLE\PRODUCT\10.2.
0\ORADATA\DB101\USERS01.DBF
channel ORA_DISK_1: starting piece 1 at 01-DEC-05
channel ORA_DISK_1: finished piece 1 at 01-DEC-05
piece handle=C:\FRA\DB101\BACKUPSET\2005_12_01\O1_MF_NNNDF_
TAG20051201T152314_1RYPYP5C_.
BKP tag=TAG20051201T152314 comment=NONE
channel ORA_DISK_1: backup set complete, elapsed time: 00:00:16
channel ORA_DISK_1: starting full datafile backupset
channel ORA_DISK_1: specifying datafile(s) in backupset
including current control file in backupset
including current SPFILE in backupset
channel ORA_DISK_1: starting piece 1 at 01-DEC-05
channel ORA_DISK_1: finished piece 1 at 01-DEC-05
piece handle=C:\FRA\DB101\BACKUPSET\2005_12_01\O1_MF_NCSNF_
TAG20051201T152314_1RYPZ71G_.
BKP tag=TAG20051201T152314 comment=NONE
channel ORA_DISK_1: backup set complete, elapsed time: 00:00:03
Finished backup at 01-DEC-05
RMAN>
```

6. Observe the output generated by RMAN. Three backupsets are created this time.
7. The first backupset contains a single piece containing the blocks of SYSTEM01.DBF. The second backupset contains a single piece containing the blocks from the remaining datafiles. The third backupset contains a single piece consisting of the control file and spfile.
8. In Figure 2-11, you can see the three backup pieces created in the flash recovery area.

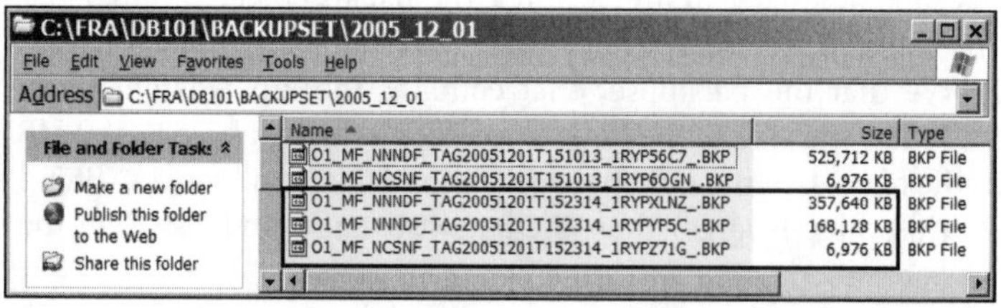

FIGURE 2-11 Three backupsets created by using the MAXSETSIZE clause

9. Exit RMAN.

The BACKUP TABLESPACE command may be used to back up one or more tablespaces. Multiple tablespaces may be backed up using a single command by separating the tablespace name with commas.

Practice 4: Backing Up Tablespaces

In this practice you will perform the steps to back up the SYSTEM tablespace.

NOTE

When the SYSTEM tablespace is backed up, the controlfile and spfile are also backed up automatically by RMAN.

1. Launch RMAN. Connect to the target database and to the recovery catalog database if you have created one. See Step 1 of Practice 3.
2. Backup the SYSTEM tablespace by using the BACKUP TABLESPACE command. In the output generated by RMAN, observe the automatic backup of the control file and spfile being done.

```
RMAN> BACKUP TABLESPACE SYSTEM;
Starting backup at 02-DEC-05
using target database control file instead of recovery catalog
allocated channel: ORA_DISK_1
channel ORA_DISK_1: sid=131 devtype=DISK
channel ORA_DISK_1: starting full datafile backupset
channel ORA_DISK_1: specifying datafile(s) in backupset
input datafile fno=00001 name=C:\ORACLE\PRODUCT\10.2.
0\ORADATA\DB101\SYSTEM01.DBF
channel ORA_DISK_1: starting piece 1 at 02-DEC-05
channel ORA_DISK_1: finished piece 1 at 02-DEC-05
piece handle=C:\FRA\DB101\BACKUPSET\2005_12_02\O1_MF_NNNDF_
TAG20051202T111816_1SOWY8VC_.
BKP tag=TAG20051202T111816 comment=NONE
channel ORA_DISK_1: backup set complete, elapsed time: 00:00:25
channel ORA_DISK_1: starting full datafile backupset
channel ORA_DISK_1: specifying datafile(s) in backupset
including current control file in backupset
including current SPFILE in backupset
channel ORA_DISK_1: starting piece 1 at 02-DEC-05
channel ORA_DISK_1: finished piece 1 at 02-DEC-05
piece handle=C:\FRA\DB101\BACKUPSET\2005_12_02\O1_MF_NCSNF_
TAG20051202T111816_1SOWZ3X9_.
BKP tag=TAG20051202T111816 comment=NONE
channel ORA_DISK_1: backup set complete, elapsed time: 00:00:02
Finished backup at 02-DEC-05
```

3. You can backup multiple tablespaces using a single command, as in:

```
RMAN> BACKUP TABLESPACE USERS,SYSAUX;
```

4. To specify a location for the backup use the FORMAT option. In this example the USERS tablespace is being backed up. You are providing the location and naming format "db_%N_%T_%s_%p" for the backup pieces. The tag USERBKP is a user-defined string to identify this backup.

```
RMAN> BACKUP TABLESPACE USERS FORMAT
      'C:\RMAN\BACKUPS\db_%N_%T_%s_%p' tag usersbkp;
```


In Figure 2-12, the output file called DB_USERS_20051202_18_1 is generated in C:\RMAN\BACKUPS and its size is 376K.

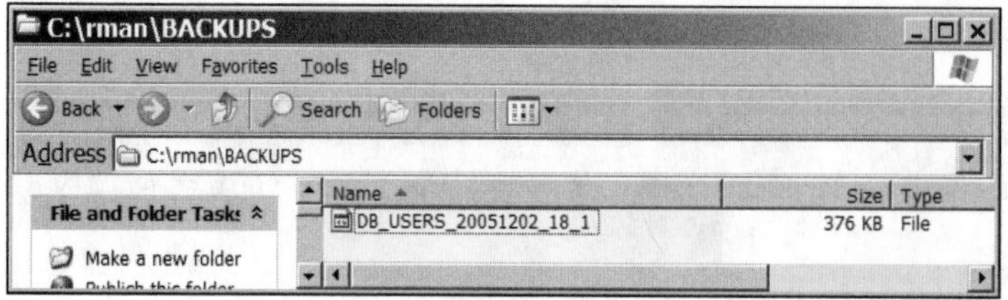

FIGURE 2-12 The output file generated by backing up the USERS tablespace

5. The MAXPIECESIZE influences the size of the backup pieces. The MAXPIECESIZE option can be specified in the CONFIGURE CHANNEL DEVICE TYPE command. It will establish the size of a backup piece created by an automatic channel. To set the maximum size of the backup piece as 100 K, type the following CONFIGURE command at the RMAN prompt.

```
RMAN> configure channel device type disk maxpiecesize=100k;
```

Now upon re-issuing the command to backup the USERS tablespace, RMAN creates 6 backup pieces within the same backupset. In the sample output shown, notice all backup pieces belong to backupset number 20, but have different backup piece numbers. The backup piece numbers run serially from 1 to 6. The number of backup pieces created may vary on your machine, however all the backup pieces must be less than 100K in size.

```
RMAN> BACKUP TABLESPACE USERS FORMAT
      'C:\RMAN\BACKUPS\DB_%N_%T_%S_%P';
STARTING BACKUP AT 02-DEC-05
ALLOCATED CHANNEL: ORA_DISK_1
CHANNEL ORA_DISK_1: SID=131 DEVTYPE=DISK
CHANNEL ORA_DISK_1: STARTING FULL DATAFILE BACKUPSET
CHANNEL ORA_DISK_1: SPECIFYING DATAFILE(S) IN BACKUPSET
INPUT DATAFILE FNO=00004 NAME=C:\ORACLE\PRODUCT\10.2.
0\ORADATA\DB101\USERS01.DBF
CHANNEL ORA_DISK_1: STARTING PIECE 1 AT 02-DEC-05
CHANNEL ORA_DISK_1: FINISHED PIECE 1 AT 02-DEC-05
PIECE HANDLE=C:\RMAN\BACKUPS\DB_USERS_20051202_20_
1 TAG=TAG20051202T113107 COMMENT=NONE
CHANNEL ORA_DISK_1: STARTING PIECE 2 AT 02-DEC-05
CHANNEL ORA_DISK_1: FINISHED PIECE 2 AT 02-DEC-05
PIECE HANDLE=C:\RMAN\BACKUPS\DB_USERS_20051202_20_
2 TAG=TAG20051202T113107 COMMENT=NONE
CHANNEL ORA_DISK_1: STARTING PIECE 3 AT 02-DEC-05
CHANNEL ORA_DISK_1: FINISHED PIECE 3 AT 02-DEC-05
PIECE HANDLE=C:\RMAN\BACKUPS\DB_USERS_20051202_20_
3 TAG=TAG20051202T113107 COMMENT=NONE
CHANNEL ORA_DISK_1: STARTING PIECE 4 AT 02-DEC-05
CHANNEL ORA_DISK_1: FINISHED PIECE 4 AT 02-DEC-05
```

```
PIECE HANDLE=C:\RMAN\BACKUPS\DB_USERS_20051202_20_
4 TAG=TAG20051202T113107 COMMENT=NONE
CHANNEL ORA_DISK_1: STARTING PIECE 5 AT 02-DEC-05
CHANNEL ORA_DISK_1: FINISHED PIECE 5 AT 02-DEC-05
PIECE HANDLE=C:\RMAN\BACKUPS\DB_USERS_20051202_20_
5 TAG=TAG20051202T113107 COMMENT=NONE
CHANNEL ORA_DISK_1: STARTING PIECE 6 AT 02-DEC-05
CHANNEL ORA_DISK_1: FINISHED PIECE 6 AT 02-DEC-05
PIECE HANDLE=C:\RMAN\BACKUPS\DB_USERS_20051202_20_
6 TAG=TAG20051202T113107 COMMENT=NONE
CHANNEL ORA_DISK_1: BACKUP SET COMPLETE, ELAPSED TIME: 00:00:06
FINISHED BACKUP AT 02-DEC-05
```

Figure 2-13 displays the backup pieces that were created. The backup pieces are all within 100 K.

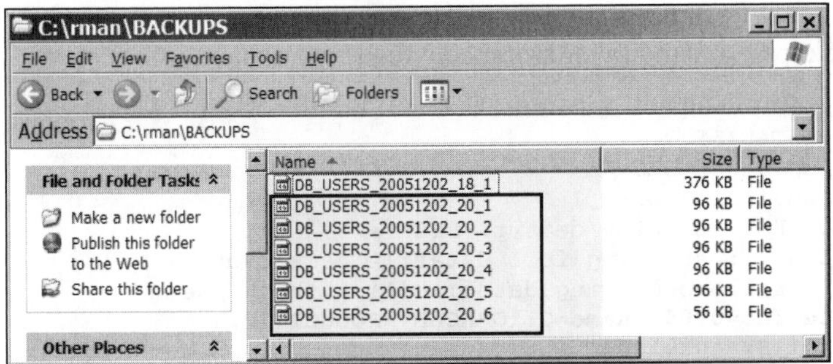

FIGURE 2-13 The backup pieces are below 100 K.

6. Clear the MAXPIECESIZE configuration by issuing the command:

   ```
   RMAN> CONFIGURE CHANNEL DEVICE TYPE DISK CLEAR;
   ```

7. Exit RMAN.

The RMAN command to back up datafiles is BACKUP DATAFILE. The name or number of the datafile can be specified. Multiple names/numbers may be specified in a single command separated by commas.

Practice 5: Backing up a datafile

In this practice example, you will back up some datafiles. If you are unsure about the datafile numbers; issue the REPORT SCHEMA command from the RMAN prompt.

1. Launch RMAN. Connect to the target database and to the recovery catalog database if you have created one. See Step 1 of Practice 3.
2. You can find the datafile number and name from within RMAN by using the REPORT SCHEMA command. In the output displayed by RMAN, observe the datafile number of the datafile called SYSAUX01.dbf is 3.

   ```
   RMAN> REPORT SCHEMA;
   REPORT OF DATABASE SCHEMA
   LIST OF PERMANENT DATAFILES
   ===========================
   FILE SIZE(MB) TABLESPACE RB SEGS
   DATAFILE NAME
   ```

```
---- -------- ---------- ------- ------------------------
1    470      SYSTEM    *** C:\ORACLE\PRODUCT\10.2.
0\ORADATA\DB101\SYSTEM01.DBF
2    25       UNDOTBS1           ***     C:\ORACLE\PRODUCT\10.
2.0\ORADATA\DB101\UNDOTBS01.DBF
3    240      SYSAUX             ***     C:\ORACLE\PRODUCT\10.
2.0\ORADATA\DB101\SYSAUX01.DBF
4    5        USERS              ***     C:\ORACLE\PRODUCT\10.
2.0\ORADATA\DB101\USERS01.DBF
List of Temporary Files
=======================
File Size(MB) Tablespace           Maxsize(MB)
Tempfile Name
---- -------- -------------------- ----------- ------------
1    20       TEMP                 32767        C:
\ORACLE\PRODUCT\10.2.0\ORADATA\DB101\TEMP01.DBF
```

3. To back up the datafile 3, issue the BACKUP DATAFILE command. You can specify the backup command by either specifying the datafile number or the name.

```
RMAN> BACKUP DATAFILE 3;
Starting backup at 02-DEC-05
allocated channel: ORA_DISK_1
channel ORA_DISK_1: sid=159 devtype=DISK
channel ORA_DISK_1: starting full datafile backupset
channel ORA_DISK_1: specifying datafile(s) in backupset
input datafile fno=00003 name=C:\ORACLE\PRODUCT\10.2.
0\ORADATA\DB101\SYSAUX01.DBF
channel ORA_DISK_1: starting piece 1 at 02-DEC-05
channel ORA_DISK_1: finished piece 1 at 02-DEC-05
piece handle=C:\FRA\DB101\BACKUPSET\2005_12_02\O1_MF_NNNDF_
TAG20051202T114449_1S0YJ25V_.
BKP tag=TAG20051202T114449 comment=NONE
channel ORA_DISK_1: backup set complete, elapsed time: 00:00:16
Finished backup at 02-DEC-05
```

NOTE

The command could have also been written using the datafile name.

```
RMAN> BACKUP DATAFILE
      'C:\ORACLE\PRODUCT\10.2.0\ORADATA\DB101\SYSAUX01.DBF';
```

4. Next, to backup two or more datafiles using a single command specify the datafile numbers one after another separated by a comma. To backup datafile 2 and 4, type:

```
RMAN> backup datafile 2,4;
```

5. Exit RMAN.

The current control file may be backed up using the BACKUP CURRENT CONTROLFILE command.

Practice 6: Backing up the current controlfile

This practice demonstrates a backup of the current controlfile.

1. Launch RMAN. Connect to the target database and to the recovery catalog database if you have created one. See Step 1 of Practice 3.
2. From the RMAN prompt, issue the command BACKUP CURRENT CONTROLFILE. A backupset containing the current controlfile will be created.

```
RMAN> BACKUP CURRENT CONTROLFILE;
Starting backup at 02-DEC-05
using channel ORA_DISK_1
channel ORA_DISK_1: starting full datafile backupset
channel ORA_DISK_1: specifying datafile(s) in backupset
including current control file in backupset
channel ORA_DISK_1: starting piece 1 at 02-DEC-05
channel ORA_DISK_1: finished piece 1 at 02-DEC-05
piece handle=C:\FRA\DB101\BACKUPSET\2005_12_02\O1_MF_NCNNF_
TAG20051202T114924_1S0YRO4D_.
BKP tag=TAG20051202T114924 comment=NONE
channel ORA_DISK_1: backup set complete, elapsed time: 00:00:02
Finished backup at 02-DEC-05
```

3. Exit RMAN.

Compressed backupsets occupy less space than uncompressed backupsets. Compressed backupsets were introduced in Oracle 10g. Compression is not possible on image copies.

Practice 7: Creating Compressed Backups

In this practice example you will create a compressed backup of the datafile 3.

1. Launch RMAN. Connect to the target database and to the recovery catalog database if you have created one. See Step 1 of Practice 3.
2. To create a compressed backupset of the datafile 3, type the command displayed below at the RMAN prompt.

```
RMAN> BACKUP AS COMPRESSED BACKUPSET DATAFILE 3;
Starting backup at 02-DEC-05
using channel ORA_DISK_1
channel ORA_DISK_1: starting compressed full datafile backupset
channel ORA_DISK_1: specifying datafile(s) in backupset
input datafile fno=00003 name=C:\ORACLE\PRODUCT\10.2.
0\ORADATA\DB101\SYSAUX01.DBF
channel ORA_DISK_1: starting piece 1 at 02-DEC-05
channel ORA_DISK_1: finished piece 1 at 02-DEC-05
piece handle=C:\FRA\DB101\BACKUPSET\2005_12_02\O1_MF_NNNDF_
TAG20051202T115230_1S0YYGWB_.
BKP tag=TAG20051202T115230 comment=NONE
channel ORA_DISK_1: backup set complete, elapsed time: 00:00:15
Finished backup at 02-DEC-05
```

In Figure 2-14, notice the sizes of the uncompressed (created in Practice 5) and compressed backupsets created for datafile 3. The compressed backupset has a size of 12,128 KB whereas the uncompressed backupset has a size of 148,280 KB.

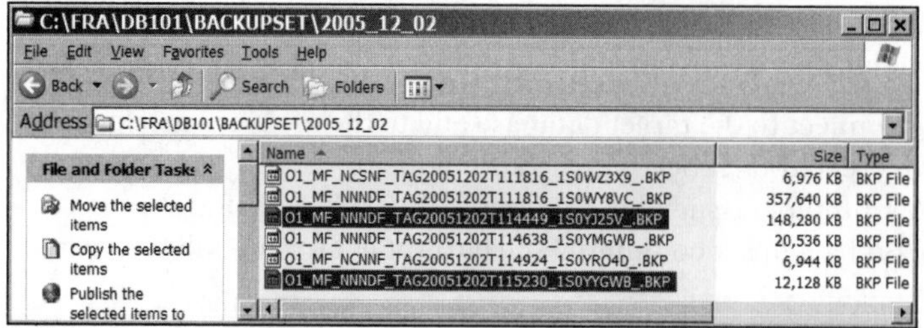

FIGURE 2-14 Comparing the sizes of compressed and uncompressed backupsets

3. Exit RMAN.

The BACKUP ARCHIVELOG command may be used to back up archivelog files. The DELETE INPUT clause may also be specified when backing up the archivelog files. This clause results in the deletion of archivelog files after they have been backed up. This frees up space for new archive log files that will be generated. To backup archivelog files that were created within a certain time frame use the BACKUP ARCHIVELOG... FROM TIME ... UNTIL TIME command.

Practice 8: Backing up Archivelog Files

This practice example displays the BACKUP ARCHIVELOG command along with a number of different options.

1. Launch RMAN. Connect to the target database and to the recovery catalog database if you have created one. See Step 1 of Practice 3.
2. From the RMAN prompt, issue the BACKUP ARCHIVELOG ALL command to back up all the archivelog files.

```
RMAN> BACKUP ARCHIVELOG ALL;
Starting backup at 02-DEC-05
current log archived
using channel ORA_DISK_1
channel ORA_DISK_1: starting archive log backupset
channel ORA_DISK_1: specifying archive log(s) in backup set
input archive log thread=1 sequence=8 recid=6 stamp=575985348
channel ORA_DISK_1: starting piece 1 at 02-DEC-05
channel ORA_DISK_1: finished piece 1 at 02-DEC-05
piece handle=C:\FRA\DB101\BACKUPSET\2005_12_02\O1_MF_ANNNN_
TAG20051202T115548_1S0Z4P00_.
BKP tag=TAG20051202T115548 comment=NONE
channel ORA_DISK_1: backup set complete, elapsed time: 00:00:02
Finished backup at 02-DEC-05
```

3. You will now issue a BACKUP ARCHIVELOG command with the DELETE INPUT clause to delete the archivelog files after they have been backed up.

```
RMAN> BACKUP ARCHIVELOG ALL DELETE INPUT;
Starting backup at 02-DEC-05
current log archived
using channel ORA_DISK_1
channel ORA_DISK_1: starting archive log backupset
channel ORA_DISK_1: specifying archive log(s) in backup set
```

```
input archive log thread=1 sequence=8 recid=6 stamp=575985348
input archive log thread=1 sequence=9 recid=7 stamp=575985452
channel ORA_DISK_1: starting piece 1 at 02-DEC-05
channel ORA_DISK_1: finished piece 1 at 02-DEC-05
piece handle=C:\FRA\DB101\BACKUPSET\2005_12_02\O1_MF_ANNNN_
TAG20051202T115732_1S0Z7XM1_.
BKP tag=TAG20051202T115732 comment=NONE
channel ORA_DISK_1: backup set complete, elapsed time: 00:00:02
channel ORA_DISK_1: deleting archive log(s)
archive log filename=C:\FRA\DB101\ARCHIVELOG\2005_12_02\O1_MF_1_
8_1S0Z4N2G_.ARC
recid=6 stamp=575985348
archive log filename=C:\FRA\DB101\ARCHIVELOG\2005_12_02\O1_MF_1_
9_1S0Z7VSW_.ARC
recid=7 stamp=575985452
Finished backup at 02-DEC-05
```

The output shows you how the archive logs are deleted one by one, after the backupset has been created.

4. To backup archivelog files generated in the past two days, execute:

```
RMAN> BACKUP ARCHIVELOG
      FROM TIME 'SYSDATE-2' UNTIL TIME 'SYSDATE';
```

5. Exit RMAN.

Incremental backups allow the database administrator, to create smaller backups that take less time to complete. When implementing an incremental backup strategy, you can choose from either differential (the default) or cumulative backups. The first backup that you must take in either case should be a level 0 backup. This backup acts as a base against which all other incremental backups can be applied.

Practice 9: Performing Incremental Backups

This practice example demonstrates the creation of incremental backups using RMAN.

1. Launch RMAN. Connect to the target database and to the recovery catalog database if you have created one. See Step 1 of Practice 3.
2. Create a Level 0 incremental backup of the entire database. At the RMAN prompt type:

```
RMAN> BACKUP INCREMENTAL LEVEL 0 DATABASE;
Starting backup at 02-DEC-05
using channel ORA_DISK_1
channel ORA_DISK_1:
 starting incremental level 0 datafile backupset
channel ORA_DISK_1: specifying datafile(s) in backupset
input datafile fno=00001 name=C:\ORACLE\PRODUCT\10.2.
0\ORADATA\DB101\SYSTEM01.DBF
input datafile fno=00003 name=C:\ORACLE\PRODUCT\10.2.
0\ORADATA\DB101\SYSAUX01.DBF
input datafile fno=00002 name=C:\ORACLE\PRODUCT\10.2.
0\ORADATA\DB101\UNDOTBS01.DBF
input datafile fno=00004 name=C:\ORACLE\PRODUCT\10.2.
0\ORADATA\DB101\USERS01.DBF
channel ORA_DISK_1: starting piece 1 at 02-DEC-05
channel ORA_DISK_1: finished piece 1 at 02-DEC-05
```

```
piece handle=C:\FRA\DB101\BACKUPSET\2005_12_02\O1_MF_NNND0_
TAG20051202T120039_1S
0ZFR3F_.BKP tag=TAG20051202T120039 comment=NONE
channel ORA_DISK_1: backup set complete, elapsed time: 00:00:45
channel ORA_DISK_1:
 starting incremental level 0 datafile backupset
channel ORA_DISK_1: specifying datafile(s) in backupset
including current control file in backupset
including current SPFILE in backupset
channel ORA_DISK_1: starting piece 1 at 02-DEC-05
channel ORA_DISK_1: finished piece 1 at 02-DEC-05
piece handle=C:\FRA\DB101\BACKUPSET\2005_12_02\O1_MF_NCSN0_
TAG20051202T120039_1S
0ZH7TV_.BKP tag=TAG20051202T120039 comment=NONE
channel ORA_DISK_1: backup set complete, elapsed time: 00:00:03
Finished backup at 02-DEC-05
```

3. Incremental backups may be taken at a tablespace or datafile level also. To take a Level 0 incremental backup of the datafiles 2 and 4, execute:

```
RMAN> BACKUP INCREMENTAL LEVEL 0 DATAFILE 2,4;
```

4. To create a Level 0 incremental backup of the USERS tablespace, execute:

```
RMAN> BACKUP INCREMENTAL LEVEL 0 TABLESPACE USERS;
```

5. To create a Level 1 incremental backup of the USERS tablespace, execute:

```
RMAN> BACKUP INCREMENTAL LEVEL 1 TABLESPACE USERS;
```

6. To create a cumulative Level 1 backup use the word CUMULATIVE. A cumulative Level 1 backup of the USERS tablespace can be taken by issuing:

```
RMAN> BACKUP INCREMENTAL LEVEL 1 CUMULATIVE TABLESPACE USERS;
```

7. Exit RMAN.

In Oracle 10*g*, image copies of the entire database, a tablespace, or a datafile can be created using a single command. The BACKUP AS COPY command is used to create image copies. When the DATABASE keyword is used, RMAN creates an image copy of every datafile in the database. It finally creates an image copy of the controlfile and a backupset containing the spfile.

Practice 10: Creating Image Copies

In the following practice, you will create a number of image copies. The backup options such as TAG and FORMAT may be applied to image copies as well.

1. Launch RMAN. Connect to the target database and to the recovery catalog database if you have created one. See Step 1 of Practice 3.
2. From the RMAN prompt issue the BACKUP AS COPY command. The keyword DATABASE indicates you wish to take a full database backup.

```
RMAN> BACKUP AS COPY DATABASE;
Starting backup at 02-DEC-05
using channel ORA_DISK_1
channel ORA_DISK_1: starting datafile copy
input datafile fno=00001 name=C:\ORACLE\PRODUCT\10.2.
0\ORADATA\DB101\SYSTEM01.DBF
```

```
output filename=C:\FRA\DB101\DATAFILE\O1_MF_SYSTEM_1S0ZOL4W_.
DBF tag=TAG20051202T120449 recid=1 stamp=575985914
channel ORA_DISK_1: datafile copy complete, elapsed time: 00:
00:25
channel ORA_DISK_1: starting datafile copy
input datafile fno=00003 name=C:\ORACLE\PRODUCT\10.2.
0\ORADATA\DB101\SYSAUX01.DBF
output filename=C:\FRA\DB101\DATAFILE\O1_MF_SYSAUX_1S0ZPCGN_.
DBF tag=TAG20051202T120449 recid=2 stamp=575985927
channel ORA_DISK_1: datafile copy complete, elapsed time: 00:
00:15
channel ORA_DISK_1: starting datafile copy
input datafile fno=00002 name=C:\ORACLE\PRODUCT\10.2.
0\ORADATA\DB101\UNDOTBS01.DBF
output filename=C:\FRA\DB101\DATAFILE\O1_MF_UNDOTBS1_1S0ZPTWB_.
DBF tag=TAG20051202T120449 recid=3 stamp=575985932
channel ORA_DISK_1: datafile copy complete, elapsed time: 00:
00:03
channel ORA_DISK_1: starting datafile copy
input datafile fno=00004 name=C:\ORACLE\PRODUCT\10.2.
0\ORADATA\DB101\USERS01.DBF
output filename=C:\FRA\DB101\DATAFILE\O1_MF_USERS_1S0ZPY5C_.
DBF tag=TAG20051202T120449 recid=4 stamp=575985934
channel ORA_DISK_1: datafile copy complete, elapsed time: 00:
00:01
channel ORA_DISK_1: starting datafile copy
copying current control file
output filename=C:\FRA\DB101\CONTROLFILE\O1_MF_
TAG20051202T120449_1S0ZPZB8_.
CTL tag=TAG20051202T120449 recid=5 stamp=575985935
channel ORA_DISK_1: datafile copy complete, elapsed time: 00:
00:01
channel ORA_DISK_1: starting full datafile backupset
channel ORA_DISK_1: specifying datafile(s) in backupset
including current SPFILE in backupset
channel ORA_DISK_1: starting piece 1 at 02-DEC-05
channel ORA_DISK_1: finished piece 1 at 02-DEC-05
piece handle=C:\FRA\DB101\BACKUPSET\2005_12_02\O1_MF_NNSNF_
TAG20051202T120449_1S0ZQ1J3_.
BKP tag=TAG20051202T120449 comment=NONE
channel ORA_DISK_1: backup set complete, elapsed time: 00:00:02
Finished backup at 02-DEC-05
```

In the output of the command notice for every input file there is a corresponding output file. Directories called DATAFILE and CONTROLFILE are also automatically created in the flash recovery area to hold the image copies of the datafiles and control files respectively.

Figure 2-15 displays the different directories created in the flash recovery area to separate the different kinds of backups.

3. To create image copies of all the files belonging to the USERS tablespace, and give the backup a tag "USERS_WLY_BKP", execute:

```
RMAN> BACKUP AS COPY TAG "USERS_WKLY_BKP" TABLESPACE USERS;
```

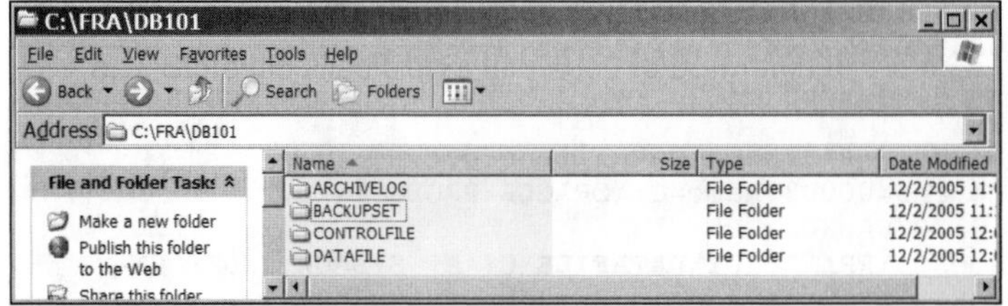

FIGURE 2-15 Directories created in the flash recovery area

4. To create an image copy of a single datafile, use the DATAFILE keyword. To create an image copy of the datafile 4, type:

   ```
   RMAN> BACKUP AS COPY DATAFILE 4;
   ```

5. Exit RMAN.

The RUN Command

The RUN command can be used to group a sequence of RMAN commands and then execute them as a single block. The commands to be executed must be enclosed within curly braces {}. The RUN command allows you to run daily, weekly, or monthly backups in the form of a sequence of commands. If you are using a recovery catalog database the RUN block may be saved to a script for repetitive use.

Practice 11: Using the RUN command

The creation of a RUN block that backs up the entire database followed by the archivelog files has been presented in this practice example.

1. Launch RMAN. Connect to the target database and to the recovery catalog database if you have created one. See Step 1 of Practice 3.
2. From the RMAN prompt, write the block shown below. You are first backing up the entire database and then all the archivelog files.

   ```
   RMAN> RUN
         {ALLOCATE CHANNEL C1 TYPE DISK;
         BACKUP DATABASE FORMAT 'db_%d_%s_%u'
         TAG MONTHLY_BACKUP;
         BACKUP FORMAT 'arch_%t_%s_%p'
         (ARCHIVELOG ALL);}
         released channel: ORA_DISK_1
         allocated channel: C1
         channel C1: sid=159 devtype=DISK
         Starting backup at 02-DEC-05
         channel C1: starting full datafile backupset
         channel C1: specifying datafile(s) in backupset
         input datafile fno=00001 name=C:\ORACLE\PRODUCT\10.2.
         0\ORADATA\DB101\SYSTEM01.DBF
         input datafile fno=00003 name=C:\ORACLE\PRODUCT\10.2.
         0\ORADATA\DB101\SYSAUX01.DBF
         input datafile fno=00002 name=C:\ORACLE\PRODUCT\10.2.
         0\ORADATA\DB101\UNDOTBS01.DBF
   ```

```
input datafile fno=00004 name=C:\ORACLE\PRODUCT\10.2.
0\ORADATA\DB101\USERS01.DBF
channel C1: starting piece 1 at 02-DEC-05
channel C1: finished piece 1 at 02-DEC-05
piece handle=C:\ORACLE\PRODUCT\10.2.0\DB_1\DATABASE\DB_
DB101_42_1AH59MH9 tag=MONTHLY_BACKUP comment=NONE
channel C1: backup set complete, elapsed time: 00:00:45
channel C1: starting full datafile backupset
channel C1: specifying datafile(s) in backupset
including current control file in backupset
including current SPFILE in backupset
channel C1: starting piece 1 at 02-DEC-05
channel C1: finished piece 1 at 02-DEC-05
piece handle=C:\ORACLE\PRODUCT\10.2.0\DB_1\DATABASE\DB_
DB101_43_1BH59MIM tag=MONTHLY_BACKUP comment=NONE
channel C1: backup set complete, elapsed time: 00:00:03
Finished backup at 02-DEC-05
Starting backup at 02-DEC-05
current log archived
channel C1: starting archive log backupset
channel C1: specifying archive log(s) in backup set
input archive log thread=1 sequence=10 recid=8 stamp=575986269
channel C1: starting piece 1 at 02-DEC-05
channel C1: finished piece 1 at 02-DEC-05
piece handle=C:\ORACLE\PRODUCT\10.2.0\DB_1\DATABASE\ARCH_
575986269_44_1 tag=TAG20051202T121109 comment=NONE
channel C1: backup set complete, elapsed time: 00:00:02
Finished backup at 02-DEC-05
released channel: C1
RMAN>
```

The ALLOCATE CHANNEL command manually allocates a channel called C1 for the backup job. The channel C1 creates a backupset containing all the datafiles, followed by a backupset containing the controlfile and spfile. The archivelog files are put in a separate backupset. The location of the backup is automatically chosen as C:\ORACLE\PRODUCT\10.2.0\DB_1\DATABASE because you did not specify a location in the FORMAT command.

3. Exit RMAN.

Creating a Script

Scripts are a sequence of RMAN commands that are stored under a name and may be used repetitively. The ability to create and maintain scripts is possible only when using a recovery catalog. A script is created and stored in the recovery catalog using a CREATE SCRIPT command. It may be executed whenever required by the EXECUTE SCRIPT command.

Practice 12: Creating and Executing an RMAN script

This practice example demonstrates the creation and execution of an RMAN script called "monthly_backup" that is used to back up the entire database and all the archivelog files.

1. Launch RMAN; connect to the target database and to the recovery catalog database.

```
C:\> RMAN
RMAN> CONNECT TARGET
RMAN> CONNECT CATALOG RMANUSER/RMANUSER@RCDB
```

2. Type the following CREATE SCRIPT command at the RMAN prompt. A script called monthly_backup that performs backup of the entire database/ archivelogs will be created in the recovery catalog database.

```
RMAN> CREATE SCRIPT MONTHLY_BACKUP
      {BACKUP DATABASE FORMAT 'db_%d_%s_%u'
      TAG MONTHLY_BACKUP;
      BACKUP FORMAT 'arch_%t_%s_%p'
      (ARCHIVELOG ALL);}
```

3. To execute the script, create a run block and type the EXECUTE SCRIPT command.

```
RMAN> RUN
      {EXECUTE SCRIPT MONTHLY_BACKUP;}
```

4. Exit RMAN.

Setting Duration and Throttling

The amount of time taken to complete a backup may be influenced by the RATE option of the ALLOCATE CHANNEL or CONFIGURE CHANNEL command. This option specifies how many bytes an RMAN channel can read per second per file. For example, if Ryan had created a backup job for a file of size 600 K, with a RATE of 1 KB per second, the backup would have taken 600 seconds or 10 minutes to complete. The RATE option has been made obsolete in Oracle 10*g* and has been replaced with the DURATION command.

The DURATION command allows the database administrator to specify a time limit within which the backup job must complete. If the job does not complete in the allotted time, an error is displayed and the job is aborted. You can also provide a longer time frame for the backup job. This will allow RMAN to control the throttling speed accordingly and control the use of system resources.

The syntax for the DURATION command is:

```
DURATION <hours>:<minutes>[PARTIAL][MINIMIZE<TIME>|<LOAD>]
```

An explanation of the syntax is given in the following section:

PARTIAL: If the backup does not complete within the allotted time specified by DURATION, an "abort" error is not reported. However, the backup job will be terminated. All backup pieces created within the time frame will be cataloged. If you do not specify the PARTIAL keyword and the job does not complete in the allotted time, a "job aborted" error will be displayed and none of the backup pieces will be cataloged.

MINIMIZE TIME: This command indicates that Recovery Manager should minimize the time taken to complete the backup. This will cause RMAN to run at full speed, using all the system resources it requires to finish the backup job.

MINIMIZE LOAD: This command indicates that Recovery Manager should minimize the load on the system resources. Using this option causes RMAN to automatically self-monitor its speed and reduce its speed if it determines that the backup can be completed in less than the allotted time. This option is not available when writing to tape drives.

Practice 13: Specifying Duration and Throttling during Backup

In this practice you will execute a number of backup commands using the DURATION clause.

1. Launch RMAN and connect to the target database.
2. First, take a backup of the database, without using the DURATION clause to see how long a typical backup of the database will take. At the RMAN prompt, type:

```
RMAN> BACKUP DATABASE;
Starting backup at 02-DEC-05
using channel ORA_DISK_1
channel ORA_DISK_1: starting full datafile backupset
...
handle=C:\FRA\DB101\BACKUPSET\2005_12_02\O1_MF_NNNDF_
TAG20051202T102319_1BXT2S60_.BKP comment=NONE
channel ORA_DISK_1: backup set complete, elapsed time: 00:01:06
...
piece handle=C:\FRA\DB101\BACKUPSET\2005_12_02\O1_MF_NCSNF_
TAG20051202T102319_1BXT4TL7_.BKP comment=NONE
channel ORA_DISK_1: backup set complete, elapsed time: 00:00:02
Finished backup at 02-DEC-05
```

From the output above, notice that the first backupset was created in 1 minute and 6 seconds and the second backupset was created in 2 seconds.

3. Next, issue a backup command with a duration of 2 minutes. Use the MINIMIZE LOAD clause so that RMAN self-regulates its speed to complete the job within 2 minutes. If you recieve an error indicating that the backup job was aborted, repeat the command with a longer time duration.

```
RMAN> BACKUP DURATION 0:02 MINIMIZE LOAD DATABASE;
Starting backup at 02-DEC-05
allocated channel: ORA_DISK_1
channel ORA_DISK_1: sid=137 devtype=DISK
channel ORA_DISK_1: starting full datafile backupset
channel ORA_DISK_1: specifying datafile(s) in backupset
input datafile fno=00001 name=C:\ORACLE\PRODUCT\10.2.
0\ORADATA\DB101\SYSTEM01.DBF
input datafile fno=00003 name=C:\ORACLE\PRODUCT\10.2.
0\ORADATA\DB101\SYSAUX01.DBF
input datafile fno=00002 name=C:\ORACLE\PRODUCT\10.2.
0\ORADATA\DB101\UNDOTBS01.DBF
input datafile fno=00004 name=C:\ORACLE\PRODUCT\10.2.
0\ORADATA\DB101\USERS01.DBF
channel ORA_DISK_1: starting piece 1 at 02-DEC-05
channel ORA_DISK_1: finished piece 1 at 02-DEC-05
piece handle= C:\FRA\DB101\BACKUPSET\2005_12_02\O1_MF_NNNDF_
TAG20051202T101832_1BXSST9X_.BKP comment=NONE
channel ORA_DISK_1: backup set complete, elapsed time: 00:01:45
channel ORA_DISK_1: throttle time: 0:00:55
channel ORA_DISK_1: starting full datafile backupset
channel ORA_DISK_1: specifying datafile(s) in backupset
including current controlfile in backupset
including current SPFILE in backupset
channel ORA_DISK_1: starting piece 1 at 02-DEC-05
channel ORA_DISK_1: finished piece 1 at 02-DEC-05
piece handle= C:\FRA\DB101\BACKUPSET\2005_12_02\O1_MF_NCSNF_
TAG20051202T101832_1BXSX3P4_.BKP comment=NONE
channel ORA_DISK_1: backup set complete, elapsed time: 00:00:16
channel ORA_DISK_1: throttle time: 0:00:06
Finished backup at 02-DEC-05
```

The backup job took longer this time. The first backupset was completed in 1 minute and 45 seconds. The second backupset was created in 16 seconds. Throttle time was 55 seconds for the first backupset and 6 seconds for the second one.

4. In this next example, you are giving RMAN only 1 minute to complete the backup. RMAN runs at a default speed to complete the job in the allotted time. However, because the PARTIAL keyword is not specified an error is generated and the job aborted.

```
RMAN> BACKUP DURATION 0:01 DATABASE;
Starting backup at 02-DEC-05
using channel ORA_DISK_1
channel ORA_DISK_1: starting full datafile backupset
channel ORA_DISK_1: specifying datafile(s) in backupset
input datafile fno=00001 name=C:\ORACLE\PRODUCT\10.2.
0\ORADATA\DB101\SYSTEM01.DBF
input datafile fno=00003 name=C:\ORACLE\PRODUCT\10.2.
0\ORADATA\DB101\SYSAUX01.DBF
input datafile fno=00002 name=C:\ORACLE\PRODUCT\10.2.
0\ORADATA\DB101\UNDOTBS01.DBF
input datafile fno=00004 name=C:\ORACLE\PRODUCT\10.2.
0\ORADATA\DB101\USERS01.DBF
channel ORA_DISK_1: starting piece 1 at 02-DEC-05
RMAN-00571:
 ===========================================================
RMAN-00569: ===== ERROR MESSAGE STACK FOLLOWS =======
RMAN-00571:
 ===========================================================
RMAN-03009: failure of backup command on ORA_DISK_
1 channel at 12/02/2005 10:27:51
ORA-19591:
 backup aborted because job time exceeded duration time
```

5. Next, issue a backup using the PARTIAL keyword. If RMAN is unable to complete the backup, an "abort" error will not be displayed.

```
RMAN> BACKUP DURATION 0:01 PARTIAL MINIMIZE LOAD DATABASE;
Starting backup at 02-DEC-05
using channel ORA_DISK_1
channel ORA_DISK_1: starting full datafile backupset
channel ORA_DISK_1: specifying datafile(s) in backupset
input datafile fno=00001 name=C:\ORACLE\PRODUCT\10.2.
0\ORADATA\DB101\SYSTEM01.DBF
input datafile fno=00003 name=C:\ORACLE\PRODUCT\10.2.
0\ORADATA\DB101\SYSAUX01.DBF
input datafile fno=00002 name=C:\ORACLE\PRODUCT\10.2.
0\ORADATA\DB101\UNDOTBS01.DBF
input datafile fno=00004 name=C:\ORACLE\PRODUCT\10.2.
0\ORADATA\DB101\USERS01.DBF
channel ORA_DISK_1: starting piece 1 at 02-DEC-05
channel ORA_DISK_1: finished piece 1 at 02-DEC-05
piece handle= C:\FRA\DB101\BACKUPSET\2005_12_02\O1_MF_NNNDF_
TAG20051202T104231_1BXV6RKQ_.BKP comment=NONE
channel ORA_DISK_1: backup set complete, elapsed time: 00:01:05
backup of controlfile was cancelled
RMAN-00571:
 ===========================================================
RMAN-00569: ========= ERROR MESSAGE STACK FOLLOWS =====
```

```
RMAN-00571:
===========================================================
RMAN-00601: fatal error in recovery manager
RMAN-03004: fatal error during execution of command
RMAN-00600: internal error, arguments [12106] [SPFILE] [] [] []
```

Note that even though the backup job did not complete, the backup piece that was created called O1_MF_NNNDF_TAG20051202T104231_1BXV6RKQ_.BKP is cataloged in the RMAN repository.

6. Exit RMAN.

Block Change Tracking

This is a new feature introduced in Oracle 10*g* that reduces the amount of time taken for incremental backups. As you are already aware, during incremental backups only those blocks that were modified since the most recent incremental backup are backed up.

Prior to Oracle 10*g*, before performing an incremental backup the entire datafile had to be read to determine which blocks were modified. This process could take a considerable amount of time depending on the size of the file and the number of changes made. As a solution to this problem, Oracle 10*g* has provided the block change tracking feature.

NOTE

The Block Change Tracking feature is also known as Fast Incremental Backups

In block change tracking, the Oracle Database tracks the physical location of all database changes in a separate file called the **Change Tracking File**. When an incremental backup needs to be done, it reads this file to determine which blocks need to be backed up. This eliminates reading the entire datafile, which was a time-consuming step.

When a change occurs to a block, the **Change Tracking Writer (CTWR)** background process writes the change to the change tracking file. The minimum size of the change tracking file is 10 MB, and additional space is allocated to it in 10 MB increments.

You can enable block change tracking for your database explicitly by a SQL command or using Enterprise Manager. The V$BLOCK_CHANGE_TRACKING data dictionary view can be queried to see the details of block change tracking. By default, block change tracking is disabled in a database. The ALTER DATABASE ENABLE BLOCK CHANGE TRACKING USING FILE '*change_tracking_filename*'; command is used to enable block change tracking using SQL.

Practice 14: Enabling Block Change Tracking using SQL*Plus

The steps in this practice describe how you can enable block change tracking within the DB101 database using SQL*Plus.

1. Launch SQL*Plus and connect as a privileged user, such as DB_ADMIN.

```
SQL> CONNECT DB_ADMIN/DB_ADMIN
```

2. Issue a SELECT command on the V$BLOCK_CHANGE_TRACKING view to display the current status of block change tracking in the database. (See Figure 2-16.)

```
SQL> SELECT * FROM V$BLOCK_CHANGE_TRACKING;
```

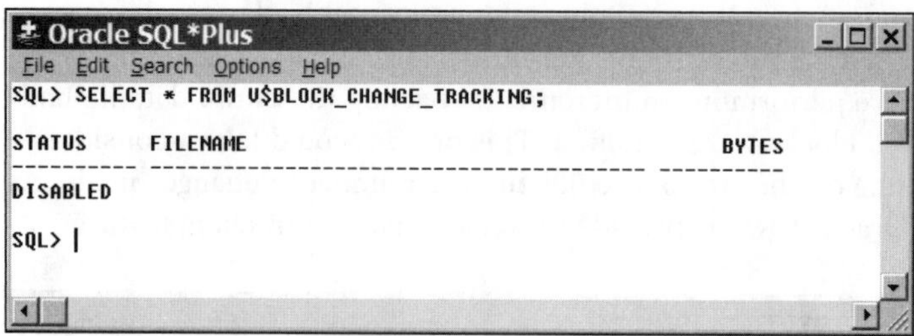

FIGURE 2-16 Viewing the status of block change tracking

3. In the C:\>drive create a folder called BCT. Use the ALTER DATABASE command to enable block change tracking. The USING FILE clause is used to indicate the location and name of the block change tracking file. The example creates the file in the C:\BCT directory. Choose an appropriate location to create the block change tracking file on your machine (see Figure 2-17).

```
SQL> ALTER DATABASE ENABLE BLOCK CHANGE TRACKING
     USING FILE 'C:\BCT\BCTFILE.CHG';
```

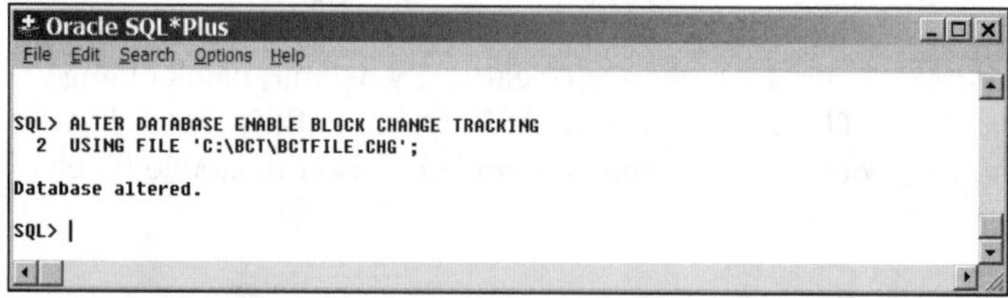

FIGURE 2-17 Enabling block change tracking

Figure 2-18 displays the file BCTFILE.CHG that is created in the C:\BCT directory.

4. Re-issue the SELECT * FROM V$BLOCK_CHANGE_TRACKING command to view the status of block change tracking in the database (see Figure 2-19).

```
SQL> SELECT * FROM V$BLOCK_CHANGE_TRACKING;
```

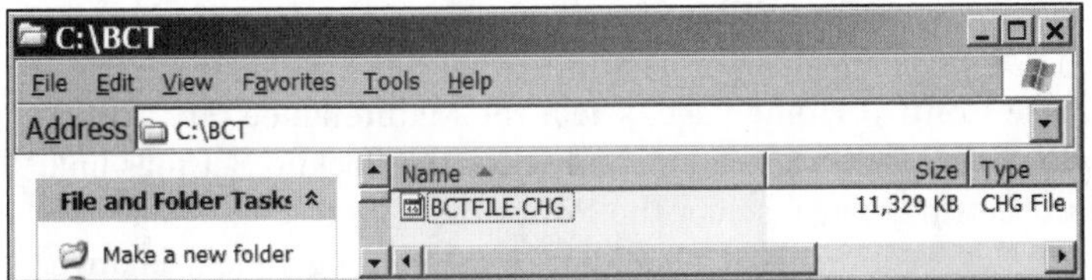

FIGURE 2-18 The block change tracking file

```
SQL> SELECT * FROM V$BLOCK_CHANGE_TRACKING;

STATUS               FILENAME                                    BYTES
-------------------- ---------------------------------------- ----------
ENABLED              C:\BCT\BCTFILE.CHG                         11599872

SQL>
```

FIGURE 2-19 Status of block change tracking after enabling it

5. You can use the DISABLE option of the ALTER DATABASE command to disable block change tracking. Upon re-querying the V$BLOCK_CHANGE_TRACKING view, the STATUS column will now indicate DISABLED (see Figure 2-20).

   ```
   SQL> ALTER DATABASE DISABLE BLOCK CHANGE TRACKING;
   ```

6. Re-issue the SELECT * FROM V$BLOCK_CHANGE_TRACKING command to view the status of block change tracking in the database.

   ```
   SQL> SELECT * FROM V$BLOCK_CHANGE_TRACKING;
   ```

```
SQL> SELECT * FROM V$BLOCK_CHANGE_TRACKING;

STATUS     FILENAME                  BYTES
---------- -------------------- ----------
DISABLED

SQL>
```

FIGURE 2-20 Status of block change tracking after disabling it

7. Exit SQL*Plus.

Practice 15: Configuring Block Change Tracking using Enterprise Manager

This practice example demonstrates the configuration of block change tracking using Enterprise Manager.

1. Launch a browser and enter the URL to access the Oracle Enterprise Manager. When prompted, log in as a user with SYSDBA privileges.
2. From the **Database Control Home** page, select the **Maintenance** tab.
3. Go the **Backup/Recovery Settings** section, and select the **Backup Settings** link.
4. From the **Backup Settings** page, select the **Policy** tab.
5. Under **Backup Policy** section, is a **checkbox** for Enabling Block Change tracking. You can also specify the **name of the block change tracking file** (see Figure 2-21).

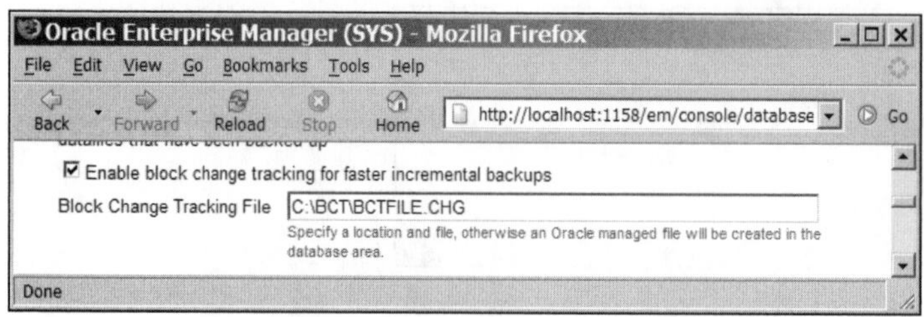

FIGURE 2-21 Enabling block change tracking from Oracle Enterprise Manager

6. **Uncheck** Enable Block Change Tracking for faster incremental backup. This will disable block change tracking. Select the **OK** button at the bottom of the page.
7. Log out of Enterprise Manager.

BACKUPS USING ENTERPRISE MANAGER

You can schedule backups from Enterprise Manager. This process of scheduling backups is relatively simple and it may be performed automatically at a scheduled time based on your selections. In EM, you can schedule two kinds of backups, **Oracle Suggested Backup Method** and a **Customized** backup.

The Oracle Suggested method of backup is an out-of-the-box backup strategy that is based on the backup destination. By default, Oracle 10g uses the retention policy of "recovery window of 1 day" for this backup method. Also, if you were backing to disk, a full backup is first done, followed by incremental backups. The backups on disk will be retained so that you can always perform a full database recovery or point in time recovery to any time within the past 1 day.

In the customized method, you have more control over the backup and can specify how and when you want the backups to be performed. You can select what kind of backup you wish to perform, such as, the whole database, specific tablespaces, datafiles, archivelogs, or archivelogs that have not already been backed to tape.

You may also choose between a full and incremental backup. The backup can be either an online or offline backup in which case the database will be mounted. When backing up archive files you can choose to delete the original archive files after the backup is done.

The backup job you create will be assigned a name. Finally, you can schedule the backup job to run immediately or at a later time. A repeat sequence may also be specified.

Practice 16: Performing Backups using Enterprise Manager

This practice example demonstrates a complete backup of the database including archivelog files using Enterprise Manager.

1. Launch a browser and enter the URL to start Oracle Enterprise Manager. Log in as a user with SYSDBA privileges.
2. From the **Database Control Home** page, select the **Maintenance** tab.
3. Under the **Backup/Recovery** section, select the **Schedule Backup** link.
4. The **Schedule Backup** page will be displayed. Figure 2-22 displays the Schedule Backup page. Two distinct sections Oracle-Suggested Backup and Customized Backup are available on this page.

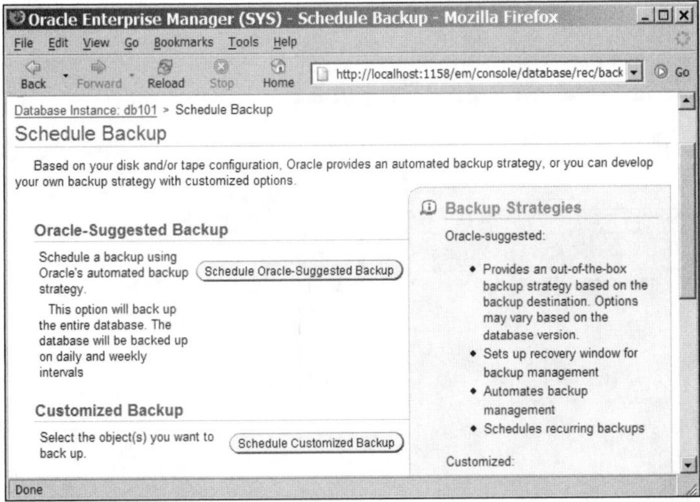

FIGURE 2-22 The Schedule Backup Page

5. Scroll to the **Customized Backup** section.
6. Select the option **Whole Database**.
7. Enter the operating system **Host Credentials** and **Password**, if you are unsure about what you are to enter please ask your instructor.
8. Then select the **Schedule Customized Backup** button.
9. The **Schedule Customized Backup: Options** page will be displayed. Figure 2-23 displays the **Schedule Customized Backup: Options** page.
10. On this page select **Full Backup** from the Backup Type section.
11. Next select **Online Backup** from the Backup Mode section.
12. **Check** the box that says **Also back up all archived logs on disk**.
    Figure 2-23 and Figure 2-24 display the options you will select on the **Schedule Customized Backup: Options** page.
13. Select the **Next** Button to move to the next page.
14. The **Schedule Customized Backup: Settings** page will be displayed.
15. The page will display the location on the disk where the backup will be done.

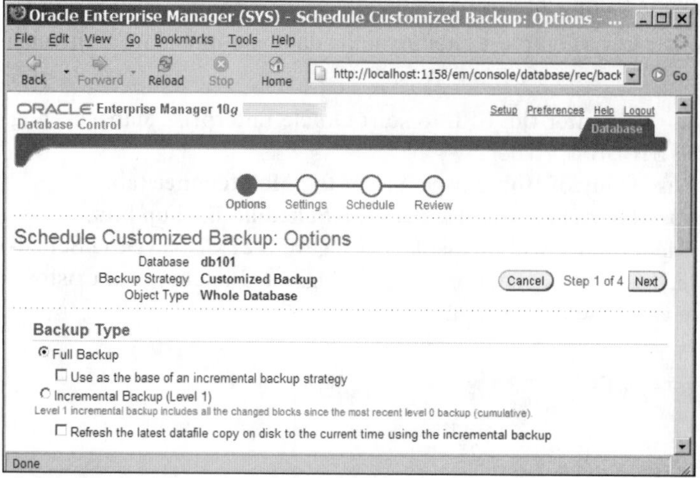

FIGURE 2-23 Setting Backup Options

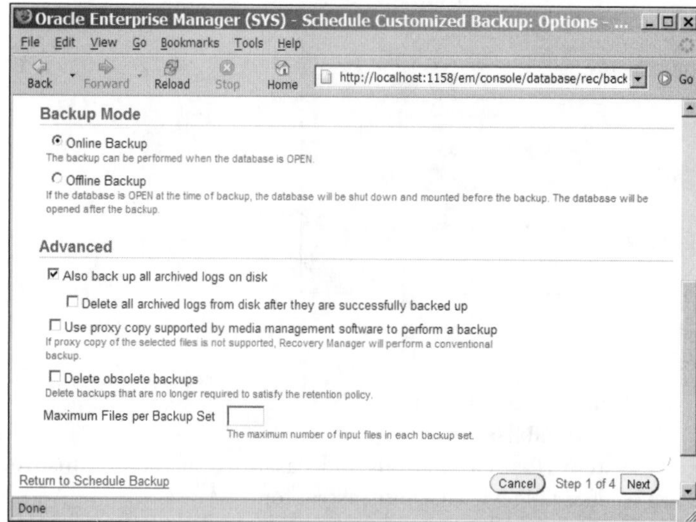

FIGURE 2-24 Setting the backup mode and other options

Figure 2-25 displays the Schedule Customized Backup: Settings page and its options. Select the **Next** button to move to the next page.

16. The **Schedule Customized Backup: Schedule** page will then be displayed. The backup will be assigned a default job name and a description (see Figure 2-26).
17. Scroll down this page to view the **Schedule** section. To perform the backup right away, leave the option **Immediately** selected under the Start section.

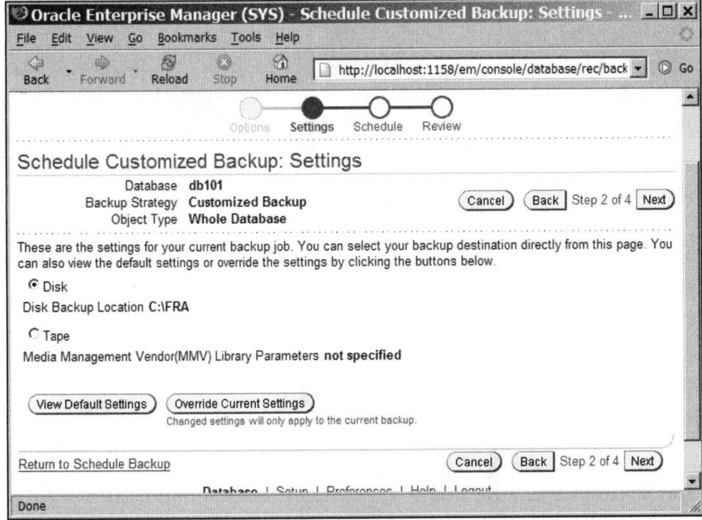

FIGURE 2-25 Step 2, indicating settings for a scheduled backup

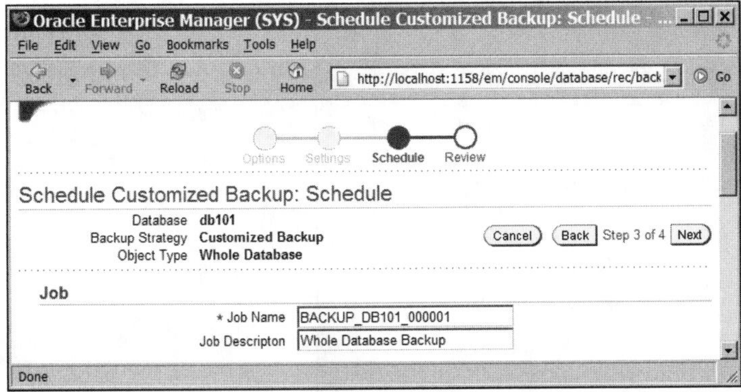

FIGURE 2-26 Step 3, specifying the job name and description

18. Under the Repeat section, leave the **One Time** option selected. Figure 2-27 displays the scheduling options available for the backup.
19. Select the **Next** button on the page to move to the **Schedule Customized Backup: Review** Page. Details about the backup in addition to the RMAN script that will be executed are displayed on this page. Figure 2-28 displays the Schedule Customized Backup: Review page.
20. Finally select the **Submit Job** button. A **Status** page will be displayed indicating that the job has been successfully submitted. **Click OK.**
21. The backup you just configured becomes a job that is to be executed. To view the details of this job go back to the Database Control page, by selecting the **Home** tab on the top right-hand corner.
22. Scroll along the Database Home Page until you reach the **Related Links** section.

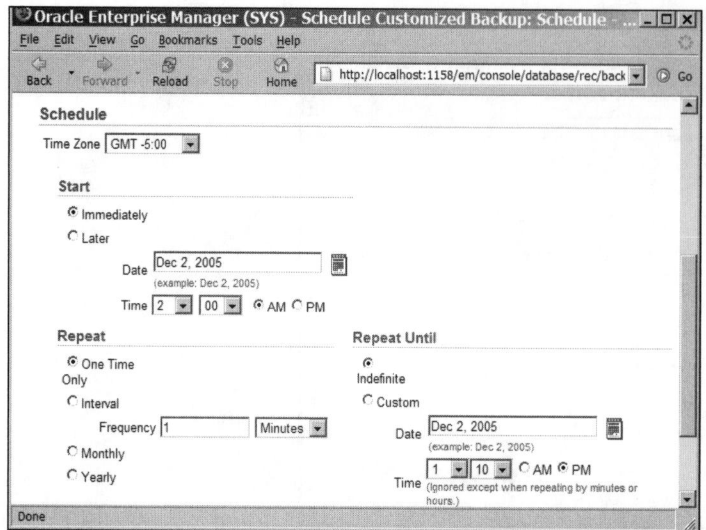

FIGURE 2-27 Scheduling the backup for a specific time

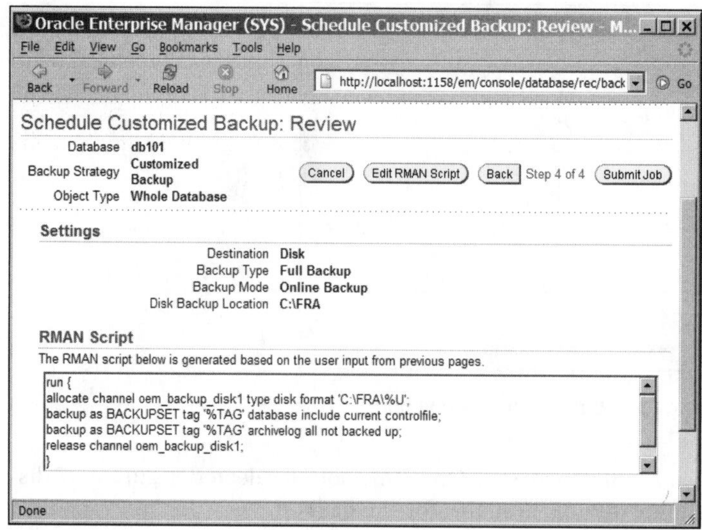

FIGURE 2-28 Step 4, Reviewing the choices

23. Select the **Jobs** link.
24. The **Job Activity** page will be displayed. Under the **Results** section is the name of the job you just created and its Status. The status could be Scheduled, Running, Succeeded, or Failed. Figure 2-29 displays the Job Activity page. From the figure you can see that the BACKUP_DB101_000001 job completed successfully.

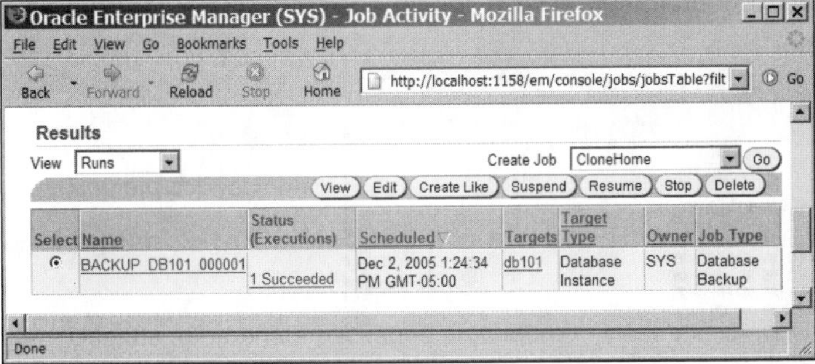

FIGURE 2-29 The Job Activity page

25. Log out of Enterprise Manager.

MONITORING RMAN BACKUPS

A DBA can view RMAN metadata regarding backups and recoveries by querying various dynamic performance views on the target database. These views display information from the control file of the target database.

Some of the commonly accessed views are displayed in the Table 2-2.

TABLE 2-2 Views that display information about RMAN backups

Data Dictionary View	Description
V$RMAN_OUTPUT	Displays messages reported by an RMAN job in progress.
V$RMAN_STATUS	Displays the status of the RMAN job, as to whether it was successful or unsuccessful.
V$SESSION_LONGOPS	Shows progress reports on RMAN backup and restores.

Practice 17: Querying the Data Dictionary

This practice demonstrates a query to display information about backup jobs that failed.

1. Start SQL*Plus and connect as a user with SYSDBA privileges.

```
SQL> CONNECT DB_ADMIN/DB_ADMIN AS SYSDBA
```

2. Issue the following query on $RMAN_STATUS to see the details of all failed RMAN jobs. To determine the backupset number, status, and the start and end times of a failed backup job, type:

```
SQL> SELECT RECID, STATUS, START_TIME, END_TIME
     FROM V$RMAN_STATUS
     WHERE STATUS='FAILED';
```

Figure 2-30 displays the output of the query on V$RMAN_STATUS.

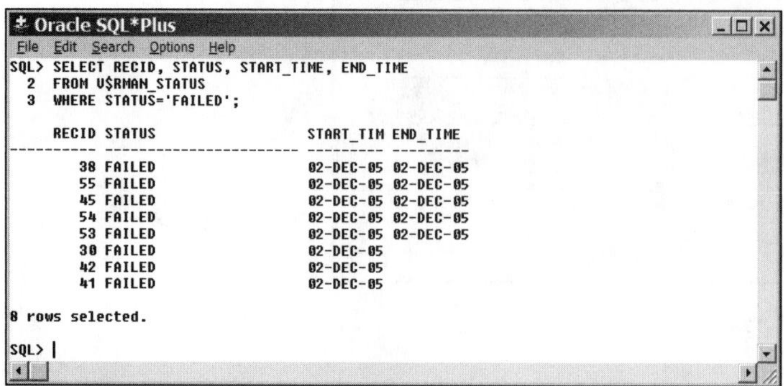

FIGURE 2-30 Viewing backup jobs from V$RMAN_STATUS

3. Exit SQL*Plus.

RMAN COMMANDS

A database administrator may want to know which files have been backed up and those that have not. This can be easily determined by querying the RMAN repository. Two very useful commands that may be used to display information about the backups already created and the files that need backup are the LIST and REPORT commands respectively.

The LIST command

This command may be used to determine which backups are currently available. The command can display details of backups of the database, tablespaces, datafiles, archived logs, and control files. The LIST INCARNATION command may also be used to display the incarnations of the target database. A new incarnation of a database is created whenever the RESETLOGS option is used when opening a database—when an incomplete recovery is done on a database.

The options of the LIST command are BY BACKUP or BY FILE. The BY BACKUP clause displays the output based on the backupsets stored by RMAN. The BY FILE option displays a listing at a file level. The BY BACKUP clause is the default. The keywords SUMMARY or VERBOSE may also be mentioned to indicate whether a summarized or verbose output is desired. VERBOSE is the default.

Practice 18: The LIST command

In this practice, you will issue the LIST command in various ways to display information about backups created in the database.

1. Launch RMAN if it is not already open and connect to the target database.

```
C :\> RMAN
RMAN> CONNECT TARGET
```

2. Issue the command below to display backupsets present in the database, you may use either of the commands: LIST BACKUP or LIST BACKUPSET. The BY

BACKUP option displays the output based on the backupsets stored by RMAN. The list of files included in each backupset is also displayed. The backupset key, the type of backup, the device on which the backup exists, its size, the time it was taken, its status, tag, and so on are included in the output. The output by default is verbose. Figure 2-31 displays the output of the LIST BACKUP BY BACKUP command.

```
RMAN> LIST BACKUP BY BACKUP;
or
RMAN> LIST BACKUPSET BY BACKUP;
or
RMAN> LIST BACKUP BY BACKUP VERBOSE;
```

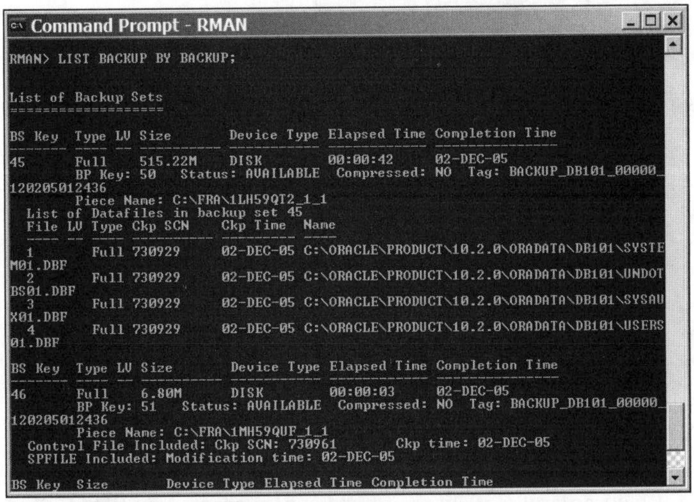

```
Command Prompt - RMAN
RMAN> LIST BACKUP BY BACKUP;

List of Backup Sets
===================

BS Key  Type LV Size       Device Type Elapsed Time Completion Time
------- ---- -- ---------- ----------- ------------ ---------------
45      Full    515.22M    DISK        00:00:42     02-DEC-05
        BP Key: 50   Status: AVAILABLE  Compressed: NO  Tag: BACKUP_DB101_00000_
120205012436
        Piece Name: C:\FRA\1LH59QT2_1_1
  List of Datafiles in backup set 45
  File LV Type Ckp SCN    Ckp Time  Name
  ---- -- ---- ---------- --------- ----
  1       Full 730929     02-DEC-05 C:\ORACLE\PRODUCT\10.2.0\ORADATA\DB101\SYSTE
M01.DBF
  2       Full 730929     02-DEC-05 C:\ORACLE\PRODUCT\10.2.0\ORADATA\DB101\UNDOT
BS01.DBF
  3       Full 730929     02-DEC-05 C:\ORACLE\PRODUCT\10.2.0\ORADATA\DB101\SYSAU
X01.DBF
  4       Full 730929     02-DEC-05 C:\ORACLE\PRODUCT\10.2.0\ORADATA\DB101\USERS
01.DBF

BS Key  Type LV Size       Device Type Elapsed Time Completion Time
------- ---- -- ---------- ----------- ------------ ---------------
46      Full    6.80M      DISK        00:00:03     02-DEC-05
        BP Key: 51   Status: AVAILABLE  Compressed: NO  Tag: BACKUP_DB101_00000_
120205012436
        Piece Name: C:\FRA\1MH59QUF_1_1
  Control File Included: Ckp SCN: 730961       Ckp time: 02-DEC-05
  SPFILE Included: Modification time: 02-DEC-05

BS Key  Size       Device Type Elapsed Time Completion Time
```

FIGURE 2-31 The BY BACKUP option of the LIST command

3. By using the SUMMARY option, you get summarized information about the backupsets in the database. Figure 2-32 displays summarized information about the backupsets.

   ```
   RMAN> LIST BACKUP BY BACKUP SUMMARY;
   ```

```
Command Prompt - RMAN
RMAN> LIST BACKUP BY BACKUP SUMMARY;

List of Backups
===============
Key     TY LV S Device Type Completion Time #Pieces #Copies Compressed Tag
------- -- -- - ----------- --------------- ------- ------- ---------- ---
45      B  F  A DISK        02-DEC-05       1       1       NO         BACKUP_DB
101_00000_120205012436
46      B  F  A DISK        02-DEC-05       1       1       NO         BACKUP_DB
101_00000_120205012436
47      B  A  A DISK        02-DEC-05       1       1       NO         BACKUP_DB
101_00000_120205012436

RMAN>
```

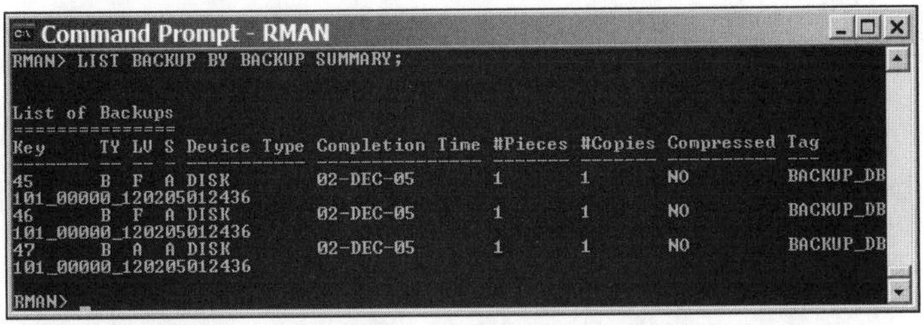

FIGURE 2-32 The SUMMARY option of the LIST command

4. The BY FILE option gives a listing at a file level. If you do not specify an object, RMAN displays a list of all datafiles, archived logs, control files, and parameter files and the corresponding backupsets containing their backup (see Figure 2-33).

```
RMAN> LIST BACKUP BY FILE;
```

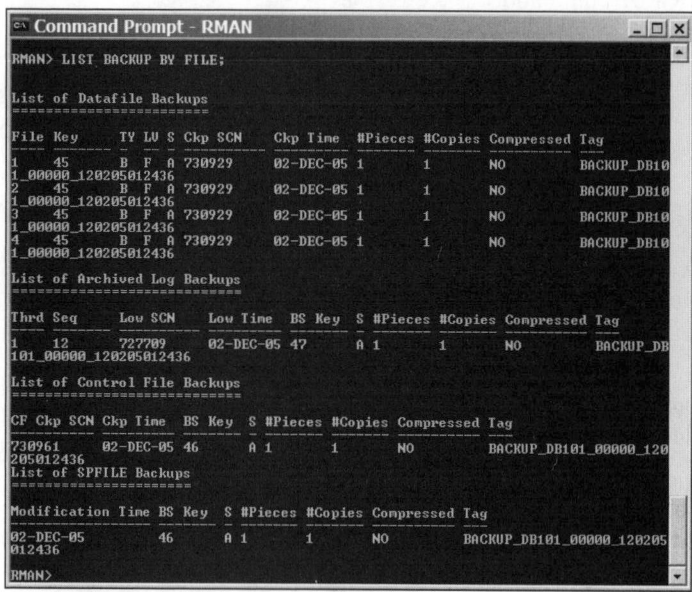

```
Command Prompt - RMAN
RMAN> LIST BACKUP BY FILE;

List of Datafile Backups
========================

File Key     TY LV S Ckp SCN    Ckp Time  #Pieces #Copies Compressed Tag
---- ------- -  -- - ---------- --------- ------- ------- ---------- ---
1    45      B  F  A 730929     02-DEC-05 1       1       NO         BACKUP_DB10
1_00000_120205012436
2    45      B  F  A 730929     02-DEC-05 1       1       NO         BACKUP_DB10
1_00000_120205012436
3    45      B  F  A 730929     02-DEC-05 1       1       NO         BACKUP_DB10
1_00000_120205012436
4    45      B  F  A 730929     02-DEC-05 1       1       NO         BACKUP_DB10
1_00000_120205012436

List of Archived Log Backups
============================

Thrd Seq     Low SCN    Low Time  BS Key  S #Pieces #Copies Compressed Tag
---- ------- ---------- --------- ------- - ------- ------- ---------- ---
1    12      727709     02-DEC-05 47      A 1       1       NO         BACKUP_DB
101_00000_120205012436

List of Control File Backups
============================

CF Ckp SCN Ckp Time  BS Key  S #Pieces #Copies Compressed Tag
---------- --------- ------- - ------- ------- ---------- ---
730961     02-DEC-05 46      A 1       1       NO         BACKUP_DB101_00000_120
205012436
List of SPFILE Backups
======================

Modification Time BS Key  S #Pieces #Copies Compressed Tag
----------------- ------- - ------- ------- ---------- ---
02-DEC-05         46      A 1       1       NO         BACKUP_DB101_00000_120205
012436

RMAN>
```

FIGURE 2-33 The BY FILE option of the LIST command

5. Use the LIST COPY command to view the image copies created by RMAN. You can specify the options as DATABASE, TABLESPACE, or DATAFILE. For example, using the word DATABASE will display all the image copies created for all the database files of the database, as well as the control file and spfile.

```
RMAN> LIST COPY OF DATABASE;
RMAN> LIST COPY OF TABLESPACE USERS;
RMAN> LIST COPY OF DATAFILE 3;
```

6. The LIST INCARNATION command is used to view the different incarnations of the target database.

```
RMAN> LIST INCARNATION;
```

7. Exit RMAN.

The REPORT Command

The REPORT command is also another useful command of RMAN. It helps a database administrator answer questions that are relevant to the backup and recovery strategy being implemented. Some questions that are answered by the REPORT command are:

- Which files are in need of a backup?
- Which files are obsolete and may be deleted?
- What is the current physical structure of the database, and what was it at a previous point in time?

The REPORT NEED BACKUP command

The REPORT NEED BACKUP command may be used to find out the names of files that are in need of a backup.

In Chapter 1 you were introduced to the REDUNDANCY option of the CONFIGURE command. It established the minimum number of backups that RMAN must maintain as valid. For example, if REDUNDANCY has been set to 2 and only a single backup of the USERS tablespace currently exists, then the USERS tablespace would need one more backup to match the value specified by REDUNDANCY. If three backups exist for the USERS tablespace, then it exceeds the REDUNDANCY of 2 and the first backup may be considered OBSOLETE.

Practice 19: Identifying files that are in need of backup

This practice example demonstrates how to display the names of files that are in need of backup because they do not satisfy the redundancy value.

1. Launch RMAN if it is not already open and connect to the target database.

   ```
   C :\> RMAN
   RMAN> CONNECT TARGET
   ```

2. At the RMAN prompt, type the following CONFIGURE command to set REDUNDANCY to 2. If you already have a minimum of 2 backups this command will not display the names of any datafiles. If you do not have a minimum of 2 backups an output similar to Figure 2-34 may be displayed.

   ```
   RMAN>CONFIGURE RETENTION POLICY TO REDUNDANCY 2;
   ```

3. Issue the REPORT NEED BACKUP to display all those datafiles that do not have a minimum of 2 backups.

   ```
   RMAN>REPORT NEED BACKUP;
   ```

   Figure 2-34 indicates that the SYSTEM01.DBF, UNDOTBS01.DBF, SYSAUX01.DBF and USERS01.DBF datafiles are in need of backup.

   You may also use the DAYS *n* clause with the REPORT NEED BACKUP command, where *n* is a numeric value representing days. When the REPORT... DAYS command is executed, the names of all files that require more than the specified number of DAYS worth of archived logs for recovery will be displayed.
4. To find the names of files in the database that need a minimum of 7 days of log files to be applied in the event of recovery, you can issue:

   ```
   RMAN> REPORT NEED BACKUP DAYS=7 DATABASE;
   ```

5. Exit RMAN.

```
Command Prompt - RMAN
RMAN> CONFIGURE RETENTION POLICY TO REDUNDANCY 2;

new RMAN configuration parameters:
CONFIGURE RETENTION POLICY TO REDUNDANCY 2;
new RMAN configuration parameters are successfully stored

RMAN> REPORT NEED BACKUP;

RMAN retention policy will be applied to the command
RMAN retention policy is set to redundancy 2
Report of files with less than 2 redundant backups
File #bkps Name
---- ----- -----------------------------------------------------
1    1     C:\ORACLE\PRODUCT\10.2.0\ORADATA\DB101\SYSTEM01.DBF
2    1     C:\ORACLE\PRODUCT\10.2.0\ORADATA\DB101\UNDOTBS01.DBF
3    1     C:\ORACLE\PRODUCT\10.2.0\ORADATA\DB101\SYSAUX01.DBF
4    1     C:\ORACLE\PRODUCT\10.2.0\ORADATA\DB101\USERS01.DBF

RMAN>
```

FIGURE 2-34 Reporting the names of files that are in need of backup

The REPORT OBSOLETE command

The REPORT OBSOLETE command may be used to display the backups that are obsolete and are no longer needed for recovery. Files are considered obsolete if they do not meet the RETENTION POLICY. If the RETENTION POLICY has been set to REDUNDANCY 3, then the fourth backup taken for a file will render its oldest backup obsolete. RMAN does not automatically delete obsolete backups unless 100% of space in the flash recovery area has been consumed. However, the database administrator may manually delete them by using the DELETE OBSOLETE command.

Practice 20: Displaying the names of obsolete backups and deleting them

1. In this practice example you will execute commands to report and delete obsolete backups.
2. Launch RMAN if it is not already open and connect to the target database.

   ```
   C :\> RMAN
   RMAN> CONNECT TARGET
   ```

3. Issue the REPORT OBSOLETE command to display all the backups that RMAN considers obsolete.

   ```
   RMAN> REPORT OBSOLETE;
   ```

   Figure 2-35, displays a number of backupsets that are currently obsolete.

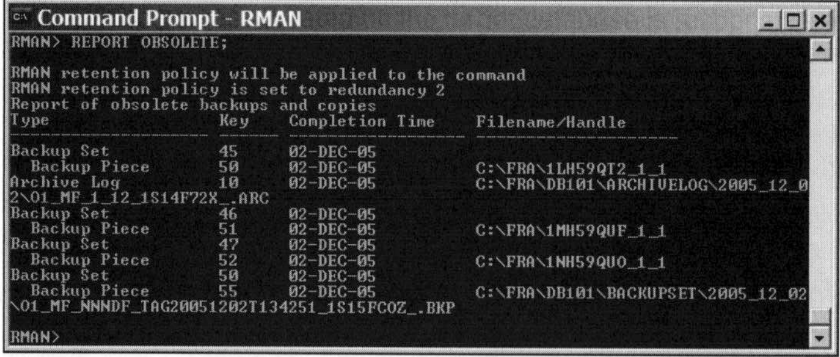

```
Command Prompt - RMAN
RMAN> REPORT OBSOLETE;

RMAN retention policy will be applied to the command
RMAN retention policy is set to redundancy 2
Report of obsolete backups and copies
Type                 Key    Completion Time    Filename/Handle
-------------------- ------ ------------------ --------------------
Backup Set           45     02-DEC-05
  Backup Piece       50     02-DEC-05          C:\FRA\1LH59QT2_1_1
Archive Log          10     02-DEC-05          C:\FRA\DB101\ARCHIVELOG\2005_12_0
2\O1_MF_1_12_1S14F72X_.ARC
Backup Set           46     02-DEC-05
  Backup Piece       51     02-DEC-05          C:\FRA\1MH59QUF_1_1
Backup Set           47     02-DEC-05
  Backup Piece       52     02-DEC-05          C:\FRA\1NH59QUO_1_1
Backup Set           50     02-DEC-05
  Backup Piece       55     02-DEC-05          C:\FRA\DB101\BACKUPSET\2005_12_02
\O1_MF_NNNDF_TAG20051202T134251_1S15FCOZ_.BKP

RMAN>
```

FIGURE 2-35 Displaying obsolete backups

4. Next issue the DELETE OBSOLETE command and confirm the deletion by typing Y when prompted for confirmation. Figure 2-36 displays the output of the DELETE OBSOLETE command.

   ```
   RMAN> DELETE OBSOLETE;
   ```

```
Command Prompt - RMAN
RMAN> DELETE OBSOLETE;

RMAN retention policy will be applied to the command
RMAN retention policy is set to redundancy 2
using channel ORA_DISK_1
Deleting the following obsolete backups and copies:
Type                 Key    Completion Time    Filename/Handle
-------------------- ------ ------------------ --------------------
Backup Set           45     02-DEC-05
  Backup Piece       50     02-DEC-05          C:\FRA\1LH59QT2_1_1
Archive Log          10     02-DEC-05          C:\FRA\DB101\ARCHIVELOG\2005_12_0
2\O1_MF_1_12_1S14F72X_.ARC
Backup Set           46     02-DEC-05
  Backup Piece       51     02-DEC-05          C:\FRA\1MH59QUF_1_1
Backup Set           47     02-DEC-05
  Backup Piece       52     02-DEC-05          C:\FRA\1NH59QUO_1_1
Backup Set           50     02-DEC-05
  Backup Piece       55     02-DEC-05          C:\FRA\DB101\BACKUPSET\2005_12_02
\O1_MF_NNNDF_TAG20051202T134251_1S15FCOZ_.BKP

Do you really want to delete the above objects (enter YES or NO)? Y
deleted backup piece
backup piece handle=C:\FRA\1LH59QT2_1_1 recid=50 stamp=575990690
deleted archive log
archive log filename=C:\FRA\DB101\ARCHIVELOG\2005_12_02\O1_MF_1_12_1S14F72X_.ARC
 recid=10 stamp=575990743
deleted backup piece
backup piece handle=C:\FRA\1MH59QUF_1_1 recid=51 stamp=575990737
deleted backup piece
backup piece handle=C:\FRA\1NH59QUO_1_1 recid=52 stamp=575990745
deleted backup piece
backup piece handle=C:\FRA\DB101\BACKUPSET\2005_12_02\O1_MF_NNNDF_TAG20051202T13
4251_1S15FCOZ_.BKP recid=55 stamp=575991771
Deleted 5 objects


RMAN>
```

FIGURE 2-36 The output of the DELETE OBSOLETE command

5. Exit RMAN.

The REPORT SCHEMA command

The REPORT SCHEMA command may be used to display the physical and logical structure of the database. The other options the command can take are AT TIME or AT SCN to display the structure at a previous point in time.

Practice 21: Displaying the structure of the target database from RMAN

The following section lists a series of commands you can execute to view the current/previous structure of the DB101 database.

1. Launch RMAN, connect to the target and recovery catalog database.

   ```
   C:\> RMAN
   RMAN>CONNECT TARGET
   RMAN> CONNECT CATALOG RMANUSER/RMANUSER@RCDB
   ```

2. At the RMAN prompt, issue REPORT SCHEMA to display the current structure of the target database (see Figure 2-37).

   ```
   RMAN> REPORT SCHEMA;
   ```

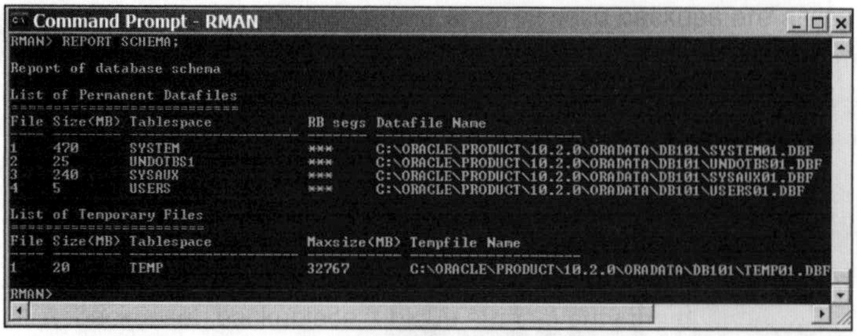

```
Command Prompt - RMAN
RMAN> REPORT SCHEMA;

Report of database schema

List of Permanent Datafiles
===========================
File Size(MB) Tablespace           RB segs Datafile Name
---- -------- -------------------- ------- ------------------------
1    470      SYSTEM               ***     C:\ORACLE\PRODUCT\10.2.0\ORADATA\DB101\SYSTEM01.DBF
2    25       UNDOTBS1             ***     C:\ORACLE\PRODUCT\10.2.0\ORADATA\DB101\UNDOTBS01.DBF
3    240      SYSAUX               ***     C:\ORACLE\PRODUCT\10.2.0\ORADATA\DB101\SYSAUX01.DBF
4    5        USERS                ***     C:\ORACLE\PRODUCT\10.2.0\ORADATA\DB101\USERS01.DBF

List of Temporary Files
=======================
File Size(MB) Tablespace           Maxsize(MB) Tempfile Name
---- -------- -------------------- ----------- --------------------
1    20       TEMP                 32767       C:\ORACLE\PRODUCT\10.2.0\ORADATA\DB101\TEMP01.DBF

RMAN>
```

FIGURE 2-37 The schema of the target database

3. To display the schema structure of the database, as it was a week ago, use the AT TIME clause.

   ```
   RMAN> REPORT SCHEMA AT TIME 'SYSDATE-7';
   ```

4. To display the schema structure of the database, as it was at, say, SCN 900000 use the AT SCN clause.

   ```
   RMAN> REPORT SCHEMA AT SCN 900000;
   ```

5. Exit RMAN.

In this chapter you learned how to perform different types of backups using Recovery Manager and Enterprise Manager. The syntax of the BACKUP command and a number of options were reviewed. You also learned how to simplify incremental backups by using the Block Change Tracking file. Finally a review of some useful RMAN commands related to the backups was illustrated. In Chapter 3, you will learn about the types of failures that can occur in a database and the recovery options available using Recovery Manager and Enterprise Manager.

Chapter Summary

- The Recovery Manager is the preferred and recommended method for performing backups.
- The Flash Recovery Area introduced in the Oracle 10*g* database is a centralized location for the management of backup and recovery related files.
- The DB_RECOVERY_FILE_DEST and DB_RECOVERY_FILE_DEST_SIZE initialization parameters are used to configure the flash recovery area.
- In noarchivelog mode, RMAN backups are taken only when the database is mounted.
- In archivelog mode, RMAN backups may be taken when the database is open.
- Backupsets and image copies may be created using RMAN.
- A backupset is a backup created in an RMAN-specific format created using the BACKUP command.
- A backupset is made up of backup pieces. A backup piece can contain blocks from multiple files. This feature is known as multiplexing.
- A database administrator can choose to implement an incremental backup strategy. Incremental backups can either be Differential and Cumulative.
- A Level 0 backup acts as a base backup against which Level 1 backups can be applied.
- A differential backup is a Level 1 backup that backs up all blocks that have been modified since the most recent incremental level 0 or 1 backup.
- A cumulative backup is a Level 1 backup that backs up blocks that have been modified since the most recent incremental Level 0 backup.
- Backupsets are created using the BACKUP command.
- Image copies are similar to files created using the operating system copy command. Image copies are created using the BACKUP AS COPY command.
- Backup options such as TAG, MAXSETSIZE, FORMAT, and RATE may be specified in the BACKUP command.
- Backups of the entire database, tablespaces, individual datafiles, the current control file, and archivelog files may be taken using the BACKUP command.
- Backups of the entire database, tablespaces, and individual datafiles may be created using the BACKUP AS COPY command.
- The RUN command is used to run a sequence of RMAN commands together as a single unit.
- Scripts are created for repetitive use and stored in the recovery catalog database.
- New in Oracle 10*g* is a feature that allows the DBA to control the amount of time and throttling speed of a backup. It is performed using the DURATION command.
- New in Oracle 10*g* is the block change tracking feature that decreases the time taken for incremental backups.
- The Oracle database tracks the physical location of all database changes in a separate file called the Change Tracking File.

- The Change Tracking Writer (CTWR) background process is responsible for writing to the Change Tracking File.

- The LIST command is used to determine which backups are available in the database.
- The REPORT command is used find out the current schema structure of the target database as well as files in the need of backup.

Syntax Guide

SYNTAX GUIDE		
Command	**Description**	**Example**
Configuring the Flash Recovery Area		
DB_RECOVERY_FILE_DEST	Indicates the location of the flash recovery area.	`ALTER SYSTEM SET DB_RECOVERY_FILE_ DEST = 'C:\FRA' SCOPE=BOTH;`
DB_RECOVERY_FILE_DEST_SIZE	Indicates the maximum amount of space that the flash recovery area is allowed to utilize.	`ALTER SYSTEM SET DB_RECOVERY_FILE_DEST_ SIZE=20G SCOPE=BOTH;`
Options of the BACKUP Command		
TAG	A user-defined string that can be specified to identify a backup easily.	`BACKUP CURRENT CONTROLFILE TAG CFTAG;`
MAXSETSIZE	Specifies the maximum size (in bytes) for a backup set.	`BACKUP FULL DATABASE MAXSETSIZE=300M;`
MAXPIECESIZE	Specifies the maximum size of a backup piece.	`CONFIGURE CHANNEL DEVICE TYPE DISK MAXPIECESIZE=500K;`
FORMAT	Used to indicate the format of the name to be assigned to the output file.	`BACKUP FORMAT 'C:\ARCHIVE\%d_%s_%p_ %T' (DATAFILE 2)`
RATE	The option can limit the I/O resources consumed by a backup job.	`CONFIGURE CHANNEL DEVICE TYPE DISK FORMAT 'C:\FRA' RATE 5M;`
DURATION	Used to specify a time frame for the backup job and throttling speed. RMAN controls throttling speed based on the amount of time specified.	`BACKUP DURATION 1:30 MINIMIZE TIME TABLESPACE USERS;`

SYNTAX GUIDE		
Command	**Description**	**Example**
The BACKUP command		
DATABASE	Indicates a full database backup, including all the datafiles and the control file.	`BACKUP DATABASE;`
TABLESPACE	Indicates a tablespace level backup.	`BACKUP TABLESPACE USERS;`
DATAFILE	Indicates a backup at an individual datafile level.	`BACKUP DATAFILE 'C:\ORACLE\PRODUCT\10.2.0\ORADATA\DB101\users01.dbf';` `BACKUP DATAFILE 2;`
INCLUDE CURRENT CONTROLFILE	Backs up the control file along with the rest of the backup.	`BACKUP (TABLESPACE USERS INCLUDE CURRENT CONTROLFILE);`
CURRENT CONTROLFILE	Backs up the current control file.	`BACKUP CURRENT CONTROLFLE;`
COMPRESSED BACKUPSET	Creates a compressed backupset that is smaller in size than an uncompressed backupset.	`BACKUP AS COMPRESSED BACKUPSET DATABASE;`

ARCHIVELOG	Used to create backups of archivelog files. The keywords ALL, FROM TIME..UNTIL TIME, can be used with this command.	`BACKUP ARCHIVELOG ALL;`
		
		`BACKUP ARCHIVELOG FROM TIME 'SYSDATE-2' UNTIL TIME 'SYSDATE';`

INCREMENTAL LEVEL = *n* [CUMULATIVE]	*n* can take a value of 0 or 1. A differential backup is the default. The cumulative keyword is used to create cumulative incremental backups.	`BACKUP INCREMENTAL LEVEL 0 TABLESPACE SYSAUX;` `BACKUP INCREMENTAL LEVEL 1 CUMULATIVE DATABASE;`

AS COPY	Used to create image copies. The options you could specify are DATABASE, TABLESPACE, DATAFILE.	`BACKUP AS COPY DATABASE;`
		`BACKUP AS COPY TABLESPACE USERS;`
		`BACKUP AS COPY DATAFILE 3;`

SYNTAX GUIDE		
Command	**Description**	**Example**
RMAN Commands		

RUN	Used to execute a sequence of RMAN command as a single unit.	`RUN {`
		`ALLOCATE CHANNEL C1 TYPE DISK;`
		`BACKUP DATABASE;`
		`BACKUP (ARCHIVELOG ALL);`
		`}`

CREATE SCRIPT	Command available when using a recovery catalog database. Can be used to create scripts for repetitive use.	`CREATE SCRIPT MONTHLY_BACKUP {BACKUP DATABASE; BACKUP (ARCHIVELOG ALL);}`
EXECUTE SCRIPT	Used to execute a script.	`EXECUTE MONTHLY_ BACKUP;`
Options for BLOCK CHANGE TRACKING		
ENABLE BLOCK CHANGE TRACKING	Command to enable block change tracking. The feature optimizes incremental backups.	`ALTER DATABASE ENABLE BLOCK CHANGE TRACKING;`
DISABLE BLOCK CHANGE TRACKING	Used to disable block change tracking causing RMAN to read the entire datafile while performing incremental backups.	`ALTE DATABASE DISABLE BLOCK CHANGE TRACKING;`
Options for the LIST command		
BACKUP BY BACKUP	Display backupsets created.	`LIST BACKUP BY BACKUP;`
VERBOSE	Displays a verbose output.	`LIST BACKUP BY BACKUP VERBOSE;`
SUMMARY	Displays a summarized output.	`LIST BACKUP BY BACKUP SUMMARY;`
BY FILE	Displays a listing at a file level. Shows all the backups that contain the file.	`LIST BACKUP BY FILE;`
INCARNATION	Displays the current incarnation of the database.	`LIST INCARNATION;`

SYNTAX GUIDE		
Command	Description	Example
Options for the REPORT command		
NEED BACKUP	Displays a listing of files in need of backup because they do not meet the retention policy.	`REPORT NEED BACKUP;`
SCHEMA	Displays the structure of the target database.	`REPORT SCHEMA;`
OBSOLETE	Displays a listing of the backups that are obsolete.	`REPORT OBSOLETE;`

Review Questions

1. The ________________ is a centralized location for backup and recovery related files.
2. The ________________ command can be used to dynamically change the value of initialization parameters.
3. The ________________ option can be used to indicate that the change to an initialization parameter should affect the current and future instances of the database.
4. The ________________ and ________________ parameters are used to configure the flash recovery area.
5. A ________________ value for the ________________ initialization parameter disables the flash recovery area.
6. The ________________ data dictionary view can be queried to display recommendations made by Oracle regarding space usage in the flash recovery area.
7. RMAN allows you to create two types of backups, they are ________________ and ________________ .
8. A ________________ backup should be created as a base backup when implementing an incremental backup strategy.
9. A ________________ incremental backup is a level 1 backup that backups up all blocks that have been modified since the most recent level 0 backup.
10. The ________________ option of the BACKUP command can be used to specify the location of the backupsets.
11. A user-defined string can be specified to name a backup. It is called a
    a. STRING
    b. TAG
    c. LIST
    d. LABEL

12. The clause that can be specified when the backup media places limitations on file size is:
    a. MAXSIZE
    b. MAXFILESIZE
    c. MAXSETSIZE
    d. MAXPIECESIZE
13. Name the feature of RMAN that allows blocks from different datafiles to be interspersed.
14. Identify the difference between a full backup and a level 0 backup taken by RMAN.
15. The DBA creates a format using 'DB_%N_%T_%s_%p', while backing up the SYSTEM tablespace. Which of the following is true?
    a. Two backupsets will be created.
    b. The backupsets will have the names DB_SYSTEM_20050606_12_1 and DB_SYSTEM_20050606_12_1 respectively.
    c. The backupsets will have the names DB_SYSTEM_20050606_12_1 and DB_SYSTEM_20050606_12_2 respectively.
    d. The first backup will be created successfully but the second will display an error, because the format cannot be used while backing up the control file.
16. Parallelism of channels can be obtained by which of the following CONFIGURE commands?
    a. CONFIGURE DEVICE TYPE DISK PARALLELISM 2;
    b. CONFIGURE CHANNEL DEVICE TYPE DISK PARALLELISM 2;
    c. CONFIGURE DISK PARALLELISM 2;
    d. None of the above.
17. When backing up the SYSTEM tablespace, which database file is also backed up?
18. The DBA issues the following command while trying to perform a backup.

    ```
    BACKUP TABLESPACE USERS, TOOLS, SYSAUX.
    ```

    [Choose the correct answer]
    a. The backup will generate an error.
    b. The control file will be backed up after backing the datafiles of the three tablespaces.
    c. The backup will succeed provided all three tablespaces exist in the database.
    d. The SYSAUX tablespace cannot be backed along with other tablespaces.
    e. The SYSAUX tablespace must be backed up only with the SYSTEM tablespace.
19. Which command can be used to display current structure of the target database?
20. Which command can be used to display the current incarnation of the target database?
21. Which option can you specify that will cause RMAN to automatically delete the archivelog files after they have been backed up?
22. Identify the data dictionary view that can be queried to determine the STATUS of block change tracking.
    a. V$CHANGE_TRACKING
    b. DBA_CHANGE_TRACKING

c. V$BLOCK_CHANGE_TRACKING

d. DBA_BLOCK_CHANGE_TRACKING

23. When using the MINIMIZE LOAD option of the DURATION command, which additional statement will be displayed in the RMAN output?

a. Elapsed time

b. Piece handle

c. Throttle Time

d. Completed Time

24. The ________________ keyword can be used to inform RMAN that even if the entire backup does not complete, backup pieces that are completed within the time frame must be cataloged.

25. The background process that performs block tracking to the block change tracking file is called:

a. DBWR

b. CTWR

c. CTRW

d. DBCT

e. None of the above

26. The ________________ performance view can be used to display backup jobs that failed.

27. The ________________ option of the LIST command displays a summarized output. The default mode is ________________ .

28. The ________________ option of the REPORT NEED BACKUP command can be used to display datafiles that have not been backed up in the last *n* days.

29. A database administrator manually deletes old backups that do not satisfy the retention policy using the command:

a. REPORT OBSOLETE

b. DELETE OBSOLETE

c. RMAN automatically deletes old backups; the DBA does not have to do any manual deletion.

d. You have to set the RETENTION POLICY TO REDUNDANCY 2 for a deletion to be successful.

30. The ________________ feature that was introduced in Oracle 10*g* speeds up the process of taking incremental backups.

Hands-On Assignments

Assignment 2-1 Viewing the Initialization Parameters associated with the Flash Recovery Area.

1. Open SQL*Plus and connect as a user with SYSDBA privileges
2. Issue the command to display all parameters that contain DB_RECOVERY in them.
3. View the archiving mode of the database.
4. Identify the archiving destination.
5. Exit SQL*Plus.

Assignment 2-2 Setting the Flash Recovery Area.

1. Start SQL*Plus and connect as a user with SYSDBA privileges.
2. Query the V$RECOVERY_FILE_DEST view to determine whether a flash recovery area has been configured.
3. If it has already been configured, issue the command to disable it and once again query the V$RECOVERY_FILE_DEST view to see that your change has taken place. If it is not configured, go to step 4.
4. Using the appropriate ALTER SYSTEM commands, set the parameters that will configure the flash recovery area. If you are unsure about the location to specify you may ask your instructor. Set the size of the destination large enough to hold all the backups that you may take.
5. Exit SQL*Plus.

Assignment 2-3 Displaying the current structure of the target database from RMAN

1. Start RMAN and connect to the target database.
2. Issue the command to display the current schema of the target database.
3. Make a note of the datafile number of the SYSTEM and SYSAUX tablespaces.
4. Exit RMAN.

Assignment 2-4 Displaying the names of datafiles that have not been backed up in the past one week.

1. Start RMAN and connect to the target database.
2. If you have created a recovery catalog database, connect to it.
3. Issue the SHOW command to display the current retention policy.
4. Issue the REPORT command to display the names of datafiles that have not been backed up in the past 7 days.
5. Exit RMAN.

Assignment 2-5 Backing up the entire database

1. Start RMAN and connect to the target database and the recovery catalog database if you have created one.
2. Issue the command to backup the entire database. Give this backup a tag of COMPBKP.

3. Navigate to the Flash Recovery area and make sure you can identify the backup pieces that were created for this backup run.
4. Look at the RMAN output of the backup job and see how many backupsets and backup pieces were created.
5. Exit RMAN.

Assignment 2-6 Configuring Parallel Channels

1. Start RMAN and connect to the target database and the recovery catalog database if you have created one.
2. Issue the CONFIGURE command to configure automatic channels to a parallelism of 2.
3. Issue a backup command to back up the datafiles belonging to the SYSTEM and SYSAUX tablespaces.
4. Are the backups being done in parallel? What are the names of the automatic channels being created?
5. Configure automatic channels to the default parallelism of 1.
6. Exit RMAN.

Assignment 2-7 Backing up Tablespaces

1. Start RMAN and connect to the target and recovery catalog database if you have created one.
2. Issue the REPORT SCHEMA command to display the names of all the tablespaces in the database.
3. Record the names of any two tablespaces from the output displayed.
4. Issue the BACKUP command to back up the two tablespaces. Also specify a location different from the flash recovery area for creating these backups, using the FORMAT option. Let the name of the backup piece(s) generated contain the tablespace name followed by the backup set number followed by the backup piece number.
5. After the backup has been created, go to the location specified in the BACKUP command and make sure the backup piece(s) were created in the desired manner.
6. Exit RMAN.

Assignment 2-8 Backing up the Current Control File

1. Start RMAN and connect to the target database.
2. Issue a BACKUP command that will create a backup of the current control file.
3. Exit RMAN.

Assignment 2-9 Creating Compressed Backupsets

1. Start RMAN and connect to the target database.
2. Issue the BACKUP command that will create a backup of the entire database, in the form of a compressed backupset.
3. After the backup has completed. Go to the location of the backupset and make sure it is smaller than the backup that you created in Assignment 2-5.
4. Exit RMAN.

Assignment 2-10 Backing Archivelog Files

1. Start RMAN and connect to the target database.
2. Issue the command to back up all the archivelog files.
3. Open the flash recovery area and locate the backupsets created by this backup job. Observe a folder called ARCHIVELOG within the flash recovery area. This folder is automatically created.
4. Exit RMAN.

Assignment 2-11 Creating a Level 0 incremental backup of a tablespace

1. Start RMAN and connect to the target database and recovery catalog database if you have created one.
2. Issue the BACKUP command that will create a Level 0 backup of the SYSAUX tablespace.
3. Exit RMAN.

Assignment 2-12 Creating Level 1 incremental backups

1. Start RMAN and connect to the target database and recovery catalog database if you have created one.
2. Issue the BACKUP command that will create a Level 1 differential backup of the SYSAUX tablespace.
3. Issue the BACKUP command that will create a Level 1 cumulative backup of the SYSAUX tablespace.
4. Exit RMAN.

Assignment 2-13 Creating a RUN block to backup a tablespace and all archivelog files.

1. Start RMAN and connect to the target database and recovery catalog database if you have created one.
2. Within a RUN block:
   a. Manually allocate a channel called T1
   b. Issue the backup command to backup the SYSAUX tablespace, specify a tag of SYSABKP.
   c. Issue the command to back up all the archivelog files that were generated in the past three days. Also delete the archivelog files from their original location after the backup has been done.
3. Exit RMAN.

Assignment 2-14 Specifying a duration for the Backup job

1. Start RMAN and connect to the target database and recovery catalog database if you have created one.
2. Issue a BACKUP command that will back up the entire database. Indicate that RMAN must complete the backup in 4 minutes. Also indicate that RMAN need not run at full speed, but regulate its speed to complete it in the allotted time.

3. If RMAN was successfully able to complete the backup, what was the throttle time for the first backupset?
4. Exit RMAN.

Assignment 2-15 Enabling Block Change Tracking

1. Start SQL*Plus and log in using an administrative account such as SYSTEM.
2. Query the V$BLOCK_CHANGE_TRACKING view to display the status of block change tracking in the database.
3. If it is currently DISABLED, issue the ALTER DATABASE command that could enable block change tracking. Name the block change tracking file bctfile.chg.
4. Once again query the V$BLOCK_CHANGE_TRACKING view to display the status of block change tracking in the database.
5. Issue the command to disable block change tracking.
6. Exit SQL*Plus.

Assignment 2-16 Creating an Image copy of the SYSAUX tablespace.

1. Start RMAN and connect to the target database.
2. Issue an appropriate command that will create an image copy of a datafile belonging to the SYSAUX tablespace.
3. Exit RMAN.

Assignment 2-17 Displaying information about Backups created.

1. Start RMAN and connect to the target database.
2. Issue the command to display a verbose listing of all the backupsets created by RMAN.
3. Issue the command to display a summarized listing of all the backupsets created in RMAN.
4. Issue the command to display a verbose listing of all the files and the backupsets that contain them.
5. Issue the command to display all the image copies created for the datafiles of the database.
6. Exit RMAN.

Assignment 2-18 Configuring retention policy to a redundancy

1. Start RMAN and connect to the target database.
2. Issue the appropriate CONFIGURE command that will set the retention policy to a redundancy of 3.
3. Issue a REPORT command to display the names of all datafiles that do not satisfy the redundancy you have just set.
4. Exit RMAN.

Case Study

Ryan has been assigned the job of developing an appropriate incremental backup strategy for the database with some prerequisites. Restoration time should be minimized. Backups taken on a daily basis should not take long. On Sunday, the backup should incorporate all the backups that were performed on a daily basis. Reports are generated at the end of the month, so it is a time of high activity for the IT department. At the beginning of the month, things slow down for a while, during which a backup should be performed that includes all the used blocks of the database. Based on the information provided, what kind of strategy do you think Ryan can implement?

CHAPTER 3

RECOVERY IN ORACLE 10*g*

LEARNING OBJECTIVES

After completing this chapter, you should be able to:

- Identify the different types of failures that occur in the database
- Perform complete recovery
- Perform incomplete recovery
- Perform recovery of non-critical files

ORACLE CERTIFICATION EXAM OBJECTIVES COVERED IN THIS CHAPTER INCLUDE:

- Explain reasons for incomplete recovery
- Perform incomplete recovery using EM
- Perform incomplete recovery using RMAN
- Perform incomplete recovery using SQL
- Perform database recovery following a RESETLOGS operation
- Recover temporary tablespaces
- Recover a redo log group member
- Recover index tablespaces
- Recover read-only tablespaces
- Recreate the password file
- Recover the control file

INTRODUCTION

Different types of errors can occur in an Oracle database. Some are critical and some are not. Critical errors are those that need the intervention of the DBA to resolve them. Non-critical errors on the other hand, need little or no DBA intervention. In this chapter you will learn about the different kinds of errors and failures that may occur in the Oracle database and the methods available to an administrator to resolve them. Recovering from failures is a tricky task and should be done with utmost care and planning. An administrator should have tested various backup and recovery scenarios and be very sure of a well-tested recovery procedure when a problem arises. A fundamental element in recovery is the archiving mode of the database. Options for recovery from a loss or failure vary depending on the archiving mode of the database. This chapter considers the archiving mode of the database when presenting the recovery methods available within in the database.

The chapter discusses recovery based on two main categories: recovery of critical files and non-critical files. Critical files are those that are vital to the database itself and their loss can adversely affect the availability of the database. Non-critical files are not so vital and their loss may be tolerated to some extent. The chapter reviews complete and incomplete recovery with an emphasis on incomplete recovery and recovery from non-critical errors.

The chapter approaches the subject using a hands-on approach by presenting a number of practice examples that simulate failures that usually occur and demonstrate the recovery procedure.

THE CURRENT CHALLENGE AT KELLER MEDICAL CENTER

Anita is the senior database administrator at Keller Medical Center. As the DBA her primary goal is to ensure that the database is available and running optimally at all times. She has organized the DB101 database in such a manner that user data is stored in the USERS tablespace, temporary data in the TEMP tablespace, undo segments in the UNDOTBS tablespace, and index data in the INDX tablespace. In addition, she has other tablespaces to store data for various applications.

Since the database operates nonstop, she and Ryan (the recently hired junior DBA) have developed a method by which RMAN performs scheduled backups. This has made backing up the database much easier than it was previously.

Anita is also responsible for handling emergency situations at the IT department. One Friday afternoon, the datafile containing patient information was lost due to a hard disk failure. The situation needed immediate attention and Anita was called in to recover the datafile. Being the only DBA responsible for critical tasks has been very stressful and she is hoping Ryan will soon learn the methods available in Oracle 10g for recovery.

In this chapter Ryan will learn about media failure and the various methods available within Oracle that may be used to resolve them.

SETUP FOR THIS CHAPTER

In order to successfully complete the practice examples and hands-on tasks presented in this chapter, please execute the **ch03setup.sql** script available in the Chapter03 folder of the student datafiles. This script creates a user called MEDUSER whose password is MEDUSER. You may be required to login as this user during a number of hands-on tasks throughout this book.

1. Start SQL*Plus, and connect as a user with SYSDBA privileges.

   ```
   SQL>CONNECT SYS/ORACLE AS SYSDBA;
   ```

2. Execute the ch03setup.sql script.

   ```
   SQL><PATH>\ch03setup.sql
   ```

3. Exit SQL*Plus.

RECOVERY OPTIONS

As mentioned in a previous chapter, all production databases must operate in archivelog mode. When operating the database in this mode, Oracle creates an offline file using the contents of the redo log files. This is done every time a log switch occurs. Running a database in archivelog mode ensures that complete and incomplete recovery of the database is possible in the event of failure.

In noarchivelog mode, the options for recovery are limited. Since archive logs are not created, the only option available to the DBA in the event of a failure is restore the lost files or missing data from an existing backup. The database will be taken back in time and all the changes made since that backup will have to be re-entered manually.

NOTE

Complete Recovery is not possible when operating the database in noarchivelog mode.

An important decision as to whether it is necessary to be able to recover without any loss of data or some loss is tolerable must be made by the database administrator. If no loss can be tolerated, the database must be operated in archivelog mode. If some loss is tolerable then the database may operate in noarchivelog mode.

Media failure arises when there is a problem during input/output (I/O) operations to a file that is a part of the Oracle database. Media errors cannot be resolved by a user and require administrator intervention. Media failure can occur if there is a failure or damage to a disk on which files belonging to the database existed, or if a physical file of the database is accidentally deleted. To be able to recover from such errors a well-tested recovery strategy must be in place. Further, the backups that are available will determine the recovery options.

A database administrator's primary task is to ensure that in the event of media failure, complete recovery is possible. There are three methods of recovery available to an administrator of an Oracle database. They are user-managed recovery, RMAN recovery, and recovery using Enterprise Manager. In user-managed recovery, recovery is done manually by issuing commands. In RMAN recovery, recovery is performed by Recovery Manager, by the execution of a sequence of RMAN commands. This method is more reliable and less prone to error. Finally, there is the graphical interface of Enterprise Manager that makes selection of choices easy and recovery straightforward. In this chapter all three methods are discussed, with a specific focus of recovery using RMAN and Enterprise Manager.

Recovering the database in Noarchivelog Mode

It should be noted that complete recovery is not possible when the database is running in noarchivelog mode. Recovery is only possible up to the last backup that was taken. Consider a database running in noarchivelog mode. A complete closed backup was taken last night at 23:00 hours. In the morning a disk failure occurs causing a certain Oracle datafile that existed on the disk to become inaccessible. As part of the recovery the database administrator must restore all the files from the backup taken last night. All changes made to the database since the backup was taken are lost and have to be manually re-entered. This is the only option available when operating in noarchivelog mode whether you are performing recovery manually or using a tool such as RMAN or Enterprise Manager.

Recovering the database in Archivelog Mode

When the database is running in archivelog mode, a DBA can perform both complete and incomplete recovery. Complete recovery allows recovery right up to the time of failure. There is no loss of data. Incomplete recovery may be performed when you are unable to recover right up to the time of failure; however you are able to recover some changes beyond the last backup. This kind of recovery will be discussed in length in the section "Incomplete Recovery".

RECOVERY IN THE DATABASE

Recovery in an Oracle database involves two main steps. The first step is called **restoration**. In this step, the administrator or RMAN will use the files that exist in backup and replace the missing or damaged files. Restoration to the original location is possible if the disk on which the file existed is not damaged. In situations where the original location is not intact the files must be restored to another location. Restoration may be done manually using operating system commands or using the RMAN **RESTORE** command. The second step in recovery involves the application of archivelog and redo log files and is known as **recovery**. The appropriate archive and redo logs must be applied on the backup that was restored to recreate all the changes that occurred in the database since the backup.

In complete recovery, all the changes made to the database, existing in archivelogs taken since the backup and current redo log files need to be applied during this step. During incomplete recovery, you will apply changes in the archive log files to a point before the occurrence of the failure. Recovery is done by issuing a **RECOVER** command. The syntax of this command varies in complete and incomplete recovery.

Complete recovery may be a closed database or open database recovery. Closed database recovery is performed when the database is mounted. Open database recovery is performed when the database is open. Closed database recovery has to be done when you are recovering a file belonging to the system tablespace, a file containing active undo segments or when the entire database needs to be recovered. Open database recovery can be done on a datafile that does not belong to the SYSTEM tablespace. In open database recovery the datafile that needs to be recovered must be taken offline. All other datafiles can be accessed during the recovery process. Incomplete recovery is always done when the database is closed.

In the next few sections of this chapter you will learn about recovery options that are available when operating the database in archivelog mode. The methods will be discussed using either the manual method, RMAN or Enterprise Manager.

Performing Complete Recovery Manually

As you are already aware, complete recovery is recovery right up to the time of failure. There is no data loss in complete recovery.

If complete recovery is to be done manually, the restoration step is accomplished by copying the files from the backup media to their original location. This may be done using an operating system "copy" command.

In the recovery step you use the RECOVER command. When performing a closed database recovery, the DATABASE and DATAFILE options of the RECOVER command may be used. When performing an open database recovery, the DATABASE, TABLESPACE, or DATAFILE options of the RECOVER command may be used. The syntax of the RECOVER command is displayed below. The RECOVER command is issued from the SQL prompt.

```
RECOVER [DATABASE|TABLESPACE tablespace_name|{DATAFILE number|name}]
```

RMAN Commands for Complete Recovery

When using RMAN, both restoration and recovery is done by issuing commands. The RESTORE command is used for restoration and the RECOVER command for recovery.

The options of the RESTORE command will vary depending on whether you are performing an open or closed database restoration. A closed database restoration is done when the database is mounted and not opened.

During a complete recovery only the missing files need to be restored.

Restoration using RMAN

Open database restoration using RMAN: Open database restoration is done when a file that does not belong to the SYSTEM tablespace or does not contain active undo segments is being restored. You can use the DATABASE, TABLESPACE, or DATAFILE options of the RESTORE command when performing an open database restoration. The syntax of the RMAN RESTORE command in an open database restoration is:

```
RESTORE [DATABASE| TABLESPACE tablespace_name|{DATAFILE number | name}]
```

Closed database restoration using RMAN: Closed database restoration is done when a file belonging to the SYSTEM tablespace or one that contains active undo segments is being restored. You can use the DATABASE or DATAFILE option of the RESTORE command when performing a closed database recovery such as the recovery of the datafile belonging to the SYSTEM tablespace. The syntax of the RESTORE command in a closed database restoration is:

```
RESTORE [DATABASE |{DATAFILE number | name}]
```

Specifying an Alternate Location Using RMAN: When the original media on which the file(s) existed is damaged, an alternate location must be specified. The RMAN command to restore to an alternate location is the SET NEWNAME command. It informs RMAN of the new location of the file. After restoration, the control file of the database must be updated with the new location of the file. This is done using the SWITCH DATAFILE ALL command. The sequence of RMAN commands are:

```
SET NEWNAME FOR DATAFILE {'<original path>/datafilename' | datafile#}
TO '<new path>/datafilename';
RESTORE DATAFILE datafile# ;
SWITCH DATAFILE ALL;
```

For example if the datafile SYSAUX01.DBF (File# 3) that was originally on the C:\ drive is to be restored to say the D:\ drive. The commands you would issue are:

```
SET NEWNAME FOR DATAFILE 'C:\sysaux01.dbf' TO 'D:\sysaux01.dbf';
RESTORE DATAFILE 3;
SWITCH DATAFILE ALL;
```

Recovering the Database Using RMAN

Open database recovery using RMAN: Open database recovery may be done when recovering file(s) that do not belong to the SYSTEM tablespace or do not contain active undo segments. The RECOVER command may be used for this purpose. The options of this command include DATABASE, TABLESPACE, or DATAFILE. The DATABASE keyword may be used when a number of files are lost. The TABLESPACE option may be used when one or more datafiles of a certain tablespace are lost. The DATAFILE option may be used when a datafile is lost. The syntax of the RECOVER command is:

```
RECOVER [DATABASE| TABLESPACE tablespace_name| {DATAFILE number | name}]
```

Closed database recovery using RMAN: A closed database recovery must be done when trying to recover files that belong to the SYSTEM tablespace or that contain active undo segments. You may use the DATABASE or DATAFILE options of the RECOVER command when performing a closed database recovery. The syntax of the RECOVER command is:

```
RECOVER [DATABASE| DATAFILE {number | name}]
```

Examples of Recovering the Database Using RMAN

Closed database recovery must be performed when a datafile that belongs to the SYSTEM tablespace or one that contains active undo segments is lost. The database must be mounted during the recovery.

Practice 1: Complete closed database recovery using RMAN when operating the database in archivelog mode

Consider the following scenario. It is 12:30 p.m. Users have been accessing the database as usual. A sudden power surge occurs, causing a hard disk to fail. The datafile belonging to the SYSTEM tablespace was on the failed disk. This datafile contained the data dictionary. A closed database recovery needs to be performed. The name of the missing datafile is *system01.dbf*. Recovery has to be performed immediately.

Upon investigating the problem, you realize that it is not possible to restore the file to the original location.

Please make sure your database is running in archivelog mode by issuing the ARCHIVE LOG LIST command. Practice 1 of Chapter 1 describes how a database may be put in archivelog mode. Also, before you perform the recovery procedures described in this lesson, please perform a complete backup of the database. This is particularly necessary if you have not performed any of the backups described in Chapter 2.

In this practice you will simulate the error that might have occurred. Because it is not possible to intentionally simulate the loss of the hard disk, we will simulate only the loss of the datafile. You must choose a datafile belonging to the SYSTEM tablespace in your database.

Part 1: Simulating a scheduled backup of the database

1. Launch RMAN and connect to the target database. You may optionally connect to the recovery catalog database if you have created one.

```
C:\> RMAN
RMAN> CONNECT TARGET
RMAN> CONNECT CATALOG RMANUSER/RMANUSER@RCDB
```

2. Write the block displayed below to take a complete backup of the database and archivelogs.

```
RMAN> RUN{
      BACKUP DATABASE;
      BACKUP ARCHIVELOG ALL;
      }
```

3. Exit RMAN.

Part 2: Simulating the loss of a file belonging to the SYSTEM tablespace

4. Connect to SQL*Plus as a user with SYSDBA privileges.
5. Shutdown the DB101 database.

```
SQL> SHUTDOWN IMMEDIATE;
```

6. From the operating system, navigate to the folder that contains the datafile *system01.dbf* or a file belonging to the SYSTEM tablespace. The file will typically be in the %ORACLE_BASE%\oradata\db101 directory. Figure 3-1 indicates that the SYSTEM01.DBF file is located in `C:\ORACLE\PRODUCT\10.2.0\ORADATA\DB101`.

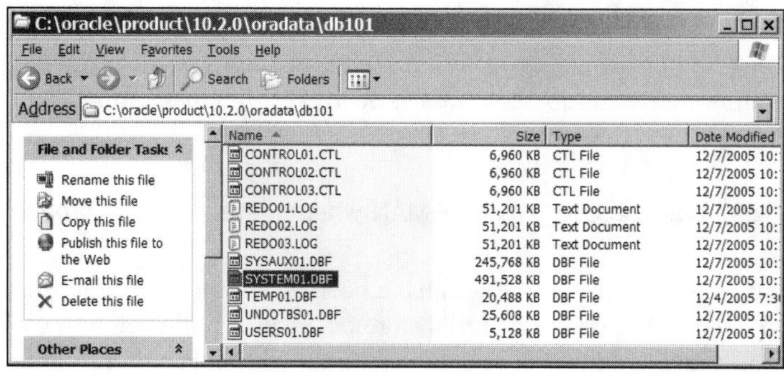

FIGURE 3-1 The location of the SYSTEM01.DBF file

7. Delete the SYSTEM01.DBF file using an operating system command.
8. Go back to SQL*Plus and try to startup the database. You will receive an error when trying to open the database. The database will remain in a mounted state. Figure 3-2 displays the error indicating the datafile (File 1) could not be found. Note the datafile number as displayed on your machine.

```
SQL> STARTUP
```

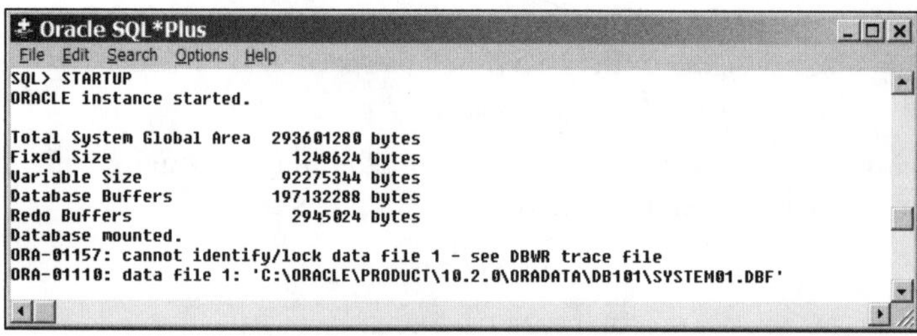

FIGURE 3-2 The STARTUP command fails indicating the SYSTEM01.DBF datafile is missing.

Part 3: Performing a complete closed recovery using RMAN

Because the file belongs to the SYSTEM tablespace, a closed database recovery must be performed.

9. Launch RMAN and connect to the target database. Connect to the recovery catalog database if you have created one.
10. Type the RUN block displayed below at the RMAN prompt to perform the recovery. In the block a channel called T1 is first allocated. Because our findings indicated the original location was damaged an alternate location is specified. In the

example it has been restored to F:\. You may substitute F:\ with any alternate drive letter that is on your machine. If not, you can use the same drive letter that the file was originally located in. The file is restored to the F:\ drive using the SET NEWNAME command. The RESTORE command then restores the lost file from backup. The control file is then updated with the new location using the SWITCH DATAFILE ALL command. The archivelogs are finally applied to the restored datafile by the RECOVER command. Please substitute in place of "1" the datafile number of the file belonging to the SYSTEM tablespace. This was noted in step 8. The output of the RUN block is displayed in Figure 3-3.

NOTE

When performing a complete recovery in archivelog mode, only the missing datafile needs to be restored.

```
RMAN> RUN{
      ALLOCATE CHANNEL T1 TYPE DISK;
      SET NEWNAME FOR DATAFILE 1 TO 'F:\SYSTEM01.DBF';
      RESTORE DATAFILE 1;
      SWITCH DATAFILE ALL;
      RECOVER DATAFILE 1;
      }
```

11. Finally, open the database from the RMAN prompt. Figure 3-3 displays the output of the complete closed recovery done using RMAN.

```
RMAN> ALTER DATABASE OPEN;
```

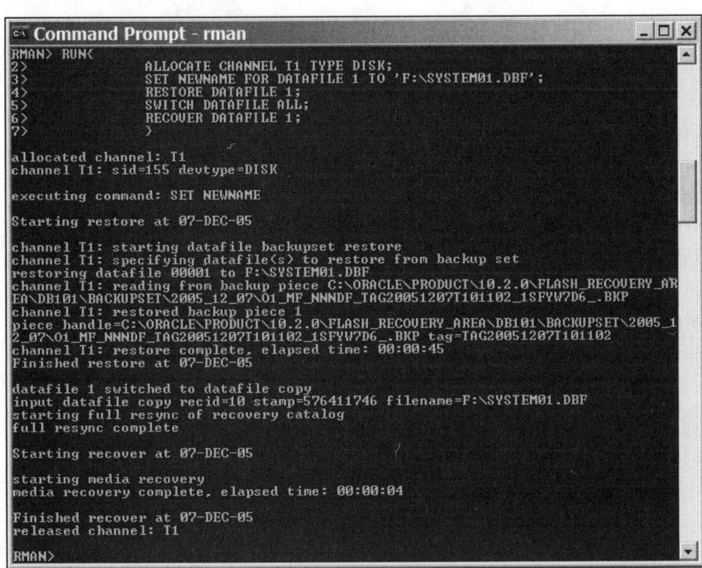

FIGURE 3-3 The RMAN block that performs recovery to an alternate location

12. Exit RMAN.

NOTE

Once you have completed this practice example, you may want to restore the file SYSTEM01.DBF to the same location as other datafiles of the database. Performing these steps is optional, but recommended so that all the datafiles of the database are in a single folder, making it easier for you to go through other exercises in this chapter.

```
C:\>RMAN
RMAN> CONNECT TARGET
RMAN> SHUTDOWN IMMEDIATE;
RMAN> STARTUP MOUNT;
RMAN> RUN{
      SET NEWNAME FOR DATAFILE 1 TO '<original_ path> \
      SYSTEM01.DBF';
      RESTORE DATAFILE 1;
      SWITCH DATAFILE ALL;
      RECOVER DATABASE;
      SQL 'ALTER DATABASE OPEN';
      }
RMAN> EXIT
```

Open database recovery may be performed when a datafile that does not belong to the SYSTEM tablespace or one that does not contain active undo segments is lost. Before performing the recovery you will need to take the missing datafile offline. The rest of the database may be opened during the recovery process.

Practice 2: Complete open database recovery using RMAN when operating the database in archivelog mode

Consider the following scenario. It is 8:30 a.m. The database administrator has mounted the database to perform some maintenance tasks. Upon opening the database an error is displayed indicating that the *users01.dbf* file is not available. The datafile contained many important tables and must be recovered right away. The original location of the file is intact.

In this practice example we will first take a complete backup of the database and then simulate the error that might have occurred by deleting the users01.dbf datafile. If this datafile does not exist on your machine, choose an alternate datafile. However, do not choose one that belongs to either the SYSTEM tablespace or the datafiles of the active undo tablespace. You will then perform open database recovery using RMAN.

Part 1: Performing a complete backup of the database using RMAN

Perform a complete backup or all datafiles and archivelogs using RMAN before you begin with this recovery. This backup will simulate a scheduled backup of the database.

1. Launch RMAN and connect to the target database. You may optionally connect to the recovery catalog database if you have created one.
2. Issue the RUN block displayed below to take a complete backup of the database, followed by a backup of all archive files.

```
RMAN> RUN{
      BACKUP DATABASE;
      BACKUP ARCHIVELOG ALL;
      }
```

3. Exit RMAN.

Part 2: Simulating the loss of the datafile:

4. Connect to SQL*Plus as a user with SYSDBA privileges.
5. Shutdown the database.

```
SQL> SHUTDOWN IMMEDIATE;
```

6. From the operating system, navigate to the folder that contains the datafile *users01.dbf* and delete it. If you do not have a datafile called *users01.dbf* choose a datafile that does not belong to the SYSTEM tablespace. If you are unsure about the datafile to select, please ask your instructor. Figure 3-4 displays the physical files of the DB101 database as the `%ORACLE_BASE%\oradata\DB101` directory.

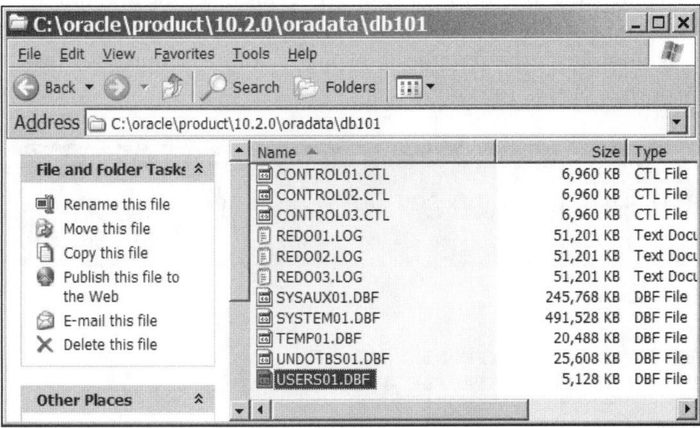

FIGURE 3-4 The location of the physical file of the DB101 database

7. Go back to SQL*Plus and try to startup the database. You will receive an error when trying to open the database. The database will be in a mounted state. The error displays the datafile number and name of the missing file. Note the name and number. The datafile number will be required in step 10 of this practice. In Figure 3-5, the datafile number is 4 and datafile name is C:\ORACLE\PRODUCT\10.2.0\ORADATA\DB101\USERS01.DBF.

```
SQL> STARTUP
```

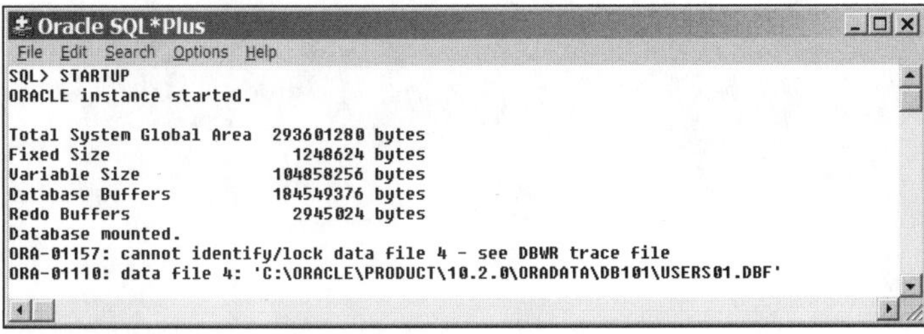

FIGURE 3-5 The RMAN block that performs recovery

8. Exit SQL*Plus.

Part 3: Performing a complete open recovery using RMAN:

Since the file does not belong to the SYSTEM tablespace, an open database recovery may be performed.

9. Launch RMAN and connect to the target database. Connect to the recovery catalog database if you have created one.
10. Type the RUN block, displayed below, at the RMAN prompt to perform the recovery. In the block a channel called T1 is allocated. The missing datafile (# 4) is then taken offline. The datafile number was identified in Step 7. This is done using the ALTER DATABASE ... OFFLINE command. The database is then opened so that the rest of database is accessible. The RESTORE command restores the missing file from backup. The archivelogs are finally applied to the restored datafile by the RECOVER DATAFILE command. After media recovery is complete, the datafile is brought online. Figure 3-6 displays the RMAN output of this recovery.

NOTE

When issuing SQL commands from RMAN, use the prefix SQL, before executing the command. Enclose the SQL command in single quotes.

```
RMAN> RUN{
      ALLOCATE CHANNEL T1 TYPE DISK;
      SQL 'ALTER DATABASE DATAFILE 4 OFFLINE';
      SQL ' ALTER DATABASE OPEN';
      RESTORE DATAFILE 4;
      RECOVER DATAFILE 4;
      SQL 'ALTER DATABASE DATAFILE 4 ONLINE';
      }
```

NOTE

Note: In an open database recovery you may use the TABLESPACE keyword instead of DATAFILE, as shown in this command block:

```
RMAN> RUN
 {SQL 'ALTER DATABASE DATAFILE 4 OFFLINE';
  SQL 'ALTER DATABASE OPEN';
  RESTORE TABLESPACE USERS;
  RECOVER TABLESPACE USERS;
  SQL 'ALTER TABLESPACE USERS ONLINE';
  }
```

11. Exit RMAN.

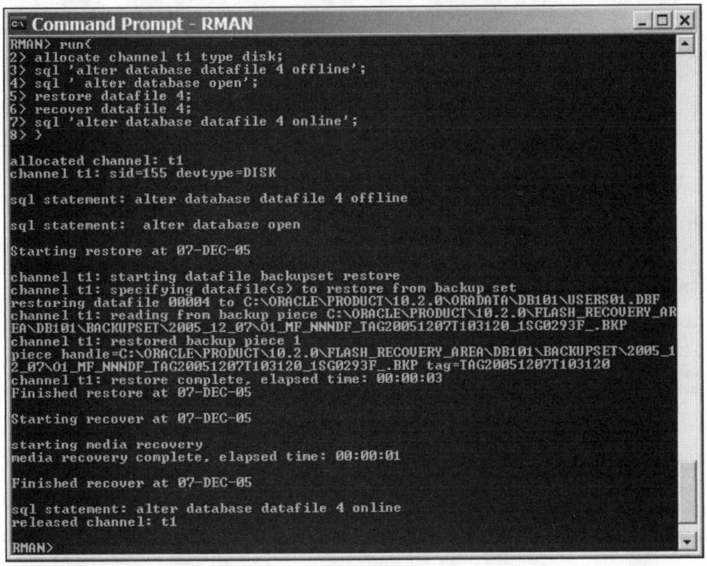

```
Command Prompt - RMAN
RMAN> run{
2> allocate channel t1 type disk;
3> sql 'alter database datafile 4 offline';
4> sql ' alter database open';
5> restore datafile 4;
6> recover datafile 4;
7> sql 'alter database datafile 4 online';
8> }

allocated channel: t1
channel t1: sid=155 devtype=DISK

sql statement: alter database datafile 4 offline

sql statement:  alter database open

Starting restore at 07-DEC-05

channel t1: starting datafile backupset restore
channel t1: specifying datafile(s) to restore from backup set
restoring datafile 00004 to C:\ORACLE\PRODUCT\10.2.0\ORADATA\DB101\USERS01.DBF
channel t1: reading from backup piece C:\ORACLE\PRODUCT\10.2.0\FLASH_RECOVERY_AR
EA\DB101\BACKUPSET\2005_12_07\O1_MF_NNNDF_TAG20051207T103120_1SG0293F_.BKP
channel t1: restored backup piece 1
piece handle=C:\ORACLE\PRODUCT\10.2.0\FLASH_RECOVERY_AREA\DB101\BACKUPSET\2005_1
2_07\O1_MF_NNNDF_TAG20051207T103120_1SG0293F_.BKP tag=TAG20051207T103120
channel t1: restore complete, elapsed time: 00:00:03
Finished restore at 07-DEC-05

Starting recover at 07-DEC-05

starting media recovery
media recovery complete, elapsed time: 00:00:01

Finished recover at 07-DEC-05

sql statement: alter database datafile 4 online
released channel: t1

RMAN>
```

FIGURE 3-6 The RMAN block for recovery

INCOMPLETE RECOVERY

Sometimes, a database administrator may not be able to perform complete recovery even when the database is operating in archivelog mode. For example if a user accidentally drops an important table and the approximate time that the table was dropped is known, the DBA can recover from the loss of the table by performing incomplete recovery up to that time. All changes from the time of recovery to the present time will be lost and have to be manually re-entered. Another example of an incomplete recovery could be the loss of one or more archivelog files. If a certain archivelog file is missing, then you cannot apply it during complete recovery and you would have to terminate the recovery when Oracle tries to apply it.

There are three kinds of Incomplete Recovery. You would choose the appropriate method based on the error condition. The Table 3-1 displays the different types of incomplete recovery methods available in the Oracle database.

TABLE 3-1 Incomplete recovery methods and their description

Incomplete Recovery Method	Description
Time-based Incomplete Recovery	This method is used to recover the database up to a certain time in the past.
SCN based Incomplete Recovery	This method is used to recover the database up to a certain System Change Number (SCN). See the note below.
Sequence based Incomplete Recovery	This method is used to recover the database up to the application of a certain log file (archive or redo log).

NOTE

When a user commits a transaction, the transaction is assigned a system change number (SCN), which Oracle records along with the transaction's redo entries in the redo log file.

Guidelines When Performing Incomplete Recovery

When performing incomplete recovery, Oracle recommends taking a complete backup of the database, before and after the recovery. The backup you perform before the incomplete recovery should be done so that if for any reason the incomplete recovery does not succeed as expected, you can at least return to the point of failure.

NOTE

The backup that is taken before the incomplete recovery must be done manually and not using RMAN. The steps to take to complete closed backup manually are:
1. Shutdown the database.
2. Copy all the physical files of the database to a backup folder using operating system commands. (Refer to Case-Study 1 in Chapter 1).

The second backup should be performed after the recovery is completed successfully. This backup may be taken using RMAN. In earlier versions of Oracle, this was a mandatory step. However in Oracle 10g, backups taken prior to the incomplete recovery can be used even after an incomplete recovery of the database is done. This point has been explained under the topic Simplified Recovery through Resetlogs.

NOTE

It is important to restore all the datafiles during incomplete recovery, not just the missing datafiles.

You must also remember to open your database using the RESETLOGS clause after performing the incomplete recovery. This resets the log sequence numbers to begin with 0. A new incarnation of the database is created after an incomplete recovery.

Basic steps for performing an Incomplete Recovery

The steps presented below are common to all incomplete recoveries. Only the RECOVER command will vary depending on the kind of incomplete recovery. The steps include:

- Query the V$DATAFILE view and make sure all datafiles are currently ONLINE. OFFLINE datafiles cannot be recovered after an incomplete recovery.
- Shut down the database and perform a complete closed backup using a method other than RMAN. Backup to some other location, without overwriting already existing backups.
- Mount the database.
- Indicate the new location if the original location is damaged or unavailable.
- Restore all the datafiles, not just the missing file.

- If you performed step 5, update the control file about the new location of the file.
- Recover the database by using UNTIL TIME, UNTIL SEQUENCE, or UNTIL SCN.
- Open the database using the RESETLOGS option.
- Perform a whole database backup, either online or offline, using any method.

Incomplete Recovery Methods

User–Managed Incomplete Recovery

When performing incomplete recovery, you will perform two main steps. You will first restore all the datafiles of the database using an operating system "copy" command. You will recover the database using the SQL RECOVER command.

The RECOVER command When performing incomplete recovery manually the syntax of the RECOVER command is slightly different. An optional keyword AUTOMATIC may be specified to indicate that the required archive log files should be automatically applied by Oracle. Omitting the keyword causes Oracle to prompt you for the name of archivelog file. The RECOVER command takes one of the following forms depending on the type of incomplete recovery being performed.

- For time-based incomplete recovery:

  ```
  RECOVER [AUTOMATIC] DATABASE UNTIL TIME 'DD-MON-YYYY HH:MI:SS'
  ```

- For cancel-based incomplete recovery:

  ```
  RECOVER DATABASE UNTIL CANCEL
  ```

- For change-based incomplete recovery

  ```
  RECOVER [AUTOMATIC] DATABASE UNTIL SCN n;
  ```

Where *n* is the system change number up to which you wish to recover (*n* not inclusive).

NOTE

Note: The automatic option should not be used during cancel-based recovery since you would need to control when incomplete recovery must be terminated.

Practice 3: Performing Time-Based Incomplete Recovery using the User-Managed Method

This kind of recovery may be performed when the approximate time the error occurred is known. The present time is 3:30 p.m. Jenny, the staff nurse has been using the PATIENT_TAB table all morning looking up patient information. She rushes to the database administrator saying that she might have accidentally dropped the PATIENT_TAB table while running one of the scripts. She had been away from her desk for the past two hours, and the last time she accessed the PATIENT_TAB table was around 1:10 p.m. At that time, when querying the table, she got all her results without a problem. Before she went out for lunch, she had deleted some temporary tables, and wasn't quite sure if it was then that she accidentally deleted the PATIENT_TAB table. Anita, the senior DBA decides to perform an incomplete recovery. She has to restore the database to the state it was in at 1:10 p.m. All changes made to the database from 1:10 p.m. to the present time will be lost.

In this practice example you will first simulate the problem and then perform the steps required to perform the incomplete recovery.

Part 1: Simulate the accidental loss of the PATIENT_TAB table

1. Open SQL*Plus and log in as a user with SYSDBA privileges.
2. Shut down the database and take a complete backup of the database, **manually**. See the note in section Guidelines When Performing Incomplete Recovery. This backup simulates a regular backup taken at Keller Medical Center. We shall refer to this backup as BACKUP1. This backup will be used during restoration.
3. Startup the database.

   ```
   SQL> STARTUP
   ```

4. Go the Chapter03 folder included as part of the datafiles of this book. Run the script called **ch03time.sql** from the SQL prompt. This script creates a table called PATIENT_TAB, adds some rows to the table and commits the changes.

   ```
   SQL> START <PATH>\CH03TIME.SQL
   ```

5. Describe or query the PATIENT_TAB table to make sure it was created.

   ```
   SQL> SELECT * FROM PATIENT_TAB;
   ```

6. Note the exact date and time maintained by the Oracle Server. You can use the SELECT statement displayed below to obtain it. We shall refer to this time as T1.

   ```
   SQL> SELECT TO_CHAR(SYSDATE,'DD-MON-YYYY HH24:MI:SS') FROM DUAL;
   ```

   For the sake of this example, the time T1 is "07-DEC-2005 10:49:51".
7. Wait for a few minutes.
8. Go to the Chapter03 folder and execute the script called **ch03drop.sql** from the SQL prompt. This script deletes the PATIENT_TAB table, created in the step 4. Query the PATIENT_TAB table to make sure it no longer exists. Figure 3-7 indicates that the query on the PATIENT_TAB fails because the table has been dropped.

   ```
   SQL> START <PATH>\CH03DROP.SQL
   SQL> SELECT * FROM PATIENT_TAB;
   ```

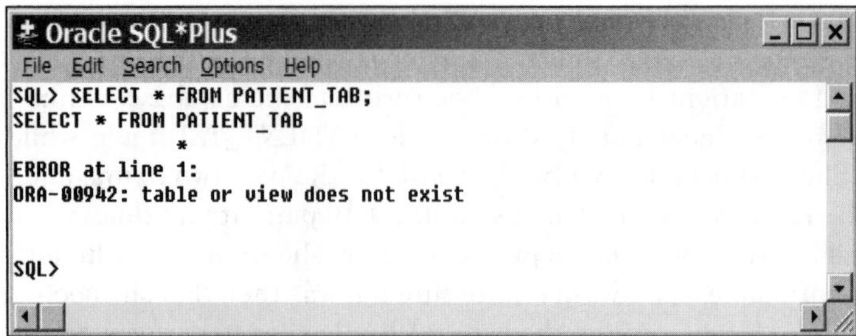

FIGURE 3-7 The PATIENT_TAB table has been dropped.

9. Note the exact date and time maintained by the Oracle Server. You can use the SELECT statement displayed below to obtain it. We shall refer to this time as T2.

```
SQL> SELECT TO_CHAR(SYSDATE,'DD-MON-YYYY HH24:MI:SS') FROM DUAL;
```

For the sake of this example, the time T2 is "07-DEC-2005 10:58:45".

Part 2: Performing the Incomplete Recovery Manually

10. Before performing an incomplete recovery, it is important to bring all offline datafiles online. Offline datafiles cannot be recovered after an incomplete recovery. Query the V$DATAFILE view and make sure all the datafiles of the database are currently ONLINE. For example, if the PHYAPP01.DBF (file# 6) is offline you can bring it online using ALTER DATABASE DATAFILE 6 ONLINE. This command is only an example and need not be executed if none of your datafiles are currently offline. Figure 3-8 indicates that all the files are currently online.

```
SQL> SELECT NAME, STATUS FROM V$DATAFILE;
```

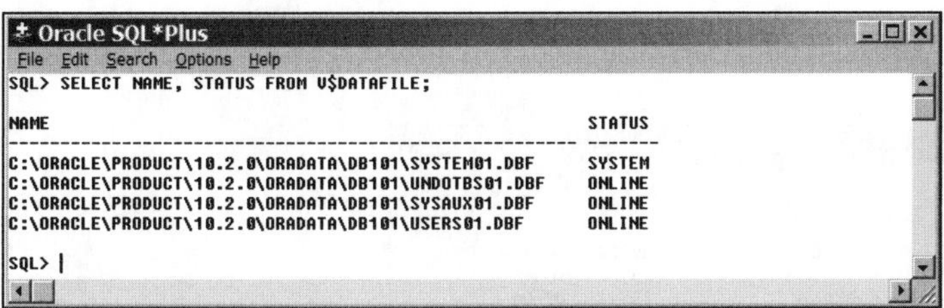

FIGURE 3-8 Querying the V$DATAFILE view to display the online status.

11. Shutdown the database.

```
SQL>SHUTDOWN IMMEDIATE;
```

12. Perform a complete closed backup, by manually copying the files of the database to another location. See the note in the section Guidelines When Performing Incomplete Recovery. This backup should not overwrite any previously taken backups and will be used if there is an error during the recovery process. We shall refer to this backup as BACKUP2. This is the backup that must be taken before performing the incomplete recovery.
13. Restore *all* the datafiles to the original location using an operating system "copy" command—%ORACLE_BASE%\ORADATA\DB101—using a backup taken prior to the time of failure. You will use the datafiles from the backup identified as BACKUP1.
14. Mount the database, from SQL*Plus using:

```
SQL> STARTUP MOUNT;
```

15. The next step is optional. You may issue this so that you make sure you do not encounter an error with recovery because of an incorrect time format. Issue the ALTER SESSION command to set the NLS_DATE_FORMAT parameter to interpret the date using a 24-hour format.

```
SQL> ALTER SESSION SET NLS_DATE_FORMAT='DD-MON-YYYY HH24:MI:SS':
```

16. Issue the RECOVER DATABASE command using UNTIL TIME option. The time that you specify is the time T1 you noted in Step 6.

```
SQL> RECOVER DATABASE UNTIL TIME '07-DEC-2005 10:49:51';
```

17. Open the database by using the RESETLOGS open of the ALTER DATABASE command.

```
SQL>ALTER DATABASE OPEN RESETLOGS;
```

18. Verify that you have recovered the database as desired. Using SQL*Plus and issue a SELECT statement to retrieve data from the PATIENT_TAB table. Figure 3-9 indicates that the PATIENT_TAB table has been successfully recovered.

```
SQL>SELECT * FROM PATIENT_TAB;
```

```
Oracle SQL*Plus
File Edit Search Options Help
SQL> SELECT * FROM PATIENT_TAB;

PATIENT_NO PATIENT_NAME              PHYSICIAN     WARD_NO DATE_IN
---------- ------------------------- ---------- ---------- ---------
1          FRED                      MARYANN T          10 14-JAN-06
2          BRYAN                     DR. RAJ            20 22-FEB-06
3          PAULA                     DR.GREG            20 21-FEB-06

SQL>
```

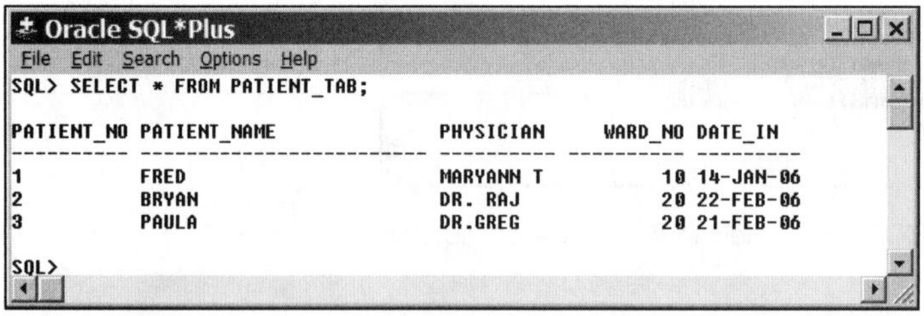

FIGURE 3-9 The PATIENT_TAB table has been recovered.

19. Exit SQL*Plus.

Once you have confirmed that your table now exists, you may take a backup of the database, either manually, using RMAN or Enterprise Manager.

Incomplete Recovery Using RMAN

The SET UNTIL command in RMAN The SET UNTIL command is used when using RMAN to perform incomplete recovery. Instead of using a RECOVER DATABASE UNTIL clause as shown in the manual method, you use the SET UNTIL statement to inform RMAN about the kind of incomplete recovery it must perform. The SET UNTIL command can take one of the following forms.

- For Time-based incomplete recovery:

```
SET UNTIL TIME 'DD MON YYYY HH:MI:SS'
```

- For Cancel-based incomplete recovery:

```
SET UNTIL LOG SEQUENCE n
```

- For SCN-based incomplete recovery:

```
SET UNTIL SCN n
```

We will now learn the different recovery procedures based on a number of different scenarios. The method of recovery may be manual, done using RMAN or using Enterprise Manager. You must be familiar with all the methods.

Practice 4: Performing Change-Based Incomplete Recovery using Recovery Manager

The present time is 3:30 p.m. Jenny, the staff nurse has been using the CHANGE_REC table all morning to look up patient information. She has been working with the table since 9 a.m. During the course of the day, she has been dropping various tables and feels she might have accidentally dropped the CHANGE_REC table.

In the scenario presented, the approximate time of error is not known and would be a suitable scenario for a change-based recovery. Every transaction is assigned an SCN number that is recorded in the redo log files. For example, if you issue a DROP TABLE command, Oracle will assign it an SCN number. If you wish to recover to the point just before the DROP TABLE command, you can perform a change-based incomplete recovery using its SCN number. To successfully perform change-based recovery you must determine the SCN number of the statement up to which you want to perform recovery. This can be done by analyzing the log files using the **Logminer** utility.

The Logminer is a tool provided by Oracle that may be used to analyze the contents of the redo/archive log files. The DBMS_LOGMNR and DBMS_LOGMNR_D Oracle-supplied packages may be used with Logminer. The output of Logminer may be viewed using the V$LOGMNR_CONTENTS view.

In this practice example we will perform the steps required to use the Logminer utility to find out the SCN of a DROP TABLE command.

Part 1: Simulating the loss of the CHANGE_REC table

1. Open SQL*Plus and login as a user with SYSDBA privileges.
2. Take a complete backup of the database. This simulates a regular backup taken at Keller Medical Center. We shall refer to this backup as BACKUP1. This backup may be taken using RMAN.
3. Go the Chapter03 folder and run the script called **ch03change.sql** from the SQL prompt. This script creates a table called CHANGE_REC and then drops it. We will have to find out the SCN number of the DROP TABLE CHANGE_REC; command.

```
SQL> START <PATH>\CH03CHANGE.SQL
```

4. Verify that the table no longer exists by querying it. Figure 3-10 indicates that the CHANGE_REC table does not exist.

```
SQL> SELECT * FROM CHANGE_REC;
```

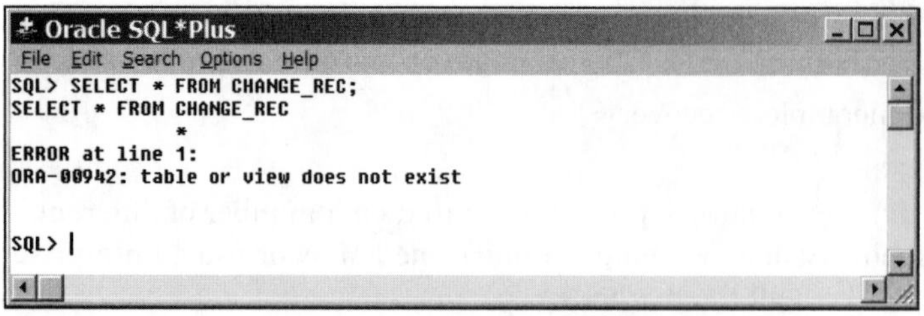

```
Oracle SQL*Plus
File Edit Search Options Help
SQL> SELECT * FROM CHANGE_REC;
SELECT * FROM CHANGE_REC
              *
ERROR at line 1:
ORA-00942: table or view does not exist

SQL> |
```

FIGURE 3-10 The CHANGE_REC table has been dropped.

Part 2: Using the LogMiner utility to determine the SCN.

5. The LogMiner utility is used specifically to analyze redo log files. Redo log files contain a record of all the changes made to a database. The following steps describe how you can read the contents of the redo log files. The first step is to set the value of the initialization parameter UTL_FILE_DIR to a directory on your machine. This is the location where Oracle can create a flat file containing the contents of the data dictionary. The flat file is required by Logminer.
6. Open SQL*Plus, connect as a user with SYSDBA privileges.
7. Issue the following command to set the value of the UTL_FILE_DIR parameter in the initialization parameter file (spfile). In the example, the location of the data dictionary file is set to C:\LOGMINER.

```
SQL> ALTER SYSTEM SET UTL_FILE_DIR='C:\LOGMINER' SCOPE=SPFILE;
```

8. Shut down the database.

```
SQL> SHUTDOWN IMMEDIATE;
```

9. Start up the database.

```
SQL>STARTUP
```

10. Create a directory called LOGMINER in the C:\ drive using an operating system command.
11. You will now create a data dictionary file on the operating system. You use the DBMS_LOGMNR_D.BUILD packaged procedure to do so. The first argument of the procedure is the name of the data dictionary file (call it LOGDICT.ORA) you are creating and the second argument is the location where the file it to be created. The value of the second argument should be the same as the value set for the UTL_FILE_DIR parameter.

```
SQL> EXECUTE DBMS_LOGMNR_D.BUILD('LOGDICT.ORA','C:\LOGMINER');
```

12. The next step is to create a list of redo log files that Logminer can analyze. The redo logs contain the SCN that you are trying to determine. Use the DBMS_LOGMNR.ADD_LOGFILE packaged procedure to do so. The procedure receives two parameters. The first is the name of the redo log file, specifying its complete path. The second parameter indicates whether it is the first log file (DBMS_LOGMNR.NEW) or a subsequent redo log file (DBMS_LOGMNR.ADDFILE). The ADDFILE option will be repeated for all redo log and archive

logs that you add to the list other than the first. Figure 3-11 displays the output of adding the redo log files to the list.

```
SQL> EXECUTE DBMS_LOGMNR.ADD_LOGFILE(LOGFILENAME =>
     '<path>\redo01.log', OPTIONS => DBMS_LOGMNR.NEW);
SQL> EXECUTE DBMS_LOGMNR.ADD_LOGFILE(LOGFILENAME =>
     '<path>\redo02.log', OPTIONS=> DBMS_LOGMNR.ADDFILE);
```

```
Oracle SQL*Plus
File Edit Search Options Help
SQL> EXECUTE DBMS_LOGMNR.ADD_LOGFILE(-
> LOGFILENAME => 'C:\ORACLE\PRODUCT\10.2.0\ORADATA\DB101\REDO01.LOG', -
> OPTIONS => DBMS_LOGMNR.NEW);

PL/SQL procedure successfully completed.

SQL> EXECUTE DBMS_LOGMNR.ADD_LOGFILE(-
> LOGFILENAME => 'C:\ORACLE\PRODUCT\10.2.0\ORADATA\DB101\REDO02.LOG',-
> OPTIONS => DBMS_LOGMNR.ADDFILE);

PL/SQL procedure successfully completed.

SQL>
```

FIGURE 3-11 Adding the redo logs to the list for log mining.

13. Next, start the mining process using the DBMS_LOGMNR.START_LOGMNR procedure. The DDL_DICT_TRACKING option indicates that you wish to track DDL commands in the redo log file.

```
SQL> EXECUTE DBMS_LOGMNR.START_LOGMNR(OPTIONS=>
      DBMS_LOGMNR.DDL_DICT_TRACKING);
```

14. You can now query the V$LOGMNR_CONTENTS view to determine the SCN number. The columns that will give you the SCN and the original statement that was issued are SCN and SQL_REDO. Type the following SELECT statement to display all the SCN numbers assigned to the DDL commands issued on the CHANGE_REC table.

```
SQL> SELECT SCN, SQL_REDO FROM V$LOGMNR_CONTENTS
      WHERE SEG_NAME='CHANGE_REC';
```

Figure 3-12 displays the SCN number for the DROP TABLE CHANGE_REC as 804223.

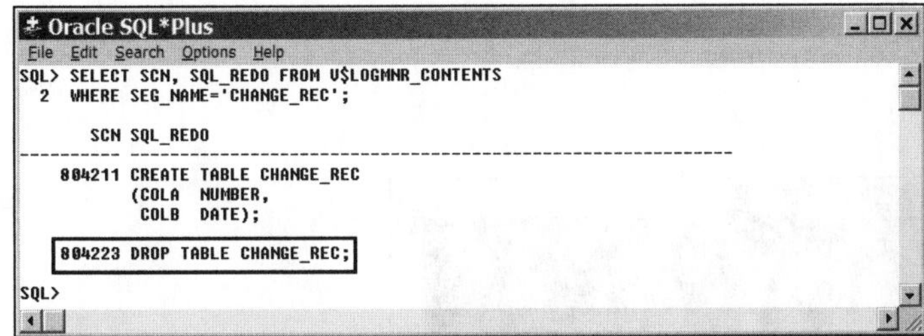
Oracle SQL*Plus
File Edit Search Options Help
SQL> SELECT SCN, SQL_REDO FROM V$LOGMNR_CONTENTS
2 WHERE SEG_NAME='CHANGE_REC';
SCN SQL_REDO
804211 CREATE TABLE CHANGE_REC
(COLA NUMBER,
COLB DATE);
804223 DROP TABLE CHANGE_REC;
SQL>

FIGURE 3-12 Querying the V$LOGMNR_CONTENTS to obtain the SCN

15. Now that you have determined the desired SCN number, note the SCN, since you will need it in Step 21 of this practice. You can stop the mining session, by executing:

```
SQL> EXECUTE DBMS_LOGMNR.END_LOGMNR;
```

Part 3: Performing the Incomplete Recovery using RMAN:

16. Launch SQL*Plus, query the V$DATAFILE view and make sure all datafiles are currently ONLINE.

```
SQL> SELECT FILE#, STATUS FROM V$DATAFILE;
```

17. If any of the files are offline, bring them online, using the `ALTER DATABASE DATAFILE <file#> ONLINE;` command.
18. Shutdown the database and perform a complete closed backup *manually*. See the note in the section Guidelines When Performing Incomplete Recovery. Perform the backup to some other location, without overwriting already existing backups. This backup can be used to restore the database back to this point in case the incomplete recovery fails. We shall refer to this backup as BACKUP2.
19. Connect to RMAN and to the target database. You may connect to the recovery catalog database if you have created one.
20. Mount the target database.

```
RMAN> STARTUP MOUNT;
```

21. Type the RMAN block displayed to perform the change-based incomplete recovery to recover the table CHANGE_REC. The SET UNTIL SCN command tells RMAN the SCN number (not inclusive) up to which recovery must be done. The RESTORE DATABASE instructs RMAN to pick up all the datafiles from the appropriate backup. The RECOVER DATABASE command instructs RMAN to apply the archive log files. The ALTER DATABASE OPEN RESETLOGS command creates a new incarnation of the database after incomplete recovery is performed. Figure 3-13 displays the RMAN block that you must type to perform an SCN-based incomplete recovery.

```
RMAN> RUN{
      ALLOCATE CHANNEL C1 TYPE DISK;
      SET UNTIL SCN 804223;
      RESTORE DATABASE;
      RECOVER DATABASE;
      ALTER DATABASE OPEN RESETLOGS;
      }
```

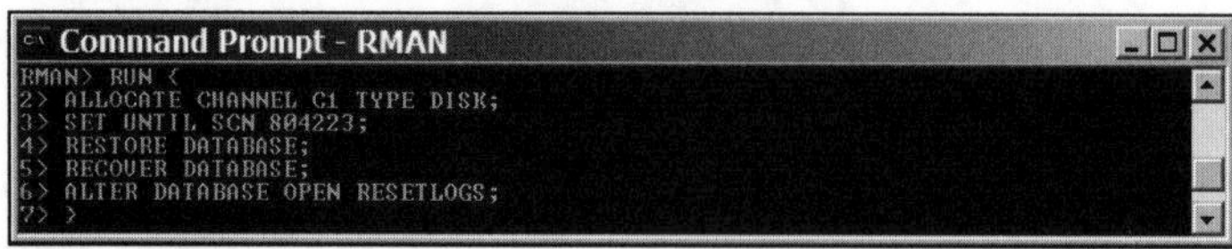

FIGURE 3-13 Performing recovery using RMAN.

22. Verify that you have recovered the database as desired. Open SQL*Plus and issue a SELECT statement to retrieve data from the CHANGE_REC table. Figure 3-14 displays the contents of the CHANGE_REC table indicating it was successfully recovered.

```
SQL> SELECT * FROM CHANGE_REC;
```

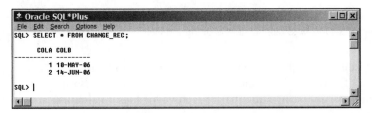

FIGURE 3-14 The CHANGE_REC table has been recovered.

23. Exit SQL*Plus and RMAN.

Once you have confirmed that your table now exists, you may take a backup of the database, either manually, using RMAN or from Oracle Enterprise Manager.

Practice 5: Performing Cancel-Based Incomplete Recovery using Recovery Manager

Cancel-based recovery is also referred to as sequence-based recovery. In this type of incomplete recovery the DBA cancels the recovery some time during the application of archived or redo log files. This method can be used when a specific archivelog file required for recovery is missing. It can also be used if a current redo log file that has not been archived is missing. The steps in the following practice example demonstrate the loss of a current unarchived redo log file and the recovery steps that need to be done.

Part 1: Simulating a scheduled backup using RMAN.

1. Launch in to RMAN and connect to the target database and recovery catalog database if you have created one.
2. Start up the database if it has not already been started.

```
RMAN> STARTUP
```

3. Perform a complete backup of the database. This simulates a scheduled backup of the database taken at Keller Medical Center. The backup may be performed using RMAN.

Part 2: Simulating the loss of the current redo log file:

4. Start SQL*Plus and log in as a user with SYSDBA privileges.
5. Issue the command displayed to query the V$LOG performance view to retrieve the log sequence numbers of the current redo log files. Log sequence number may vary on your machine. Figure 3-15 displays the output of the query on the V$LOG view.

```
SQL> SELECT GROUP#, SEQUENCE#, ARCHIVED, STATUS FROM V$LOG;
```

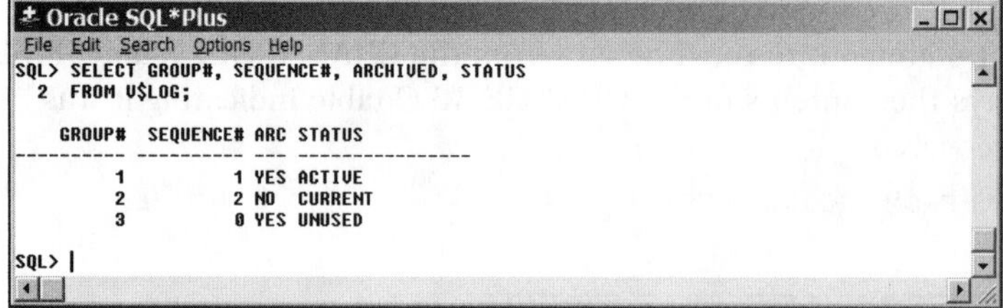

FIGURE 3-15 Querying the V$LOG view to display details of the log files.

6. Run the script **ch03seq.sql** from the Chapter03 folder. This script creates a table called LOG_REC, inserts some rows into the table, and performs a number of log switches generating a number of archive log files, to simulate activity in the database.

```
SQL> START <PATH>\CH03SEQ.SQL
```

7. Re-issue the query to display the group#, log sequence number, and archival status of the log files. Note the sequence number of the *current* redo log file that has *not* yet been archived. In our example it is group 1 with a log sequence number of 4. Figure 3-16 indicates that the Group 1, with a log sequence number 4 is the current redo log file.

```
SQL> SELECT GROUP#, SEQUENCE#, ARCHIVED, STATUS FROM V$LOG;
```

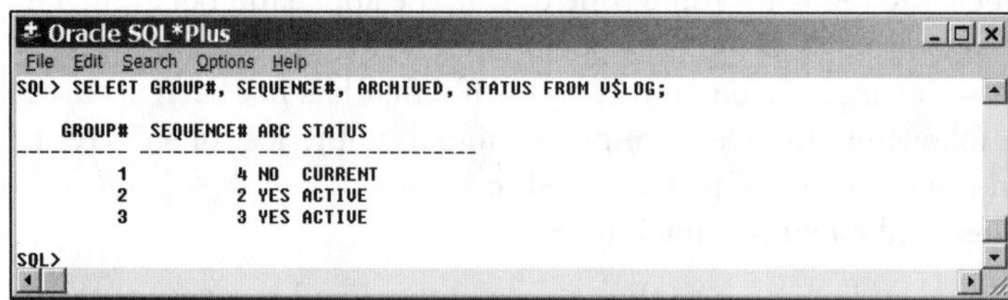

FIGURE 3-16 Querying the V$LOG to display information about the log files.

8. Next, determine the name of the redo log files that belong to the current group by querying the V$LOGFILE view. Substitute the group# you noted down in place of the 1 in our example. Figure 3-17 displays the name of the redo log files belonging to the current redo group as `C:\ORACLE\PRODUCT\10.2.0\ORADATA\DB101\REDO01.LOG`.

```
SQL> SELECT MEMBER FROM V$LOGFILE WHERE GROUP#=1;
```

9. Shutdown the database.

```
SQL> SHUTDOWN IMMEDIATE;
```

10. Using Windows Explorer, locate the redo log file belonging to the current group and delete it using an operating system command. This simulates the loss of the current unarchived redo log file.

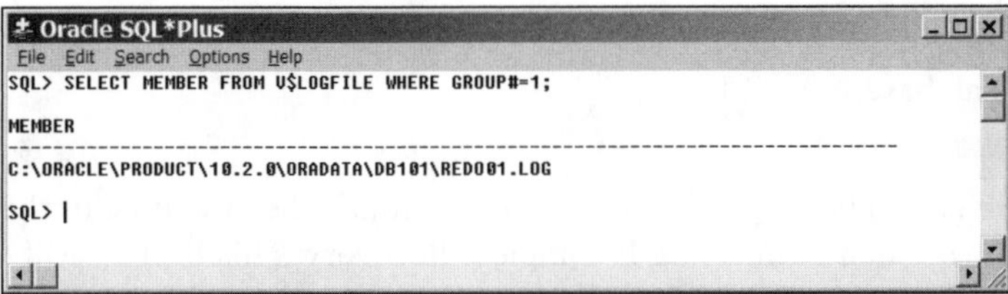

```
SQL> SELECT MEMBER FROM V$LOGFILE WHERE GROUP#=1;

MEMBER
--------------------------------------------------------------------------------
C:\ORACLE\PRODUCT\10.2.0\ORADATA\DB101\REDO01.LOG

SQL>
```

FIGURE 3-17 Displaying the members of the current redo log group

11. Start up the database. The database will be mounted. Upon trying to open the database an error will be generated indicating it was unable to open the online log file. Figure 3-18 displays the error generated when a redo log file is missing.

    ```
    SQL> STARTUP
    ```

```
SQL> STARTUP
ORACLE instance started.

Total System Global Area  293601280 bytes
Fixed Size                  1248624 bytes
Variable Size             104858256 bytes
Database Buffers          184549376 bytes
Redo Buffers                2945024 bytes
Database mounted.
ORA-00313: open failed for members of log group 1 of thread 1
ORA-00312: online log 1 thread 1:
'C:\ORACLE\PRODUCT\10.2.0\ORADATA\DB101\REDO01.LOG'
```

FIGURE 3-18 The STARTUP command fails displaying an error about the missing log file.

12. You will now have to determine whether the missing redo log file has already been archived. Repeat the query on the V$LOG view to determine this information. From Figure 3-19 you will notice that group 1 is the current and unarchived redo log file, which requires you to perform an incomplete recovery.

    ```
    SQL> SELECT GROUP#, SEQUENCE#, ARCHIVED, STATUS FROM V$LOG;
    ```

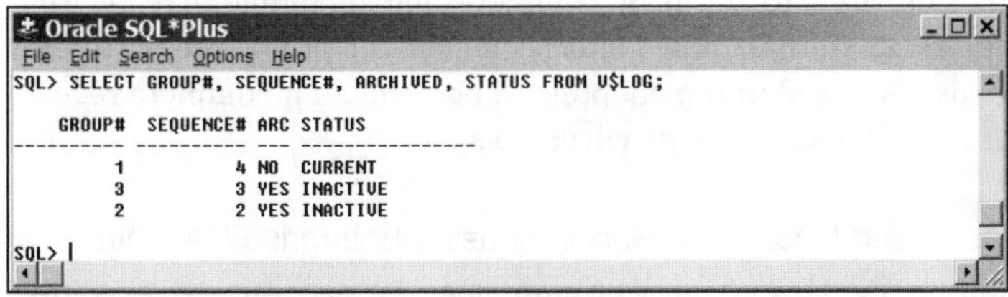

```
SQL> SELECT GROUP#, SEQUENCE#, ARCHIVED, STATUS FROM V$LOG;

    GROUP#  SEQUENCE# ARC STATUS
---------- ---------- --- ----------------
         1          4 NO  CURRENT
         3          3 YES INACTIVE
         2          2 YES INACTIVE

SQL>
```

FIGURE 3-19 Querying the V$LOG to display information about log files.

Part 3: Performing an incomplete recovery using RMAN to recover from the loss:

13. Shutdown the database.

```
SQL> SHUTDOWN IMMEDIATE;
```

14. Take a complete closed backup of the database, *manually*. See the note in the section Guidelines When Performing Incomplete Recovery. This backup will restore the datafiles in the event that the incomplete recovery fails. Do not overwrite an existing backup with this backup. We will refer to this backup as BACKUP2.
15. Start RMAN and connect to the target database and recovery catalog database if you have created one.

```
C:\>RMAN
RMAN> CONNECT TARGET
```

16. Mount the target database.

```
RMAN> STARTUP MOUNT
```

17. Type in the run block displayed below to perform an incomplete recovery up to log sequence number 4. The SET UNTIL LOGSEQ command instructs RMAN that recovery must be cancelled prior to the application of the log file with a sequence of 4.

```
RMAN>RUN{
     ALLOCATE CHANNEL C1 TYPE DISK;
     SET UNTIL LOGSEQ 4;
     RESTORE DATABASE;
     RECOVER DATABASE;
     ALTER DATABASE OPEN RESETLOGS;
     }
```

18. Exit SQL*Plus and RMAN.

Optionally, take a complete backup of the database using any method. You have successfully performed the incomplete recovery at this point. You may navigate to the location where the physical files of the database reside, to view the recovered redo log file.

Incomplete Recovery Using Enterprise Manager

The Enterprise Manager may be used to perform complete and incomplete recovery procedures. The graphical interface of Enterprise Manager makes the procedure quite easy compared to the other methods discussed in the chapter. To perform an incomplete recovery you must log in to Enterprise Manager as a privileged user.

Practice 6: Performing a Time-Based Incomplete Recovery using Enterprise Manager

This practice example demonstrates the sequence of sequence of steps you may execute to perform a time-based incomplete recovery using EM. You will first create a backup, simulate the loss of a table called PATIENT_TAB and then perform the incomplete recovery to a point prior to the loss of the table. The backup simulates a scheduled backup taken at Keller Medical Center prior to the failure.

Part 1: Taking a backup of the database using EM.

1. Start a browser and launch Enterprise Manager. Login as a user with SYSDBA privileges. Using Enterprise Manager takes a complete backup of the database as described in the following steps. This simulates a scheduled backup taken at Keller Medical Center.
2. From the **Database Home** page, select the **Maintenance** tab.
3. Select the **Schedule Backup** link in the Backup / Recovery section.
4. From the **Schedule Backup** page, navigate to the **Customized Backup** section. Figure 3-20 displays the Schedule Backup page and its options.
5. Select **Whole Database**.
6. Specify the **Host Credentials**, this will be the Operating System username and password that you used when logging on to the machine.
7. Select the **Schedule Customized Backup** button.

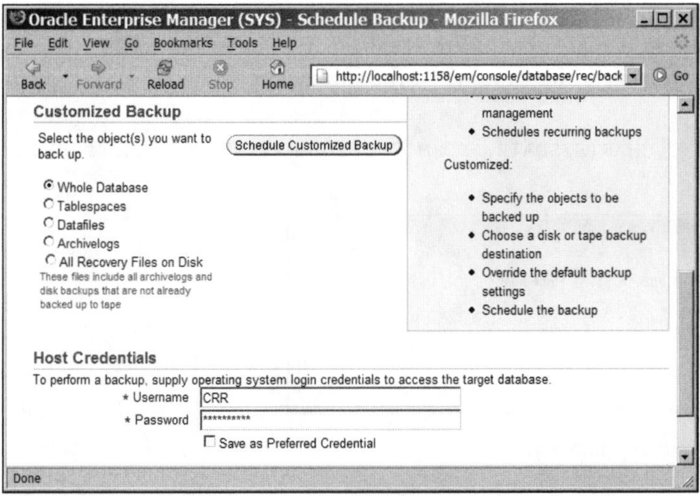

FIGURE 3-20 Taking a customized backup using Enterprise Manager

8. From the **Schedule Customized Backup: Options** page, select **Full Backup** from Backup Type.
9. Select **Online Backup** from Backup Mode.
10. Check **Also backup all archived logs on disk**.
11. Click **Next** to go to the **Schedule Customized Backup: Settings** page.
12. Select **Disk** if you are backing up to disk.
13. Click **Next** to go to the **Schedule Customized Backup: Schedule** page
14. The **Job name** and **Job description** will be displayed.
15. Schedule it to **start immediately**, with a **repeat of only one time**.
16. Click **Next** and go to the **Schedule Customized Backup: Review** page.
17. Select the **Submit Job** button.
18. The **Status** page will be displayed. You may click **OK**.

19. You may return to the Database Home page and view the **Job Activity** section. When Scheduled Executions and Running Executions display the value 0, you know that the backup has completed.
20. Log out of Enterprise Manager

Part 2: Simulating the loss of the PATIENT_TABLE at a certain time

21. Start SQL*Plus and login as a user with SYSDBA privileges.
22. Run the script called **ch03time.sql** from the Chapter03 folder that is a part of the student datafiles available with this book. This script creates a table called PATIENT_TAB.

```
SQL> START <PATH>\CH03TIME.SQL
```

23. Describe or query the PATIENT_TAB table to make sure it was created. Three rows will be displayed.

```
SQL> SELECT * FROM PATIENT_TAB;
```

24. Note the exact date and time maintained by the Oracle Server. You can use the SELECT statement displayed below to obtain it. We shall refer to this time as T1. Figure 3-21 displays the time when the table existed as "07-DEC-2005 12:47:29".

```
SQL> SELECT TO_CHAR(SYSDATE,'DD-MON-YYYY HH24:MI:SS') FROM DUAL;
```

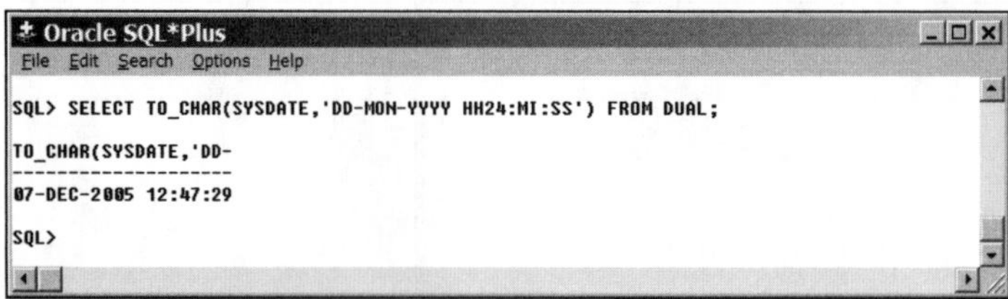

FIGURE 3-21 Displaying the current date and time

25. Go to the Chapter03 folder and execute the script called **ch03drop.sql** from the SQL prompt. This script drops the PATIENT_TAB table.
26. Describe or query the PATIENT_TAB table to verify that it no longer exists.
27. Note the exact date and time maintained by the Oracle Server. You can use the SELECT statement displayed below to obtain it. We shall refer to this time as T2. This is the time after the table was dropped.

```
SQL> SELECT TO_CHAR(SYSDATE,'DD-MON-YYYY HH24:MI:SS') FROM DUAL;
```

Part 3: Performing the time-based incomplete recovery

28. Connect to SQL*Plus as a user with SYSDBA privileges.
29. Query the V$DATAFILE view and make sure all datafiles are currently ONLINE. OFFLINE datafiles cannot be recovered after an incomplete recovery. You can also query the V$DATAFILE view to find out the status.

```
SQL> SELECT FILE#, STATUS FROM V$DATAFILE;
```

30. Shutdown the database.

```
SQL>SHUTDOWN IMMEDIATE;
```

31. Perform a complete closed backup of the database *manually* by copying the files of the database to another location. See the note in the section Guidelines When Performing Incomplete Recovery. This backup should not overwrite any previously taken backups and used in the event that there is a problem during the recovery process. We shall refer to this backup as BACKUP2.
32. Mount the database.

```
SQL> STARTUP MOUNT;
```

33. Launch Enterprise Manager.
34. You will be prompted to Startup the database or Perform Recovery. Select the **Perform Recovery** Button. Figure 3-22 displays the Database Control page when the database is not opened.

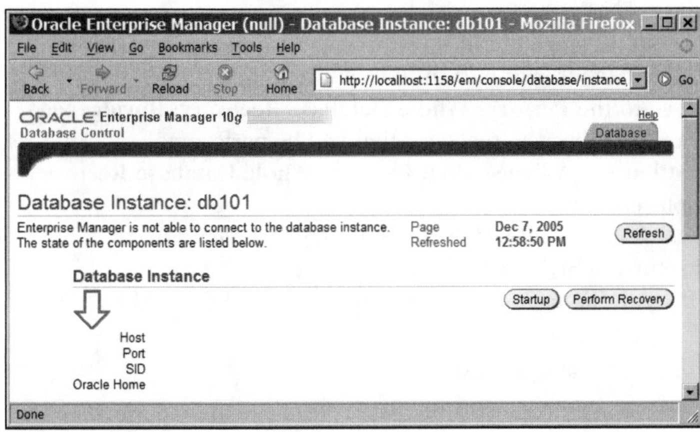

FIGURE 3-22 The Database Control Home Page

35. The **Perform Recovery: Credentials** page is displayed. Enter the username and password of the host user. Select the **Continue** button.
36. The **Database Login** page is displayed. Login as a user with SYSDBA privileges.
37. The **Perform Recovery** page is displayed
38. From the Whole Database Recovery section, select **Recover to the current time or a previous point in time.**
39. Enter the **Host Credentials.**
40. Select the **Perform Whole Database Recovery** button.
41. The **Perform Whole Database Recovery: Point-in-time** page is displayed. Figure 3-23 displays the scheduling options available on this page.
42. Select the option **Recover to a prior point-in-time**.
43. Against date, enter the date that you noted down as T1.
44. Select the **Next** button to go to the **Perform Whole Database Recovery: Rename** page.

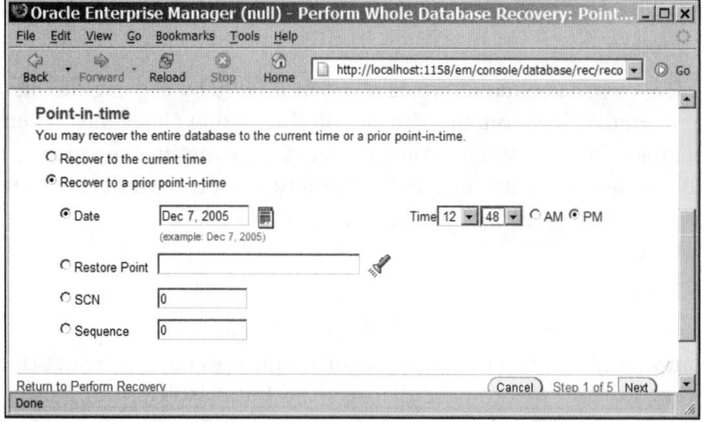

FIGURE 3-23 Performing point-in-time recovery using Enterprise Manager.

45. Leave the option **No. Restore the files to the default location** as selected. You can select the Edit RMAN script button to view the RMAN script.
46. Select **Next** and go to the **Perform Whole Database Recovery: Review** page.
47. This RMAN script describes the recovery that will be performed.
48. Click the **Submit** button. A **Processing: Perform Whole Database Recovery** page will be displayed.
49. The **Perform Recovery: Result** page will be displayed. Select **OK**.
50. Exit OEM, and return to SQL*Plus.
51. Log in as the DB_ADMIN user. Open the database using the RESETLOGS option.

    ```
    SQL> ALTER DATABASE OPEN RESETLOGS;
    ```

52. Verify if the PATIENT_TAB exists. If it exists, you successfully performed the incomplete recovery using Enterprise Manager. Figure 3-24 displays the contents of the PATIENT_TAB table indicating it was successfully recovered.

    ```
    SQL> SELECT * FROM PATIENT_TAB;
    ```

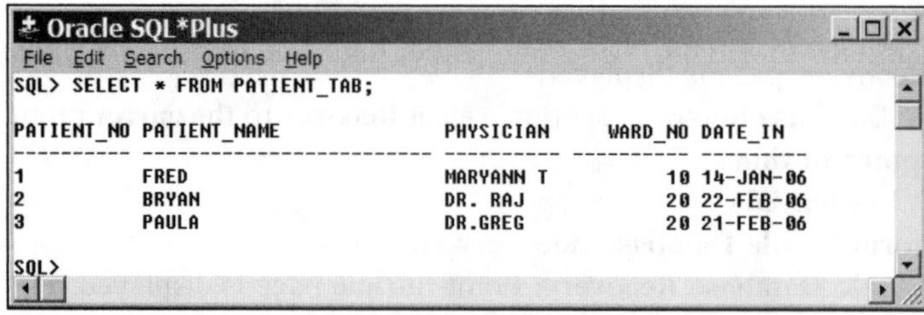

FIGURE 3-24 The PATIENT_TAB table has been recovered.

53. Exit SQL*Plus.

You have just performed all the steps involved in performing a time-based recovery using Enterprise Manager.

Recovery of the Control File

The control file is one of the most important files of the database. It maintains important information about the database such as the database name, the date the database was created, synchronization information, log sequence numbers, the names of the other files in the database, and backup and recovery information. This file is vital to the functioning of the database. Without the control file the database cannot be mounted. It is important to multiplex control files.

The control file may be manually backed up in two ways. The first is by issuing an ALTER DATABASE BACKUP CONTROLFILE TO ... command that will create a copy of the control file as it is—a binary copy. It can be done by issuing:

```
ALTER DATABASE BACKUP CONTROLFILE TO 'controlfilename';
```

Practice 7: Backing up the control file using a SQL command

This practice example demonstrates the creation of a backup control file. The current control file is backed up to a folder called 'C:\CFILEBACK with the name CFILE.CTL.

1. Start SQL*Plus and connect as an administrator.
2. Using the Operating System, create a folder called CFILEBACK in the C:\ drive.
3. Back up the control file to the C:\CFILEBACK folder with the name CFILE.CTL.

   ```
   SQL> ALTER DATABASE BACKUP CONTROLFILE
        TO 'C:\CFILEBACK\CFILE.CTL';
   ```

4. Exit SQL*Plus

The second method is by creating a text version of the control file. This text file can be used to recreate a control file in the event of a loss of *all* the control files. The text may be edited to make sure that the control file being recreated has the same description of the current database structure. The text version of the control file is created in the location specified by the USER_DUMP_DEST initialization parameter.

Practice 8: Recovering from the loss of all control files by using a text version of the current control file.

In this practice you will determine the value of the USER_DUMP_DEST parameter and create a text version of the contents of the current control file. You will then simulate a loss of all the control files and use the text version of the control file for recovery.

Part 1: Creating the text version of the control file

1. Open SQL*Plus and connect as a user with SYSDBA privileges.
2. Use the SHOW PARAMETER command to display the value of the USER_DUMP_DEST initialization parameter. Figure 3-25 displays the value of the USER_DUMP_DEST parameter as C:\ORACLE\PRODUCT\10.2.0\ADMIN\DB101\UDUMP.

   ```
   SQL> SHOW PARAMETER USER_DUMP_DEST
   ```

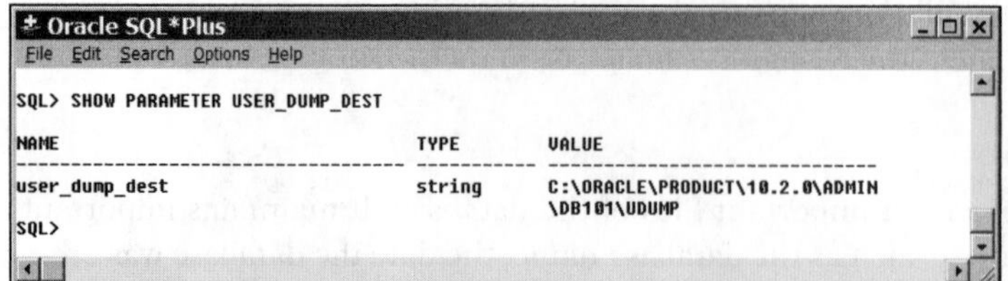

FIGURE 3-25 Displaying the value of the USER_DUMP_DEST parameter

3. Create a text version of the current control file by typing in the following command.

```
SQL> ALTER DATABASE BACKUP CONTROLFILE TO TRACE;
```

4. Using Windows Explorer, navigate to the location specified by the USER_DUMP_DEST parameter and view the text version of the control file. It would have a name like *<sid>_ora_pid.trc*, where SID is the system identifier and PID is a process ID. In Figure 3-26, the trace file that has been generated is called *db101_ora_2672.trc*.

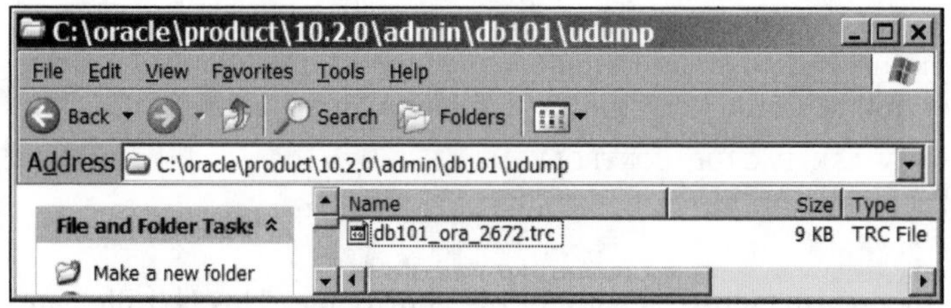

FIGURE 3-26 Identifying the trace file on the Operating System.

5. Open the file using an editor.
6. You will observe two CREATE CONTROLFILE commands in it. One can be used when you need to open the database with a RESETLOGS option. The other when the database is to be opened normally (NORESETLOGS). This file can be edited and used in the event of a loss of all the control files to recreate it. Now save this file as ***controlscript.sql*** and quit the editor.

Part 2: Simulating the loss of all the controlfiles

7. Return to SQL*Plus and issue a query against V$CONTROLFILE to determine the names of all the controlfiles being used by database. Note the names and locations since you may need to delete them. Figure 3-27 displays the names and locations of the current controlfiles.

```
SQL> SELECT NAME FROM V$CONTROLFILE;
```

8. Connect as a user with SYSDBA privileges, and shut down the database.

```
SQL> SHUTDOWN IMMEDIATE;
```

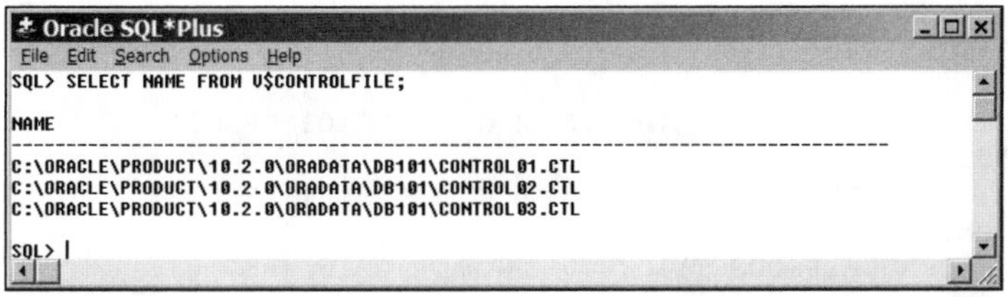

```
Oracle SQL*Plus
File Edit Search Options Help
SQL> SELECT NAME FROM V$CONTROLFILE;

NAME
--------------------------------------------------------------------------------
C:\ORACLE\PRODUCT\10.2.0\ORADATA\DB101\CONTROL01.CTL
C:\ORACLE\PRODUCT\10.2.0\ORADATA\DB101\CONTROL02.CTL
C:\ORACLE\PRODUCT\10.2.0\ORADATA\DB101\CONTROL03.CTL

SQL>
```

FIGURE 3-27 Displaying the names of the control files in the database

9. Using Windows Explorer, navigate to the location where the control files are located and using an operating system command delete all of them.
10. Return to SQL*Plus and try to open the database. The instance will be created however, when trying to mount the database you will receive an error saying it is unable to locate the control file. Figure 3-28 displays the error that is displayed when a control file is missing.

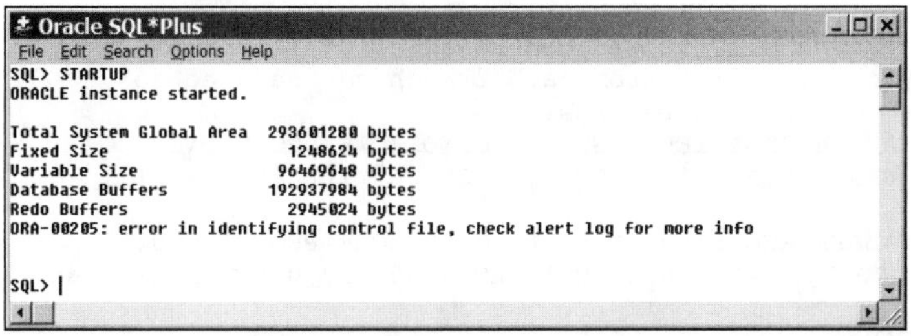

```
Oracle SQL*Plus
File Edit Search Options Help
SQL> STARTUP
ORACLE instance started.

Total System Global Area  293601280 bytes
Fixed Size                  1248624 bytes
Variable Size              96469648 bytes
Database Buffers          192937984 bytes
Redo Buffers                2945024 bytes
ORA-00205: error in identifying control file, check alert log for more info

SQL>
```

FIGURE 3-28 The STARTUP generates an error indicating the control files are missing.

Part 3: Recovering the missing control files

11. Open the file called *controlscript.sql* using an editor.
12. Remove all the lines from the text except the lines shown below.

```
--      Set #1. NORESETLOGS case
--
-- The following commands will create a new control file and
use it
-- to open the database.
-- Data used by Recovery Manager will be lost.
-- Additional logs may be required for media recovery of offline
-- Use this only if the current versions of all online logs are
-- available.
-- After mounting the created controlfile, the following SQL
-- statement will place the database in the appropriate
-- protection mode:
--  ALTER DATABASE SET STANDBY DATABASE TO MAXIMIZE PERFORMANCE
STARTUP NOMOUNT
CREATE CONTROLFILE REUSE DATABASE "DB101" NORESETLOGS  ARCHIVELOG
    MAXLOGFILES 16
    MAXLOGMEMBERS 3
    MAXDATAFILES 100
```

```
    MAXINSTANCES 8
    MAXLOGHISTORY 292
LOGFILE
  GROUP 1 'C:\ORACLE\PRODUCT\10.2.0\ORADATA\DB101\REDO01.
LOG'  SIZE 50M,
  GROUP 2 'C:\ORACLE\PRODUCT\10.2.0\ORADATA\DB101\REDO02.
LOG'  SIZE 50M,
  GROUP 3 'C:\ORACLE\PRODUCT\10.2.0\ORADATA\DB101\REDO03.
LOG'  SIZE 50M
-- STANDBY LOGFILE
DATAFILE
  'C:\ORACLE\PRODUCT\10.2.0\ORADATA\DB101\SYSTEM01.DBF',
  'C:\ORACLE\PRODUCT\10.2.0\ORADATA\DB101\UNDOTBS01.DBF',
  'C:\ORACLE\PRODUCT\10.2.0\ORADATA\DB101\SYSAUX01.DBF',
  'C:\ORACLE\PRODUCT\10.2.0\ORADATA\DB101\USERS01.DBF'
CHARACTER SET WE8MSWIN1252
;
-- Configure RMAN configuration record 1
VARIABLE RECNO NUMBER;
EXECUTE :RECNO := SYS.DBMS_BACKUP_RESTORE.
SETCONFIG('RETENTION POLICY','TO REDUNDANCY 3');
-- Commands to re-create incarnation table
-- Below log names MUST be changed to existing filenames on
-- disk. Any one log file from each branch can be used to
-- re-create incarnation records.
-- ALTER DATABASE REGISTER LOGFILE 'C:\ORACLE\PRODUCT\10.2.
0\FLASH_RECOVERY_AREA\DB101\ARCHIVELOG\2005_12_07\O1_MF_1_1_%U_.
ARC';
-- ALTER DATABASE REGISTER LOGFILE 'C:\ORACLE\PRODUCT\10.2.
0\FLASH_RECOVERY_AREA\DB101\ARCHIVELOG\2005_12_07\O1_MF_1_1_%U_.
ARC';
-- ALTER DATABASE REGISTER LOGFILE 'C:\ORACLE\PRODUCT\10.2.
0\FLASH_RECOVERY_AREA\DB101\ARCHIVELOG\2005_12_07\O1_MF_1_1_%U_.
ARC';
-- ALTER DATABASE REGISTER LOGFILE 'C:\ORACLE\PRODUCT\10.2.
0\FLASH_RECOVERY_AREA\DB101\ARCHIVELOG\2005_12_07\O1_MF_1_1_%U_.
ARC';
-- ALTER DATABASE REGISTER LOGFILE 'C:\ORACLE\PRODUCT\10.2.
0\FLASH_RECOVERY_AREA\DB101\ARCHIVELOG\2005_12_07\O1_MF_1_1_%U_.
ARC';
-- ALTER DATABASE REGISTER LOGFILE 'C:\ORACLE\PRODUCT\10.2.
0\FLASH_RECOVERY_AREA\DB101\ARCHIVELOG\2005_12_07\O1_MF_1_1_%U_.
ARC';
-- Recovery is required if any of the datafiles are restored
backups,
-- or if the last shutdown was not normal or immediate.
RECOVER DATABASE
-- All logs need archiving and a log switch is needed.
ALTER SYSTEM ARCHIVE LOG ALL;
-- Database can now be opened normally.
ALTER DATABASE OPEN;
-- Commands to add tempfiles to temporary tablespaces.
-- Online tempfiles have complete space information.
-- Other tempfiles may require adjustment.
ALTER TABLESPACE TEMP ADD TEMPFILE 'C:\ORACLE\PRODUCT\10.2.
0\ORADATA\DB101\TEMP01.DBF'
```

```
    SIZE 20971520  REUSE AUTOEXTEND ON NEXT 655360  MAXSIZE
32767M;
-- End of tempfile additions.
```

13. Shut down the database and the SQL prompt, run the CONTROLSCRIPT. SQL script. Figure 3-29 displays the output generated by executing the text-version of the control file.

```
SQL> SHUTDOWN IMMEDIATE;
SQL> START <PATH>\CONTROLSCRIPT.SQL
```


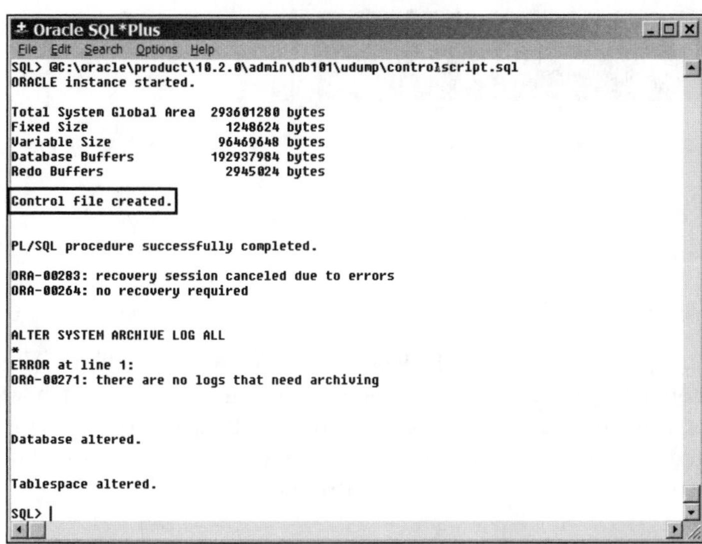

FIGURE 3-29 The control files were recreated upon running the script.

The missing control files have been recreated and you have successfully performed an incomplete recovery from the loss of all the control files.

14. Exit SQL*Plus.

In Chapter 1, we discussed the CONTROLFILE AUTOBACKUP feature of RMAN, where control files are backed up automatically whenever a complete backup or a file belonging to the SYSTEM tablespace is backed up. The CONFIGURE command can be used to force a control file autobackup after all backup and run commands that contain a BACKUP command. The RESTORE CONTROLFILE command may be issued from RMAN to recover from the loss of all control files.

Practice 9: Recovering from the loss of all control files using RMAN

In this practice example you will see how RMAN may be used to restore control files.

Part 1: Configuring CONTROLFILE AUTOBACKUP

1. Launch RMAN and connect to the target database and recovery catalog database if you have created one.

2. Issue the command to automatically back up control files.

```
RMAN> CONFIGURE CONTROLFILE AUTOBACKUP ON;
```

3. Take a complete backup of the database. The control file will automatically be backed up. Figure 3-30 displays the message displayed by RMAN when it automatically backs up of the control file during a backup of the database.

```
RMAN> BACKUP DATABASE;
```

```
Command Prompt - rman
Starting Control File and SPFILE Autobackup at 07-DEC-05
piece handle=C:\ORACLE\PRODUCT\10.2.0\FLASH_RECOVERY_AREA\DB101\AUTOBACKUP\2005_
12_07\O1_MF_S_576425937_1SGFF2CQ_.BKP comment=NONE
Finished Control File and SPFILE Autobackup at 07-DEC-05

RMAN>
```

FIGURE 3-30 Performing an automatic backup of the control file

4. Shut down the database and exit RMAN.

```
RMAN> SHUTDOWN IMMEDIATE;
RMAN> EXIT
```

Part 2: Simulate the loss of all the control files

5. Using Windows Explorer, navigate to the location where the control files of the database are stored and delete all of them using operating system commands.
6. Start SQL*Plus, connect as a SYSDBA, and try to start the database. An error will be generated indicating that the control file is not found. Figure 3-31 displays the error that is generated when the control file is missing.

```
SQL>CONNECT DB_ADMIN/DB_ADMIN AS SYSDBA
SQL> STARTUP
```

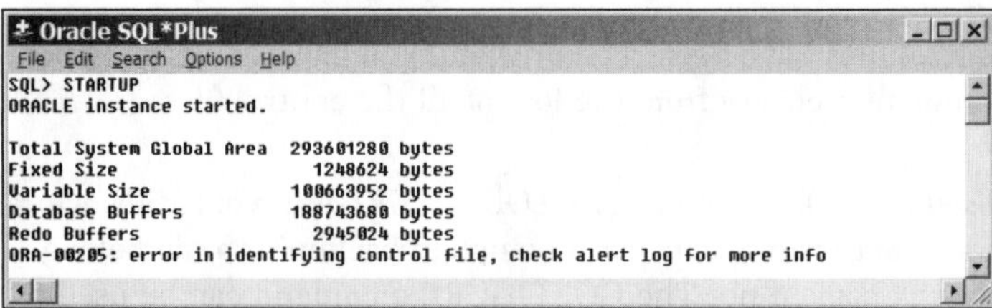

FIGURE 3-31 The STARTUP displays an error indicating the control file is missing.

Step 3: Recovering the Control file using RMAN

7. Launch RMAN and connect to the target database and the recovery catalog database if you have created one.
8. Issue the RESTORE CONTROLFILE command from the RMAN prompt. This will restore the control files. Figure 3-32 displays the RMAN output generated when the restoration is done.

```
RMAN> RESTORE CONTROLFILE FROM AUTOBACKUP;
```

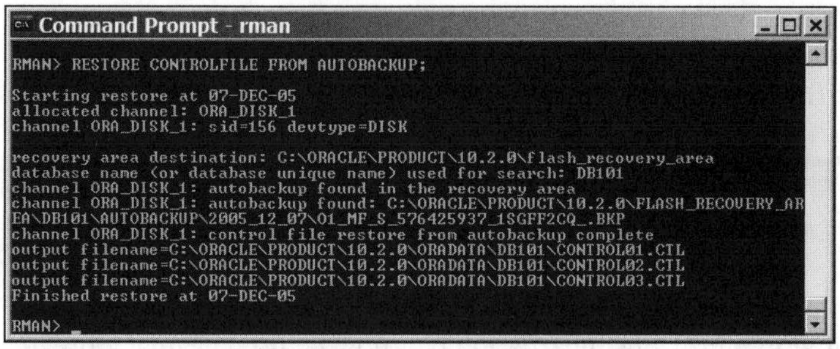

```
Command Prompt - rman
RMAN> RESTORE CONTROLFILE FROM AUTOBACKUP;

Starting restore at 07-DEC-05
allocated channel: ORA_DISK_1
channel ORA_DISK_1: sid=156 devtype=DISK

recovery area destination: C:\ORACLE\PRODUCT\10.2.0\flash_recovery_area
database name (or database unique name) used for search: DB101
channel ORA_DISK_1: autobackup found in the recovery area
channel ORA_DISK_1: autobackup found: C:\ORACLE\PRODUCT\10.2.0\FLASH_RECOVERY_AR
EA\DB101\AUTOBACKUP\2005_12_07\O1_MF_S_576425937_1SGFF2CQ_.BKP
channel ORA_DISK_1: control file restore from autobackup complete
output filename=C:\ORACLE\PRODUCT\10.2.0\ORADATA\DB101\CONTROL01.CTL
output filename=C:\ORACLE\PRODUCT\10.2.0\ORADATA\DB101\CONTROL02.CTL
output filename=C:\ORACLE\PRODUCT\10.2.0\ORADATA\DB101\CONTROL03.CTL
Finished restore at 07-DEC-05

RMAN> _
```

FIGURE 3-32 Restoring the control file using RMAN

9. Mount the target database.

   ```
   RMAN> ALTER DATABASE MOUNT;
   ```

10. Recover the database, using the RECOVER DATABASE command.

    ```
    RMAN> RECOVER DATABASE;
    ```

11. Open the database with the RESETLOGS option. Figure 3-33 displays the RMAN output generated when a database is opened using the RESETLOGS option.

    ```
    RMAN> ALTER DATABASE OPEN RESETLOGS;
    ```

```
Command Prompt - rman
RMAN> ALTER DATABASE OPEN RESETLOGS;

database opened
new incarnation of database registered in recovery catalog
starting full resync of recovery catalog
full resync complete

RMAN>
```

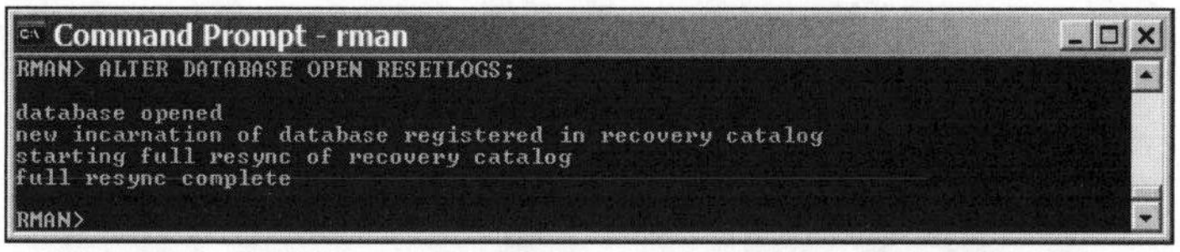

FIGURE 3-33 Opening the database with the RESETLOGS option.

12. Exit RMAN and SQL*Plus.

You have just performed a recovery from the loss of all the control files using RMAN.

Simplified Recovery through RESETLOGS

In all the incomplete recoveries that you have performed so far, after the recovery process was completed, the database was opened with the RESETLOGS option. This resulted in the creation of a new incarnation of the database. Information pertaining to this new incarnation such as the System Change Number (SCN) and timestamp will be recorded in the headers of the datafiles, control files, redo log files, and archived log files and RMAN backup pieces.

Prior to Oracle 10*g*, after opening the database with the RESETLOGS option, a complete backup of the database had to be performed. This was mandatory so that future recoveries performed could use this backup. This was necessary because previous backups taken before the incomplete recovery were no longer valid against this new incarnation.

Oracle 10*g*, has introduced a new feature called Simplified Recovery through Resetlogs. This feature allows the use of backups taken prior to the RESETLOGS to be used for recovering a new incarnation of the database.

NOTE

A backup after a RESETLOGS is no longer a mandatory step.

Archived log files created in a previous incarnation can now be used against a previous backup. A new naming format specification for archived redo log files has been introduced to avoid overwriting archived redo log files with the same sequence number across all incarnations. It ensures that unique names are constructed for the archived redo log files taking into account a resetlogs identifier. On Windows, the archive log format is ARC%S_%R.%T, where %S stands for log sequence number %R is the Resetlogs identifier and %T stands for thread number. Figure 3-34 displays the naming format for archive log formats as viewed from Enterprise Manager.

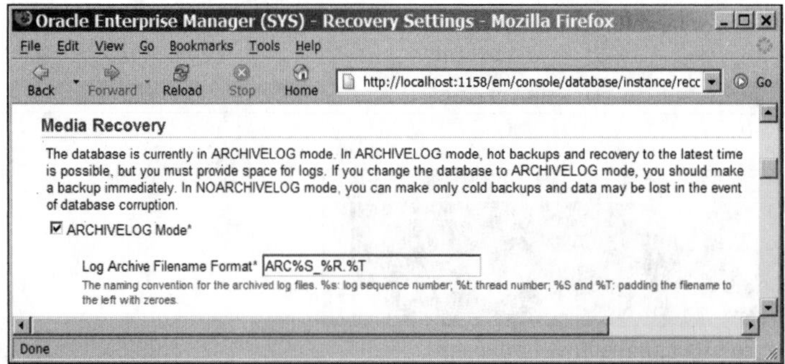

FIGURE 3-34 Setting LOG_ARCHIVE_FORMAT in Enterprise Manager

RECOVERY OF NON-CRITICAL FILES

The second part of this chapter deals with recovery of non-critical files. Though these files are required for various purposes during the normal functioning of the database their loss does not result in an inability to continue operating the database. A database administrator may perform recovery of such files with minimum effect on access to the database.

Some of the non-critical files of the database include the password file, datafiles of the temporary tablespace, inactive archived redo log files, an index tablespace, or a read-only tablespace. The loss of these non-critical files will be demonstrated in this chapter followed by the steps you would perform to recover them.

Re-creating the password file

The password file of the database is used to store the names and passwords of users who have been granted the SYSDBA and SYSOPER roles. These roles are privileged roles and a user who is granted these roles can perform actions like a STARTUP or SHUTDOWN of a database. Whenever a user logs in to the database using SYSDBA privileges the password file is referenced to authenticate the user. The password file on a Windows platform exists in the %ORACLE_HOME%\database directory or on UNIX platforms in the $ORACLE_HOME/dbs directory. The file has a naming format of PWD<SID>.ora on a Windows based platform. In Figure 3-35, the password for the DB101 database is located in C:\ORACLE\PRODUCT\10.2.0\DB_1\DATABASE\ and is called PWDdb101.ora.

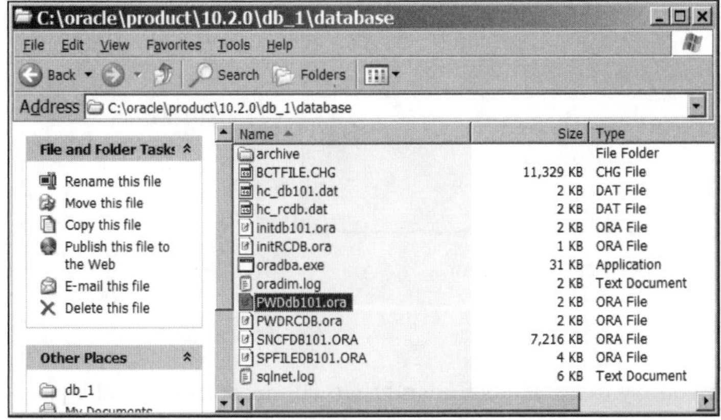

FIGURE 3-35 Viewing the password file on the Operating System.

If this file is accidentally deleted from the operating system it may be recreated using the ORAPWD utility. This utility is invoked from an operating system command prompt. The syntax of re-creating the password file is:

```
C:\> orapwd file=<passwordfile name> password=<password> entries=<n>
```

where:

`Passwordfile name:` is the complete path and name of the password file that you are creating.

`Password:` is the password of the SYS user.

`Entries:` indicates a total number of users who will be granted the SYSDBA or SYSOPER role.

Practice 10: Re-creating the Password File

In this practice example you will delete and recreate the password file. Please run the script called **ch03scott.sql** before trying this practice. The script creates a user called SCOTT whose password also is SCOTT.

Part 1: Simulating the loss of the password file

1. Open SQL*Plus, connect as a user with SYSDBA privileges.

```
SQL> CONNECT DB_ADMIN/DB_ADMIN AS SYSDBA
```

2. Shut down the database.

```
SQL> SHUTDOWN IMMEDIATE;
```

3. Using Windows Explorer, navigate to the location of the password file and delete it.
4. From SQL*Plus, try to startup the database. Figure 3-36 displays that the STARTUP command does not generate an error.

```
SQL> STARTUP;
```

```
Oracle SQL*Plus
File Edit Search Options Help
SQL> STARTUP
ORACLE instance started.

Total System Global Area  293601280 bytes
Fixed Size                  1248624 bytes
Variable Size             109052560 bytes
Database Buffers          180355072 bytes
Redo Buffers                2945024 bytes
Database mounted.
Database opened.
SQL> |
```

FIGURE 3-36 The STARTUP does not display any error.

Part 2: Recovering the password file

5. However, when you try to issue a command that will need access to the password file you will receive an error. Figure 3-37 displays the error that is generated when the user SCOTT is assigned the SYSDBA privilege.

```
SQL> GRANT SYSDBA TO SCOTT;
```

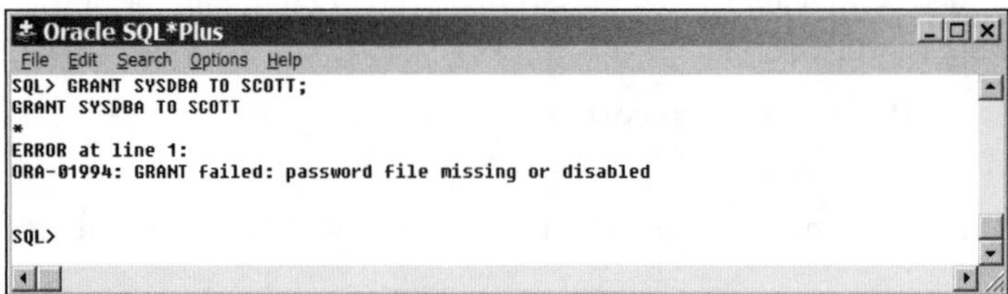
Oracle SQL*Plus
File Edit Search Options Help
SQL> GRANT SYSDBA TO SCOTT;
GRANT SYSDBA TO SCOTT
*
ERROR at line 1:
ORA-01994: GRANT failed: password file missing or disabled
SQL>

FIGURE 3-37 The GRANT SYSDBA command fails with an error.

6. To recreate the password file for the DB101 database, type the following command at the operating system command prompt. Specify the password of the SYS user appropriately. Figure 3-38 displays the execution of the ORAPWD command from the Windows command prompt.

```
C:\> ORAPWD FILE=<PATH>\PWDDB101.ORA PASSWORD=<PASSWORD> ENTRIES=5;
```

You will have to re-grant the SYSDBA and SYSOPER privileges to all the users who had it before the file was deleted. For example the command to grant user DB_ADMIN the SYSDBA privilege should be executed from SQL*Plus as: GRANT SYSDBA TO DB_ADMIN;

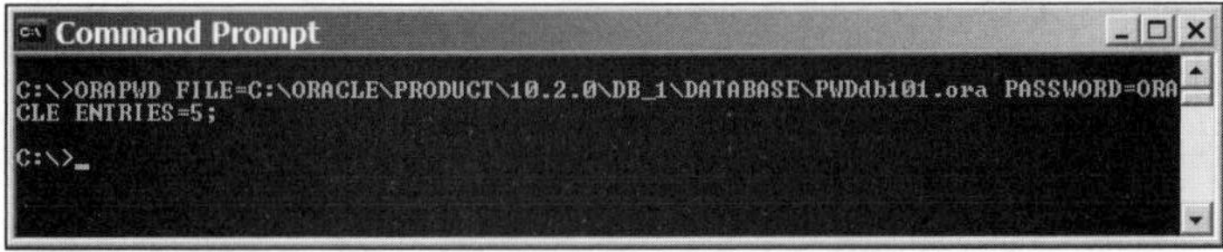
```
C:\>ORAPWD FILE=C:\ORACLE\PRODUCT\10.2.0\DB_1\DATABASE\PWDdb101.ora PASSWORD=ORA
CLE ENTRIES=5;

C:\>_
```

FIGURE 3-38 Re-creating the password file using the ORAPWD utility

7. Issue the command to grant the SYSDBA privilege to the user SCOTT. In Figure 3-39 the command to grant the SYSDBA privilege to the user SCOTT succeeded this time.

   ```
   SQL> GRANT SYSDBA TO SCOTT;
   ```

```
SQL> GRANT SYSDBA TO SCOTT;

Grant succeeded.

SQL>
```

FIGURE 3-39 The GRANT SYSDBA command is successful.

8. Exit SQL*Plus.

Recovery of the temporary tablespace

The temporary tablespace holds temporary segments. These segments are created by Oracle whenever a user requires a temporary workspace for operations like sorting. If sorts are large they cannot be completed in memory and Oracle will need to use space on disk. A separate tablespace may be created by a DBA to hold these segments on disk. Temporary segments are highly volatile in nature and cause fragmentation of disk space. A database administrator may create a default temporary tablespace for a database. In the absence of a default temporary tablespace, users who are not assigned a temporary tablespace, will automatically be assigned the SYSTEM tablespace resulting in fragmentation of the SYSTEM tablespace. Since objects in the temporary tablespace are temporary, in the event of the loss of the temporary tablespace, it is not important to recover the temporary segments. If a file belonging to the temporary tablespace is accidentally lost, then there is no recovery required. Oracle automatically recreates the file and writes a message to the Alert Log file of the database.

Practice 11: Recovering from the loss of a temporary tablespace

This practice example demonstrates the loss and recovery of a tempfiles belonging to a temporary tablespace.

Part 1: Simulating the loss of the temporary tablespace and recovering it.

1. Start SQL*Plus and connect as a user with SYSDBA privileges.

2. Query the V$TEMPFILE view to display the names of the tempfiles in the database.

```
SQL> SELECT NAME FROM V$TEMPFILE;
```

3. Create a temporary tablespace by typing the following CREATE TABLESPACE command. Change the path for the file based on your machine configuration.

```
SQL> CREATE TEMPORARY TABLESPACE tempa
     TEMPFILE 'c:\oracle\product\10.2.0\oradata\db101\tempa01.dbf'
     SIZE 10M
     EXTENT MANAGEMENT LOCAL;
```

4. Re-query the V$TEMPFILE view to display the names of the tempfiles in the database. Figure 3-40 displays the name of the newly created tempfile in addition to other tempfiles of the database.

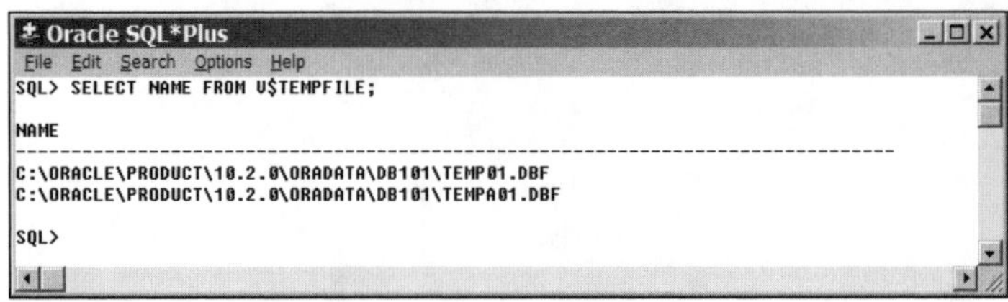

FIGURE 3-40 Viewing the names of the tempfiles.

5. Shut down the database.

```
SQL> SHUTDOWN IMMEDIATE;
```

6. Using Windows Explorer, navigate to the file called TEMPA01.DBF and delete it. From the SQL prompt, issue the STARTUP command. The database will be opened even though the tempfile was deleted as displayed by Figure 3-41.

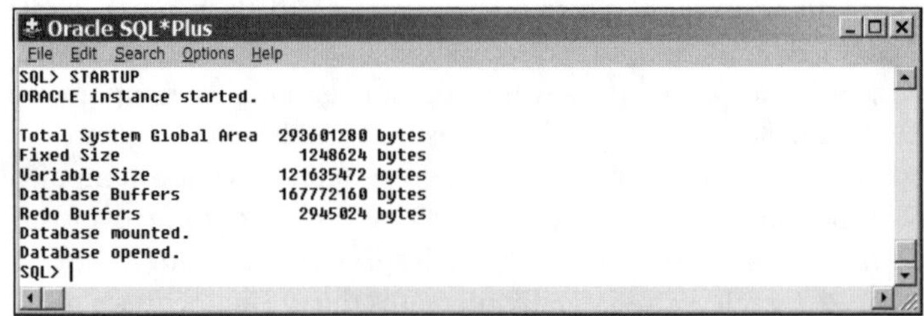

FIGURE 3-41 The STARTUP succeeds even with a missing tempfile.

7. Upon querying the DBA_TEMP_FILES data dictionary view, you will see the name of the file that you deleted in step 6. Figure 3-42 displays the tempa01.dbf file as a tempfile of the database.

```
SQL> SELECT FILE_NAME FROM DBA_TEMP_FILES;
```

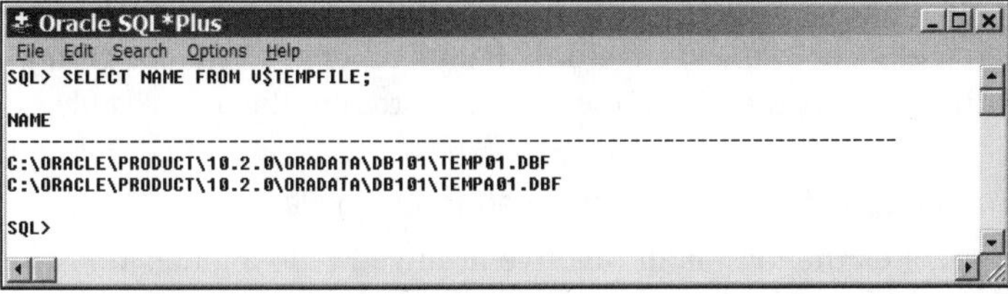

FIGURE 3-42 Querying the DBA_TEMP_FILES view

8. The alert log is the file containing messages and errors generated by Oracle. The alert log file is located in the location specified by the BACKGROUND_DUMP_DEST parameter. You may view the location of the alert log by displaying the value of the parameter. Figure 3-43 displays the location of the alert log file as `C:\ORACLE\PRODUCT\10.2.0\ADMIN\DB101\BDUMP`.

```
SQL> SHOW PARAMETER BACKGROUND_DUMP_DEST
```

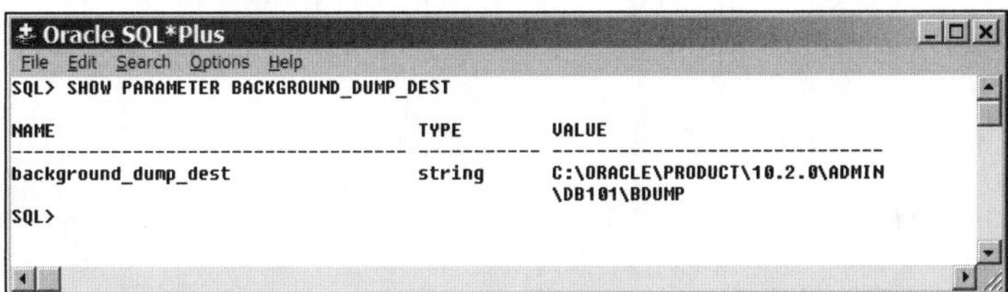

FIGURE 3-43 Displaying the value of the BACKGROUND_DUMP_DEST parameter.

The alert log file has a naming format of alert_<SID> and the alert log file for the DB101 database is called alert_db101. This file will contain messages indicating that the tempfile was recreated during startup. Figure 3-44 displays lines from the Alert Log file that indicate that the tempfile was recreated.

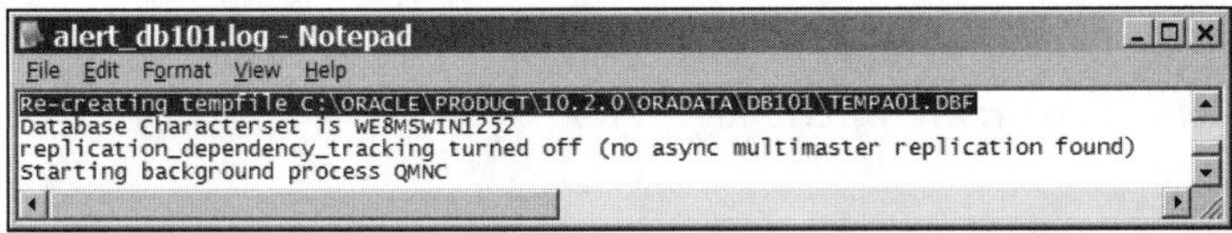

FIGURE 3-44 The ALERT file indicating that the temporary file was automatically recreated.

9. Exit SQL*Plus.

Recreating a redo log file

The redo log file contains all the changes made in the database. Redo logs files must be multiplexed by creating additional members. The recovery of redo logs files would be a non-critical recovery if an archived and inactive redo log file is missing or lost. A non-critical recovery may also be performed if one of the members of a redo log group is missing or damaged, and there are other valid members in the same group. If a member of a redo log group is damaged, the database continues to operate and a message is written to the alert log file.

Practice 12: Recovering from the loss of an inactive archived redo log file

This practice example demonstrates the loss of an inactive archived redo log file. You will first simulate the loss and then perform the recovery.

Part 1: Simulating the loss of an inactive archived redo log file

1. Start SQL*Plus and connect as a user with SYSDBA privileges.
2. Run the script called **redorecov.sql** in the Chapter03 folder. This script creates a table, adds rows, and generates a number of log switches. The script simulates changes occurring in the database.

```
SQL> <PATH>\REDORECOV.SQL
```

3. Query the v$LOG and v$LOGFILE dynamic views to display the GROUP#, MEMBER, STATUS, and ARCHIVED columns. Figure 3-45 displays the output of the query. Group 1 is currently inactive and archived. If none of the redo log files display an INACTIVE status, issue the SQL command: ALTER SYSTEM CHECKPOINT;

```
SQL> SELECT GROUP#, MEMBER, L.STATUS, ARCHIVED
     FROM V$LOG L JOIN V$LOGFILE
     USING (GROUP#);
```

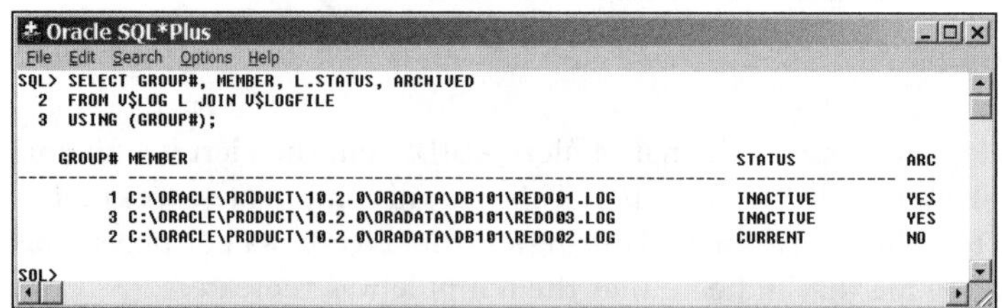

FIGURE 3-45 Querying the data dictionary to display the archived and inactive redo log files.

Part 2: Simulating the loss of an archived redo log group

4. Shut down the database.

```
SQL> SHUTDOWN IMMEDIATE;
```

5. Using Windows Explorer, navigate to the location of the redo log file belonging to the log group 1. In this example it is `C:\ORACLE\PRODUCT\10.2.0\ORADATA\DB101\REDO01.LOG`.
6. Delete the file using an operating system command.
7. Go back to SQL*Plus and try to start up the database. Figure 3-46 displays the error generated during startup.

```
SQL> STARTUP
```

```
Oracle SQL*Plus
File Edit Search Options Help
SQL> STARTUP
ORACLE instance started.

Total System Global Area  293601280 bytes
Fixed Size                  1248624 bytes
Variable Size             130024080 bytes
Database Buffers          159383552 bytes
Redo Buffers                2945024 bytes
Database mounted.
ORA-00313: open failed for members of log group 1 of thread 1
ORA-00312: online log 1 thread 1: 'C:\ORACLE\PRODUCT\10.2.0\ORADATA\DB101\REDO01.LOG'
```

FIGURE 3-46 The STARTUP fails indicating the loss of the redo log files

8. You will first need to investigate the status of the redo log file after the last shutdown. Upon querying the V$LOG dynamic view you find it to be an archived inactive group. The output of the query is displayed in Figure 3-47.

```
SQL> SELECT GROUP#, STATUS, ARCHIVED FROM V$LOG;
```

```
Oracle SQL*Plus
File Edit Search Options Help
SQL> SELECT GROUP#, STATUS, ARCHIVED
  2  FROM V$LOG;

    GROUP# STATUS           ARC
---------- ---------------- ---
         1 INACTIVE         YES
         3 INACTIVE         YES
         2 CURRENT          NO

SQL> |
```

FIGURE 3-47 Querying the V$LOG to display the status of the missing files.

Part 3: Recovering from the loss of an inactive archived redo log group:

9. To recover from this situation, you will have to first drop this redo log group.

```
SQL> ALTER DATABASE DROP LOGFILE GROUP 1;
```

10. Finally recreate again using the ALTER DATABASE ADD LOGFILE command as shown in Figure 3-48.

```
SQL> ALTER DATABASE ADD LOGFILE GROUP 1
     ('C:\ORACLE\PRODUCT\10.2.0\ORADATA\DB101\REDO01.LOG')
     SIZE 10M;
```

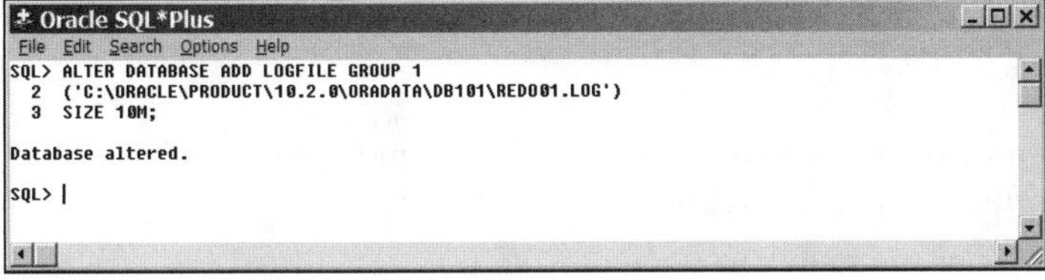

FIGURE 3-48 Adding a new log member to Group 1.

11. Open the database. The database must open successfully without any error.

```
SQL> ALTER DATABASE OPEN;
```

12. Exit SQL*Plus.

Practice 13: Recovering from the loss of a redo log member

Additional members may be added to a redo log group. Members of a group contain the same redo information. This is known as multiplexing of redo log files. Additional members of a group should be created on a different disk so that in the event of disk failure, other members are still available. If a member of a redo log group becomes unavailable when the database is running, Oracle will continue to function and an error message will be logged in the alert log file.

Anita, the senior database administrator, has been doing some routine administrative tasks. One task she does regularly is view the contents of the alert log files. This is the file that contains errors and messages generated by Oracle. As she goes through the messages she notices a message:

```
ORA-0313: open failed for members of log group 1 of thread 1.
```

She had no problems when she started the server.

In this practice example we will simulate the loss of a redo log member. You will first add an additional member to a redo log group since the DB101 database currently has groups with a single member only.

Part 1: Adding a member to a redo log group:

1. Start SQL*Plus and connect as a user with SYSDBA privileges.
2. From the SQL prompt, add a member to GROUP 1 using the ALTER DATABASE command. The output of the command is displayed in Figure 3-49.

```
SQL>ALTER DATABASE ADD LOGFILE
    MEMBER '<path>\REDO011.LOG' TO GROUP 1;
```

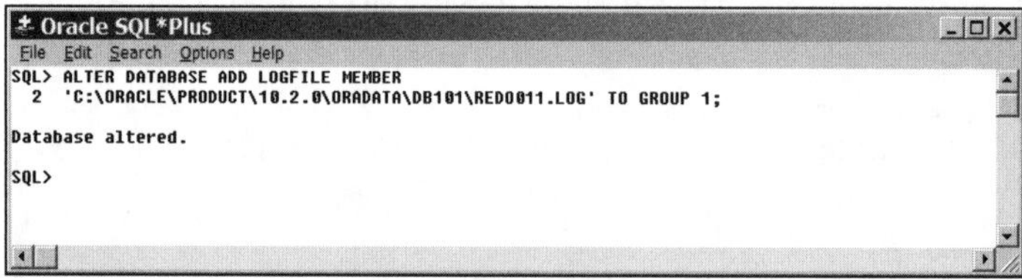

FIGURE 3-49 Adding a log member to redo log group 1.

3. Run the **redorecov.sql** script again to generate a few more log switches. This will ensure the new member is written to.

Part 2: Simulating the loss of the member:

4. From the SQL prompt shutdown the database.

```
SQL> SHUTDOWN IMMEDIATE;
```

5. Using Windows Explorer, navigate to the location of the redo log files belonging to the log group 1, in this example it is REDO01.LOG or REDO011.log.
6. Delete one of them, using operating system commands. We will delete REDO011.log.
7. At the SQL prompt, issue the command to startup the database. The database will be opened, even though one of the log members was deleted. In Figure 3-50, notice the database was started without an error.

```
SQL> STARTUP
```

```
Oracle SQL*Plus
File Edit Search Options Help
SQL> STARTUP
ORACLE instance started.

Total System Global Area  293601280 bytes
Fixed Size                  1248624 bytes
Variable Size             134218384 bytes
Database Buffers          155189248 bytes
Redo Buffers                2945024 bytes
Database mounted.
Database opened.
SQL>
```

FIGURE 3-50 The STARTUP succeeds even with a missing redo log member.

8. The information about the missing redo log member will be written to the alert log file. Open the *alert_db101* file and scroll down to the bottom. You should see an entry similar to the contents of Figure 3-51.

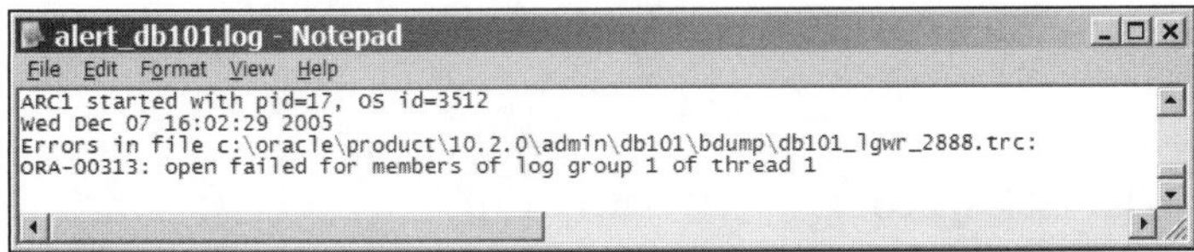

FIGURE 3-51 The ALERT log file displays information about the missing redo log file.

Part 3: Recovering from the loss of the log member:

9. To recover from the loss of the log member, you must first drop the log member using an ALTER DATABASE DROP LOGFILE MEMBER command. Figure 3-52 displays the output generated by the command.

```
SQL> ALTER DATABASE DROP LOGFILE MEMBER '<PATH>\REDO011.LOG';
```

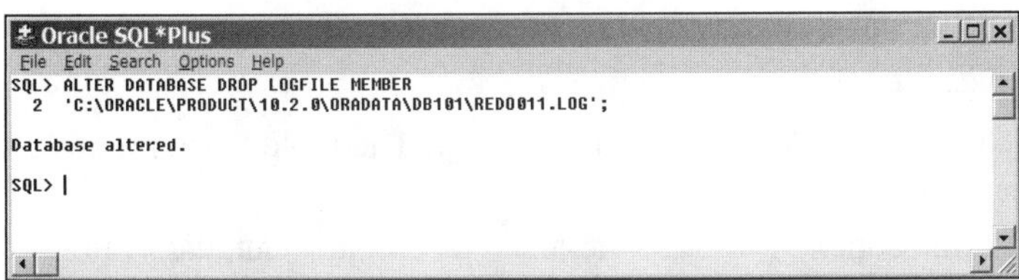

FIGURE 3-52 Dropping the missing log member.

10. Recreate the second member of redo log group 1 using the ALTER DATABASE ADD LOGFILE MEMBER command. Figure 3-53 displays the output of the command.

```
SQL>ALTER DATABASE ADD LOGFILE
    MEMBER '<path>\REDO011.LOG' TO GROUP 1;
```

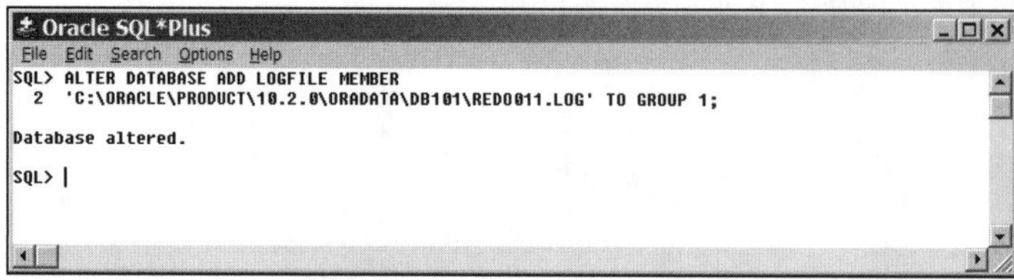

FIGURE 3-53 Recreating the redo log member

11. Exit SQL*Plus.

You have just performed the steps to recover from the loss of a redo log member.

Recovering an index tablespace

An index tablespace may be created by the database administrator for users to create indexes in. An index is an object that is created to increase the speed of query execution. A good practice is to create a script whenever you create an index. The recovery of an index tablespace is a non-critical recovery if users have the scripts that they used to create the indexes. In the event of the loss of an index tablespace the tablespace may be recreated and repopulated with indexes.

Practice 14: Recovering an index tablespace

In this practice example you will create a table and a script that holds the command to create an index on a column of the table.

Part 1: Simulating the creation of an index tablespace and an index

1. Start SQL*Plus and connect as a user with SYSDBA privileges. Execute the script **ch03indx.sql** to create a tablespace called INDX in the database. You will have to edit the script to set the path of the datafile correctly. The script can be found the Chapter03 folder of the student datafiles.

```
SQL> @<PATH>\CH03INDX.SQL
```

2. Connect as the user MEDUSER whose password is MEDUSER. This user was created by executing the script ch03setup.sql.

```
SQL> CONNECT MEDUSER/MEDUSER
```

3. Create a table called DOCDATA as displayed below. The table has a numeric and a character column.

```
SQL> CREATE TABLE DOCDATA (DOCID NUMBER, DOCNAME  VARCHAR2(40));
```

4. Create a non-unique index on the DOCNAME column of the DOCDATA table in the INDX tablespace that was created in Step 1.

```
SQL> CREATE INDEX DOCINDX ON DOCDATA(DOCNAME) TABLESPACE INDX;
```

5. To save this file to a script file in SQL*Plus you can use the save command, as:

```
SQL> SAVE DOCINDX.SQL
```

You can use this file whenever you want to recreate the index called DOCINDX.

Part 2: Simulating the loss of the index tablespace:

In this part of the practice example, the index tablespace will be dropped. This simulates an accidental loss of the index tablespace.

6. Connect to the database as a user with administrative privileges.
7. Drop the tablespace called INDX and all its contents.

```
SQL> DROP TABLESPACE INDX INCLUDING CONTENTS AND DATAFILES;
```

8. Once the tablespace has been dropped, all the indexes that existed in the tablespace are also dropped. Your option for recovering from this situation is to recreate the index and run all the scripts that you and the users of the database have created to recreate the indexes that existed in the INDX tablespace.

```
SQL> CREATE TABLESPACE INDX
     DATAFILE '<path> \INDX01.DBF' SIZE 1M;
```

9. Connect as the MEDUSER to rerun the script docindx.sql script that creates the index on the DOCDATA table, in the INDX tablespace.

```
SQL> CONNECT MEDUSER/MEDUSER
```

10. Run the script to recreate the index.

```
SQL> START DOCINDX.SQL
```

11. Exit SQL*Plus.

You will have to recreate all the indexes that existed in this tablespace in this manner. It is a good practice to maintain scripts that contain the CREATE command while creating tables, indexes, and other objects in the database.

Recovering a read-only tablespace

A read-only tablespace is one that does not permit changes to it. The objects in a read-only tablespace may be queried but cannot be modified in any way. A tablespace is made read only by issuing the ALTER TABLESPACE *tablespacename* READ ONLY command. We will consider three different scenarios.

The first arrow in Figure 3-54 depicts the scenario in which a failure occurs to a tablespace that is in a read-only mode. The tablespace was read only when the last backup was taken. Recovery involves a simple restoration of the file from the backup. There is no need to apply any redo information.

The second arrow in Figure 3-54 depicts the scenario in which a failure occurs to a tablespace that is in a read-write mode. The tablespace was in a read-only mode when the last backup was taken. Recovery in this case involves restoring from backup followed by

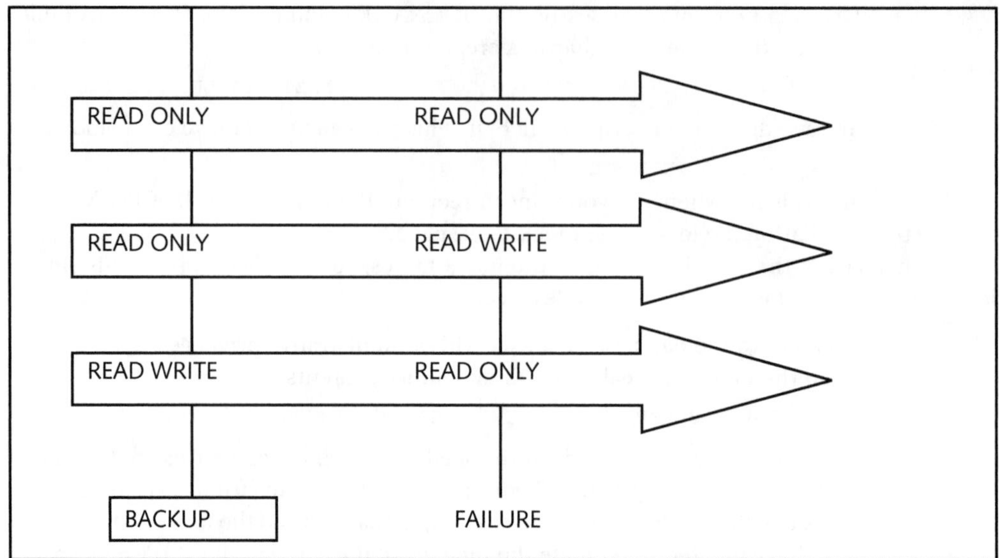

FIGURE 3-54 Displaying the read status of the tablespace during the last backup and time of failure.

recovering the tablespace by applying archived redo logs. The archived logs will contain the redo information from the point at which the tablespace was made read-write.

The third arrow in Figure 3-54 depicts the scenario when a failure occurs to a tablespace that is in a read-only mode. The tablespace was in a read-write mode when the last backup was taken. Recovery in this case involves restoring from backup followed by recovering the tablespace by applying archived redo logs. The archived logs will contain the redo information from the tablespace when it was read-write.

Practice 15: Recovering a read-only tablespace

In this practice example, you will perform a simple restoration of a tablespace that is read only when the backup is taken and is read only when the failure occurs.

Part 1: Making a tablespace read only

1. Log in to SQL*Plus as a user with SYSDBA privileges.
2. Make the USERS tablespace read only by issuing the following ALTER TABLESPACE command.

   ```
   SQL> ALTER TABLESPACE USERS READ ONLY;
   ```

3. Next launch RMAN and connect to the target database and recovery catalog database if you have created one.
4. Using RMAN take a backup of the USERS tablespace.

   ```
   RMAN> BACKUP TABLESPACE USERS;
   ```

5. Return to SQL*Plus and run the **readact.sql** script in the Chapter03 folder. This script simulates some activity in the database.

   ```
   SQL> <PATH>\READACT.SQL
   ```

Part 2: Simulating the loss of the file belonging to the read-only tablespace:

6. Now shutdown the database.

```
SQL> SHUTDOWN IMMEDIATE;
```

7. Using Windows Explorer, navigate to the location where the datafiles of the USERS tablespace are located. Delete the USERS01.DBF file.
8. Return to SQL*Plus and try to startup the database. Figure 3-55 displays the error that is generated during startup indicating that the USERS01.DBF file is missing.

```
SQL> STARTUP;
```

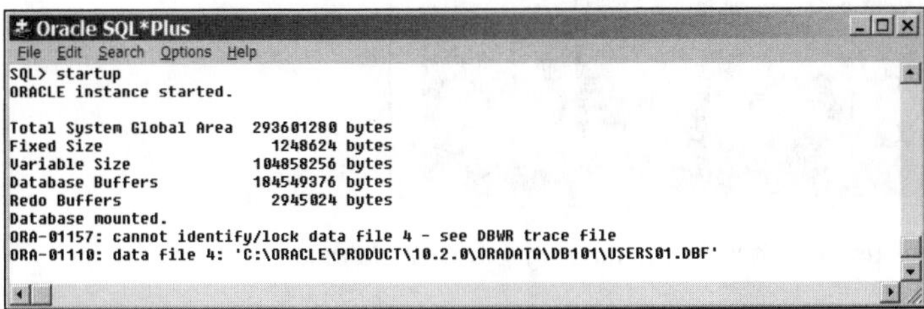

FIGURE 3-55 The STARTUP fails, displaying an error that the USERS01.DBF file is missing.

Part 3: Recovering the read-only tablespace:

9. To recover from this situation, determine the mode of the datafile by querying the FILE# AND ENABLED columns of the V$DATAFILE view. Figure 3-56 displays that file 4 has a status of read only.

```
SQL> SELECT  FILE#, ENABLED FROM V$DATAFILE;
```

```
Oracle SQL*Plus
File Edit Search Options Help
SQL> SELECT FILE#, ENABLED FROM V$DATAFILE;

     FILE# ENABLED
---------- ----------
         1 READ WRITE
         2 READ WRITE
         3 READ WRITE
         4 READ ONLY
         5 READ WRITE

SQL>
```

FIGURE 3-56 Identifying the read status of the missing datafile.

10. Type in the following RUN block. You first take the read-only datafile online and open the rest of the database. Then restore the tablespace and bring it back up online. Return to RMAN and perform the restoration of the read-only tablespace. Figure 3-57 displays the RMAN output generated when recovering the read-only tablespace.

```
RMAN>  RUN
      {SQL 'ALTER DATABASE DATAFILE 4 OFFLINE';
       SQL 'ALTER DATABASE OPEN';
```

```
RESTORE TABLESPACE USERS;
SQL 'ALTER TABLESPACE USERS ONLINE';}
```

```
Command Prompt - rman
RMAN> RUN
2> {SQL 'ALTER DATABASE DATAFILE 4 OFFLINE';
3> SQL 'ALTER DATABASE OPEN';
4> RESTORE TABLESPACE USERS;
5> SQL 'ALTER TABLESPACE USERS ONLINE';
6> }

sql statement: ALTER DATABASE DATAFILE 4 OFFLINE

sql statement: ALTER DATABASE OPEN

Starting restore at 08-DEC-05
allocated channel: ORA_DISK_1
channel ORA_DISK_1: sid=146 devtype=DISK

channel ORA_DISK_1: starting datafile backupset restore
channel ORA_DISK_1: specifying datafile(s) to restore from backup set
restoring datafile 00004 to C:\ORACLE\PRODUCT\10.2.0\ORADATA\DB101\USERS01.DBF
channel ORA_DISK_1: reading from backup piece C:\ORACLE\PRODUCT\10.2.0\FLASH_REC
OVERY_AREA\DB101\BACKUPSET\2005_12_08\O1_MF_NNNDF_TAG20051208T083955_1SJFXCWB_.B
KP
channel ORA_DISK_1: restored backup piece 1
piece handle=C:\ORACLE\PRODUCT\10.2.0\FLASH_RECOVERY_AREA\DB101\BACKUPSET\2005_1
2_08\O1_MF_NNNDF_TAG20051208T083955_1SJFXCWB_.BKP tag=TAG20051208T083955
channel ORA_DISK_1: restore complete, elapsed time: 00:00:01
Finished restore at 08-DEC-05

sql statement: ALTER TABLESPACE USERS ONLINE

RMAN> _
```

FIGURE 3-57 The RMAN block used to recover the missing read-only datafile.

The USERS tablespace has been restored.

11. From SQL*Plus, return the USERS tablespace to its READ WRITE status by typing:

    ```
    SQL> ALTER TABLESPACE USERS READ WRITE;
    ```

12. Exit SQL*Plus and RMAN.

In this chapter you learned about different types of recovery procedures and methods available in the Oracle Database. The chapter also provided a complete review of recovery options available using RMAN and Enterprise Manager. The chapter also discussed recovery of non-critical files in the Oracle database. In Chapter 4 you will learn about a new feature available in the database—the Flashback Database feature. This feature can be used for incomplete recovery in the Oracle database. Using the flashback database feature is faster than the traditional incomplete recovery steps explained in this lesson.

Chapter Summary

- An administrator should test the backup and recovery strategies to ensure they are valid and usable in the event of a failure.
- A database administrator's primary task is to ensure that in the event of media failure, complete recovery is possible.
- Complete recovery is not possible when the database is running in noarchivelog mode. Recovery is only possible up to the last backup that was taken.
- Recovery in an Oracle database always involves two main steps. The first step is called Restoration, and the second is called Recovery.
- Recovery is done by issuing a RECOVER command.
- There are three kinds of Incomplete Recovery.
    - Time-based Incomplete Recovery: This method is used to recover the database up to a certain time in the past.
    - SCN-based Incomplete Recovery: This method is used to recover the database up to a certain System Change Number.
    - Sequence-based Incomplete Recovery: This method is used to recover the database up to the application of a certain log file.
- A database must be opened using the RESETLOGS clause after performing the incomplete recovery.
- A new incarnation of the database will be created after the database is opened with RESETLOGS.
- The LOGMINER utility is used to analyze redo log files.
- A backup after a RESETLOGS is no longer a mandatory step.
- The password file of the database is used to store the names and passwords of users who have been granted the SYSDBA and SYSOPER roles.
- The temporary tablespace is a tablespace that is used to hold temporary objects.
- Redo logs files must be multiplexed by creating additional members.
- A read-only tablespace is one that does not permit changes to it.

Syntax Guide

SYNTAX GUIDE		
Command	Description	Example
SET NEWNAME FOR DATAFILE	Specifies a new location for a datafile during restoration.	`SET NEWNAME FOR DATAFILE 'E:\system01.dbf' TO 'D:\system01.dbf';`
SQL	Specifies that an SQL statement is to be executed in RMAN	`SQL 'ALTER DATABASE DATAFILE 4 ONLINE';`
SWITCH	Updates the control file with the new location of a data file	`SWITCH DATAFILE ALL;`
Commands for Complete Recovery	**Description**	**Example**

RECOVER [DATABASE | TABLESPACE tablespace name |{DATAFILE number | name }]	Recovers the database after restoration by applying archived and redo log files	`RECOVER DATABASE;`
		`RECOVER TABLESPACE USERS;`
		`RECOVER DATAFILE 'E:\PRODUCT\10.2.0\ORADATA\DB101\sysaux01.dbf';`

Commands for Incomplete Recovery	**Description**	**Example**
RECOVER [AUTOMATIC] DATABASE UNTIL TIME	Used to perform time based incomplete recovery	`RECOVER DATABASE UNTIL TIME '12-MAY-2006 13:10:00';`
RECOVER DATABASE UNTIL CANCEL		`RECOVER DATABASE UNTIL CANCEL`
RECOVER [AUTOMATIC] DATABASE UNTIL SCN *n*;		`RECOVER DATABASE UNTIL SCN 7557;`
SET UNTIL TIME 'dd mon yyyy hh:mi:ss'		`SET UNTIL TIME '12 MAY 2006 13:10:00'`
SET UNTIL LOG SEQUENCE n		`SET UNTIL LOG SEQUENCE 75;`
SET UNTIL SCN n		`SET UNTIL SCN 7557;`
RESETLOGS		`ALTER DATABASE OPEN RESETLOGS;`

SYNTAX GUIDE		
Command	Description	Example
Commands for Logminer	Description	Example
UTL_FILE_DIR	Initialization parameter used to specify the destination of the extracted data dictionary	`UTL_FILE_DIR= 'E:\LOGMINER'`
DBMS_LOGMNR_D. BUILD	Used to extract information from the data dictionary for analysis	`SQL> EXECUTE DBMS_LOGMNR_D.BUILD('logdict. ora','E:\LOGMINER);`
DBMS_LOGMNR.ADD_ LOGFILE	Adds log files o a list for analysis by Log Miner.	`EXECUTE DBMS_LOGMNR.ADD_ LOGFILE(LOGFILENAME=>'C:\oracle\ product\ 10.2.0\db101\redo02. log', OPTIONS=> DBMS_LOGMNR. ADDFILE);`
DBMS_LOGMNR. START_LOGMNR	Used to start the redo log analysis process. The DDL_DICT_ TRACKING option must be used to include DDL operations in the analysis.	`EXECUTE DBMS_LOGMNR.START_LOGMNR (OPTIONS=> DBMS_LOGMNR.DDL_DICT_ TRACKING);`
DBMS_LOGMNR. END_LOGMNR	Used to end the LogMiner session and release all resources held by the session.	`EXECUTE DBMS_LOGMNR.END_LOGMNR;`

Review Questions

1. Identify the keyword that is used to manually stop the recovery process.
2. Tom is the user of the database. He has been working all day with a table called REGROUPS. At around 6:40 p.m., while deleting some indexes he accidentally deleted the REGROUPS table. He rushes to the database administrator, who decides to perform a recovery. Identify the method(s) of recovery possible.
   a. A complete recovery of the database
   b. A time-based incomplete recovery
   c. A sequence-based incomplete recovery
   d. SCN-based incomplete recovery.
   e. RMAN recovery
3. Before using LogMiner for the first time, the DBA must edit the spfile or pfile of the database to include the ________________ parameter.

4. The database at TONY'S PIZZERIA is running in NOARCHIVELOG mode. The disk containing the DATA1 datafile is damaged. Which of the following commands can be used during recovery?
   a. RESTORE
   b. RECOVER
   c. REPAIR
   d. REJOIN
5. The command to update the control file with the new location of a datafile is _________________ .
   a. ALTER DATABASE DATAFILE LOCATION
   b. SWITCH DATAFILE ALL
   c. SET NEWNAME FOR DATAFILE
   d. None of the above.
6. In Oracle 10*g*, the 'simplified recovery through resetlogs' feature, implies:
   a. Backups are automatically taken by RMAN after a recovery.
   b. Backups need not be taken in a database, recovery is done without restoring files.
   c. A backup after an incomplete recovery is not mandatory.
   d. A backup after an incomplete recovery is mandatory.
   e. A backup after a complete recovery is not mandatory.
   f. A backup after a complete recovery is mandatory.
7. John is the database administrator of a production database called PROD. He has just performed a cancel-based incomplete recovery. How should he open the database after recovery?
   a. ALTER DATABASE OPEN RESETLOGS
   b. ALTER DATABASE OPEN
   c. ALTER DATABASE OPEN NORESETLOGS
   d. ALTER DATABASE RESETLOGS
   e. ALTER DATABASE NORESETLOGS
8. Identify the methods of incomplete recovery (choose three)?
   a. Time-based
   b. Cancel-based
   c. Change-based
   d. Tablespace recovery
9. In which database state can you recreate a control file?
   a. NOMOUNT
   b. MOUNT
   c. OPEN
   d. RESTRICTED
   e. RECREATE

10. John is the database administrator of a database called PROD. When he started the database this morning, an error was generated indicating a certain datafile was missing. This datafile does not belong to the SYSTEM tablespace. To minimize the downtime he issues:

```
STARTUP MOUNT;
ALTER DATABASE DATAFILE ... OFFLINE;
```

    What should he do next?

    a. Restore the corrupted data file
    b. Alter database open
    c. Recover data file
    d. Apply the archived logs before the crash
    e. Recreate the control files

11. To be able to perform complete recovery, which mode should the database be running in:
    a. ARCHIVELOG
    b. NOARCHIVELOG
    c. It does not matter.

12. Which type of recovery will take the database back in time. Choose three.
    a. Time-based
    b. Complete
    c. Closed
    d. SCN-based
    e. Cancel-based

13. The ________________ keyword in the ALTER DATABASE BACKUP CONTROLFILE TO command creates a text version of the Control file.
    a. TEXT
    b. TRACE
    c. TEXTFILE
    d. TRACEONLY
    e. TRACEFILE

14. One of the redo log members is suddenly unavailable. What will happen?
    a. The database will automatically shut down.
    b. A log switch will be performed.
    c. A message will be written to the alert log file.
    d. All users will be notified that the database will be going down in 10 minutes.

15. The loss of the password file is a non-critical failure in a database. Which utility would you use to recreate it.
    a. ORAPWD from within SQL.
    b. ORAPWD from the Operating System Prompt

c. RECOVER PASSWORD
d. RESTORE from the RMAN prompt.

16. If the non-default temporary tablespace is accidentally dropped. The easiest method to recover is ________________ and ________________ it.
17. A tablespace called HISTORICAL is made read only. How many backups of this tablespace are required.
    a. Every time other tablespaces are backed up, you should backup this one too.
    b. Only one backup after it was made read only is needed.
    c. A backup of the HISTORICAL tablespace is taken automatically when the SYSTEM tablespace is backed up.
    d. None of the above.
18. The password file contains the names of all users who have possess the ________________ and ________________ roles.
19. The ________________ utility is used to analyze redo log files.
20. When changing the location of a datafile you should specify the SET NEWNAME command, prior to the ________________ command.
    a. RECOVER
    b. RESTORE
    c. OPEN
    d. RESETLOGS

Hands-On Assignments

Assignment 3-1 Putting the database in NOARCHIVELOG mode

1. Start SQL*Plus and log in as a user with SYSDBA privileges.
2. Shut down the database with the immediate option.
3. Mount the database.
4. Issue the `ALTER DATABASE NOARCHIVELOG` command to put the database in NOARCHIVELOG mode.
5. Open the database.
6. Verify that it is in NOARCHIVELOG mode.
7. Exit SQL*Plus.

Assignment 3-2 Simulating an error and Recovering the database in NOARCHIVELOG mode.

1. Connect as a user with SYSDBA privileges
2. Shut down and mount the database.
3. Launch RMAN and connect to the target database.
4. Take a complete backup of the database using RMAN.
5. Delete or rename the datafile called USERS01.dbf.

6. Open the database. You will receive an error.
7. Using RMAN restore the database. When writing the run command you will only use the RESTORE command. The RECOVER command is not used since there are no archivelogs to apply.
8. Open the database.
9. Exit SQL*Plus and RMAN.

Assignment 3-3 Putting the database in Archivelog mode.

1. Start SQL*Plus and log in as a user with SYSDBA privileges
2. Shut down the database with the immediate option.
3. Mount the database.
4. Issue the `ALTER DATABASE ARCHIVELOG;` command to put the database in ARCHIVELOG mode.
5. Open the database.
6. Verify that it is in ARCHIVELOG mode with automatic archiving enabled.
7. Exit SQL*Plus.

Assignment 3-4 Re-creating the control file from a Trace File

1. Start SQL*Plus and log in as a user with SYSDBA privileges.
2. Issue the command to create a text version of the current control file. This file is created in the location specified by the USER_DUMP_DEST parameter.
3. Query the V$CONTROLFILE view to display the names of all the control files in the database.
4. Shut down the database.
5. Delete all copies of the control file from the operating system.
6. Start the database. You should receive an error indicating that there was an error identifying the control file.
7. Make the necessary changes to the trace file created in step 2; and rename it as **contrace.sql**
8. Perform the steps necessary to recreate the control files using SQL*Plus.
9. Bounce the database to make sure the recovery was successful.

Assignment 3-5 Performing a Cancel-Based Recovery Manually

In this assignment you will perform a cancel-based recovery manually. The error is the creation of a table called PATTAB. After recovery, the database will be in the state it was prior to the creation of this table.

1. Start SQL*Plus, log in as a SYSDBA and shutdown the database using the IMMEDIATE option.
2. Create a cold backup of the database. This backup should not overwrite other backups created. (Hint: copy all the physical files of the database to a folder)
3. Start up the database.
4. Query the V$LOG view to determine the sequence number of the current redo log file.

5. Run the **ch03script1.sql** script in the Chapter03 folder. This script creates a table called PATTAB and adds 3 rows to it. Query the PATTAB table to make sure it was created.
6. Issue the `ALTER SYSTEM SWITCH LOGFILE` command to force a log switch.
7. Query the NAME column of the V$ARCHIVED_LOG view to determine the name of the archive log file generated in step 4.This will be last name in the list. Note this name.
8. Shut down the database using the IMMEDIATE option.
9. Mount the database.
10. Restore all the datafiles using the cold backup created in step 2.
11. Perform a cancel-based incomplete recovery by canceling the recovery as soon as the archived log file generated in step 4 will be applied.
12. Open the database using the RESETLOGS option.
13. Verify that the PATTAB table no longer exists. If it does not exist, then you successfully performed the cancel-based incomplete recovery.
14. Shut down the database.
15. Exit SQL*Plus.

Assignment 3-6 Simulating the loss of a table and determining the SCN using Logminer

1. Start SQL*Plus and log in as a user with SYSDBA privileges.
2. Shut down the database if it is open and take a complete backup of the database using RMAN. (Note: To take a complete backup of the database using RMAN, the database must be mounted.)
3. Open the database.
4. Start SQL*Plus, connect as a SYSDBA and run the script **ch03script2.sql** in the Chapter03 folder. The script creates a table called TAB1, adds a few rows into it and then drops it.
5. Issue a SELECT statement to verify that the table TAB1 no longer exists.
6. Create a folder called LOGM in the C:\ of your machine using an operating system command.
7. Issue an ALTER SYSTEM command to set the UTL_FILE_DIR parameter to C:\LOGM. Make sure to use the SCOPE=SPFILE so that the change is persistent for future instances.
8. Shut down the database.
9. Start up the database.
10. Use the DBMS_LOGMNR_D.BUILD procedure to extract data dictionary information to a flat file called *ddbuild.ora*. It should be created in the same location specified by UTL_FILE_DIR.
11. Add the online redo log files for analysis by means of the DBMS_LOGMNR.ADD_LOGFILE procedure.
12. Start the mining process using `DBMS_LOGMNR.START_LOGMNR`. Use the option to track DDL commands.

13. Query the V$LOGMNR_CONTENTS view to determine the SCN of all DDL statements performed on the segment called TAB1.
14. Note the SCN number of the `DROP TABLE TAB1` command.
15. End the mining process using `DBMS_LOGMNR.END_LOGMNR.`

Assignment 3-7 Performing an SCN based incomplete recovery using EM

In this assignment you will perform an incomplete recovery using Enterprise Manager. You have identified the SCN number up to which recovery has to be done in the previous assignment (3–6).

1. Shut down and mount the database.
2. Perform the restore and recover until SCN using OEM.
3. Using SQL*Plus, verify the existence of the table called TAB1, by querying the table.
4. Exit SQL*Plus and EM.

Assignment 3-8 Performing a time-based incomplete recovery using RMAN.

1. Launch RMAN and connect to the target database.
2. Using RMAN, shut down the database and then mount it.
3. Take a complete backup of the database using RMAN.
4. Open the database. Exit RMAN.
5. Connect to SQL*Plus as the MEDUSER with a password MEDUSER.
6. Create a table called TAB2 with a single char column as shown below:
   ```
   CREATE TABLE TAB2(A1 CHAR(20));
   ```
7. Verify that the table exists.
8. Issue the query `SELECT CURRENT_TIMESTAMP FROM DUAL;` to determine the current date and time on the computer. Note down the date and time. We shall identify this time as T1.
9. Wait for a few minutes and then issue the command `DROP TABLE TAB2;` to drop the table you created.
10. Re-issue the query `SELECT CURRENT_TIMESTAMP FROM DUAL;` to determine the current date and time on the computer. Note the date and time. We shall identify the time as T2. You have simulated the loss of a table. You will recover the database to the point prior to the drop.
11. Connect as a privileged user and shut down the database.
12. Take a complete backup of the database manually. Do not overwrite existing backups. This backup can be used in case the incomplete recovery does not succeed.
13. Using RMAN, connect to and mount the target database.
14. Write a RUN block that includes all the steps necessary to perform recovery up to time T1.
15. Connect as MEDUSER and verify that the table TAB2 exists.
16. Exit RMAN and SQL*Plus.

Assignment 3-9 Displaying the LOG_ARCHIVE_FORMAT

1. Start SQL*Plus and connect as an administrator.
2. Issue the SHOW PARAMETER command to view the value of the LOG_ARCHIVE_FORMAT initialization parameter.
3. In the format that is displayed, identify the different elements and what they represent.
4. Exit SQL*Plus.

Assignment 3-10 Re-creating the Password file

1. Start SQL*Plus and connect as a user with SYSDBA privileges.
2. Shut down the database using the IMMEDIATE option.
3. Using Windows Explorer, navigate to the location of the password file and using an operating system command delete the password file of the database.
4. Start up the database. No error will be reported.
5. Open a command prompt window and using the ORAPWD utility recreate the password file.

Assignment 3-11 Recreating the temporary file

1. Connect to SQL*Plus as a user with SYSDBA privileges.
2. Start SQL*Plus and create a temporary tablespace called TEMP3. Name the tempfile *temp03.dbf*.
3. Query the FILE_NAME column of the DBA_TEMP_FILES view to make sure the file was created.
4. Shut down the database using the IMMEDIATE option.
5. Using Windows Explorer, navigate to the location of temp03.dbf and delete it.
6. Start up the database.
7. Query the FILE_NAME column of the DBA_TEMP_FILES view. Was the file recreated automatically?
8. Which file will contain information about the recreation of the temporary file?

Assignment 3-12 Recovering from the loss of a redo log member.

1. Start SQL*Plus and connect as a user with SYSDBA privileges.
2. Issue the query SELECT GROUP#, MEMBERS FROM V$LOG; to determine the number of members in each redo log group.
3. Add a member called **redo02b.log** to the GROUP2.
4. Issue the command ALTER SYSTEM SWITCH LOGFILE *four* times.
5. Shut down the database using the IMMEDIATE option.
6. Using Windows Explorer, navigate to the location of the redo log file called redo02b.log and delete it.
7. Start up the database. You will not receive any error.
8. Perform the steps necessary to recover from the loss of the redo log member. (Hint: Drop the log file member and add it again to the group.)

9. Issue the query SELECT GROUP#, MEMBER FROM V$LOGFILE to ensure that the redo log file was recovered.
10. Exit SQL*Plus.

Assignment 3-13 Making a tablespace read only and recovering from its loss.

1. Start SQL*Plus and connect as a user with SYSDBA privileges.
2. Issue the query `SELECT TABLESPACE_NAME, STATUS FROM DBA_TABLESPACES;` to determine the names and status of the tablespaces.
3. Put the tablespace called INDX in a read only mode.
4. Re-query the DBA_TABLESPACES data dictionary view and verify that the tablespace is read only.
5. Launch RMAN, connect to the target database and take a backup of the INDX tablespace. (The INDX tablespace was created in Practice 14 of this chapter.)
6. Shut down the database.
7. Delete or move the datafile belonging to the INDX tablespace from the operating system. The name of the datafile is INDX01.DBF.
8. Start SQL*Plus, connect as a SYSDBA and start up the database. You should receive an error indicating that the file (indx01.dbf) is missing. Note the datafile number from the error displayed.
9. Issue the query SELECT FILE#, ENABLED FROM V$DATAFILE; to see the status of the datafile belonging to the INDX tablespace. It should be read only.
10. From RMAN, perform the steps necessary to recover the READ ONLY datafile. Perform an open database recovery by taking the INDX01.DBF file offline.
11. Change the status of the INDX tablespace to READ WRITE.

Case Study

1. Ryan has created a database called MEDDB. He has decided to mirror the control files but not the online redo logs. He created the database with three log groups with one member each. The backup strategy includes taking a full level 0 backup on Monday and a level 1 incremental backup every day of the week. A power surge caused the database to crash and also caused a media failure, destroying all the online log files. Based on the information provided, what method do you recommend Ryan should use to recover from this situation. Simulate a similar situation for the current database you are working on and perform the recovery based on the solution you have provided.
2. On Saturday morning Ryan, receives a call from the nurse in charge of the outpatient department. She has been trying to add information about some patients who were ready to be discharged but when she was attempting to add the data, the OUT_PATIENTS table was not available. Ryan logs on to the database and tries to issue the SELECT * FROM OUT_PATIENTS table an error is generated indicating the table or view does not exist. In this case Ryan has no time reference to determine when the table was dropped. What is the best option available to Ryan for recovering the table?
3. Note the step-by-step instructions of how incomplete recovery is performed in the Oracle Database 10*g*.

CHAPTER 4

FLASHBACK DATABASE

LEARNING OBJECTIVES

After completing this chapter, you should be able to do the following:

- Understand the Flashback Database feature
- Understand the components of Flashback Database
- Understand the guidelines and restrictions of Flashback Database
- Configure, maintain, and monitor the Flashback Database
- Perform Flashback Database using SQL, RMAN, and Enterprise Manager
- Understand how to resolve errors that may occur during the Flashback Database operation
- Manage and monitor Flashback Database

EXAM OBJECTIVES COVERED IN THIS CHAPTER:

- Flashback Database
- Configure and use Flashback Database
- Monitor the Flashback Database
- Use the Enterprise Manager Recovery Wizard to flashback database

INTRODUCTION

Studies indicate that more than 40 percent of errors that occur in the database occur as a result of human error. Errors of this kind may occur due to logical corruption of the data, accidental deletion, modification of important data, or the loss of important tables. These errors can be difficult to resolve and recovering from them will need a considerable amount of planning. Further, recovery from such errors can be tricky, time consuming, and may result in a considerable loss of business productivity. Traditional incomplete recovery was discussed in detail in Chapter 3. The incomplete recovery methods already reviewed have been available in previous versions of the Oracle database.

The "Flashback Query" feature was introduced in Oracle 9*i*. It provided the user the ability to query and view data as it existed at a previous point in time. The feature used the undo data in the undo segments that were being maintained for undo retention. The Oracle 10*g* database provides us, in addition to Flashback Query, a suite of new features collectively known as Flashback Technologies, which provide the user with an ability to view and rewind data as it existed in the past.

The Flashback Technologies include Flashback Database, Flashback Table, Flashback Drop, Flashback Versions Query, and Flashback Transaction Query. These features provide fast and easy recovery of data at a database, table, row, and transaction level by using undo data.

This chapter discusses the first feature—the Flashback Database. It is an enhancement to traditional incomplete recovery. Flashback Database provides the ability to perform incomplete recoveries such as time-based, SCN-based, or change-based recovery, as you did in the Chapter 3, with the advantage of less downtime. By using this feature, the time taken to recover from the error is equal to the time taken for the error itself. The feature allows you to quickly rewind a database to a previous time, previous SCN, or previous log sequence number. The chapter explains the components of the Flashback Database as well as guidelines for its use and its restrictions. A complete review of its configuration and maintenance is also provided. The views available in the Oracle database that may be used to monitor the Flashback Database will also be discussed. The chapter covers the Flashback Database feature using SQL commands, RMAN, and Enterprise Manager.

THE CURRENT CHALLENGE AT KELLER MEDICAL CENTER

Sharon is a junior web developer at Keller Medical Hospital. She has been experimenting with transactions, by issuing INSERT, UPDATE, and DELETE statements, on what she assumed was her personal database. However, she has inadvertently been applying the changes to a number of tables on the production database and has accidentally deleted and committed several records to various tables. In the course of her practice she accidentally drops the PATIENT_HISTORY table. Realizing her mistake she rushes to Anita the senior DBA for help. Anita who has recently been reading a lot about enhancements in Oracle 10g thinks it is a good opportunity to try the Flashback Database feature created primarily for recovery from such logical errors. In this chapter we will simulate a similar problem and see how Anita can rectify Sharon's error.

OVERVIEW OF FLASHBACK DATABASE

Flashback Database is a new feature introduced in Oracle Database 10g. This feature is a powerful new tool in the database administrator's recovery toolbox. Using this feature the DBA can rewind the database to a state it was in the past. It is particularly useful to reverse the effects of undesirable changes caused by user errors such as the accidental drop of an important table or the committing of incorrect data.

The Flashback Database cannot be used to recover from media failures such as the loss of a file. Media failures would require a traditional method of recovery. For logical user failures the Flashback Database is relatively faster than the traditionally incomplete recovery methods that were discussed Chapter 3. The traditional methods of recovery required the use of backups and log files for the recovery process, and the time to restore the database was proportional to the size of the database. If the database was large then the recovery time would proportionately be long. In Flashback Database the recovery time is dependent on the number of changes that need to be rolled back or backed out. A new type of log file is known as **Flashback Logs** is used for the recovery. The Flashback Database feature reduces the time required to recover a database because it does not require restoring datafiles from backup and requires fewer changes from flashback logs to be applied.

COMPONENTS FOR FLASHBACK DATABASE

By default the Flashback Database functionality is disabled and must be explicitly enabled in the database. You can query the FLASHBACK_ON column of the V$DATABASE dynamic view to display the status of the feature. Once enabled, the Flashback Database feature creates and maintains a new type of log known as **Flashback Logs**. Flashback logs are always created only in the *Flash Recovery Area*. It is therefore, necessary that you configure the flash recovery area if you plan to enable Flashback Database. Flashback logs contain the before image of the data blocks. Since the before images are stored only for modified blocks, the size of the logs is dependent on the number of changes that occur in the database. The before images are stored in the System Global Area (SGA) in flashback buffers and are periodically written to the flashback logs by the new **RVWR (Recovery Writer)** background process. A new flashback log is written on a regular basis, usually hourly, even if nothing has occurred in the database. Flashback logs are typically smaller than archived redo log files and have an extension .FLB. It is also important to note that flashback logs are not archived. Figure 4-1 describes how the RVWR process writes to the flashback logs.

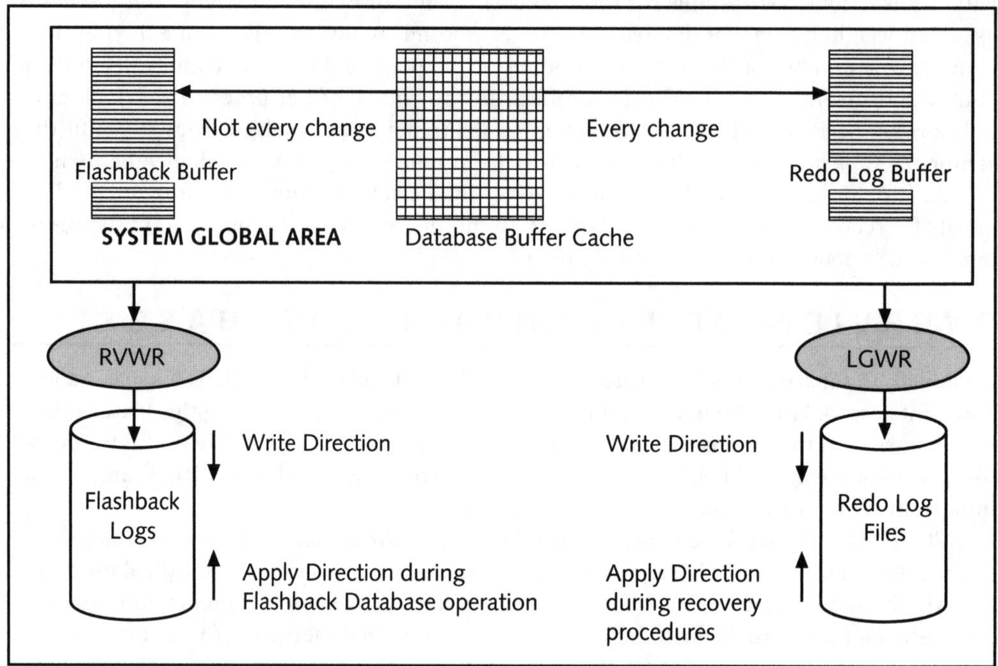

FIGURE 4-1 The RVWR background process is responsible for storing before images of changed blocks in the Flashback logs

As previously mentioned a flash recovery area must be configured if you want to implement the Flashback Database feature. The flash recovery area is a centralized location for backup and recovery related files and may be configured by the DB_RECOVERY_FILE_DEST and DB_RECOVERY_FILE_DEST_SIZE initialization parameters. A detailed discussion on the flash recovery area and its configuration is presented in Chapter 2 of this book.

When an administrator issues a Flashback Database request, Oracle reconstructs the state of the database to or before the requested point using the contents of the flashback logs.

There is a very small performance overhead incurred upon enabling Flashback Database. It is less than 2 percent. The trade off is worthwhile as it enables recovery in minutes instead of hours.

GUIDELINES OF FLASHBACK DATABASE

The Flashback Database procedure may be performed using SQL*Plus, RMAN, or Enterprise Manager. You can flashback the database to a point in time, to a specific System Change Number (SCN), or to a log sequence number.

The database must be mounted to perform a flashback of the database.

When you request a flashback of the database, the Oracle server uses the flashback logs to back out the changes. After completing the Flashback Database operation, it is recommended that you open the database in read-only mode to verify that the correct target time or SCN was used. After confirming that the flashback was successful you must open the database using a **RESETLOGS** clause.

RESTRICTIONS OF FLASHBACK DATABASE

There are some restrictions imposed by the Flashback Database feature. The Flashback Database functionality cannot be used under certain circumstances. If any of the following situations occur during the time frame that you wish to restore the database to, you will have to perform a traditional incomplete recovery operation rather than a Flashback Database operation. Flashback Database cannot be performed if:

- The control file has been restored or recreated.
- A tablespace has been dropped.
- An incomplete recovery has occurred and the database was opened with a RESETLOGS option.
- A datafile has been shrunk using a RESIZE command.

CONFIGURING FLASHBACK DATABASE

The Flashback Database feature may be configured using SQL*Plus or Enterprise Manager. The two main pre-requisites that must be satisfied are:

- The flash recovery area must be configured for the database.
- The database must be in *archivelog* mode.

The SQL command to enable Flashback Database is:

```
ALTER DATABASE FLASHBACK ON;
```

You must also configure the DB_FLASHBACK_RETENTION_TARGET initialization parameter. It determines the amount of flashback data that will be stored in the flashback logs. It is a value (in minutes) that signifies the upper limit on how far back you can flashback the database. Flashback Database must be enabled when the database is mounted.

Practice 1: Enabling the Flashback Database Feature in the Database

This practice demonstrates the steps that may be performed to enable the Flashback Database functionality in the DB101 database.

1. Start SQL*Plus and log in as a user with SYSDBA privileges.
2. Ensure that the flash recovery area has been enabled. Use the SHOW PARAMETER command to view the values of the DB_RECOVERY_FILE_DEST and

DB_RECOVERY_FILE_DEST_SIZE parameters. Figure 4-2 displays the current values of the parameters associated with the flash recovery area.

```
SQL> SHOW PARAMETER DB_RECOVERY
```


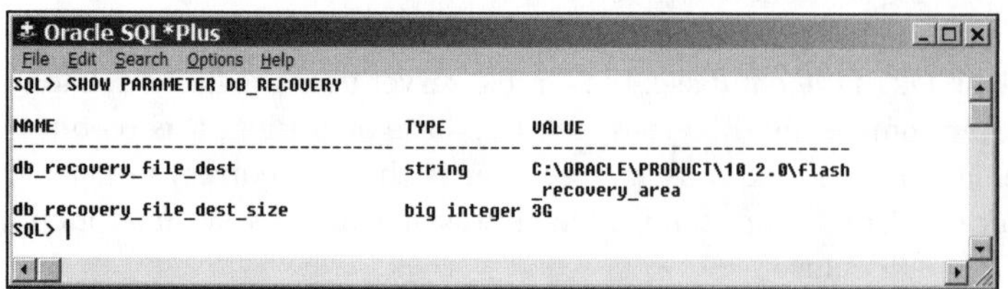

FIGURE 4-2 Parameters used to configure the flash recovery area

3. If the parameters to configure the flash recovery area parameters display null values in step 2, then configure them using the following ALTER SYSTEM commands. You may skip this step if the flash recovery area is already configured.

```
SQL> ALTER SYSTEM SET
     DB_RECOVERY_FILE_DEST='<location>' SCOPE=BOTH;
SQL> ALTER SYSTEM SET
     DB_RECOVERY_FILE_DEST_SIZE=<size in bytes>;
```

4. Next, type the ARCHIVE LOG LIST; command to view the archiving mode of the database. The database must be in archivelog mode.

```
SQL> ARCHIVE LOG LIST;
```

5. If the database is in noarchivelog mode you must perform step 7.
6. To enable Flashback Database, shut down the database and mount it.

```
SQL> SHUTDOWN IMMEDIATE;
SQL> STARTUP MOUNT;
```

7. This step may be omitted if your database is in archivelog mode. If the database is running in noarchivelog mode (Step 4) then change the archiving mode by issuing:

```
SQL> ALTER DATABASE ARCHIVELOG;
```

8. Issue the ALTER DATABASE command to enable Flashback Database.

```
SQL> ALTER DATABASE FLASHBACK ON;
```

9. Next, set the DB_FLASHBACK_RETENTION_TARGET initialization parameter. The parameter indirectly determines how much flashback log data the database will retain. Set the value of the parameter to 2880 minutes or 48 hours. Figure 4-3 displays the output of the statements issued.

```
SQL> ALTER SYSTEM SET DB_FLASHBACK_RETENTION_TARGET= 2880;
```

10. Open the database.

```
SQL> ALTER DATABASE OPEN;
```

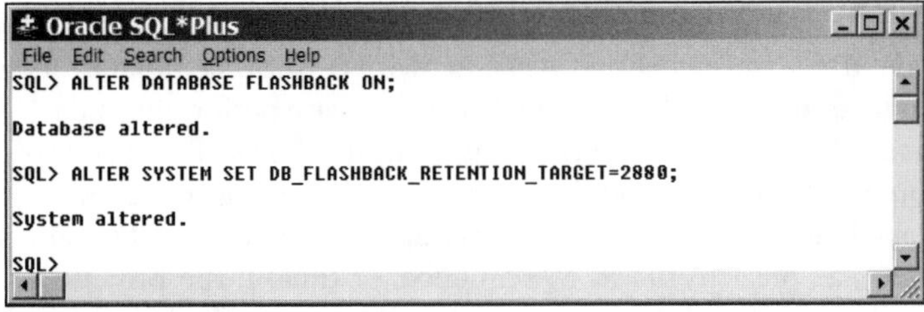

FIGURE 4-3 Commands to enable Flashback Database

11. Query the V$DATABASE view to determine if Flashback Database has been enabled. Figure 4-4 displays the status of Flashback Database after it has been enabled as YES.

    ```
    SQL> SELECT FLASHBACK_ON FROM V$DATABASE;
    ```

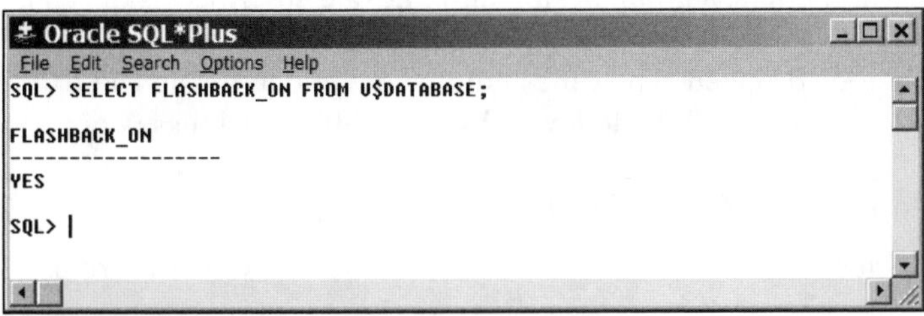

FIGURE 4-4 Querying the Flashback Database status

12. Exit SQL*Plus.

PERFORMING THE FLASHBACK DATABASE

The Flashback Database allows you to rewind the database to a previous point in time. The previous point in time may be identified using a timestamp, a system change number, or a log sequence number. The Flashback Database operation may be done using SQL commands, RMAN, or Enterprise Manager. This section provides a review of Flashback Database using all three methods.

The FLASHBACK DATABASE Command in SQL

The Flashback Database operation is done from SQL*Plus using the FLASHBACK DATABASE command. The options available with the command are TIMESTAMP and SCN number.

The syntax of the FLASHBACK DATABASE is:

```
FLASHBACK DATABASE TO {[TIMESTAMP]| [SCN number]}
```

The FLASHBACK DATABASE Command in RMAN

The following section displays the syntax of the FLASHBACK DATABASE command in Recovery Manager. The command may take the SCN directive if you are performing a flashback based on an SCN number, TIME if you are performing a flashback based on a timestamp, and SEQUENCE if you are flashing back the database based on a log sequence number. In the syntax displayed below, a BEFORE directive may be used to flash the database back to the point in time just prior to the SCN, sequence, or time. If the BEFORE directive is not specified then the flashback will be done until (inclusive) the SCN, sequence, or time.

```
FLASHBACK DATABASE
TO [BEFORE] SCN = <scn>
TO [BEFORE] SEQUENCE = <sequence>
TO [BEFORE] TIME = '<timestamp>'
```

Practice 2: Performing a Flashback Database operation using SQL

In this practice example you will simulate a problem similar to the one described as the challenge at Keller Medical Center. You will simulate the addition of some rows to the PATIENT_HISTORY table which will then be dropped. The timestamp before and after the DROP command will be noted. The simulation will be followed by a Flashback Database operation using SQL.

Part 1: Simulating the loss of the PATIENT_HISTORY table

1. Log in to SQL*Plus. Connect as the user MEDUSER whose password is MEDUSER.

```
SQL> CONNECT MEDUSER/MEDUSER
```

2. Execute the script **ch04_sim21.sql** that is in the Chapter04 folder of the student datafiles. This script creates the table called PATIENT_HISTORY and adds 10 rows to it. Query the table to verify its existence. The contents of the table are displayed in Figure 4-5.

```
SQL> START <PATH>\CH04_SIM21.SQL
SQL> SELECT * FROM PATIENT_HISTORY;
```

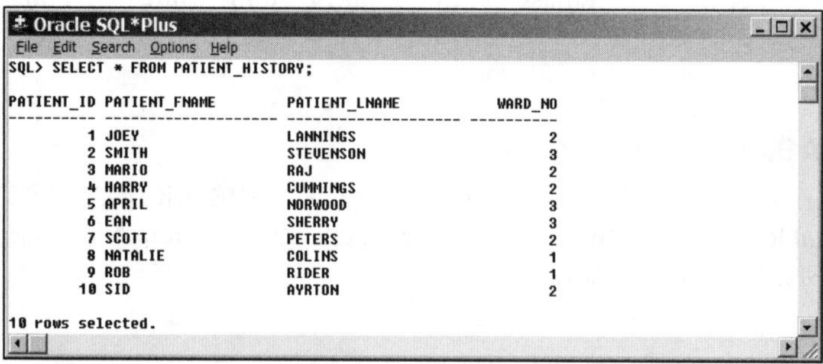

```
Oracle SQL*Plus
File Edit Search Options Help
SQL> SELECT * FROM PATIENT_HISTORY;

PATIENT_ID PATIENT_FNAME        PATIENT_LNAME           WARD_NO
---------- -------------------- -------------------- ----------
         1 JOEY                 LANNINGS                      2
         2 SMITH                STEVENSON                     3
         3 MARIO                RAJ                           2
         4 HARRY                CUMMINGS                      2
         5 APRIL                NORWOOD                       3
         6 EAN                  SHERRY                        3
         7 SCOTT                PETERS                        2
         8 NATALIE              COLINS                        1
         9 ROB                  RIDER                         1
        10 SID                  AYRTON                        2

10 rows selected.
```

FIGURE 4-5 The contents of the PATIENT_HISTORY table

3. Issue the following command to determine the current timestamp. Note the date and time. This timestamp will be referred to as T1. Figure 4-6 displays the time as "14-DEC-05 08.47.11."

```
SQL> SELECT CURRENT_TIMESTAMP FROM DUAL;
```

```
Oracle SQL*Plus
File Edit Search Options Help
SQL> SELECT CURRENT_TIMESTAMP FROM DUAL;

CURRENT_TIMESTAMP
---------------------------------------------------------------------------
14-DEC-05 08.47.11.781000 AM -05:00

SQL> |
```

FIGURE 4-6 Displaying the current date and time

4. Wait a few minutes and run the **ch04_sim22.sql** script in Chapter04 folder. This script contains a DROP command that will simulate the loss of the PATIENT_HISTORY table.

```
SQL> START <PATH>\CH04_SIM22.SQL
```

5. Issue the command to determine the current timestamp. Note the date and time. This timestamp will be referred to as T2. Figure 4-7 displays the time as "14-DEC-05 08.51.31."

```
SQL> SELECT CURRENT_TIMESTAMP from dual;
```

6. Exit SQL *Plus.

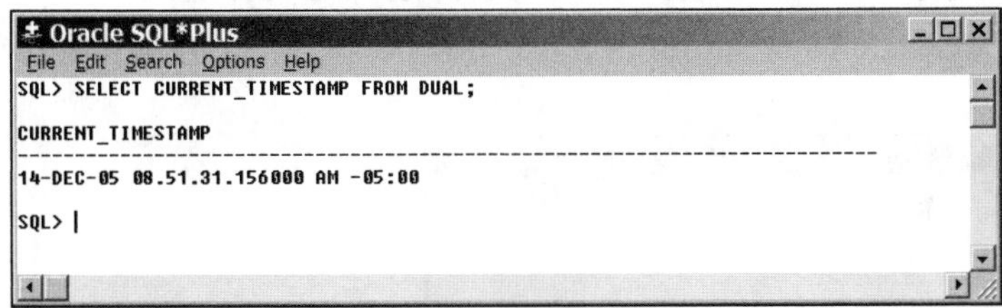

FIGURE 4-7 Displaying the current date and time

Part 2: Performing a Flashback Database operation using a SQL command

7. Based on the timestamps you noted, you will now perform the flashback database operation using SQL to the point in time when the table existed.
8. Start SQL*Plus and connect as a user with SYSDBA privileges.
9. Shut down and mount the database.

```
SQL> SHUTDOWN IMMEDIATE
SQL> STARTUP MOUNT
```

10. To ensure that the date format you specify in flashback command is accepted, set the following NLS_DATE_FORMAT parameter.

```
SQL> ALTER SESSION SET NLS_DATE_FORMAT='DD-MON-YY HH24:MI:SS';
```

11. Type the following command to perform a flashback of the database to a time prior to the dropping of the PATIENT_HISTORY table. In the command displayed, substitute the time you noted down as T1 (Use a 24-hour clock format when specifying the hours).

```
SQL> FLASHBACK DATABASE TO TIMESTAMP(TO_DATE('14-DEC-05 08:47:
11'));
```

12. Open the database in a read-only mode. Figure 4-8 displays the outputs of the last three statements issued.

```
SQL> ALTER DATABASE OPEN READ ONLY;
```

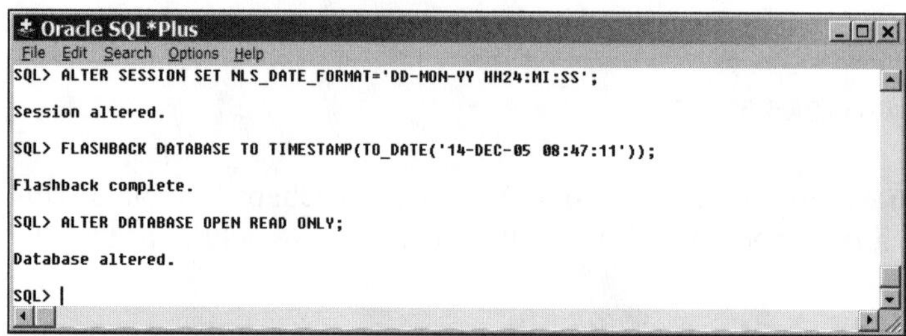

FIGURE 4-8 Issuing the FLASHBACK DATABASE command from SQL

13. Make sure the PATIENT_HISTORY table exists with the data. If the table exists with the 10 rows then the Flashback Database operation was performed successfully. If it does not exist, mount the database, adjust the time, and re-issue the FLASHBACK DATABASE using the correct time. Figure 4-9 displays the 10 rows of the PATIENT_HISTORY table indicating recovery was successful.

```
SQL> SELECT * FROM MEDUSER.PATIENT_HISTORY;
```

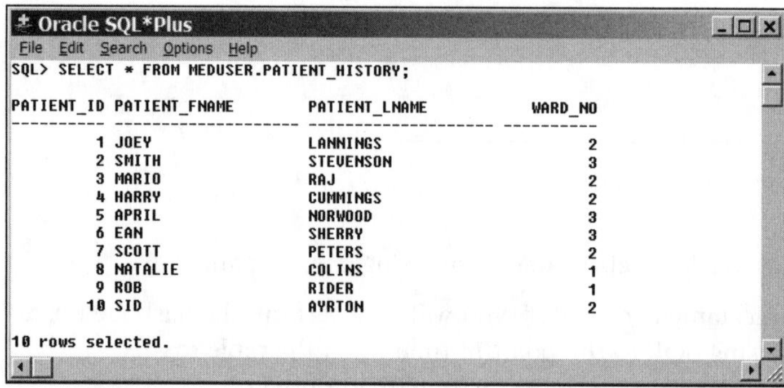

FIGURE 4-9 The contents of the PATIENT_HISTORY table after the Flashback Database

14. Shut down the database and mount it.

```
SQL> SHUTDOWN IMMEDIATE;
SQL> STARTUP MOUNT;
```

15. Open the database with the RESETLOGS option.

```
SQL> ALTER DATABASE OPEN RESETLOGS;
```

16. To view details about the flashback database operation that you just performed you may view the contents of the ALERT log file. Figure 4-10 displays a portion of the alert log file that provides information about the Flashback Database operation that was just performed.

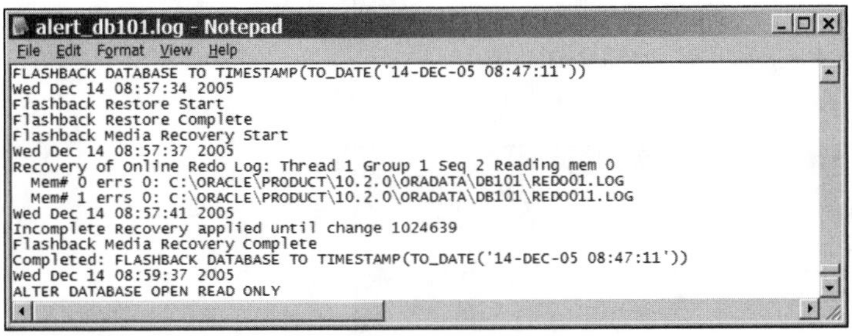

```
alert_db101.log - Notepad
File Edit Format View Help
FLASHBACK DATABASE TO TIMESTAMP(TO_DATE('14-DEC-05 08:47:11'))
Wed Dec 14 08:57:34 2005
Flashback Restore Start
Flashback Restore Complete
Flashback Media Recovery Start
Wed Dec 14 08:57:37 2005
Recovery of Online Redo Log: Thread 1 Group 1 Seq 2 Reading mem 0
  Mem# 0 errs 0: C:\ORACLE\PRODUCT\10.2.0\ORADATA\DB101\REDO01.LOG
  Mem# 1 errs 0: C:\ORACLE\PRODUCT\10.2.0\ORADATA\DB101\REDO011.LOG
Wed Dec 14 08:57:41 2005
Incomplete Recovery applied until change 1024639
Flashback Media Recovery Complete
Completed: FLASHBACK DATABASE TO TIMESTAMP(TO_DATE('14-DEC-05 08:47:11'))
Wed Dec 14 08:59:37 2005
ALTER DATABASE OPEN READ ONLY
```

FIGURE 4-10 The alert log file entries related to the Flashback Database operation

17. Exit SQL*Plus.

Practice 3: Flashback of the Database using RMAN

In this practice example you will simulate a problem similar to the one described as the challenge at Keller Medical Center. You will simulate the addition of some rows to the PATIENT_HISTORY table which will then be dropped. The timestamp before and after the DROP command will be noted. The simulation will be followed by a Flashback Database operation using RMAN.

Part 1: Simulating the loss of the PATIENT_HISTORY table

1. Start SQL*Plus. Connect as the user MEDUSER whose password is MEDUSER.

```
SQL> CONNECT MEDUSER/MEDUSER
```

2. Execute the script **ch04_sim31.sql** that is in the Chapter04 folder of the student datafiles. This script creates the table called PATIENT_HISTORY and adds 5 rows to it. Query the table to verify its existence. The contents of the table are displayed in Figure 4-11.

```
SQL> START <PATH>\CH04_SIM31.SQL
SQL> SELECT * FROM PATIENT_HISTORY;
```

3. Issue the following command to determine the current timestamp. Note the date and time. This timestamp will be referred to as T1. Figure 4-12 displays the timestamp as "13-DEC-05 10.58.20."

```
SQL> SELECT CURRENT_TIMESTAMP FROM DUAL;
```

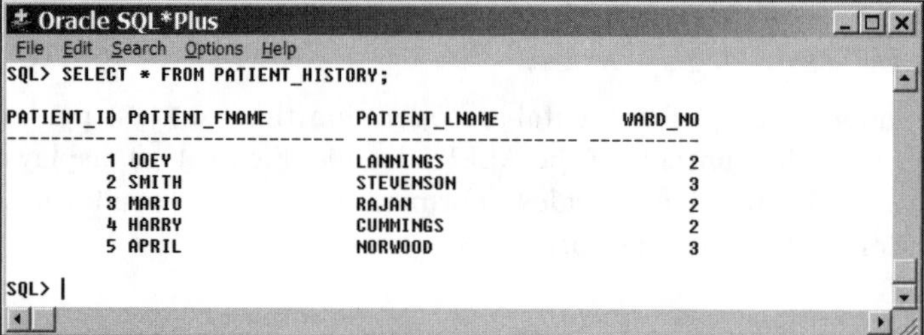

FIGURE 4-11 The contents of the PATIENT_HISTORY table

```
Oracle SQL*Plus
File Edit Search Options Help
SQL> SELECT CURRENT_TIMESTAMP FROM DUAL;

CURRENT_TIMESTAMP
---------------------------------------------------------------------------
13-DEC-05 10.58.20.343000 AM -05:00

SQL>
```

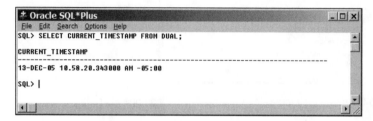

FIGURE 4-12 Displaying the current date and time when the table exists

4. Wait for a few minutes and run the **ch04_sim32.sql** script in Chapter04 folder. This script contains a DROP command that will simulate the loss of the PATIENT_HISTORY table.

```
SQL> START <PATH>\CH04_SIM32.SQL
```

5. Issue the command to determine the current timestamp. Note the date and time. This timestamp will be referred to as T2. Figure 4-13 displays the time as "13-DEC-05 11.01.33."

```
SQL> SELECT CURRENT_TIMESTAMP from dual;
```

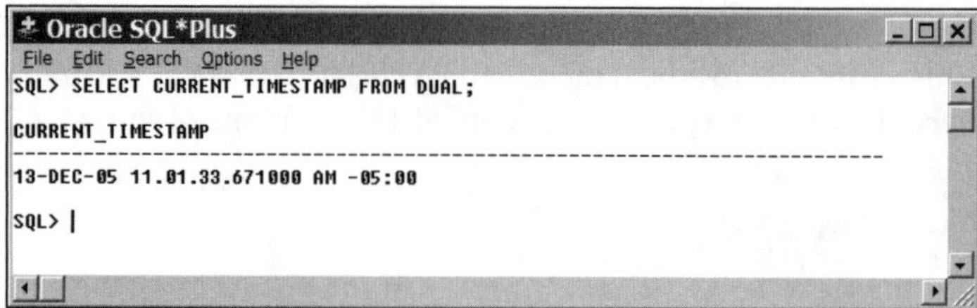

FIGURE 4-13 Displaying the current date and time after the table has been dropped

Part 2: Flashback Database operation using RMAN

6. Using SQL*Plus connect as a user with SYSDBA privileges.
7. Shutdown and mount the database.

```
SQL> SHUTDOWN IMMEDIATE;
SQL> STARTUP MOUNT;
```

8. Launch RMAN and connect to the target database.

```
C:\>RMAN
RMAN>CONNECT TARGET
```

9. To ensure that RMAN can interpret the date and time format correctly you may want to issue the SQL command to set the NLS_DATE_FORMAT initialization parameter as shown below.

```
RMAN> SQL 'ALTER SESSION SET NLS_DATE_FORMAT="DD-MON-YY HH24:MI:
SS"';
```

10. Type the following command to perform a flashback of the database to a time prior to the dropping of the PATIENT_HISTORY table. In the command displayed, substitute the time you noted as T1 (Use a 24-hour clock format when specifying the hours). Figure 4-14 displays the RMAN output generated after issuing the FLASHBACK DATABASE command.

```
RMAN> FLASHBACK DATABASE TO TIME = '13-DEC-05 10:58:20';
```

```
Command Prompt - RMAN
RMAN> FLASHBACK DATABASE TO TIME='13-DEC-05 10:58:20';

Starting flashback at 13-DEC-05
allocated channel: ORA_DISK_1
channel ORA_DISK_1: sid=154 devtype=DISK


starting media recovery
media recovery complete, elapsed time: 00:00:07

Finished flashback at 13-DEC-05

RMAN>
```

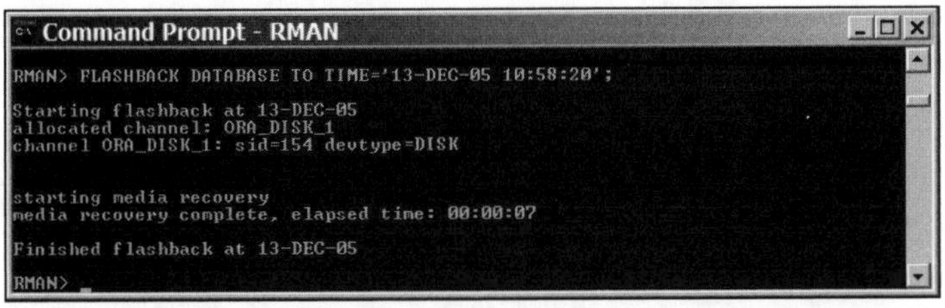

FIGURE 4-14 Performing the Flashback Database from RMAN

11. Open the database in a read-only mode.

```
RMAN> SQL 'ALTER DATABASE OPEN READ ONLY';
```

12. Open another SQL*Plus session and connect as the MEDUSER user. Make sure the PATIENT_HISTORY table exists with its data as shown in Figure 4-15. If the table exists with the 5 rows then the flashback database operation was done successfully. If it does not exist, mount the database, adjust the time, and re-issue the FLASHBACK DATABASE command using the correct time.

```
SQL> CONNECT MEDUSER/MEDUSER
SQL> SELECT * FROM PATIENT_HISTORY;
```

13. Return to the RMAN prompt, shut down the database, and mount it.

```
RMAN> SHUTDOWN IMMEDIATE;
RMAN> STARTUP MOUNT;
```

14. Open the database using the RESETLOGS option.

```
RMAN> ALTER DATABASE OPEN RESETLOGS;
```

15. Exit SQL*Plus and RMAN.

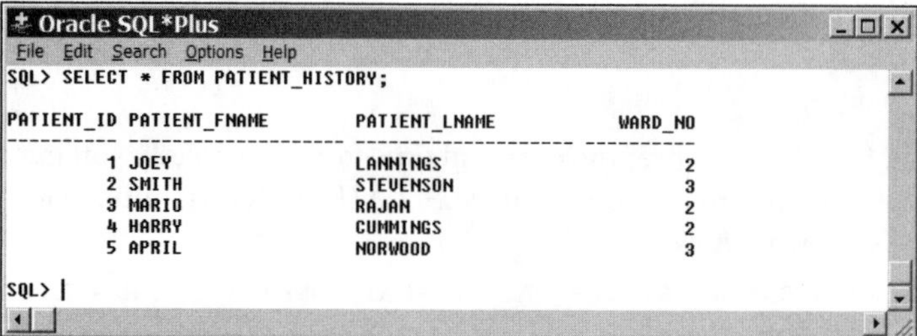

FIGURE 4-15 The contents of the PATIENT_HISTORY table after the Flashback Database

Practice 4: Flashback of the Database using Enterprise Manager

In this practice example you will simulate a problem similar to the one described as the challenge at Keller Medical Center. You will simulate the addition of some rows to the PATIENT_HISTORY table which will then be dropped. The timestamp before and after the DROP command will be noted. The simulation will be followed by a Flashback Database operation using Enterprise Manager.

Part 1: Simulating the loss of the PATIENT_HISTORY table

1. Log in to SQL*Plus. Connect as the user MEDUSER whose password is MEDUSER.

```
SQL> CONNECT MEDUSER/MEDUSER
```

2. Execute the script **ch04_sim41.sql** that is in the Chapter04 folder of the student datafiles. This script creates the table called PATIENT_HISTORY and adds 7 rows to it. Query the table to verify its existence. The contents of the table are displayed in Figure 4-16.

```
SQL> START <PATH>\CH04_SIM41.SQL
SQL> SELECT * FROM PATIENT_HISTORY;
```

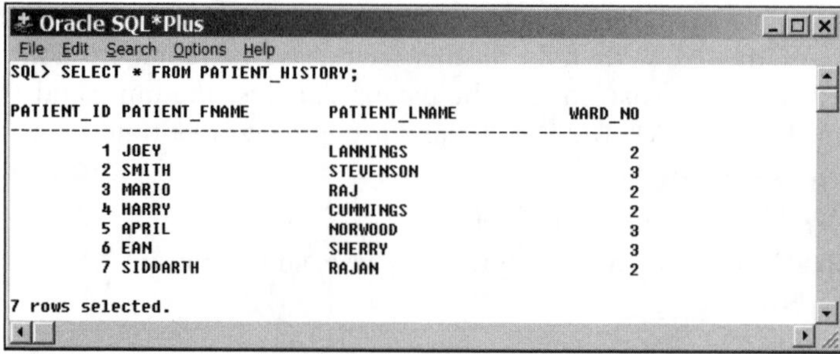

FIGURE 4-16 The contents of the PATIENT_HISTORY table

3. Issue the following command to determine the current timestamp. Note the date and time. This time will be referred to as T1. Figure 4-17 displays the time as "13-DEC-05 11.18.45."

```
SQL> SELECT CURRENT_TIMESTAMP FROM DUAL;
```

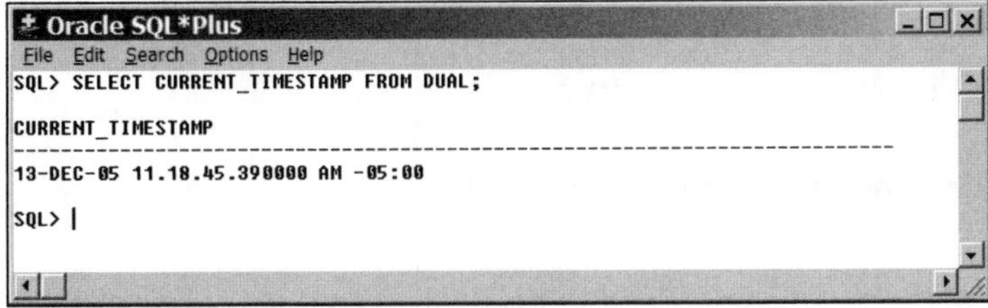

FIGURE 4-17 Displaying the current date and time when the table exists

4. Wait for a few minutes and run the **ch04_sim42.sql** script in Chapter04 folder. This script contains a DROP command that will simulate the loss of the PATIENT_HISTORY table.

   ```
   SQL> START <PATH>\CH04_SIM42.SQL
   ```

5. Issue the command to determine the current timestamp. Note the date and time. This time will be referred to as T2. Figure 4-18 displays the time as "13-DEC-05 11:22:31."

   ```
   SQL> SELECT CURRENT_TIMESTAMP from dual;
   ```

6. Exit SQL *Plus

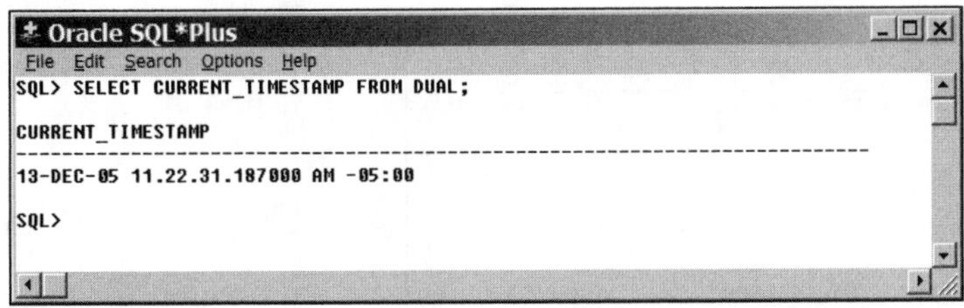

FIGURE 4-18 Displaying the current date and time after the table has been dropped

Part 2: Performing a flashback database operation using Enterprise Manager

7. Using SQL*Plus connect as a SYSDBA and shut down the database.

   ```
   SQL> SHUTDOWN IMMEDIATE;
   ```

8. Mount the database.

   ```
   SQL> STARTUP MOUNT
   ```

9. Launch a browser and enter the URL to launch Enterprise Manager. Log in as a SYSDBA.
10. From the **Database Control Home** page select the **Perform Recovery** button. Figure 4-19 displays the Perform Recovery button that may be selected.
11. The **Perform Recovery: Credentials** page will be displayed. Enter the **Host Credentials.** Select the **Continue** button.
12. From the **Database Login** page, select the login button and enter the username and password of a SYSDBA.

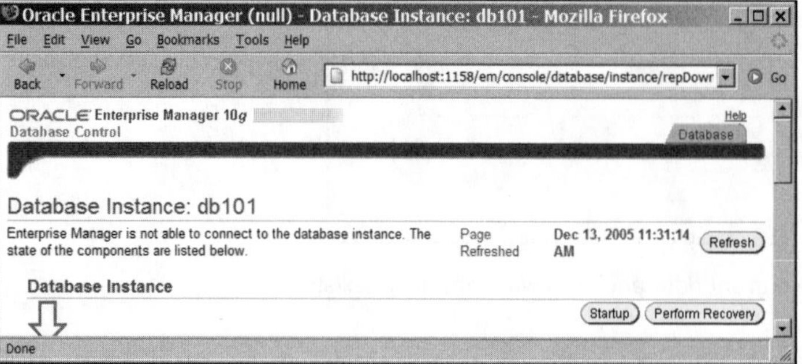

FIGURE 4-19 The Database Control Home page when the database is mounted

13. The **Perform Recovery** page is displayed.
14. Select **Recover to the current time or a previous point-in-time**.
15. Then select the **Perform Whole Database Recovery** button.
16. The **Perform Whole Database Recovery: Point-in-time** page is displayed.
17. Select **Recover to a prior point-in-time** from the **Point-in-time** section.
18. In the date area, enter the date and select the time (noted as T1) as shown in Figure 4-20. Select the **Next** button.

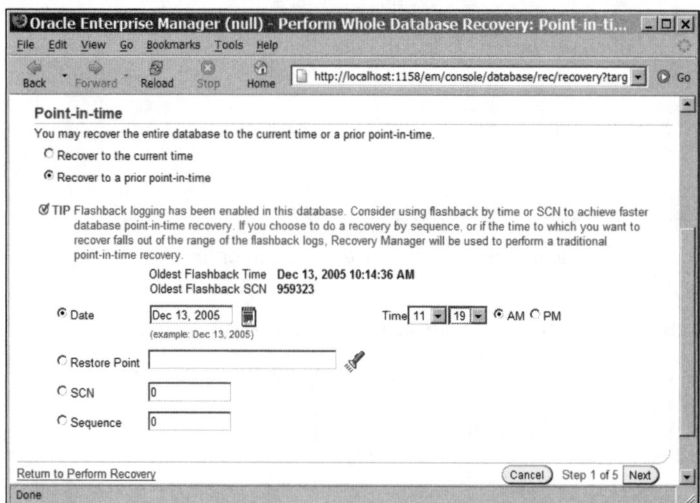

FIGURE 4-20 Entering the date and time for Flashback Database

19. The **Perform Whole Database Recovery: Flashback** page is displayed.
20. Select the **Yes, use flashback to bring the database back to the specified point-in-time** option. Select the **Next** button.
21. The **Perform Whole Database Recovery: Review** page is will be displayed. Select the **Edit RMAN Script** button to view the RMAN script that is generated (Figure 4-21) based on the choices you have made.

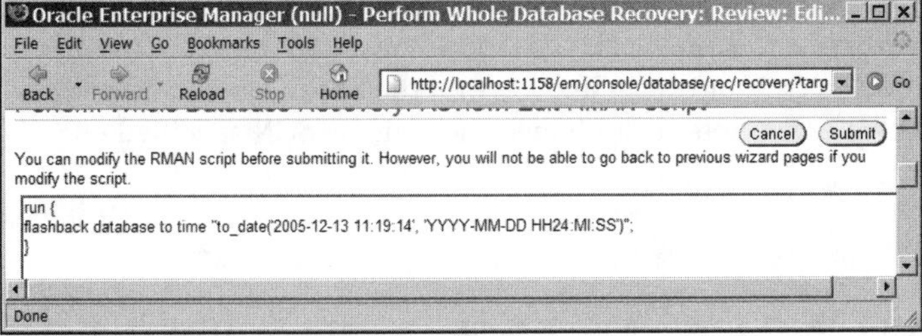

FIGURE 4-21 The RMAN script that will be executed

22. Using the **Submit** button.
23. After a few minutes the **Operation Succeeded page** will appear. You have successfully performed a flashback database operation using Enterprise Manager.
24. Select the **OK** button. Exit Enterprise Manager.
25. Using SQL*Plus, connect as a user with SYSDBA privileges.
26. Open the database using the READ ONLY option.

```
SQL>ALTER DATABASE OPEN READ ONLY;
```

27. Issue a query on the MEDUSER.PATIENT_HISTORY to see it is was successfully recovered. The table must contain 7 rows as displayed in Figure 4-22.

```
SQL> SELECT * FROM MEDUSER.PATIENT_HISTORY;
```

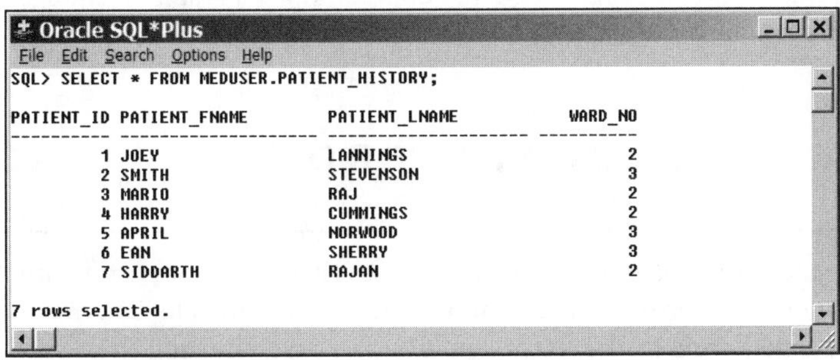

```
SQL> SELECT * FROM MEDUSER.PATIENT_HISTORY;

PATIENT_ID PATIENT_FNAME        PATIENT_LNAME           WARD_NO
---------- -------------------- -------------------- ----------
         1 JOEY                 LANNINGS                      2
         2 SMITH                STEVENSON                     3
         3 MARIO                RAJ                           2
         4 HARRY                CUMMINGS                      2
         5 APRIL                NORWOOD                       3
         6 EAN                  SHERRY                        3
         7 SIDDARTH             RAJAN                         2

7 rows selected.
```

FIGURE 4-22 The contents of the PATIENT_HISTORY table after the Flashback Database

28. Shut down the database, mount it, and open it with the RESETLOGS option.

```
SQL> SHUTDOWN IMMEDIATE;
SQL> STARTUP MOUNT;
SQL> ALTER DATABASE OPEN RESETLOGS;
```

29. Exit SQL*Plus.

FAILURES THAT MAY OCCUR DURING A FLASHBACK OPERATION

If an instance failure occurs during the Flashback Database operation all you would need to do is mount the database and begin the Flashback Database operation again.

Another error that may occur is lack of flashback database log data, causing failure to complete the flashback. An error like the one displayed below may be generated. This error may occur if you have specified an SCN or timestamp beyond the flashback database recovery window. In the event of this error, you must change the time or SCN specified.


```
SQL> FLASHBACK DATABASE TO SCN 78000;
ERROR at line 1:
ORA-38729: Not enough flashback database log data to do FLASHBACK.
```

OPTIONS AVAILABLE AFTER A FLASHBACK DATABASE

After you have performed the flashback, if you realize that you used the wrong time, SCN, or log sequence number you may do one of the following.

If the target time you chose was after the actual restore point, you can re-issue the flashback database to the earlier restore point. To rewind the database further in time you would issue:

```
RMAN> FLASHBACK DATABASE TO SCN n; #earlier than current SCN
```

If you chose a time or SCN too far in the past, you may mount the database and use the RECOVER DATABASE UNTIL to wind the database forward in time to the desired point.

```
RMAN> RECOVER DATABASE UNTIL SCN n;  #later than current SCN
```

Finally, if you wish to undo the effect of the Flashback Database command, you may perform a complete recovery using the `RECOVER DATABASE` command. As a result all changes will be re-applied to the database returning it to the current SCN.

```
RMAN> RECOVER DATABASE;
```

EXCLUDING A TABLESPACE FROM FLASHBACK

There may be certain tablespaces such as temporary tablespaces that need not participate in the Flashback Database operation because their contents are not worthwhile. You may exclude a tablespace from participating in the flashback of a database by using the `ALTER TABLESPACE tablespace_name FLASHBACK OFF;` command.

The FLASHBACK OFF attribute may be set when the tablespace is created. By default, all tablespaces have this attribute turned ON. Shown below is a CREATE TABLESPACE command with the attribute turned OFF.

```
CREATE TABLESPACE user_temp_data
DATAFILE '<path>/datafile_name '
...
FLASHBACK OFF;
```

Alternatively, if you do not want a tablespace to participate in a Flashback Database operation, you may take it offline. The tablespace may be dropped and the offline datafiles recovered using traditional incomplete recovery methods.

The flashback status of a tablespace may be viewed by querying the FLASHBACK_ON column of the V$TABLESPACE view.

Practice 5: Determining the Flashback Status of a tablespace

This practice demonstrates querying the flashback status of a tablespace.

1. Start SQL*Plus and log in as a SYSDBA.
2. Retrieve the NAME and FLASHBACK_ON columns of the V$TABLESPACE view. Figure 4-23 indicates all the tablespaces of the DB101 database have the flashback status as enabled.

   ```
   SQL> SELECT NAME, FLASHBACK_ON FROM V$TABLESPACE;
   ```

```
Oracle SQL*Plus
File Edit Search Options Help
SQL> SELECT NAME, FLASHBACK_ON FROM V$TABLESPACE;

NAME                           FLA
------------------------------ ---
SYSTEM                         YES
UNDOTBS1                       YES
SYSAUX                         YES
USERS                          YES
INDX                           YES
TEMP                           YES
TEMPA                          YES
TEMP3                          YES

8 rows selected.
```

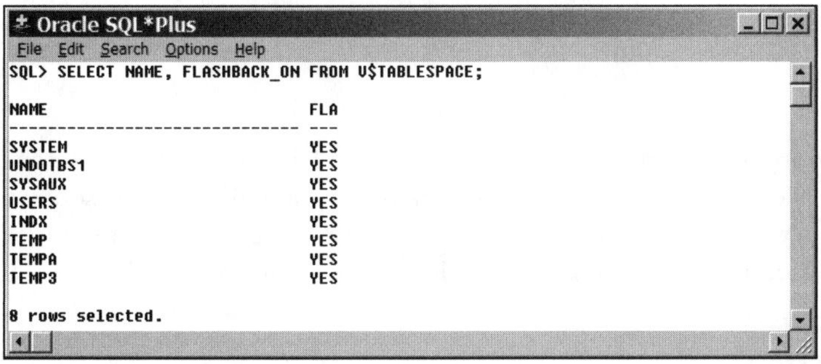

FIGURE 4-23 Determining the flashback database status of tablespaces

3. If any of the tablespaces display a status of OFF, enable flashback logging for the tablespace. You need not do this step if all values in the FLASHBACK_ON column display the value YES.

   ```
   SQL> ALTER TABLESPACE tablespace_name FLASHBACK ON;
   ```

4. Exit SQL*Plus.

MANAGING FLASHBACK DATABASE

The range of SCNs for which there is currently enough flashback log data to support the Flashback Database operation is known as the Flashback Database Window. If the amount of space in the flash recovery area is low, then old flashback logs may be deleted to free space for backup files required by the configured retention policy and new flashback logs. If you recall, the flash recovery area is the area that is used for storing backups of the database. Because flashback logs cannot be created outside of the flash recovery it is important to ensure that the flash recovery area has sufficient space.

The V$FLASHBACK_DATABASE_LOG performance view may be used to help you estimate how much space is required in the flash recovery area for flashback logs based on the activity in the database. This view can also help you determine how much of flashback data is currently in the flashback logs. Table 4-1 displays the various columns of the view and the kind of information they contain.

TABLE 4-1 The columns of the V$FLASHBACK_DATABASE_LOG view

Column Name	Description
OLDEST_FLASHBACK_SCN	Lowest SCN up to which you can flashback.
OLDEST_FLASHBACK_TIME	Earliest time to which you can flashback.
RETENTION_TARGET	Target retention time in minutes.
FLASHBACK_SIZE	Current size of flashback data in bytes.
ESTIMATED_FLASHBACK_SIZE	Estimated size of flashback data needed for the current target retention.

After you have enabled logging for the flashback database and set the flashback retention target, allow the database to run under a normal workload for a while. A representative sample of flashback logs will be generated. You may then view the estimated amount of flashback space required based on the workload using the following query:

```
SELECT * FROM V$FLASHBACK_DATABASE_LOG;
```

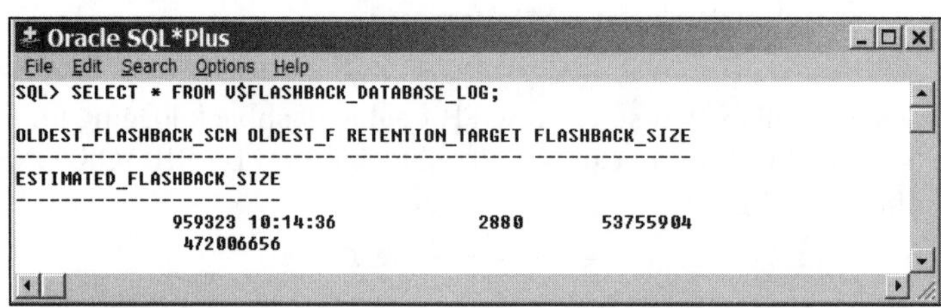

FIGURE 4-24 Viewing the V$FLASHBACK_DATABASE_LOG view

The output of the query displayed in Figure 4-24 indicates that the database may be flashed back to an earliest SCN of 959323 or a timestamp "10:14:36." The flashback retention is 2880 minutes. This value was set, as part of Practice 1, for the DB_FLASHBACK_RETENTION_TARGET initialization parameter. The current flashback data in the flash recovery area amounts to 53755904 bytes and based on the workload the ESTIMATED_FLASHBACK_SIZE is about 472006656 bytes. The value of the ESTIMATED_FLASHBACK_SIZE column will help you estimate of the amount of disk space needed to meet the current flashback retention target based on the database workload. Using the estimated values, you may choose to add space to the flash recovery area to hold the expected database flashback logs.

To make space for flashback logs, you may also back up the existing contents of the flash recovery area to tape.

MONITORING FLASHBACK LOGS

The V$FLASHBACK_DATABASE_STAT view may be used to monitor the overhead of logging flashback data in the flashback logs. The view contains estimated flashback space needed based on previous workloads. The view contains 24 hours of information with each row representing a one-hour interval specified by begin and end times and shows you how much flashback information has been collected so far. Table 4-2 displays the structure of the V$FLASHBACK_DATABASE_STAT view and a description of its columns.

TABLE 4-2 The columns of the V$FLASHBACK_DATABASE_STAT view

Column Name	Description
BEGIN_TIME	Beginning of the time interval
END_TIME	End of the time interval
FLASHBACK_DATA	Number of bytes of flashback data written during the time interval
DB_DATA	Number of bytes of database data read and written during the time interval
REDO_DATA	Number of bytes of redo data written during the time interval
ESTIMATED_FLASHBACK_SIZE	Value of ESTIMATED_FLASHBACK_SIZE in V$FLASHBACK_DATABASE_LOG at the end of the time interval.

The contents of the view can help you understand the nature of flashback log generation and estimate the size of the recovery area. Based on the information presented you may need to adjust the target retention time or the size of the flash recovery area.

Practice 6: Monitoring the Flashback Logs by querying V$FLASHBACK_DATABASE_STAT

This practice example demonstrates monitoring of the Flashback Logs. The NLS_DATE_FORMAT parameter has been modified in the practice to help you view the values of the BEGIN_TIME and END_TIME columns.

1. Launch SQL*Plus and connect as a user with SYSDBA privileges.
2. Set the NLS_DATE_FORMAT initialization parameter for the current session.

   ```
   SQL>ALTER SESSION SET NLS_DATE_FORMAT='HH24:MI:SS';
   ```

3. Query the V$FLASHBACK_DATABASE_STAT view to display the view that can be used to monitor the flashback logs. Figure 4-25 displays the output of the V$FLASHBACK_DATABASE_STAT view. In the output of the command notice that during the time interval 13:11:01 to 14:17:35, the amount of data read or written was 19906560 bytes. This I/O resulted in generating 14598144 bytes

of flashback data and 8980992 bytes of redo data. At the end of that time interval, the estimated flashback size was 631554048. If the output contained a number of rows, the values of the last column would display the trend in estimated flashback size. This trend will help you determine if the current size of the flash recovery area is sufficient or not.


```
SQL> SELECT * FROM V$FLASHBACK_DATABASE_STAT;
```

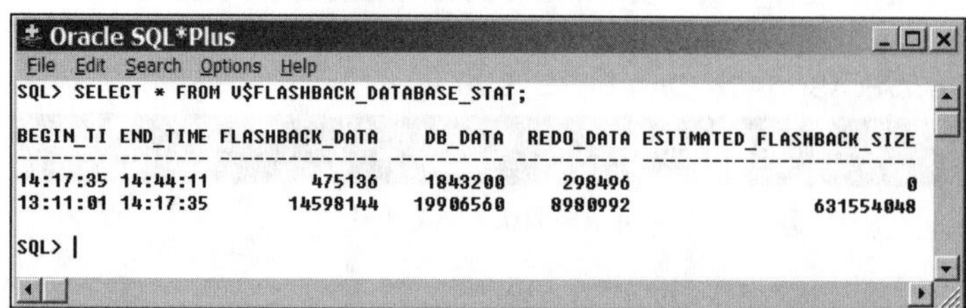

FIGURE 4-25 Viewing the V$FLASHBACK_DATABASE_STAT view

4. Exit SQL*Plus.

FLASHBACK AND DATAFILE OPERATIONS

Earlier in this chapter certain restrictions imposed by the Flashback Database feature were discussed. If a datafile was dropped during the Flashback Database window, then during the flashback database operation the dropped datafile will be added to the control file and marked offline. It will not be flashed back. After the Flashback Database operation has completed you may restore and recover the datafile using a traditional recovery method.

If a datafile is shrunk using the RESIZE command, the flashback database cannot flashback this datafile. You must take the datafile offline before beginning the Flashback Database operation. After the flashback is completed, you can restore and recover the datafile to the same time as the rest of your database using a traditional recovery method.

DISABLING FLASHBACK DATABASE

The Flashback Database feature may be disabled using a SQL command or using Enterprise Manager. The ALTER DATABASE FLASHBACK OFF command issued in SQL may be used to disable Flashback Database.

NOTE

When the flashback database feature is disabled, all the existing flashback logs are automatically deleted.

You can also enable and disable flashback database using Enterprise Manager.

Practice 7: Disabling Flashback Database using Enterprise Manager.

This practice example demonstrates how the Flashback Database functionality may be disabled using Enterprise Manager.

1. Launch a browser, enter the URL to access Enterprise Manager, and log in as a SYSDBA.
2. From the **Database Control Home** page, select the **Maintenance** tab.
3. From the **Backup/Recovery Settings** section select the **Recovery Settings**.
4. The **Recovery Settings** page will be displayed.
5. Navigate along this page to the **Flash Recovery** section.
6. To disable flashback database you will need to deselect **Enable flashback Database – flashback logging can be used for fast database point-in-time recovery**. Please do not deselect the option since you will need the Flashback Database feature enabled for the hands-on assignments (Figure 4-26).
7. Exit Enterprise Manager.

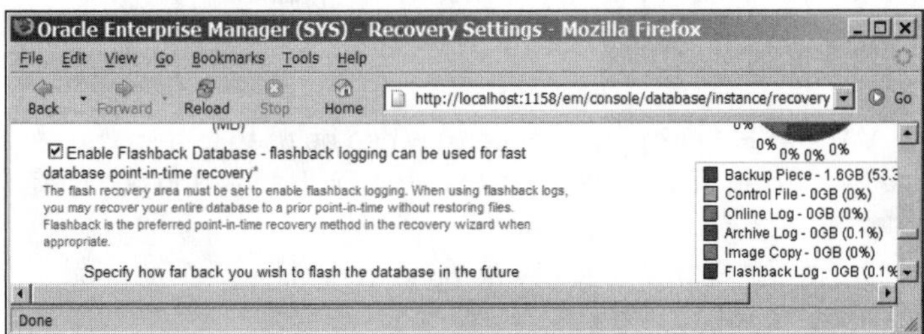

FIGURE 4-26 Disabling Flashback Database using Enterprise Manager

In this chapter you learned about the Flashback Database feature in Oracle 10*g*. You learned how to configure and implement Flashback Database. In Chapter 5, the other Flashback Technology features—Flashback Table, Flashback Versions Query, Flashback Transactions Query and Flashback Drop—will be discussed.

Chapter Summary

- The Flashback Database feature is new in Oracle 10*g*.
- Flashback Database can help you to rewind the entire database to a state it was in the past.
- The Flashback Database feature may be used to recover from logical errors such as the accidental drop of a table or the accidental committing of inaccurate data in the database.
- The database must be in archivelog mode and the flash recovery area configured before enabling this feature.
- The Flashback Database is implemented by using a new type of log file known as Flashback Logs.
- The before images of changed blocks are stored in Flashback buffers and are periodically transferred by the RVWR background process to the flashback log files.
- The DB_FLASHBACK_RETENTION_TARGET initialization parameter determines in minutes the upper limit to how far back you may flashback the database.
- You may perform the Flashback Database procedure using the either SQL*Plus, RMAN, or Enterprise Manager.
- The V$FLASHBACK_DATABASE_LOG performance view can be used to help you estimate how much space is required in the flash recovery area for flashback logs based on the activity in the database.
- The V$FLASHBACK_DATABASE_STAT view may be used to monitor the overhead of logging flashback data in the flashback logs.

Syntax Guide

SYNTAX GUIDE		
Command	**Description**	**Example**
`ALTER DATABASE FLASHBACK [ON|OFF]`	To enable or disable the Flashback Database feature	`ALTER DATABASE FLASHBACK ON;` `ALTER DATABASE FLASHBACK OFF;`
`ALTER SESSION SET NLS_DATE_FORMAT='date format'`	To modify the default date format for the current session.	`ALTER SESSION SET NLS_DATE_FORMAT='DD-MON-YY HH24:MI:SS';`
`ALTER DATABASE OPEN [READ ONLY | RESETLOGS];`	The open read-only option is used to open a database in read-only mode. Only queries on the database will be allowed. The RESETLOGS option must be used for incomplete recovery.	`ALTER DATABASE OPEN READ ONLY;` `ALTER DATABASE OPEN RESETLOGS;`

SYNTAX GUIDE		
Command	**Description**	**Example**
`ALTER TABLESPACE... FLASHBACK [ON|OFF];`	To set the Flashback Database status of a tablespace.	`ALTER TABLESPACE USERS FLASHBACK ON;` `ALTER TABLESPACE USERS FLASHBACK OFF;`
Flashback Database Command in SQL		
`FLASHBACK DATABASE TO [BEFORE] {[TIMESTAMP]|[SCN number] }`	The Flashback Database command in SQL can take parameters timestamp, SCN, or SEQUENCE number. The timestamp option indicates a time to which you want to flashback the database. The SCN option indicates an SCN number up to which you want to flashback the database.	`FLASHBACK DATABASE TO SCN 46963;` `FLASHBACK DATABASE TO TIMESTAMP (SYSDATE-1/24);` `FLASHBACK DATABASE TO TIMESTAMP to_timestamp('2002-11-11 16:00:00', 'YYYY-MM-DD HH24:MI:SS');`
Flashback Database Command in RMAN		
`FLASHBACK DATABASE TO {[TIME= 'date string'] | [SCN= number ] | [SEQUENCE= sequence] }`	Use the TIME='datestring' option to flashback to a specific date and time. Use the SCN =number option to flashback up to but not including the specific SCN. Use the sequence=sequence_number to flashback up to but not including a specific sequence number.	`RMAN> FLASHBACK DATABASE TO TIME = '2005-07-11 15:06:23';` `RMAN> FLASHBACK DATABASE TO SCN = 712223;` `RMAN> FLASHBACK DATABASE UNTIL SEQUENCE=185;`

Review Questions

1. The Flashback Database is similar to the traditional ________________ recoveries.
   a. Complete
   b. Incomplete
   c. Tablespace
   d. None of the above
2. When enabling the Flashback Database feature the database must be in ________________ mode.
   a. Noarchivelog
   b. Archivelog
   c. It does not matter.
   d. Flashback

3. The ________________ view can be queried to determine if Flashback Database has been enabled.
   a. V$DATABASE
   b. V$FLASHBACK_ON
   c. V$FLASHBACK_MODE
   d. DBA_DATABASE

4. Enabling Flashback Database has a small impact on performance. However the trade off is ________________ .
5. The ________________ background process is responsible for performing logging before images to the logs.
   a. RVWR
   b. RWRV
   c. RWVR
   d. DBWR
6. The ________________ store before images of changed blocks.
7. The initialization parameter that indirectly determines the amount of flashback data that will be stored in the flashback logs is ________________ .
   a. DB_FLASHBACK_RETENTION_TARGET
   b. DB_FLASHBACK_TARGET
   c. DB_RECOVERY_FILE_DEST
   d. None of the above
8. After the flashback database has been done the database must be opened using the ________________ keyword.
9. The ________________ log file can be viewed to obtain information regarding the flashback database operation.
10. To exclude a tablespace from being flashed back you can use the ________________ clause during tablespace creation.
11. To view the flashback status of a tablespace, which view would you query?
    a. V$DATABASE
    b. V$INSTANCE
    c. V$TABLESPACE
    d. DBA_DATA_FILES
12. Identify the view that can be queried to help you estimate how much space is required in the flash recovery area for flashback logs based on the activity of the database.
    a. V$DATABASE
    b. V$FLASHBACK_DATABASE
    c. V$FLASHBACK_DATABASE_LOG
    d. DBA_TABLESPACES

13. The view that you can query to monitor the overhead of logging flashback data in the flashback logs is ________________.
    a. V$FLASHBACK_DATABASE_LOG
    b. V$DATABASE
    c. V$FLASHBACK_MONITOR
    d. V$FLASHBACK_DATABASE_STAT
14. When performing a flashback database operation using RMAN, the database must be .
    a. In a nomount mode
    b. Mounted
    c. Opened
    d. It does not matter
15. The two important pre-requisites for enabling the Flashback Database feature are: (Choose 2)
    a. The database must be in noarchivelog mode.
    b. The database must be in archivelog mode.
    c. The flash recovery area must be configured.
    d. The RVWR background process must be explicitly started.
    e. The flashback logs need to be created.
16. Your Oracle 10*g* database is running in ARCHIVELOG mode, and a flash recovery area is configured. The database is in the MOUNT EXCLUSIVE state. Which steps would you follow to configure Oracle Flashback Database? (Choose all that apply.)
    a. Open the database in read-only mode.
    b. Set the retention target with the DB_FLASHBACK_RETENTION_TARGET initialization parameter.
    c. Execute the ALTER DATABASE FLASHBACK ON command.
    d. Enable block change tracking.
17. You have configured the Oracle Flashback Database feature for your database. Which statements are correct in this scenario? (Choose all that apply.)
    a. Flashback logs will be generated for all the tablespaces by default.
    b. When you disable the Oracle Flashback Database feature, flashback logs are automatically deleted.
    c. You can use the Oracle Flashback Database feature for recovery if your database is physically corrupted.
    d. Flashback logs are archived by default.
18. You are required to flash back your database. You need to determine the approximate time and the oldest SCN to which you can flash back. How would you calculate this information?
    a. Query the V$FLASHBACK_DATABASE_LOG view.
    b. Query the V$FLASHBACK_DATABASE_STAT view.

c. Check the value set for the DB_FLASHBACK_RETENTION_TARGET initialization parameter.

d. Query the V$RECOVERY_FILE_DEST view.

19. The ________________ column of the V$FLASHBACK_DATABASE_STAT view displays the time at which the query was executed.

20. You have disabled the Flashback Database feature. Which of the following statements are true?

a. The Flashback logs will be archived and automatically deleted.

b. The Flashback logs will be automatically deleted.

c. The database will have to be restarted.

d. The Flashback logs will be backed up for future use.

Hands-On Assignments

Assignment 4-1 Flashback Database using SQL

In this assignment you will be performing a flashback of the database using SQL. You will simulate an incorrect flashback database operation to the wrong time and then repeat the flashback database to the correct time. This is done to demonstrate the ease with which it is possible to change the flashback time. In the practice the objective is to flashback to a time when the table contained only 10 rows.

1. Open SQL*Plus and connect as a user with SYSDBA privileges.
2. Run the script **chass4-1.sql** from the Chapter04 folder of the student datafiles. The script creates a table called TAB41 and populates it with 10 rows. Query the table to confirm its existence.
3. Retrieve the current_timestamp. Identify this as time T1.
4. Run the script **chass4-1b.sql**. This script adds another 10 rows to the table TAB41.
5. Retrieve the current timestamp. Identify this as time T2.
6. Shut down and mount the database.
7. Issue an ALTER SESSION command to set the date format to DD-MON-YY HH24:MI:SS.
8. Flash back the database to the time indicated by T2. This simulates the flashback to the incorrect time.
9. Open the database in a read-only mode.
10. Query the table TAB41. If it contains 20 rows then you have flashed back to the wrong time. You need to re-issue the flashback command.
11. Shut down and mount the database.
12. Flash back the database to the time indicated by T1. This simulates the flashback to the correct time.
13. Open the database in read-only mode.
14. Query the TAB41 table and view the number of rows in the table. There should be 10 rows. You have re-issued the flashback command to the correct time.

15. Shut down and mount the database.
16. Open the database using the RESETLOGS option.
17. Launch RMAN, connect to the target database, and take a complete backup of the database.
18. Exit RMAN and SQL*Plus.

Assignment 4-2 Flashback Database using RMAN

In this practice you will simulate the loss of an important table. You will then use RMAN to perform a time-based flashback database to recover to a point prior to the drop command.

1. Launch RMAN, connect to the target database, and take a complete backup of the database. Exit RMAN after taking the backup.
2. Open SQL*Plus and connect as a user with SYSDBA privileges.
3. Run the script **chass4-2.sql**. This script creates a table called TAB42 and adds 10 rows to it. Query the table to make sure it was created successfully.
4. Display the current timestamp.
5. Wait for a few minutes and run the script **chass4-2b.sql**. This script drops the table called TAB42.
6. Display the current timestamp.
7. Launch RMAN and connect to the target database.
8. Shut down and mount the database.
9. Issue a command to and set the NLS_DATE_FORMAT parameter to "DD-MON-YY HH24:MI:SS" for the current session.
10. Perform a flashback of the database to the time T1.
11. Using SQL*Plus, connect as a SYSDBA and open the database as READ ONLY.
12. Query the TAB42 table to see if it exists with 10 rows.
13. Shut down, mount, and open the database with the RESETLOGS option.
14. Exit SQL*Plus and RMAN.

Assignment 4-3 Performing an flashback database operation using the SCN number

In the following assignment you will perform a flashback using Enterprise Manager. You will first create a table called TAB43, and then drop it. You will use the methods learned earlier (LOGMINER) to determine the SCN number. You will then perform a flashback using the SCN.

1. Launch SQL*Plus and connect as a user with SYSDBA privileges.
2. Start RMAN, connect to the target database, and perform a backup of the entire database. Exit RMAN.
3. Run the script **chass4-3.sql** from the Chapter04 folder. The script creates a table called TAB43, inserts 10 rows to it and then drops it.
4. Query the TAB43 table. It should not exist.
5. Start the process of analyzing the redo logs to determine the SCN number of the DROP TABLE TAB43 command. (Follow the steps described in Chapter 3: Practice 4: Step 2.)
6. Shut down and mount the database. Exit SQL*Plus.

7. Launch Enterprise Manager and perform the steps required to perform a flashback operation until the SCN number you just determined.
8. Using SQL*Plus, connect as a SYSDBA and open the database as READ ONLY.
9. Query the TAB43 table. If it exists with 10 rows the flashback was successful.
10. Shut down, mount, and open the database using the RESETLOGS option.
11. Exit SQL*Plus and Enterprise Manager.

Assignment 4-4 Disable the Flashback Database feature

1. Using the steps described in Practice 7, disable the Flashback Database feature using Enterprise Manager.

Case Study

1. Ryan has been assigned the responsibility of assisting the developers in the creation of the ELECTRONIC MEDICAL RECORD SYSTEMS application. The system is a designed to allow easy access of patient information at any time. He has been helping developers create tables with appropriate columns, sizes, and keys. He has also been working with the quality assurance (QA) managers and testers to ensure that the application works with all sorts of test data. Because there are some records that act as baseline data, he has been looking for a way to restore baseline data for repetitive reuse without re-entering the data every time. Suggest a method and the steps you would perform to accomplish this task with speed and least effort.
2. On Friday evening a DBA drops a user account without realizing the schema of the user had important tables. Identify the various ways in which you could determine information about when the account was dropped, or the SCN associated with the dropping of the account. If you had to suggest a solution, clearly define your investigation strategy and provide an appropriate solution.

CHAPTER 5

RECOVERING FROM USER ERRORS

LEARNING OBJECTIVES

After completing this chapter, you should be able to do the following:

- Understand the new Flashback Technology features available in Oracle Database 10*g*
- Understand the configuration and implementation of Flashback Drop
- Understand the recycle bin
- Understand the configuration and implementation of Flashback Query
- Understand the configuration and implementation of Flashback Versions Query
- Understand the configuration and implementation of Flashback Transaction Query
- Understand the configuration and implementation of Flashback Table

EXAM OBJECTIVES COVERED IN THIS CHAPTER:

- Recover a dropped table using Flashback technology
- Perform Flashback table operation
- Manage the recycle bin
- Recover from user errors using Flashback versions query
- Perform transaction level recovery using Flashback Transaction query

INTRODUCTION

Chapter 4 introduced you to the Flashback Database feature. This feature was an excellent alternative to traditional incomplete procedures. In this chapter you will be introduced to the other flashback technology features introduced in Oracle 10*g*.

Human errors are one of the primary causes of downtime, accounting for nearly 40 percent of errors that may occur in the database. These errors occur in an unpredictable manner and need to be resolved without delay. Using the Flashback Technologies, a database administrator can quickly resolve these errors as soon as they occur with no impact on other users and the performance of the database.

In this chapter the various Flashback Technologies will be discussed. We begin with the Flashback Drop feature, which helps a user quickly recover from the accidental loss of a table. We will then look at the Flashback Query feature that allows a user to issue simple queries to view data as it existed in the past. This is followed by the Flashback Versions Query that may be used to view different versions of the data during a certain time frame as well as reverse the changes. The Flashback Transaction Query will then be discussed. This feature may be used to view changes made to the database at the level of a transaction and undo the effects of undesirable changes. Finally, a review of the Flashback Table will be done, which is extremely useful for recovering from accidental and undesirable changes made to a table.

With the new Flashback Table, Flashback Drop, and Flashback Database capabilities, erroneous changes in multiple tables, accidentally dropped tables, and logical data corruptions can be instantly rolled back with a single SQL command instead of performing complex media recovery procedures.

THE CURRENT CHALLENGE AT KELLER MEDICAL CENTER

The doctors and nurses at Keller Medical Center have requested an easier method of auditing changes in medications prescribed to patients. Further, the staff have also requested a feature in the database that will signal if a patient is assigned the wrong medication. Since the DB101 database was upgraded from *9i* to 10*g*, the database administrators at Keller Medical Center have been trying to find ways to simplify the tasks they normally perform. Errors such as the accidental loss of tables have also been a major concern. Since the database must be constantly available, using long and error-prone recovery procedures is becoming increasingly unacceptable. In this chapter you will see how the Flashback Technology features can be used to solve many of the problems caused by human error as well analyze, diagnose, and audit transactions.

SETUP FOR THE CHAPTER

To successfully complete the practice examples and hands-on assignments presented in this chapter you will have to execute various scripts from the Chapter05 folder of the student datafiles. The script to be executed is mentioned in the specific practice.

FLASHBACK DROP

Dropping the wrong table accidentally is something most of us have done at some time or another. There are various methods of recovering from this situation. In earlier versions of Oracle, prior to 10*g*, you could import the table if a logical backup was available in a dump file. You could also perform a rather complex point-in-time recovery procedure. In Oracle 10*g*, recovering from such errors is a trivial task. The Flashback Drop may be used to recover from a table that has been accidentally dropped. The Flashback Drop feature is a part of the new Flashback Technologies introduced in Oracle Database 10*g*.

The Flashback Drop feature makes use of a **RECYCLE BIN**. It is the location where a table is placed when it is dropped using a DROP TABLE command. As long as the object is in the RECYCLE BIN it can be recovered.

The RECYCLE BIN

In Oracle 10*g*, the Oracle server maintains a recycle bin. The recycle bin is a part of the Oracle database and acts like a container of dropped objects. Every time an object is dropped, a reference of the object is placed in the recycle bin and the object is renamed with a globally unique name. The naming convention takes the form BIN$unique_id. For example, the name of a table in the recycle bin could be BIN$Eo82hIYhSceR0IQc01hI3g==$1.

The objects that are dropped continue to occupy space in their original tablespace. The extents remain in the datafile and they continue to count toward the space quota the user has been allotted in the tablespace and the used space of the tablespace. All indexes, triggers, constraints, and dependent objects created on the dropped object are retained and renamed with a prefix of BIN$. As long as a table is in the recycle bin it can be "undropped." These objects can be queried from the recycle bin as they could prior to the drop, except that you need to reference them by the new name assigned to them when they were put into the recycle bin. Users continue to hold their privileges on the objects in the recycle bin as they did prior to the drop.

The dropped object remains in the recycle bin until one of the following situations occurs:

- The tablespace that contains the dropped object cannot accommodate any more data and needs additional space.
- The datafile that contains the objects extends automatically.

It should be noted that there is no guarantee as to how long an object remains in the recycle bin. Reclamation of space for objects in the recycle bin is dependent on the space utilization in the tablespace. The objects that were the first to enter the recycle bin are the first to leave. When there is no space left in a tablespace, or when a user's quota on a tablespace is met, the oldest objects of the tablespace currently in the recycle bin are automatically purged. A user may permanently delete objects from the recycle bin by using the PURGE command.

The contents of the recycle bin may be viewed by querying the USER_RECYCLEBIN or RECYCLEBIN data dictionary views. The views display the objects that were dropped and are currently in the recycle bin. The DBA may query the DBA_RECYCLEBIN to query all objects that were dropped system-wide.

Performing a Flashback Drop

The Flashback Drop operation may be performed using SQL*Plus or Enterprise Manager. The Flashback Drop operation is performed from SQL*Plus using the FLASHBACK TABLE... DROP command.

The syntax of the command is:

```
FLASHBACK TABLE tablename TO BEFORE DROP [RENAME TO newname];
```

The `RENAME TO` *`newname`* clause allows you to rename the table after restoring it from the recycle bin. If the clause is omitted, the table is restored with its original name. The clause is useful if another table by the original name has been created in the schema between the drop and recovery operation.

Practice 1: Performing a Flashback Drop operation

In this practice example you will simulate the creation of a table called PHY_FD. The table will then be dropped. You will then simulate a restoration of the table using the FLASHBACK TABLE...DROP command.

1. Start SQL*Plus and connect to the database as the MEDUSER user.

   ```
   SQL> CONNECT MEDUSER/MEDUSER
   ```

2. Run the script called **ch5_fdcreate.sql**. The script creates a table called PHY_FD and populates it with 10 rows.

   ```
   SQL>START <PATH>\CH5_FDCREATE.SQL
   ```

3. Query the USER_TABLES view to confirm the PHY_FD table's creation in the MEDUSER schema. (See Figure 5-1.)

   ```
   SQL> SELECT TABLE_NAME FROM USER_TABLES;
   ```

```
Oracle SQL*Plus
File Edit Search Options Help
SQL> SELECT TABLE_NAME FROM USER_TABLES;

TABLE_NAME
------------------------------
DOCDATA
TAB2
PATIENT_HISTORY
PHY_FD

SQL> |
```

FIGURE 5-1 Confirm the creation of the PHY_FD table by querying USER_TABLES

4. Next, run the script called **ch5_fddrop.sql**. This script drops the PHY_FD table created in the previous step.

```
SQL> START <PATH>\CH5_FDDROP.SQL
```

5. Query the USER_RECYCLEBIN data dictionary view to retrieve information about the table that was just dropped.

```
SQL> SELECT *
     FROM USER_RECYCLEBIN
     WHERE ORIGINAL_NAME='PHY_FD';
```

```
Oracle SQL*Plus
File Edit Search Options Help
SQL> SELECT * FROM USER_RECYCLEBIN
  2  WHERE ORIGINAL_NAME='PHY_FD';

OBJECT_NAME                    ORIGINAL_NAME                    OPERATION
------------------------------ -------------------------------- ---------
TYPE                      TS_NAME                          CREATETIME
------------------------- -------------------------------- -------------------
DROPTIME               DROPSCN PARTITION_NAME                   CAN CAN
------------------- ---------- -------------------------------- --- ---
   RELATED BASE_OBJECT PURGE_OBJECT      SPACE
---------- ----------- ------------ ----------
BIN$bH+0079GTl6YskWrq2zjkQ==$0 PHY_FD                           DROP
TABLE                     USERS                            2005-12-19:08:50:01
2005-12-19:08:51:40    1064378                                  YES YES
     51576       51576        51576          8

SQL> |
```

FIGURE 5-2 The contents of the RECYCLE BIN after dropping the PHY_FD table

Figure 5-2 displays a lot of information about the table that is currently dropped and in the recycle bin. The new name of the table is BIN$bh+0079GT16YskWrq2zjkQ==$0. The original name was PHY_FD. The operation that was performed was a DROP. The tablespace the table belongs to is USERS. The timestamp of table creation is 2005-12-19 08:50:01. The timestamp when the table was dropped is 2005-12-19 08:51:40. The SCN number of the DROP table command is 1064378.

6. Issue the FLASHBACK TABLE command to recover the table. Do not rename the table. (See Figure 5-3.)

```
SQL> FLASHBACK TABLE PHY_FD TO BEFORE DROP;
```

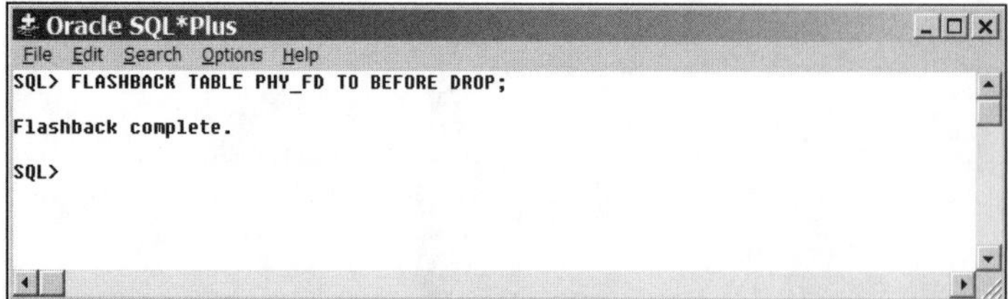

FIGURE 5-3 Recovering the dropped table using the FLASHBACK DROP command.

7. Retrieve data from the PHY_FD table. The table should be displayed with 10 rows.

```
SQL>SELECT * FROM PHY_FD;
```

8. Query the TABLE_NAME and DROPPED columns of the USER_TABLES view to see if the table exists in the MEDUSER schema. The value of the DROPPED column should be NO.

```
SQL> SELECT TABLE_NAME, DROPPED FROM USER_TABLES;
```

9. Query the recycle bin to confirm that the table was "undropped." The view will no longer hold information about the PHY_FD table.

```
SQL> SELECT * FROM USER_RECYCLEBIN;
```

NOTE

The SHOW RECYCLEBIN command may also be used to display the contents of the recycle bin.

10. Exit SQL*Plus.

The Flashback Drop operation may also be done using Enterprise Manager.

Practice 2: Dropping a Table and Recovering It Using Enterprise Manager

In this practice a table called PHY2_FD will be created by executing a script and will then be dropped. The recovery of the table will be performed using the Flashback Drop feature from Enterprise Manager.

1. Start SQL*Plus and connect to the database as the MEDUSER user.

```
SQL> CONNECT MEDUSER/MEDUSER
```

2. Run the script called **ch52_fdcreate.sql**. The script creates a table called PHY2_FD and populates it with 10 rows. Query the PHY2_FD table to confirm its creation.

```
SQL>START <PATH>CH52_FDCREATE.SQL
SQL> SELECT * FROM PHY2_FD;
```

3. Next, run the script called **ch52_fddrop.sql**. This script drops the PHY2_FD table created in the previous step. Minimize the SQL*Plus window.

```
SQL> START <PATH>\CH52_FDDROP.SQL
```

4. Open a web browser and enter the URL to launch Enterprise Manager. Log in as a user with SYSDBA privileges.
5. From the **Database Control Home** page, select the **Maintenance** tab.
6. From the **Backup/Recovery** section, select the **Perform Recovery** link.
7. Navigate to the **Object Level Recovery** section. Select **Tables** from the **Object Type** list. (See Figure 5-4.)
8. The page will be refreshed. Select the **Flashback Dropped Tables** option.

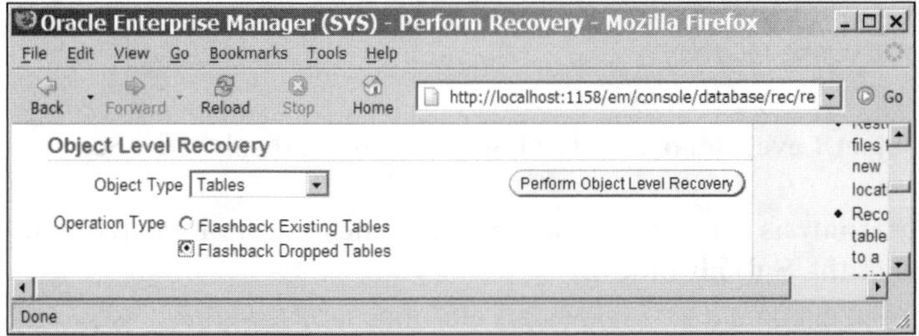

FIGURE 5-4 The Object Level Recovery option

9. Enter the Host User Credentials. Select the **Perform Object Level Recovery** button.
10. The **Perform Object Level Recovery: Dropped Objects Selection** page will be displayed. Under Schema Name, type MEDUSER and select the **Go** button under the Table Option.
11. Under the Results section the name of the table that was dropped will appear, namely PHY2_FD along with other dropped tables. (See Figure 5-5.)

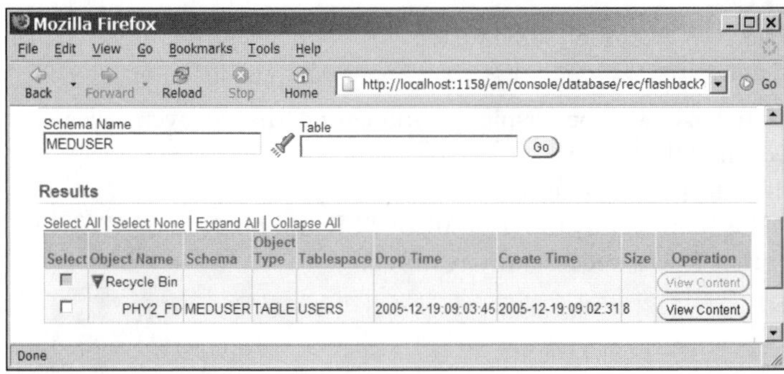

FIGURE 5-5 Selecting the object to be "undropped"

12. **Select** the checkbox (√) against the table to be restored and click **Next**.
13. The **Perform Object Level Recovery: Rename** page will be displayed.
14. If you wish to rename the table upon restoration, you can enter the new name in the textbox provided.
15. Do not rename the table; leave it as PHY2_FD. Click on **Next**. (See Figure 5-6.)

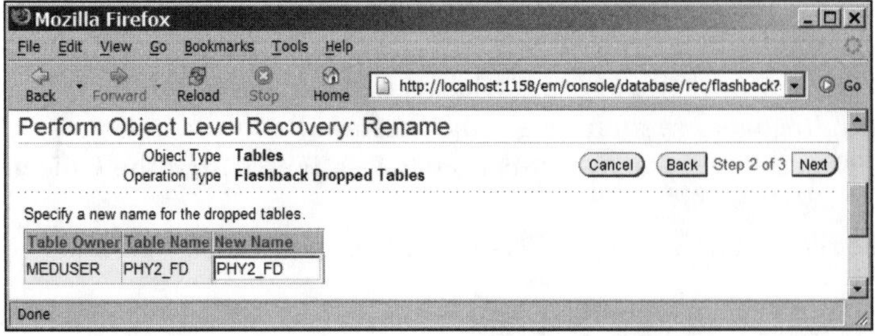

FIGURE 5-6 Renaming the table during recovery

16. The **Perform Object Level Recovery: Review** page will be displayed. (See Figure 5-7.)
17. View the **Impact Analysis** section. It displays the names of all tables that will be restored. Select the **Submit** button.

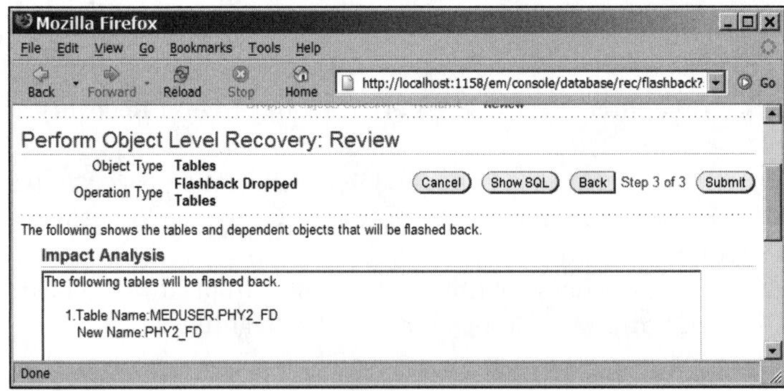

FIGURE 5-7 The Perform Object Level Recovery: Review page

18. The **Confirmation** page will be displayed indicating the recovery was successful. Select the OK button.
19. Log out and exit Enterprise Manager.
20. Return to SQL*Plus, connect as the user MEDUSER and query the PHY2_FD table to confirm that it was successfully restored.
21. Exit SQL*Plus.

Purging a table

In Oracle 10g, the DROP TABLE command can also take a PURGE directive. This directive results in a permanent deletion of the object. The table will not be sent to the recycle bin and the extents of the object are immediately released as free space that may be utilized by other objects.

The command to purge a table is:

```
DROP TABLE tablename PURGE;
```

Another command in Oracle 10g that may be used to permanently remove an object from the recycle bin is the PURGE TABLE command. The purge command should follow a DROP TABLE command. When the PURGE TABLE command is issued, all the extents of the object will be released and can be reused in the datafile. The object will be removed from the recycle bin. The command to permanently delete an object is:

```
PURGE TABLE table_name;
```


To delete all objects present in the recycle bin that belong to a specific tablespace, you may issue the PURGE TABLESPACE command. The command takes the form:

```
PURGE TABLESPACE tablespacename;
```

To permanently drop all the objects belonging to a particular user in a specific tablespace, you may use the PURGE TABLESPACE...USER command. The command takes the form:

```
PURGE TABLESPACE tablespacename USER username;
```

To permanently delete all the objects currently in the recycle bin you can issue:

```
PURGE RECYCLEBIN;
```

Practice 3: Purging a table

In this practice example, the usage of the PURGE command will be demonstrated.

1. Start SQL*Plus if it is not already opened and connect to the database as the MEDUSER user.

   ```
   SQL> CONNECT MEDUSER/MEDUSER
   ```

2. In this part of the practice, the DROP TABLE... PURGE command will be demonstrated. Execute the **ch5_fpcreate.sql** script. This script creates a table called PHYFP, containing 10 rows.

   ```
   SQL> START <PATH>\CH5_FPCREATE.SQL
   ```

3. Query the PHYFP table and display its contents to confirm that it was created successfully. The table should be displayed with 10 rows.

   ```
   SQL> SELECT * FROM PHYFP;
   ```

4. Issue the DROP TABLE command using the PURGE clause to permanently drop the PHYFP table.

   ```
   SQL> DROP TABLE PHYFP PURGE;
   ```

5. Query the USER_RECYCLEBIN view to see if the table was sent to the recycle bin. It should not exist. The output of the command is “no rows selected.”

   ```
   SQL> SELECT * FROM USER_RECYCLEBIN
        WHERE ORIGINAL_NAME = 'PHYFP';
   ```

6. In this part of the practice the usage of the PURGE TABLE command will be demonstrated. Re-run the script **ch5_fpcreate.sql**. This script will recreate the table called PHYFP, containing 10 rows.

   ```
   SQL> START <PATH>\CH5_FPCREATE.SQL
   ```

7. Display the contents of the PHYFP table to confirm that it was created successfully. The contents of the table are displayed in Figure 5-8.

```
SQL> SELECT * FROM PHYFP;
```

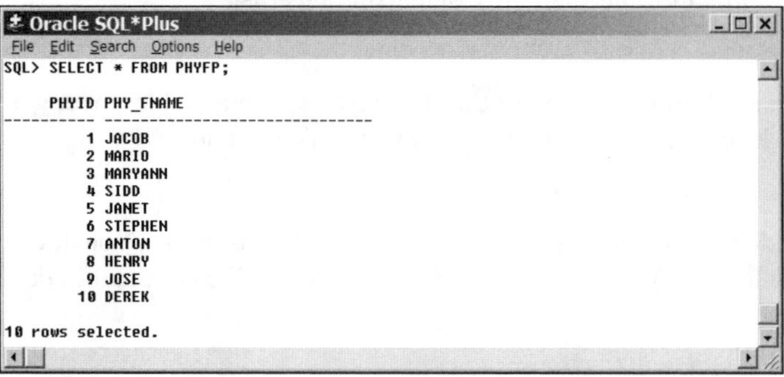

FIGURE 5-8 The contents of the PHYFP table.

8. Issue the PURGE command to delete the PHYFP table permanently. An error will be generated because the object does not exist in the recycle bin. (See Figure 5-9.)

```
SQL> PURGE TABLE PHYFP;
```

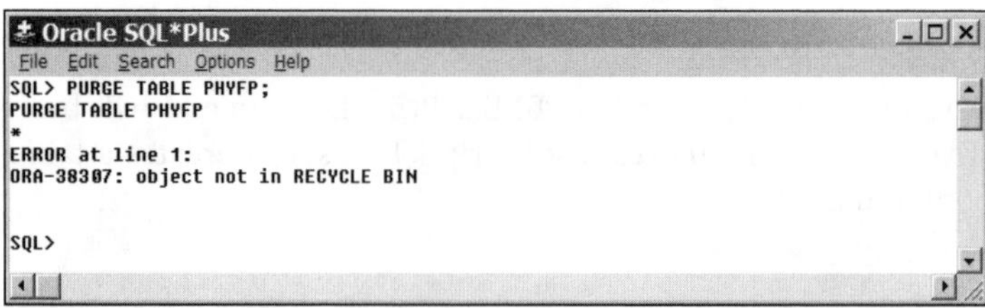

FIGURE 5-9 The PURGE TABLE command must follow a DROP TABLE command

9. Issue the DROP TABLE command to drop the PHYFP table. The table will be sent to the recycle bin.

```
SQL> DROP TABLE PHYFP;
```

10. Now, issue the PURGE command to delete the PHYFP table permanently. (See Figure 5-10.)

```
SQL> PURGE TABLE PHYFP;
```

11. Query the USER_RECYCLEBIN view to see if the table was sent to the recycle bin. It should not exist.

```
SQL> SELECT * FROM USER_RECYCLEBIN
     WHERE ORIGINAL_NAME = 'PHYFP';
```

```
Oracle SQL*Plus
File Edit Search Options Help
SQL> PURGE TABLE PHYFP;

Table purged.

SQL> |
```


FIGURE 5-10 Once purged the object is deleted from the recycle bin

12. To display all objects currently in the recycle bin you can also issue the SHOW RECYCLEBIN command, as in:

    ```
    SQL> SHOW RECYCLEBIN;
    ```

13. Issue the command to permanently delete all the objects stored in the recycle bin.

    ```
    SQL> PURGE RECYCLEBIN;
    ```

14. Exit SQL*Plus.

Dropping a Tablespace or User

If all the objects of a tablespace are to be dropped, the DROP TABLESPACE command may be used. When a tablespace is dropped, objects that existed in the tablespace and are currently in the recycle bin will be automatically purged. A tablespace containing objects may be dropped using the DROP TABLESPACE *tablespacename* INCLUDING CONTENTS command. The tablespace will be dropped and all objects belonging to it will be purged without being sent to the recycle bin.

If a user is dropped using the DROP USER username CASCADE command, the user will be dropped from the database and all objects belonging to the user will be permanently deleted or purged.

Practice 4: Dropping a tablespace or a user

In this practice, a user called TUSER will be created. Two tables called TAB51 and TAB52 will be created in the TUSER schema. You will then simulate the deletion of the user and view the contents of the recycle bin.

1. Start SQL*Plus and connect as a user with SYSDBA privileges.
2. Run the script **ch5_ucreate.sql**. This script creates the TUSER user and the two tables TAB51 and TAB52, in the TUSER schema.

    ```
    SQL> START <PATH>\CH5_UCREATE.SQL
    ```

3. Connect as TUSER with a password of TUSER. Then, query the USER_TABLES data dictionary view to confirm the existence of TAB51 and TAB52 in the TUSER schema. Figure 5-11 displays both tables with a DROPPED status of NO.

    ```
    SQL> CONNECT TUSER/TUSER
    SQL> SELECT TABLE_NAME, DROPPED FROM USER_TABLES;
    ```

4. Issue the command to drop the table TAB51.

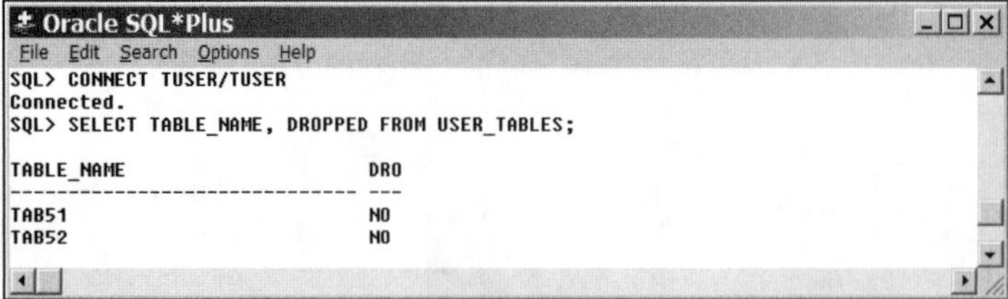

FIGURE 5-11 The contents of the TUSER schema

```
SQL> DROP TABLE TAB51;
```

5. View the contents of the recycle bin. The table TAB51 should exist in the recycle bin.

```
SQL> SELECT * FROM USER_RECYCLEBIN;
```

6. Connect as a user with administrative privileges and drop the user TUSER and all the objects in the TUSER schema.

```
SQL> CONNECT DB_ADMIN/DB_ADMIN
SQL> DROP USER TUSER CASCADE;
```

7. Query the DBA_USERS view to display details of the user TUSER. The user must not exist. (See Figure 5-12.)

```
SQL> SELECT * FROM DBA_USERS WHERE USERNAME='TUSER';
```

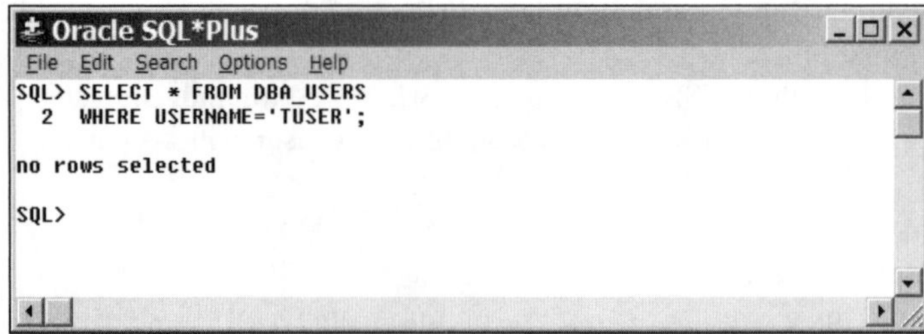

FIGURE 5-12 User TUSER has been dropped.

8. Query the DBA_RECYCLEBIN view to display any objects belonging to the user TUSER currently in the recycle bin. No rows should be selected. (See Figure 5-13.)

```
SQL> SELECT * FROM DBA_RECYCLEBIN WHERE OWNER='TUSER';
```

9. Exit SQL*Plus.

In this section of the chapter you were introduced to the Flashback Drop feature of the Oracle 10*g* database. It is extremely useful to recover from user errors that result in the accidental loss of tables. Recovery involves a simple command that may be issued without affecting other users who are currently connected to the database.

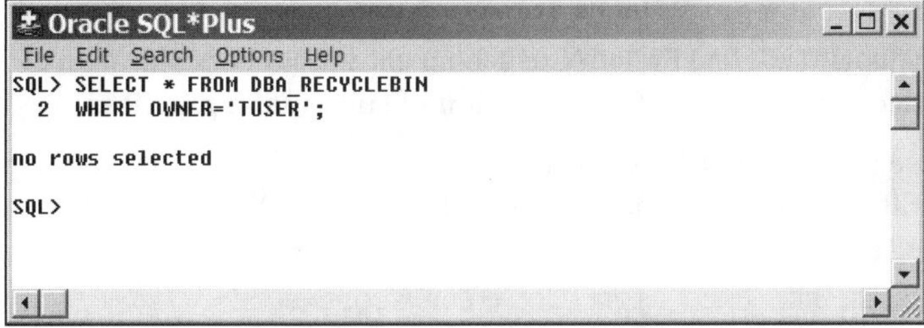

FIGURE 5-13 The recycle bin does not hold any objects belonging to TUSER.

THE FLASHBACK QUERY FEATURE

The Flashback Query feature was the first to be introduced as part of the Flashback Technologies in Oracle 9*i*. The feature may be used by users to view the contents of a table as it existed at a time in the past, as long as the past data exists in the undo segments.

To use the Flashback Query feature you must configure automatic undo management (see Appendix A) by setting the UNDO_ MANAGEMENT initialization parameter to AUTO. The DBA must set the UNDO_TABLESPACE parameter to the name of an existing undo tablespace. Once defined, the Oracle server will create and manage the undo segments in the undo tablespace. The undo tablespace that is defined must be large enough to hold undo data generated in the database as well as hold undo data for the time period defined by undo retention.

Understanding Undo Retention

The UNDO_RETENTION initialization parameter (a value in seconds) may be configured to ensure that undo data continues to remain in the undo segments even after the transaction(s) that generated it is completed. Undo data that remains in the undo segments for the time period defined by UNDO_RETENTION and then released, is referred to as "expired." Although the UNDO_RETENTION specifies how long undo data may be retained, it does not guarantee it. When undo segments cannot extend and require space for new undo data, the oldest inactive extent will be reused to satisfy the requirements of the current transaction. This may result in some long-running queries failing with an ORA-1555 – Snapshot Too Old error. This problem is resolved in Oracle 10*g* by the use of the RETENTION GUARANTEE clause of an UNDO TABLESPACE command. This clause causes the undo tablespace to guarantee the retention of unexpired undo extents. A new undo tablespace may be created in the following way:

```
CREATE UNDO TABLESPACE tablespacename
DATAFILE '<location>\datafilename' SIZE n
RETENTION GUARANTEE;
```

An existing undo tablespace may be re-configured as:

```
ALTER TABLESPACE tablespacename RETENTION GUARANTEE;
```

The Flashback Query utilizes the "unexpired" undo data, retained for the purpose of retention, to display data as it existed in the past.

Practice 5: Setting the Undo Retention

In this practice you will set the UNDO_RETENTION to 1 hour or 3600 seconds. It is necessary to perform this practice for the successful completion of subsequent practices.

1. Connect as a user with SYSDBA privileges.
2. Issue the ALTER SYSTEM command to set UNDO_RETENTION to 3600 seconds.


```
SQL> ALTER SYSTEM SET UNDO_RETENTION=3600 SCOPE=BOTH;
```

3. Exit SQL*Plus.

Performing a Flashback Query

The Flashback Query operation may be performed using the SELECT... AS OF TIMESTAMP TO_TIMESTAMP statement or the Oracle-supplied DBMS_FLASHBACK package. Users who need to perform Flashback Query must be granted the FLASHBACK privilege or possess execute privileges on the DBMS_FLASHBACK package.

Practice 6: Performing a Flashback Query operation

This practice demonstrates how Flashback Query is performed in an Oracle database.

1. Start SQL*Plus and connect as the MEDUSER user.

```
SQL> CONNECT MEDUSER/MEDUSER
```

2. Create a table called FLASHQ having a single numeric column called COLA.

```
SQL> CREATE TABLE FLASHQ(COLA  NUMBER);
```

3. Insert the value 101 as the first row of the table and commit the row.

```
SQL> INSERT INTO FLASHQ VALUES (101);
SQL> COMMIT;
```

4. The value 101 represents valid data in the table. Display the current timestamp. This time will be referenced later in the practice as T1. (See Figure 5-14.)

```
SQL> SELECT CURRENT_TIMESTAMP FROM DUAL;
```

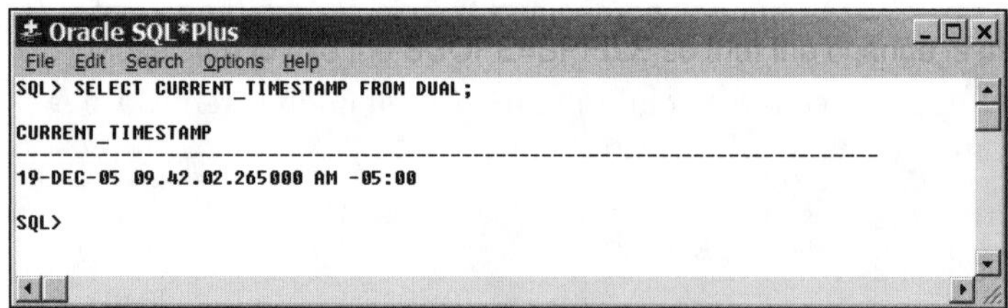

```
SQL> SELECT CURRENT_TIMESTAMP FROM DUAL;

CURRENT_TIMESTAMP
---------------------------------------------------------------------------
19-DEC-05 09.42.02.265000 AM -05:00

SQL>
```


FIGURE 5-14 The time when the table contained correct data

5. Wait for a few minutes and perform and modify the value 101 to -1. This simulates an incorrect update being done to a table. Commit the change you make.

```
SQL> UPDATE FLASHQ SET COLA= -1 WHERE COLA=101;
SQL> COMMIT;
```

6. In this step you will perform a Flashback Query operation using the SELECT ... AS OF TIMESTAMP TO_TIMESTAMP clause to display the contents of a table or row at a certain time. When issuing the command, substitute the time you noted in Step 4. Figure 5-15 displays the value 101 from the FLASHQ table at time T1.

```
SQL>SELECT * FROM FLASHQ AS OF TIMESTAMP
      TO_TIMESTAMP('19-DEC-05 09:42:02','DD-MON-YY HH24:MI:SS');
```


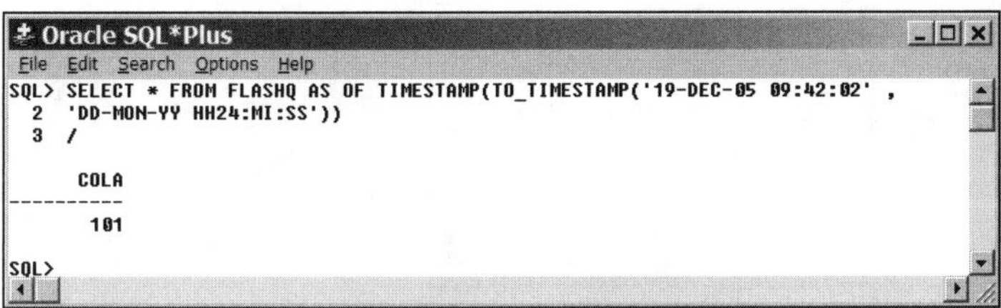

FIGURE 5-15 Performing a Flashback Query

7. The Flashback Query operation can also be performed using the ENABLE_AT_TIME procedure of the DBMS_FLASHBACK package. Substitute the timestamp value, T1 when executing the command. (See Figure 5-16.) If you receive an error similar to the one displayed in Figure 5-17 when executing the EXECUTE command displayed below please read the following note.

```
SQL> EXECUTE DBMS_FLASHBACK.ENABLE_AT_TIME('19-DEC-05 09:42:
02');
```

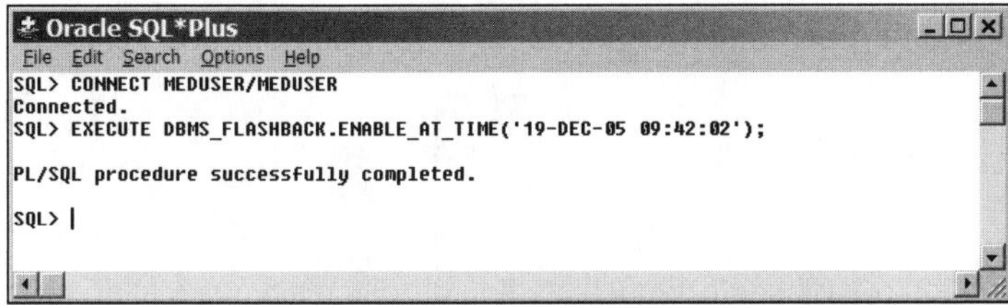

FIGURE 5-16 Performing a Flashback Query using the DBMS_FLASHBACK package

8. Now, if you query the FLASHQ table, you will view the data as it existed at time T1. The value 101 will be displayed from the undo segments.

```
SQL> SELECT * FROM FLASHQ;
```

NOTE

If the error shown in Figure 5-17 is displayed when you execute the DBMS_FLASHBACK package, it implies the user does not execute privileges on the DBMS_FLASHBACK package.

You must connect as an administrator and grant the user the privilege as:

```
SQL> CONNECT DB_ADMIN/DB_ADMIN AS SYSDBA
SQL> GRANT EXECUTE ON DBMS_FLASHBACK TO MEDUSER
SQL> CONNECT MEDUSER/MEDUSER
SQL> Re-execute the command in step 7.
```



```
Oracle SQL*Plus
File Edit Search Options Help
SQL> EXECUTE DBMS_FLASHBACK.ENABLE_AT_TIME('19-DEC-05 09:42:02');
BEGIN DBMS_FLASHBACK.ENABLE_AT_TIME('19-DEC-05 09:42:02'); END;

      *
ERROR at line 1:
ORA-06550: line 1, column 7:
PLS-00201: identifier 'DBMS_FLASHBACK' must be declared
ORA-06550: line 1, column 7:
PL/SQL: Statement ignored


SQL>
```

FIGURE 5-17 The user does not possess the EXECUTE privilege on the DBMS_FLASHBACK package

9. When you have finished with Flashback Query, you may disable the feature using the DISABLE procedure of DBMS_FLASHBACK.

   ```
   SQL> EXECUTE DBMS_FLASHBACK.DISABLE;
   ```

10. If you issue a query to retrieve the information from the FLASHQ table, the current value held by the column COLA (-1) will be displayed. (See Figure 5-18.)

   ```
   SQL>SELECT * FROM FLASHQ;
   ```

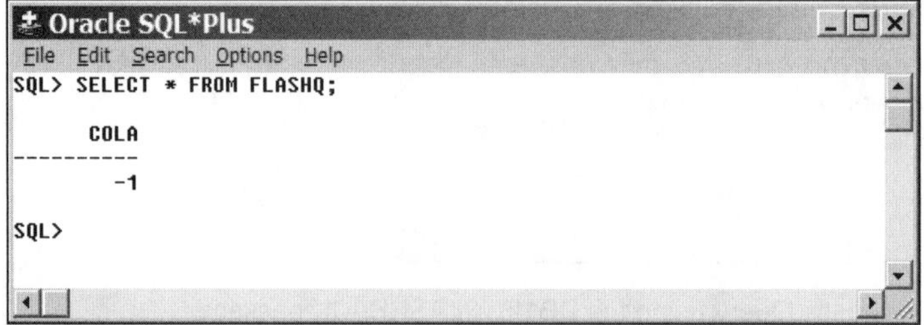

FIGURE 5-18 The current contents of the FLASHQ table

11. Exit SQL*Plus.

The following scenario presents a practical application of the Flashback Query feature.

Cathy, the senior developer at Keller Medical Center has been updating and deleting patient insurance records from the PATIENT_INSURANCE table. She accidentally deletes a number of records instead of updating them and commits. The mistake was made at 9:35 A.M. and was discovered only at around 11:05 A.M. Because the database cannot be made unavailable and the loss of changes made between 9:35 A.M. and 11:05 A.M. is not acceptable, the DBA decides to use the Flashback Query in an INSERT statement. The INSERT statement shown below re-inserts the records that were deleted by using the rows returned by the Flashback Query operation. The statement that the DBA issues is:


```
INSERT INTO PATIENT_INSURANCE
(SELECT * FROM PATIENT_INSURANCE
 AS OF TIMESTAMP
 TO_TIMESTAMP('19-DEC-05 9:35:00','DD-MON-YY HH24:MI:SS')
 MINUS
 SELECT * FROM PATIENT_INSURANCE);
```

In this section of the chapter you were introduced the Flashback Query feature. The feature may be used to view data as it existed in the past and to recover from incorrect changes that are made to the database.

FLASHBACK VERSIONS QUERY FEATURE

The functionality of Flashback Query has been expanded in Oracle 10g. The Flashback Versions Query feature enables you to see the values of table data as it changes over time. You can view different versions of data as it existed and exists between two points of time or between two system change numbers (SCNs). The new version of a row is generated only when the change is committed.

To use the Flashback Versions Query feature, the DBA must configure automatic undo management. The UNDO_RETENTION parameter must also be configured to ensure that undo data continues to remain in the undo segments even after the transaction that generated it, is completed. The undo segment retained, is used to generate the different versions of committed data.

This feature is implemented using the VERSIONS BETWEEN clause of the SELECT statement. The output of a Flashback Versions Query is a list of all committed changes made to the rows of the table across transactions, excluding the current transaction. A Flashback Versions Query gives you a history of all changes made to rows without any additional setup. There are certain restrictions imposed by the VERSIONS BETWEEN clause. The VERSIONS BETWEEN cannot produce versions of rows across structural changes made to the table. For example, if you add a column or drop a column, versions of rows before the structural changes cannot be obtained. The VERSIONS BETWEEN clause cannot be used against a view; however, you can use the clause in the definition of the view during its creation.

A number of psuedocolumns have been introduced in Oracle 10g that can be used with the Flashback Versions Query feature. The Table 5-1 displays the names of these psuedocolumns along with a brief description.

TABLE 5-1 The psuedocolumns that may be used for flashback versions query

Column Name	Description
VERSIONS_XID	The transaction ID that created the row version.
VERSIONS_STARTTIME	Timestamp when the row version was created.
VERSIONS_ENDTIME	Timestamp when the row version expired.
VERSIONS_STARTSCN	System Change Number (SCN) when the row version was created.
VERSION_ENDSCN	System Change Number (SCN) when the row version expired.
VERSIONS_OPERATION	The operation performed by the transaction. The letter I represents INSERT, U represents UPDATE and D represents DELETE.

Performing the Flashback Versions Query

To use the Flashback Versions Query functionality, a user must have the FLASHBACK and SELECT object privileges on the table being queried. A user with the FLASHBACK ANY TABLE privileges can query all tables in the database.

The following is the syntax that you can use to implement the flashback versions query feature.

```
SELECT column, column
FROM table
VERSIONS BETWEEN SCN minvalue AND maxvalue [WHERE condition];
```

Or

```
SELECT column, column,...
FROM table
VERSIONS BETWEEN TIMESTAMP timestamp1 AND timestamp2
[WHERE condition];
```

where

`SCN minvalue and maxvalue`: refers to the starting and ending SCN respectively.

`TIMESTAMP timestamp1 AND timestamp2`: refers to the starting time and ending time. All versions of the rows between timestamp1 and timestamp2 will be displayed. In the syntax above, timestamp1 and timestamp2 may take a timestamp value in a format similar to TO_TIMESTAMP('25-12-2005 10:10:00','DD-MON-YY HH24:MI:SS');

Before you begin with the practice examples in this topic, ensure that you have set UNDO_RETENTION to at least 1 hour. If it is not already set, execute the steps described in Practice 5.

Practice 7: Performing the Flashback Version Query operation

In this practice, the Flashback Versions Query feature will be demonstrated. A table called PATIENT_MEDS will be created containing three columns, namely PATIENT_ID, PRESCRIBED_MEDS, and REFILLS. During the course of the practice a number of transactions will be executed resulting in the modification and deletion of rows. Finally, queries will be performed on the table using the SELECT...VERSIONS BETWEEN statement to demonstrate the functionality of the Flashback Versions Query feature.

1. Start SQL*Plus and connect to the database as the user MEDUSER.

   ```
   SQL>CONNECT MEDUSER/MEDUSER
   ```

2. Run the script **ch5_fvq.sql**. This script creates a table called PATIENT_MEDS.

   ```
   SQL> START <PATH>\CH5_FVQ.SQL
   ```

3. Run the script **ch5_fvq1.sql**. This script inserts five rows into the PATIENT_MEDS table. The five rows inserted indicate the first version of these rows.

   ```
   SQL> START <PATH>\CH5_FVQ1.SQL
   ```

4. Query the PATIENT_MEDS table to confirm its creation and the addition of the 5 rows. (See Figure 5-19.)

   ```
   SQL> SELECT * FROM PATIENT_MEDS;
   ```

```
Oracle SQL*Plus
File Edit Search Options Help
SQL> SELECT * FROM PATIENT_MEDS;

PATIEN PRESCRIBED_MEDS         REFILLS
------ -------------------- ----------
INP001 MED1001                       2
INP002 MED1010                       4
INP003 MED2000                       1
INP004 MED2002                       4
INP005 MED3000                       2

SQL>
```

FIGURE 5-19 The contents of the PATIENT_MEDS table

5. Note the current timestamp by issuing the following query. We will refer to this time as T1. Figure 5-20 displays the timestamp as 19-DEC-05 10:17:16.

   ```
   SQL> SELECT CURRENT_TIMESTAMP FROM DUAL;
   ```

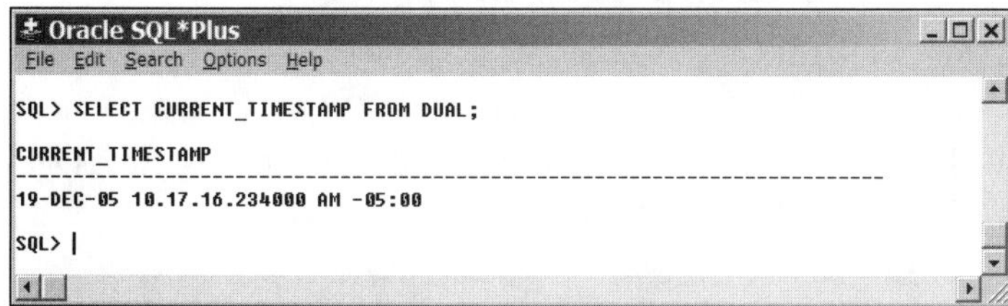

FIGURE 5-20 The timestamp prior to the changes

6. In this step, a number of transactions will be executed. These transactions simulate changes occurring to the PATIENT_MEDS table resulting in the creation of different versions of its rows. Execute the following changes to the rows of the table.

This update results in the second version of the row with PATIENT_ID INP003.

```
SQL> UPDATE PATIENT_MEDS SET REFILLS=3
     WHERE PATIENT_ID='INP003';
SQL> COMMIT;
```

This update results in the second version of the row with PATIENT_ID INP001.


```
SQL> UPDATE PATIENT_MEDS SET REFILLS=1
     WHERE PATIENT_ID='INP001';
SQL> COMMIT;
```

This update results in the third version of the row with PATIENT_ID INP003.

```
SQL> UPDATE PATIENT_MEDS SET
     PRESCRIBED_MEDS='MED2003'
     WHERE PATIENT_ID='INP003';
SQL> COMMIT;
```

This update results in the third version of the row with PATIENT_ID INP001.

```
SQL> DELETE FROM PATIENT_MEDS WHERE PATIENT_ID = 'INP001';
SQL> COMMIT;
```

7. Query the PATIENT_MEDS tabs to verify the changes occurred successfully. The output you see should be similar to that displayed by Figure 5-21.

```
SQL> SELECT * FROM PATIENT_MEDS;
```

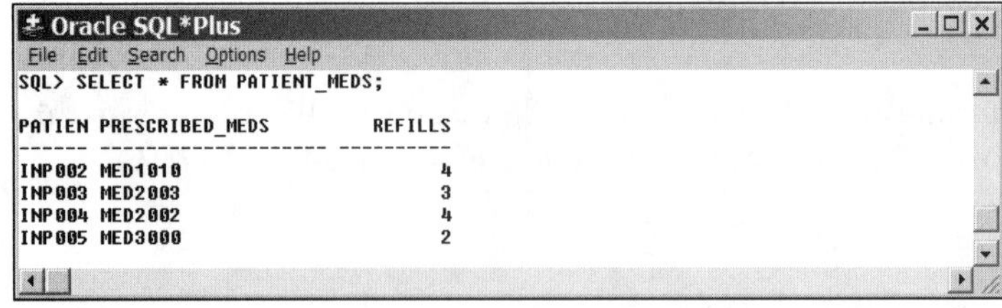

FIGURE 5-21 The contents of PATIENT_MEDS after the changes

8. Note the current timestamp. We will refer to this time as T2. Figure 5-22 displays this timestamp as 19-DEC-05 10:29:32.

```
SQL> SELECT CURRENT_TIMESTAMP FROM DUAL;
```

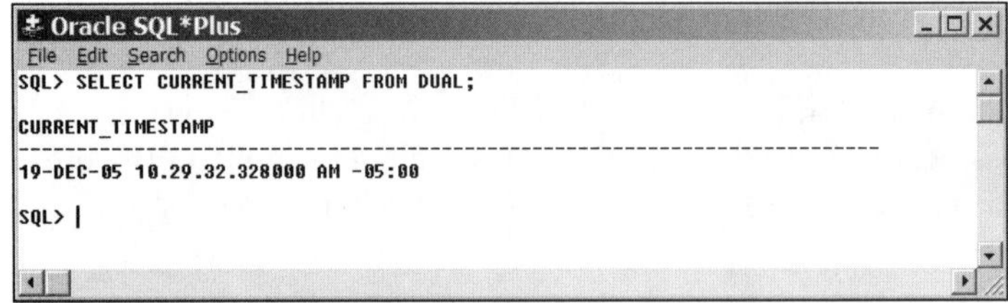

FIGURE 5-22 The TIMESTAMP after the changes

9. Execute a VERSIONS_BETWEEN query on the PATIENT_MEDS table to display the different versions of the rows between the first and last changes made to the table. In the Figure 5-23, notice that the first set of INSERT statements are part of transaction ID 05001100B4010000, or have the same start SCN number 1070557. The last row's version (from the Figure 5-23) ended when transaction 07000E00B8010000 was executed and the row was updated. This version of the row also ended when transaction 07001000B8010000 was executed, resulting in its deletion.

```
SQL> SELECT VERSIONS_XID, VERSIONS_STARTSCN,VERSIONS_ENDSCN,
     VERSIONS_OPERATION, PATIENT_ID, PRESCRIBED_MEDS, REFILLS
     FROM PATIENT_MEDS
     VERSIONS BETWEEN TIMESTAMP MINVALUE AND MAXVALUE;
```

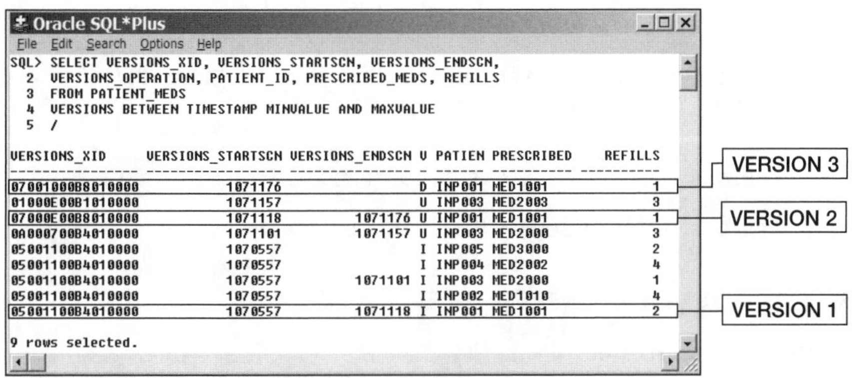

FIGURE 5-23 The output of the VERSIONS BETWEEN statement

10. Execute a VERSIONS_BETWEEN query on the PATIENT_MEDS table to display the different versions of the rows between the timestamps T1 and T2, noted earlier. In the query when specifying the time T1, modify the time T1 to a value a few seconds or a minute prior to the time noted down for an accurate output. The output will be the same as in Figure 5-23.

```
SQL> SELECT VERSIONS_XID, VERSIONS_STARTSCN, VERSIONS_ENDSCN,
     VERSIONS_OPERATION, PATIENT_ID, PRESCRIBED_MEDS, REFILLS
     FROM PATIENT_MEDS
     VERSIONS BETWEEN TIMESTAMP
     TO_TIMESTAMP('19-DEC-05 10:15:00,'DD-MON-YY HH24:MI:SS')
     AND TO_TIMESTAMP('19-DEC-05 10:30:00','DD-MON-YY HH24:MI:SS');
```

11. Execute a VERSIONS BETWEEN query on the PATIENT_MEDS tables retrieving all versions of the rows of the PATIENT_MEDS table between the lowest SCN number and highest SCN number of changes made to the table. The output will be same as in Figure 5-23.

```
SQL> SELECT VERSIONS_XID, VERSIONS_STARTSCN, VERSIONS_ENDSCN,
 VERSIONS_OPERATION, PATIENT_ID, PRESCRIBED_MEDS, REFILLS
 FROM PATIENT_MEDS
VERSIONS BETWEEN SCN MINVALUE AND MAXVALUE;
```

12. You can also find out the SCN numbers corresponding to the timestamps T1 and T2. This may be done using a new Oracle 10g function, **TIMESTAMP_TO_SCN**. The TIMESTAMP_TO_SCN function takes as an argument a timestamp value and returns the approximate SCN associated with that timestamp. A similar query will now be executed to determine the committed changes that occurred to the table between timestamps T1 and T2, but this time using SCN numbers. Please substitute the timestamps T1 and T2 in the first and second query respectively. Figure 5-24 displays the SCN numbers as 1070541 and 1071365 for timestamps T1 and T2 respectively. Then execute the SELECT...VERSIONS BETWEEN SCN statement, substituting the SCNs that were generated on your machine. The output of the statement will be the same as in Figure 5-23.

```
SQL> SELECT TIMESTAMP_TO_SCN(TO_DATE('19-DEC-05 10:15:00',
     'DD-MON-YY HH24:MI:SS')) FROM DUAL;

SQL> SELECT TIMESTAMP_TO_SCN(TO_DATE('19-DEC-05 10:30:00',
     'DD-MON-YY HH24:MI:SS')) FROM DUAL;

SQL> SELECT VERSIONS_XID, VERSIONS_STARTSCN, VERSIONS_ENDSCN,
     VERSIONS_OPERATION, PATIENT_ID, PRESCRIBED_MEDS, REFILLS
     FROM PATIENT_MEDS
     VERSIONS BETWEEN SCN 1070541 AND 1071365;
```

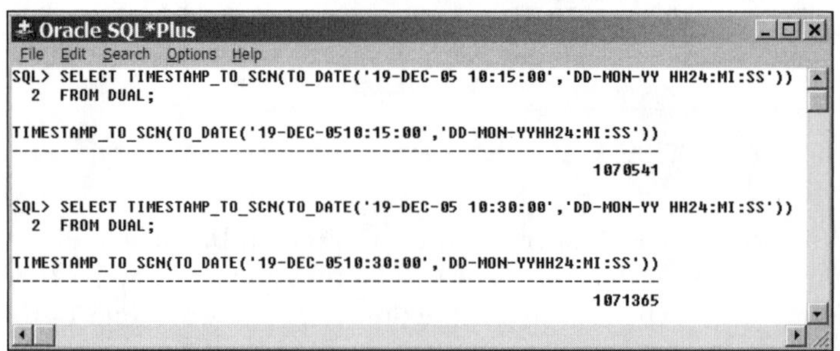

FIGURE 5-24 The TIMESTAMP_TO_SCN function

13. Next, create a table called PATIENT_MEDS_VERS that can store the output of the SELECT VERSIONS BETWEEN statement. (See Figure 5-25.)

```
SQL> CREATE TABLE PATIENT_MEDS_VERS
     AS
     SELECT VERSIONS_XID, VERSIONS_STARTSCN, VERSIONS_ENDSCN,
     VERSIONS_OPERATION, PATIENT_ID, PRESCRIBED_MEDS, REFILLS
     FROM PATIENT_MEDS
     VERSIONS BETWEEN SCN 1070541 AND 1071365;
```

14. Exit SQL*Plus.

The Flashback Versions Query operation may also be performed using Enterprise Manager. The following practice describes the steps for this operation.

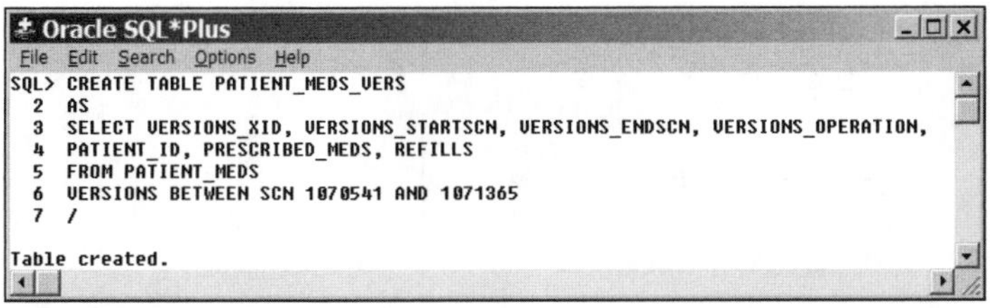

```
Oracle SQL*Plus
File Edit Search Options Help
SQL> CREATE TABLE PATIENT_MEDS_VERS
  2  AS
  3  SELECT VERSIONS_XID, VERSIONS_STARTSCN, VERSIONS_ENDSCN, VERSIONS_OPERATION,
  4  PATIENT_ID, PRESCRIBED_MEDS, REFILLS
  5  FROM PATIENT_MEDS
  6  VERSIONS BETWEEN SCN 1070541 AND 1071365
  7  /

Table created.
```


FIGURE 5-25 The SELECT..VERSIONS BETWEEN clause in a CREATE TABLE command

Practice 8: Performing Flashback Versions Query using Enterprise Manager

1. Start SQL*Plus and connect to the database as the user MEDUSER.

   ```
   SQL>CONNECT MEDUSER/MEDUSER
   ```

2. Run the script **ch5_fvq.sql**. This script creates a table called PATIENT_MEDS.

   ```
   SQL> START <PATH>\CH5_FVQ.SQL
   ```

3. Run the script **ch5_fvq1.sql**. This script inserts five rows into the PATIENT_MEDS table. The five rows inserted indicate the first version of these rows.

   ```
   SQL> START <PATH>\CH5_FVQ1.SQL
   ```

4. In this step, a number of transactions will be executed. These simulate changes occurring in the database resulting in different versions of rows. Execute the following changes to the rows of the table. The update results in the second version of the row with PATIENT_ID INP003.

   ```
   SQL> UPDATE PATIENT_MEDS SET REFILLS=3
        WHERE PATIENT_ID='INP003';
   SQL> COMMIT;

   SQL> DELETE FROM PATIENT_MEDS WHERE PATIENT_ID = 'INP001';
   SQL> COMMIT;
   ```

5. Open a web browser and enter the URL to launch Enterprise Manager. Log in as the SYS user with SYSDBA privileges.
6. From the **Database Control Home** page, select the **Maintenance** tab.
7. From the **Backup/Recovery** section, select the **Perform Recovery** link.
8. Navigate to the **Object Level Recovery** section and select **Tables** from the **Object Type** list.
9. The page will be refreshed. Select **Flashback Existing Tables** option. Select the **Perform Object Level Recovery** button.
10. The **Perform Object Level Recovery: Point-in-time** page is displayed.
11. Select **Evaluate rows changes and transactions to decide on a point in time**
12. If you know the name of the table, enter it in the text box, otherwise select the Icon of the Flashlight. Within the textbox type, **MEDUSER.PATIENT_MEDS**. Select the **Next** button.
13. The **Perform Object Level Recovery: Flashback Versions Query Filter** page is displayed.
14. From the **Step 1. Choose Columns** section, move all the Columns in the Available Columns section to the Selected Columns by selecting the Move All button. (See Figure 5-26.)

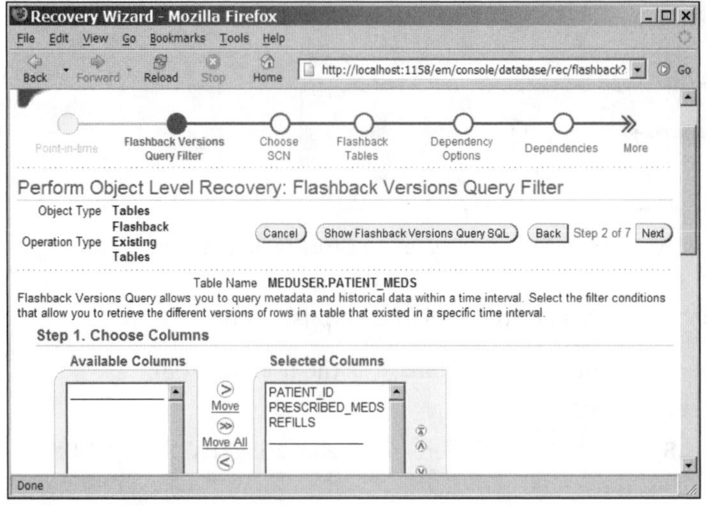

FIGURE 5-26 Choosing the columns to be displayed

15. Scroll down and in the textbox provided in the **Step 2. Bind the Row Value** section, type **WHERE REFILLS > -1**
16. Under the **Step 3. Select Time Interval,** select **Show all row history**. (See Figure 5-27.)

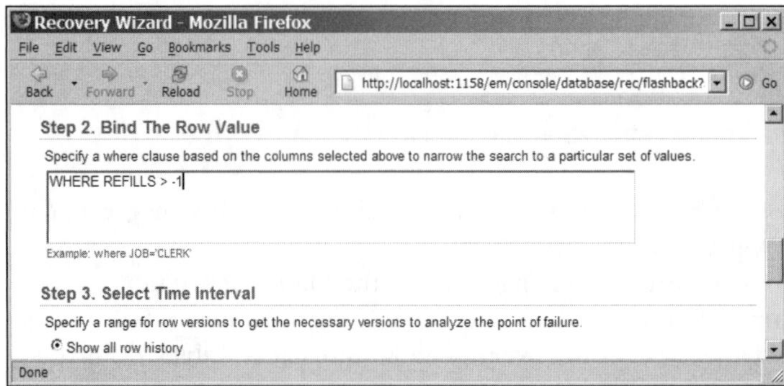

FIGURE 5-27 Specifying the WHERE clause to narrow the search to a particular set of values

17. Select **Next** to display the **Perform Object Level Recovery: Choose SCN** page. On this page you will see the changes that were made to the different rows of the PATIENT_MEDS table. Observe and note the Transaction ID corresponding to the INSERT statements. In Figure 5-28 it is 0A000B00B5010000. This value will be needed in Practice 9.
18. Exit Enterprise Manager and SQL*Plus.

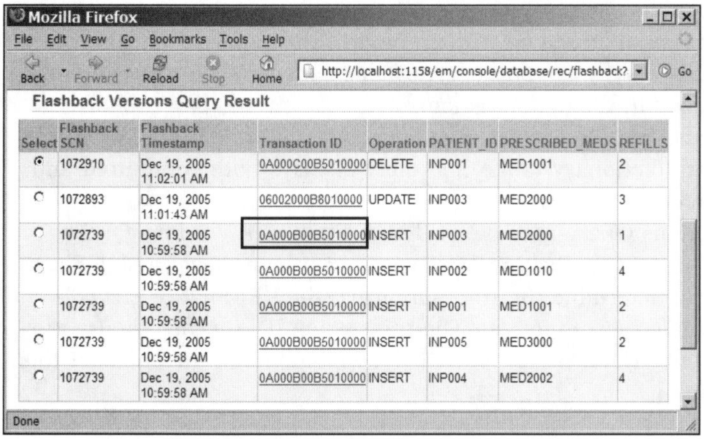

Mozilla Firefox

File Edit View Go Bookmarks Tools Help

Back Forward Reload Stop Home http://localhost:1158/em/console/database/rec/flashback? Go

Flashback Versions Query Result

Select	Flashback SCN	Flashback Timestamp	Transaction ID	Operation	PATIENT_ID	PRESCRIBED_MEDS	REFILLS
◉	1072910	Dec 19, 2005 11:02:01 AM	0A000C00B5010000	DELETE	INP001	MED1001	2
○	1072893	Dec 19, 2005 11:01:43 AM	06002000B8010000	UPDATE	INP003	MED2000	3
○	1072739	Dec 19, 2005 10:59:58 AM	0A000B00B5010000	INSERT	INP003	MED2000	1
○	1072739	Dec 19, 2005 10:59:58 AM	0A000B00B5010000	INSERT	INP002	MED1010	4
○	1072739	Dec 19, 2005 10:59:58 AM	0A000B00B5010000	INSERT	INP001	MED1001	2
○	1072739	Dec 19, 2005 10:59:58 AM	0A000B00B5010000	INSERT	INP005	MED3000	2
○	1072739	Dec 19, 2005 10:59:58 AM	0A000B00B5010000	INSERT	INP004	MED2002	4

Done

FIGURE 5-28 The Flashback Versions Result

Errors that may occur during flashback transaction query In case you try to use the VERSIONS BETWEEN clause to display changes that occurred beyond the undo retention period, an error similar to the output displayed by Figure 5-29 may occur.

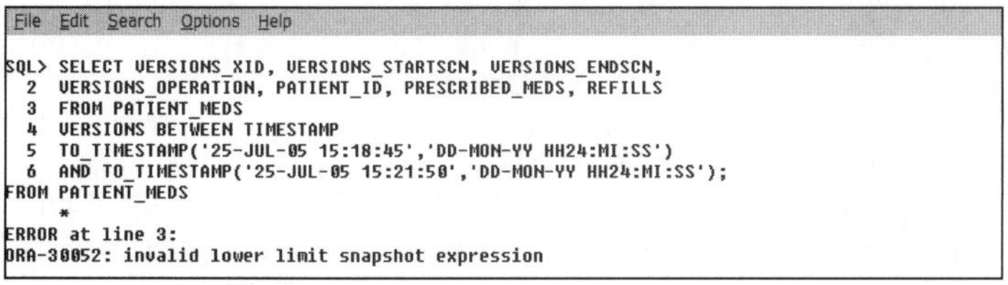

File Edit Search Options Help

```
SQL> SELECT VERSIONS_XID, VERSIONS_STARTSCN, VERSIONS_ENDSCN,
  2  VERSIONS_OPERATION, PATIENT_ID, PRESCRIBED_MEDS, REFILLS
  3  FROM PATIENT_MEDS
  4  VERSIONS BETWEEN TIMESTAMP
  5  TO_TIMESTAMP('25-JUL-05 15:18:45','DD-MON-YY HH24:MI:SS')
  6  AND TO_TIMESTAMP('25-JUL-05 15:21:50','DD-MON-YY HH24:MI:SS');
FROM PATIENT_MEDS
     *
ERROR at line 3:
ORA-30052: invalid lower limit snapshot expression
```

FIGURE 5-29 The VERSIONS BETWEEN clause cannot display the output, undo data does not exist

In this section of the chapter you learned how the Flashback Versions Query can be used to view different versions of the data across transactions along with all the metadata of the changes. It may be used to diagnose incorrect changes made to the rows of a table.

FLASHBACK TRANSACTION QUERY FEATURE

Flashback Transaction Query is another new feature in Oracle 10*g*. Its main purpose is to view changes made by a transaction or all transactions to the database at a transaction level during a specified time. It is particularly useful for diagnosing, analyzing, and auditing changes made by transactions within a specified time. Using Flashback Transaction Query you can determine the statement that may be used to reverse the effect of changes made within a transaction (UNDO_SQL).

Just as in Flashback Versions Query, the Flashback Transaction Query feature is also implemented by configuring automatic undo management in the database. The UNDO_RETENTION parameter must be set to an appropriate value depending on how much time the undo data must be retained in the undo segments.

The output of a Flashback Transactions Query may be viewed using the FLASHBACK_TRANSACTION_QUERY data dictionary table. The table displays both committed and active transactions in the undo segments.

The Flashback Transactions Query may be used with Flashback Versions Query to recover the database from user or application errors at a transaction level. Using Flashback Versions Query you can determine the transaction ID (the VERSIONS_XID column) that modified the specific row of interest. The transaction ID can then be used to determine the changes made by the transaction. This type of auditing is much faster than using the LOGMINER utility.

Performing the Flashback Transaction Query

Before you begin with the practice examples in this section, ensure that you have set UNDO_RETENTION to at least 1 hour. If it is not already set, execute the steps displayed in Practice 5.

Practice 9: Performing a Flashback Transaction Query Operation

This practice example demonstrates the Flashback Transaction Query feature. The table FLASHBACK_TRANSACTION_QUERY will be queried and the Transaction ID and UNDO_SQL for the statements displayed.

1. Start SQL*Plus and connect as a user with SYSDBA privileges.
2. To display the transaction ID (XID), operation performed (OPERATION), and the statement that may be used to undo the operation (UNDO_SQL) statements issued on the PATIENT_MEDS table belonging to MEDUSER, you may execute the following query. From Figure 5-30, notice a listing of all transactions issued against the PATIENT_MEDS table are displayed.

```
SQL> SELECT XID, OPERATION, UNDO_SQL
     FROM FLASHBACK_TRANSACTION_QUERY
     WHERE TABLE_NAME='PATIENT_MEDS'
     AND TABLE_OWNER='MEDUSER';
```

3. In step 17 of Practice 8, you noted the transaction ID corresponding to the five rows that were inserted into the table. It was 0A000B00B501000 in the Figure 5-28. This transaction ID may be used to determine the statements that can be issued to reverse the changes made by it. To view the UNDO_SQL statements that correspond to the transaction, issue a statement similar to the one displayed below. Substitute the Transaction ID you noted in the command.

```
SQL> SELECT * FROM FLASHBACK_TRANSACTION_QUERY
     WHERE XID='0A000B00B501000';
```

4. Exit SQL*Plus.

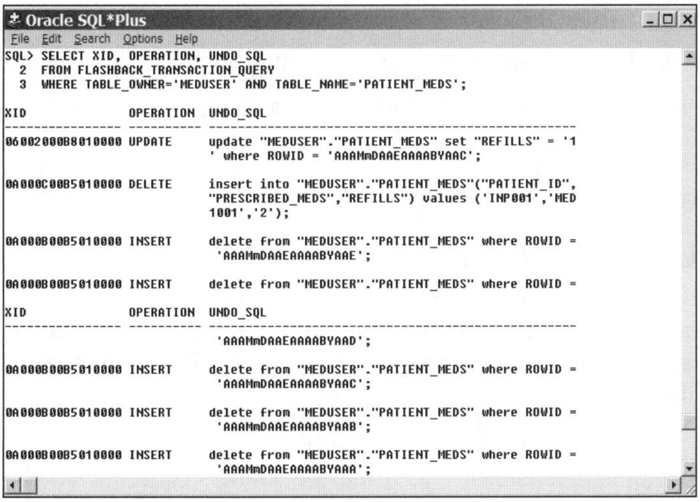

```
Oracle SQL*Plus
File Edit Search Options Help
SQL> SELECT XID, OPERATION, UNDO_SQL
  2  FROM FLASHBACK_TRANSACTION_QUERY
  3  WHERE TABLE_OWNER='MEDUSER' AND TABLE_NAME='PATIENT_MEDS';

XID              OPERATION  UNDO_SQL
---------------- ---------- --------------------------------------------------
06002000B8010000 UPDATE     update "MEDUSER"."PATIENT_MEDS" set "REFILLS" = '1
                            ' where ROWID = 'AAAMmDAAEAAAABYAAC';

0A000C00B5010000 DELETE     insert into "MEDUSER"."PATIENT_MEDS"("PATIENT_ID",
                            "PRESCRIBED_MEDS","REFILLS") values ('INP001','MED
                            1001','2');

0A000B00B5010000 INSERT     delete from "MEDUSER"."PATIENT_MEDS" where ROWID =
                             'AAAMmDAAEAAAABYAAE';

0A000B00B5010000 INSERT     delete from "MEDUSER"."PATIENT_MEDS" where ROWID =

XID              OPERATION  UNDO_SQL
---------------- ---------- --------------------------------------------------
                             'AAAMmDAAEAAAABYAAD';

0A000B00B5010000 INSERT     delete from "MEDUSER"."PATIENT_MEDS" where ROWID =
                             'AAAMmDAAEAAAABYAAC';

0A000B00B5010000 INSERT     delete from "MEDUSER"."PATIENT_MEDS" where ROWID =
                             'AAAMmDAAEAAAABYAAB';

0A000B00B5010000 INSERT     delete from "MEDUSER"."PATIENT_MEDS" where ROWID =
                             'AAAMmDAAEAAAABYAAA';
```

FIGURE 5-30 The output of querying the FLASHBACK_TRANSACTION_QUERY table

In this part of the chapter, you were introduced to the Flashback Transaction Query feature of Oracle 10*g* database. This feature is useful for diagnosing, analyzing, and auditing transactions. It gives the user the ability to view the statements that were issued and the statements that can reverse or undo the changes that were made within a transaction.

FLASHBACK TABLE

In this last topic, the Flashback Table functionality will be discussed. Flashback Table may be used to recover a table to a previous point in time. If a table has been accidentally modified, then the Flashback Table feature alleviates the need to perform complicated point in time recovery operations. It allows you to restore data in a table to a previous point in time using a timestamp or SCN. It is important to note that after the Flashback Table operation has completed, the data in the table (prior to the Flashback) continues to exist, allowing you to revert to this state if necessary. Flashback Table is done using the undo data in the undo segments to restore the data. There are a number of pre-requisites you must be aware of regarding the Flashback Table functionality.

- To perform a FLASHBACK TABLE operation, you must possess the FLASHBACK ANY TABLE system privilege or have the FLASHBACK object privilege on the table.
- You must have the SELECT, INSERT, DELETE, and ALTER privileges on the table.
- The undo data in the undo segments must go as far back in time as required by the FLASHBACK TABLE operation.
- The integrity constraints specified on the table must not be violated after the flashback.
- Row movement on the table must be enabled. This can be done by issuing the command `ALTER TABLE table ENABLE ROW MOVEMENT;`

Performing the Flashback Table

The commands that may be used to perform a Flashback Table are:

```
FLASHBACK TABLE tablename TO TIMESTAMP TO_TIMESTAMP(timestamp);
```

or

```
FLASHBACK TABLE tablename TO SCN scn_number;
```


Practice 10: Performing a Flashback Table Operation

In this practice example the Flashback Table feature will be demonstrated. A table called PHYFT containing four rows will be created by executing a script. The table will then be updated, simulating an erroneous change to the table. The PHYFT table will then be recovered using the Flashback Table feature.

1. Start SQL*Plus and connect as the user MEDUSER.

   ```
   SQL> CONNECT MEDUSER/MEDUSER
   ```

2. Execute the script **ch5_ft.sql**. The script creates a table called PHYFT and inserts four rows into the table.

   ```
   SQL> START <PATH>\CH5_FT.SQL
   ```

3. Query the table to view its contents. (See Figure 5-31.)

   ```
   SQL> SELECT * FROM PHYFT;
   ```

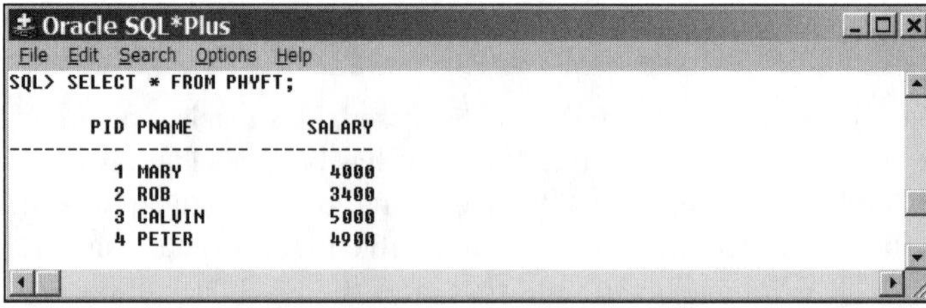

FIGURE 5-31 The contents of the PHYFT table

4. Issue a comment to display the current timestamp. We will refer to this timestamp as T1. In Figure 5-32 the timestamp value is 20-DEC-05 12:49:54.

   ```
   SQL> SELECT CURRENT_TIMESTAMP FROM DUAL;
   ```

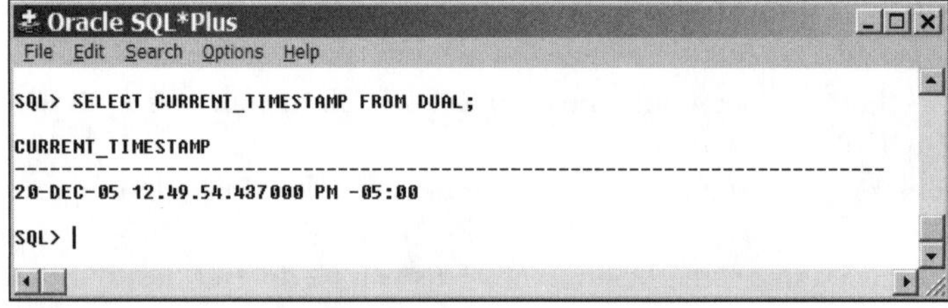

FIGURE 5-32 The timestamp (T1) when the data was correct

5. Wait for a couple of minutes and issue the UPDATE statement followed by a COMMIT statement. The update modifies the salaries of Physicians 1 and 3 to 6000. This update simulates the erroneous change made to the table.

```
SQL>UPDATE PHYFT SET SALARY=6000 WHERE PID IN (1,3);
SQL>COMMIT;
```

6. Once again display the current timestamp. We will refer to this timestamp as T2. In Figure 5-33 the timestamp value is 20-DEC-05 12:54:43.

```
SQL>SELECT CURRENT_TIMESTAMP FROM DUAL;
```


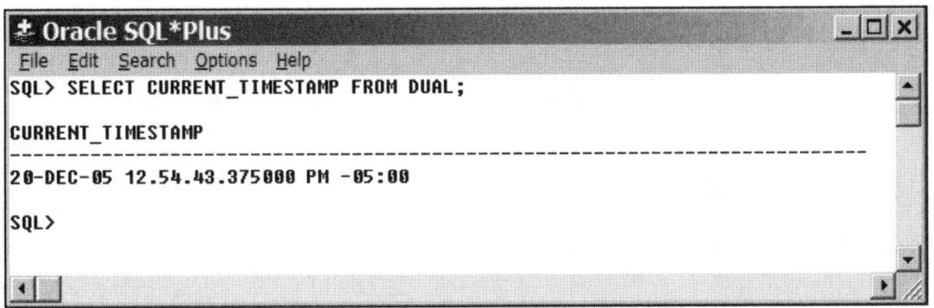

FIGURE 5-33 The timestamp (T2) when the data was incorrect

7. We now recover the table to its state at time T1. First, enable row movement in the table PHYFT.

```
SQL>ALTER TABLE PHYFT ENABLE ROW MOVEMENT;
```

8. Next issue the FLASHBACK TABLE command using the timestamp you noted as T1. (See Figure 5-34.)

```
SQL>FLASHBACK TABLE PHYFT TO TIMESTAMP
    TO_TIMESTAMP('20-DEC-05 12:49:54','DD-MON-YY HH24:MI:SS');
```

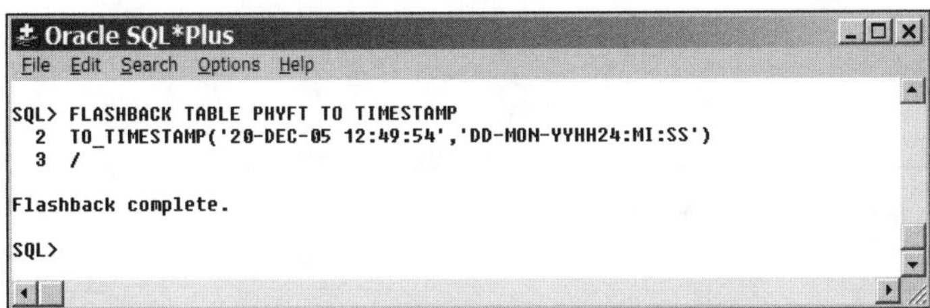

FIGURE 5-34 The FLASHBACK TABLE command using the TIMESTAMP clause

9. Query the table PHYFT to display its contents. The original data should be displayed as in Figure 5-31.

```
SQL>SELECT * FROM PHYFT;
```

10. In this part of the practice you will see how to determine the SCN using a timestamp (TIMESTAMP_TO_SCN function) and how easy it is to return to the time

represented by T2 by re-issuing the FLASHBACK TABLE command. Issue the following SELECT statement to determine the SCN corresponding to time T2. Figure 5-35 displays the SCN as 1121535. Note the value displayed on your machine.

```
SQL>SELECT TIMESTAMP_TO_SCN(TO_DATE('20-DEC-05 12:54:43','DD-MON-YY HH24:MI:SS')) FROM DUAL;
```


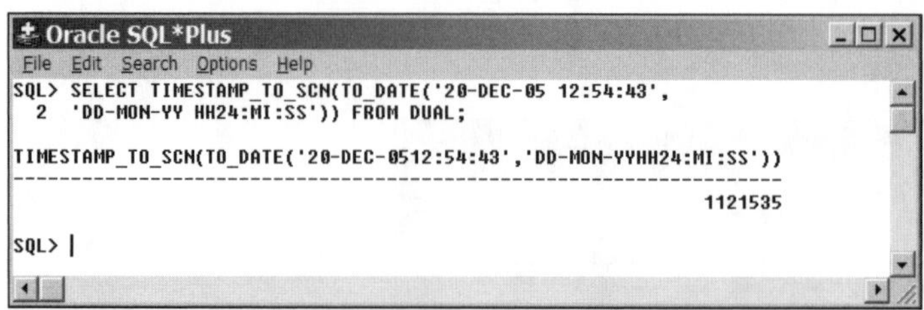

FIGURE 5-35 Determining the SCN using a TIMESTAMP

11. Issue a FLASHBACK TABLE command using the SCN you noted in the previous step.

    ```
    SQL>FLASHBACK TABLE PHYFT TO SCN 1121535;
    ```

12. Re-query the PHYFT to display its contents. The output would be as it was after the update was done. (See Figure 5-36.)

    ```
    SQL>SELECT * FROM PHYFT;
    ```

```
Oracle SQL*Plus
File Edit Search Options Help
SQL> SELECT * FROM PHYFT;

       PID PNAME          SALARY
---------- ---------- ----------
         1 MARY             6000
         2 ROB              3400
         3 CALVIN           6000
         4 PETER            4900
```

FIGURE 5-36 The contents of the table at the time T2.

13. Exit SQL*Plus.

In this part of the chapter the Flashback Table feature was discussed. The topic explained how the DBA can restore the state of one or more tables to a point in time when a human or application error occurs.

This chapter completely reviewed the Flashback Technology features in Oracle 10g including Flashback Database, Flashback Drop, Flashback Query, Flashback Versions Query, Flashback Transactions Query, and Flashback Table. They are used primarily in the recovery from human and logical errors. In Chapter 6 you will learn how to detect and correct block corruption in the Oracle 10g database.

Chapter Summary

- Based on recent surveys, approximately 40 percent of errors generated in the database are the result of human error.
- The Flashback Technologies in Oracle 10*g* include Flashback Database, Flashback Drop, Flashback Query, Flashback Versions Query, and Flashback Transactions Query.
- The Flashback Drop feature is used to "undrop" a table if it was accidentally deleted using the DROP TABLE command.
- The Flashback Drop feature utilizes a "virtual container" known as the RECYCLE BIN.
- When objects are deleted, they are put into the recycle bin and renamed.
- To delete a table permanently you can use the PURGE option.
- When a tablespace is dropped, all its objects are purged before it is dropped.
- When a user is dropped, all objects created by the user are purged before the user is dropped.
- The Flashback Query, Flashback Versions Query, and Flashback Transactions Query make use of automatic undo management.
- The undo retention is the period of time data is retained in the undo segments even after the transaction that generated it has completed.
- The Flashback Version Query feature is an enhancement of the Flashback Query feature.
- The Flashback Query feature allows a user to see data as it existed at a time in the past.
- The Flashback Versions query feature allows a user to see all versions of data during a time frame.
- The Flashback Transactions Query allows a user to see changes made at a transaction level.
- The Flashback Table command allows the user to restore previous contents of a table without complicated point-in-time recovery steps.

Syntax Guide

SYNTAX GUIDE		
Command	Description	Example
FLASHBACK TABLE... TO BEFORE DROP [RENAME TO newname]	To recover a table that is currently in the recycle bin. The RENAME TO clause may be used to rename the table during recovery.	SQL> FLASHBACK TABLE PATIENTS TO BEFORE DROP; SQL> FLASHBACK TABLE PATIENTS TO BEFORE DROP RENAME TO PATIENTS_CPY;
DROP TABLE ... PURGE	To permanently delete a table without sending it to the recycle bin.	SQL> DROP TABLE PATIENTS_TEMP PURGE;

SYNTAX GUIDE		
Command	**Description**	**Example**
`PURGE TABLE tablename`	To delete a table currently in the recycle bin, permanently.	`SQL> PURGE TABLE PATIENTS;`
`PURGE TABLESPACE ...`	To permanently drop all objects belonging to a tablespace from the recycle bin.	`SQL> PURGE TABLESPACE USERS;`
`DROP TABLESPACE ... INCLUDING CONTENTS;`	To permanently drop a tablespace and purge all its contents.	`SQL> DROP TABLESPACE DATA INCLUDING CONTENTS;`
`SHOW RECYCLEBIN`	To display all objects currently in the recycle bin and can be undropped.	`SQL> SHOW RECYCLEBIN;`
`PURGE RECYCLEBIN`	To permanently delete all objects currently in the recycle bin.	`SQL> PURGE RECYCLEBIN;`
`DROP USER ... CASCADE`	To drop a user and purge all objects belonging to the user.	`SQL> DROP USER JOHNDOE CASCADE;`
`SELECT ... AS OF TIMESTAMP`	To perform a flashback query operation.	`SQL> SELECT * FROM FLASHQ AS OF TIMESTAMP TO_TIMESTAMP('25-JUL-05 14:30:00 DD-MON-YY HH24:MI:SS');`
`EXECUTE DBMS_FLASHBACK. ENABLE_AT_TIME`	To perform a flashback query operation using the DBMS_FLASHBACK package.	`SQL> EXEC DBMS_FLASHBACK. ENABLE_AT_TIME( '25-JUL-05 14:30:00');`
`EXECUTE DBMS_FLASHBACK.DISABLE`	To disable the flashback query operation.	`SQL> EXEC DBMS_FLASHBACK.DISABLE;`
`SELECT column, column FROM table VERSIONS BETWEEN SCN minvalue AND maxvalue;`	To perform a flashback versions query operation. To view all versions of the rows of a table within a specified SCN window.	`SQL>SELECT VERSIONS_XID, PATIENT_ID, REFILLS FROM PATIENT_MEDS VERSIONS BETWEEN SCN 100 AND 200;`

SYNTAX GUIDE		
Command	Description	Example
`SELECT column, column, ... FROM table VERSIONS BETWEEN TIMESTAMP timestamp1 AND timestamp2;`	To view all versions of the rows of the table within a specified time frame.	`SQL> SELECT * FROM PATIENT_MEDS VERSIONS BETWEEN TIMESTAMP TO_TIMESTAMP('25-JUL-05 15:39:03','DD-MON-YY HH24:MI:SS') AND TO_TIMESTAMP('25-JUL-05 15:44:27','DD-MON-YY HH24:MI:SS');`

`FLASHBACK TABLE .. TO TIMESTAMP |SCN`	To undo undesirable changes made to a table by restoring a table to a state it was in the past.	`FLASHBACK TABLE PHYFT TO SCN 1121535;`
		
		`FLASHBACK TABLE PHYFT TO TIMESTAMP TO_TIMESTAMP('20-DEC-05 12:49:54','DD-MON-YY HH24:MI:SS');`

Review Questions

1. The _______________ feature allows you to undrop tables that you have accidentally dropped.
2. The _______________ holds all objects that have been dropped until the tablespace requires additional space.
3. The _______________ feature allows you to view table data as it existed five minutes ago.
4. The _______________ feature allows you to view all versions of the rows created between 10:10 A.M. and 10:30 A.M.
5. The _____________ option of the DROP TABLE command is used to permanently delete objects from the recycle bin.
6. A user who desires to use the Flashback Query feature must possess the ____________ and _____________ privileges.
7. The ____________________ Oracle supplied package can be used to perform a flashback query operation.
8. The ____________________________ clause of the SELECT statement allows a user to perform a flashback versions query.

9. A tablespace called USER_DATA is currently empty. Two tables—T1 and T2—that existed in the tablespace, are deleted and currently reside in the recycle bin. The database administrator issues the DROP TABLESPACE USER_DATA INCLUDING CONTENTS command. What do you think would be the outcome of this command?
    a. The tablespace will be deleted and the objects will be renamed in the recycle bin.
    b. The tablespace will be deleted and the objects will not be renamed in the recycle bin.
    c. The tablespace will be deleted and the objects belonging to the tablespace, currently residing in the recycle bin, will be deleted.
    d. An error will be generated.
10. The database administrator has performed an erroneous transaction (XID 020020000004C000). The database administrator wishes to view all the changes made by the transaction. Which view would the administrator query?
    a. FLASHBACK_VERSIONS_QUERY
    b. FLASHBACK_TRANSACTION_QUERY
    c. FLASHBACK_DROP_QUERY
    d. FLASBACK_XID_QUERY
11. The PHYSICIANS table has been dropped. It existed in the DATA tablespace. Which of the following statements are true? [Choose 2].
    a. The table is sent to the recycle bin and renamed.
    b. The extents of the table continue to be allocated in the datafile belonging to the DATA tablespace.
    c. The extents are immediately released and can be re-used for new objects.
    d. The indexes and constraints created on the table are also dropped automatically.
    e. The DATA tablespace is automatically dropped, and the PHYSICIANS table purged.
12. The PATIENT_LABS table was dropped yesterday. Another table was re-created a few hours later using the same name. The database administrator wishes to restore the original table that was dropped. What options does the administrator have? [Choose 2].
    a. The table cannot be recovered because when a new table was created with the same name, the original table was automatically purged.
    b. The table can be restored using the FLASHBACK TABLE... TO BEFORE DROP command.
    c. The table can be restored using the FLASHBACK TABLE... TO BEFORE DROP RENAME TO... command.
    d. The table will be restored but all the rows will be deleted.
    e. The table can be restored as long as it is in the recycle bin.

13. The DBA created a table T1 with a single column COLA. She issued the following statements.

```
SQL> INSERT INTO T1 VALUES (10);
SQL> INSERT INTO T1 VALUES (20);
SQL> COMMIT;
SQL> INSERT INTO T1 VALUES (30);
SQL> ROLLBACK;
SQL> UPDATE T1 SET COLA=11 WHERE COLA=10;
SQL> COMMIT;
```


She then issued a Flashback Versions query statement. Which of the operations mentioned above will appear in the output?

a. The INSERT of values 10, 20, 30 and the update.

b. The INSERT of values 10, 20 and the update.

c. The insert of values 10, 20, 30 and not the update.

d. The insert of values 10, 20, 30 and 11.

e. All the above.

14. The XRAYS table has been modified and a certain row from the table accidentally deleted. The administrator has to identify the statement that can be used to undo the action. Which of the options given below would he use?

a. ROLLBACK;

b. The Flashback UNDO_SQL feature.

c. The Flashback versions query feature only.

d. The Flashback versions query and Flashback Transaction Query feature.

e. None of the above.

15. The table XRAYS_2003 was dropped last night at 3:00 AM. It belonged to the PAT_XRAYS tablespace. At 5:00 AM the datafile belonging to the PAT_XRAYS tablespace extended as a result of its AUTOEXTEND ON property. At 6:30 AM the database administrator realized that he was supposed to delete the XRAYS_2001 table and had accidentally deleted the wrong table. What are his options for recovery?

a. The XRAYS_2003 table can be restored from the recycle bin.

b. The XRAYS_2003 table can be restored but must be renamed to XRAYS_2001.

c. The XRAYS_2003 table can be queried from the undo segments as long as the undo retention is met.

d. The XRAYS_2003 table cannot be restored because the datafile extended automatically.

e. The XRAYS_2003 wasn't dropped because of the automatic datafile extension.

16. The table LAB_OP table was dropped at 2:30 P.M. The database administrator issues a command to create a table LAB_OP. What is the outcome of this action?

    a. Another table with the same name cannot be created because the table still exists in the user's schema.

    b. The table must be created with the RENAME clause.

    c. The table in the recycle bin must be purged before another table with the same name can be created.

    d. The table will be created.

    e. None of the above.

17. The user JOHN was dropped using the command :

    ```
    DROP USER JOHN CASCADE;
    ```

    Which of the following statements about the command are true?

    a. The user will be dropped and all the objects will be sent to the recycle bin.

    b. The user can be dropped only if the tablespace is also dropped.

    c. The user will be dropped and all the objects belonging to the user will be purged.

    d. The tables will be de-allocated and the user dropped.

    e. A user must be dropped using the PURGE clause.

18. Identify the pseudocolumns that can be used to for the flashback versions query feature. [Choose 6].

    a. VERSIONS_XID

    b. VERSIONS_TRANSID

    c. VERSIONS_STARTTIME

    d. VERSIONS_ENDTIME

    e. VERSIONS_STARTSCN

    f. VERSIONS_ENDSCN

    g. VERSIONS_TIMESTAMP

    h. VERSIONS_OPERATION

19. Why would you use the following FLASHBACK TABLE command?

    FLASHBACK TABLE phyft TO TIMESTAMP('10:10','hh:mi');

    a. To view the changes made to the to the PHYFT table since 10:10.

    b. To view the data as it existed at 10:10.

    c. To undo the changes made to the PHYFT table since the 10:10 A.M.

    d. To view the changes made to the PHYFT table for specific rows.

20. The DBA issues the command TRUNCATE TABLE PHYSICIAN; He can issue the FLASHBACK TABLE command to revert the table to its previous state. True or False?

Hands-On Assignments

Assignment 5-1 Setting the undo retention parameter

1. Connect as a user with SYSDBA privileges.
2. Dynamically increase the size of the UNDO_RETENTION parameter to four hours.
3. Exit SQL*Plus.

Assignment 5-2 Performing a Flashback Drop operation

1. Start SQL*Plus, connect as the user MEDUSER.
2. Create a table called BDROP, containing a single numeric column COL1.
3. Insert the values 99 and 100 into the table.
4. Drop the table BDROP.
5. Issue the SHOW RECYCLEBIN command to view the contents of the recycle bin. Is the BDROP table in the recycle bin?
6. Issue the command to restore the BDROP table.
7. Re-execute the SHOW RECYCLEBIN command to view the contents of the recycle bin. Does the BDROP table exist in the recycle bin?
8. Query the BDROP table to make sure it has been restored.
9. Exit SQL*Plus.

Assignment 5-3 Performing a Flashback Drop operation with rename

1. From SQL*Plus, connect as the MEDUSER.
2. If the BDROP table does not exist in the MEDUSER schema, perform steps 2 and 3 of Assignment 5-2.
3. Query the BDROP table. It should contain two rows, with values 99 and 100.
4. Drop the BDROP table.
5. Create a table called BDROP having a single numeric column called COL2.
6. Now try to restore the table using the Flashback Drop feature. Try to do it without the RENAME clause. Notice the error generated.
7. Now execute the FLASHBACK DROP command with the RENAME option and rename the table as BDROPOLD
8. Query the BDROPOLD table to confirm it was restored successfully.
9. View the contents of the recycle bin. The BDROP table should not exist in it.
10. Remain connected to SQL*Plus.

Assignment 5-4 Dropping a tablespace and the Flashback Drop command

1. Using SQL*Plus, connect as a user with SYSDBA privileges.
2. Run the **ch5_4a.sql** script. This script creates a tablespace called DATATAB. You may need to modify the script and change the path of the datafile.
3. Run the **ch5_4b.sql** script. This script creates a user called USERT with a password USERT. The user's default tablespace is DATATAB. The user is then granted privileges to connect and create objects in the database.

4. Connect as the USERT with the password USERT.
5. Run the **ch5_4c.sql** script. This script creates two tables called UA and UB.
6. Verify the tables UA and UB exist.
7. Connect as a user with SYSDBA privileges.
8. Drop the tablespace DATATAB and all its contents.

9. Query the OBJECT_NAME, ORIGINAL_COLUMNS of DBA_RECYCLEBIN view to determine if any table belonging to USERT was moved to the recycle bin. The output should be "no rows."
10. Connect as the USERT and display the contents of the recycle bin. It must be empty.
11. Try to query the UA and UB tables. They should not exist.
12. Exit SQL*Plus.

Assignment 5-5 Purging a table

1. Connect as the MEDUSER.
2. Create a table called CH52, with a single numeric column.
3. Insert the value 100 into the table and issue a commit.
4. Issue the command to permanently delete the table without sending it to the recycle bin.
5. View the recycle bin to verify the deletion. It should not exist in the recycle bin.
6. Exit SQL*Plus.

Assignment 5-6 Performing a Flashback Query

1. From SQL*Plus connect as the MEDUSER user.
2. Run the script **ch5_6a.sql**. The script creates a table called CH56 having a single numeric column. Two rows with values 10 and 20 are also inserted into the table.
3. Note the current timestamp.
4. Wait for about three minutes.
5. Issue the following UPDATE statement.
   ```
   SQL> UPDATE CH56 SET C1=99;
   SQL> COMMIT;
   ```
6. Using the timestamp you noted down in step 3, issue a SELECT... AS OF TIMESTAMP query to perform a flashback query and display data as it existed at that time. The values 10 and 20 must be displayed.
7. Issue a SELECT * FROM CH56 to view data at the current time.
8. Exit SQL*Plus.

Assignment 5-7 Performing Flashback Versions Query

1. Using SQL*Plus, connect as the user MEDUSER.
2. Run the script **ch5_7a.sql**. The script creates a table called CH57 having a single numeric column.
3. Run the script **ch5_7b.sql**. Two rows with values 10 and 20 are also inserted into the CH57 table.

4. Query the table called CH57 to view its contents.
5. Issue a command to update the row where the column C1 takes the value 10. Set the value to 100. Commit the change.
6. Issue a query to display all versions of the rows of the table CH57. Display the transaction ID, the type of operation performed, and the values of the table. Use the timestamp option. Note the transaction ID for the INSERT statements.
7. Issue a query to display all versions of the rows of the table CH57. Display the transaction ID, version start time, version end time, and the values of the table. Use the SCN option.
8. Exit SQL*Plus.

Assignment 5-8 Performing a Flashback Transaction query

1. Using SQL*Plus, connect to the database as a user with administrative privileges.
2. Query the FLASHBACK_TRANSACTION_QUERY table to determine the statement issued under the transaction whose ID you noted in step 5 of Assignment 5-7. Retrieve the OPERATION, TABLE_NAME, TABLE_OWNER, and UNDO_SQL columns of the table.
3. Remain connected to SQL*Plus.

Assignment 5-9 The outcome of a Flashback Drop across multiple drops of a table.

1. Using SQL*Plus, connect as the user MEDUSER.
2. Create a table called CH59 with a single numeric column called C1.
3. Insert the value 5 into the table CH59. Commit the change.
4. Drop the table CH59.
5. Recreate the table CH59 as you did in step 2.
6. Insert the value 15 into the table CH59. Commit the change.
7. Drop the table CH59.
8. Recreate the table CH59 as you did in step 2.
9. Insert the value 25 into the table CH59. Commit the change.
10. Drop the table CH59.
11. Issue the command to restore the table CH59 from the recycle bin.
12. Which table version do you think was restored? Verify your answer by querying the CH59 table.
13. Exit SQL*Plus.

Assignment 5-10 Understanding purging of tables

1. Using SQL*Plus, connect as the user MEDUSER.
2. Create a table called CH510 with a single numeric column called N1.
3. Drop the table CH510.
4. Create the table called CH510 with a single date column called D1.
5. Drop the table CH510.
6. View the contents of the recycle bin.
7. Issue the command to purge the table CH510.

8. Which of the tables do you think was purged? Was it the table with the column N1 or D1?
9. Verify your answer.

Case Study

Keller Medical Center has established many detailed procedures and policies for managing their data. However, because no environment—however well managed—can be free of user errors, the database administrators at Keller Medical Center are keen on building a safety net with the new Flashback Technologies. They plan to identify the most common user errors in the database and see how the Flashback Technologies may be used to recover from them. As part of this case, you must help identify as many user errors as you can and note the steps you would perform to recover from them.

CHAPTER **6**

HANDLING BLOCK CORRUPTION

LEARNING OBJECTIVES

After completing this chapter, you should be able to do the following:

- Understand block corruption
- Identify block corruption
- Resolve block corruption
- Understand the ANALYZE command
- Become familiar with the DBVERIFY utility
- Utilize the DB_BLOCK_CHECKING parameter
- Execute the DBMS_REPAIR package
- Block Media Recovery using RMAN

EXAM OBJECTIVES COVERED IN THIS CHAPTER:

- Handling Block Corruption
- Dealing with Database Corruption
- What is block corruption?
- The ANALYZE command
- How to Handle Corruptions
- The DBMS_REPAIR Package
- Block Media Recovery (BMR)
- Detecting and Interpreting Database Corruptions Using DBVERIFY
- Using RMAN to Repair Corrupt Blocks

INTRODUCTION

In the earlier chapters of this book, we discussed media failures in the database and how recovery could be performed manually, using RMAN and Oracle Enterprise Manager. This chapter introduces another type of corruption that might occur and the recovery options that are available to the DBA. The focus of this chapter is block corruption in an Oracle database. Block corruption is a rare phenomenon within the Oracle database. However, when it does occur, it is one of the most dreaded errors. All database administrators unanimously agree that recovering from block corruptions is one of their most challenging tasks. Recovery is not always possible and often the help of Oracle Worldwide Support is required. In this chapter you will learn about the Oracle block, input/output operations on a block, and how corruption may be introduced into the block. This is followed by a complete discussion of the recovery options available that may be used by the administrator to identify block corruptions and resolve them, if possible.

THE CURRENT CHALLENGE AT KELLER MEDICAL CENTER

Ryan was querying the LABS_2005 table when he received an error that nearly made him choke. The error displayed to him was as follows:

```
SQL> SELECT * FROM LABS_2005;

select * from labs_2005
*
ERROR at line 1:

ORA-01578: ORACLE data block corrupted (file #8, block #730)
ORA-01110: data file 8: 'C:\oracle\product\10.2.0\db101\medlabs01.dbf'
```

Seeing the error message he was quite sure this was a case of block corruption. The LABS_2005 table was an important table and its loss was unacceptable. A backup of datafile 8 had been taken last night using Recovery Manager. The DB101 database operates in archivelog mode. Quickly gathering his thoughts the first thing he did was ANALYZE the object for integrity. The same error was generated. He then began to think of other ways in which he could recover it. Because he did not have a copy of the table in the form of an export, an import of the object was not an option. In his study of Recovery Manager, Ryan had read how the BLOCKRECOVER command of RMAN may be used to recover one or more corrupted blocks. He was excited about trying the command because block corruption is something he didn't encounter often. He carefully issued the BLOCKRECOVER command and re-issued the SELECT * FORM LABS_2005. The command went through without an error.

In addition to learning how Ryan recovered the corrupt block, this chapter explains the other techniques available to help a database administrator detect and correct corrupt blocks.

SETUP FOR THE CHAPTER

Before performing the practice and hands-on exercises in this chapter you must run the script called **ch6_setup.sql** that is in the Chapter06 folder of the student datafiles. This script creates a table called C6_PHY and an index called C6_INDX_PNAME.

1. Start SQL*Plus, and connect as the user MEDUSER.

   ```
   SQL> CONNECT MEDUSER/MEDUSER
   ```

2. From the SQL prompt execute the script ch6_setup.sql.

   ```
   SQL> START <PATH>\CH6_SETUP.SQL
   ```

3. Exit SQL*Plus.

BLOCKS AND BLOCK CORRUPTION

Before you can learn about block corruption it is important to understand the concept of an Oracle Block. An Oracle block is the smallest unit that the Oracle Server can read or write. Oracle blocks have a pre-defined format. The Oracle server expects to find a block in this format during Input/Output (I/O) operations. The default size of an Oracle block is defined during the creation of the database or during tablespace creation. The default block size for an Oracle database is defined by the DB_BLOCK_SIZE initialization parameter. A tablespace with a non-standard block size is defined by the BLOCKSIZE size clause during tablespace creation. An Oracle block is made up of one or more operating system blocks and the Oracle block size must always be a multiple of the operating system block size—if the operating system block size is 2 K, the Oracle block may be defined as 2 K, 4 K, 8 K, 16 K, 32 K, or 64 K.

An Oracle block consists of different parts. It has a data block header containing valuable information about the block such as block address known as the Data Block Address (DBA). The block address is a 48-bit integer that is referenced when checking the integrity of the block. It consists of a file number and a relative block number. The file number represents the datafile the block belongs to (file# column of V$DATAFILE) and the relative block number represents the position of the block relative to the beginning of the file. The block header also holds table directory and row directory along with the locking status of the rows in the block. Apart from the block header, an Oracle block contains free space and row data. The row data is made up of the actual rows stored in the block. Row data grows in a bottom-up fashion, decreasing the amount of free space between itself and the block header as it grows.

Figure 6-1 displays an Oracle block and its relationship with an operating system block. In the figure, the Oracle block is made up of four operating system blocks. The operating system is aware of the Oracle block format.

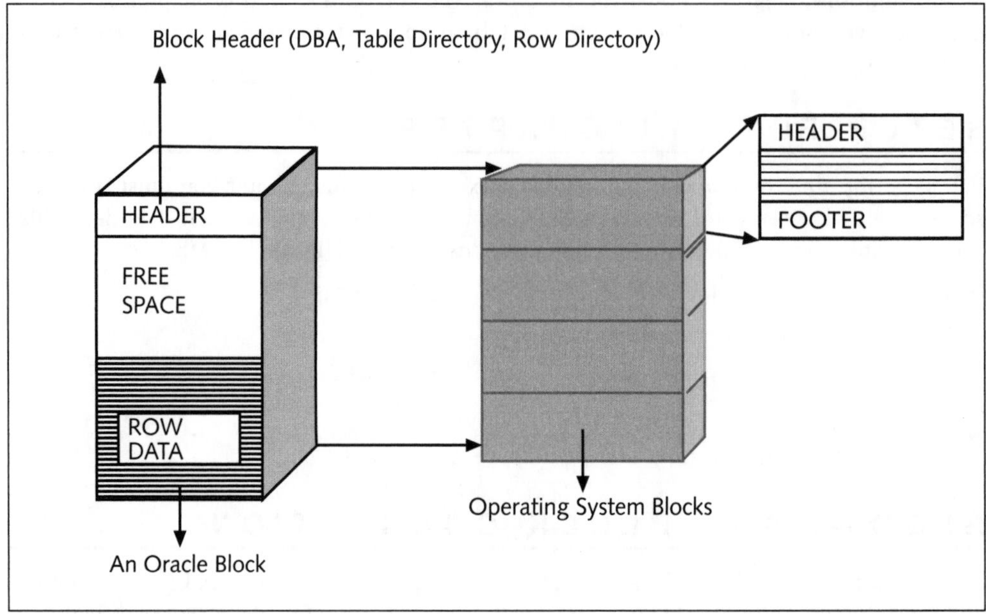

FIGURE 6-1 Relationship between an Oracle block and an Operating system block

When inserts, updates, or deletes are performed on the rows of a table, they are performed on the rows maintained in the Oracle blocks. The changes are made to the blocks in the Database Buffer Cache of the System Global Area (SGA) which is created in real memory or RAM when the database is started. The modified blocks are written back to disk periodically by the Database Writer (DBWn) background process. The Oracle block passes through different system layers before it is successfully written to disk. Some of the communication points along the way include:

- The SGA in Memory
- The UNIX buffer cache in Memory (On a UNIX machine)
- The Disk Controller Cache
- The disk containing the datafile that holds the block.

As the block passes through these various layers before reaching its final destination, corruptions may creep into the block along the way. A block can be corrupted due to memory or caching problems, bad hardware or firmware, mechanical problems in the disk, problems with device drivers as well as operating system software and Oracle software bugs.

Figure 6-2 shows the different layers that the block must pass through before it can reach the datafile that resides on the hard disk. Layers may typically include the operating system file system, the logical volume manager (LVM), the I/O driver, the operating system, the host bus adapter, and the disk controller.

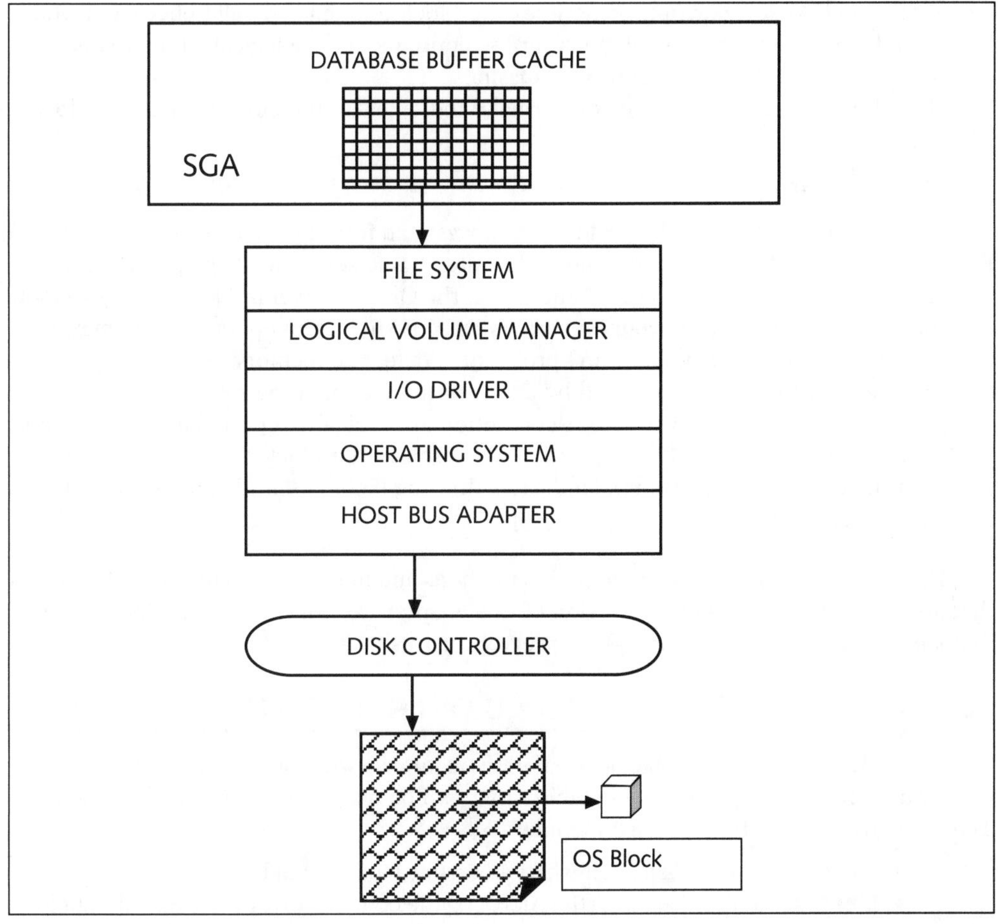

FIGURE 6-2 The different communications points that a block has to traverse before reaching the datafile

Block corruption can be of two types namely "Hard Corruption" and "Soft Corruption". Hard corruption also known as physical corruption or media corruption occurs when the block cannot be read as a result of a problem with the media. The structure of the block cannot be recognized at all. Oracle recognizes a media corrupt block in various ways. The checksum may be invalid, the block may contain all zeroes, and the header and footer of the block may not match. A problem with the media can result in the block becoming inaccessible.

Soft corruption occurs when the block format is different from the Oracle default block format. Soft corruption is also known as logical or software corruption. Oracle marks a block soft corrupt when reading the block from disk into the database memory cache. As mentioned earlier in this chapter, errors can be introduced by any of the layers that the block must pass through before it is written to disk. Such errors are not detected until the next read on the block is performed. If any inconsistencies are found the Oracle Server marks the block as soft corrupt. Sometimes the block may have a valid checksum, the header and footer may even match however the contents may be logically inconsistent. An example would be if the row directory is missing.

The ORA-600 [3339] Oracle error normally indicates a problem with the data block address:

```
ORA-00600: internal error code, arguments: [3339],[RBA1],[RBA2],[]...
```


In the error, RBA1 is the block address that was read from the block header (DBA), and RBA2 is the physical address of the block that the Oracle server was trying to access. If there are discrepancies between RBA1 and RBA2, the Oracle Server marks the blocks as soft corrupt. Such differences can occur for various reasons such as an operating system repair attempt after a system crash, faulty I/O processing, defective memory modules, or even as a result of an inaccurate block read by an overstressed operating system.

Oracle errors associated with block corruption are typically reported as ORA-600 and ORA-1578 errors. The ORA-1578 error usually displays the block that is corrupted as shown in the example. This example indicates that the block 98 in file 161 is corrupt.

```
ORA-1578: ORACLE data block corrupted (file #161,block #98)
```

The Oracle Server provides a number of methods and techniques to help identify blocks that are corrupt. In the following section of this chapter we will closely examine some of the popular tools provided by the Oracle server for this task.

IDENTIFYING BLOCK CORRUPTION

With an understanding of how block corruption occurs we will now look into the different techniques provided in the Oracle database that can be used to identify corrupt blocks. The methods that will be discussed include:

- Error Messages displayed when a corrupt block is read
- Log files and Trace Files (the Alert Log file contains error messages about block corruption)
- The ANALYZE command
- The DBVERIFY utility
- Using the DB_BLOCK_CHECKSUM and DB_BLOCK_CHECKING initialization parameters
- The V$DATABASE_BLOCK_CORRUPTION data dictionary view that lists corrupt blocks in the database detected during the backup operation
- The V$BACKUP_CORRUPTION and V$COPY_CORRUPTION views that list block corruption in backups

Error Messages

When a corrupt block is read by a server process, the Oracle server often displays an ORA-1578 error, specifying the location of the corrupt block. The file# and block# where the problem was encountered is reported. The information is also written to the alert log file and server process trace files. This is the most obvious method by which a database administrator is made aware of a corrupt block. A typical error is displayed in the following manner when a corrupt block is read:

```
SQL> SELECT COUNT(*) FROM MED_RECS;

ERROR:
ORA-01578: ORACLE data block corrupted (file #4, block #89779)
ORA-01110: data file 4: 'C:\oracle\product\10.2.0\oradata\db101\data01.
dbf'
```


The Alert Log File and Trace Files

The alert log file is the file containing a chronological listing of all errors and messages generated in the Oracle database. If a block corruption error is generated it is written to the alert log file and to a Database Writer trace file. The error that will be written to the alert log file is the ORA-1578 error.

The ANALYZE command

The ANALYZE ...VALIDATE STRUCTURE command can be used to check the integrity of a schema object. The command can be used on a table or an index.
The syntax for the ANALYZE command is:

```
ANALYZE TABLE tablename VALIDATE STRUCTURE [CASCADE];
or
ANALYZE INDEX indexname VALIDATE STRUCTURE;
```

where:
tablename – The name of the table that is having its structure validated.
indexname – The name of the index that is having its structure validated.
CASCADE – Indicates that all dependent indexes on the table must also be validated and verifies if the tables and its indexes are in sync.

If the object is free of errors a message confirming validation is returned; otherwise an error message is returned. An *ORA-1498: block check failure* error is displayed if the ANALYZE command detects block corruption. If an error is generated when analyzing a table you would need to use some method to recreate the corrupt block. If the failure occurs when analyzing an index, simply rebuilding the index can eliminate the problem. If corruption has affected a subset of the rows you can attempt to create a new table using the CREATE TABLE... AS SELECT statement to create the table excluding the corrupt rows. Other options include the use of the DBMS_REPAIR package, the BLOCKRECOVER command of RMAN, or if nothing else works drop and recreate it.

Practice 1: The ANALYZE command

In this practice example, you will see how the ANALYZE command is performed on tables and indexes.

1. Log on to SQL*Plus and connect as the MEDUSER.

   ```
   SQL> CONNECT MEDUSER/MEDUSER
   ```

2. Issue the ANALYZE command to validate the structure of the table C6_PHY. (See Figure 6-3.)

```
SQL> ANALYZE TABLE C6_PHY VALIDATE STRUCTURE;
```

Oracle SQL*Plus
File Edit Search Options Help

```
SQL> CONNECT MEDUSER/MEDUSER
Connected.
SQL> ANALYZE TABLE C6_PHY VALIDATE STRUCTURE;

Table analyzed.

SQL>
```


FIGURE 6-3 Analyzing a table

3. Issue the ANALYZE command to validate the structure of the index C6_INDX_PNAME. (See Figure 6-4.)

```
SQL> ANALYZE INDEX C6_INDX_PNAME VALIDATE STRUCTURE;
```

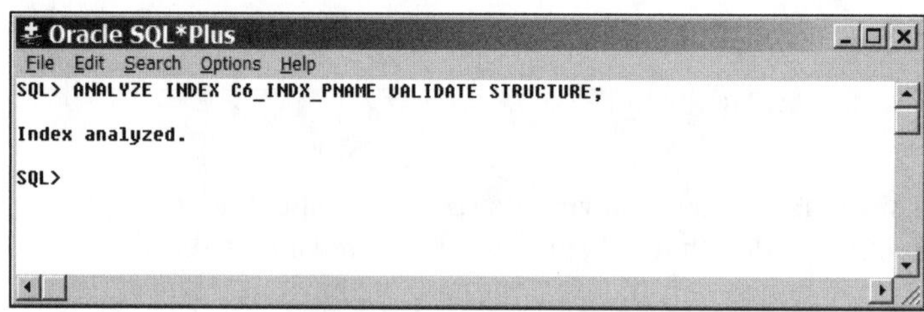

FIGURE 6-4 Analyzing an Index

NOTE

If corruption is found in an index it can be rebuilt using the following command from the SQL*Plus prompt:

```
SQL> ALTER INDEX indexname  REBUILD [ONLINE];
```

If you use the ONLINE option, users can access the index during the rebuilding process.

4. Exit SQL*Plus.

The DBVERIFY utility

The DBVERIFY utility is a command line utility that may be used as a diagnostic aid for detection of block corruption in datafiles. This command line tool is invoked from an operating system prompt such as the command prompt on Windows or a terminal window on a UNIX platform. The utility is used to check the integrity of all or some of the data blocks within a datafile. The utility is used only against cache-managed blocks—datafiles—and not on control files and redo log files. It can be used on online datafiles, offline datafiles, or backups of datafiles. The DBVERIFY tool is most often used for checking the validity of backups before they can be used for restoration during a recovery procedure.

The DBVERIFY utility can also be used to verify the integrity of a segment regardless of the number of datafiles it spans.

The DBVERIFY utility takes the following format:

```
Command prompt> dbv [keyword=value][keyword=value]...
```

where:

dbv – The name of the executable used to invoke the DBVERIFY utility

keyword – Refers to an option of the DBVERIFY utility. The different options for the DBVERIFY command have been displayed in the Table 6-1.

value – The value of the parameter

Table 6-1 describes some of the commonly used parameters of the DBVERIFY utility.

TABLE 6-1 The options of the DBVERIFY command

Keyword	Description
HELP	Provides with a complete listing of all parameters that can be issued to the DBVERIFY tool. The parameter can take the value YES or NO.
USERID	Specifies a username and password. Must be specified when verifying ASM files, optional in the case of regular datafiles.
FILE	The name of the datafile to verify. You must specify the entire path, filename, and extension of the datafile being verified.
START	If you want to verify a portion of a datafile you can specify a starting and ending block address. The START option indicates the starting block within the datafile where verification must begin. If this option is not specified then the default value is the first block of the datafile.
END	This option indicates the last block that must be verified. If the option is not specified then verification will be performed until the last block of the datafile.
BLOCKSIZE	This option must be specified if the block size of blocks in the datafile being verified is a value other than 2 K. You can determine the block size for the datafile by querying the BLOCK_SIZE column of the V$DATAFILE view.
LOGFILE	This option is the name of a file that can be used to hold the output of the DBVERIFY run. If you do not specify the option, the output will be displayed on the screen.
FEEDBACK	This option acts as a progress indicator. For example, if you set this value of the option to 5, then a dot or period (.) will be displayed on the screen after every 5 blocks are verified.

TABLE 6-1 The options of the DBVERIFY command (continued)

Keyword	Description
PARFILE	The PARFILE option can take the name of a file that holds all the options for a DBVERIFY run. It is created primarily for repetitive use of the DBVERIFY command. Once it is created the PARFILE can be used any time datafile verification needs to be done.
SEGMENT_ID	This option allows you to scan a segment. The extents of the segment may span multiple datafiles. The format of the value specified for the parameter is **ts#.segfile.segblock** where ts# is the tablespace number, segfile is the header file, and segblock is the header block. When this option is invoked the USERID option must also be specified for enabling a connection with the database.

Practice 2: The DBVERIFY utility

In this practice example you will invoke the DBVERIFY utility using some of the options mentioned in Table 6-1. The DBVERIFY utility is invoked using the *dbv* executable.

1. From the SQL*Plus prompt, connect as a user with administrative privileges.

```
SQL> CONNECT DB_ADMIN/DB_ADMIN AS SYSDBA
```

2. Determine the names of all the datafiles and their block sizes in the database by querying the NAME and BLOCK_SIZE columns from the V$DATAFILE view. Choose any datafile to be verified. In the example displayed, the USERS01. DBF file is being verified. Choose an alternate datafile if the USERS01.DBF file does not exist on your machine. Figure 6-5 displays the complete path and name of the datafile USERS01.DBF and its blocksize.

```
SQL> SELECT NAME, BLOCK_SIZE FROM V$DATAFILE
     WHERE NAME LIKE '%USERS01.DBF';
```

FIGURE 6-5 Displaying the blocksize of a datafile by querying the V$DATAFILE view

3. Invoke the command prompt on the operating system. This would be the command prompt on a Windows-based machine.

```
Start -> All Programs -> Accessories -> Command Prompt
```

4. At the command prompt invoke the DBV command. When specifying the FILE option, type in the complete path of the datafile you identified in step 2. The FEEDBACK option indicates that a dot be displayed after verification of every 250 blocks. The BLOCKSIZE option has been specified because the blocksize

of the datafile was not 2 K. The output of the DBVERIFY run will be displayed on the screen.

```
C:\> DBV FILE=<PATH>\USERS01.DBF FEEDBACK=250 BLOCKSIZE=8192
```



```
Command Prompt
C:\>DBV FILE=C:\ORACLE\PRODUCT\10.2.0\ORADATA\DB101\USERS01.DBF FEEDBACK=250 BLO
CKSIZE=8192

DBVERIFY: Release 10.2.0.1.0 - Production on Thu Dec 29 17:19:55 2005

Copyright (c) 1982, 2005, Oracle.  All rights reserved.

DBVERIFY - Verification starting : FILE = C:\ORACLE\PRODUCT\10.2.0\ORADATA\DB101
\USERS01.DBF
...

DBVERIFY - Verification complete

Total Pages Examined         : 640
Total Pages Processed (Data) : 85
Total Pages Failing   (Data) : 0
Total Pages Processed (Index): 4
Total Pages Failing   (Index): 0
Total Pages Processed (Other): 83
Total Pages Processed (Seg)  : 0
Total Pages Failing   (Seg)  : 0
Total Pages Empty            : 468
Total Pages Marked Corrupt   : 0
Total Pages Influx           : 0
Highest block SCN            : 1151786 (0.1151786)

C:\>
```

FIGURE 6-6 The output of the DBVERIFY utility

Figure 6-6 indicates that 640 blocks were examined. Of these, 85 data blocks were examined, and 4 index blocks and 83 blocks containing other data were verified. 468 blocks were empty or unused. Not a single corrupt block was found. A detailed explanation of the output is provided in The Output of the DBVERIFY Command section.

5. To examine a particular segment for block corruption using the DBVERIFY utility, the tablespace name, the header file, and header block of the segment must be determined. This information can be obtained by joining the V$TABLESPACE and DBA_SEGMENTS dictionary views. (See Figure 6-7.) To determine this information about the C6_PHY table execute the following query:

```
SQL> SELECT T.TS#, S.HEADER_FILE, S.HEADER_BLOCK
     FROM V$TABLESPACE T, DBA_SEGMENTS S
     WHERE S.SEGMENT_NAME='C6_PHY'
     AND T.NAME=S.TABLESPACE_NAME;
```

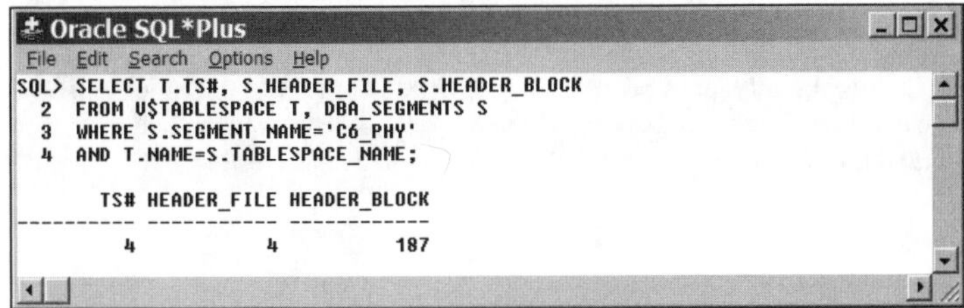

```
Oracle SQL*Plus
File Edit Search Options Help
SQL> SELECT T.TS#, S.HEADER_FILE, S.HEADER_BLOCK
  2  FROM V$TABLESPACE T, DBA_SEGMENTS S
  3  WHERE S.SEGMENT_NAME='C6_PHY'
  4  AND T.NAME=S.TABLESPACE_NAME;

       TS# HEADER_FILE HEADER_BLOCK
---------- ----------- ------------
         4           4          187
```

FIGURE 6-7 Displaying information about the segment

The output indicates that the tablespace number is 4, the segment header file number is 4 and the segment header block number is 187.

6. Next, invoke the DBVERIFY utility to verify the object. While executing the command shown below please substitute the tablespace number, segment header file number, and segment header block number appropriately. (See Figure 6-8.)

```
C:\> DBV USERID=MEDUSER/MEDUSER SEGMENT_ID=4.4.187
```



```
Command Prompt
C:\>DBV USERID=MEDUSER/MEDUSER SEGMENT_ID=4.4.187

DBVERIFY: Release 10.2.0.1.0 - Production on Thu Dec 29 17:30:38 2005

Copyright (c) 1982, 2005, Oracle.  All rights reserved.

DBVERIFY - Verification starting : SEGMENT_ID = 4.4.187


DBVERIFY - Verification complete

Total Pages Examined         : 8
Total Pages Processed (Data) : 5
Total Pages Failing   (Data) : 0
Total Pages Processed (Index): 0
Total Pages Failing   (Index): 0
Total Pages Processed (Other): 2
Total Pages Processed (Seg)  : 1
Total Pages Failing   (Seg)  : 0
Total Pages Empty            : 0
Total Pages Marked Corrupt   : 0
Total Pages Influx           : 0
Highest block SCN            : 1151046 (0.1151046)
```

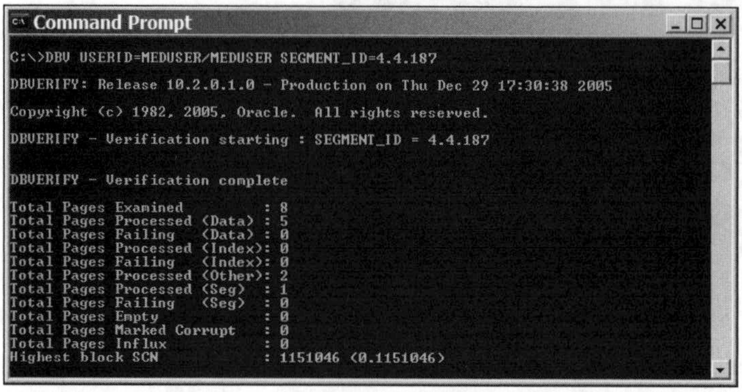

FIGURE 6-8 The output of the DBVERIFY using the SEGMENT_ID option

7. Exit the command prompt window and SQL*PLus.

The output of the DBVERIFY command In the output of the DBVERIFY command the word "pages" represent blocks. An explanation of the output has been displayed in Table 6-2.

TABLE 6-2 The output of the DBVERIFY command

Output of DBVERIFY	Description
Total Pages Examined	The number of blocks in the file.
Total Pages Processed	The number of formatted blocks that were verified.
Total Pages Failing (Data)	The number of blocks that failed the data block checking routine.
Total Pages Failing (Index)	The number of blocks that failed the index block checking routine.
Total Pages Marked Corrupt	The number of blocks for which the data block header was invalid as a result of block corruption.
Total Pages Influx	The number of blocks being read and written to at the same time. This can occur if the datafile being verified is online and the block had to be read multiple times by DBVERIFY to obtain a consistent image.

The DB_BLOCK_CHECKSUM and DB_BLOCK_CHECKING Initialization Parameters

The DB_BLOCK_CHECKSUM initialization parameter has been around since Oracle 9*i* and has a default value of TRUE. When set to TRUE, the Database Writer (DBW*n*) calculates a checksum based on the contents of the block and stores this checksum in the data block header (DBA) whenever a modified block is written back to the datafile. A checksum is a number calculated from all the bytes stored in a block. Once a checksum has been stored in the header, the checksum is once again verified when the block is read the next time. We are already aware that blocks may be corrupted during their journey to the datafiles. The checksum can be a valuable tool to verify if the contents are still intact. Upon reading the block, the checksum will once again be computed based on the contents and the checksums compared.

It should be noted that checksums are always computed for blocks that belong to the SYSTEM tablespace. This happens even if the DB_BLOCK_CHECKSUM parameter is set to FALSE. This parameter can be changed dynamically when the database is running.

If checksum verification fails the ORA-1578 error is usually raised and a message about the corruption is written to the alert log file.

The DB_BLOCK_CHECKING initialization parameter is another parameter that is associated with block corruption. This parameter by default is set to FALSE. By setting DB_BLOCK_CHECKING to TRUE the Database Writer background process verifies the entire contents of data and index blocks every time they are modified. The blocks are verified for consistency. When set to FALSE this verification is done only for the blocks of the SYSTEM tablespace. The value of the parameter can be modified dynamically. Setting it to TRUE is definitely an overhead on system performance resulting in a 1–10 percent overhead depending on the workload. Figure 6-9 illustrates a SHOW PARAMETER command that displays the current values of these parameters.

```
Oracle SQL*Plus
File  Edit  Search  Options  Help
SQL> SHOW PARAMETER DB_BLOCK

NAME                                 TYPE        VALUE
------------------------------------ ----------- ------------------------------
db_block_buffers                     integer     0
db_block_checking                    string      FALSE
db_block_checksum                    string      TRUE
db_block_size                        integer     8192
SQL>
```

FIGURE 6-9 Initialization parameters associated with blocks

The V$ Views

The V$ views that can be used to identify corrupt blocks are the V$DATABASE_BLOCK_CORRUPTION, V$BACKUP_CORRUPTION and V$COPY_CORRUPTION views. These views are used when backups are performed using Recovery Manager. If a corrupt block is found during the process of backup, information about the block will be written to the V$DATABASE_BLOCK_CORRUPTION view.

A historical record of all corrupt blocks found during the creation of backupsets can be viewed using the V$BACKUP_CORRUPTION view. A record of all corrupt blocks found during the creation of images copies can be obtained from the V$COPY_CORRUPTION view. These views obtain their information from the control file.

RECOVERING FROM BLOCK CORRUPTION

When corruption has been identified it is important to resolve it; otherwise the block may become unusable. Recovering from block corruption is one of the hardest and most challenging tasks performed by a database administrator. The Oracle Database provides different methods to eliminate or recover from block corruption. They include:

- Restoring and Recovering from backup
- The DBMS_REPAIR package
- Block Media Recovery feature of Recovery Manager
- Dropping and Re-creating the object

Restoring and Recovering Corrupt Blocks Using a Backup

This is one of the most commonly used options for resolving block corruption errors. It is widely used in the event of a hard corruption or if many blocks are corrupted. If the database is running in archivelog mode and a good backup exists that contains the blocks that have been corrupted, then this method can be used.

For example, consider a situation where many blocks on a certain disk are corrupted and the disk is inaccessible. If a backup taken before the blocks were corrupted, exists, then you can restore the datafiles using the backup to an alternate disk and perform recovery using the archivelog files. This option known as "Complete Recovery" was discussed in detail in Chapter 3 and is suitable only if you are running the database in archivelog mode. The recovery may be performed using the user-managed method, RMAN, or Enterprise Manager. However, it can be a time-consuming operation if a large number of datafiles need to be restored.

The DBMS_REPAIR Package

The DBMS_REPAIR is an Oracle-supplied package that can be used to detect and repair block corruption in specific objects of an Oracle database. The DBMS_REPAIR utility can detect corrupt blocks in tables and indexes. The package consists of a number of useful procedures that perform its functions. Table 6-3 describes some procedures of the DBMS_REPAIR package.

TABLE 6-3 Procedures included in the DBMS_REPAIR package

Procedure Name	Description
ADMIN_TABLES	Allows you to perform administrative functions on the repair and orphan key tables.
CHECK_OBJECT	Detects and reports corruptions in a table or index.
FIX_CORRUPT_BLOCKS	Marks blocks that were identified as corrupt, as "Software corrupt."

TABLE 6-3 Procedures included in the DBMS_REPAIR package (continued)

Procedure Name	Description
SKIP_CORRUPT_BLOCKS	Allows you to skip the corrupt blocks during table and index scans. If the procedure is not invoked, there is the possibility of the ORA-1578 error being generated.
DUMP_ORPHAN_KEYS	Reports the index entries that point to rows in the corrupt blocks. These index entries are populated into the orphan key table.
REBUILD_FREELISTS	Rebuilds the freelist of the object.

The ADMIN_TABLES procedure Before you can make use of the DBMS_REPAIR package you must create two tables called REPAIR_TABLE and ORPHAN_TABLE. The REPAIR_TABLE is used to hold details of all tables that have corrupt blocks. The ORPHAN_TABLE contains information about the index entries that point to corrupt data blocks.

The REPAIR_TABLE and ORPHAN_TABLE can be created by invoking the ADMIN_TABLES procedure of the DBMS_REPAIR package.

The syntax of the ADMIN_TABLES procedure is:

```
DBMS_REPAIR.ADMIN_TABLES (
table_name  IN   VARCHAR2,
table_type  IN   BINARY_INTEGER,
action      IN   BINARY_INTEGER,
tablespace  IN   VARCHAR2 DEFAULT NULL);
```

where:

table_name – The name of the REPAIR_TABLE. You may use any name of your choice.

table_type –The type of table being created. The options are REPAIR_TABLE or ORPHAN_TABLE.

action – This directive indicates the kind of action being performed on the table. The values the directive can take are CREATE_ACTION, PURGE_ACTION, or DROP_ACTION. CREATE_ACTION specifies that the table is to be created. PURGE_ACTION specifies that the rows of the table are to be deleted. DROP_ACTION specifies that the table needs to be dropped.

tablespace – The name of the tablespace in which the REPAIR_TABLE will reside.

Practice 3: The ADMIN_TABLES procedure of DBMS_REPAIR

In this practice the REPAIR_TABLE and ORPHAN_TABLE will be created using the ADMIN_TABLES procedure of the DBMS_REPAIR package.

1. Log on to SQL*Plus as a user with SYSDBA privileges.

   ```
   SQL> CONNECT DB_ADMIN/DB_ADMIN AS SYSDBA
   ```

2. Write the following PL/SQL block that creates the REPAIR_TABLE with the name REPAIR_MED in the USERS tablespace.

   ```
   SQL> BEGIN
        DBMS_REPAIR.ADMIN_TABLES (
        TABLE_NAME => 'REPAIR_MED',
        TABLE_TYPE => DBMS_REPAIR.REPAIR_TABLE,
        ACTION     => DBMS_REPAIR.CREATE_ACTION,
        TABLESPACE => 'USERS'
        );
   ```

```
END;
/
PL/SQL procedure successfully completed.
SQL>
```

3. Next, create the orphan table called ORPHAN_MED in the USERS tablespace.

```
SQL> BEGIN
     DBMS_REPAIR.ADMIN_TABLES (
     TABLE_NAME => 'ORPHAN_MED',
     TABLE_TYPE => DBMS_REPAIR.ORPHAN_TABLE,
     ACTION     => DBMS_REPAIR.CREATE_ACTION,
     TABLESPACE => 'USERS'
     );
     END;
     /
PL/SQL procedure successfully completed.
SQL>
```

4. Remain connected to SQL*Plus for the next practice.

The CHECK_OBJECTS procedure The CHECK_OBJECTS procedure of the DBMS_REPAIR package may be invoked to search the blocks for corruption. The CHECK_OBJECTS procedure accepts a number of parameters and sends out a numeric value representing the number of corrupt blocks found (CORRUPT_COUNT). The procedure accepts many arguments; however, we will discuss some of the commonly used arguments.

The syntax of the CHECK_OBJECT procedure is displayed:

```
DBMS_REPAIR.CHECK_OBJECT
(schema_name        IN  VARCHAR2,
 object_name        IN  VARCHAR2,
 object_type        IN  BINARY_INTEGER DEFAULT TABLE_OBJECT,
 repair_table_name IN  VARCHAR2  DEFAULT 'REPAIR_TABLE',
 corrupt_count      OUT BINARY_INTEGER);
```

where:

schema_name – The schema name of the object being checked for block corruption.

object_name – The name of the object being checked for block corruption.

object_type – The type of object being checked. The values of the parameter can either be TABLE_OBJECT or INDEX_OBJECT.

repair_table_name – The name of repair table that was created by using the ADMIN_TABLES procedure.

corrupt_count – The output of the CHECK_OBJECT procedure containing the number of blocks that were found corrupt.

Practice 4: The CHECK_OBJECTS procedure of DBMS_REPAIR

In this practice you will execute the CHECK_OBJECT procedure of the DBMS_REPAIR package. The procedure checks the C6_PHY table belonging to MEDUSER for corrupt blocks.

1. Write the following PL/SQL block to detect corrupt blocks in the C6_PHY table.

```
SQL> SET SERVEROUT ON
SQL> DECLARE
     CORR_CNT     NUMBER := 0;
     BEGIN
```

```
        DBMS_REPAIR.CHECK_OBJECT (
        SCHEMA_NAME       => 'MEDUSER',
        OBJECT_NAME       => 'C6_PHY',
        OBJECT_TYPE       => DBMS_REPAIR.TABLE_OBJECT,
        REPAIR_TABLE_NAME => 'REPAIR_MED',
        CORRUPT_COUNT     => CORR_CNT);
        DBMS_OUTPUT.PUT_LINE('Corrupt Blocks ='|| CORR_CNT);
        END;
        /
Corrupt Blocks = 0
PL/SQL procedure successfully completed.
SQL>
```

If any corrupt blocks were found they would have been displayed by the CORR_CNT variable. The variable holds the value 0 after the execution of the CHECK_OBJECT procedure indicating that no corrupt blocks were found in the C6_PHY table.

2. Remain connected to SQL*Plus.

The FIX_CORRUPT_BLOCKS procedure The next step after checking blocks for corruption is to fix the corrupt blocks. The Oracle database does not actually fix or repair corrupt blocks but marks them as "software corrupt". If the corruption detected is a bad row in a block the entire block is marked corrupt. This is achieved by means of the FIX_CORRUPT_BLOCKS procedure.

The FIX_CORRUPT_BLOCKS procedure receives a number of arguments and sends out a single value in the form of the OUT parameter. This is a count of the number of blocks that were fixed. This number should be the same as the number of corrupt blocks found. The syntax of the FIX_CORRUPT_BLOCKS procedure is:

```
DBMS_REPAIR.FIX_CORRUPT_BLOCKS (
   schema_name       IN  VARCHAR2,
   object_name       IN  VARCHAR2,
   object_type       IN  BINARY_INTEGER DEFAULT TABLE_OBJECT,
   repair_table_name IN  VARCHAR2 DEFAULT 'REPAIR_TABLE',
   fix_count         OUT BINARY_INTEGER);
```

where:

fix_count – The output of the procedure indicating the number of blocks that were fixed or marked corrupt.

All other clauses have the same meaning as they did in the procedures already explained.

Practice 5: The FIX_CORRUPT_BLOCKS procedure of DBMS_REPAIR

In this practice you will execute the FIX_CORRUPT_BLOCKS procedure of the DBMS_REPAIR package.

1. In this step you will execute the FIX_CORRUPT_BLOCKS procedure. The PL/SQL block fixes corrupt blocks into the C6_PHY table belonging to MEDUSER and displays the count using of the FIXCNT variable.

```
SQL> DECLARE
     FIXCNT    NUMBER := 0;
     BEGIN
```

```
    DBMS_REPAIR.FIX_CORRUPT_BLOCKS(
    SCHEMA_NAME        => 'MEDUSER',
    OBJECT_NAME        => 'C6_PHY',
    REPAIR_TABLE_NAME => 'REPAIR_MED',
    FIX_COUNT          => FIXCNT);
    DBMS_OUTPUT.PUT_LINE('The number of blocks fixed='
|| FIXCNT);
    END;
    /
The number of blocks fixed = 0
PL/SQL procedure successfully completed.
SQL>
```


2. Remain connected to SQL*Plus.

After the execution of the FIX_CORRUPT_BLOCKS procedure the variable FIXCNT holds a count of the number of blocks that were repaired. In the example code, the variable holds a value 0 indicating that no blocks were fixed.

The SKIP_CORRUPT_BLOCKS procedure After the corrupt blocks have been marked "software corrupt" you can then execute the SKIP_CORRUPT_BLOCKS procedure of the DBMS_REPAIR package. When a skip is set, the corrupt blocks will be skipped during table and index scans.

The syntax of the SKIP_CORRUPT_BLOCKS procedure is:

```
DBMS_REPAIR.SKIP_CORRUPT_BLOCKS (
schema_name IN VARCHAR2,
object_name IN VARCHAR2,
object_type IN BINARY_INTEGER DEFAULT TABLE_OBJECT,
flags       IN BINARY_INTEGER DEFAULT SKIP_FLAG);
```

where:

flags – Can take the value SKIP_FLAG or NOSKIP_FLAG. SKIP_FLAG indicates the blocks must be skipped when a read is done. If NOSKIP_FLAG is specified and corrupt blocks are read, an ORA-1578 error will be generated.

Practice 6: The SKIP_CORRUPT_BLOCKS procedure of DBMS_REPAIR

In this practice you will execute the SKIP_CORRUPT_BLOCKS procedure of the DBMS_REPAIR package.

1. The following PL/SQL block will ensure that the Oracle server will skip corrupt blocks when reading the C6_PHY table.

```
SQL> BEGIN
     DBMS_REPAIR.SKIP_CORRUPT_BLOCKS(
     SCHEMA_NAME => 'MEDUSER',
     OBJECT_NAME => 'C6_PHY',
     FLAGS       => DBMS_REPAIR.SKIP_FLAG);
     END;
     /
PL/SQL procedure successfully completed.
```

2. Remain connected to SQL*Plus.

The DUMP_ORPHAN_KEYS procedure If the object that was fixed was a table then the index entries that point to rows in the corrupt blocks would need to be identified. The DUMP_ORPHAN_KEYS procedure can be used to identify these index entries. The index entries (key value, ROWID) that point to rows in corrupt blocks are inserted into the orphan key table that was also created by executing the ADMIN_TABLES procedure. An index that points to corrupt blocks can be rebuilt using the ALTER INDEX...REBUILD command.

The syntax of the DUMP_ORPHAN_KEYS procedure of the DBMS_REPAIR package is displayed below. The procedure accepts a number of arguments but sends out only one value which is the KEY_COUNT. This parameter indicates the number of orphaned index entries.


```
DBMS_REPAIR.DUMP_ORPHAN_KEYS (
schema_name        IN  VARCHAR2,
object_name        IN  VARCHAR2,
object_type        IN  BINARY_INTEGER DEFAULT INDEX_OBJECT,
repair_table_name  IN  VARCHAR2 DEFAULT 'REPAIR_TABLE',
orphan_table_name  IN  VARCHAR2 DEFAULT 'ORPHAN_KEYS_TABLE',
key_count          OUT BINARY_INTEGER);
```

where:

orphan_table_name – The name of the orphan table created in the first step.

key_count – The output the procedure holding a count of the number of orphaned index entries.

All the other clauses have the same meaning as they did in the already discussed procedures of the DBMS_REPAIR package.

Practice 7: The DUMP_ORPHAN_KEYS procedure of DBMS_REPAIR

In this practice example you will execute the DUMP_ORPHAN_KEYS procedure.

1. The PL/SQL block shown below identifies the number of index entries that point to corrupt blocks and displays a count of the orphaned index entries in KEY_CNT variable.

```
SQL> DECLARE
     KEYCNT     NUMBER := 0;
     BEGIN
     DBMS_REPAIR.DUMP_ORPHAN_KEYS(
     SCHEMA_NAME       => 'MEDUSER',
     OBJECT_NAME       => 'C6_INDX_PNAME',
     OBJECT_TYPE       => DBMS_REPAIR.INDEX_OBJECT,
     REPAIR_TABLE_NAME => 'REPAIR_MED',
     ORPHAN_TABLE_NAME => 'ORPHAN_MED',
     KEY_COUNT         => KEYCNT);
     DBMS_OUTPUT.PUT_LINE('The number of orphaned index entries
are = '||KEYCNT);
     END;
     /
The number of orphaned index entries are = 0
PL/SQL procedure successfully completed.
SQL>
```

2. Remain connected to SQL*Plus.

The REBUILD_FREELISTS procedure If certain blocks have been marked as corrupt by the DBMS_REPAIR, the freelist of the table has to be rebuilt. The freelist is the data structure maintained by Oracle containing all blocks of a table into which new rows can be inserted. The REBUILD_FREELISTS procedure of DBMS_REPAIR is used for this purpose. The syntax of the procedure is shown below:

```
DBMS_REPAIR.REBUILD_FREELISTS (
   schema_name   IN VARCHAR2,
   object_name   IN VARCHAR2,
   object_type   IN BINARY_INTEGER DEFAULT TABLE_OBJECT);
```


where:

object_type – The type of object being processed. The values the parameter can take are either TABLE_OBJECT or INDEX_OBJECT.

Practice 8: The REBUILD_FREELISTS procedure of DBMS_REPAIR

In this practice you will execute the REBUILD_FREELISTS procedure.

1. The PL/SQL block accepts the object details and rebuilds the freelist of the object.

```
SQL> BEGIN
     DBMS_REPAIR.REBUILD_FREELISTS(
     SCHEMA_NAME => 'MEDUSER',
     OBJECT_NAME => 'C6_PHY',
     OBJECT_TYPE => DBMS_REPAIR.TABLE_OBJECT);
     END;
     /

PL/SQL Procedure Completed Successfully
SQL>
```

2. Exit SQL*Plus.

NOTE

When executing the REBUILD_FREELISTS procedure you may receive an ORA-10614 error. This error is displayed when the object is created in a tablespace that has its SEGMENT SPACE MANAGEMENT property set to AUTO. When set to AUTO, Oracle manages free blocks automatically without the use of freelists. An example of the error has been displayed in the Figure 6-10.

In this part of the chapter you learned how the DBMS_REPAIR package and its procedures give you the ability to detect and repair blocks in tables and indexes. The advantage of this method is that you can address corruption in the blocks and continue to use the object during the process of repair.

```
Oracle SQL*Plus
File Edit Search Options Help
SQL> BEGIN
  2  DBMS_REPAIR.REBUILD_FREELISTS(
  3  SCHEMA_NAME => 'MEDUSER',
  4  OBJECT_NAME => 'C6_PHY',
  5  OBJECT_TYPE => DBMS_REPAIR.TABLE_OBJECT);
  6  END;
  7  /
BEGIN
*
ERROR at line 1:
ORA-10614: Operation not allowed on this segment
ORA-06512: at "SYS.DBMS_REPAIR", line 400
ORA-06512: at line 2
```

FIGURE 6-10 Error generated when segment exists in a tablespace that uses automatic segment space management

RMAN and Block Corruption

In the earlier chapters of this book Recovery Manager was discussed extensively. We learned how useful RMAN can be for performing backup and recovery operations. Another useful feature provided by RMAN is the ability to detect block corruption in datafiles during the process of backup. This applies to physical and logical corruption in blocks. RMAN also provides a feature that helps eliminate corruption by making use of previous backups of the corrupt blocks and applying redo using log files.

You are already familiar with how block corruption occurs and that corrupt blocks may be found in datafiles as a result of memory and I/O errors. When RMAN performs backups, the server process performing the backup reads the datafiles and generates backup files either in the form of backupsets or image copies. During the process of reading the datafiles the server process may detect corrupt blocks in the datafiles. The server process immediately writes information about the corrupt block(s) into the control file or recovery catalog. (See Figure 6-11.) The information about the corrupt blocks found during the process of backup can then be viewed by querying the V$DATABASE_BLOCK_CORRUPTION view.

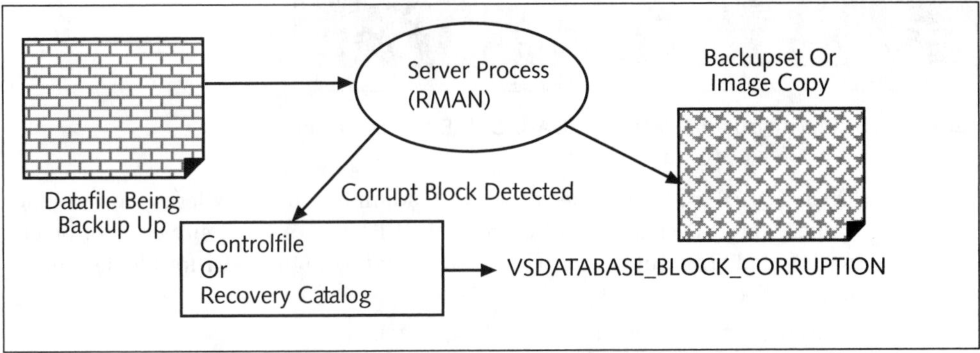

FIGURE 6-11 The V$DATABASE_BLOCK_CORRUPTION is populated with corrupt blocks during an RMAN backup

This process is done whenever a BACKUP command or a BACKUP VALIDATE command is issued.

The BACKUP VALIDATE command

The BACKUP VALIDATE command in RMAN allows you to check a datafile for physical or logical corruption without taking a backup—an output file is not generated. It is useful to verify files for corruption before they are backed up. The command can be used on datafiles and archivelog files. The commands that can be issued from the RMAN prompt are:


```
RMAN> BACKUP VALIDATE DATABASE;
RMAN> BACKUP VALIDATE ARCHIVELOG ALL;
```

Practice 9: The BACKUP VALIDATE command of RMAN

In this practice example, the BACKUP VALIDATE command will be executed on the datafiles of the database followed by the archivelog files of the database. Once the verification is done, you can query the V$DATABASE_BLOCK_CORRUPTION view to view the blocks that were identified as corrupt. (See Figure 6-12.)

1. Open RMAN and connect to the target database.

   ```
   C:\> RMAN
   RMAN> CONNECT TARGET
   ```

2. Issue the command to perform a backup validation of entire database. If you look at the output closely you will notice that the piece handle is not generated, indicating that the physical file was not created.

   ```
   RMAN> BACKUP VALIDATE DATABASE;
   ```

```
Command Prompt - RMAN
RMAN> BACKUP VALIDATE DATABASE;

Starting backup at 29-DEC-05
using channel ORA_DISK_1
channel ORA_DISK_1: starting full datafile backupset
channel ORA_DISK_1: specifying datafile(s) in backupset
input datafile fno=00001 name=C:\ORACLE\PRODUCT\10.2.0\ORADATA\DB101\SYSTEM01.DBF
input datafile fno=00003 name=C:\ORACLE\PRODUCT\10.2.0\ORADATA\DB101\SYSAUX01.DBF
input datafile fno=00002 name=C:\ORACLE\PRODUCT\10.2.0\ORADATA\DB101\UNDOTBS01.DBF
input datafile fno=00004 name=C:\ORACLE\PRODUCT\10.2.0\ORADATA\DB101\USERS01.DBF
input datafile fno=00005 name=C:\ORACLE\PRODUCT\10.2.0\ORADATA\DB101\INDX01.DBF
channel ORA_DISK_1: backup set complete, elapsed time: 00:00:25
Finished backup at 29-DEC-05
```

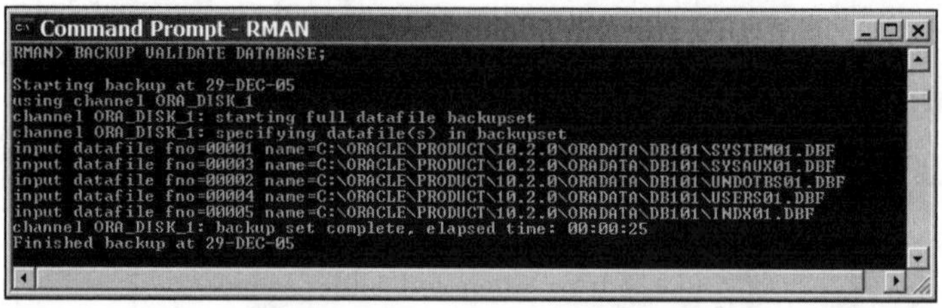

FIGURE 6-12 Performing a BACKUP VALIDATE DATABASE operation

3. Open SQL*Plus, connect as a user with administrative privileges, and execute a query on V$DATABASE_BLOCK_CORRUPTION to see if any corrupt blocks were found. The output returns no rows, indicating no corrupt blocks were found. (See Figure 6-13.)

   ```
   SQL>CONNECT DB_ADMIN/DB_ADMIN AS SYSDBA
   SQL> SELECT * FROM V$DATABASE_BLOCK_CORRUPTION;
   ```

4. Exit RMAN and SQL*Plus.

RMAN also gives you the ability to recover the corrupt blocks. This process is known as Block Media Recovery. The next section of the chapter discusses block media recovery.

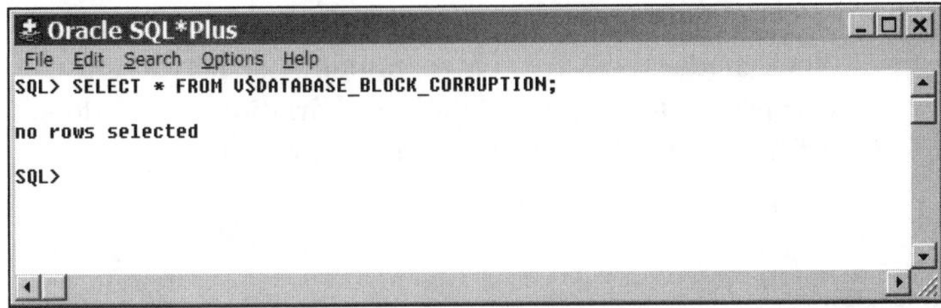

FIGURE 6-13 Displaying the contents of V$DATABASE_BLOCK_CORRUPTION

Block Media Recovery

Block Media Recovery is provided by Recovery Manager to help you restore and recover corrupt data blocks. However, keep in mind that this method is most useful when the number of blocks to be recovered are few. If many of the blocks are corrupt, then the method of completely restoring and recovering the entire file is a better option. Block media recovery can be performed only on a database running in archivelog mode. It can be performed on a mounted or open database and the datafile containing the corrupt blocks may be online during the process. However, the corrupt block(s) cannot be accessed during the process. The recovery of the corrupt block is done only using full backups of the blocks that were previously created by RMAN; this could be either backupsets or image copies. Incremental backups are not used. Redo is then applied to these blocks to recover them completely. Block Media Recovery can be done only using the BLOCKRECOVER command of RMAN.

NOTE

Only complete media recovery of individual blocks is supported. Point-in-time recovery of individual blocks cannot be performed.

In most cases of block corruption the file# and block# of the corrupt block is known when the error is reported. For example, a trace file may contain the following error message about a corrupt block.

```
ORA-01578: ORACLE data block corrupted (file # 3, block # 66)
ORA-01110: data file 3: C:\> oracle\product\10.2.0\db101\users01.dbf
```

If the file number and block number are known, the BLOCKRECOVER command can be invoked from the **RMAN** prompt to perform recovery.

The syntax of the BLOCKRECOVER command is:

```
BLOCKRECOVER DATAFILE m1 BLOCK n1 [,n2...] [DATAFILE m2 BLOCK n,[n ...]]...
```

where:

m1, m2... – The datafile number

n, n1, n2... – The block number of the corrupt block(s)

Practice 10: Block Media Recovery using RMAN

In this practice, you will perform block media recovery. The commands displayed may be issued even if you do not have corrupt blocks in your database. Variations and additional clauses of the BLOCKRECOVER command have also been demonstrated.

1. Start RMAN and connect to the target database.

```
C:\> RMAN
RMAN> CONNECT TARGET
```


2. Issue the BLOCKRECOVER command to recover three blocks (4, 32, and 75) in file #2 and two blocks (33, 68) in file #5. (See Figure 6-14.)

```
RMAN> BLOCKRECOVER DATAFILE 2 BLOCK 4, 32, 75 DATAFILE 5 BLOCK 33, 68;
```

```
Command Prompt - RMAN
RMAN> BLOCKRECOVER DATAFILE 2 BLOCK 4, 32, 75 DATAFILE 5 BLOCK 33, 68;

Starting blockrecover at 29-DEC-05
using target database control file instead of recovery catalog
allocated channel: ORA_DISK_1
channel ORA_DISK_1: sid=133 devtype=DISK

starting media recovery
media recovery complete, elapsed time: 00:00:00

Finished blockrecover at 29-DEC-05

RMAN>
```

FIGURE 6-14 The BLOCKRECOVER command issued in RMAN

During a BLOCKRECOVER operation you can also specify if the block must be recovered using an image copy (DATAFILECOPY) or backupset (BACKUPSET).

3. Using the BLOCKRECOVER command recover the block 55 and 67 of file #2 using an image copy.

```
RMAN>BLOCKRECOVER DATAFILE 2 BLOCK 55, 67 FROM DATAFILECOPY;
```

You can also instruct RMAN to restore the corrupt block using a backup that was made at a specific time. The RESTORE UNTIL TIME option of the BLOCKRECOVER command is used.

4. If you wish to perform a block recover operation on the block 5 in file 2, using a backup that was made 4 days ago, you can issue:

```
RMAN>BLOCKRECOVER DATAFILE 2 BLOCK 5 RESTORE UNTIL TIME
     'SYSDATE - 4';
```

When RMAN detects corrupt blocks during a BACKUP or BACKUP VALIDATE operation, information about the corrupt blocks is written to the V$DATABASE_BLOCK_CORRUPTION view. The corrupt blocks identified in the view can be recovered by using the CORRUPTION LIST clause of the BLOCKRECOVER command.

5. To repair all corrupt blocks identified in the V$DATABASE_BLOCK_CORRUPTION view, you can issue the following command from the RMAN prompt.

```
RMAN>BLOCKRECOVER CORRUPTION LIST;
```

6. Exit RMAN.

A record all of corrupt blocks can also be viewed using the V$BACKUP_CORRUPTION and V$COPY_CORRUPTION views. These views get their information from the control file and display corrupt blocks detected during the process of backupset creation and image copy creation respectively.

Dropping and Re-creating the Object

Finally, if nothing else works to help resolve the block corruption and if no previous backup of the object exists (such as an export), the only option the database administrator would have is to drop and re-create the object. The database administrator may also try using the CREATE TABLE... AS SELECT command to salvage some rows of the table that reside in the good blocks.

In this chapter, we learned how corruption can creep into an Oracle database block and the different techniques available to help administrators detect and resolve them. In Chapter 7, we will move into another area of administering an Oracle 10g database commonly known as the Common Manageability Infrastructure.

Chapter Summary

- An Oracle block is the smallest unit of input/output that the Oracle database can read or write.
- Block corruption is a rarely occurring error that may be very difficult to recover from.
- The address of the block is in its header in an area known as the data block address (DBA).
- When a modified block is written back to disk from the database buffer cache it has to pass through memory modules and disk components.
- A block can become corrupt due to memory or caching problems, bad hardware or firmware, mechanical problems, and even operating system software or Oracle software errors.
- Block corruption can be of two kinds: media corruption and logical corruption. Media corruption occurs when the blocks are written to defective media devices. Logical corruption occurs when the Oracle block format is no longer consistent.
- The methods available to help detect corrupt blocks include Error Messages, The ANALYZE command, the DBVERIFY utility, DB_BLOCK_CHECKSUM, and DB_BLOCK_CHECKING initialization parameters and the V$DATABASE_BLOCK_CORRUPTION views.
- The methods available to help resolve corrupt blocks include the recovery methods, the DBMS_REPAIR package and Block Media Recovery using RMAN.

Syntax Guide

SYNTAX GUIDE		
Command	**Description**	**Example**
ANALYZE TABLE tablename VALIDATE STRUCTURE [CASCADE]	Used to validate or verify a table for data integrity. The CASCADE option will result in a validation of all dependent objects.	SQL> ANALYZE TABLE C6_PHY VALIDATE STRUCTURE;
ANALYZE INDEX indexname VALIDATE STRUCTURE	Used to validate or verify an index for integrity.	SQL> ANALYZE INDEX C6_PHY_IDX VALIDATE STRUCTURE;
C:\> DBV	Executable used to invoke the DBVERIFY executable.	C:\> DBV FILE=C:\DATA01.DBF BLOCKSIZE=4K
DB_BLOCK_CHECKSUM= [TRUE | FALSE]	If the parameter is TRUE, a checksum is calculated based on the blocks contents and will be stored in the data block header. If set to FALSE, the checksumming feature is turned off.	Init<sid>.ora DB_BLOCK_CHECKSUM = TRUE
DB_BLOCK_CHECKING =[TRUE | FALSE]	If the parameter is set to TRUE, checksumming is done for all datafile blocks.	Init<sid>.ora DB_BLOCK_CHECKING =TRUE

SYNTAX GUIDE		
Command	Description	Example
BACKUP VALIDATE	A command executed in RMAN to perform a validation of all data blocks. The backup file will not be generated; however it can be used to verify the integrity of the datafile prior to backup.	RMAN> BACKUP VALIDATE;
BLOCKRECOVER DATAFILE m1 BLOCK n1	An RMAN command to perform recovery of one or more individual blocks.	RMAN> BLOCKRECOVER DATAFILE 5 BLOCK 35, 78;
BLOCKRECOVER CORRUPTION LIST	An RMAN command to recover corrupt blocks that have been identified and have been populated in the V$ views.	RMAN> BLOCKRECOVER CORRUPTION LIST;

Review Questions

1. Identify the characteristics of an Oracle Block. [Choose 4]
   a. The default size of an Oracle block is 2 K.
   b. The default size of an Oracle block is OS dependent.
   c. The size of an Oracle block is determined by the DB_BLOCK_SIZE initialization parameter.
   d. The Oracle block size must be a multiple of the OS block size.
   e. The OS block size must be a multiple of the Oracle block size.
   f. An Oracle block is the smallest unit of I/O.
2. Free space in an Oracle block is used for ________________ and ________________. [Choose 2]
   a. New rows being inserted.
   b. Updates to existing rows.
   c. Deletions of existing rows.
   d. Modifications made to the structure of the table.
3. Hard corruption also known as media corruption occurs when ________________.
   a. The contents of an Oracle block do not match the default Oracle format.
   b. A media failure results in the block becoming unusable.
   c. The DBWR writes inconsistent changes into the block.
   d. None of the above.

4. Soft corruption also known as logical corruption occurs when ________________.
   a. A read operation fails because the contents of the block are inconsistent with the format Oracle expects it to be in.
   b. The disk on which the file exists has bad sectors.
   c. The write operation fails because the database writer cannot identify the correct location of the block.
   d. All the above.
5. Block corruption errors are displayed as ________________ or ________________ oracle errors. [Choose 2]
   a. ORA-700
   b. ORA-600
   c. ORA-1578
   d. ORA-1568
   e. All of the above.
6. Which of the following can be used to identify block corruption? [Choose 3]
   a. The ANALYZE...COMPUTE STATISTICS command.
   b. The ANALYZE...VALIDATE STRUCTURE command.
   c. The DBVERIFY utility.
   d. The Alert Log file.
   e. The BLOCKRECOVER command.
7. The default value for the BLOCKSIZE parameter of the DBVERIFY utility is ________________.
   a. 4 K
   b. 2 K
   c. 8 K
   d. 32 K
   e. Any size.
8. Identify the characteristics of the DBVERIFY utility. [Choose 4]
   a. It is an operating system utility.
   b. It is invoked from the SQL prompt.
   c. It can be used to verify the contents of offline files only.
   d. It can be used to verify the contents of offline and online files.
   e. It can be used to verify a portion of a datafile.
   f. It can be used to verify a segment.

9. The initialization parameters that are related to block corruption include:
   a. DB_BLOCK_CHECKSUM
   b. DATABASE_BLOCK_CORRUPTION
   c. V$DATABASE_BLOCK_CORRUPTION
   d. DB_BLOCK_CHECKING
10. The default value of the DB_BLOCK_CHECKSUM is ________________.
   a. TRUE
   b. FALSE

11. The DB_BLOCK_CHECKSUM initialization parameter has been set to FALSE. Which of the following statements is TRUE?
   a. A checksum will be computed for all blocks by the DBWR process during a write.
   b. A checksum will be computed for all blocks by the DBWR process during a read.
   c. A checksum will be computed for all blocks by the server process during a read.
   d. A checksum will be computed for blocks belonging to the SYSTEM tablespace.
   e. A checksum will be computed and stored along with row data.
12. Mary is the database administrator of a database called SALES. She is in the process of identifying corrupt blocks in certain important tables of the database. She is using the DBMS_REPAIR package. Identify the order in which she will execute the procedures of the package.
   a. FIX_CORRUPT_BLOCKS
   b. ADMIN_TABLES
   c. CHECK_OBJECT
   d. SKIP_CORRUPT_BLOCKS
13. Which of the following procedures of DBMS_REPAIR is used to delete the contents of the REPAIR and ORPHAN tables?
   a. CHECK_OBJECT
   b. ADMIN_TABLES
   c. REBUILD_FREELISTS
   d. SKIP_CORRUPT_BLOCKS
   e. DUMP_ORPHAN_TABLES
14. The output of the CHECK_OBJECT procedure is the ________________ of the corrupt blocks.
   a. data block address
   b. corrupt rows
   c. count
   d. object ID
   e. object name

15. Which of the following statements about Block Media Recovery is TRUE?
    a. Can be performed using SQL*Plus.
    b. Can be performed using RMAN.
    c. Can be performed using both SQL*Plus and RMAN.
    d. Can be performed on all blocks.
16. Josh is the senior database administrator at ABC, Inc. He is responsible for managing two large databases. While going through the log files he notices an error associated with block corruption. What two pieces of information does he need to know to perform a recovery of the corrupt blocks using the BLOCKRECOVER command?
    a. The relative datafile number.
    b. The absolute datafile number.
    c. The absolute block number.
    d. The relative block number.
    e. The object ID of the segment containing the corruption.
    f. The tablespace number with the corrupt blocks.
17. Identify the different ways in which blocks can be recovered in Oracle. [Choose 3]
    a. Restoring and recovering corrupt blocks using backups.
    b. Importing a table from a valid export.
    c. The block media recovery feature of SQL*Plus.
    d. Dropping and re-creating the object.
    e. The ANALYZE command.
18. The ________________ command can be used to verify if a backup will be free of corrupt blocks without actually taking a backup.
19. The ________________ data dictionary view holds a count of all corrupt blocks found during the process of taking a backup.
20. The ________________ option of the BLOCKRECOVER command can be used to recover corrupt blocks that were identified using the BACKUP VALIDATE command.

Hands-On Assignments

Assignment 6-1 Determining the database block size

1. Open SQL*Plus and connect as the user DB_ADMIN.
2. Using the SHOW PARAMETER command display the current default block size.
3. Issue a query on the V$DATAFILE view, to determine the names of the datafiles (NAME) and their block sizes (BLOCK_SIZE) for all the datafiles of the database. Note: Since Oracle 9*i* it is possible to create tablespaces with non-standard block sizes.
4. Exit SQL*Plus.

Assignment 6-2 Analyzing tables in the MEDUSER schema

1. Using SQL*Plus, connect as the user MEDUSER.
2. Using a query on the USER_TABLES data dictionary view, display the names of all tables (TABLE_NAME) that belong to the user MEDUSER.
3. From the list of table names that are displayed in the output, choose any one name and issue the ANALYZE command to verify it for block corruption.
4. Exit SQL*Plus.

Assignment 6-3 Analyzing indexes in the MEDUSER schema

1. Using SQL*Plus, connect as the user MEDUSER.
2. Using a query on the USER_INDEXES data dictionary view, display the names of all indexes that are created on the tables belonging to MEDUSER. (Hint: Describe the USER_INDEXES view to identify the column that will contain the index names.)
3. From the list of index names displayed in the output, choose any one index name and issue the ANALYZE command to verify it for block corruption.
4. Issue the command to rebuild the index that you analyzed.
5. Exit SQL*Plus.

Assignment 6-4 Using DBVERIFY to verify datafiles for block corruption

1. From SQL*Plus, connect as a user with SYSDBA privileges.
2. Issue a query on the V$DATAFILE data dictionary view to display the names and block sizes of the datafiles in your database. Note the name and blocksize of any one of them.
3. Shut down the database using the IMMEDIATE option.
4. Open the operating system command prompt.
5. Issue the DBVERIFY command to verify the datafile you noted in step 2. Make sure you specify the entire path. This datafile is currently offline. Use the option that displays a dot on the screen after every 25 blocks are verified. Send the output of the DBVERIFY command to a file called DBV64.log. Specify the blocksize parameter if it is not 2 K.
6. View the output of the DBVERIFY command by opening the file DBV64.LOG. (You can use the **TYPE *filename*** command at the command prompt to view its contents.)
7. Were any corrupt blocks detected?
8. Exit the command prompt window.
9. Return to the SQL*Plus window and startup the database.
10. Exit SQL*Plus.

Assignment 6-5 Modifying parameters associated with Checksumming

1. From SQL*Plus, connect as a user with SYSDBA privileges.
2. Using the SHOW PARAMETER commands, display the values of DB_BLOCK_CHECKSUM and DB_BLOCK_CHECKING initialization parameters.
3. If the value of the DB_BLOCK_CHECKING is currently FALSE, issue an ALTER SYSTEM command to change it to TRUE. The change you make should affect only the current instance (set SCOPE=MEMORY).

4. Issue the SHOW PARAMETER command to confirm the change in value.
5. Exit SQL*Plus.

Assignment 6-6 Creating the ADMIN tables required for detecting block corruption using the DBMS_REPAIR package

1. Using SQL*Plus, connect as a user with SYSDBA privileges.
2. Using the appropriate procedure of the DBMS_REPAIR package, create a repair table called REPAIR_66 in the SYSTEM tablespace.

3. Using the appropriate procedure of the DBMS_REPAIR package, create an orphan table called ORPHAN_66 in the SYSTEM tablespace.
4. Remain connected to SQL*Plus for the next practice.

Assignment 6-7 Checking an object for corruption using the DBMS_REPAIR package

1. From SQL*Plus, connect as a user with SYSDBA privileges.
2. Issue the following query on the TABLE_NAME column of the DBA_TABLES data dictionary view and display the names of all tables belonging to the user MEDUSER. Note any one of the names displayed.

   ```
   SQL>SELECT TABLE_NAME FROM DBA_TABLES WHERE OWNER='MEDUSER';
   ```

3. Write a PL/SQL block to check the object for corruption using the DBMS_REPAIR package. Use the name that you noted in step 2 of this assignment.
4. Were any corrupt blocks identified?
5. Remain connected to SQL*Plus for the next practice.

Assignment 6-8 Fixing corrupt blocks using the DBMS_REPAIR package

1. From SQL*Plus, connect as a user with administrative privileges.
2. Write a PL/SQL block to fix any blocks that were identified corrupt in Assignment 6-7.
3. Were any corrupt blocks fixed?
4. Remain connected to SQL*Plus for the next practice.

Assignment 6-9 Dumping orphan keys for corrupt blocks found in the table

1. From SQL*Plus, connect as a user with SYSDBA privileges.
2. Write a query on the DBA_INDEXES view to obtain the names of all indexes in the MEDUSER schema that exist on the table you noted in Step 2 of Assignment 6-7.

   ```
   SQL>SELECT INDEX_NAME FROM DBA_INDEXES WHERE OWNER='MEDUSER'
   AND TABLE_NAME=<tablename>;
   ```

3. Select an index from the output displayed and write a PL/SQL block that will identify all the index entries corresponding to the corrupt blocks found on the table that was checked in Assignment 6-7.
4. How many orphaned keys were detected?
5. Remain connected to SQL*Plus for the next practice.

Assignment 6-10 Skipping corrupt blocks found in the table.

1. From SQL*Plus, connect as a user with SYSDBA privileges.
2. Write a PL/SQL block that will instruct reads and writes to skip the corrupt blocks found in the table.
3. Remain connected to SQL*Plus for the next practice.

Assignment 6-11 Rebuilding the freelists of the table

1. From SQL*Plus, connect as a user with SYSDBA privileges.
2. Write a PL/SQL block that will rebuild freelists of the table with corrupt blocks. An error may be generated indicating the operation cannot succeed in case the tablespace in which the table exists makes use of AUTO SEGMENT SPACE MANAGEMENT.
3. Exit SQL*Plus.

Assignment 6-12 Performing a backup validate operation using RMAN

1. Open RMAN and connect to the target database.
2. Issue the command to verify if all the datafiles of the database can be backed up. Do not generate an output backupset.
3. Issue the command to verify if all the datafiles belonging to the USERS tablespace can be backed up. Do not generate an output backupset. (Use the TABLESPACE tablespacename directive.)
4. Issue the command to verify if all the archivelog files of the database can be backed up. Do not generate an output backupset. (Use the ARCHIVELOG ALL directive.)
5. Remain connected to RMAN for the next practice.

Assignment 6-13 Performing Block Media Recovery

1. Open RMAN if it is not already open and connect to the target database.
2. Issue the command to recover the block 56 and 93 of the datafile number 2.
3. Issue the command to recover the block 73 of file# 3 using a datafilecopy during the restoration step.
4. Issue the command to recover the block 44 and 32 of datafile number 2. Instruct RMAN to use a backup that was created more than a week ago during the restoration process.
5. Exit RMAN.

Case Study

1. The database administrators at Keller Medical Center wish to prepare themselves for all types of errors they may encounter with the database. A major concern is block corruption. Draft a memo indicating the type of error you may encounter and outline the method you would use to resolve the error. Identify the tools available to detect block corruption and what methods in the database can help eliminate the error if it occurs.

2. Identifying errors using DBVERIFY and performing a recovery using RMAN
   a. Connect as the user DB_ADMIN with SYSDBA privileges enabled.
   b. Create a tablespace called BREC, with a datafile called BREC01.DBF having a size of 500K.
   c. Create a table called TREC in the tablespace BREC having a single column.
   d. Insert some rows into the table TREC.
   e. Using RMAN take a backup of the tablespace BREC.
   f. Open the file BREC01.DBF using the Notepad editor.
   g. Select some of the content visible in the file and delete it. Save the file and replace its contents with the change you just made.
   h. Bounce the database.
   i. Did you receive an error upon starting the database?
   j. View the contents of the DBWR trace file that holds information about the error. The error indicates a file size mismatch.
   k. Run the DBVERIFY utility on the file to see if any blocks were marked corrupt.
   l. Using RMAN, recover from the error.

CHAPTER 7

AUTOMATIC DATABASE MANAGEMENT

LEARNING OBJECTIVES

After completing this chapter, you should be able to understand the following:

- Performance Tuning
- Common Manageability Infrastructure
- Automatic Workload Repository
- Advisory Framework
- SQL Tuning Advisor
- SQL Access Advisor
- Automatic Undo Retention Tuning

EXAM OBJECTIVES COVERED IN THIS CHAPTER INCLUDE:

- Automatic Database Management
- Use the Database Advisors to gather information about your database
- Use the SQL Tuning Advisor to improve database performance
- Use automatic undo retention tuning

INTRODUCTION

The earlier chapters of this book focused on backup and recovery related functions of a database administrator. In this chapter we move to another area of a database administrator's job function—performance tuning. Performance tuning involves making sure the applications are well tuned, the database is responsive and running optimally, and the resources required for smooth operation are available. This job function requires knowledge, experience, and keen attention to detail. It is also one of the most demanding tasks performed by the DBA.

In this chapter, you will see how this new release of the Oracle 10*g* software has made this challenging task relatively simple. A database administrator is no longer burdened with constantly monitoring the database to identify and track problems. Performing tuning is now largely a function of the Oracle database itself. A large number of tasks that were performed manually in earlier versions of Oracle have now become automatic. This chapter focuses on automatic database management. You will be able to appreciate the many new features in the Oracle 10*g* database that automatically perform tuning-related activities without the manual intervention of the DBA.

We will discuss the components the Common Manageability Infrastructure of Oracle 10*g*, with emphasis on the Automatic Workload Repository (AWR) and the Advisory Framework. The advisors that will be discussed in detail include the Automatic Database Diagnostic Monitor (ADDM), the SQL Tuning Advisor, and the SQL Access Advisor. The chapter concludes with a discussion on automatic undo retention tuning.

THE CURRENT CHALLENGE AT KELLER MEDICAL CENTER

On Monday morning, Ryan receives an email from the DBA on weekend duty indicating that a certain report that normally takes about 20 minutes took a little over 3 hours to complete. Users have been complaining that the database has been responding slowly. Ryan tries to recall what change(s) were made to the report and recalls that some of the reports had been modified because some new tables had been added to the database. Ryan draws out an action plan to resolve the problem and presents it to Anita, the senior DBA at Keller Medical Center. He has decided to come in on the following Saturday and monitor the database and guarantees a solution within 10 days. Anita, however, reminds him that they were now using an Oracle 10g database. The database would have a record of the events that occurred on Saturday and all Ryan would have to do is examine the advisory framework to help him in his troubleshooting.

SETUP FOR THE CHAPTER

To successfully complete the hands-on practice examples demonstrated in the chapter, execute the following steps.

1. Start SQL*Plus and connect as the user MEDUSER.

   ```
   SQL> CONNECT MEDUSER/MEDUSER
   ```

2. Execute the **c7_setup.sql** script from the Chapter07 folder of the student datafiles. The script creates three tables, C7_PATIENT, C7_PHYSICIAN, and PHYSICIAN_SPECIALITY, with some rows in them.

   ```
   SQL> START <PATH>\C7_SETUP.SQL
   ```

3. Exit SQL*Plus.

AN OVERVIEW OF PERFORMANCE TUNING

An important task performed by the DBA involves configuring, maintaining, and ensuring that the database is running optimally. The administrator must ensure that the database is available, the applications are able to access the data, and the required resources are available at all times. This requires the DBA to not only perform day-to-day maintenance tasks, but keep the database well tuned as well. The database must run at peak performance at all times. This requires extensive knowledge, skill, and experience on the part of the administrator.

The task of tuning a database is not an easy one, because a problem is usually created by multiple factors. Tuning one aspect may result in performance degradation elsewhere, and the administrator must be aware of the trade-offs. Performance tuning is classified into two categories: proactive and reactive. Proactive performance tuning involves preparing, planning, designing, and developing the performance architecture during the initial stages of implementation. This involves proper hardware and software selection, capacity planning, understanding user requirements, average workload on the system, and tailoring the system carefully based on the needs of the application and system.

Reactive tuning is done once your system is in place. It involves maintaining and tuning the system within the boundaries of the existing components. In most environments, administrators spend their time reacting to problems after they are observed. A typical example could be a complaint from a user that a certain report takes too much time to complete. Reports are generated by querying on one or more tables. Queries may be written in many ways, some more efficient than others. A developer with a limited knowledge of SQL may not be aware of SQL's finer points and may write an inefficient query. A database administrator analyzing the poorly executing report needs to be aware of the tools and methods available in the Oracle database to come up with an appropriate solution. This is reactive tuning. Proactive tuning could have been accomplished if the developer, with the help of the administrator in some cases, had designed the query optimally in the first place.

Performance tuning should always be done in a systematic and methodical manner, with a complete documentation of all changes made. Addition of hardware and memory is rarely an answer to performance problems.

Further, surveys suggest that more than 50 percent of the administrators' time is spent monitoring and tuning the database—a difficult task to perform properly. Some positive news amidst the problems posed by performance tuning lies in Oracle's claim that the Oracle Database 10*g* is a self-managing database. The Oracle Database 10*g* comes preconfigured with intelligence to guide an administrator when problems arise. Many of the tedious database and tuning tasks are performed automatically. All this is achieved by the Oracle 10*g* feature popularly known as Common Manageability Infrastructure.

COMMON MANAGEABILITY INFRASTRUCTURE

Prior to Oracle 10*g*, a major part of a database administrator's responsibility involved determining solutions to various issues regarding the functioning of the Oracle database. These issues are associated with space, object performance analysis, optimizer statistics collection, segment space management, response times, disk configuration, datafile sizing, backup methods and strategy, memory structures, and growth trend analysis to name just a few. The Oracle Database 10*g* has a new manageability architecture that automatically informs an administrator about the health of the database. The Oracle database is able to monitor and provide an administrator with useful recommendations regarding the performance, memory management, space management, and disk and resource allocation issues. This is done through intelligence that is built into the Oracle software. This self-tuning capability is achieved by four major components that together form the Common Manageability Infrastructure.

The Common Manageability Infrastructure in Oracle 10*g* consists of:

- Automatic Workload Repository (AWR)
- Server-Generated Alerts
- Advisory Framework
- Automated Routine Administrative Tasks

In this chapter we will concentrate on the third component, the Advisory Framework. An overview of the Automatic Workload Repository has been presented because it forms the core of the Common Manageability Infrastructure. The Advisory Framework may use the data from the Automatic Workload Repository to analyze and generate valuable recommendations about problem areas.

Automatic Workload Repository (AWR)

Automatic Workload Repository (AWR) forms the core of the manageability infrastructure. It consists of a collection of tables—referred to as a *repository*—that holds performance-related statistical data that is gathered when the database is running based on the current workload and activity. The statistical data gathered is very precise and granular and is used by the other components of the Common Manageability Infrastructure.

The AWR data is available in memory and in repository tables. The AWR gathers raw data known as base statistics in memory. The amount of statistics gathered is dependent on the STATISTICS_LEVEL initialization parameter. This parameter controls the type of statistics collected and stored. It can take one of the following values: BASIC, TYPICAL, or ALL. When set to BASIC, the gathering of some statistics and metrics is turned off.

When set to TYPICAL, some important statistics are collected that can be used by advisories. When set to ALL, all possible statistics are captured.

Statistics gathered may belong to the following five categories:

- **Base statistics**—Raw statistics that are based on a time-model, indicating the amount of time taken to perform a certain action such as connection time. This includes time spent compiling a PL/SQL block, time taken for read and write operations, database time, CPU time, and so on. Statistics could be based on CPU and memory utilization, read/write activity on objects, and object space utilization.
- **Metrics**—Derived from the base statistics, metrics track the rate of change of activities in the database such as the average number of physical reads performed in the past 10 minutes. Metrics are particularly useful for tuning purposes. Prior to Oracle 10g, computing metrics was a job of the administrator.
- **SQL statistics**—This category is associated with SQL statements. Statistical data about a SQL statement could be the number of logical reads performed during the execution of the statement.
- **Contents of active session history**—Active session history refers to a historical record of currently active sessions. It is useful for analyzing system performance based on current activity in the database.
- **Advisor results**—Results generated by the expert analysis done by advisories, such as the SQL Tuning advisor, SQL Access advisor, Memory advisor, and the Undo advisor.

The AWR also consists of a set of persistent data dictionary views. Statistical and metric data from the in-memory location are transferred to disk every 60 minutes in the form of a snapshot that is taken by the **MMON** background process. An interval determines how often snapshots are taken. A snapshot is identified by an identifier (SNAP_ID). Snapshots may be taken manually by a database administrator if necessary. Snapshot information is accessible by means of data dictionary views. The default retention period for snapshots is seven days, after which they are automatically purged. An administrator may interact with the AWR using the Oracle Supplied DBMS_WORKLOAD_REPOSITORY package. This package can be used to create snapshots manually, as well as modify the settings such as the snapshot interval or retention period. Table 7-1 describes some of the important subprograms of the DBMS_WORKLOAD_REPOSITORY repository package.

TABLE 7-1 Subprograms of the DBMS_WORKLOAD_REPOSITORY package

Subprogram	Description
CREATE_SNAPSHOT	Used to create a manual snapshot
MODIFY_SNAPSHOT_SETTINGS	Used to configure the snapshot interval and retention period for snapshots

Statistics maintained in the repository persist through instance crashes and can be used to generate baselines. If an administrator identifies a certain snapshot pair that signifies a point of time when the database was running optimally, the administrator could create a baseline using the snapshot pair. Baselines are a means of specifying a tag to statistical data that can be referenced in the future to identify, diagnose, and track deviations from the baseline. Historical statistics are also useful for identifying trends.

The AWR is created in a system-defined **WR** schema that resides in the SYSAUX tablespace and is owned by the SYS user. The repository tables may be of two kinds, metadata tables and historical tables. The metadata tables store information about the behavior of the WR repository such as when snapshots need to be captured and what needs to be captured. The metadata tables are prefixed with WRM$. The historical tables store statistical data generated within the database. The historical statistical tables are prefixed with WRH$. Data dictionary views may be used to query the workload repository. A data dictionary view containing the historical information from the AWR has a prefix of DBA_HIST_.

An administrator may generate reports using the statistical and metric data currently stored in the workload repository. This can be done by executing the **awrrpt.sql** script. Reports can be in either text or HTML format.

Practice 1: Interacting with the Automatic Workload Repository

This practice example demonstrates the creation of a manual snapshot, modification to snapshot parameters, and the generation of a report using the awrrpt.sql script.

1. Start SQL*Plus and connect as a user with SYSDBA privileges.

```
SQL> CONNECT DB_ADMIN/DB_ADMIN AS SYSDBA
```

2. Write a query for the DBA_HIST_SNAPSHOT data dictionary view to determine the snapshots available (SNAP_ID) and when they were taken (STARTUP_TIME). Figure 7-1 displays a number of snapshots with IDs that range from 51 through 55.

```
SQL> COLUMN STARTUP_TIME FORMAT A40
SQL> SELECT SNAP_ID, STARTUP_TIME FROM
     DBA_HIST_SNAPSHOT
     ORDER BY 1, 2;
```

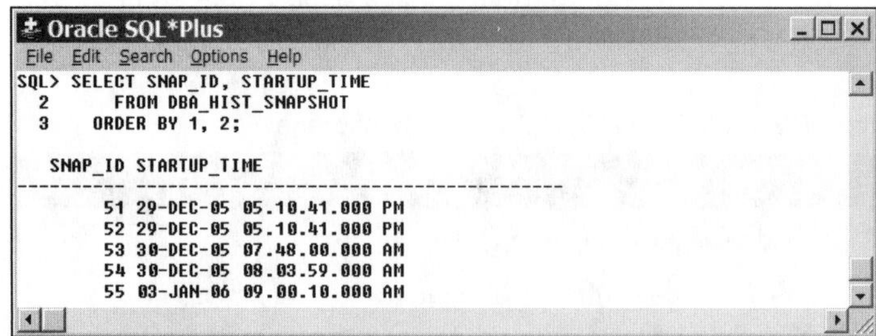

FIGURE 7-1 The snapshots available in the database

3. Take a manual snapshot of the database, using the DBMS_WORKLOAD_REPOSITORY.CREATE_SNAPSHOT packaged procedure.

```
SQL> EXECUTE DBMS_WORKLOAD_REPOSITORY.CREATE_SNAPSHOT;
```

4. Next, type the PL/SQL block shown to retain snapshots in the repository for 2 days (i.e., 2880 minutes) and set the snapshot interval to 15 minutes.

```
SQL> BEGIN
     DBMS_WORKLOAD_REPOSITORY.MODIFY_SNAPSHOT_SETTINGS
     (RETENTION => 2880, INTERVAL => 15);
     END;
     /
```


5. Take another snapshot of the database manually using the CREATE_SNAPSHOT procedure.

```
SQL> EXECUTE DBMS_WORKLOAD_REPOSITORY.CREATE_SNAPSHOT;
```

6. Rewrite the query on the DBA_HIST_SNAPSHOT data dictionary view to determine the SNAP_ID of the snapshots that you created manually. Figure 7-2 displays the snapshots that are currently available in the database. The manual snapshots taken are the last two listed in the output, 56 and 57. Note the last two SNAP_IDs displayed on your machine.

```
SQL> SELECT SNAP_ID, STARTUP_TIME FROM DBA_HIST_
     SNAPSHOT ORDER BY 1, 2;
```

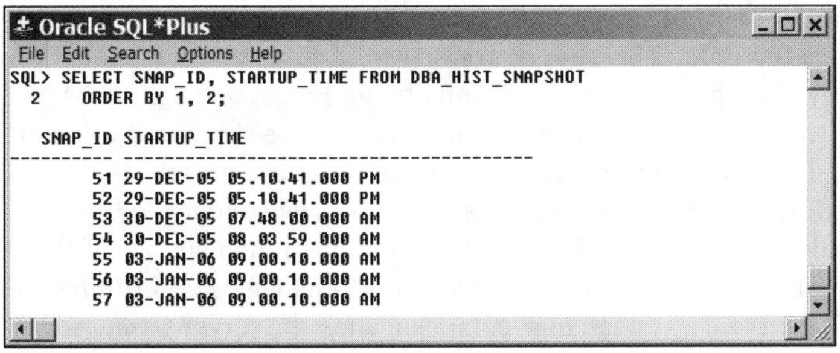

```
Oracle SQL*Plus
File Edit Search Options Help
SQL> SELECT SNAP_ID, STARTUP_TIME FROM DBA_HIST_SNAPSHOT
  2     ORDER BY 1, 2;

   SNAP_ID STARTUP_TIME
---------- ---------------------------------------
        51 29-DEC-05 05.10.41.000 PM
        52 29-DEC-05 05.10.41.000 PM
        53 30-DEC-05 07.48.00.000 AM
        54 30-DEC-05 08.03.59.000 AM
        55 03-JAN-06 09.00.10.000 AM
        56 03-JAN-06 09.00.10.000 AM
        57 03-JAN-06 09.00.10.000 AM
```

FIGURE 7-2 The snapshots available in the database

7. Execute the awrrpt.sql script from the %ORACLE_HOME%\rdbms\admin directory. A copy of the awrrpt.sql script is also provided in the Chapter07 folder of the student datafiles.

```
SQL> START <PATH>\AWRRPT.SQL
```

When prompted for the report type, type **text**.
When prompted for Enter value for num_days: **(hit the Enter key)**.
A list of all the completed snapshots will be displayed.
When prompted for the beginning snapshot, type **the snap id of the first** snapshot you noted in step 6. Continuing our example it will be 56.
When prompted for the beginning snap, type **the snap id of the second snapshot** you noted in step 6. Continuing our example it will be 57.

When prompted for the name of the report, type **AWRREP**.
The script will then run until completion.

8. Exit SQL*Plus.
9. Locate the file **AWRREP.LST** and open it using a text editor such as Notepad. View its contents. A copy of the AWRREP.LST file is available in the Chapter07 folder of the student datafiles for your reference.

The data gathered is used by the Oracle server for problem detection, self-tuning, and providing the DBA with useful recommendations. Most importantly, data collected by the AWR is used by many internal and external components of the Oracle database. The statistics also may be used by third-party applications to create customized monitoring tools and scripts.

The Advisory Framework

The statistical and metric data collected by the Automatic Workload Repository is used to analyze the activity of the database. This information is used by internal components known as advisories. Advisories provide valuable recommendations about specific problems.

Automatic Database Diagnostic Monitor (ADDM)

A common problem that database administrator's encounter is a complaint from a developer that a certain query takes too long to execute. The administrator then needs to analyze the SQL statement issued and may rewrite the statement if there is an alternate method of retrieving the desired data. The administrator would probably first view the execution plan generated by the optimizer. The columns being retrieved need to be examined to identify the need for indexes. Histograms may need to be generated to determine the way in which the data is distributed and so on. This is not always an easy task because an administrator must be aware of the various strategies available for SQL statement tuning, along with their pros and cons. This process would be much simpler if the administrator had a helper who was well versed in the art of self-managing and tuning the database. This is exactly what Oracle intended to accomplish when the server-based Advisory Framework was introduced in Oracle 10g. The advisory framework is a collection of advisories that identify bottlenecks, analyze the issue, and provide expert recommendations.

Earlier in this chapter, we saw how the AWR continuously gathers statistical data and stores it in memory. This data is useful because it is collected using the current activity of the database. We also know that the AWR takes a snapshot of the data in memory and stores it in the repository in the form of a snapshot. After a snapshot has been taken, the **Automatic Database Diagnostic Monitor (ADDM)** is automatically invoked to perform an analysis. A central component of the Advisory Framework is the ADDM. The ADDM by default analyzes the information contained in the AWR for the duration of time pertaining to the last two snapshots.

The ADDM sifts through all the data in the last two snapshots to identify bottlenecks and problems. Its main function is to identify the root causes of problems. It looks for issues related to CPU utilization, connection management, SQL and PL/SQL parsing activity, and I/O operations, to name a few.

If a certain problem is identified by the ADDM, it may invoke a specific advisor to perform a detailed analysis of the problem. For example, if a certain high-resource SQL statement is identified, the ADDM provides suggestions on how to rewrite it and directs the administrator to invoke the SQL Tuning Advisor that provides more detailed information on the problematic SQL statement. The administrator has a choice to implement or discard the suggestions.

The ADDM works in conjunction with other advisors. These advisors are specific to individual subsystems of the database. They provide detailed and comprehensive information and recommendations. For example, the Segment Advisor provides recommendations specific to space usage in segments. When a certain object is low on space, the Segment Advisor can tell the database administrator how space can be reclaimed from the object. All the advisors in the Oracle 10g database present a consistent look and feel. They are invoked in a similar manner and the results/output generated are also similar. The output of the advisors is also available through the Enterprise Manager's GUI interface, making it easy for an administrator to view the output.

The diagnosis of ADDM is displayed in the form of findings. Findings are listed in the order of their impact. Higher-impact findings are listed before those with a lower impact. When dealing with performance-related issues, an administrator must begin by viewing the findings generated by the ADDM.

As mentioned earlier, the ADDM by default analyzes the last two snapshots. If the administrator wishes to analyze statistical data between two non-adjacent snapshots, he or she may do so by invoking ADDM manually by creating an ADDM task.

To understand further how to invoke and use ADDM, a scenario is presented by Ryan. In the scenario Ryan aims to generate a large workload on a test database that will generate some I/O bottlenecks. To begin, he resizes the Database Buffer Cache to 4 megabytes, which is too small for the expected activity. He issues the command displayed below from the SQL prompt.

```
SQL> ALTER SYSTEM SET DB_CACHE_SIZE=4M;
```

The STATISTICS_LEVEL has been set to ALL, so all possible statistics will be collected. He then launches three simultaneous SQL sessions. He connects as the user DB_ADMIN within the first two sessions and MEDUSER in the third session.

Session 1: Connected as a user with SYSDBA privileges, Ryan creates a table called OBJ_DUP using the DBA_OBJECTS data dictionary view. The data from DBA_OBJECTS is then inserted multiple times into the table OBJ_DUP. These statements simulate many inserts occurring in the database.

```
SQL> CONNECT DB_ADMIN/DB_ADMIN AS SYSDBA

SQL> CREATE TABLE OBJ_DUP
     AS SELECT * FROM DBA_OBJECTS;

SQL> INSERT INTO OBJ_DUP
     SELECT * FROM DBA_OBJECTS;

SQL>/

SQL>/
```

```
SQL>/

SQL>COMMIT;
```

Session 2: Simultaneously within the next session, connected as a user with SYSDBA privileges, Ryan issues a query on the DBA_OBJECTS view. This simulates a large read occurring in the database.

```
SQL>CONNECT DB_ADMIN/DB_ADMIN AS SYSDBA
SQL>SELECT * FROM DBA_OBJECTS;
```


Session 3: Within the third SQL window, Ryan connects as the user MEDUSER and issues a PL/SQL block and displays the string 'LARGE WORKLOAD' many times. This PL/SQL block is going to keep the CPU busy for a while.

```
SQL>CONNECT MEDUSER/MEDUSER
SQL>SET SERVEROUT ON
SQL>BEGIN
    FOR I IN 1..100000 LOOP
    DBMS_OUTPUT.PUT_LINE('LARGE WORKLOAD');
    END LOOP;
    END;
    /
```

The statements issued in the three sessions generate a significant amount of I/O. The inserts will be performed in the Database Buffer Cache and would then be written to the datafiles by the Database Writer background process. The reads done would cause the blocks from the datafiles to be read into the Database Buffer Cache. The PL/SQL block results in a large amount of processing to be done by the CPU. On the whole, Ryan has tried to simulate a large workload on the machine.

In the background, during all this activity the AWR has been collecting data regarding the workload and storing it in memory. The contents of memory are then transferred to disk in the form of a snapshot. After the snapshot is taken, the ADDM is invoked automatically to identify bottlenecks, analyze the workload, and display performance findings. Ryan views the output of ADDM using Enterprise Manager.

He launches a browser, enters the URL to access Enterprise Manager, and logs on as a user with SYSDBA privileges.

The **Database Control** page is displayed. On this page, under the **Diagnostic Summary** section, a link pertaining to **Performance Findings** is displayed. The value for Performance Findings is **3**. This indicates that ADDM identified three bottlenecks during the process of analysis. (See Figure 7-3.)

Scrolling down along the page, the **Performance Analysis** section is displayed. This section describes the three performance-related issues identified by ADDM. (See Figure 7-4.)

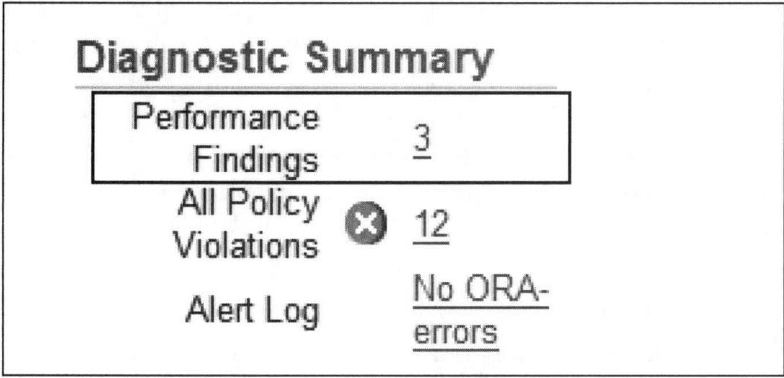

FIGURE 7-3 The Diagnostic Summary section

Related Alerts

Severity	Target Name	Target Type	Category	Name	Message	Alert Triggered	Last Value	Time
(No alerts)								

Performance Analysis

Period Start Time **Aug 16, 2005 10:59:01 AM** Period Duration (minutes) **34.88**

Impact (%)	Finding	Recommendations
30.84	The buffer cache was undersized causing significant additional read I/O.	**1** DB Configuration
30.62	SQL statements consuming significant database time were found.	**2** SQL Tuning
11.78	Hard parsing of SQL statements was consuming significant database t...	

FIGURE 7-4 The Performance Analysis section

The **Impact (%)** represents the specific impact of each problem in terms of a percentage. The **Findings** displayed by the output indicate that the size of the buffer cache was not sufficient, resulting in additional read I/O and the SQL statements that were running the database had to be tuned. Clicking the hyperlink associated with each of the findings displays the **Performance Finding Details** page. This page provides detailed information about the particular finding along with recommendations to solve the issue. (See Figure 7-5.)

Database: db101 > Advisor Central > Automatic Database Diagnostic Monitor (ADDM) > Performance Finding Details Logged in As SYS

Performance Finding Details

Database Time (minutes) **7.15** Period Start Time **Aug 16, 2005 10:59:01 AM** Period Duration (minutes) **34.88**
Task Owner **SYS** Task Name **ADDM:1031930064_1_62** Average Active Sessions **0.2**

Finding **The buffer cache was undersized causing significant additional read I/O.**
Impact (minutes) **2.2**
Impact (%) **30.84**

Recommendations

Show All Details | Hide All Details

Details	Category	Benefit (%)
Hide	DB Configuration	30.84

Message **Increase the buffer cache size by setting the value of parameter "db_cache_size" to 8 M.** (Implement)

FIGURE 7-5 The Performance Finding Details page

The ADDM suggests increasing the value of the DB_CACHE_SIZE parameter to 8 M. This would result in a 30.84% reduction in database time. The administrator is also given a choice to implement the suggestion. This can be done by selecting the **Implement** button.

The scenario presented above should give you an idea about how the ADDM identifies problems and helps the administrator to proactively manage problems in the database before they become significant.

Practice 2: Working with the Automatic Database Diagnostic Monitor

In this practice you will be able to apply the concepts that you have learned about the ADDM. The practice simulates an **application wait** problem. You will manually take a snapshot and invoke ADDM, so that you need not wait for an automatic snapshot to be taken. After the ADDM is run, you will view the findings generated by ADDM and also take corrective action to solve the wait-related issue. The practice makes use of the C7_PATIENT table that is created by executing the C7_setup.sql script.

1. Start SQL*Plus and connect as user MEDUSER.

   ```
   SQL> CONNECT MEDUSER/MEDUSER
   ```

2. Issue a command to update the records of the C7_PATIENT table so that the patients currently in ward number 10 are moved to ward number 25.

   ```
   SQL> UPDATE C7_PATIENT SET WARD_NO=25 WHERE WARD_NO=10;
   ```

   This update will result in locking all rows where the ward number is currently 10, in an exclusive mode. This implies other transactions cannot gain access to these rows for modification until the locks are released.

3. Open another SQL*Plus window, connect as MEDUSER, and delete the record of the patient with an ID of 9. This patient was in ward number 10, and the patient's row is still locked from the ongoing update. The delete will not complete until the transaction updating the row completes. This delete operation will wait, as illustrated in the cursor waiting without returning to the SQL prompt. (See Figure 7-6.)

   ```
   SQL> CONNECT MEDUSER/MEDUSER
   SQL> DELETE FROM C7_PATIENT WHERE C7_PATIENT_NO=9;
   ```

```
SQL> DELETE FROM C7_PATIENT
  2    WHERE C7_PATIENT_NO=9;
|
```

FIGURE 7-6 The DELETE statement waits for the update to complete

4. To view performance-related information regarding this activity in the database, launch **Enterprise Manager** using a browser. Log in as a user with SYSDBA privileges.
5. The **Database Control Home** page is displayed. Notice the graph in the Active Sessions Section. The WAIT on the graph will be significantly high. (See Figure 7-7.)

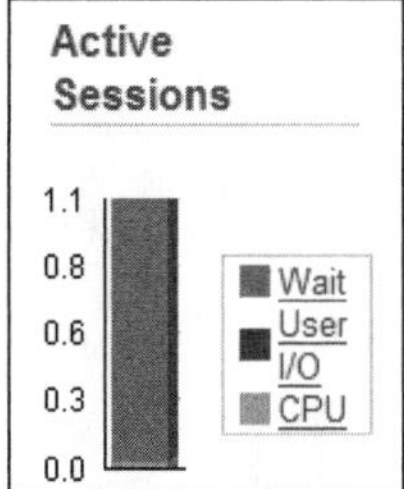

FIGURE 7-7 The Active Sessions section

6. Wait for about 5 minutes and then select the **Performance** tab from the top of the Database Control Home page.
7. The **Performance** page is displayed. On this page is the **Average Active Sessions** section that displays a graphical representation of the wait that has occurred. (See Figure 7-8.)

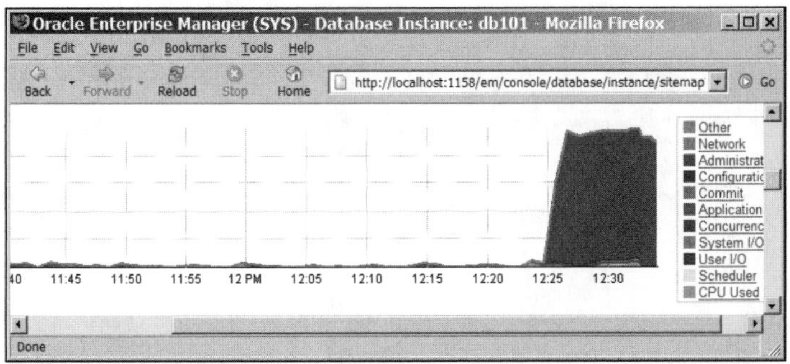

FIGURE 7-8 A graphical representation of the wait that is occurring

8. Scroll down to the bottom of the page and select the link **Snapshots** under the **Additional Monitoring Links** section.
9. To generate a performance finding for the wait that is occurring, create a snapshot of the database at this point manually. To do so select the **Create** button. A confirmation window is displayed; confirm by selecting **YES**. The snapshot will be taken.
10. After the snapshot is taken, return to the **Database Control Home** page by selecting the **Database** breadcrumb followed by the **Home** tab.
11. On this page, scroll down to the **Alerts** section. You will notice an alert **Metrics "Database Time Spent Waiting (%)" is at 91.39296 for event class "Application"** indicating SQL statements were found waiting for row lock waits. (See Figure 7-9.)

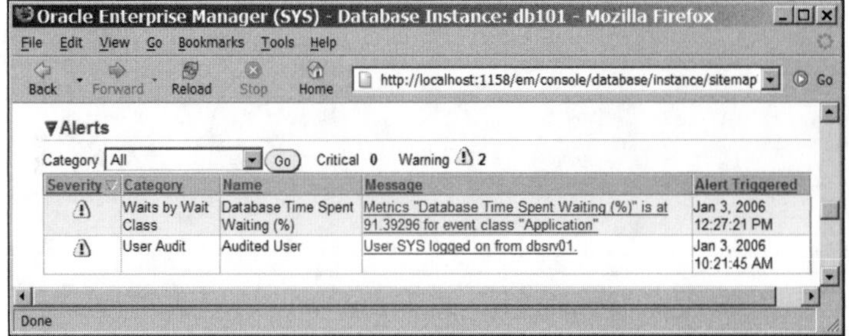

FIGURE 7-9 The wait generates an alert that is visible through Enterprise Manager

12. Select the finding that reads Metrics "Database Time Spent Waiting (%)" is at *n* for event class "Application" by clicking on its hyperlink.
13. The **Database Time Spent Waiting (%): Wait Class Application** page will be displayed. Scroll down to the **Recommendations** section. The recommended action is to run ADDM. (See Figure 7-10.)

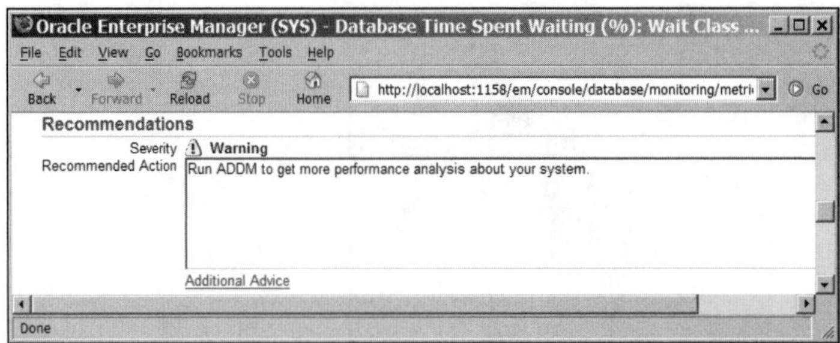

FIGURE 7-10 The recommendation is to run ADDM

14. Select the **Additional Advice** link.
15. The **Automatic Database Diagnostic Monitor (ADDM)** page will be displayed. Scroll down this page until you reach the **Performance Analysis** section. Here you will see the findings generated by ADDM. The first finding, "SQL statements were found waiting for row lock waits," is linked to the wait incurred by the second session. (See Figure 7-11.)
16. On this page, select the **View Report** button. The **View Report** page will be displayed. Go through this report.
17. Select the **Back** button of the browser to return to the **Automatic Database Diagnostic Monitor** page.
18. Select the finding "SQL statements were found waiting for row lock waits" to get further information about the error by clicking on its hyperlink.

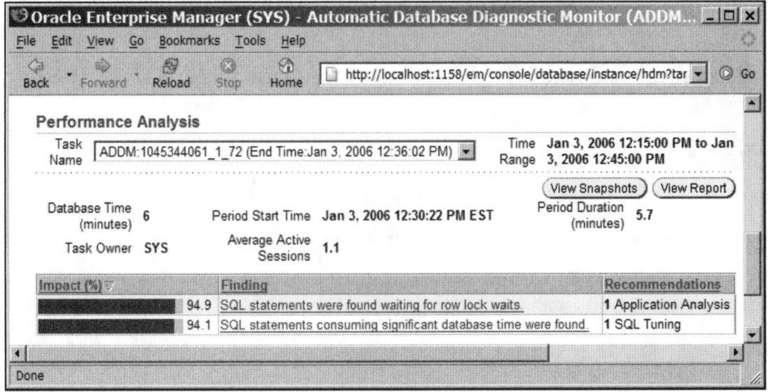

FIGURE 7-11 The Automatic Database Diagnostic Monitor page

19. The **Performance Finding Details** page is displayed and gives you further information about the wait. The Action and Rationale are displayed on this page. Figure 7-12 indicates that the SQL statement with a SQL_ID of "2cuq0yyavjtu4" was blocked.

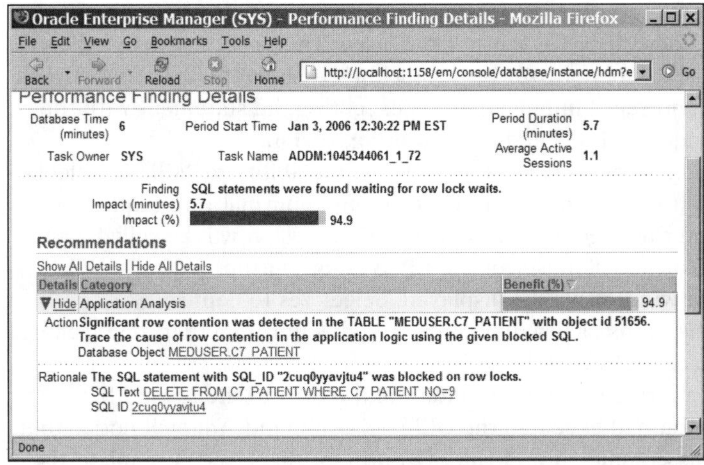

FIGURE 7-12 The Performance Finding Details page provides additional information

Knowing the SQL_ID, the database administrator can resolve the issue by performing either one of the following operations. If the SQL session that is blocking is accessible, it may be terminated by completing the transaction with either a commit or rollback. If the blocking session is not available, terminating it properly may not be feasible and the administrator may kill it.

20. Note the SQL_ID and select the **Database** breadcrumb followed by the **Home** tab to return to the **Database Control Home** page.

21. Select the **Performance** tab. Scroll along this page to the **Additional Monitoring Links** section.
22. Select the link **Blocking Sessions**. The **Blocking Sessions** page is displayed.

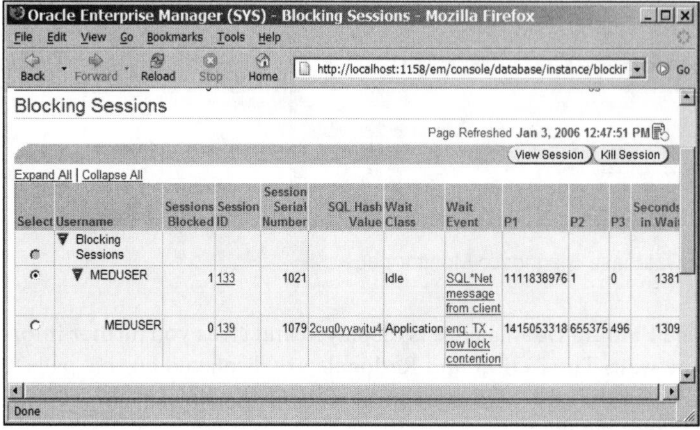

FIGURE 7-13 The Blocking Sessions page

Figure 7-13 describes the wait-related issue. The session with a session ID of 133 and serial number of 1021 is the blocking session. The session with session ID of 139 and serial number 1079 is executing the statement with the SQL_ID of "2cuq0yyavjtu4" and is the waiting session.

The Blocking Sessions page also gives you the ability to "kill" the blocking session. Killing a session would result in an abnormal termination of the user session and the ongoing transaction in that session will be rolled back.

23. To kill the blocking session, select the **Kill Session** button.
24. A **Confirmation window** will be displayed. Select **Yes** to confirm.
25. The **Blocking Sessions** page will be redisplayed confirming that the blocking session was successfully killed.
26. Minimize the Enterprise Manager window and return to the second SQL*Plus session where you had executed the DELETE command. You will notice that the deletion has completed and the SQL prompt displayed. Complete the transaction by typing a commit.

    ```
    SQL> COMMIT;
    ```

27. Return to the Enterprise Manager window. Select the **Database** breadcrumb from the upper left-hand corner, followed by the **Home** tab, and return to the **Database Control Home** page.
28. Notice that the alert under the **Alerts** section has been cleared. You may have to wait for a few minutes and refresh this page. (See Figure 7-14.)
29. Exit SQL*Plus and Enterprise Manager.

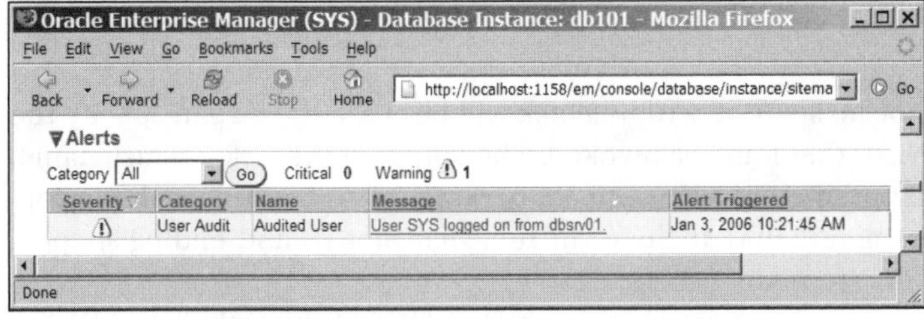

FIGURE 7-14 The wait-related alert has been cleared

In this practice exercise you created an application wait issue and successfully resolved it using ADDM.

Invoking ADDM using the DBMS_ADVISOR package

The ADDM may be invoked from the command line using the DBMS_ADVISOR package. An administrator can use the package to generate reports using non-adjacent snapshots. The package consists of various procedures that may be used to work with advisors.

NOTE

You must possess the ADVISOR system privilege to work with the subprograms of the DBMS_ADVISOR package.

Table 7-2 displays some of the commonly used subprograms of the DBMS_ADVISOR package.

TABLE 7-2 Subprograms of the DBMS_ADVISOR package

Procedure	Description
CREATE_TASK	Creates a new task in the repository
DELETE_TASK	Deletes a task from the repository
EXECUTE_TASK	Initiates execution of the task
INTERRUPT_TASK	Suspends a task that is currently executing
GET_TASK_REPORT	Generates a text report containing diagnosis and recommendations
RESUME_TASK	Resumes a suspended task
SET_TASK_PARAMETER	Modifies a task parameter
MARK_RECOMMENDATION	Marks one or more recommendations as accepted, rejected, or ignored
GET_TASK_SCRIPT	Creates a script of all the recommendations that are accepted

To configure a typical tuning session using the DBMS_ADVISOR package, execute the following steps:

- **Create an advisor task**—A new tuning task will be created. You can specify the name of the advisor that must be invoked. The output of the task is a task name.
- **Adjust the task parameters**—You can set parameters to control the behavior of the task. Parameters may include starting snapshot ID and ending snapshot ID in addition to many others.
- **Perform an analysis**—The next step involves executing the task. The ADDM advisor will analyze the statistics between the two snapshots and generate an output.
- **Review the results**—You can finally view the report to see the recommendations.

Practice 3: The DBMS_ADVSIOR package

In this practice example you will invoke the ADDM advisor using the DBMS_ADVISOR package.

1. Start SQL*Plus and log in with SYSDBA privileges.

```
SQL> CONNECT DB_ADMIN/DB_ADMIN AS SYSDBA
```

2. Write a query in the DBA_HIST_SNAPSHOT data dictionary view to determine the snapshots available (SNAP_ID) and when they were taken (STARTUP_TIME). Note the SNAP_IDs of any two non-adjacent snapshots. We will refer to the first one as *n1* and the second as *n2*.

```
SQL> COLUMN STARTUP_TIME FORMAT A40
SQL> SELECT SNAP_ID, STARTUP_TIME
     FROM DBA_HIST_SNAPSHOT
     ORDER BY 1, 2;
```

3. Using an editor, edit a script called **addman.sql** and type in the PL/SQL block displayed below. A copy of this script is available in the Chapter07 folder. The SET variables are required for displaying a formatted report. The variable TN will hold a task name, after the creation of the ADDM task. The task that you are creating will analyze all snapshots between *n1* and *n2*. When writing the code displayed, substitute the value of *n1* in place of 60 and the value *n2* in place of 66. This is followed by an execution of the task. Finally the output generated by the ADDM task is viewed using the SELECT statement.

```
SQL> EDIT <PATH>\ADDMAN.SQL

SQL> SET LONG 999999
SQL> SET LONGCHUNKSIZE 999999
SQL> VARIABLE TN VARCHAR2(50)
SQL> DECLARE
     TID       NUMBER;
     BEGIN
     DBMS_ADVISOR.CREATE_TASK('ADDM',TID,:TN);
     DBMS_ADVISOR.SET_TASK_PARAMETER(:TN,'START_SNAPSHOT',60);
     DBMS_ADVISOR.SET_TASK_PARAMETER(:TN,'END_SNAPSHOT',66);
     DBMS_ADVISOR.EXECUTE_TASK(:TN);
     END;
     /
```

```
SQL> SELECT DBMS_ADVISOR.GET_TASK_REPORT(:TN) FROM DUAL;
```

4. Save the script and exit the editor.
5. Execute the script **addman.sql**. The report will be displayed at the end. Any findings and recommendations will be presented. Go through the output displayed.

```
SQL> START <PATH>\ADDMAN.SQL
```

6. Exit SQL*Plus.

In this part of the chapter you have learned about the Automatic Database Diagnostic Monitor, its function, and the different ways to work with it. In the next section we will look at some other advisors available in the Oracle 10*g* database.

Other Important Advisors

In addition to the ADDM there are a number of other advisors available in the Oracle database that provide valuable information about problems that can occur in specific subsystems of the Oracle database. All these advisors have a uniform interface and may share information if necessary. These advisors use the AWR for their input. They may be invoked individually or from within an ADDM run.

A brief overview of the different advisors is given below. A complete discussion of the SQL Tuning Advisor and SQL Access Advisor follows. In subsequent chapters of this book other advisors will be discussed.

SQL Tuning Advisor—This advisor provides tuning recommendations for SQL statements executed in the database. Suggestions include how the statement could be rewritten to perform more efficiently.

SQL Access Advisor—This advisor provides valuable recommendations about schema objects, especially in relation to identifying optimal ways to access data by the addition and removal of indexes and materialized views.

Memory Advisor—The Memory Advisor presents recommendations on how system memory and the memory associated with the Oracle instance can be optimized. It provides recommendations on how specific memory structures such as the Database Buffer Cache must be sized to optimally handle the current activity in the database. The recommendations presented by the Memory Advisor are useful only when automatic memory management is not enabled for the database. The Memory Advisor consists of the SGA Advisor and the PGA Advisor.

SGA Advisor—It provides advice on the proper sizing of memory structures such as the Buffer Cache and Library cache.

The Buffer Cache Advisor provides advice on how to size the Database Buffer Cache to obtain optimal cache hit ratios. Consider a user issuing a SELECT statement. To satisfy the query, the block(s) containing the requested rows needs to be retrieved. If the requested blocks already exist in memory then the datafiles do not have to be accessed, thereby reducing I/O. A read request satisfied from memory is known as a *hit*. The ratio of the blocks read from memory compared to the total number of blocks read is the *cache hit ratio*. The more blocks that are found in memory, the better the Database Buffer Cache hit ratio. The size of the cache plays an important role in attaining a good hit ratio that is close to 100 percent.

The Library Cache is the area in memory where SQL statements and their parsed representations are stored. When two identical statements are executed in the database, the SQL text, its parse code and execution plan can be shared. Sharing, results in a hit eliminating the need to reparse, resulting in faster statement execution. The Library Cache Advisor provides recommendations on the proper sizing of this cache to ensure that the hit ratio remains high and close to a 100 percent.

PGA advisor—PGA memory is memory that holds the data and control information of a server process. The amount of memory allocated as PGA memory is particularly important for sorting operations. Sorts are done when users issue SQL statements that contain clauses, such as ORDER BY, DISTINCT, GROUP BY, CONNECT BY, UNION, MINUS, CREATE INDEX, and so on. If the sorting operation involves a large amount of data, space on disk may be used to complete it. Ideally, the entire sort operation must be completed in memory. The PGA Advisor provides advice and recommendations on sizing PGA memory based on the activity of the database.

Segment Advisor—This advisor is responsible for providing information regarding space issues in a database object. This advisor is discussed in Chapter 10.

Undo Advisor—Undo management was made automatic in Oracle 9*i*. The Oracle Server was responsible for managing the undo data within undo segments without the intervention of the DBA. The database administrator was only responsible for creating an undo tablespace where undo segments could be created. However, proper sizing of the undo tablespace to handle the undo generated in the database is important. The Undo Advisor provides recommendations on the proper sizing of the undo tablespace based on current and previous workload history.

Characteristics of Advisors

Advisors can run in one of two modes, **Limited** or **Comprehensive**. In a limited mode the recommendations are general, whereas the comprehensive mode generates detailed recommendations. In comprehensive mode the advisor will use various iterations, statistics, and methods to determine optimal solutions as well as point out the deficiencies of certain solutions. When invoking an advisor you may specify a time limit indicating the maximum time that the advisor can run. Advisors are interruptible, in which case the advisor can be interrupted to display partial results. Advisors may also take user directives that could influence the recommendations provided.

The SQL Tuning Advisor

A situation that database administrator's are frequently faced with is the tuning of a problematic or poorly performing SQL query. A developer requests the assistance of the DBA with a query that takes too long to complete or is consuming too many resources. The DBA would then need to analyze the way in which the query is executing and come up with alternate ways of writing the command to produce the same output. It is important to understand that in most cases there is more than one way of writing a SQL statement. Some ways are more efficient than others. For example, when a SELECT statement is issued, one method of accessing a particular row could be by performing a full table scan on the entire table. If an index exists on the table, an index scan may be done. Making a choice between performing a full table scan and an index scan is done by the **optimizer** of the Oracle database.

There is one more important aspect to SQL statement tuning that you should be aware of. The optimizer analyzes various factors and statistics to generate an optimal execution plan. These statistics should be made available to the optimizer. If statistics are not available or are outdated, the optimizer may not be able to generate optimal plans.

Oracle provides some guidelines and best practices that may be followed by the administrator during the process of tuning SQL statements. However, database administrators may not be completely knowledgeable about SQL best practices. To simplify the task of SQL tuning, the Oracle 10g database has provided the SQL Tuning Advisor to help the administrator with this task.

The SQL Tuning Advisor can receive as its input poorly executing SQL statements, and after an evaluation that is based on resource consumption, provide the administrator with advice on how to optimize the execution plans.

After diagnosis, the advisor reports findings about objects that do not have valid statistics, on the addition and removal of certain SQL clauses and creation of data structures such as indexes or materialized views. It may even point the database administrator toward invoking the SQL Access Advisor for further analysis.

The SQL Tuning advisor may be invoked using the command-line Oracle-supplied DBMS_SQLTUNE package or Enterprise Manager. Either way, a SQL Tuning task would first need to be created and executed. The output of the advisor is available in the form of a report. The report displays various findings identified by the advisor with recommendations that may be implemented by the administrator.

A description of some subprograms available in the DBMS_SQLTUNE package is given in Table 7-3. These subprograms may be used to interact with the SQL Tuning advisor.

TABLE 7-3 Subprograms of the DBMS_SQLTUNE package

Description	Function
CREATE_TUNING_TASK	Used to initiate the task of tuning a SQL statement
DROP_TUNING_TASK	Drops a tuning task that has been created
EXECUTE_TUNING_TASK	Executes a previously executed tuning task
RESET_TUNING_TASK	Used to reset a currently executing task to its initial state
REPORT_TUNING_TASK	Used to display the results of the tuning operation

Practice 4: The DBMS_SQLTUNE package

In this practice example, you will learn how to invoke the SQL Advisor using the DBMS_SQLTUNE package. You will also view the output of the advisor and implement the recommendations presented.

1. Start SQL*Plus and connect as a user with SYSDBA privileges.

   ```
   SQL> CONNECT DB_ADMIN/DB_ADMIN AS SYSDBA
   ```

2. Grant to user MEDUSER the ADVISOR privilege. This system privilege is required to invoke and use the advisors.

   ```
   SQL> GRANT ADVISOR TO MEDUSER;
   ```

3. Issue the following ALTER SYSTEM commands to clear the contents of the Shared Pool and Database Buffer Cache.

```
SQL> ALTER SYSTEM FLUSH SHARED_POOL;
SQL> ALTER SYSTEM FLUSH BUFFER_CACHE;
```

4. Connect as the user MEDUSER.

```
SQL> CONNECT MEDUSER/MEDUSER
```


5. To understand how the SQL Tuning Advisor is invoked, you will create a tuning task using the CREATE_TUNING_TASK packaged procedure. In the code displayed below, a procedure called SQLTUNE_TASK is being created that will create a new SQL tuning task called C7_SQLAD. This taskname will be referenced in subsequent steps of this practice. The SQL statement being analyzed is `"SELECT * FROM C7_PHYSICIAN WHERE PHYSICIAN_ID=1003"`. The statement is stored in a variable called SQLSTMT, which is the input to the CREATE_TUNING_TASK procedure. The task is launched in a comprehensive mode and allowed to run for a maximum of 30 seconds. The variable TASK_ID will hold a system-generated task identifier.

```
SQL> CREATE OR REPLACE PROCEDURE SQLTUNE_TASK IS
     TASK_ID        VARCHAR2(50);
     SQLSTMT     VARCHAR2(150);
     BEGIN
     SQLSTMT        := 'SELECT * FROM C7_PHYSICIAN
                       WHERE PHYSICIAN_ID=1003';
     TASK_ID        := DBMS_SQLTUNE.CREATE_TUNING_TASK(
     SQL_TEXT       => SQLSTMT,
     USER_NAME      => 'MEDUSER',
     SCOPE          => 'COMPREHENSIVE',
     TIME_LIMIT     => 30,
     TASK_NAME      => 'C7_SQLAD',
     DESCRIPTION    => 'SQL TUNING EXAMPLE');
     END SQLTUNE_TASK;
     /
```

6. The next step is to execute the procedure that was created in step 5. Use the EXECUTE command from the SQL prompt to do so. The SQL Tuning task with a name C7_SQLAD will be created.

```
SQL> EXECUTE SQLTUNE_TASK
```

7. Next, execute the EXECUTE_TUNING_TASK procedure of the DBMS_SQLTUNE package. Pass the taskname as an argument to the procedure. The SQL Tuning Advisor will then tune the task and identify the different ways in which the DBA could perform to improve query performance.

```
SQL> BEGIN
     DBMS_SQLTUNE.EXECUTE_TUNING_TASK(TASK_NAME => 'C7_SQLAD');
     END;
     /
```

8. To obtain a report of the SQL tuning exercise, execute the REPORT_TUNING_TASK function. This can be done using a SELECT statement. Make sure you issue the following SET commands or the output may not be displayed properly.

```
SQL> SET LONG 999999
SQL> SET LONGCHUNKSIZE 999999
SQL> SET LINESIZE 100
SQL> SELECT DBMS_SQLTUNE.REPORT_TUNING_TASK
     ('C7_SQLAD') FROM DUAL;
```

The report generated by the advisor contains various sections. The first section is the header that describes the details of the tuning task that you created, such as the mode in which the task was run and the timestamp of when the task was started and completed. The next section is the SQL statement that was executed followed by a findings section. In the output notice, two findings are reported. The first finding indicates that the table does not have any statistics because the optimizer needs statistics to come up with optimal execution plans. A recommendation is also provided as to how statistics can be gathered. The recommendation suggests the use of the Oracle-supplied DBMS_STATS.GATHER_TABLE_STATS packaged procedure. The second finding indicates that an index on the C7_PHYSICIAN should be created. The CREATE INDEX command that can be executed is displayed. The last section displays the execution plan that was generated by the optimizer for the execution of the query. The output of the report has been formatted to improve readability.

Report generated by the SQL Tuning Task.

```
DBMS_SQLTUNE.REPORT_TUNING_TASK
-----------------------------------------------------------------
GENERAL INFORMATION SECTION
-----------------------------------------------------------------
Tuning Task Name                    : C7_SQLAD
Tuning Task Owner                   : MEDUSER
Scope                               : COMPREHENSIVE
Time Limit(seconds)                 : 30
Completion Status                   : COMPLETED
Started at                          : 01/06/2006 10:58:58
Completed at                        : 01/06/2006 10:58:59
Number of Statistic Findings        : 1
Number of Index Findings            : 1

DBMS_SQLTUNE.REPORT_TUNING_TASK
-----------------------------------------------------------------
Schema Name: MEDUSER
SQL ID     : 3d6xnjwp54gr2
SQL Text   : SELECT * FROM C7_PHYSICIAN
                                WHERE PHYSICIAN_ID=1003
-----------------------------------------------------------------
FINDINGS SECTION (2 findings)
-----------------------------------------------------------------
DBMS_SQLTUNE.REPORT_TUNING_TAS
-----------------------------------------------------------------
1- Statistics Finding
---------------------
```

```
  Table "MEDUSER"."C7_PHYSICIAN" was not analyzed.

Recommendation
--------------
Consider collecting optimizer statistics for this table.
execute dbms_stats.gather_table_stats(ownname => 'MEDUSER',
tabname => 'C7_PHYSICIAN', estimate_percent => DBMS_STATS.AUTO_
SAMPLE_SIZE,
method_opt => 'FOR ALL COLUMNS SIZE AUTO');

DBMS_SQLTUNE.REPORT_TUNING_TASK
-------------------------------------------------------------------
Rationale
---------
The optimizer requires up-to-date statistics for the table
in order to select a good execution plan.

2- Index Finding (see explain plans section below)
--------------------------------------------------
The execution plan of this statement can be improved by creating one
or more indexes.

 Recommendation (estimated benefit: 100%)

DBMS_SQLTUNE.REPORT_TUNING_TASK
-------------------------------------------------------------------
Consider running the Access Advisor to improve the physical
schema
design or creating the recommended index.
create index MEDUSER.IDX$$_034B0001 on
MEDUSER.C7_PHYSICIAN('PHYSICIAN_ID');

Rationale
---------
Creating the recommended indices significantly improves the
execution plan of this statement.
However, it might be preferable to run "Access Advisor" using a
representative SQL workload as opposed to a single statement.
This will allow you to get comprehensive index
recommendations which takes into account index maintenance
overhead and additional space consumption.

EXPLAIN PLANS SECTION
--------------------------------------------------------------------
1- Original
-----------
Plan hash value: 2190039663

DBMS_SQLTUNE.REPORT_TUNING_TAS
--------------------------------------------------------------------
| Id  | Operation           | Name           | Rows  | Bytes | Cost
(%CPU)|
Time      |
--------------------------------------------------------------------
|   0 | SELECT STATEMENT    |                |     1 |    25 |
3   (0)|
00:00:01 |
```

```
|*  1 |  TABLE ACCESS FULL| C7_
PHYSICIAN |      1 |    25 |      3   (0)|
00:00:01 |
-----------------------------------------------------------------
Predicate Information (identified by operation id):
---------------------------------------------------
   1 - filter("PHYSICIAN_ID"=:SYS_B_0)

DBMS_SQLTUNE.REPORT_TUNING_TAS
-----------------------------------------------------------------
2- Using New Indices
--------------------
Plan hash value: 3031426769
-----------------------------------------------------------------
| Id  | Operation                        | Name             | Rows
| Bytes |
Cost (%CPU)| Time     |
-----------------------------------------------------------------
|   0 | SELECT STATEMENT                 |                  |     1
|    25 |
3   (0)| 00:00:01 |
|   1 |  TABLE ACCESS BY INDEX ROWID| C7_
PHYSICIAN    |      1 |    25 |
3   (0)| 00:00:01 |
|*  2 |   INDEX RANGE SCAN             | IDX$$_
034B0001 |      1 |       |
1   (0)| 00:00:01 |

DBMS_SQLTUNE.REPORT_TUNING_TAS
-----------------------------------------------------------------
Predicate Information (identified by operation id):
---------------------------------------------------
   2 - access("PHYSICIAN_ID"=:SYS_B_0)
```

9. Using the recommendation of the SQL Advisor, execute the DBMS_STATS. GATHER_TABLE_STATS procedure against the C7_PHYSICIAN table.

```
SQL> BEGIN
     DBMS_STATS.GATHER_TABLE_STATS(
     OWNNAME => 'MEDUSER',
     TABNAME => 'C7_PHYSICIAN',
     ESTIMATE_PERCENT => DBMS_STATS.AUTO_SAMPLE_SIZE);
     END;
     /
```

10. Next, create the index recommended.

```
SQL> CREATE INDEX MEDUSER.IDX$$_034B0001 ON
     MEDUSER.C7_PHYSICIAN('PHYSICIAN_ID');
```

11. After implementing the suggestion, reset the tuning task using the RESET_ TUNING_TASK procedure.

```
SQL> BEGIN
     DBMS_SQLTUNE.RESET_TUNING_TASK(TASK_NAME => 'C7_SQLAD');
     END;
     /
```

12. Now, execute the tuning task once again. The taskname continues to be C7_SQLAD.

```
SQL> BEGIN
     DBMS_SQLTUNE.EXECUTE_TUNING_TASK(TASK_NAME=> 'C7_SQLAD');
     END;
     /
```

13. Once again display the report using the REPORT_TUNING_TASK function. Notice this time there are no recommendations displayed. In Oracle 10*g* Release 1, the report generated will indicate no recommendations. However, in Oracle 10*g* Release 2, the report may continue to display a finding even after the creation of the indexes.


```
SQL> SELECT DBMS_SQLTUNE.REPORT_TUNING_TASK('C7_SQLAD')
     FROM  DUAL;

DBMS_SQLTUNE.REPORT_TUNING_TASK('C7_SQLAD')

-----------------------------------------------------------------
-------
GENERAL INFORMATION SECTION
-----------------------------------------------------------------
-------
Tuning Task Name    : C7_SQLAD
Scope               : COMPREHENSIVE
Time Limit(seconds): 30
Completion Status   : COMPLETED
Started at          : 01/03/2006 15:55:07
Completed at        : 01/03/2006 15:55:07
-----------------------------------------------------------------
-------
SQL ID  : 526smjyvx3kzh
DBMS_SQLTUNE.REPORT_TUNING_TASK('C7_SQLAD')
-----------------------------------------------------------------
SQL Text: SELECT * FROM C7_PHYSICIAN
          WHERE PHYSICIAN_ID=1003
-----------------------------------------------------------------
There are no recommendations to improve the statement.
```

14. After having completed the tuning exercise you must drop the tuning task. This can be accomplished using the DROP_TUNING_TASK procedure of the DBMS_SQLTUNE package.

```
SQL>BEGIN
    DBMS_SQLTUNE.DROP_TUNING_TASK('C7_SQLAD');
    END;
    /
```

15. Exit SQL*Plus.

In this section of the chapter, you learned about the SQL Tuning Advisor and its value to a DBA for SQL Tuning.

The SQL Access Advisor

The SQL Tuning Advisor discussed in the previous section of this chapter is an extremely powerful tool for tuning poorly written SQL statements. The SQL Tuning Advisor may also indicate that an index on a column(s) may improve query response. It may point the administrator toward invoking the SQL Access Advisor separately for further information about how the index could help.

The SQL Access Advisor is another advisor that helps achieve higher performance with regard to SQL statement tuning. It can be used to analyze some or all the statements in an application workload. Upon analysis it may suggest the addition or removal of indexes and materialized views.

Indexes are database objects that can be created on one or more columns of a table to speed up query execution. Indexes must be created carefully on columns that are frequently accessed in the WHERE clause of SELECT statements. Once an index is created the Oracle Server may or may not choose to use the index. This decision is made by the optimizer and is based on a number of factors such as the structure, size of the table, and statistics.

Materialized views, on the other hand, are summary tables that contain the results of a query. They are particularly useful when a local copy of data that is located remotely needs to be maintained. Such a copy is also known as a *snapshot*. Materialized views are read-only and can be queried in the same way a table or view is accessed. The contents of a materialized view may be refreshed periodically based on the refresh rate option. A materialized view is similar to a view, with the primary difference being that data is actually stored within a materialized view. A regular view, on the other hand, has no data of its own and always derives its data from a base table. If materialized views exist, the optimizer can dramatically improve the speed with which it accesses data.

The SQL Access Advisor can be invoked using the Oracle-supplied DBMS_ADVISOR package or the Enterprise Manager. The input to the SQL Access Advisor can be a SQL Tuning Set, a user-defined workload, the SQL cache that contains the most recently executed SQL statements, or a hypothetical workload using one or more tables. A SQL Tuning set can be created using existing SQL statements in the AWR, such as the top SQL statements.

Practice 5: Accessing SQL Access Advisor using Enterprise Manager

This practice example demonstrates the SQL Access Advisor. The advisor will be invoked from Enterprise Manager to analyze some SELECT statements issued by MEDUSER on the C7_PATIENT table. The SELECT statements are available in the **c7saa.sql** script in the Chapter07 folder. Please go through the script before executing it. In this practice the ANALYZE TABLE...COMPUTE STATISTICS command has been introduced. The command is used to gather statistics on objects. The statistics are used by the cost-based optimizer to identify optimal execution plans. The optimizer and statistics gathering are discussed in Chapter 9.

1. Start SQL*Plus and connect as a user with SYSDBA privileges.

   ```
   SQL> CONNECT DB_ADMIN/DB_ADMIN AS SYSDBA
   ```

2. Issue the following ALTER SYSTEM command to clear the contents of the shared pool. This may be necessary for the successful completion of this practice.

   ```
   SQL> ALTER SYSTEM FLUSH SHARED_POOL;
   SQL> ALTER SYSTEM FLUSH BUFFER_CACHE;
   ```

3. Also, issue the following ALTER SYSTEM command to ensure that cursor sharing is performed only when identical statements are issued.

   ```
   SQL> ALTER SYSTEM SET CURSOR_SHARING=EXACT;
   ```

4. Connect as the user MEDUSER.

```
SQL> CONNECT MEDUSER/MEDUSER
```

5. Issue an ANALYZE table command to ensure that statistics are gathered for the C7_PATIENT table.

```
SQL> ANALYZE TABLE C7_PATIENT COMPUTE STATISTICS;
```

6. Run the script **c7saa.sql** that is in the Chapter07 folder of the student datafiles. The script queries different rows of the C7_PATIENT table.

```
SQL> START <PATH>\C7SAA.SQL
```


After this script is run, the SQL cache will contain the SQL statements. Now to view the recommendations presented by SQLAccess Advisor based on this workload we will invoke SQL Access Advisor from the Enterprise Manager.

7. Launch a browser and enter the correct URL to invoke Enterprise Manager. Log in as a user with SYSDBA privileges.
8. From the **Database Control Home** page, scroll down to the Related Links section and select the **Advisor Central** link.
9. The **Advisor Central** page will be displayed.
10. From the **Advisors** section, select the **SQL Access Advisor**. (See Figure 7-15.)

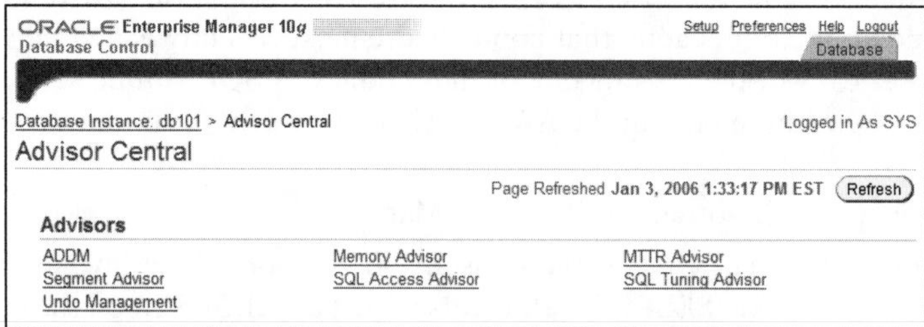

FIGURE 7-15 The Advisor Central page may be used to access all the other advisors

11. The **SQL Access Advisor: Initial Options** page will be displayed. Select the option **Use Default Options**. Select the **Continue** button.
12. The **SQL Access Advisor: Workload Source** page will be displayed. On this page you can indicate what needs to be analyzed. Because we just generated the workload as the MEDUSER, the statements to be analyzed are currently in the SQL cache. Choose the option **Current and Recent SQL Activity**. (See Figure 7-16.)

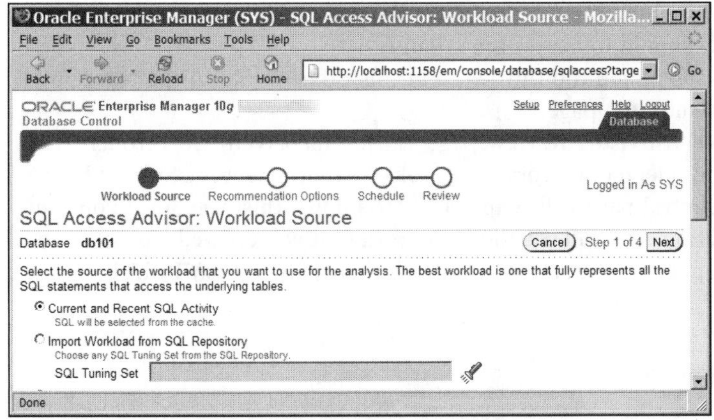

FIGURE 7-16 Selecting the input for SQL Access Advisor

13. On this page, expand the option **Filter Options**.
14. Select **Filter Workload Based on these Options**.
15. From the Users Section, select **Include only SQL statements executed by these users**. In the text box provided, type **MEDUSER**. (See Figure 7-17.)

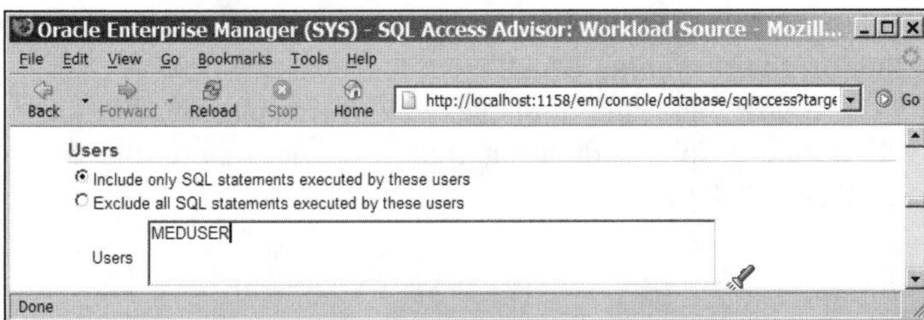

FIGURE 7-17 Setting the filter options

16. You have just completed the first step of the process. Scroll to the bottom of the page and select the **Next** button.
17. The **SQL Access Advisor: Recommendation Options** page is displayed. On this page you can specify what type of recommendations you want SQL Access Advisor to generate. You can choose between Indexes, Materialized Views, or both Indexes and Materialized Views. Select the option **Both Indexes and Materialized Views**.
18. At this point you have completed the second step of this process. Select the **Next** button.
19. The **SQL Access Advisor: Schedule** page will be displayed.
20. Under the Advisor Task Name section, type **SAAP** as the Task Name.
21. Leave the Task Description as **SQL Access Advisor**.
22. For Scheduling Options, from the Schedule Type list, select the option **Standard**.

23. The Repeat value should indicate **Do not Repeat**.
24. The Start value should indicate **Immediately**.
25. You have now completed the third step in this process. Select the **Next** button at the bottom of the page.
26. The **SQL Access Advisor: Review** page will be displayed. Go through the options that you selected. If everything looks correct, select the **Submit** button.
27. The **Advisor Central** page will reappear. Scroll down this page until you see the **Results** section. You will see the SAAP task that you created. You may need to **Refresh** this page for the status of the task to display as **COMPLETED**. (See Figure 7-18.)

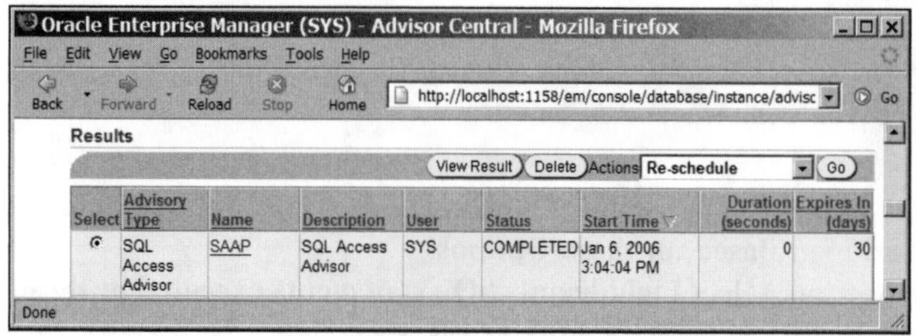

FIGURE 7-18 Viewing the output of SQL Access Advisor

28. Select the hyperlink on the taskname **SAAP**.
29. The **Results for Task: SAAP** page will be displayed. On this page in the Summary tab you will notice graphs indicating that there is a potential for improvement. (See Figure 7-19.)

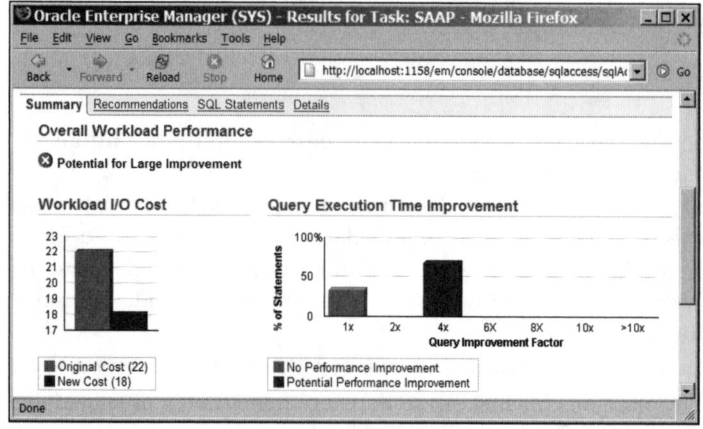

FIGURE 7-19 The results of the task

30. Scroll down to the **Recommendations** section. Notice there is one recommendation. (See Figure 7-20.)

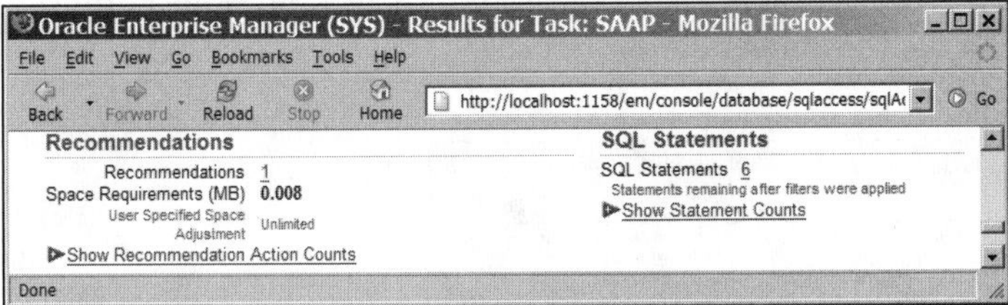

FIGURE 7-20 Viewing the recommendations of SQL Access Advisor

31. Select the hyperlink on Recommendation **1**.
32. The **Recommendation** tab will be displayed. Scroll along this page until you reach the Select Recommendations for Implementation Section. Select the hyperlink on the ID 1. The **Recommendation: 1** page will be displayed. (See Figure 7-21.)

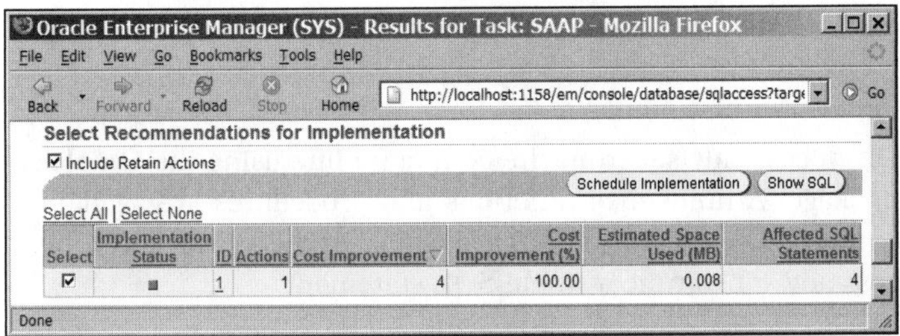

FIGURE 7-21 The recommendations for Implementation

33. Scroll to the **Actions** section. Notice the recommendation to create an INDEX on the C7_PATIENT_NO column of the C7_PATIENT table. Below this section is a listing of all the statements that will benefit from the creation of the index. (See Figure 7-22.)

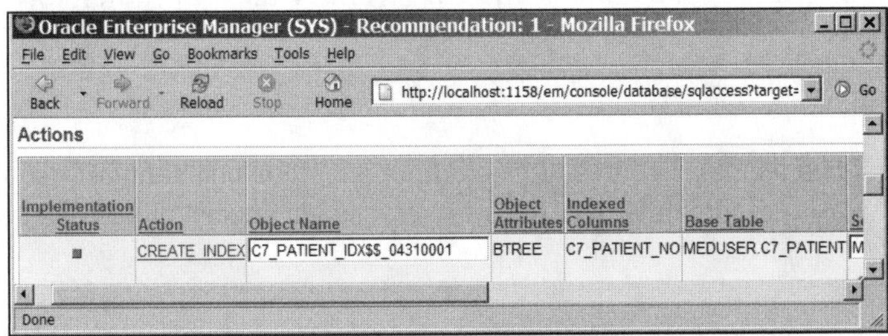

FIGURE 7-22 The recommendation was to create an index

285

34. On selecting the hyperlink on the CREATE INDEX action, the **Show SQL** page will be displayed with the CREATE INDEX command that may be issued to create the index. The suggestion was to create an index on the C7_PATIENT_NO column of the C7_PATIENT table. (See Figure 7-23.) Select the **Done** button. You will return to the **Recommendation: 1** page.

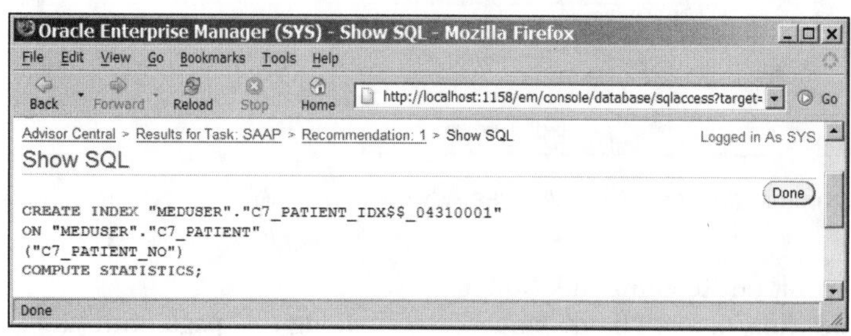

FIGURE 7-23 The CREATE INDEX command that can implement the recommendation

35. Select the **OK** button to return to the **Results for Task: SAAP** page. Do not create the index yet. It will be done in the next practice.
36. You can now return to the **Database Control Home** page and log out of Enterprise Manager.
37. Exit SQL*Plus and Enterprise Manager.

You may also invoke SQL Access Advisor from the command line using the Oracle-supplied DBMS_ADVISOR package. A number of functions and procedures are available with the DBMS_ADVISOR package. The QUICK_TUNE procedure of this package can be used to invoke the SQL Access advisor to tune a single SQL statement.

Practice 6: Accessing SQL Access Advisor using the DBMS_ADVISOR package

This practice example demonstrates how the SQL Access Advisor can be invoked using the DBMS_ADVISOR package. The recommendations are then viewed using Enterprise Manager.

1. Start SQL*Plus and connect as the user MEDUSER.

```
SQL> CONNECT MEDUSER/MEDUSER
```

2. Issue an ANALYZE TABLE command on the C7_PATIENT table to gather statistics on the table.

```
SQL> ANALYZE TABLE C7_PATIENT COMPUTE STATISTICS;
```

3. At the SQL prompt, type the following PL/SQL block that executes the QUICK_TUNE procedure of the DBMS_ADVISOR package. The inputs to the procedure include the advisor being invoked which is SQLACCESS_ADVISOR, a taskname (SQT), and the SELECT statement that will be analyzed.

```
SQL> BEGIN
     DBMS_ADVISOR.QUICK_TUNE (
     DBMS_ADVISOR.SQLACCESS_ADVISOR,
     'SQT',
     'SELECT C7_PATIENT_NAME FROM C7_PATIENT
     WHERE C7_PATIENT_NO=3');
     END;
     /
```


4. The recommendation generated can be viewed from Enterprise Manager.
5. Minimize the SQL*Plus window, we will return to it in step 13 of this practice.
6. Launch a browser and enter the correct URL to start Enterprise Manager. Log in as a user with SYSDBA privileges.
7. From the **Database Control Home** page, scroll to the **Related Links** section. Select the **Advisor Central** link.
8. Under the **Results** section you will be able to see the **SQT** task that you created. (See Figure 7-24.)

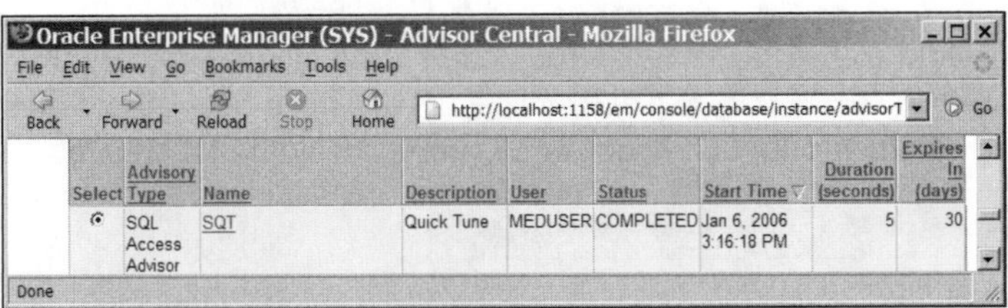

FIGURE 7-24 The output of the SQT task

9. Select the task **SQT** by selecting the link on it.
10. The **Results for Task: SQT** page will be displayed. This page contains information about potential for improvement.
11. Scroll to the Recommendations section on this page. You will see one recommendation. (See Figure 7-25.)

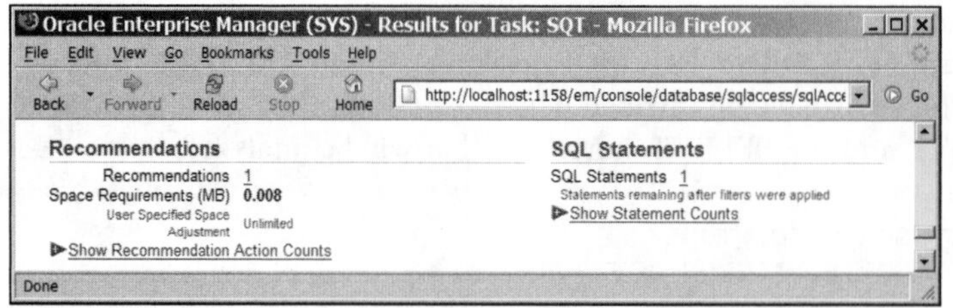

FIGURE 7-25 The recommendation for the SQT task

12. Select the hyperlink on **1**. From the Select **Recommendations for Implementation** section, once again select the hyperlink on **1**, to view recommendation. On the **Recommendation: 1** page you will see the actions you may take (CREATE INDEX) as well as the statement that will be affected by implementing the recommendation. (See Figure 7-26.)

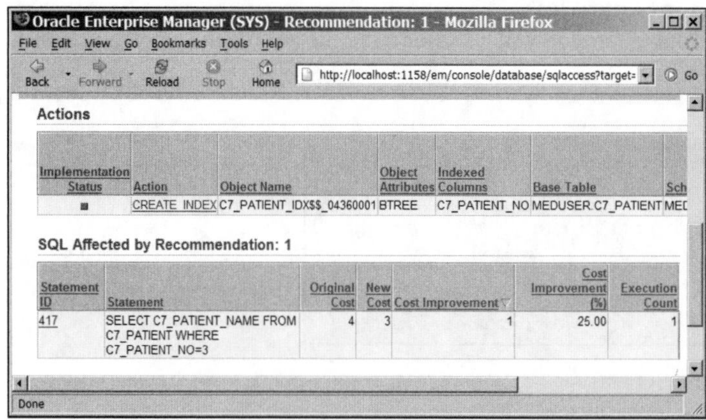

Implementation Status	Action	Object Name	Object Attributes	Indexed Columns	Base Table	Sch
■	CREATE INDEX	C7_PATIENT_IDX$$_04360001	BTREE	C7_PATIENT_NO	MEDUSER.C7_PATIENT	MEL

Statement ID	Statement	Original Cost	New Cost	Cost Improvement	Cost Improvement (%)	Execution Count
417	SELECT C7_PATIENT_NAME FROM C7_PATIENT WHERE C7_PATIENT_NO=3	4	3	1	25.00	1

FIGURE 7-26 The actions that may be implemented for the SQT task

13. From the Actions section, select the hyperlink on CREATE INDEX. The **SHOW SQL** page will be displayed. The CREATE INDEX command will be displayed. Copy this CREATE command and paste it in the SQL*Plus window.
14. Now create the index by executing the command.
15. Connect as a user with SYSDBA privileges, and clear the contents of the SHARED_POOL.

```
SQL> ALTER SYSTEM FLUSH SHARED_POOL;
```

16. Connect as the user MEDUSER, and repeat steps 3 through 8 to confirm if implementing the index helped the performance of the query. You will need to specify another taskname when executing step 3. This time the recommendation displayed by Oracle will be to retain the index on the C7_PATIENT_NO column.
17. Exit Enterprise Manager and SQL*Plus.

In this part of the chapter, we discussed the SQL Access Advisor and how it can be used as part of your SQL statement tuning strategy. The advisor is extremely useful for tuning third-party applications, where you do not have access to the SQL code. By running the application, the SQL workload will be available in the cache. This workload can then be analyzed using the SQL Access advisor for achieving better performance.

AUTOMATIC UNDO RETENTION TUNING

To understand how and what recommendations are provided by the undo advisor, it is important that you first know what is meant by undo data. Undo data refers to previous values. When a user issues an update statement to modify existing values in a table, the previous values that existed in the table is undo data. Undo data is required for three main purposes, namely transaction rollback, instance recovery, and read consistency. If the user who made the update decides that he or she does not want to make the change permanent. By performing a rollback, the undo data can be used to restore the previous values. This operation is referred to as *transaction rollback*.

When a user updates a row, the undo data is kept in undo segments. The undo data can be used to satisfy read requests for the data currently being modified. Because a user always has an option to rollback the change, other users must not see the data in the state of change. Therefore, users performing queries on rows currently being modified view data from the undo segments. This is referred to as *read consistency*.

If an instance failure occurs because of an improper termination of the instance, *instance recovery* will be performed. At the time of failure, there may have been some ongoing transactions. Other transactions that were completed may not have been written back to disk. During the next startup of the database, the System Monitor (SMON) background process will perform instance recovery. During instance recovery, all committed changes will be made permanent and uncommitted changes will be rolled back. The rollback step during instance recovery is done by making use of the undo data that was stored prior to the instance failure.

Undo segments that store undo data are created in undo tablespaces. In an Oracle database, a system undo segment is created during database creation time. This system undo segment holds undo data generated for the system tablespace only. If additional tablespaces are created in the database for storing data in an organized manner, the database administrator has to create a separate undo tablespace. Once an undo tablespace has been created, the Oracle Server automatically creates 10 undo segments in the undo tablespace where the undo data will be stored. The size of the undo tablespace created must be large enough to store the entire undo generated by the applications accessing the database, especially during periods of peak activity.

There is one more aspect to be aware of when dealing with undo data. The undo data stored in undo segments may need to be retained even after the transaction that generated it has completed. This may be required for queries that are currently reading the undo data from the undo segments and have not finished yet. We discussed this as read consistency. If the undo tablespace is not large enough for the current workload, the undo space occupied by completed transactions may be required right away by new transactions. If the undo data is released before the query completes, the session that issued the query will receive a "Snapshot too old" error. If the undo data had remained in the undo segments even after the transaction was done, the error might not have been generated. This problem can be minimized to some extent using a feature known as Undo Retention.

Undo Retention is defined in terms of time and specifies the amount of time that undo data might be retained even after the transaction that generated it has completed. Undo Retention is also used by the Flashback features discussed in Chapter 5. Undo Retention is specified using the UNDO_RETENTION initialization parameter. The value of the parameter is defined in terms of seconds. The default is 900 seconds. Specifying an appropriate value for undo retention is an important aspect when tuning undo segments.

Prior to Oracle 10*g*, a database administrator had to specify this value in the initialization parameter file. If the value was set too low, space in the undo segments could be wasted. If set too high, there is a problem of running out of free space in the undo tablespace. As a result, the administrator would have to determine the appropriate value based on trial and error. This problem has been somewhat resolved in Oracle 10*g* by means of the automatic undo retention tuning feature. The value for Undo Retention is automatically managed by the Oracle 10*g* server. The Oracle server sets the value for undo retention by collecting database statistics based on workload history. An administrator may set a low threshold value for the UNDO_RETENTION parameter, so that the system retains the undo for at least the value specified by the parameter. However, if space constraints exist, undo retention may be lower than the threshold value. If surplus undo space exists, the Oracle server may choose to retain the undo data for as long as necessary. This reduces the chances of a query generating a *Snapshot too old* error.

In this chapter we discussed different ways in which the Oracle 10*g* Database automatically manages many aspects related to performance tuning. Our main focus was on difficult tuning issues. We began with a discussion of what was involved in tuning the Oracle database and then looked at the different ways that the Oracle 10*g* Server performs self-tuning. All the functionalities discussed in this chapter substantiate Oracle's claim of being a *self-managing* database.

In Chapter 8 we will discuss another aspect related to administering the Oracle 10*g* database. It deals with the Databse Resource Manager which is a tool that is specifically used for managing limited system resources more efficiently.

Chapter Summary

- An important function of the database administrator is to ensure that the database is running smoothly at all times. This is done by monitoring the database, identifying bottlenecks, and taking corrective action to eliminate the problem.
- In Oracle 10*g*, this function has largely been taken over by the Oracle database. The Oracle database, monitors, identifies bottlenecks, and provides the administrator with suggestions on what corrective action may be taken to alleviate the problem.
- The self-managing capability of the Oracle 10*g* database is achieved by the new Common Manageability Infrastructure, which has four main components: the Automatic Workload Repository, the Advisory Framework, Server Alerts, and Automatic Tasks.
- The AWR forms the core of the infrastructure. It is responsible for maintaining current and historical tuning-related information in the form of statistics and metrics.
- The data in the AWR is available for identifying deviations from baseline statistics as well as analyzing growth trends and patterns.
- The statistical data maintained in the AWR is used by the internal and external components of the Oracle database.
- The Advisory Framework consists of a group of advisories that provides tuning recommendations about different subsystems of the Oracle database.
- The main advisory that is automatically invoked to analyze the last two snapshots in the AWR is the Automatic Database Diagnostic Monitor.
- Specific advisories may be invoked by the ADDM or manually by the administrator.
- All advisories present a similar look and feel for consistency purposes. Their main purpose is to analyze specific problem areas and provide valuable recommendations that the administrator may or may not choose to implement.
- The SQL Tuning Advisor helps in tuning SQL statements. It provides recommendations on how the statement could be rewritten or what actions may be taken to help the optimizer create a more efficient execution plan.
- The SQL Access Advisor primarily focuses on the improvement in query performance by the addition or removal of indexes, materialized logs, and materialized views.
- In Oracle 10*g*, specifying an appropriate value for undo retention is performed automatically by the Oracle Server. Based on current and past workload the undo retention value will be set to ensure maximum retention that may help alleviate the occurrence of the Snapshot too old error.

Syntax Guide

SYNTAX GUIDE		
Command	**Description**	**Example**
Subprograms of the DBMS_SQLTUNE package		

`CREATE_TUNING_TASK`	Prepares the tuning of a single SQL statement or a set of statements. The procedure creates a tuning task with the name defined by the task_name parameter.	`SQL> CREATE OR REPLACE PROCEDURE TUNING_TASK1 IS`
		`TASK_ID  VARCHAR2(50);`
		`SQLTEXT  VARCHAR2(250);`
		`BEGIN`
		`SQLTEXT := 'SELECT * FROM PATIENT WHERE PATIENT_ID=101';`
		`TASK_ID :=`
		`DBMS_SQLTUNE.CREATE_TUNING_TASK(`
		`SQL_TEXT   => SQLTEXT,`
		`USER_NAME  => 'MEDUSER',`
		`SCOPE      => 'LIMITED',`
		`TIME_LIMIT => 30,`
		`TASK_NAME  => 'TASK1');`
		`END TUNING_TASK1;`
		`/`

`EXECUTE_TUNING_TASK`	Executes a previously created tuning task.	`SQL> BEGIN`
		`DBMS_SQLTUNE.EXECUTE_TUNING_TASK(`
		`TASK_NAME => 'TASK1');`
		`END;`
		`/`

`REPORT_TUNING_TASK`	Displays the results of a tuning task.	`SQL>SELECT`
		`DBMS_SQLTUNE.REPORT_TUNING_TASK`
		`('TASK1') FROM DUAL;`

`RESET_TUNING_TASK`	Resets the currently executing tuning task to its initial state.	`SQL> BEGIN`
		`DBMS_SQLTUNE.RESET_TUNING_TASK (`
		`TASK_NAME => 'TASK1');`
		`END;`
		`/`

`DROP TUNING TASK`	To drop a previously created tuning task.	`SQL> BEGIN`
		`DBMS_SQLTUNE.DROP_TUNING_TASK(`
		`'TASK1');`
		`END;`
		`/`

Subprograms of the DBMS_STATS package used for the purpose of statistics gathering		

`GATHER_TABLE_STATS`	Used to gather current statistics for tables, to be used by the optimizer.	`BEGIN`
		`DBMS_STATS.GATHER_TABLE_STATS (`
		`OWNNAME => 'MEDUSER',`
		`TABNAME => 'PATIENT' );`
		`END;`
		`/`

SYNTAX GUIDE		
Command	Description	Example
Other commands		
`CREATE INDEX`	Used to create an index on a column(s) of a table.	`SQL> CREATE INDEX INDX_C7 ON C7_PATIENT(PATIENT_ID);`
`ALTER SYSTEM FLUSH SHARED_POOL;`	Used to clear the contents of the shared pool.	`SQL> ALTER SYSTEM FLUSH SHARED_POOL;`
`ALTER SYSTEM FLUSH BUFFER_CACHE`	Used to clear the contents of the database buffer cache.	`SQL> ALTER SYSTEM FLUSH BUFFER_CACHE;`
`ANALYZE TABLE.. COMPUTE STATISTICS;`	Used to gather statistics on a table, for use by the optimizer.	`SQL> ALTER TABLE t1 COMPUTE STATISTICS;`

Review Questions

1. The common manageability infrastructure consists of:
   a. AWR
   b. Server Alerts
   c. Workload Alerts
   d. Automatic Tasks
   e. Advisory Framework
   f. Advisory Repository
   g. Server Framework
2. Information gathered by the Automatic Workload Repository includes _______________ . [Choose all that apply.]
   a. Base statistics
   b. Metrics
   c. SQL statistics
   d. Active Session History
   e. Past Session History
   f. Advisor Results
   g. All the above
   h. None of the above

3. The Oracle-supplied package used to invoke and access the SQL Tuning advisor is ________________.
   a. DBMS_SQL
   b. DBMS_TUNE
   c. DBMS_SQLTUNE
   d. DBMS_STATS
   e. DBMS_ADVISOR

4. The amount of statistics gathered by the AWR is dependent on the ________________ initialization parameter.
   a. STATISTICS_GATHERED
   b. STATISTICS_LEVEL
   c. AWR_LEVEL
   d. AWR_STATISTICS
   e. None of the above
5. The AWR computes ________________ using the statistical data it collects. These determine the rate of change of activities in the database.
   a. Raw statistics
   b. Metrics
   c. Active Session History
   d. Growth trends
6. The advisories included in the Advisory Framework include ________________. [Choose 5.]
   a. Growth Trend Advisor
   b. Memory Advisor
   c. ADDM
   d. SQL Tuning Advisor
   e. SQLAccess Advisor
   f. MTTR Advisor
7. The AWR is created in the ________________ schema.
   a. AWR
   b. SYS
   c. SYSTEM
   d. SYSAUX
   e. WR

8. The SQL Access Advisor is invoked in the following ways: ________________ . [Choose 2.]
    a. DBMS_ADVISOR
    b. DBMS_SQLTUNE
    c. DBMS_STATS
    d. DBMS_SQLACCESS
    e. Enterprise Manager
9. The ________________ advisor provides recommendations regarding sizing the undo tablespace properly.
10. The database administrator at Tom's Pizzeria needs to tune a SQL statement to try to reduce its execution time. Identify the different advisors he can use for the purpose. [Choose 2.]
    a. SQL Tuning Advisor
    b. ADDM
    c. SQLAccess Advisor
    d. Segment Advisor
    e. SQLApp Advisor
11. The SQL Access Advisor provides recommendations regarding ________________ . [Choose 2.]
    a. Indexes
    b. Materialized Views
    c. Rewriting SQL statistics
    d. Gathering statistics
    e. All the above
12. The __________ background process is responsible for taking a snapshot of the statistics in memory and transferring to repository tables in disk.
    a. MMON
    b. MMAN
    c. PMON
    d. SMON
    e. MMNL
13. A hashed representation of a SQL statement can be referenced in the database using its ________________ .
    a. SQLID
    b. SQL_ID
    c. SQL_NO
    d. SQL_HASH
    e. SQL_TEXT

14. A database administrator is operating the SQL Access Advisor in PARTIAL mode. Which of the recommendations given below will *not* be provided in this mode? [Choose 2.]
    a. Adding a new index to a table
    b. Dropping an unused index
    c. Modifying an index by adding columns to the end
    d. Adding new materialized view logs
    e. Modifying an existing index by changing the index type
15. The SQL Tuning Advisor can receive its input from the following sources: ________________. [Choose 4.]
    a. ADDM
    b. SQL Cache
    c. AWR
    d. SQL Profile
    e. Custom Workload
    f. SQL Access Advisor
16. The ADDM is primarily used to identify bottlenecks that occur in an Oracle database. Identify three of its characteristics.
    a. It provides recommendations to the DBA.
    b. Its output can be viewed by using the Enterprise Manager.
    c. It is an add-on that needs to be purchased additionally for its functionality as a performance expert.
    d. The DBA has to implement the recommendations generated by the ADDM.
    e. It performs analysis using a top-down approach identifying the symptoms and then refining them to reach the root causes.
17. Identify the statements that are true with respect to Automatic Undo Management in Oracle 10*g*. [Choose 3.]
    a. The optimal value of undo retention is automatically determined based on the size of the undo tablespace.
    b. The database can dynamically adjust itself to change undo requirements based on system activity.
    c. The segment advisor provides undo recommendations, which can be used to size the undo tablespace properly.
    d. The Oracle 10*g* database remembers optimal undo settings for future use.

18. The ADDM analysis results are represented in the form of ________________.
    a. OUTPUTS
    b. FINDINGS
    c. RESULTS
    d. ANALYSIS
    e. DIAGNOSIS
    f. None of the above.
19. A DBA wishes to change the interval between snapshots. He wishes to take the snapshot every 6 minutes. What action would he perform to achieve this?
    a. It is not possible to change the interval.
    b. It is not possible to change the interval below 10 minutes.
    c. Use the MODIFY_SNAPSHOT_SETTINGS procedure of the DBMS_WORKLOAD_REPOSITORY package.
    d. Turn off automatic capturing of statistics.
20. Which Oracle 10*g* advisor is responsible for determining the most appropriate method to access data?
    a. SQL Tuning Advisor
    b. Memory Advisor
    c. ADDM
    d. SQL Access Advisor
    e. Segment Advisor

Hands-On Assignments

Assignment 7-1 Viewing the value of the STATISTICS_LEVEL initialization parameter

1. Start SQL*Plus and log in as a user with SYSDBA privileges.
2. Display the value of the STATISTICS_LEVEL initialization parameter using the SHOW PARAMETER command.
3. If it is currently set to TYPICAL, modify it to ALL using an ALTER SYSTEM command.
4. Verify your change by re-issuing the statement you issued in step 2.
5. Exit SQL*Plus.

Assignment 7-2 Modifying the retention period of snapshots using the DBMS_WORKLOAD_REPOSITORY package

1. Start SQL*Plus and connect as a user with SYSDBA privileges.
2. Type the following PL/SQL block to modify the snapshot settings. The retention should be set to a value 900 minutes.

```
SQL> BEGIN
  2  DBMS_WORKLOAD_REPOSITORY.MODIFY_SNAPSHOT_SETTINGS
  3  (RETENTION => 900);
  4  END;
  5  /
```

3. Did you receive an error? What are the limits for the retention period?
4. Exit SQL*Plus.

Assignment 7-3 Modifying the snapshot interval using the DBMS_WORKLOAD_REPOSITORY package

1. Start SQL*Plus and connect as a user with SYSDBA privileges.
2. Type in the following PL/SQL block to modify the snapshot settings. The interval should be set to a value 8 minutes.

```
SQL> BEGIN
  2  DBMS_WORKLOAD_REPOSITORY.MODIFY_SNAPSHOT_SETTINGS
  3  (INTERVAL => 8);
  4  END;
  5  /
```

3. Did you receive an error? What is the minimum value for the interval?
4. Exit SQL*Plus.

Assignment 7-4: Viewing Metrics from Enterprise Manager

1. Launch the browser and start Enterprise Manager. Log in as a user with SYSDBA privileges.
2. From the Database Control Home page, scroll down to the Related Links section.
3. Select the link All Metrics to display the All Metrics page.
4. Select the Expand All link.
5. Scroll down the page until you see all the metrics associated with Efficiency. Select the link Sorts in Memory (%). The Sorts in Memory (%) page will be displayed. What is the percentage of sorts being done in memory? Is it close or equal to 100 percent? If so, the PGA memory on your machine has been configured well.
6. Go through some more metrics so that you get an idea of what metrics are used for.
7. Exit Enterprise Manager.

Assignment 7-5 Using the Automatic Database Diagnostic Monitor

1. Open SQL*Plus and connect as a user with SYSDBA privileges.
2. Issue and ALTER SYSTEM command to set the size of the Database Buffer Cache to 4 M.
3. Open another SQL*Plus session and log in as a user with administrative privileges, like the SYSTEM user.

4. Open a third session of SQL*Plus and log in as a user with administrative privileges, like the SYSTEM user.
5. Launch Enterprise Manager using a browser and connect as a user with SYSDBA privileges.
6. From the Database Control Home page, select the Performance tab and navigate to the Additional Monitoring Links section.
7. Select the Snapshots link. From the Snapshots page choose to create a snapshot. We refer to this snapshot as 1.
8. Next perform steps 4a, 4b, and 4c simultaneously from the three SQL*Plus windows. You are simulating a large workload on the database.

   a. From the first SQL*Plus session, issue the following sequence of statements:

```
SQL> CREATE TABLE C7WORK
     AS SELECT * FROM DBA_SEGMENTS;
SQL> INSERT INTO C7WORK
     SELECT * FROM DBA_SEGMENTS;
SQL>/
SQL>/
SQL>/
SQL> COMMIT;
```

   b. Now, from the second SQL*Plus window, issue a query to view the entire DBA_OBJECTS table.

```
SQL> SELECT * FROM DBA_OBJECTS;
```

   c. Now, from the third SQL*Plus window, issue a query to view the entire DBA_OBJECTS table.

```
SQL> SELECT * FROM DBA_OBJECTS;
```

9. As the sessions are running, open the Enterprise Manager browser, navigate to the Performance tab, and examine the various graphs displayed. Notice spikes in the graphs reflecting increased I/O and CPU utilization.
10. Wait until all sessions complete.
11. Scroll down the Performance page to the Additional Monitoring Links section.
12. Select the Snapshots link. From the Snapshots page choose to create a snapshot.
13. Confirm the creation of the manual snapshot. Name this snapshot Snapshot 2.
14. After the creation of the manual snapshot, from the Snapshots page, choose Run ADDM from within the Actions list. Select the Go button.
15. Make the beginning snapshot Snapshot 1 and ending snapshot Snapshot 2. This can be done by selecting the radio button corresponding to Snapshot 2.
16. Select the OK button to initiate the creation of an ADDM task from the Run ADDM page. (The ending snapshot is Snapshot 2.)
17. The Processing: Run ADDM page will be displayed. After processing has completed, the Automatic Database Diagnostic page will be displayed.
18. Scroll to Performance Analysis section on this page. ADDM may have identified some findings. Findings will vary depending on the machine configuration.
19. Go through the different findings by selecting on each of the links to get further information about the finding.

20. Try to understand as many recommendations as you can.
21. Exit all three SQL*Plus sessions and log out of Enterprise Manager.

Assignment 7-6 Tuning a SQL statement using the SQL Tuning Advisor

1. Start SQL*Plus and connect as the user MEDUSER.
2. Execute the script c7_setup.sql from the Chapter07 folder.
3. Open an editor, and create a script called PRO76.sql. Within the script, write a procedure called EX76, that will create a SQL tuning task, for the following query:

   ```
   'SELECT COUNT(*) FROM C7_PHYSICIAN'
   ```


   Name the task TUNE76.
4. Create the procedure by executing the script.

   ```
   SQL> START PRO76.SQL
   ```

5. Execute the procedure EX76 so that the SQL tuning task is created.

   ```
   SQL> EXECUTE EX76
   ```

6. Next execute the tuning task, using the DBMS_SQLTUNE.EXECUTE_TUNING_TASK packaged procedure.
7. Display the output of the tuning task, using the DBMS_SQLTUNE.REPORT_TUNING_TASK packaged procedure. Make sure you require SET commands to make sure the output is displayed.
8. How many findings were generated?
9. Implement the recommendation(s).
10. Reset the tuning task.
11. Execute the tuning task again.
12. Invoke the REPORT_TUNING_TASK procedure to display the tuning report.
13. Are any more recommendations presented?
14. Using the DBMS_SQLTUNE.DROP_TUNING_TASK procedure, drop the existing tuning task.
15. Exit SQL*Plus.

Assignment 7-7 Performing a quick tune operation using the SQL Access Advisor

1. Start SQL*Plus and connect as a user with SYSDBA privileges.
2. Issue the commands to flush the buffer cache and shared pool.
3. Connect as the user MEDUSER.

   ```
   SQL> CONNECT MEDUSER/MEDUSER
   ```

4. Issue the following CREATE TABLE command to create a table called T1.

   ```
   SQL> CREATE TABLE T1 (COL1 NUMBER, COLB  DATE);
   ```

5. Execute the following PL/SQL block to insert 5000 rows into the table T1.

   ```
   SQL> BEGIN
     2  FOR I IN 1..5000
     3  LOOP
     4  INSERT INTO T1 VALUES(I, SYSDATE);
     5  END LOOP;
     6  END;
        /
   ```

6. Issue an ANALYZE statement to collect statistics on the T1 table.
7. Write a PL/SQL block that will create a SQL Access Advisor task called S7. Using the DBMS_ADVISOR.QUICK_TUNE function, determine the recommendations that can be implemented on the following query.

```
SELECT COUNT(*) FROM T1 WHERE COL1=550;
```

8. Launch Enterprise Manager, log in as a SYSDBA and view the recommendations that were generated for the query. From the Database Control Home page, scroll to the Advisor Central link. Select it.
9. From the Advisor Central page, go to the Results section.
10. Select the link under the task called S7.
11. Are there any recommendations? If so, view the recommendation(s).
12. Exit SQL*Plus and Enterprise Manager.

Assignment 7-8 Viewing Undo Tablespace and Undo Retention Information using Enterprise Manager

1. Launch Enterprise Manager and log in as a user with SYSDBA privileges.
2. Select the Administration tab.
3. From the Database Configuration section, select the Undo Management link.
4. From the Undo Management page, select the Undo Advisor button.
5. What is the current value of the Auto-tuned Undo Retention (minutes). This value is what the Oracle Server has identified as the undo retention for the database, based on workload history.
6. Set the New Undo Retention to 10 minutes. What is the change in the Tablespace Size for the New Undo Retention?
7. Log out and exit Enterprise Manager.

Case Study

1. Read the challenge that was faced by Ryan once again, and write down the steps you would use to find a solution to the problem. Also, clearly mention the tools you would use.
2. A new DBA has joined the organization and needs guidance about the Advisory Framework in the Oracle 10*g* database. He was working on an Oracle 9*i* database at his previous job and is aware of what is involved in tuning the database. To help him understand the advisory framework, create a chart with the following headings: Name of advisory, Function, Methods to Invoke, and Type of recommendations. Under each heading list the name of the advisory and the other information required to help him understand the function of the new advisors in Oracle 10*g*.

CHAPTER **8**

DATABASE RESOURCE MANAGER

LEARNING OBJECTIVES

After completing this lesson you should be able to understand:

- The purpose of Database Resource Manager
- Components of the Database Resource Manager
- Creating Consumer groups
- Creating Resource Plans
- Creating Resource Plan Directives
- Associating the different components of Database Resource Manager
- Automatic Mapping of user sessions with Consumer Groups
- Obtaining information about the Database Resource Manager

ORACLE CERTIFICATION EXAM OBJECTIVES COVERED IN THIS CHAPTER INCLUDE:

- Manage Resources
- Configure the Resource Manager
- Assign users to Resource Manager Groups
- Create Resource Plans within groups
- Specify directives for allocating resources to Consumer Groups

INTRODUCTION

In any computing environment, database administrators need to make sure that the resources for applications and users are available and adequate. Inadequate resources can lead to an overstressed database. Further, the resources that are available must be shared between the users in an efficient manner. This is especially true in environments that have a mixed workload. In certain production environments at certain times of the day, specific applications need to run and all the available resources must be allocated to them with higher priority. You must not have trivial applications consuming system resources at this time. It is also worth mentioning that in production environments it is preferable to have the database(s) on host machines that are not running other applications.

In this chapter you will learn about the Database Resource Manager (DRM). This tool may be used to make resource management easier for the administrator. The chapter covers the important components of DRM and how they work together to accomplish better resource management. The chapter focuses on environments that run a mixed workload handling both online transactions and long-running queries. The DRM tool will be discussed using both command-line and Enterprise Manager. You will also learn how to automatically map user sessions with consumer groups. Finally, the data dictionary views that contain DRM information will be reviewed.

THE CURRENT CHALLENGE AT KELLER MEDICAL CENTER

The administrators at Keller Medical Center have been receiving complaints from the medical staff that the database tends to be slow between 9:30 and 11:00 A.M. Upon closer examination of the activity, Ryan notices that around 9:30 A.M. a large report is run. The report is run by a junior administrator who generates the report first thing in the morning, so she does not forget. However, morning hours are also peak activity hours when the demands on the database are greatest. Ryan also observes that certain metrics on the database indicate that CPU time is utilized to 100% every time such reports are run. Ryan wonders if a solution to this problem could be implemented using the Database Resource Manager.

SETUP FOR THE CHAPTER

Before performing the practice and hands-on exercises in this chapter, you must run the script called **c8_setup.sql** in the Chapter08 folder of the student datafiles.

1. Start SQL*Plus, and connect as a user with SYSDBA privileges.

```
SQL> CONNECT DB_ADMIN/DB_ADMIN AS SYSDBA
```

2. Execute the c8_setup.sql script.

```
SQL> START <PATH>\C8_SETUP.SQL
```

3. Exit SQL*Plus.

TERMINOLOGY

There are some terms that you must be familiar with before you proceed with this chapter.

Online Transaction Processing (OLTP)—This is an environment that is predominantly characterized by many concurrent short transactions, such as a reservation or order entry system.

Decision Support System (DSS)—This is an environment that is characterized by long-running queries for the purpose of analyzing the data.

Hybrid Environment—This is an environment that runs both OLTP and DSS type applications. Hybrid environments are often known as Mixed Workload environments.

OVERVIEW OF DATABASE RESOURCE MANAGER

The Database Resource Manager (DRM) was introduced in Oracle 8*i* and has since had many significant enhancements. The DRM is an invaluable tool for database administrators who have to manage an Oracle database with a limited amount of hardware resources. Often, in production environments, different types of applications run at different times of the day. For instance, during normal business hours, users may be accessing the database to make changes. After office hours users may access the database primarily to generate reports and perform backups. During normal business hours, the users accessing the database to make changes must receive higher priority and must be allocated more system resources. For example, a user issuing a report at 9:30 A.M. must be given the least priority and must be allocated resources only after the requirements of other active sessions have been met. On the same note, after office hours, priority must be given to user sessions that are running reports, taking backups or performing exports.

The DRM has been created primarily for such environments, where both OLTP and DSS applications may need to run simultaneously with a priority assigned to either of them at certain times of the day. The database administrator has a lot more control of resource utilization using the DRM tool than is normally possible using operating system resource management alone. The DRM guarantees certain users a minimum amount of resources regardless of the load on the database.

Using Database Resource Manager a database administrator can:

- **Manage CPU usage**—Total CPU usage may be shared among the different users sessions based on percentages. For example, OLTP users during the day may be granted 80% of CPU time, whereas DSS users may be granted only 20%. If the operating system were to manage CPU time, all active sessions would be given an equal amount of CPU time. It will not prioritize one task over another.
- **Specify a Degree of Parallelism**—You can specify a limit to the number of parallel processes that are started within user sessions. This is particularly useful for DSS environments in which users issue long-running queries. Queries can complete faster if parallel query processes are started.
- **Create an Active Session Pool**—A collection of users with similar needs is known as a consumer group (discussed in the next section of this chapter). Using DRM you can limit the number of active sessions within a consumer group. This feature is used to control available resources more efficiently. Consider a consumer group called OLTP consisting of 10 members. To conserve system resources the administrator may choose to create the active session pool as 7 users. This will limit the number of concurrent OLTP user sessions to 7. When the 8th user session tries to connect, the session will be queued.
- **Specify Undo Space Limits**—Undo data is generated when data manipulation statements (DML) are issued. The amount of undo data generated by a consumer group can be controlled by specifying a user-defined limit. If the amount of undo generated exceeds the specified threshold, members of the consumer group will not be able to continue DML operations until undo space is made available.
- **Enable Automatic Consumer Group Switching**—DRM allows automatic switching of users from one consumer group to another based on some user-defined criteria. For example, if a user performs an action that takes more than a specified amount of time, the user can be assigned to a lower priority group for the rest of the session or for the duration of the statement being executed.
- **Specify a Maximum Estimated Execution Time**—This feature prevents long-running operations such as a time-consuming query from being started during periods of high activity. If the optimizer determines that a certain operation may take longer than a specified amount of time, it will not be started at all.

DRM enables the effective prioritization of database operations by applying system resources to user-defined business requirements. The use of DRM requires the configuration of a number of components.

CONFIGURING DRM

When implementing a solution for effective resource management using DRM, a number of components need to be configured individually. Table 8-1 lists some of the main components of DRM.

TABLE 8-1 The main components of Database Resource Manager

DRM Component	Description
Consumer Group	A logical grouping of users with similar resource needs.
Resource Plan	A method of allocating resources. For example, an administrator may create a DAYPLAN that may be implemented during the day and a NIGHTPLAN to be implemented at night.
Resource Plan Directives	They define how resources should be distributed among the various consumer groups or subplans. For example, a plan directive can ensure OLTP users 80% of CPU consumption during business hours.

A user who wishes to use the DRM must posses the ADMINISTER_RESOURCE_MANAGER system privilege.

The DRM tool can be administered using the DBMS_RESOURCE_MANAGER and DBMS_RESOURCE_MANAGER_PRIVS packages. The subprograms of these packages have been described in various parts of the chapter.

Consumer Groups

A consumer group consists of a logical grouping of users with similar resource requirements. User sessions are assigned to consumer groups. A user may be assigned to multiple consumer groups; however for a given session created by the user, the user will belong to only one group. Users may switch from one consumer group to another during a session. A number of consumer groups come pre-configured with the Oracle 10g database. When creating a consumer group you may specify the method by which CPU is shared between members of the group. This is done by using the CPU_MTH parameter. The default value of CPU_MTH is ROUND_ROBIN which ensures all users an equal amount of CPU time. You can also choose RUN_TO_COMPLETION in which case the most active sessions are scheduled to run ahead of other sessions. Table 8-2 displays the names of the pre-defined consumer groups and their descriptions.

TABLE 8-2 Pre-defined consumer groups in the database

Consumer Group	Description
SYS_GROUP	A group consisting of the SYS and SYSTEM user.
OTHER_GROUPS	This group consists of users who are assigned to other consumer groups that are a not part of the active plan. When creating plan directives for plans and subplans a directive for OTHER_GROUPS must always be included.
LOW_GROUP	A group with lower priority than SYS_GROUP and OTHER_GROUPS in the SYSTEM_PLAN. You must decide which user sessions will be part of LOW_GROUP. Initially no user is associated with this consumer group.
DEFAULT_CONSUMER_GROUP	The default group for all user sessions that have not been assigned an initial consumer group.

To manage consumer groups the administrator can use the subprograms (listed in Table 8-3) of the DBMS_RESOURCE_MANAGER package.

TABLE 8-3 Subprograms associated with consumer groups

Subprogram Name	Description
CREATE_CONSUMER_GROUP	Creates a consumer group. The consumer group must be given a unique name and a description.
UPDATE_CONSUMER_GROUP	Updates a consumer group's comment.
DELETE_CONSUMER_GROUP	Deletes a consumer group.
SET_INITIAL_CONSUMER_GROUP	Sets the initial resource consumer group for a user.
SWITCH_CONSUMER_GROUP_FOR_SESS	Dynamically switches the consumer group for a connected session.
SWITCH_CONSUMER_GROUP_FOR_USER	Dynamically switches the consumer group of all sessions belonging to a specific user.
SET_CONSUMER_GROUP_MAPPING	Allows you to map a user session to a consumer group based on either login or run-time attributes.
SET_CONSUMER_GROUP_MAPPING_PRI	Prioritizes mappings when there are multiple attribute mappings associated with a consumer group.

Example: If an administrator wants to create a consumer group called NURSE_CG for all sessions created by nurses at Keller Medical Center, the following block may be executed.

```
SQL> BEGIN
     DBMS_RESOURCE_MANAGER.CREATE_CONSUMER_GROUP
     ('NURSE_CG', 'Nurse Consumer Group');
     END;
     /
```

The procedure accepts the name of the consumer group as NURSE_CG and a comment Nurse Consumer Group.

Examples of the other subprograms related to consumer groups have been presented in other sections of this chapter as well as in the syntax guide.

Resource Plans

A resource plan is a method of allocating system resources. A plan is given a name during creation. A plan known as the SYSTEM_PLAN comes pre-defined in the Oracle database. A plan may have a subplan. A subplan must be created before the parent plan.

The subprograms of the DBMS_RESOURCE_MANAGER package that are associated with creating and managing resource plans are displayed in Table 8-4.

TABLE 8-4 Subprograms of associated with resource plans

Subprogram	Description
CREATE_PLAN	To create a resource plan.
UPDATE_PLAN	To update a resource plan's comment.
DELETE_PLAN	To delete a resource plan and its directives.
CREATE_SIMPLE_PLAN	To create a single level plan based on CPU usage.

Example: If an administrator wanted to create a resource plan for Keller Medical Center that will be active during the day, a plan called KELLER_DAYPLAN may be created as shown:

```
SQL>BEGIN
    DBMS_RESOURCE_MANAGER.CREATE_PLAN
    ('KELLER_DAYPLAN', 'Day Plan for KMC');
    END;
    /
```

Examples of the other subprograms related to resource plans have been presented in other sections of this chapter as well as in the syntax guide.

Resource Plan Directives

Consumer groups and subplans are associated with resource plans by means of resource plan directives. Resource plan directives may be created with many different options or directives.

The following plan directives exist for the pre-defined SYSTEM_PLAN of the database.

- The SYS_GROUP consumer group is assigned 100% CPU at a Level 1.
- The OTHER_GROUPS consumer group is assigned 100% CPU at a Level 2.
- The LOW_GROUPS consumer group is assigned 100% CPU at a Level 3.

CPU levels are discussed under the topic Managing CPU.

The subprograms of the DBMS_RESOURCE_MANAGER package that are associated with the creation and management of resource plan directives are displayed in Table 8-5.

TABLE 8-5 Subprograms of associated with resource plan directives

Subprogram	Description
CREATE_PLAN_DIRECTIVE	To create a plan directive, by associating a consumer group or a subplan to a parent plan.
UPDATE_PLAN_DIRECTIVE	To updates plan directives.
DELETE_PLAN_DIRECTIVE	To delete plan directives.

A detailed discussion of the various resource plan directives available in DRM is presented under the topic Resource Plan Directives in Detail.

In addition to the subprograms mentioned above, the DBMS_RESOURCE_MANAGER package has some other important subprograms. These subprograms are used to create and manage a staging area when implementing a solution using DRM. Table 8-6 describes these subprograms.

TABLE 8-6 Additional procedures of the DBMS_RESOURCE_MANAGER package

Subprogram	Description
CREATE_PENDING_AREA	To create a staging area. It is an area where the different elements of DRM are created and managed.
VALIDATE_PENDING_AREA	To verify changes that are applied to the pending area.
SUBMIT_PENDING_AREA	Submits the pending area for completion by the DRM.
CLEAR_PENDING_AREA	To clear a pending area without submitting the changes.

Another package called the DBMS_RESOURCE_MANAGER_PRIVS package is also available for managing resources using DRM. The package contains the subprograms (Table 8-7) required to grant privileges to users who need to use DRM. You must possess the ADMINISTER_RESOURCE_MANAGER privilege to administer DRM.

TABLE 8-7 Subprograms of the DBMS_RESOURCE_MANAGER_PRIVS package.

Subprogram	Description
GRANT_SYSTEM_PRIVILEGE	Grants the ADMINISTER_RESOURCE_MANAGER system privilege to a user or role.
REVOKE_SYSTEM_PRIVILEGE	Revokes the ADMINISTER_RESOURCE_MANAGER system privilege from a user or role.
GRANT_SWITCH_CONSUMER_GROUP	Grants a user, role, or PUBLIC the permission to switch to another consumer group dynamically.
REVOKE_SWITCH_CONSUMER_GROUP	Revokes the permission from a user, role, or public to switch to a specified resource consumer group.

Resource Plan Directives in Detail

Resource plan directives are a means of associating resource plans, consumer groups, and the system resources. When creating plan directives you can specify how different resources such as CPU, undo space, execution time, and active session pool are to be allocated. Plan directives are created using the CREATE_PLAN_DIRECTIVE procedure. The procedure accepts many parameters depending on the options you wish to set. When creating plan directives you must specify the name of the plan, the name of the group, or subplan for whom the directives are being created, a comment, and the plan directives.

Table 8-8 displays the different parameters available for managing plan directives for both subplans and consumer groups.

TABLE 8-8 Parameter options for managing the plan directives of subplans or consumer groups

Parameter	Description
PLAN	Name of the resource plan.
GROUP_OR_SUBPLAN	Name of the consumer group or subplan.
COMMENT	User-defined remark.
CPU_P*n*	Specification of CPU usage at a priority level *n*. Value is specified in percentages.

Table 8-9 displays other additional parameter options that may be specified when creating plan directives. These options are applicable to consumer groups only:

TABLE 8-9 Parameter options that are specific to consumer groups

Parameter	Description
ACTIVE_SESS_POOL_P1	Specifies the maximum number of concurrent active sessions for a resource consumer group. The default value is UNLIMITED.
QUEUEING_P1	Specifies the time-out value in seconds for a queued session. After the time-out exceeds, the session will be aborted. Default value is UNLIMITED.
PARALLEL_DEGREE_LIMIT_P1	Specifies the degree of parallelism for an operation. Default value is UNLIMITED.
SWITCH_GROUP	Specifies the consumer group to which this session is switched if other switch criteria are met. Default value is NULL.
SWITCH_TIME	Specifies time (in seconds) that a session can execute before an action is taken. The action involves moving the session to another lower-priority consumer group. Default is UNLIMITED.
SWITCH_ESTIMATE	Can be set to TRUE or FALSE. A value TRUE, tells the database to use its "execution time estimate" to automatically switch the consumer group of an operation prior to beginning its execution. The default is FALSE.
MAX_EST_EXEC_TIME	Specifies the maximum execution time (in seconds) allowed for a session. If the optimizer estimates that an operation will take longer than this value the operation is not started and ORA-07455 is issued. Default is UNLIMITED.
UNDO_POOL	Defines the total amount of undo that can be generated by a consumer group in Kilobytes (K). Default is UNLIMITED.
MAX_IDLE_TIME	Indicates the maximum session idle time in seconds. Default is NULL, implying UNLIMITED.

TABLE 8-9 Parameter options that are specific to consumer groups (continued)

Parameter	Description
MAX_IDLE_BLOCKER_TIME	Indicates the maximum session idle time of a blocking session. Default is NULL, implying UNLIMITED.
SWITCH_TIME_IN_CALL	Specifies the time (in seconds) that a session can execute before an action is taken. The action may involve moving the session to a lower-priority consumer group for the duration of the current call. After completion of the call, the session is restored to its original consumer group. Default is UNLIMITED. You cannot specify both SWITCH_TIME_IN_CALL and SWITCH_TIME.

Managing CPU Utilization CPU time is an important and expensive resource that can be managed using the DRM. Resource plans have two options regarding CPU allocation–EMPHASIS and RATIO. The EMPHASIS method is more commonly used and in this method the CPU usage is allocated in terms of percentages. The method may be used for both single and multi-level plans. The RATIO method is used only in single-level plans and CPU usage is expressed in terms of a weight.

Within a consumer group, all user sessions share CPU time in a round-robin fashion. When specifying plan directives, a consumer group or subplan may divide CPU usage at different levels. Up to 8 levels can be created using DRM. These levels provide a priority ranking within a plan, where the needs of Level 1 must be met before that of Level 2, the needs of Level 2 must be met before Level 3, and so on. A directive for CPU utilization is specified using CPU_Pn. When *n* takes a value of 1, it indicates the highest priority level of 1, when *n* takes a value 2, it represents a lower priority compared to level 1 and so on.

Example: If a database administrator wishes to allocate 80% of the CPU to members of the OLTP consumer group, at a level 1, under the KELLER_DAYPLAN, the following resource plan directive may be created.

```
SQL>DBMS_RESOURCE_MANAGER.CREATE_PLAN_DIRECTIVE (
    PLAN => 'KELLER_DAYPLAN',
    GROUP_OR_SUBPLAN => 'OLTP',
    CPU_P1 => 80);
```

Degree of Parallelization In data-warehousing environments where large queries are executed to analyze the data, parallelization of query processes may be performed to achieve faster performance. Using DRM, the maximum number of parallel processes that may be started are specified by the PARALLEL_DEGREE_LIMIT_P1 plan directive.

Example: If the database administrator wants to limit the members of the REPORTS_CG consumer group from initiating more than 5 parallel query processes during queries, a plan directive may be created in the following manner:

```
SQL>DBMS_RESOURCE_MANAGER.CREATE_PLAN_DIRECTIVE (
    PLAN => 'KELLER_DAYPLAN',
    GROUP_OR_SUBPLAN => 'REPORT_CG',
    PARALLEL_DEGREE_LIMIT_P1 => 5);
```

The Active Session Pool As a database administrator you may want to control the amount of resources that a particular consumer group uses. This is to ensure that no single consumer group is consuming all the available system resources. Using DRM, the database administrator can limit the number of active sessions started by a consumer group. This is the active session pool.

For example, if you define the active pool to 5, when a 6th session tries to connect, it will be assigned to a queue. The queue may be managed by specifying a timeout value. If a session waits in the queue beyond the time-out value, the session will be automatically aborted. However, if one of the active sessions completes, it will free up space for the oldest queued session.

Parameters associated with the active session pool are ACTIVE_SESS_POOL_P1 and QUEUEING_P1. An active session pool is defined by the ACTIVE_SESS_POOL_P1 parameter. The QUEUEING_P1 parameter can be used to indicate how long any session will wait in the queue before being terminated. This time-out value is specified in seconds and has a default value of UNLIMITED.

Example: To define the active session pool for the REPORT_CG consumer group to be 6 and a time-out value for the sessions in the queue as 300 seconds, the following plan directive may be created.

```
SQL>DBMS_RESOURCE_MANAGER.CREATE_PLAN_DIRECTIVE
    (PLAN=> 'KELLER_DAYPLAN',
    GROUP_OR_SUBPLAN => 'REPORT_CG',
    COMMENT => 'ACTIVE SESSION POOL EXAMPLE',
    ACTIVE_SESS_POOL_P1 => 6,
    QUEUEING_P1=> 300);
```

Maximum Estimated Execution Time During periods of high activity in a database, administrators may not wish to allow long-running jobs to be started until activity slows. This may be because long-running jobs consume excessive system resources. When a statement is issued, the optimizer calculates the amount of time the execution of the statement is likely to take. Using this value the DRM prevents execution of statements that are likely to take longer than a user-defined threshold. The threshold value for the maximum time a statement can take may be specified by means of the MAX_EST_EXEC_TIME parameter. For example, if you specify MAX_EST_EXEC_TIME to 180 seconds (3 minutes), then any statement that the optimizer determines will take more than 3 minutes to complete, will not be started. If the SWITCH_ESTIMATE directive is set to TRUE, and the optimizer estimates the amount of time an operation will take to exceed MAX_EST_EXEC_TIME, an error will be displayed and the operation will not start. If SWITCH_ESTIMATE is FALSE, Oracle will start the operation even if it exceeds the maximum estimated time.

Example: To ensure that the REPORT_CG consumer group cannot execute a statement that will take more than 180 seconds or 3 minutes, the following code may be executed.

```
SQL>DBMS_RESOURCE_MANAGER.CREATE_PLAN_DIRECTIVE
    (PLAN              => 'KELLER_DAYPLAN',
    GROUP_OR_SUBPLAN  => 'REPORT_CG',
    COMMENT           => 'MAX EST EXEC TIME EXAMPLE',
    MAX_EST_EXEC_TIME => 180
    SWITCH_ESTIMATE   => TRUE);
```

Automatic Consumer Group Switching Often in a hybrid environment, where the database may see both Online Transaction Processing (OLTP) and Decision Support System (DSS) type activity, the DBA may choose to separate the activity based on the time of day. Users may issue OLTP transactions during the early part of day and run their reports and backups later. However, if for any reason, batch jobs have to run alongside OLTP transactions, then the long-running batch job that monopolizes CPU time may be switched to a lower priority consumer group dynamically. This feature is achieved by setting parameters when defining plan directives.

The SWITCH_GROUP parameter specifies the group to switch to. The SWITCH_TIME parameter is a limit in seconds that a session can be active. By active we mean the session is running and consuming resources. When using the SWITCH_TIME directive a session that has been put into a different consumer group remains there until the session ends.

Oracle 10g introduced another parameter, SWITCH_TIME_IN_CALL. It is similar to SWITCH_TIME except that a session that has moved to another consumer group is returned to its original consumer group after the SQL call is completed. The SWITCH_TIME and SWITCH_TIME_IN_CALL parameters are mutually exclusive and cannot be specified together.

The SWITCH_ESTIMATE is another parameter that is associated with the automatic switching of user session to other consumer groups. The value of the parameter can be TRUE or FALSE. If set to TRUE, the DRM uses a predicted estimate of how long a certain operation is likely to take. If the predicted value exceeds the SWITCH_TIME or SWITCH_TIME_IN_CALL parameters, the session will be switched to the SWITCH_GROUP even before the operation begins.

Example: In the following example the user sessions of the REPORT_CG consumer group, can issue a call that can run for a maximum of 180 seconds (3 minutes). Upon exceeding this time limit, they will be automatically switched to the OTHER_GROUPS consumer group. However after the completion of the SQL call, they will be returned to their original group.

```
SQL>DBMS_RESOURCE_MANAGER.CREATE_PLAN_DIRECTIVE
    (PLAN                => 'KELLER_DAYPLAN',
    GROUP_OR_SUBPLAN     => 'REPORT_CG',
    COMMENT              => 'AUTOMATIC SWITCHING EXAMPLE',
    SWITCH_GROUP         => 'OTHER_GROUPS',
    SWITCH_TIME_IN_CALL=> 180);
```

Undo Quota The DRM also provides a directive of limiting the amount of undo data generated by consumer groups. The UNDO_POOL parameter may be specified to indicate the maximum amount (in Kilobytes) of the undo space that can be used by consumer groups. When a consumer group exceeds this limit, user sessions of this consumer group can continue to issue SELECT statements but cannot issue DML statements (INSERT, UPDATE, DELETE) that generate undo entries. If a consumer group exceeds its quota during the execution of a DML statement, the operation will abort with an error. The consumer group can execute DML statements again when undo space is freed by another session of the same group or the undo quota is increased.

Example: The example displays how the DBA may set the undo quota for the REPORT_CG consumer group to 600K.

```
SQL> DBMS_RESOURCE_MANAGER.CREATE_PLAN_DIRECTIVE
     (PLAN              => 'KELLER_DAYPLAN',
     GROUP_OR_SUBPLAN => 'REPORT_CG',
     COMMENT            => 'UNDO POOL EXAMPLE',
     UNDO_POOL          => 600);
```

Maximum Idle Time Introduced in Oracle 10g, this directive limits the amount of time (in seconds) a user session may be idle. This is achieved by the MAX_IDLE_TIME directive. When a session exceeds the limit, the PMON background process forcibly kills the session and cleans up resources that it may be holding.

Example: In the following example the user sessions of the REPORT_CG consumer group can remain idle for a maximum of 480 seconds, after which they will be automatically terminated.


```
SQL> DBMS_RESOURCE_MANAGER.CREATE_PLAN_DIRECTIVE
     (PLAN              => 'KELLER_DAYPLAN',
     GROUP_OR_SUBPLAN => 'REPORT_CG',
     COMMENT            => 'UNDO POOL EXAMPLE',
     MAX_IDLE_TIME      => 480);
```

Maximum Idle Blocker Time Introduced in Oracle 10g, this directive specifies the maximum number of seconds that a session may remain idle while blocking another session. A blocking session is one that is currently locking resources in an exclusive mode, while there are other sessions waiting for their release. This is done by the MAX_IDLE_BLOCKER_TIME plan directive. The blocking session will be forcibly killed by the PMON background process, releasing all resources held by it.

Example: In the following example, user sessions of the REPORT_CG consumer group, can remain idle when blocking other sessions for a maximum of 600 seconds.

```
SQL> DBMS_RESOURCE_MANAGER.CREATE_PLAN_DIRECTIVE
     (PLAN                  => 'KELLER_DAYPLAN',
     GROUP_OR_SUBPLAN     => 'REPORT_CG',
     COMMENT                => 'UNDO POOL EXAMPLE',
     MAX_IDLE_BLOCKER_TIME=> 600);
```

Putting the Pieces Together

The objective of using the DRM is to effectively manage system resources within the database. We have learned the different elements that need to be configured when implementing a solution using DRM. In this section you will be able to understand how the different elements are put together to achieve a complete solution.

A database administrator can create two kinds of plans using DRM. Simple single-level plans that involve only CPU usage can be easily created using the CREATE_SIMPLE_PLAN packaged procedure. A complex plan must be created if it is a multi-level plan or if it involves plan directives for resources other than CPU time.

Creating Simple Plans

Using the DRM, simple and complex plans can be created. A simple plan is one that involves CPU consumption at only one level (level 1). It can be created by using the CREATE_SIMPLE_PLAN procedure of the DBMS_RESOURCE_MANAGER package. When creating a plan, the name of the plan, the name of the consumer group, and the CPU consumption in terms of a percentage must be mentioned. This implies that the consumer groups must be created, and the users assigned to the consumer groups before creating the simple plan. The procedure allows for the specification of up to eight consumer groups and their CPU allocations.

Example: In the example, the CPU consumption for the consumer group ALLSTAFF is limited to 35%, DSS_STAFF is limited to 65%, and OTHER_GROUPS will get 100% CPU resources at Level 1.

```
SQL> BEGIN
     DBMS_RESOURCE_MANAGER.CREATE_SIMPLE_PLAN (
     SIMPLE_PLAN       => 'KELLER_NIGHTPLAN',
     CONSUMER_GROUP1 => 'ALLSTAFF',
     GROUP1_CPU        => 35,
     CONSUMER_GROUP2 => 'DSS_STAFF',
     GROUP2_CPU        => 65);
     END;
     /
```


Creating Complex Plans

Complex Plans are those that involve system resources other than CPU. The options for creating complex plans are more flexible but require additional steps. It provides a means of creating multi-level plans by nesting subplans.

A complex plan can be created using the DRM, by following a number of steps, as listed in the following section.

1. **Create a pending area.** This is a staging area, where resource plans, consumer groups, and directives will be created. This is done using the CREATE_PENDING_AREA procedure.
2. **Create the resource plans.** Every plan has a name. If the plan has a subplan, the subplan must be created first. This is done using the CREATE_RESOURCE_PLAN procedure.
3. **Create the consumer groups.** Every consumer group must have a name. This is done using the CREATE_CONSUMER_GROUPS procedure.
4. **Create the resource plan directives.** These directives associate a consumer group or subplan to the parent plan. This is done using the CREATE_PLAN_DIRECTIVES procedure.
5. **Validate the pending area.** This involves verifying the changes made in the pending area. This is done using the VALIDATE_PENDING_AREA procedure.
6. **Submit the validated plan.** This involves submitting the pending area for completion. This is done using the SUBMIT_PENDING_AREA procedure.
7. **Assign users to the consumer groups.** In this step you associate the database user with the consumer group. This is done using the SET_INITIAL_CONSUMER_GROUP procedure.
8. **Make the plan active for the instance.** After the plan has been created, it may be made active for the current/future instance by modifying the RESOURCE_PLAN initialization parameter. This is done using the ALTER SYSTEM SET RESOURCE_PLAN=<*plan name*> command.

Practice 1: Implementing a Complex Plan

The steps discussed in the previous section for the creation of a complex plan will be demonstrated in a practice example. You will create consumer groups, resource plans, and resource plan directives based on some business requirements. This example will give you an opportunity to both understand and learn how to configure the components of the DRM tool.

Figure 8-1 depicts a plan that needs to be implemented at Keller Medical Center. The plan must be active during normal office hours. Following Figure 8-1 is a description of the desired business requirements. This will be followed by a solution using the DRM.

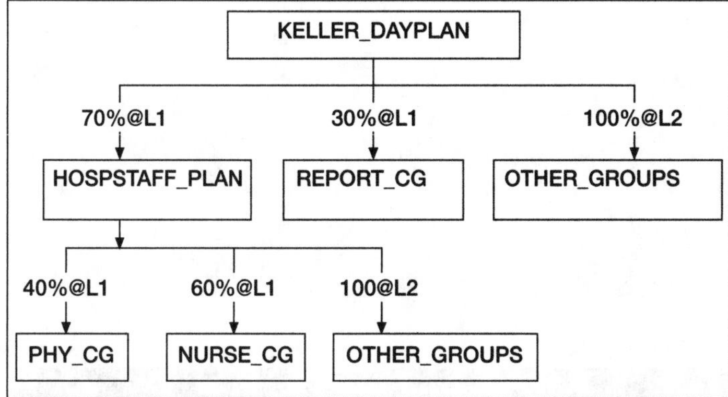

FIGURE 8-1 An overview of the KELLER_DAYPLAN that must be created.

In Figure 8-1, you can see a number of plans, subplans, consumer groups, and plan directives for CPU utilization in terms of percentages at different levels. To understand the requirements, a further breakdown of the scenario is given in Tables 8-10 through 8-12.

Plan Name: KELLER_DAYPLAN

Subplans: HOSPSTAFF_PLAN

Consumer Groups: REPORT_CG, PHY_CG, NURSE_CG, OTHER_GROUPS

TABLE 8-10 Resource Plan Directives for CPU utilization

Consumer Group/Subplan	Parent Plan	CPU% at Level 1	CPU% at Level 2
HOSPSTAFF_PLAN	KELLER_DAYPLAN	70%	
REPORT_CG	KELLER_DAYPLAN	30%	
OTHER_GROUPS	KELLER_DAYPLAN		100%
PHY_CG	HOSPSTAFF_PLAN	40% of 70%= 28%	
NURSE_CG	HOSPSTAFF_PLAN	60% of 70%= 42%	
OTHER_GROUPS	HOSPSTAFF_PLAN		100%

TABLE 8-11 Other Resource Plan Directives for Consumer Groups

Consumer Group	REPORT_CG	PHY_CG	NURSE_CG
Plan Directives			
ACTIVE_SESS_POOL_P1			1
QUEUEING_P1			1
PARALLEL_DEGREE_LIMIT_P1	10		
SWITCH_GROUP		OTHER_GROUPS	
SWITCH_TIME			
SWITCH_ESTIMATE	TRUE		
MAX_EST_EXEC_TIME	3		
UNDO_POOL			50
MAX_IDLE_TIME	120		
MAX_IDLE_BLOCKER_TIME		120	
SWITCH_TIME_IN_CALL		15	

TABLE 8-12 Users and their consumer groups..

Username(s)	Consumer Group
Tammy / Tanya	PHY_CG
Toby / Rick	NURSE_CG
Zaira	REPORT_CG
Steve	-

Explanation: The KELLER_DAYPLAN is the plan that is made active during the day. At 100% CPU utilization, the HOSPSTAFF_PLAN utilizes 70% of the CPU and the remaining 30% is utilized by REPORT_CG consumer group. If 100% of CPU is not allocated, the remaining CPU time after consumption by the HOSPSTAFF_PLAN and the REPORT_CG consumer group will be given to the OTHER_GROUPS consumer groups. This is done because the OTHER_GROUPS consumer group is allocated 100% CPU at a level 2.

The PHY_CG and NURSE_CG consumer groups have plan directives under the HOSPSTAFF_PLAN. Out of the 70% allocated to the HOSPSTAFF_PLAN, 40% will be allocated to the PHY_CG consumer group. This makes it 28% of CPU at a Level 1. Out of the 70% allocated to the HOSPSTAFF_PLAN, 60% will be allocated to the NURSE_CG consumer group. This makes it 42% of CPU at a Level 1. If the total 70% allocated to the HOSPSTAFF_PLAN is not consumed, all of the remaining (100%) will be given to the OTHER_GROUPS consumer group.

To create this multi-level complex plan you will create a pending area; create the resource plans, the consumer groups, and the resource plan directives. You will also assign users to their consumer groups and finally make the KELLER_DAYPLAN active.

Make sure you run the script **C8_setup.sql** script mentioned under the section "Setup for the chapter." This script creates the six users TAMMY, TANYA, TOBY, RICK, ZAIRA, and STEVE. It also grants the users certain privileges necessary for the practice. Please go through the contents of the script before performing these steps.

1. Connect as a user with SYSDBA privileges.

```
SQL> CONNECT DB_ADMIN/DB_ADMIN AS SYSDBA
```

2. Using the CREATE_PENDING_AREA procedure of the DBMS_RESOURCE_MANAGER package, establish a pending area.


```
SQL> BEGIN
     DBMS_RESOURCE_MANAGER.CREATE_PENDING_AREA;
     END;
     /
```

3. Create the three consumer groups, namely REPORT_CG, PHY_CG, and NURSE_CG. The OTHER_GROUPS consumer group already exists in the database and must not be created.

```
SQL> BEGIN
     DBMS_RESOURCE_MANAGER.CREATE_CONSUMER_GROUP ('REPORT_
     CG', 'Report Consumer Group');
     DBMS_RESOURCE_MANAGER.CREATE_CONSUMER_GROUP ('PHY_
     CG', 'Physicians Consumer Group');
     DBMS_RESOURCE_MANAGER.CREATE_CONSUMER_GROUP ('NURSE_
     CG', 'Nurse Consumer Group');
     END;
     /
```

4. Create the resource plans and subplans. Create subplans before you create the parent plan.

```
SQL> BEGIN
     DBMS_RESOURCE_MANAGER.CREATE_PLAN ('HOSPSTAFF_
     PLAN',' Plan for hospital staff');
     DBMS_RESOURCE_MANAGER.CREATE_PLAN
     ('KELLER_DAYPLAN',' Plan for KMC');
     END;
     /
```

5. Create the resource plan directives for the subplans HOSPSTAFF and consumer groups based on the business requirements described.

```
SQL>  -- Plan Directives for the HOSPSTAFF Plan
SQL> BEGIN
     DBMS_RESOURCE_MANAGER.CREATE_PLAN_DIRECTIVE (
     PLAN             => 'KELLER_DAYPLAN',
     GROUP_OR_SUBPLAN => 'HOSPSTAFF_PLAN',
     COMMENT          => 'PLAN FOR HOSPITAL STAFF',
     CPU_P1           => 70);
     END;
     /

SQL>-- Plan Directives for REPORT_CG
```

```
SQL> BEGIN
     DBMS_RESOURCE_MANAGER.CREATE_PLAN_DIRECTIVE (
     PLAN                 => 'KELLER_DAYPLAN',
     GROUP_OR_SUBPLAN  => 'REPORT_CG',
     COMMENT              => 'PLAN DIRECTIVES FOR REPORT_CG',
     CPU_P1                      => 30,
     PARALLEL_DEGREE_LIMIT_P1 => 10,
     MAX_EST_EXEC_TIME           => 3,
     SWITCH_ESTIMATE             => TRUE,
     MAX_IDLE_TIME               => 120);
     END;
     /

SQL> -- Plan Directives for OTHER_GROUPS
SQL> BEGIN
     DBMS_RESOURCE_MANAGER.CREATE_PLAN_DIRECTIVE(
     PLAN                   => 'KELLER_DAYPLAN',
     GROUP_OR_SUBPLAN     => 'OTHER_GROUPS',
     COMMENT => 'PLAN DIRECTIVES FOR OTHER GROUPS',
     CPU_P2                 => 100);
     END;
     /

SQL> -- Plan Directives for PHY_CG
SQL>BEGIN
    DBMS_RESOURCE_MANAGER.CREATE_PLAN_DIRECTIVE(
    PLAN                      => 'HOSPSTAFF_PLAN',
    GROUP_OR_SUBPLAN          => 'PHY_CG',
    CPU_P1                    => 40,
    COMMENT                   =>'PLAN DIRECTIVES FOR PHY_CG',
    SWITCH_GROUP              => 'OTHER_GROUPS',
    SWITCH_TIME_IN_CALL         => 15,
    MAX_IDLE_BLOCKER_TIME       => 120  );
    END;
    /

SQL> -- Plan Directives for NURSE_CG
SQL> BEGIN
     DBMS_RESOURCE_MANAGER.CREATE_PLAN_DIRECTIVE(
     PLAN                     => 'HOSPSTAFF_PLAN',
     GROUP_OR_SUBPLAN       => 'NURSE_CG',
     COMMENT                  => 'PLAN DIRECTIVES FOR NURSE_CG',
     CPU_P1                   => 60,
     ACTIVE_SESS_POOL_P1    => 1,
     QUEUEING_P1              => 1,
     UNDO_POOL                => 50);
     END;
/

SQL> -- Plan Directive for OTHER_GROUPS
SQL>BEGIN
    DBMS_RESOURCE_MANAGER.CREATE_PLAN_DIRECTIVE(
    PLAN                => 'HOSPSTAFF_PLAN',
    GROUP_OR_SUBPLAN => 'OTHER_GROUPS',
    COMMENT             => 'PLAN DIRECTIVES FOR OTHER_GROUPS',
    CPU_P2              => 100);
    END;
  /
```

6. Validate the pending area, using the VALIDATE_PENDING_AREA packaged procedure.

```
SQL> BEGIN
     DBMS_RESOURCE_MANAGER.VALIDATE_PENDING_AREA;
     END;
     /
```

7. Submit the pending area using the SUBMIT_PENDING_AREA packaged procedure.

```
SQL> BEGIN
     DBMS_RESOURCE_MANAGER.SUBMIT_PENDING_AREA;
     END;
     /
```


8. Using the GRANT_SWITCH_CONSUMER_GROUP, grant the users the privilege to switch to consumer groups. Do not allow the grantee or user to grant the switch privilege to other users.

```
SQL> -- ASSIGNING USERS TO CONSUMER GROUPS
SQL> BEGIN
     DBMS_RESOURCE_MANAGER_PRIVS.GRANT_SWITCH_CONSUMER_GROUP(
     'TAMMY','PHY_CG',FALSE);

     DBMS_RESOURCE_MANAGER_PRIVS.GRANT_SWITCH_CONSUMER_GROUP(
     'TANYA','PHY_CG',FALSE);

     DBMS_RESOURCE_MANAGER_PRIVS.GRANT_SWITCH_CONSUMER_GROUP(
     'TOBY','NURSE_CG',FALSE);

     DBMS_RESOURCE_MANAGER_PRIVS.GRANT_SWITCH_CONSUMER_GROUP(
     'RICK','NURSE_CG',FALSE);

     DBMS_RESOURCE_MANAGER_PRIVS.GRANT_SWITCH_CONSUMER_GROUP(
     'ZAIRA','REPORT_CG',FALSE);

     END;
     /
```

9. Assign the users to their initial consumer groups by using the SET_INITIAL_CONSUMER_GROUP procedure.

```
SQL> BEGIN
     DBMS_RESOURCE_MANAGER.SET_INITIAL_CONSUMER_GROUP('TAMMY',
     'PHY_CG');
     DBMS_RESOURCE_MANAGER.SET_INITIAL_CONSUMER_GROUP('TANYA',
     'PHY_CG');
     DBMS_RESOURCE_MANAGER.SET_INITIAL_CONSUMER_GROUP('TOBY',
     'NURSE_CG');
     DBMS_RESOURCE_MANAGER.SET_INITIAL_CONSUMER_GROUP('RICK',
     'NURSE_CG');
     DBMS_RESOURCE_MANAGER.SET_INITIAL_CONSUMER_GROUP('ZAIRA',
     'REPORT_CG');
     END;
     /
```

10. The last step in this procedure is to establish the KELLER_DAYPLAN as the active resource plan for the current instance. This is done using the following ALTER SYSTEM command.

```
SQL> ALTER SYSTEM SET RESOURCE_MANAGER_PLAN = KELLER_DAYPLAN;
```

11. Exit SQL*Plus.

Practice 2: Testing the Complex Plan

In this exercise, you will test the various plan directives that were created for the consumer groups.

Testing the MAX_BLOCKER_IDLE_TIME plan directive The PHY_CG consumer group has a plan directive that controls the amount of time a blocking session can remain idle. In this test, you will simulate an idle blocking session, and see how the MAX_BLOCKER_IDLE_TIME plan directive resolves the wait.

1. Start SQL*Plus and connect as the user TAMMY, with a password of TAMMY.

```
SQL> CONNECT TAMMY/TAMMY
```

2. Issue the following UPDATE command on the EMERGENCY_ASSTS table.

```
SQL> UPDATE EMERGENCY_ASSTS
     SET ASSISTANT_NAME='VICTORIA SHAW' WHERE ASNO=2;
```

3. Start another SQL*Plus session, connect as the user TANYA, with a password of TANYA. Tanya also belongs to the PHY_CG consumer group.

```
SQL> CONNECT TANYA/TANYA
```

4. Issue the following UPDATE command on the EMERGENCY_ASSTS table belonging to TAMMY. This statement will wait. The row being updated is currently being modified by the user TAMMY.

```
SQL> UPDATE TAMMY.EMERGENCY_ASSTS
     SET ASSISTANT_NAME='VICTORIA SHAW' WHERE ASNO=2;
```

5. Wait for about 4 minutes.
6. After some time, you will notice that the second session created by TANYA will automatically display "1 row updated." This was the session that was earlier in the waiting state.
7. Return to the session created by TAMMY, and issue the command to retrieve all the data from the EMERGENCY_ASSTS table. An ORA-02396 error indicating "exceeded maximum idle time" will be displayed (Figure 8-2).

   The error is generated because the session created by TAMMY was idle and blocking TANYA's session for more than 2 minutes. The MAX_IDLE_BLOCKER_TIME plan directive has been created the members for the PHY_CG consumer group.
8. Exit both SQL*Plus sessions.

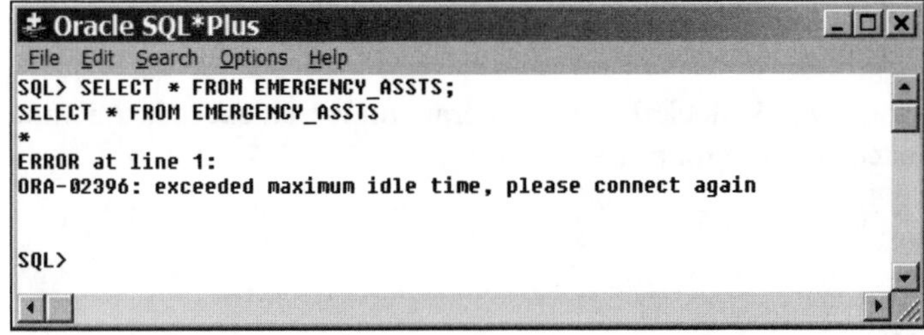
```
SQL> SELECT * FROM EMERGENCY_ASSTS;
SELECT * FROM EMERGENCY_ASSTS
*
ERROR at line 1:
ORA-02396: exceeded maximum idle time, please connect again


SQL>
```

FIGURE 8-2 The maximum blocker idle time has been exceeded

Testing MAX_IDLE_TIME plan directive The consumer group REPORT_CG has a plan directive that limits idle time to 2 minutes. In this test, you will connect as the user ZAIRA, who belongs to the REPORT_CG group. You will then perform no activity for a few minutes. The DRM will automatically disconnect ZAIRA's connection with the database.

1. Open SQL*Plus and connect as the user ZAIRA with a password ZAIRA.

   ```
   SQL> CONNECT ZAIRA/ZAIRA
   ```

2. Wait for about 3–4 minutes.
3. Issue the command, to view the names of all tables that belong to the current schema.

   ```
   SQL> SELECT TABLE_NAME FROM USER_TABLES;
   ```

   An ORA-02396 error will be generated, indicating "exceeded maximum idle time" (Figure 8-3).

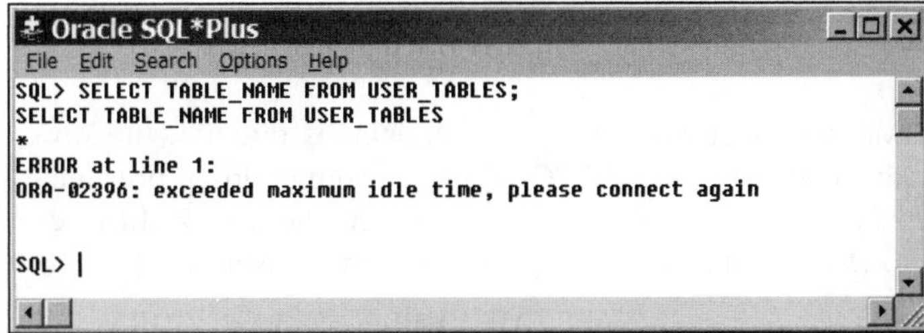
```
SQL> SELECT TABLE_NAME FROM USER_TABLES;
SELECT TABLE_NAME FROM USER_TABLES
*
ERROR at line 1:
ORA-02396: exceeded maximum idle time, please connect again


SQL> |
```

FIGURE 8-3 The maximum idle time has been exceeded

4. Exit SQL*Plus.

Testing the UNDO_POOL plan directive The NURSE_CG consumer group has a plan directive that limits undo usage to 50 bytes. In this test example, you will create a table, and start inserting rows into the table using a PL/SQL block. The insert statements will require undo space exceeding the undo quota specified for the group resulting in an error.

1. Open SQL*Plus and connect as the user RICK with a password of RICK.

   ```
   SQL> CONNECT RICK/RICK
   ```

2. Create a table called N1 containing a single numeric column.

```
SQL> CREATE TABLE N1 (C1 NUMBER);
```

3. Write the following PL/SQL block that will generate undo that exceeds the limit specified for this consumer group (Figure 8-4).

```
SQL> BEGIN
     FOR I IN 1..1000
     LOOP
     INSERT INTO N1 VALUES (1);
     END LOOP;
     END;
     /
```

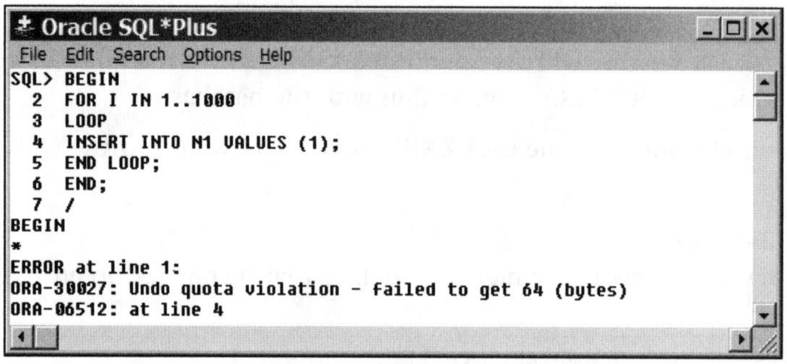

```
Oracle SQL*Plus
File Edit Search Options Help
SQL> BEGIN
  2  FOR I IN 1..1000
  3  LOOP
  4  INSERT INTO N1 VALUES (1);
  5  END LOOP;
  6  END;
  7  /
BEGIN
*
ERROR at line 1:
ORA-30027: Undo quota violation - failed to get 64 (bytes)
ORA-06512: at line 4
```

FIGURE 8-4 The undo quota has exceeded the limit

The error indicates that an undo quota violation has occurred, and it was unable to get the 64 bytes that were required for the operation to complete.

4. Exit SQL*Plus

Testing MAX_EST_EXEC_TIME plan directive This test, will demonstrate how the MAX_EST_EXEC_TIME plan directive created for the REPORT_CG consumer group prevents the execution of a query that takes longer than 3 seconds. When the user ZAIRA performs a query on the DBA_SEGMENTS data dictionary view an error is generated.

1. Start SQL*Plus and connect as the user ZAIRA with a password ZAIRA.

```
SQL> CONNECT ZAIRA/ZAIRA
```

2. Issue a statement to read the entire DBA_SEGMENTS table. Notice the error that is generated (Figure 8-5). It is a result of the MAX_EST_EXEC_TIME plan directive that has been defined for the REPORT_CG consumer group.

```
SQL> SELECT * FROM DBA_SEGMENTS;
```

The error indicates that the statement failed to execute because the estimated execution was 7 seconds and the limit specified is 3 seconds.

3. Exit SQL*Plus.

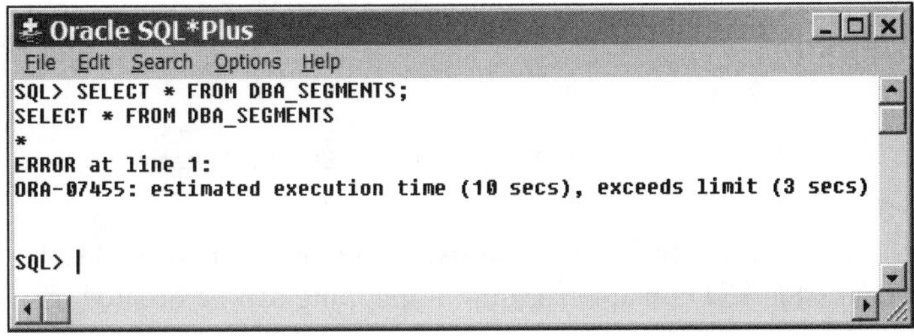

FIGURE 8-5 The maximum execution time has exceeded the limit

AUTOMATIC MAPPING OF SESSIONS TO CONSUMER GROUPS

In an earlier part of this chapter we saw how user sessions were assigned to consumer groups by means of the DBMS_RESOURCE_MANAGER.SET_INITIAL_CONSUMER_GROUP packaged procedure. In Oracle 10*g* a new feature has been introduced where a session is automatically assigned to a consumer group based on its login and run-time attributes. Table 8-13 associates the login and run-time attributes with the name they can be referenced with.

TABLE 8-13 Names assigned to run-time attributes

Attribute	Name referenced with
The Oracle Username	ORACLE_USER
The Client machine name	CLIENT_MACHINE
The client program name	CLIENT_PROGRAM
The client Operating system (OS) name	CLIENT_OS_NAME
The module name	MODULE_NAME
The module name action	MODULE_NAME_ACTION
The service name	SERVICE_NAME
The service module	SERVICE_MODULE
The service module action	SERVICE_MODULE_ACTION

One or more of these attributes can be mapped to a consumer group by using the DBMS_RESOURCE_MANAGER.SET_CONSUMER_GROUP_MAPPING packaged procedure. The procedure receives three parameters, the attribute name, the attribute value, and the consumer group name. If the third attribute is null, it results in the deletion of the mapping.

If you want a user who logs into the machine using an operating system username of PANDA to be assigned to the PHY_CG consumer group, a mapping can be created in the following manner.

```
DBMS_RESOURCE_MANAGER.SET_CONSUMER_GROUP_MAPPING (DBMS_RESOURCE_MANAGER.
CLIENT_OS_NAME,'PANDA','PHY_CG');
```

If you want a user who logs into the database using a username of HEADNURSE to be automatically assigned to the NURSE_CG consumer group, a mapping can be created as:

```
DBMS_RESOURCE_MANAGER.SET_CONSUMER_GROUP_MAPPING (DBMS_RESOURCE_MANAGER.
ORACLE_USER,'HEADNURSE','NURSE_CG');
```


In this manner, many mappings may be created, associating the run-time attributes to consumer groups. However, this may result in a situation where more than one mapping is TRUE or applicable when a user logs in to the database.

A user may log in to the operating system as the user PANDA and then to the database with the username HEADNURSE. In this case, will the user be assigned to both the PHY_CG and NURSE_CG consumer groups? To resolve this, numbers (to represent ranks) may be assigned to attributes. The number 1 has a higher priority over 2, 2 over 3, and so on.

These priorities can be assigned to attributes using the DBMS_RESOURCE_MANAGER. SET_CONSUMER_GROUP_MAPPING_PRI packaged procedure.

The following example displays the default priorities assigned to the attributes:

```
DBMS_RESOURCE_MANAGER.SET_CONSUMER_GROUP_MAPPING_PRI
(EXPLICIT=> 1, ORACLE_USER => 5,
SERVICE_NAME=> 4, CLIENT_OS_USER=> 7,
CLIENT_PROGRAM=> 6, CLIENT_MACHINE=> 8,
MODULE_NAME=> 3, MODULE_NAME_ACTION=> 2
);
```

These priorities may be modified if necessary. Using the default priorities, the user logging in to the operating system as PANDA, and to the database as HEADNURSE will be assigned the NURSE_CG consumer group because the ORACLE_USER attribute has a higher priority (5) compared to the CLIENT_OS_USER (7).

RELEVANT DATA DICTIONARY VIEWS

Information about the different elements created using the DRM is available through a number of views. Some of the important views and their descriptions are listed in Table 8-14.

TABLE 8-14 The views that provide information regarding DRM components

View Name	Description
V$RSRC_CONSUMER_GROUP	Displays cumulative information for the currently active plan. Can be used for tuning purposes.
V$RSRC_PLAN	Describes the active plan.

TABLE 8-14 The views that provide information regarding DRM components (continued)

View Name	Description
DBA_RSRC_CONSUMER_GROUPS	Lists all resource consumer groups that exist in the database.
DBA_RSRC_CONSUMER_GROUP_PRIVS	Lists all resource consumer groups and the users and roles to which they have been granted.
DBA_RSRC_MANAGER_SYSTEM_PRIVS	Lists all users and roles that have been granted DRM system privileges.
DBA_RSRC_PLANS	Lists all resource plans that exist in the database.
DBA_RSRC_PLAN_DIRECTIVES	Lists all resource plan directives that exist in the database.
V$SESSION	Lists the name of the resource consumer group of each current session.

Practice 3: Querying the Data Dictionary

In the following practice, you will view the name of the currently active plan.

1. Start SQL*Plus, and connect as a user with SYSDBA privileges.

```
SQL> CONNECT DB_ADMIN/DB_ADMIN AS SYSDBA
```

2. Query the V$RSRC_PLAN view to display information about the currently active plan(s).

```
SQL> SELECT * FROM V$RSRC_PLAN;
```

3. Exit SQL*Plus.

DRM USING ENTERPRISE MANAGER

The DRM can also be managed using the Enterprise Manager, as described in the following practice.

Practice 4: Managing DRM using Enterprise Manager

1. Start SQL*Plus, and connect as a user with SYSDBA privileges.
2. Issue an ALTER SYSTEM command to set the current RESOURCE plan to KELLER_DAYPLAN

```
SQL> ALTER SYSTEM SET RESOURCE_MANAGER_PLAN = KELLER_DAYPLAN;
```

3. Exit SQL*Plus.
4. Launch a browser and enter the URL to start Enterprise Manager. Log in as a user with SYSDBA privileges.
5. From the **Database Control Home** page, select the **Administration** tab.
6. Navigate to the **Resource Manager** section. (See Figure 8-6.)

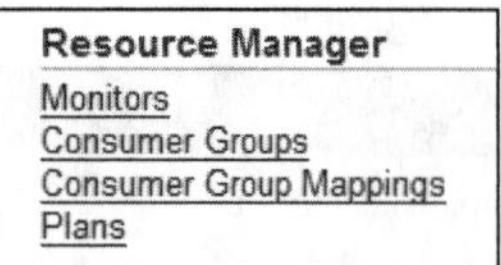

FIGURE 8-6 The Resource Manager section

7. Select the option **Monitors**. The **Resource Monitors** page will be displayed.
8. Notice the name of the active plan. It should be KELLER_DAYPLAN.
9. On this page, you can also change the active plan by selecting the plan name from the list provided against Available Resource Plans and selecting the Activate button. Do not change the current plan.
10. Select the **Back** button of the browser to return to the Administration tab.
11. Select the **Consumer Groups** link, to display the **Resource Consumer Groups** page.
12. A list of all the available consumer groups is displayed. (See Figure 8-7.) Figure 8-7 may display additional consumer groups that do not display in your output. Please ignore the ones that do not appear on your machine.

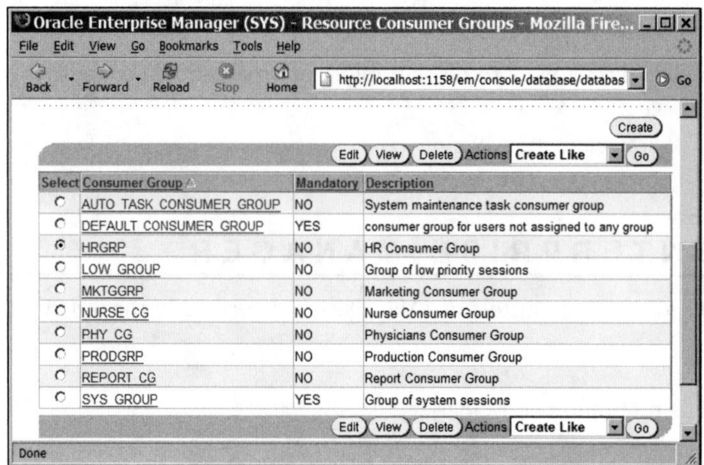

FIGURE 8-7 A list of all the available consumer groups is displayed

13. Select the link on the REPORT_CG consumer group. The **View Resource Consumer Group: REPORT_CG** page will be displayed.
14. Notice the names of users belonging to the consumer group will be displayed, as shown in Figure 8-8.

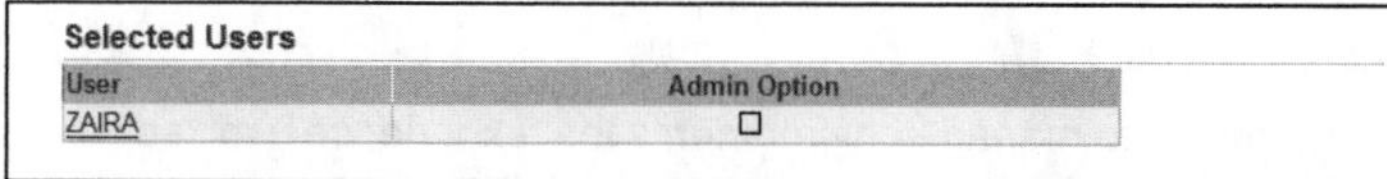

Selected Users

User	Admin Option
ZAIRA	☐

FIGURE 8-8 The names of users belonging to the REPORT_CG consumer group.

15. Click the **Back** button on the browser twice to return to the Administration tab.
16. Select the option **Consumer Group Mappings** to display the **Resource Consumer Group Mapping** page.
17. This page allows you to configure the Resource Manager to automatically assign consumer groups to sessions by providing mappings between session attributes and consumer groups. Who are the members of the SYS_GROUP consumer group?
18. Select the **Priorities** tab to view the current priorities. You may select the Up and Down arrows to change priorities if necessary.
19. Select the **Back** button of the browser to return to the Administration tab.
20. Select the **Plans** link to display the Resource Plans page.
21. A list of available plans is displayed on this page. Figure 8-9 indicates that the KELLER_DAYPLAN is currently active.

○	INTERNAL_QUIESCE		Plan to internally quiesce system
○	KELLER_DAYPLAN	ACTIVE	Plan for KMC
○	OLTPPLAN		Plan for OLTP users

FIGURE 8-9 The active plan for the current instance

22. Select the link on **KELLER_DAYPLAN**.
23. The **View Resource Plan: KELLER_DAYPLAN** page will be displayed. Go through this page, to view the resource plan directives of this plan.
24. Log out of Enterprise Manager.

In this chapter you learned how the DRM can help an administrator manage the available and limited resources more effectively. In Chapter 9 you will learn about the Scheduler that can be used to easily manage jobs created in the database.

Chapter Summary

- The DRM is a tool used primarily to manage environments that experience a mixed workload, consisting of both OLTP and DSS type applications.
- The primary elements of the DRM consist of consumer groups, resource plans, and resource plan directives.
- Consumer groups consist of users with similar processing needs in an Oracle database.
- Resource Plans are a means of allocating system resources to consumer groups. Plans may consist of subplans.
- Resource Plans can be simple or complex. Simple plans are single level and complex plans may be multilevel.
- Resource Plan directives consist of directives that specify how the resources must be allocated to the consumer groups or subplans.
- Plan directives may be created for the following resources:
    - CPU directives
    - Degree of Parallelization
    - Active Session Pool
    - Automatic Switching of User
    - Undo Space Usage
    - Maximum Estimated Execution
    - Maximum Idle
    - Maximum Idle Blocking Time
- A user session may automatically be assigned to consumer groups based on login and run-time attributes.
- If more than one attribute applies to a user session, the consumer group can be determined by assigning priorities to the attributes.
- Information regarding DRM can be obtained from the following data dictionary and performance views.
    - V$RSRC_CONSUMER_GROUP
    - V$RSRC_CONSUMER_GROUP_MTH
    - V$RSRC_PLAN
    - V$RSRC_PLAN_CPU_MTH
    - DBA_RSRC_CONSUMER_GROUPS
    - DBA_RSRC_CONUMER_GROUP_PRIVS
    - DBA_RSRC_MANAGER_SYSTEM_PRIVS
    - DBA_RSRC_PLANS
    - DBA_RSRC_PLAN_DIRECTIVES
    - V$SESSION

Syntax Guide

SYNTAX GUIDE		
Subprogram Name	**Description**	**Example**
CREATE_CONSUMER_GROUP	Creates a consumer group.	DBMS_RESOURCE_MANAGER.CREATE_ CONSUMER_GROUP('EUSRS','CG for endusers')
UPDATE_CONSUMER_GROUP	Updates a consumer group's comment.	DBMS_RESOURCE_MANAGER.UPDATE_ CONSUMER_GROUP(CONSUMER_GROUP =>'EUSRS', NEW_COMMENT =>'endusers')
DELETE_CONSUMER_GROUP	Deletes a consumer group.	DBMS_RESOURCE_MANAGER.DELETE_ CONSUMER_GROUP('EUSRS')
SET_INITIAL_CONSUMER_GROUP	Sets the initial resource consumer group for a user.	DBMS_RESOURCE_MANAGER.SET_IN ITIAL_CONSUMER_GROUP('RICK', 'NURSE_CG');
SWITCH_CONSUMER_GROUP_FOR_ SESS	Dynamically switches a consumer group for a connected session.	DBMS_RESOURCE_MANAGER.SWITCH_ CONSUMER_GROUP_FOR_SESS(SESSION_ID => '22', SESSION_SERIAL => 45', CONSUMER_GROUP => 'NEWGRP')
SWITCH_CONSUMER_GROUP_FOR_ USER	Switches the consumer group of all sessions belonging to a specific user.	DBMS_RESOURCE_MANAGER.SWITCH_ CONSUMER_GROUP_FOR_USER(USER =>'JOSE', CONSUMER_GROUP => 'NEWGRP')
SET_CONSUMER_GROUP_MAPPING	Allows you to map a user session to a consumer group based on either login or runtime attributes.	DBMS_RESOURCE_MANAGER.SET_CO NSUMER_GROUP_MAPPING(ATTRIBUTE =>'CLIENT_OS_USER', VALUE =>'TOBY', CONSUMER_GROUP=> 'OLTPGRP')
SET_CONSUMER_GROUP_MAPPING_ PRI	Prioritizes mappings when there are multiple attribute mappings associated with a consumer group.	DBMS_RESOURCE_MANAGER.SET_MA PPING_PRIORITY(EXPLICIT =>1, CLIENT_OS_USER => 2, CLIENT_MACHINE => 3 , CLIENT_PROGRAM => 4 , ORACLE_USER => 5 , MODULE_NAME => 6, MODULE_NAME_ACTION =>7 , SERVICE_NAME => 8, SERVICE_MODULE => 9, SERVICE_MODULE_ACTION =>10)
CREATE_PLAN	Creates a resource plan.	EXECUTE DBMS_RESOURCE_MANAGER.CREATE_ PLAN(PLAN=> 'DP', COMMENT => 'DAY PLAN')

SYNTAX GUIDE		
Subprogram Name	**Description**	**Example**
UPDATE_PLAN	Updates a resource plan's comment.	EXECUTE DBMS_RESOURCE_MANAGER.UPDATE _PLAN(PLAN=> 'DP', NEW_COMMENT=>'PLAN FOR DAY')
DELETE_PLAN	Deletes a resource plan.	EXECUTE DBMS_RESOURCE_MANAGER.DELETE _PLAN(PLAN=> 'DP')
CREATE_SIMPLE_PLAN	Can be used to create a single-level plan.	EXECUTE DBMS_RESOURCE_MANAGER.CREATE_ SIMPLE_PLAN (SIMPLE_PLAN => 'KNP', CONSUMER_GROUP1 => 'GROUP1', GROUP1_CPU => 25, CONSUMER_GROUP2 => 'GROUP2', GROUP2_CPU => 75)
CREATE_PLAN_DIRECTIVE	Creates a plan directive, by associating a consumer group or a subplan to a parent plan.	EXECUTE DBMS_RESOURCE_MANAGER.CREATE_ PLAN_DIRECTIVE (PLAN => 'KELLER_DAYPLAN', GROUP_OR_SUBPLAN => 'RCG', COMMENT => 'FOR REPORT_CG', CPU_P1 => 30, MAX_EST_EXEC_TIME => 3, SWITCH_ESTIMATE => TRUE, MAX_IDLE_TIME => 120)
UPDATE_PLAN_DIRECTIVE	Updates plan directives.	EXECUTE DBMS_RESOURCE_MANAGER.UPDATE _PLAN_DIRECTIVE (PLAN => 'KELLER_DAYPLAN', GROUP_OR_SUBPLAN => 'RCG', NEW_MAX_EST_EXEC_TIME=> 13)
DELETE_PLAN_DIRECTIVE	Deletes plan directives.	EXECUTE DBMS_RESOURCE_MANAGER.DELETE _PLAN_DIRECTIVE (PLAN => 'KELLER_DAYPLAN', GROUP_OR_SUBPLAN => 'RCG')
CREATE_PENDING_AREA	Creates a staging area.	EXECUTE DBMS_RESOURCE_MANAGER.CREATE _PENDING_AREA;
VALIDATE_PENDING_AREA	Verifies changes that were applied to the pending area.	EXECUTE DBMS_RESOURCE_MANAGER.VALIDA TE_PENDING_AREA;
SUBMIT_PENDING_AREA	Submits the pending area.	EXECUTE DBMS_RESOURCE_MANAGER.SUBMIT _PENDING_AREA;

SYNTAX GUIDE		
Subprogram Name	**Description**	**Example**
CLEAR_PENDING_AREA	To clear a pending area without submitting your changes.	EXECUTE DBMS_RESOURCE_MANAGER.CLEAR _PENDING_AREA;
GRANT_SYSTEM_PRIVILEGE	Used to grant the ADMINISTER_ RESOURCE_ MANAGER system privilege to a user or role.	EXECUTE DBMS_RESOURCE_MANAGER_PRIVS. GRANT_SYSTEM_PRIVILEGE('JO', 'ADMINISTER_RESOURCE_MANAGER ',TRUE)
REVOKE_SYSTEM_PRIVILEGE	Revokes the ADMINISTER_ RESOURCE_ MANAGER system privilege from a user or role.	EXECUTE DBMS_RESOURCE_MANAGER_PRIVS. REVOKE_SYSTEM_PRIVILEGE('JO', 'ADMINISTER_RESOURCE_MANAGER')
GRANT_SWITCH_CONSUMER_GROUP	Grants a user, role, or PUBLIC the permission to switch to a consumer group.	EXECUTE DBMS_RESOURCE_MANAGER_PRIVS. GRANT_SWITCH_CONSUMER_GROUP('TOBY','GROUP1',FALSE)
REVOKE_SWITCH_CONSUMER_GROUP	Revokes the permission from a user, role, or public to switch to a specified resource consumer group.	EXECUTE DBMS_RESOURCE_MANAGER_PRIVS. REVOKE_SWITCH_CONSUMER_GROUP ('TOBY','GROUP1')
ALTER SYSTEM SET RESOURCE_ MANAGER_PLAN=<plan_name>	To activate a plan for the current instance.	SQL> ALTER SYSTEM SET RESOURCE_MANAGER_PLAN = KELLER_DAYPLAN;

Review Questions

1. Name the two Oracle-supplied packages used to manage the Database Resource Manager.
2. A user, who wishes to administer the Database Resource Manager, must be granted the ________________ system privilege.
    a. GRANT
    b. ADMINISTER_RESOURCE_MANAGER
    c. RESOURCE_LIMIT
    d. ADMINISTER
    e. RESOURCE_MANAGER
    f. None of the above.

3. Jose, the database administrator, has created two resource plans called PLAN1 and PLAN2. Which of the following statements about the plans is true?
   a. The PLAN2 must be a subplan of PLAN1.
   b. The PLAN1 must be a subplan of PLAN2.
   c. Only one of the two plans can be active for an instance.
   d. The plans must be created as subplans of the SYSTEM_PLAN.
4. From the list below, identify the subprograms of the DBMS_RESOURCE_MANAGER package.
   a. CREATE_PENDING_AREA
   b. SET_INITIAL_CONSUMER_GROUP
   c. CREATE_PLAN
   d. GRANT_SYSTEM_PRIVILEGE
   e. GRANT_SWITCH_CONSUMER_GROUP
5. Jose, the administrator, wishes to create a simple plan. How many levels of CPU can he allocate?
6. A directive for the ________________ consumer group must be created for all plans and subplans.
7. Jose wishes to change the plan directive for the GROUP2, consumer group. The old UNDO_POOL value had been set to 80 bytes. The new value must be set to 100. Which of the following are applicable? Identify 2.
   a. CREATE_NEW_PLAN_DIRECTIVE
   b. UPDATE_PLAN_DIRECTIVE
   c. UNDO_POOL
   d. NEW_UNDO_POOL
   e. NEW_POOL_DIRECTIVE
8. The service name, module name, and action name attributes need to be mapped to a consumer group. Which package could be used to implement it?
   a. DBMS_SCHEDULER
   b. DBMS_MONITOR
   c. DBMS_RESOURCE_MANAGER
   d. DBMS_SERVER_ALERTS
   e. DBMS_RLS
9. The procedure used to assign priorities to attribute mappings is:
   a. SET_CONSUMER_GROUP_MAPPING
   b. SET_CONSUMER_GROUP_PRIORITIES
   c. SET_CONSUMER_GROUP_MAPPING_PRI
   d. SET_CONSUMER_ _MAPPING_PRI

10. The new Oracle 10*g* feature that automatically switches a session back to the original consumer group at the end of the call is achieved by which packaged procedure?
    a. DBMS_RESOURCE_MANAGER.CREATE_PLAN_DIRECTIVE
    b. DBMS_RESOURCE_MANAGER.CREATE_PLANS
    c. DBMS_RESOURCE_MANAGER.CREATE_SWITCH_DIRECTIVE
    d. SWITCH_TIME_IN_CALL
11. The directive whose value in seconds indicates the maximum time that a session can be idle is ________________ .
    a. MAX_IDLE_TIME
    b. MAX_SLEEP_TIME
    c. MAX_IDLE_BLOCKING_TIME
    d. IDLE_MAX_TIME

12. The procedure that is used to assign a user to their initial consumer group is ________________ .
    a. UPDATE_CONSUMER_GROUP
    b. SET_INITIAL_CONSUMER_GROUP
    c. SWITCH_CONSUMER_GROUP_FOR_SESS
    d. CREATE_INITIAL_CONSUMER_GROUP
13. A ________________ area must be created before any of the components of the Database Resource Manager can be created or updated.
14. The ________________ plan is a pre-defined plan consisting of plan directives to the SYS and SYSTEM users.
15. The ________________ view contains information about the initial consumer group that a session is assigned to.
16. The ________________ initialization parameter determines the name of the plan that will be active for the database.
17. Plan directives can be created for ________________ and ________________ components of Database Resource Manager.
18. When a user logs in to the database, the user's client machine name must determine the consumer group the user session is assigned to. If you were the administrator, how would you achieve this?
19. Jose, the DBA, does not specify a plan directive for the number of sessions that can be active for the GROUP1 consumer group. What is the result of not setting it?
20. Identify the correct order in which the following must be performed, when configuring a plan using database resource manager.
    a. Validate the pending area
    b. Create the consumer groups
    c. Create the pending area
    d. Make the plan active for the instance

Hands-On Assignments

In this assignment you will use the Database Resource Manager to implement a resource management solution, based on the diagram presented below. The main plan is called DAYPLAN that has two subplans OLTPPLAN and DSSPLAN. The consumer groups are PRODGRP, MKTGGRP, and HRGRP. Plan directives for the plans and subplans are provided as part of the assignment. (See Figure 8-10.)

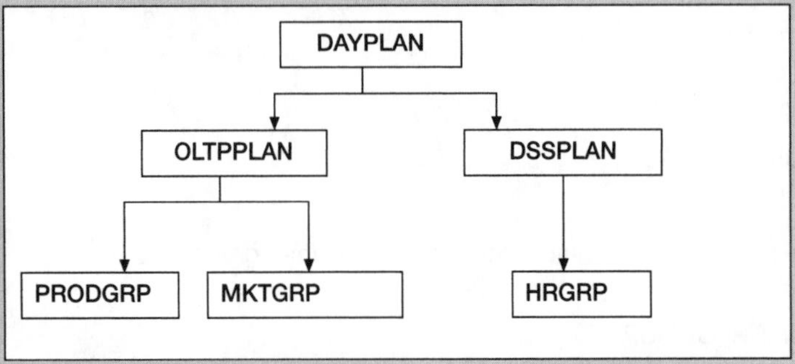

FIGURE 8-10 The DAYPLAN to be created

Assignment 8-1 Granting the ADMINISTER_RESOURCE_MANAGER system privilege

1. Start SQL*Plus and connect as a user with SYSDBA privileges.
2. Grant the ADMINISTER_RESOURCE_MANAGER system privilege to the user MEDUSER (See the syntax guide for the syntax).
3. Remain connected to SQL*Plus for the next practice.

Assignment 8-2 Creating a pending area

1. Connect as the user MEDUSER with the password MEDUSER.
2. Create a pending area.
3. Remain connected to SQL*Plus.

Assignment 8-3 Creating the consumer groups

1. Issue the commands to create the consumer groups PRODGRP, MKTGGRP, and HRGRP. You can choose comments of your own.
2. Remain connected to SQL*Plus.

Assignment 8-4 Creating the resource plans

1. Create the resource plans called DAYPLAN, OLTPPLAN, and DSSPLAN. You may write comments of your own.
2. Remain connected to SQL*Plus.

Assignment 8-5 Specifying plan directives for the OLTPPLAN

1. Create the following plan directives for the OLTPPLAN subplan.
   a. CPU at Level 1 = 60%
2. Remain connected for the next practice.

Assignment 8-6 Specifying plan directives for the DSSPLAN

1. Create the following plan directives for the DSSPLAN subplan.
   a. CPU at Level 1 = 30%
2. Remain connected for the next practice.

Assignment 8-7 Specifying plan directives for the OTHER_GROUPS under the DAYPLAN

1. Create the following plan directives for the OTHER_GROUPS consumer group subplan.
   a. CPU at Level 1 = 10%
2. Remain connected for the next practice.

Assignment 8-8 Creating Plan directives for the OLTPPLAN

1. Create the following plan directives for the PRODGRP consumer group.
   a. CPU usage at Level 1 = 25%
   b. Maximum Estimated Execution Time = 15 minutes
   c. Switch Estimate = TRUE
   d. Maximum time a session can be idle = 10 minutes
   e. Maximum time a blocking session can be idle= 8 minutes.
   f. Maximum amount of undo generated = 500 Kilobytes
2. Remain connected for next practice.

Assignment 8-9 Creating Plan directives for the MKTGGRP

1. Create the following plan directives for the MKTGGRP consumer group.
   a. CPU usage at Level 1 = 25%
   b. The session must be automatically switched to the OTHER_GROUPS consumer group when a statement that exceeds 10 minutes is initiated. The consumer group must not return to the original group after statement execution.
2. Remain connected for next practice.

Assignment 8-10 Specifying plan directives for the OTHER_GROUPS under the OLTPPLAN

1. Create the following plan directives for the OTHER_GROUPS consumer group subplan.
   a. CPU usage at Level 2 = 100%
2. Remain connected for next practice.

Assignment 8-11 Creating Plan directives for the HRGRP

1. Create the following plan directives for the HRGRP consumer group, under the DSSPLAN.
    a. CPU usage at Level 1 = 100%
    b. Maximum number of parallel processes = 12
    c. Maximum number of active sessions = 4
    d. Amount of time spent in the queue after which session is terminated = 5 minutes.
2. Remain connected for next practice.

Assignment 8-12 Specifying plan directives for the OTHER_GROUPS under the DSSPLAN

1. Create the following plan directives for the OTHER_GROUPS consumer group subplan.
    a. CPU usage at Level 2 = 100%
2. Remain connected for next practice.

Assignment 8-13 Validating and Submitting the Pending area

1. Validate the pending area.
2. Submit the pending area.
3. Remain connected for next practice.

Assignment 8-14 Creating the users and assigning initial consumer groups

1. Connect as a user with SYSDBA privileges.
2. Run the script in the Chapter08 folder of the student datafiles, called **c8as814.sql**. The script creates three users called TIM, FERN, and PETER.
3. Re-connect as the user MEDUSER.
4. Give the users the privilege to switch consumer groups as shown. Also set their initial consumer groups as shown.
    a. User TIM -> PRODGRP
    b. User FERN -> MKTGGRP
    c. User PETER-> HRGRP
5. Remain connected for next practice.

Assignment 8-15 Making the DAYPLAN the active plan

1. Connect as a user with SYSDBA privileges.
2. Issue the ALTER SYSTEM command to make the DAYPLAN the active plan for the current instance.
3. Remain connected for the next practice.

Assignment 8-16 Querying the data dictionary

1. Retrieve all the data from the V$RSRC_PLAN view. What does it display?
2. Retrieve the names of all consumer groups and the method by which CPU is allocated from the DBA_RSRC_CONSUMER_GROUPS data dictionary view.

3. Retrieve the names of all resource plans stored in the database. Query the DBA_RSRC_PLANS view.
4. Retrieve the plan directives for the consumer group called MKTGGRP from the data dictionary. Query the DBA_RSRC_PLAN_DIRECTIVES view.
5. Exit SQL*Plus.

Case Study

1. Using the official Oracle documentation, identify all the subprograms that are part of the DBMS_RESOURCE_MANAGER package.
2. The Database Resource Manager can also be accessed using the Oracle Enterprise Manager. Using the EM, implement a solution for the plan shown in Figure 8-11.

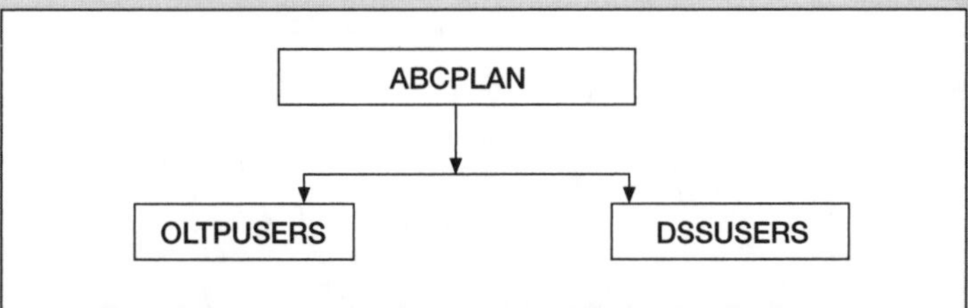

FIGURE 8-11 ABCPLAN using Enterprise Manager

Consumer Group	OLTPUSERS	DSSUSERS
Plan Directives		
CPU@L1	80%	20%
Degree of Parallelism	-	5
Active Session Pool	10	3
Undo Pool	1M	-

3. Revisit the scenario presented at the beginning of this chapter, and recommend a solution that Ryan can implement using Database Resource Manager.

CHAPTER 9

THE SCHEDULER

LEARNING OBJECTIVES

After completing this lesson you should be able to understand:

- Purpose of the Scheduler
- Basic components of the Scheduler—program, schedule, and job
- Reuse Scheduler components for similar tasks
- Advanced components of the Scheduler—job classes, windows, and window groups
- Automatic gathering of optimizer statistics using the Scheduler
- Relevant data dictionary views

ORACLE CERTIFICATION EXAM OBJECTIVES COVERED IN THIS CHAPTER INCLUDE:

- Simplify management tasks by using the Scheduler
- Create a job, program, schedule, and window
- Reuse Scheduler components for similar tasks
- View information about job executions and job instances

INTRODUCTION

Many tasks of a database administrator are repetitive. For example, administrators may need to execute a certain program or take a backup at a certain time of the day, every day. There are quite a few tasks that occur in the database such as performing daily backups, collecting table and index statistics on highly volatile tables, checking for queued events every 15 minutes, or generating daily or end-of-month reports that are repetitive as well as time consuming. Introduced in Oracle 10*g*, the Scheduler, allows an administrator to easily manage such routine tasks and time-consuming jobs.

The Scheduler is a utility provided by Oracle that can help DBAs manage jobs easily, making effective use of an organization's limited computing resources. Using the Scheduler, routine database tasks may be performed without manual intervention, thereby reducing operating costs, saving time, and minimizing human error.

This chapter will focus on the Scheduler; describe its architecture, function, and configuration. You will also learn how the Scheduler can be used to automatically gather object statistics used by the optimizer to make efficient decisions about execution plans.

THE CURRENT CHALLENGE AT KELLER MEDICAL CENTER

The number of reports that need to be printed by the IT department and sent to various departments has been steadily growing at the Keller Medical Center. On Monday morning, Ryan receives an urgent phone call from the junior administrator that he forgot to print out the monthly patient reports for Dr. Young of the cardiology department. These reports had to be printed on the last day of the month and Dr. Young will be upset that the report was not run. Ryan has been concerned about the many reports that have to be generated at various times of the month and sent to different departments for a while now. Complaints have been rising that reports are not being delivered in a timely fashion. Ryan, who has been working on Oracle 9*i* databases, thinks of the DBMS_JOB feature to help him with this problem. But he also wonders how he is going to implement it because working with DBMS_JOB is complicated. He is optimistic that Oracle 10*g* provides an easier solution.

SETUP FOR THE CHAPTER

Before performing the practice and hands-on exercises in this chapter you must run the script called **C9_setup.sql** in the Chapter09 folder of the student datafiles.

1. Start SQL*Plus, and connect as a user MEDUSER.
   ```
   SQL> CONNECT MEDUSER/MEDUSER
   ```
2. From the SQL prompt run the script C9_setup.sql.
   ```
   SQL> START <PATH>\C9_SETUP.SQL
   ```
3. Exit SQL*Plus.

THE ORACLE SCHEDULER

The Oracle Scheduler is the new feature of the Oracle 10*g* database. It comes as a replacement to the DBMS_JOB package that was available in prior versions of Oracle. The main function of the Scheduler is to simplify the management and execution of repetitive tasks without manual intervention. It offers a number of benefits, including ease of use, modularity and portability. The DBA, by means of simple configurations, can easily define jobs to be executed at specific times and repetitively. At the same time administrators have complete control over what runs in the database and when. Objects created in the Scheduler are modular; they can be reused and shared among users. Jobs created using the Scheduler can be moved from one system to another, for example, from a development to a production environment very easily with little or no modification. The Scheduler is a part of the Oracle 10g database and does not have to be purchased additionally.

The Scheduler Architecture

The main function of the Scheduler is to perform tasks or jobs at certain times. Administrators create jobs that are added to a job table maintained by the Scheduler. The job table contains a list of jobs that are enabled for execution by the Scheduler. A single job table exists for each database. The jobs are maintained in a queue and executed based on a schedule. A new background process known as the Job Coordinator (**cjqNNN**) wakes up periodically, queries the job table, and places any jobs it finds in a memory cache. The job coordinator is also responsible for managing a pool of job slaves. Job slaves are spawned by the job coordinator. When a job is to be executed it is assigned to a job slave. After the completion of the job, the slave process updates the job table with a status of completion which may either be SUCCESSFUL or FAILED. An entry is also added to the job log table. When no more jobs need to be executed, the job coordinator cleans up the job slave pool and goes to sleep. (See Figure 9-1.)

Database administrators can manage and monitor the status of jobs easily by means of the Enterprise Manager or a command-line PL/SQL interface.

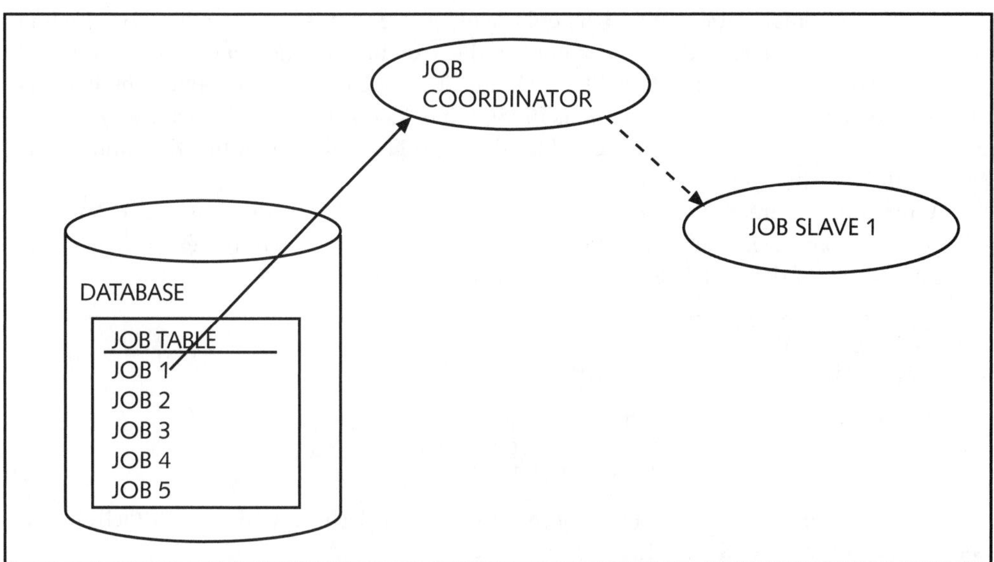

FIGURE 9-1 The Job Coordinator process coordinates jobs created in the scheduler

Working with the Scheduler

The Oracle Scheduler may be accessed and managed by means of the **DBMS_SCHEDULER** package which contains a number of procedures and functions.

Using the Scheduler, you can create jobs that need to run in the database at a certain date and time. Such jobs are referred to as transient jobs. You can also create scheduler objects known as Programs and Schedules that can be created once, stored in the database, and reused multiple times. This modular approach allows you to manage scheduler components easily as well as reuse and share them between users with little or no modification.

To use the Scheduler you must be aware of some important Scheduler objects. In this topic we will learn how to create some basic scheduler objects and how they can be associated with one another to create and simplify task management using the Scheduler.

NOTE

To use the DBMS_SCHEDULER package a user must have CREATE JOB or CREATE ANY JOB system privileges.

There are three basic components or objects that can be created using the Scheduler:

- Program
- Schedule
- Job

PROGRAM

A program holds metadata about a particular executable that is to be run by the Scheduler. It holds information regarding the name of the executable, the type of executable (EXECUTABLE or STORED_PROCEDURE), and the code of the executable. The executable may be in the form of an anonymous PL/SQL block, a stored PL/SQL, a stored JAVA procedure, or an operating system executable file. A program also identifies the number of arguments that the executable accepts.

A program is created using the CREATE_PROGRAM procedure of the DBMS_SCHEDULER package. The procedure may receive a number of parameters.

The syntax of the CREATE_PROGRAM procedure is:

```
DBMS_SCHEDULER.CREATE_PROGRAM
(PROGRAM_NAME           IN VARCHAR2,
PROGRAM_TYPE            IN VARCHAR2,
PROGRAM_ACTION          IN VARCHAR2,
NUMBER_OF_ARGUMENTS     IN BINARY_INTEGER DEFAULT 0,
ENABLED                 IN BOOLEAN DEFAULT FALSE,
COMMENTS                IN VARCHAR2 DEFAULT NULL);
```

The description of the parameters of the DBMS_SCHEDULER.CREATE_PROGRAM procedure is displayed in Table 9-1.

TABLE 9-1 Parameters of the CREATE_PROGRAM procedure

Parameter Name	Description
PROGRAM_NAME	A name given to a program.
PROGRAM_TYPE	The type of program to be executed. The valid values the parameter can take include: PLSQL_BLOCK, STORED_PROCEDURE, and EXECUTABLE.
PROGRAM_ACTION	This is the anonymous PLSQL procedure, the name of the operating system executable file, or the name of the stored procedure that is to be executed.
NUMBER_OF_ARGUMENTS	Specifies the number of arguments accepted by the stored procedure or executable.
ENABLED	Indicates whether the program must be enabled when it is created. By default it is disabled, taking a value FALSE.
COMMENTS	A user-defined comment describing the program.

To help you better understand the concept of a program, consider the following scenario.

Example: At Keller Medical Center, a table known as PATIENT contains information about all patients being treated at the center. When a patient is discharged, the STATUS column in the PATIENT table is changed to DISCHARGED for that patient record. Every night at around 10 P.M. a staff member performs the task of transferring the records of discharged patients to a PATIENT_HISTORY table. The records of discharged patients are then deleted from the PATIENT table. The process described above is performed by a stored procedure called DISPATIENTS. The DISPATIENTS procedure is displayed below.

```
CREATE OR REPLACE PROCEDURE DISPATIENTS
IS
BEGIN
INSERT INTO PATIENT_HISTORY
SELECT * FROM PATIENT
WHERE STATUS='DISCHARGED';
DELETE FROM PATIENT
WHERE STATUS='DISCHARGED';
END;
```

If this stored procedure were to be executed by the Scheduler, a program may be created as shown in the code below. The name of the program is DISPATS; the program is associated with a stored procedure called DISPATIENTS belonging to the user MEDUSER. The program is enabled during creation.

The program can be created as:

```
DBMS_SCHEDULER.CREATE_PROGRAM (
PROGRAM_NAME       => 'DISPATS',
PROGRAM_ACTION     => 'MEDUSER.DISPATIENTS',
PROGRAM_TYPE       => 'STORED_PROCEDURE',
ENABLED            => TRUE);
```

Once a program is created it is stored as an object of the database, it may be reused and shared among the users of the database. The DBMS_SCHEDULER package has a number of subprograms that are also related to programs. Table 9-2 lists some of the subprograms. Examples of the usage of these subprograms are provided in subsequent practices and in the Syntax Guide at the end of the chapter.

TABLE 9-2 Other subprograms of the DBMS_SCHEDULER that are related to programs

Subprograms	Description
DEFINE_PROGRAM_ARGUMENT	A stored program may accept arguments. When creating a program we only mention the number of arguments. The DEFINE_PROGRAM_ARGUMENT is the method by which you specify the datatype of the argument that the stored procedure receives. It can take the following parameters: PROGRAM_NAME: Specifies the name of the program. ARGUMENT_POSITION: A numeric integer value indicating the position of the argument. ARGUMENT_TYPE: The datatype of the argument.
DROP_PROGRAM_ARGUMENT	This procedure is used to drop an argument. The procedure can receive the following parameters. PROGRAM_NAME: Specifies the name of the program. ARGUMENT_NAME or ARGUMENT_POSITION: The former is the name of the argument to be dropped. The latter is the positional value of the argument.
DROP_PROGRAM	Used to drop programs created in the database. If there are any jobs that are dependent on the program, the drop will fail. You can use the FORCE option to forcefully drop the program. In which case all the dependent jobs will be disabled. The procedure receives the following arguments: PROGRAM_NAME: the name of the program to be dropped. FORCE: can take values TRUE or FALSE. TRUE results in a forceful dropping of the program, disabling all dependent jobs.

SCHEDULE

The second type of basic Scheduler object is known as a Schedule. The Schedule determines when and how often a job is to be executed. A job may be scheduled to run once or repetitively. A job may also be scheduled to run immediately or at a later time. You can also indicate a time interval for the execution of the job, in terms of well-defined start and end dates. A Schedule is saved in the database with a name and may be reused multiple times when creating jobs. An example of a schedule may be “Run every day at 12:30 PM, beginning on the 1st of Jan, 2006 and ending on 31st of Jan, 2006”.

A schedule is created using the CREATE_SCHEDULE procedure of the DBMS_SCHEDULER package.

The syntax of the CREATE_SCHEDULE procedure is:

```
DBMS_SCHEDULER.CREATE_SCHEDULE (
SCHEDULE_NAME      IN VARCHAR2,
START_DATE         IN TIMESTAMP WITH TIMEZONE DEFAULT NULL,
END_DATE           IN TIMESTAMP WITH TIMEZONE DEFAULT NULL,
REPEAT_INTERVAL    IN VARCHAR2,
COMMENTS           IN VARCHAR2 DEFAULT NULL);
```

The CREATE_SCHEDULE procedure accepts a number of parameters, described in Table 9-3.

TABLE 9-3 Parameters of the CREATE_SCHEDULE procedure

Parameter Name	Description
SCHEDULE_NAME	The name of the schedule.
START_DATE	The date and time on which the schedule becomes active. If you omit the START_DATE the job will be run immediately.
END_DATE	The date and time on which the schedule expires. If you omit the END_DATE, the job will not expire.
REPEAT_INTERVAL	Indicates when and how often the job must execute. If you omit REPEAT_INTERVAL, the job will run just once however the START_DATE must be specified.
COMMENTS	A user-defined comment describing the schedule.

Repeat Intervals The REPEAT_INTERVAL parameter controls how often a job repeats. It is an expression using either the calendaring syntax or PL/SQL syntax. The calendaring syntax for the REPEAT_INTERVAL is:

```
REPEAT_INTERVAL = FREQUENCY_CLAUSE [";" INTERVAL_CLAUSE]
                  [";" BYMONTH_CLAUSE][";" BYWEEKNO_CLAUSE]
                  [";" BYYEARDAY_CLAUSE][";" BYMONTHDAY_CLAUSE]
                  [";" BYDAY_CLAUSE][";" BYHOUR_CLAUSE]
                  [";" BYMINUTE_CLAUSE][";" BYSECOND_CLAUSE]
```

The *frequency_clause* is specified by the FREQ keyword. It indicates the type of recurrence. It can take one of the following values: YEARLY, MONTHLY, WEEKLY, DAILY, HOURLY, MINUTELY, and SECONDLY.

The *interval_clause* is specified by the INTERVAL keyword. The INTERVAL clause is a numeric value with values ranging from 1 to 99.

The other clauses displayed in the syntax have a prefix *"BY."* They indicate the time when the job is to be run. Multiple clauses with the BY prefix may be specified to create a valid repeat interval. These clauses include: BYMONTH, BYWEEKNO, BYYEARDAY, BYMONTHDAY, BYDAY, BYHOUR, BYMINUTE, and BYSECOND.

Table 9-4 provides a number of examples that may help you to better understand how a REPEAT_INTERVAL may be interpreted.

TABLE 9-4 Interpreting the REPEAT_INTERVAL clause

Repeat Frequency	REPEAT_INTERVAL clause
Every Year	REPEAT_INTERVAL => 'FREQ=YEARLY; INTERVAL=1'
Every 2 years	REPEAT_INTERVAL => 'FREQ=YEARLY; INTERVAL=2'
Every 5 years	REPEAT_INTERVAL => 'FREQ=YEARLY; INTERVAL=5'

TABLE 9-4 Interpreting the REPEAT_INTERVAL clause (continued)

Repeat Frequency	REPEAT_INTERVAL clause
Every Month	`REPEAT_INTERVAL => 'FREQ=MONTHLY; INTERVAL=1'`
Every 3 Months	`REPEAT_INTERVAL => 'FREQ=MONTHLY; INTERVAL=3'`
Every Week	`REPEAT_INTERVAL => 'FREQ=WEEKLY; INTERVAL=1'`
Every other week	`REPEAT_INTERVAL => 'FREQ=WEEKLY; INTERVAL=2'`
Every day	`REPEAT_INTERVAL => 'FREQ=DAILY; INTERVAL=1'`
Every 7 days	`REPEAT_INTERVAL => 'FREQ=DAILY; INTERVAL=7'`
Every hour	`REPEAT_INTERVAL => 'FREQ=HOURLY; INTERVAL=1'`
Every 4 hours	`REPEAT_INTERVAL => 'FREQ=HOURLY; INTERVAL=4'`
Every minute	`REPEAT_INTERVAL => 'FREQ=MINUTELY; INTERVAL=1'`
Every 5 minutes	`REPEAT_INTERVAL => 'FREQ=MINUTELY; INTERVAL=5'`
Every second	`REPEAT_INTERVAL => 'FREQ=SECONDLY; INTERVAL=1'`
Every 30 seconds	`REPEAT_INTERVAL => 'FREQ=SECONDLY; INTERVAL=30'`
Every January, April, September of a Year	`REPEAT_INTERVAL => 'FREQ=YEARLY; BYMONTH=1,4,9'`
On the 25 and 26 week of the year	`REPEAT_INTERVAL => 'FREQ=YEARLY; BYWEEKNO=25,26'`
On the 280th day of the year	`REPEAT_INTERVAL => 'FREQ=YEARLY; BYYEARDAY=280'`
On the 15th of the month	`REPEAT_INTERVAL => 'FREQ=MONTHLY; BYMONTHDAY=15'`
On the 15th of August	`REPEAT_INTERVAL => 'FREQ=YEARLY; BYMONTH=AUG BYMONTHDAY=15'`
On the last day of the month	`REPEAT_INTERVAL => 'FREQ = MONTHLY;BYMONTHDAY=-1'`
Every Friday of the week	`REPEAT_INTERVAL => 'FREQ=WEEKLY; BYDAY=FRI'`
At 8 PM every day	`REPEAT_INTERVAL => 'FREQ=DAILY; BYHOUR=20'`
At 15 minutes past the hour	`REPEAT_INTERVAL => 'FREQ=HOURLY; BYMINUTE=15'`
At 1.15.30 PM every day	`REPEAT_INTERVAL => 'FREQ=DAILY; BYHOUR = 13 BYMINUTE=15 BYSECOND=30'`

NOTE

The BYMONTHDAY clause, accepts negative values that represent a count of days from the end of the month. For example, -1 represents the last day of the month.

Repeat Intervals can also be created by using PL/SQL expressions. Because they use the PL/SQL programming language this method is robust, offering the flexibility available with programming.

An example of a PL/SQL expression in the REPEAT_INTERVAL clause could be:

Repeat Frequency	REPEAT_INTERVAL clause
Every Minute	SYSTIMESTAMP + 1/1440
Every Hour	SYSTIMESTAMP + 1/24

Example: In the example shown below, a schedule called EVERY_MIN, that starts on Sep 7, 2006 at 2:25 P.M. and ends on Sep 7, 2006 at 2:30 PM and repeats with a frequency of once every minute is being created.


```
BEGIN
DBMS_SCHEDULER.CREATE_SCHEDULE(
SCHEDULE_NAME          => 'EVERY_MIN',
START_DATE             => '07-SEP-06 02.25.00 PM',
END_DATE               => '07-SEP-06 02.30.00 PM',
REPEAT_INTERVAL        => 'FREQ=MINUTELY; INTERVAL=1');
END;
/
```

JOB

The third type of Scheduler object that can be created is known as a Job. A job refers to a user-defined task that needs to be executed. A job is a means of associating what needs to be run and when. In other words, a job associates programs and schedules. However, jobs can be created without programs and schedules. A job is created using the DBMS_SCHEDULER.CREATE_JOB packaged procedure.

The CREATE_JOB procedure accepts a number of parameters. An explanation of all acceptable parameters of this procedure is given in Table 9-5.

TABLE 9-5 Parameters of the CREATE_JOB packaged procedure

Parameter of CREATE_JOB procedure	Description
JOB_NAME	A name that uniquely identifies the job.
JOB_TYPE	Specifies the type of job being created. Valid values include PLSQL_BLOCK, STORED_PROCEDURE, and EXECUTABLE.
JOB_ACTION	Specifies the action of the job. In case the JOB_TYPE was PL/SQL block, then the JOB_ACTION will contain the entire PL/SQL block that must be executed. It is similar to the PROGRAM_ACTION clause.
PROGRAM_NAME	The name of an existing program that is executed when the job is run.
NUMBER_OF_ARGUMENTS	Indicates the number of arguments received by a STORED_PROCEDURE that is executed by the job.

TABLE 9-5 Parameters of the CREATE_JOB packaged procedure (continued)

Parameter of CREATE_JOB procedure	Description
START_DATE	The date and time on which the job should start executing.
REPEAT_INTERVAL	Indicates the frequency with which the job must be repeated. Has the same meaning as in schedules.
END_DATE	Indicates the date/time when the job must stop executing. Has the same meaning as in schedules.
SCHEDULE_NAME	The name of an already existing schedule that indicates when and how often the job is to be run.
ENABLED	Indicates if the job must be enabled on creation. By default it is disabled, i.e., takes a value FALSE.
JOB_CLASS	Specifies the name of the job class that the job is assigned to. If a job is not assigned to a job class, it is automatically assigned to a job class called the DEFAULT_JOB_CLASS, which is pre-defined in the Oracle database.
COMMENTS	A user-defined string that describes the job.

A job can be created using the Scheduler, in one of four ways, including:

1. Job without a program or schedule.
2. Job with a program and without a schedule.
3. Job with a schedule and without a program.
4. Job with a schedule and a program.

Creating a Job without a program or schedule Jobs may be created without a program name and schedule. In this case you will specify both, what needs to be run as well as timing and repeat information.

The clauses that may be mentioned are displayed in the syntax below:

```
DBMS_SCHEDULER.CREATE_JOB (
   JOB_NAME            IN VARCHAR2,
   JOB_TYPE            IN VARCHAR2,
   JOB_ACTION          IN VARCHAR2,
   NUMBER_OF_ARGUMENTS IN PLS_INTEGER              DEFAULT 0,
   START_DATE          IN TIMESTAMP WITH TIME ZONE DEFAULT NULL,
   REPEAT_INTERVAL     IN VARCHAR2                 DEFAULT NULL,
   END_DATE            IN TIMESTAMP WITH TIME ZONE DEFAULT NULL,
   JOB_CLASS           IN VARCHAR2                 DEFAULT NULL,
   ENABLED             IN BOOLEAN                  DEFAULT FALSE,
   COMMENTS            IN VARCHAR2                 DEFAULT NULL);
```

Example: A job called JOB1 is created to run an anonymous PL/SQL block on September 7th, at 6 P.M. It is executed only once, because a REPEAT_INTERVAL is not specified. The job has been enabled during creation.

```
DBMS_SCHEDULER.CREATE_JOB (
     JOB_NAME      => 'JOB1',
     JOB_TYPE      => 'PLSQL_BLOCK',
     JOB_ACTION    => 'BEGIN
                       MEDUSER.DISPATIENTS;
                       END;',
     START_DATE    => '07-SEP-06 6.00.00 PM',
     ENABLED       =>  TRUE,
     COMMENTS      => 'EXECUTE ONCE AT 6 PM ON SEPT 7, 2005');
```

Creating a Job with a program and without a schedule A job may be created using a program name and without a schedule. The PROGRAM_NAME argument will be specified instead of JOB_TYPE and JOB_ACTION. The PROGRAM_NAME argument will hold the name of an existing program. The program will contain directives about the executable to be run.

The syntax for a job with a program name, and an inline schedule is displayed.

```
DBMS_SCHEDULER.CREATE_JOB (
   JOB_NAME                IN VARCHAR2,
   PROGRAM_NAME            IN VARCHAR2,
   START_DATE              IN TIMESTAMP WITH TIME ZONE DEFAULT NULL,
   REPEAT_INTERVAL         IN VARCHAR2  DEFAULT NULL,
   END_DATE                IN TIMESTAMP WITH TIME ZONE DEFAULT NULL,
   ENABLED                 IN BOOLEAN   DEFAULT FALSE,
   COMMENTS                IN VARCHAR2  DEFAULT NULL);
```

Example: A job called JOB2 is being created. It executes the program called DISPATS that exists in the database. It is executed only once, on the 7th of September, 2005 at 6.30 P.M. and is enabled during creation.

```
DBMS_SCHEDULER.CREATE_JOB (
JOB_NAME             => 'JOB2',
PROGRAM_NAME         => 'DISPATS',
START_DATE           => '07-SEP-05 6.30.00 PM',
ENABLED              =>  TRUE,
COMMENTS             => 'JOB WITH PROGRAM NAME TO EXECUTE ONCE');
/
```

Creating a Job without a program and with a schedule A job can also be created without a program, but with a schedule. The schedule must exist in the database.

The CREATE_JOB procedure will accept the SCHEDULE_NAME argument. There will be no need to specify arguments such as START_DATE, END_DATE, and other clauses associated with timing and repeat intervals. In the syntax shown below all parameters have the same meaning as they did in procedures discussed earlier.

```
DBMS_SCHEDULER.CREATE_JOB (
   JOB_NAME                  IN VARCHAR2,
   SCHEDULE_NAME             IN VARCHAR2,
   JOB_TYPE                  IN VARCHAR2,
   JOB_ACTION                IN VARCHAR2,
   NUMBER_OF_ARGUMENTS       IN PLS_INTEGER DEFAULT 0,
   ENABLED                   IN BOOLEAN DEFAULT FALSE,
   COMMENTS                  IN VARCHAR2 DEFAULT NULL);
```

Example: A job called JOB3 is being created. The job executes an operating system executable file called *exjob.bat*. Timing is based on the schedule called EVERY_MIN.

```
DBMS_SCHEDULER.CREATE_JOB (
JOB_NAME            => 'JOB3',
SCHEDULE_NAME       => 'EVERY_MIN',
JOB_TYPE            => 'EXECUTABLE',
JOB_ACTION          => 'C:\EXJOB.BAT',
ENABLED             => TRUE,
COMMENTS            => 'EXECUTABLE RUNS EVERY MINUTE');
END;
```

Creating a Job with a program and a schedule Finally, a job can be created that references an existing program and schedule. The CREATE_JOB procedure accepts the name of the program and schedule.

Example: A job called JOB4 is being created. The job executes the program called DISPATS, using a schedule called EVERY_MIN.

```
DBMS_SCHEDULER.CREATE_JOB (
   JOB_NAME               => 'JOB4',
PROGRAM_NAME              => 'DISPATS',
SCHEDULE_NAME             => 'EVERY_MIN');
```

In addition to the CREATE_JOB procedure, there are a number of other useful subprograms that are part of the DBMS_SCHEDULER package that are related to jobs. A description of these is provided in Table 9-6. Examples for these subprograms are provided as part of the Syntax Guide.

TABLE 9-6 Other subprograms of DBMS_SCHEDULER associated with Jobs

Subprogram Name	Description
COPY_JOB	Used to copy a job. The procedure accepts two parameters: OLD_JOB: the name of the old job NEW_JOB: the name of the new job. The new job will be created in a disabled state.
RUN_JOB	Used to execute a certain job once right away. This procedure is particularly useful if you are testing a job. The RUN_JOB procedure accepts two parameters: JOB_NAME parameter: The JOB_NAME parameter is the name of the job to be run. USE_CURRENT_SESSION: The USE_CURRENT_SESSION parameter can be set to TRUE or FALSE. If set to TRUE, the job will be run within the user's session and control will be returned to the user only after the job has completed execution. If set to FALSE, the scheduler will run the job asynchronously and control will be returned to the user session immediately.
STOP_JOB	This procedure is to stop or terminate a job that is running. If the job is successfully stopped its status will be STOPPED. The procedure accepts two parameters: JOB_NAME: The name of the job to stop. FORCE: An optional parameter resulting in stopping the job faster. It can take the values TRUE or FALSE.

Other important procedures

We have discussed a number of subprograms of the DBMS_SCHEDULER package so far that are related to the basic components. This topic reviews some additional subprograms that you may use when working with the Scheduler. Table 9-7 describes some of these subprograms. Examples of these subprograms have been provided as part of the Syntax Guide.

TABLE 9-7 Other procedures of the DBMS_SCHEDULER package

Subprograms of DBMS_SCHEDULER	Description
`ENABLE`	This procedure is applicable to all scheduler objects with the exception of Schedules. It is used to indicate whether the object is eligible for use by the Scheduler.
`DISABLE`	This procedure is used to indicate that the object is not eligible for use by the Scheduler. When disabling an object, you can specify two parameters. The first is the name of the object(s) (separated by commas) and a FORCE parameter. The FORCE parameter may take the value of TRUE or FALSE. When set to TRUE, it indicates that all dependent objects must also be disabled.
`SET_ATTRIBUTE`	The procedure is used to modify or alter any of the attributes of a scheduler object. Prior to actually changing the attribute, the Scheduler will attempt to disable the object. After changing the attribute the object will be re-enabled automatically. The parameters that the procedure accepts include : NAME: the name of the object ATTRIBUTE: the specific attribute whose value is being altered VALUE: The new value.
`SET_ATTRIBUTE_NULL`	The procedure can be used to set the value of an attribute to NULL. The parameters accepted by the procedure include: NAME: the name of the object. ATTRIBUTE: the attribute whose value is to be set to null.

Practice 1: Working with the Scheduler

The Oracle-supplied DBMS_STATS package may be used to analyze objects and generate statistics on objects of the database. These statistics are used by the optimizer to generate efficient execution plans for queries that are executed on the objects. Statistics gathering on objects that are modified and accessed frequently is an important function of the database administrator.

In this practice example you will create a Scheduler job that will gather statistics for the table called C9_PATIENTS. We will create a program that will invoke the DBMS_STATS.GATHER_TABLE_STATS packaged procedure that can be used to gather statistics on a specific table. This procedure accepts two inputs, the name of schema and the name of the table to be analyzed. The exercise will be performed as the user MEDUSER. You will first grant MEDUSER the privilege to create jobs in the database. Please make sure you execute the instructions mentioned in the Setup for the Chapter section before attempting this practice.

1. Start SQL*Plus and connect as a user with SYSDBA privileges.

```
SQL> CONNECT DB_ADMIN/DB_ADMIN AS SYSDBA
```

2. Grant the user MEDUSER, the CREATE JOB privilege that is necessary for MEDUSER to create Scheduler objects.

```
SQL> GRANT CREATE JOB TO MEDUSER;
```

3. Connect as the user MEDUSER, with the password MEDUSER.

```
SQL> CONNECT MEDUSER/MEDUSER
```

4. Create a program called ANTABLE that will execute the Oracle-supplied DBMS_STATS.GATHER_TABLE_STATS package. This package gathers statistics for a table. The program type is a STORED_PROCEDURE and it receives two arguments.


```
SQL> -- Creating the program
SQL> BEGIN
     DBMS_SCHEDULER.CREATE_PROGRAM
     (PROGRAM_NAME              => 'ANTABLE',
      PROGRAM_TYPE              => 'STORED_PROCEDURE',
      PROGRAM_ACTION            => 'DBMS_STATS.GATHER_TABLE_
                                   STATS',
      NUMBER_OF_ARGUMENTS       =>  2,
      COMMENTS                  => 'GATHERING TABLE STATISTICS');
      END;
     /
```

5. Because the DBMS_STATS.GATHER_TABLE_STATS package accepts two mandatory arguments—the name of the schema and the table name—you will now define the datatypes of these program arguments. Both arguments are of a VARCHAR2 datatype.

```
SQL> -- Defining the first argument
SQL> BEGIN
     DBMS_SCHEDULER.DEFINE_PROGRAM_ARGUMENT(
     PROGRAM_NAME               => 'ANTABLE',
     ARGUMENT_POSITION          => 1,
     ARGUMENT_TYPE              => 'VARCHAR2');
     END;
     /
SQL> -- Defining the second argument
SQL> BEGIN
     DBMS_SCHEDULER.DEFINE_PROGRAM_ARGUMENT(
     PROGRAM_NAME               => 'ANTABLE',
     ARGUMENT_POSITION          => 2,
     ARGUMENT_TYPE              => 'VARCHAR2');
     END;
     /
```

6. Next, create a schedule called PM10. This schedule begins on the current date, and repeats itself daily at 10 P.M. everyday. There is no end date for the schedule.

```
SQL> -- Creating a schedule
SQL> BEGIN
     DBMS_SCHEDULER.CREATE_SCHEDULE(
     SCHEDULE_NAME              => 'PM10',
```

```
START_DATE              => SYSDATE,
REPEAT_INTERVAL         => 'FREQ=DAILY;BYHOUR=22');
END;
/
```

7. We will now create a job called ANJOB that will execute the program ANTABLE using the schedule PM10.

```
SQL> -- Creating a Job
SQL> BEGIN
     DBMS_SCHEDULER.CREATE_JOB
     (JOB_NAME              => 'ANJOB',
     PROGRAM_NAME           => 'ANTABLE',
     SCHEDULE_NAME          => 'PM10');
     END;
     /
```


8. In this next step, you will set the arguments of the job. The first argument is the schema name. Because we are analyzing the MEDUSER's table, we will specify the schema name as MEDUSER. The second argument is the name of the table being analyzed which is C9_PATIENT.

```
SQL> -- Setting the first argument which is the schema
SQL> BEGIN
     DBMS_SCHEDULER.SET_JOB_ARGUMENT_VALUE(
     JOB_NAME             => 'ANJOB',
     ARGUMENT_POSITION    =>  1,
     ARGUMENT_VALUE       => 'MEDUSER');
     END;
     /
SQL> -- Setting the second argument which is the table name
SQL> BEGIN
     DBMS_SCHEDULER.SET_JOB_ARGUMENT_VALUE(
     JOB_NAME                 => 'ANJOB',
     ARGUMENT_POSITION        =>  2,
     ARGUMENT_VALUE           => 'C9_PATIENT');
     END;
     /
```

9. Finally before executing the job, you must enable the program and the job. This is done using the ENABLE procedure of the DBMS_SCHEDULER package.

```
SQL> -- Enabling the program
SQL> BEGIN
     DBMS_SCHEDULER.ENABLE('ANTABLE');
     END;
     /
SQL> -- Enabling the job
SQL> BEGIN
     DBMS_SCHEDULER.ENABLE('ANJOB');
     END;
     /
```

10. Now that the job has been created and enabled, you may view the status of the job using the Enterprise Manager.
11. Launch a Browser, specify the URL to access the Enterprise Manager and log in with SYSDBA privileges.
12. From the **Database Control Home** page, select the **Administration** tab, scroll to the **Scheduler** section, as shown in Figure 9-2.

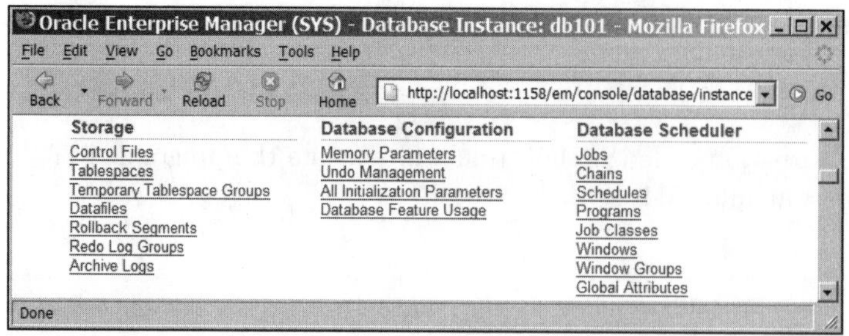

FIGURE 9-2 The Scheduler section under the Administration tab

13. Select the **Jobs** link. The **Scheduler Jobs** page will be displayed.
14. Scroll down this page until you see the details of the **ANJOB** job. Notice the time it is scheduled to run around 10 P.M. (See Figure 9-3.) It has not yet executed because the Last Run Date displays as N/A. This job belongs to a job class called DEFAULT_JOB_CLASS.

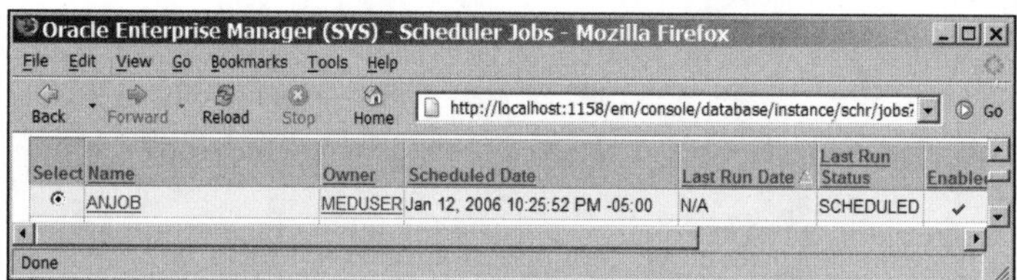

FIGURE 9-3 The ANJOB job is listed as a job to be executed

15. Select the job by clicking on the radio button next to ANJOB. (See Figure 9-4.)

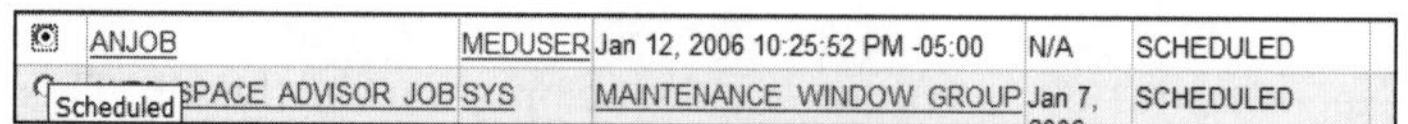

FIGURE 9-4 Selecting the ANJOB job

16. Even though the job has been scheduled to run at 10 P.M., you can run it immediately to see if the job was created successfully by selecting the **Run Now** button on the top of the page. (See Figure 9-5.)

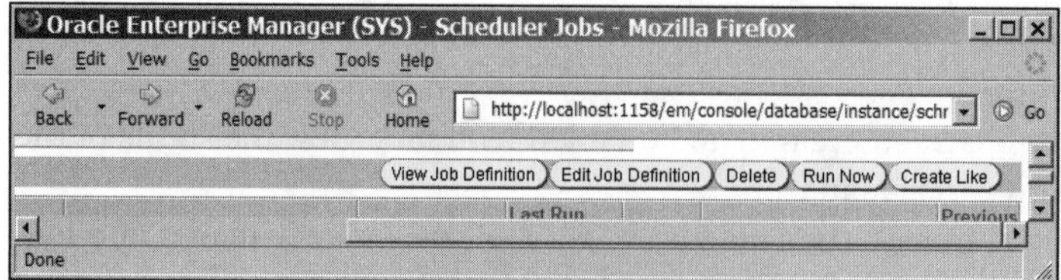

FIGURE 9-5 Running the job immediately: the RUN NOW button

17. A **Confirmation** page will be displayed, indicating that the MEDUSER.ANJOB job is running.
18. Select the **Refresh** button on the top-right corner of the page. You will be returned to the **Scheduler Jobs** page.
19. Once again scroll down to the job called ANJOB and view the information about it. A date will be displayed in the Last Run Date column and the Previous Runs displays a value of 1. (See Figure 9-6.)

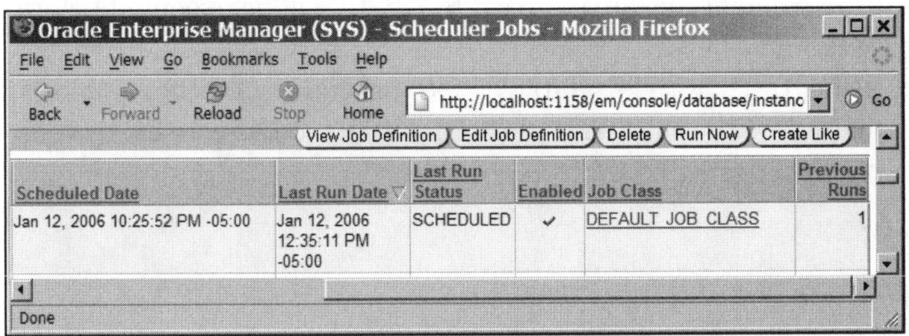

FIGURE 9-6 The job has been executed once

20. Next, move to the top of the Scheduler Jobs page, and select the **History** tab.
21. On this page you will see an entry about the job ANJOB and the status of completion. Figure 9-7 indicates that the job completed successfully on Jan 12, 2006 12:35:12 PM -05:00.

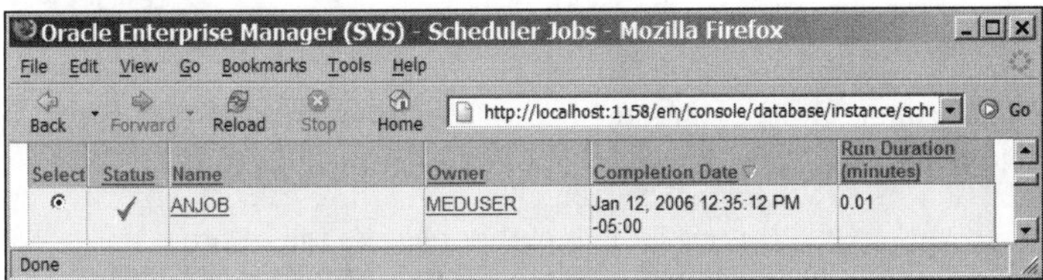

FIGURE 9-7 The history and status of the ANJOB job

22. Log out of Enterprise Manager and exit SQL*Plus.

ADVANCED SCHEDULER COMPONENTS

In addition to the basic scheduler components, there are some advanced objects that may be configured using the Scheduler. They are:

- Job Classes
- Windows
- Window Groups

Job Classes Job classes provide a method of grouping jobs into logical entities based on characteristics and system requirements. In Chapter 8 we reviewed the Database Resource Manager and understood how to group users who had similar resource requirements into consumer groups. Using the Scheduler, you can identify jobs that have similar resource needs and assign them to a consumer group. They will then be allocated resources based on the plan directives created for that consumer group under a given resource plan. A job can belong to only one job class at a time. Within a job class you can prioritize jobs by assigning some jobs more importance compared to others. The JOB_PRIORITY attribute can be assigned to a job, in such a way that a job that has the value of this attribute set to HIGH, will be executed before the job whose priority attribute is set to LOW.

A job class is created using the CREATE_JOB_CLASS procedure of the DBMS_SCHEDULER package. The syntax of the CREATE_JOB_CLASS procedure is displayed. Table 9-8 describes the parameters of the procedure.


```
DBMS_SCHEDULER.CREATE_JOB_CLASS (
   JOB_CLASS_NAME              IN VARCHAR2,
   RESOURCE_CONSUMER_GROUP     IN VARCHAR2 DEFAULT NULL,
   LOGGING_LEVEL               IN PLS_INTEGER DEFAULT NULL,
   LOG_HISTORY                 IN PLS_INTEGER DEFAULT NULL,
   COMMENTS                    IN VARCHAR2 DEFAULT NULL);
```

TABLE 9-8 Parameters of the CREATE_JOB_CLASS procedure

Parameter	Description
JOB_CLASS_NAME	Name of the job class. The name must be unique in the SYS schema.
RESOURCE_CONSUMER_GROUP	The name of the resource consumer group that the job class is associated with. Jobs assigned to the job class will be allocated resources based on the plan directives created for the consumer group.
LOGGING_LEVEL	This parameter determines the level of logging for jobs. Job logs can be maintained by the scheduler indicating the status of the job. The LOGGING_LEVEL parameter can take one of three values: LOGGING_OFF: Logging for jobs of this job class will be turned off. LOGGING_RUNS: Information about the runs of all jobs in the job class will be logged. LOGGING_FULL: Performs a detailed logging of every operation performed on every job of the job class.
LOG_HISTORY	Determines how long the logged data should be retained, after which they will be automatically purged. The default value is 30 days. Valid values are 1 through 999.
COMMENTS	A user-defined comment about the job class.

Example: A job class called DAILY_TASKS is being created. The job class is assigned to a consumer group called ADMIN_GROUP. Detailed information about all jobs assigned to the job class must be logged and retained in the database for a period of 90 days.

```
DBMS_SCHEDULER.CREATE_JOB_CLASS(
JOB_CLASS_NAME          => 'DAILY_TASKS',
RESOURCE_CONSUMER_GROUP => 'ADMIN_GROUP',
```

```
LOGGING_LEVEL              => DBMS_SCHEDULER.LOGGING_FULL,
LOG_HISTORY                => 90,
COMMENTS                   => 'Job class comprises routine tasks');
```

In addition to the CREATE_JOB_CLASS procedure, the DROP_JOB_CLASS procedure is available in the DBMS_SCHEDULER package. Table 9-9 describes the procedure.

TABLE 9-9 Other subprograms associated with Job classes

Subprogram Name	Description
DROP_JOB_CLASS	Used to drop job classes. If there are jobs that are assigned to the job class being dropped, an error will be displayed. You can, however, forcefully drop a job class that will result in all dependent jobs being disabled. The procedure receives the following arguments: JOB_CLASS_NAME: the name of the job class FORCE: can take values TRUE or FALSE. A value of TRUE results in a forceful dropping of the job class, disabling all dependent jobs.

Window A window is another scheduler object that can be created. A window is a time interval with a well-defined beginning and end time. In Chapter 8 you learned how resource plans may be created to manage system resources more efficiently. Consider the resource plans called DAYPLAN that must be activated during the day and NIGHTPLAN that must be activated at night. These plans contain different plan directives for the different consumer groups that access the database. You also learned the ALTER SYSTEM SET RESOURCE_MANAGER=<*plan_name*> command that was used to make a plan active. This command had to be manually issued by the DBA at a particular time of day. The window provides a method of activating a resource plan at a particular time of the day without the manual intervention of the administrator.

A window is a time interval; for example, you can define a window between 9 A.M. to 6 P.M. and another between 6 P.M. to 9 A.M. A window is given a name and attributes, such as the name of a resource plan, a schedule, and a repeat interval. A window is created using the CREATE_WINDOW procedure of the DBMS_SCHEDULER package.

The syntax of the command is displayed followed by Table 9-10 that describes some of the important parameters of the procedure.

```
DBMS_SCHEDULER.CREATE_WINDOW (
WINDOW_NAME               IN VARCHAR2,
RESOURCE_PLAN             IN VARCHAR2,
SCHEDULE_NAME             IN VARCHAR2,
DURATION                  IN INTERVAL DAY TO SECOND,
WINDOW_PRIORITY           IN VARCHAR2 DEFAULT 'LOW',
COMMENTS                  IN VARCHAR2 DEFAULT NULL);
```

TABLE 9-10 Parameters of the CREATE_WINDOW procedure

Window Attribute	Description
WINDOW_NAME	The name of the window which must be unique in the SYS schema.
RESOURCE_PLAN	The name of a resource plan that is made active when the window is opened. If a resource plan is not associated with a window, the currently active plan will continue to be active for the duration of the window.
START_DATE	Specifies the date when the window is to open for the first time. If it is null or a date in the past, the window will be made active immediately.
DURATION	A value that specifies how long a window will remain open. This is a mandatory attribute and the value must be specified. It does not hold a default value. The value should be specified as an INTERVAL DAY to SECOND datatype. For example, a duration can be INTERVAL '8' hour.
REPEAT_INTERVAL	This attribute indicates how often the window should repeat. If set to NULL, the window is opened only once on the specified start date. Its value can be set using a calendaring expression as explained under the topic Repeat Intervals. For example, FREQ=DAILY; INTERVAL=5 would indicate repeat every 5 days.
END_DATE	Specifies the date when the window will be disabled. If the value is set to NULL, the window will be active for the life of the program.
SCHEDULE_NAME	Is the name of an existing schedule, that will determine, when the window will open, how often it will repeat and when it will expire.
WINDOW_PRIORITY	Used to assign priorities to windows that overlap one another. In such a case, one of them can be assigned a higher priority by assigning it a window priority of HIGH and the other a window priority of LOW.
COMMENTS	A user-defined comment about the window.

Example: Consider a schedule called DAYSCH that is created in the following manner:

```
DBMS_SCHEDULER.CREATE_SCHEDULE(
SCHEDULE_NAME      => 'DAYSCH',
START_DATE         => SYSDATE,
REPEAT_INTERVAL    => 'FREQ=DAILY; BYHOUR=9',
COMMENTS           => 'SCHEDULE THAT BEGINS AT 9 AM');
```

In the code displayed, a window called DAYWIN that references the schedule DAYSCH is being created. The window will be opened between 9 A.M. and 6 P.M. When the window is started the DAYPLAN resource plan is made active. The window will be opened every day, forever.

```
DBMS_SCHEDULER.CREATE_WINDOW (
WINDOW_NAME        => 'DAYWIN',
RESOURCE_PLAN      => 'DAYPLAN',
SCHEDULE_NAME      => 'DAYSCH',
DURATION           => INTERVAL '9' HOUR,
COMMENTS           => 'Window opened during office hours');
```

In addition to the CREATE_WINDOW procedure, the DBMS_SCHEDULER package provides other subprograms that are related to managing windows. Table 9-11 describes some of the important subprograms. Examples of the usage of these procedures are presented in the Syntax Guide.

TABLE 9-11 Other subprograms associated with windows

Subprogram Name	Description
OPEN_WINDOW	Used to manually open a window. The window will be opened independent of its schedule. The resource plan associated with the window will be made active. Parameters that can be specified include: WINDOW_NAME: The name of the window to be opened. DURATION: The duration of time for which it should remain open, this value will override any value specified during window creation. FORCE: Can take a value TRUE or FALSE. The value TRUE indicates that the window must be opened even if its priority is lower than that of the active window.
CLOSE_WINDOW	Used to manually close a window. The only parameter accepted by the procedure is the name of the window (WINDOW_NAME) to be closed.

Window Group A window group may be created to group windows logically, for ease of use. If you have created windows to identify weekends, nights, and holidays, you can group these windows into a logical group. A window group is created using the CREATE_WINDOW_GROUP packaged procedure.

The syntax of the CREATE_WINDOW_GROUP packaged procedure is displayed below followed by Table 9-12, which describes its parameters.

```
DBMS_SCHEDULER.CREATE_WINDOW_GROUP (
   GROUP_NAME               IN VARCHAR2,
   WINDOW_LIST              IN VARCHAR2 DEFAULT NULL,
   COMMENTS                 IN VARCHAR2 DEFAULT NULL);
```

TABLE 9-12 Parameters of the CREATE_WINDOW_GROUP

Parameter	Description
GROUP_NAME	Name of the window group
WINDOW_LIST	A comma-separated list of windows that need to be grouped.
COMMENTS	A user-defined comment about the window group.

Example: A window group called OFFHOURS is being created that logically groups three windows (WEEKWIN, NIGHTWIN, and HOLWIN) that exist in the database.

```
DBMS_SCHEDULER.CREATE_WINDOW_GROUP
(GROUP_NAME         =>'OFFHOURS',
WINDOW_LIST         =>'WEEKWIN','NIGHTWIN','HOLWIN',
COMMENTS            =>'Creating a window group');
```

STATISTICS GATHERING IN THE ORACLE DATABASE

Object Statistics

When a user issues a query in the database, the optimizer of the Oracle database is responsible for creating an execution plan. The execution plan is a series of steps that are performed to retrieve the data that is requested. Within the database there are different methods to access data. Some methods are more efficient than others because they incur a lower cost. To determine the cost and choose the most efficient access path, the optimizer needs statistics about the object requested. Up-to-date statistics helps the optimizer identify optimal plans because it is aware of the most recent state of the object. Object statistics are particularly important for objects that are accessed and modified frequently. Prior to Oracle 9*i*, it was a database administrator's job to gather statistics for objects. The administrator had to identify volatile tables of the database and then gather statistics.

Optimizer statistics generated for a table include: the number of rows, the number of columns, the average row length, the number of distinct values in a column, the number of nulls in the column, and histograms that describe the distribution of data in the column.

There are a number of methods available to an administrator to gather statistics. The commonly used methods are the ANALYZE command and the Oracle-supplied DBMS_STATS package. The ANALYZE command is used to analyze individual tables. The DBMS_STATS package contains subprograms to analyze individual objects as well as entire schemas.

NOTE

For statistics to be generated the STATISTICS_LEVEL initialization parameter must be set to either TYPICAL or ALL.

The ANALYZE command may be used to analyze a table and generate statistics. The syntax of the ANALYZE command when analyzing a table is:

```
ANALYZE TABLE tablename [COMPUTE|ESTIMATE] STATISTICS;
```

The COMPUTE STATISTICS option results in a detailed and accurate analysis of the object, taking all rows into consideration when generating statistics. The ESTIMATE STATISTICS option is a faster process in which only a few sample rows are analyzed.

Using the DBMS_STATS package you can either gather statistics for an individual object or for an entire schema. Table 9-13 describes some of the commonly used subprograms of this package.

TABLE 9-13 Subprograms of the DBMS_STATS package

Subprogram Name	Description
GATHER_TABLE_STATS	Used to gather table, index, and column statistics.
GATHER_SCHEMA_STATS	Used to gather statistics for all objects in a schema.
DELETE_TABLE_STATS	Used to delete table, index, and column statistics.
LOCK_TABLE_STATS	Used to lock statistics on a table, index, or column to prevent modifications. Must only be used in a static environment where you can guarantee that the statistics will never change.

After analysis is done, the table statistics are populated into the data dictionary views that are related to tables such as DBA_TABLES, ALL_TABLES, USER_TABLES, and DBA_TAB_COLS, USER_TAB_COLS.

Practice 2: Gathering Statistics

In this practice example, you will gather statistics using the ANALYZE command and DBMS_STATS package on the C9PATIENT table belonging to the user MEDUSER. The C9PATIENT table was created by executing the script **c9_setup.sql** (See Setup section of this chapter).

1. Start SQL*Plus and connect as a user with SYSDBA privileges.

   ```
   SQL> CONNECT DB_ADMIN/DB_ADMIN AS SYSDBA
   ```

2. Ensure that the STATISTICS_LEVEL parameter is set to TYPICAL by issuing the ALTER SYSTEM command.

   ```
   SQL> ALTER SYSTEM SET STATISTICS_LEVEL=TYPICAL;
   ```

3. Connect as the user MEDUSER with a password of MEDUSER.

   ```
   SQL> CONNECT MEDUSER/MEDUSER
   ```

4. In this step you will perform a detailed analysis of the table called C9PATIENT, using the ANALYZE command.

   ```
   SQL> ANALYZE TABLE C9_PATIENT COMPUTE STATISTICS;
   ```

5. In this step, you will perform a detailed analysis of the table called C9PATIENT, using the DBMS_STATS.GATHER_TABLE_STATS packaged procedure.

   ```
   SQL> BEGIN
        DBMS_STATS.GATHER_TABLE_STATS('MEDUSER','C9_PATIENT');
        END;
        /
   ```

6. You will now use the DBMS_STATS.GATHER_SCHEMA_STATS package to gather statistics on all objects belonging to the user MEDUSER.

   ```
   SQL> BEGIN
        DBMS_STATS.GATHER_SCHEMA_STATS('MEDUSER');
        END;
        /
   ```

7. Exit SQL*Plus.

The Scheduler and Statistics Gathering

As already mentioned, statistics gathering is an important function of a DBA. However, it may not always be done regularly by administrators. To remove the burden of statistics gathering from the administrator, the Automatic Statistics Gathering feature has been introduced in Oracle 10*g*. The task of gathering statistics is now a job for the Scheduler.

The Oracle 10*g* database has a predefined job that is managed by the scheduler called GATHER_STATS_JOB. This job is responsible for gathering optimizer statistics on all objects that have either stale or missing statistics. The GATHER_STATS_JOB job invokes the Oracle-supplied DBMS_STATS.GATHER_DATABASE_STATS_JOB_PROC packaged procedure. The GATHER_STATS_JOB is part of a job class known as AUTO_TASKS_JOB_CLASS.

A pre-defined consumer group known as AUTO_TASKS_CONSUMER_GROUP is also created during database creation. The AUTO_TASKS_JOB_CLASS job class is assigned to the AUTO_TASKS_CONSUMER_GROUP consumer group.

Also available in the Oracle 10*g* database is a window group known as the MAINTENANCE_WINDOW_GROUP window. This window group consists of two pre-defined windows: The WEEKNIGHT_WINDOW whose time interval is 10 P.M. to 6 A.M. and the WEEKEND_WINDOW whose time interval includes 12 A.M. on Saturday to 12 A.M. on Monday. Optimizer statistics are gathered automatically by the Scheduler within the time interval specified by the MAINTENANCE_WINDOW_GROUP.

Viewing Information from Enterprise Manager You can view the GATHER_STATS_JOB and its status from within the Enterprise Manager.

Practice 3: Viewing the GATHER_STATS_JOB from Enterprise Manager

1. Launch a browser and enter the URL to invoke the Enterprise Manager. Log in as a user with SYSDBA privileges.
2. From the **Database Control Home** page, select the **Administration** tab.
3. Scroll down to the **Scheduler** section, and select the **Jobs** link.
4. The **Scheduler Jobs** page will be displayed.
5. Notice the job with the name GATHER_STATS_JOB. It is associated with the MAINTENANCE_WINDOW_GROUP. (See Figure 9-8.) The job class is AUTO_TASKS_JOB_CLASS. Figure 9-9 indicates the job has been run 2 times. The details of the GATHER_STATS_JOB continues in Figure 9-9.

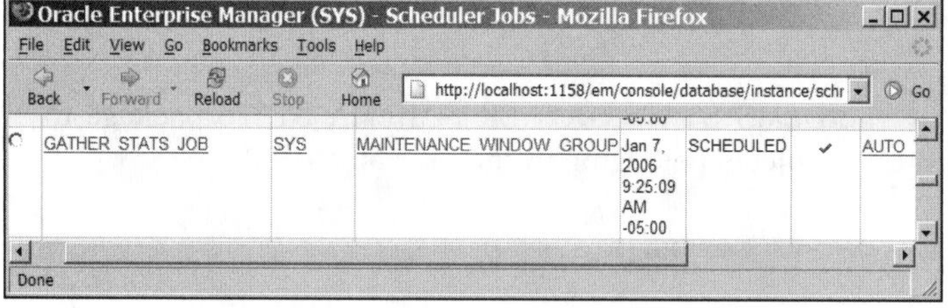

FIGURE 9-8 The GATHER_STATS_JOB job

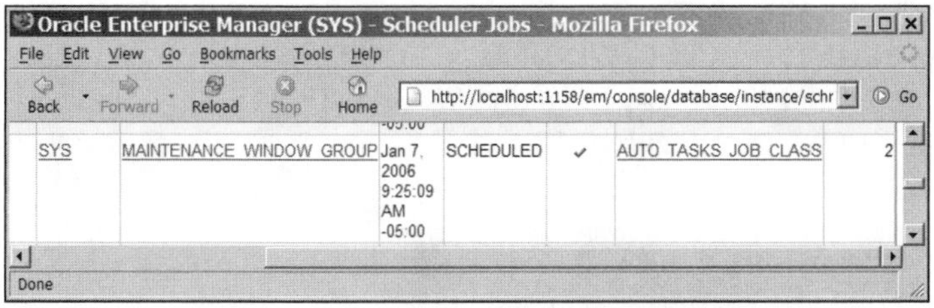

FIGURE 9-9 Details of the GATHER_STATS_JOB continued

6. Click on the **GATHER_STATS_JOB** link. The **View Job: SYS.GATHER_STATS_JOB** page will be displayed. Figure 9-10 shows you information about the job.

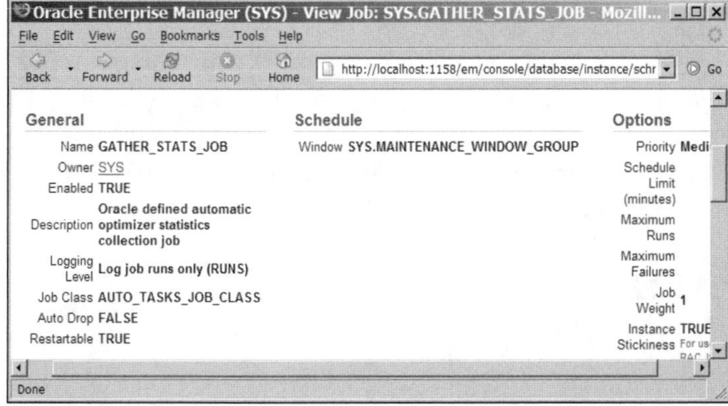

FIGURE 9-10 The View Job: SYS.GATHER_STATS_JOB page

7. You may select the **Edit** button on this page, to make changes to the job if necessary. Go through the options available on the **Edit Job: SYS.GATHER_STATS_JOB** page.
8. Select the **Scheduler Jobs** link on the top of the page as shown in Figure 9-11 to return to the Scheduler Jobs page.

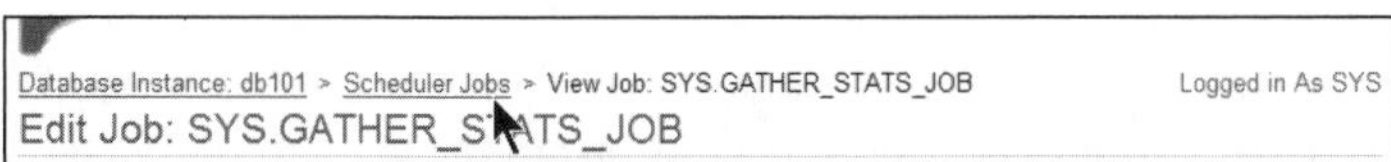

FIGURE 9-11 The Scheduler Jobs Link

9. Select the **MAINTENANCE_WINDOW_GROUP** link to display the **Edit Window Group: MAINTENTANCE_WINDOW_GROUP** page. Notice that the members are listed on the page, namely WEEKEND_WINDOW and WEEKNIGHT_WINDOW. (See Figure 9-12.)

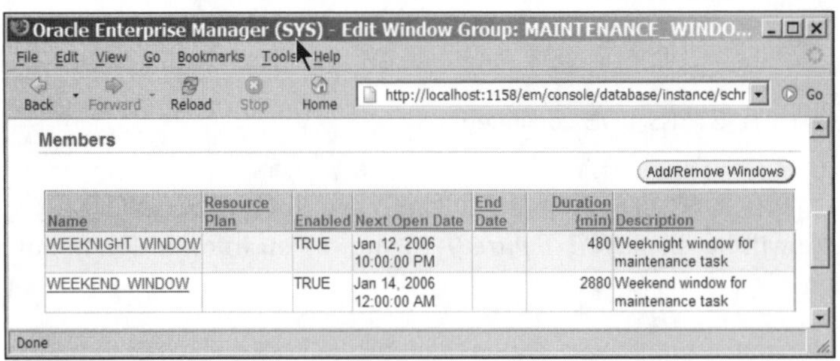

FIGURE 9-12 Members of the MAINTENANCE_WINDOW_GROUP

10. Select the **WEEKEND_WINDOW** link to display the **View Window: WEEKEND_WINDOW** page. In the Schedule section you can see the details about the schedule of this window. It repeats on a weekly basis, starting at 12 A.M. for a period of 48 hours. (See Figure 9-13.)

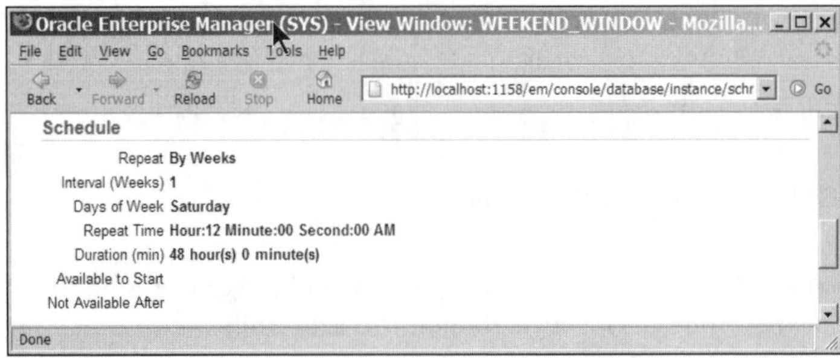

FIGURE 9-13 The schedule of the WEEKEND_WINDOW window

11. Select the **OK** button and return to the **Edit Window Group: MAINTENANCE_WINDOW_GROUP** page.
12. Select the **Database Instance: (database name)** link on the top-left corner of the page to return to the Administration tab. Once again navigate to the Scheduler section and select the Jobs link.
13. From the **Scheduler Jobs** page, select the link under the job class **AUTO_TASKS_JOB_CLASS**.
14. The **Edit Job Class: AUTO_TASKS_JOB_CLASS** page will be displayed. The page indicates that this job class is the System maintenance job class. The name of the consumer group associated with this job class is displayed as AUTO_TASK_CONSUMER_GROUP. (See Figure 9-14.)

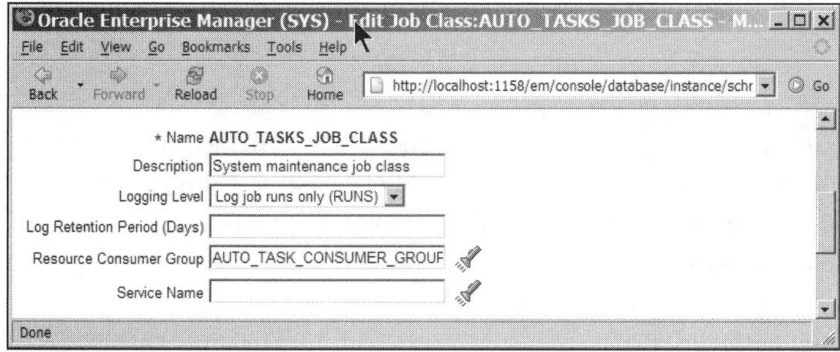

FIGURE 9-14 Details of the AUTO_TASK_CONSUMER_GROUP

15. Log out of Enterprise Manager.

RELEVANT DATA DICTIONARY VIEWS

There are a number of data dictionary views available within the database that provide information about the Scheduler. Table 9-14 describes the data dictionary views related to the Scheduler and its objects. The asterisk (*) may substituted by {DBA|ALL|USER}.

TABLE 9-14 Data Dictionary views containing scheduler information

View	Description
*_SCHEDULER_PROGRAMS	Information about programs created.
*_SCHEDULER_PROGRAM_ARGUMENTS	Displays all arguments that are registered with programs.
*_SCHEDULER_SCHEDULES	Information about schedules.
*_SCHEDULER_JOBS	Information about all jobs.
*_SCHEDULER_JOB_CLASSES	Information about all job classes.
*_SCHEDULER_WINDOWS	Information about all windows.
*_SCHEDULER_WINDOW_GROUPS	Information about window groups.
*_SCHEDULER_WINGROUP_MEMBERS	Shows all members of all window groups. One row of information is available or each group member.
*_SCHEDULER_RUNNING_JOBS	Information about currently executing jobs.
*_SCHEDULER_JOB_RUN_DETAILS	Information about all completed jobs. It includes those which completed successfully as well as failed.
*_SCHEDULER_GLOBAL_ATTRIBUTE	Displays the current values of Scheduler attributes.

Practice 4: Querying the data dictionary

In earlier practices, you created a number of scheduler objects. In this practice example, you will query some of the data dictionary views relevant to the Scheduler as the user MEDUSER.

1. Start SQL*Plus, and connect as the user MEDUSER with a password of MEDUSER.

```
SQL> CONNECT MEDUSER/MEDUSER
```

2. Issue a query to access all the data from the USER_SCHEDULER_PROGRAMS view. Information about programs created by MEDUSER will be displayed. Notice we have a program called ANTABLE, that was created in an earlier exercise. (See Figure 9-15.)

```
SQL> SELECT * FROM USER_SCHEDULER_PROGRAMS;
```


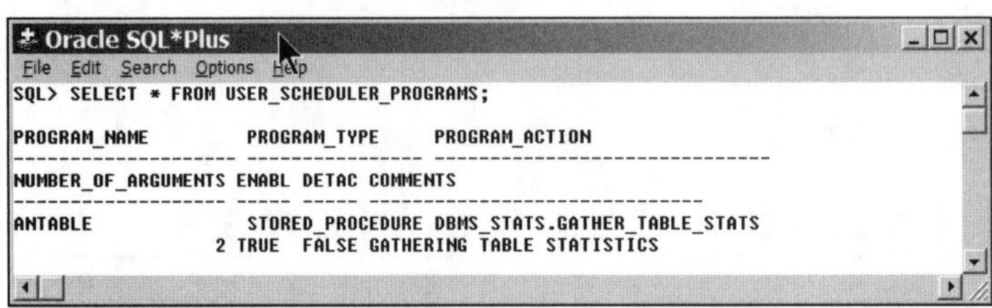

FIGURE 9-15 Querying the USER_SCHEDULER_PROGRAMS view

3. Issue a query to access all the data from the USER_SCHEDULER_PROGRAMS view. Information about the schedules created by MEDUSER will be displayed. Notice, the schedule called PM10. (See Figure 9-16.)

```
SQL> SELECT SCHEDULE_NAME, SCHEDULE_TYPE,
     START_DATE, END_DATE, REPEAT_INTERVAL
     FROM USER_SCHEDULER_SCHEDULES;
```

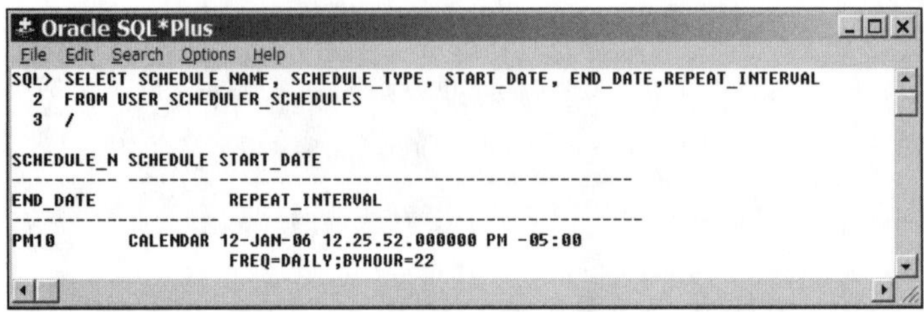

FIGURE 9-16 Querying the USER_SCHEDULER_SCHEDULES view

4. Issue a query to retrieve the JOB_NAME, JOB_CREATOR, PROGRAM_NAME, NUMBER_OF_ARGUMENTS, SCHEDULER_NAME, and JOB_CLASS columns from USER_SCHEDULER_JOBS view for the ANJOB job. Figure 9-17 displays the output of the query.

```
SQL> SELECT JOB_NAME, JOB_CREATOR, PROGRAM_NAME,
     NUMBER_OF_ARGUMENTS,
     SCHEDULE_NAME, JOB_CLASS FROM USER_SCHEDULER_JOBS
     WHERE JOB_NAME='ANJOB';
```

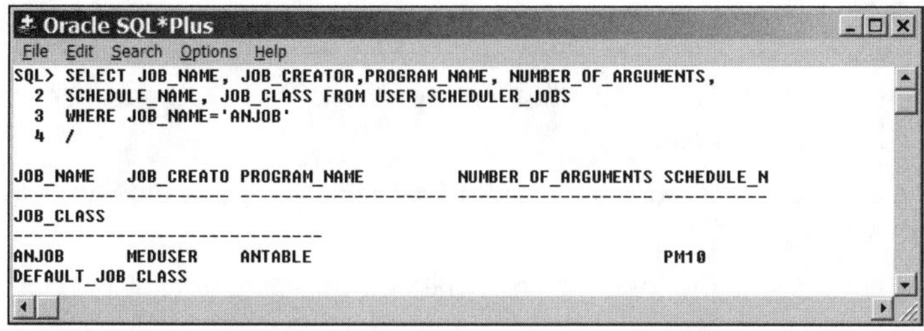
```
SQL> SELECT JOB_NAME, JOB_CREATOR,PROGRAM_NAME, NUMBER_OF_ARGUMENTS,
  2  SCHEDULE_NAME, JOB_CLASS FROM USER_SCHEDULER_JOBS
  3  WHERE JOB_NAME='ANJOB'
  4  /

JOB_NAME   JOB_CREATO PROGRAM_NAME         NUMBER_OF_ARGUMENTS SCHEDULE_N
---------- ---------- -------------------- ------------------- ----------
JOB_CLASS
------------------------------
ANJOB      MEDUSER    ANTABLE                                  PM10
DEFAULT_JOB_CLASS
```

FIGURE 9-17 Querying the USER_SCHEDULER_JOBS view

5. Next, query the USER_SCHEDULER_JOB_RUN_DETAILS view to display the JOB_NAME, STATUS, and ERROR# columns of the job called ANJOB. Notice the status displays as SUCCEEDED and the ERROR# is 0. (See Figure 9-18.)

```
SQL> SELECT JOB_NAME, STATUS, ERROR#
     FROM USER_SCHEDULER_JOB_RUN_DETAILS
     WHERE JOB_NAME='ANJOB';
```

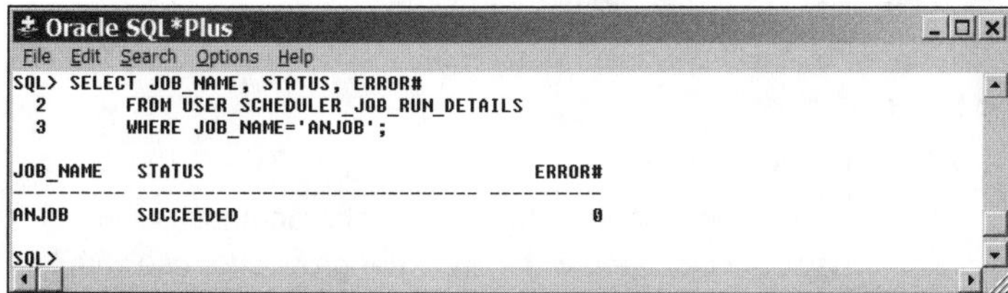
```
SQL> SELECT JOB_NAME, STATUS, ERROR#
  2       FROM USER_SCHEDULER_JOB_RUN_DETAILS
  3       WHERE JOB_NAME='ANJOB';

JOB_NAME   STATUS                             ERROR#
---------- ------------------------------ ----------
ANJOB      SUCCEEDED                               0

SQL>
```

FIGURE 9-18 Querying the USER_SCHEDULER_JOB_RUN_DETAILS

6. Exit SQL*Plus.

In this chapter you learned about the Scheduler. The Scheduler is very useful for jobs that are time consuming and repetitive. It provides the administrator the ability to configure such jobs for automatic execution, without manual intervention. In Chapter 10 you will see how an administrator can proactively manage space in an Oracle database.

Chapter Summary

- The Scheduler is a new feature in Oracle 10*g* that replaces the DBMS_JOB package available in previous versions of Oracle.
- The Scheduler may be accessed by means of the DBMS_SCHEDULER package as well as from the Enterprise Manager.
- The Scheduler uses a background process known as the Job Coordinator (cjqNNN) for managing jobs.
- A user who needs to access the Scheduler must possess the CREATE JOB system privilege.
- The basic objects of the Scheduler include:
  - Program—A collection of metadata about what must be run by the Scheduler. A program can be created once and reused many times, and can be shared among the users of the database.
  - Schedule—A collection of metadata about when and how frequently jobs must be run by the Scheduler. A schedule can be created once and reused many times, and can be shared among the users of the database.
  - Job—A task to be executed by the Scheduler. When creating a job you must indicate what needs to be run and when.
- The advanced objects of the Scheduler include:
  - Job Classes—A method of grouping jobs with similar characteristics and requirements. Job classes may be associated with consumer groups for use with the Database Resource Manager.
  - Window—A time interval with a well-defined beginning time and end time. Windows facilitate the automatic change of resource plans at different times of the day.
  - Window Group—A logical grouping of windows. They may be created to simplify management of windows.
- Table statistics may be gathered by the ANALYZE command or the DBMS_STATS.GATHER_TABLE_STATS packaged procedure.
- Using the Scheduler, the gathering of object statistics has been made automatic. The Scheduler performs the job of gathering statistics automatically after 6 P.M. every day.

Syntax Guide

SYNTAX GUIDE		
Procedures associated with Programs	**Description**	**Example**
CREATE_PROGRAM	Used to create a program.	`DBMS_SCHEDULER.CREATE_PROGRAM ( PROGRAM_NAME => 'PROGRAM1', PROGRAM_ACTION => 'USER1.PROG1', PROGRAM_TYPE =>'STORED_PROCEDURE');`
DEFINE_PROGRAM _ARGUMENT	Used to define the position and datatype of arguments sent to stored procedures.	`DBMS_SCHEDULER.DEFINE_PROGRAM _ARGUMENT( PROGRAM_NAME => 'PROGRAM1', ARGUMENT_POSITION => 1, ARGUMENT_TYPE => 'VARCHAR2');`
DROP_PROGRAM _ARGUMENT	Used to drop a program argument.	`DBMS_SCHEDULER.DROP_PROGRAM _ARGUMENT( PROGRAM_NAME => 'PROGRAM1', ARGUMENT_POSITION => 1);`
DROP_PROGRAM	Used to drop existing programs from the database.	`DBMS_SCHEDULER.DROP_PROGRAM ( PROGRAM_NAME => 'PROGRAM1', FORCE => TRUE);`
Procedures associated with Schedules	**Description**	**Example**
CREATE_SCHEDULE	Used to create a schedule.	`DBMS_SCHEDULER.CREATE_SCHEDULE (SCHEDULE_NAME => 'SCHEDULE1', START_DATE => SYSDATE, REPEAT_INTERVAL => 'FREQ=DAILY; BYHOUR=17');`
DROP_SCHEDULE	Used to drop a schedule.	`DBMS_SCHEDULER.DROP_SCHEDULE ( SCHEDULE_NAME => 'SCHEDULE1', FORCE => TRUE);`
Procedures associated with Jobs	**Description**	**Example**
CREATE_JOB	Used to create a job.	`DBMS_SCHEDULER.CREATE_JOB( JOB_NAME => 'JOB1', PROGRAM_NAME => 'PROGRAM1', SCHEDULE_NAME => 'SCHEDULE1');`
COPY_JOB	Used to copy a job.	`DBMS_SCHEDULER.COPY_JOB( OLD_JOB => 'JOB1', NEW_JOB => 'JOB1COPY');`
RUN_JOB	Used to execute a job, independent of its schedule.	`DBMS_SCHEDULER.RUN_JOB( JOB_NAME => 'JOB1', FORCE => TRUE);`

SYNTAX GUIDE		
Procedures associated with Jobs	**Description**	**Example**
SET_JOB_ARGUMENT _VALUE	Used to assign a value to an argument.	DBMS_SCHEDULER.SET_JOB _ARGUMENT_VALUE (JOB_NAME => 'JOB1', ARGUMENT_POSITION => 1, ARGUMENT_VALUE => 'MEDUSER');
STOP_JOB	Used to terminate a job that is currently running.	DBMS_SCHEDULER.STOP_JOB(JOB_NAME => 'JOB1', FORCE => TRUE);
Procedures associated with Windows	**Description**	**Example**
CREATE_WINDOW	Used to create a window.	DBMS_SCHEDULER.CREATE_WINDOW (WINDOW_NAME => 'WINDOW1', RESOURCE_PLAN => 'PLAN1', SCHEDULE_NAME => 'SCHEDULE1', DURATION => INTERVAL '6' HOUR, COMMENTS => 'A 6 HOUR WINDOW');
OPEN_WINDOW	Used to manually open a window, independent of its schedule.	DBMS_SCHEDULER.OPEN_WINDOW(WINDOW_NAME => 'WINDOW1', DURATION => INTERVAL '30' MINUTE, FORCE => TRUE);
CLOSE_WINDOW	Used to manually close a window.	DBMS_SCHEDULER.CLOSE_WINDOW(WINDOW_NAME => 'WINDOW1');
DROP_WINDOW	To drop existing window(s).	DBMS_SCHEDULER.DROP_WINDOW(WINDOW_NAME => 'WIN1, WIN2', FORCE => TRUE);
CREATE_JOB_CLASS	Used to create a job class.	DBMS_SCHEDULER.CREATE_JOB_CLASS(JOB_CLASS_NAME => 'JCLASS1', RESOURCE_CONSUMER_GROUP =>'GRP1', LOGGING_LEVEL => DBMS_SCHEDULER.LOGGING_RUNS, LOG_HISTORY => 10, COMMENTS => 'NEW JOB CLASS');
CREATE_WINDOW_GROUP	Used to create a window group.	DBMS_SCHEDULER.CREATE_WINDOW_GROUP (GROUP_NAME =>'OFFHOURS', WINDOW_LIST =>'WIN1','WIN2','WIN3', COMMENTS =>'New window group');
Other Important Procedures	**Description**	**Example**
ENABLE	To make an object eligible for use by the Scheduler.	DBMS_SCHEDULER.ENABLE('PROGRAM1');

SYNTAX GUIDE		
Other Important Procedures	**Description**	**Example**
DISABLE	To make an object ineligible for use by the Scheduler.	DBMS_SCHEDULER.DISABLE('PROGRAM1');
SET_ATTRIBUTE	To modify or alter an attribute of a Scheduler object.	DBMS_SCHEDULER.SET_ATTRIBUTE (NAME => 'JOB1', ATTRIBUTE => 'ENABLED', VALUE => TRUE);
SET_ATTRIBUTE _NULL	To set the value of an attribute to NULL.	DBMS_SCHEDULER.SET_ATTRIBUTE_NULL (NAME => 'SCHEDULE1', ATTRIBUTE => 'REPEAT_INTERVAL');
Commands and Packaged procedures associated with Statistics gathering		
ANALYZE command	Used to analyze an object to gather statistics.	ANALYZE TABLE table1 COMPUTE STATISTICS; ANALYZE TABLE table1 ESTIMATE STATISTICS;
DBMS_STATS. GATHER_TABLE_STATS	Used to gather statistics for a table.	DBMS_STATS.GATHER_TABLE_STATS('USER1','TABLE1');
DBMS_STATS. GATHER_SCHEMA_STATS	Used to gather statistics for all objects of a schema.	DBMS_STATS.GATHER_SCHEMA_STATS('USER1')
DBMS_STATS. DELETE_TABLE_STATS	Used to delete statistics for a table.	DBMS_STATS.DELETE_TABLE_STATS('USER1','TABLE1');
DBMS_STATS. LOCK_TABLE_STATS	Used to lock statistics so that they cannot be modified.	DBMS_STATS.LOCK_TABLE_STATS('USER1','TABLE1');

Review Questions

1. Identify the three basic objects that can be created using the Oracle 10*g* scheduler.
   a. JOB CLASS
   b. JOB
   c. JOB GROUP
   d. WINDOW
   e. PROGRAM
   f. SCHEDULE
   g. WINDOW GROUP
2. The ________________ system privilege is required to create a job under any schema.
3. By default a job and program are created in a disabled manner. True or False?

4. When creating a program using the DBMS_SCHEDULER package, the PROGRAM_TYPE argument received by the CREATE_PROGRAM procedure can include ________________ . [Choose 3.]
   a. SQL statements
   b. PL/SQL blocks
   c. Stored Procedures
   d. Operating System executable files
   e. Text files
5. The ________________ packaged procedure is used to enable a job that is currently disabled.
   a. DBMS_SCHEDULER.CREATE_JOB
   b. DBMS_SCHEDULER.DISABLE
   c. DBMS_SCHEDULER.ENABLE
   d. DBMS_RESOURCE_MANAGER.ENABLE_JOB
6. Identify the valid program types that can be created using the Scheduler.
   a. PLSQL_ANONYMOUS_BLOCK
   b. PLSQLBLOCK
   c. PLSQL_BLOCK
   d. STORED_PROCEDURE
   e. EXECUTABLE
   f. OS_EXECUTABLE
7. A schedule is created by a database administrator in the following manner:

```
DBMS_SCHEDULER.CREATE_SCHEDULE (
SCHEDULE_NAME           => 'NEW_SCHEDULE',
START_DATE              => SYSTIMESTAMP,
REPEAT_INTERVAL         => 'FREQ=WEEKLY; BYDAY=TUE;
                            BYHOUR=7; BYMINUTE=40');
```

   Choose the statement that best describes the above schedule:
   a. At 7:40 P.M. every Tuesday starting immediately.
   b. At 7:40 A.M. every Tuesday starting immediately.
   c. Every seven hours every Tuesday starting immediately.
   d. Every seventh hour and fortieth minute on Tuesday.
8. To create a job, schedule, or program a user needs a specific system privilege. Identify the correct privilege.
   a. MANAGE_SCHEDULER
   b. CREATE_JOB
   c. MANAGE_JOB
   d. CREATE_SCHEDULER_OBJECTS
   e. None of the above.

9. A user-defined task scheduled to run one or more times is known as a:
   a. PROGRAM
   b. SCHEDULE
   c. JOB
   d. WINDOW
   e. WINDOW GROUP
   f. JOB CLASS
10. Which of the following data dictionary views can the DBA query to determine the completed (failed/successful) jobs?
   a. DBA_SCHEDULER_JOBS
   b. DBA_SCHEDULER_RUNNING_JOBS
   c. DBA_SCHEDULER_JOB_RUN_DETAILS
   d. DBA_SCHEDULER_JOB_CLASSES
   e. DBA_SCHEDULER_JOB_ARGUMENTS
11. The Scheduler is the feature in Oracle 10*g* that permits repetitive tasks to be performed. Identify three characteristics of the Scheduler.
   a. Scheduler objects are modular and can be reused.
   b. Scheduler can be invoked using both EM Console and packaged procedures.
   c. Scheduler does not allow the same operation to be performed on multiple jobs.
   d. Jobs can be filtered and sorted for easy viewing.
   e. Jobs cannot be moved from a testing to a production environment.
12. Which procedure of the DBMS_SCHEDULER package would you execute to disable automatic statistics gathering in the database?
   a. STOP_JOB
   b. DISABLE
   c. DISABLE_STATISTICS
   d. STOP_STATISTICS_GATHERING
   e. Resumable space allocation feature
   f. NOGATHER_STATS_JOB
13. The background process that is responsible for coordinating the jobs of the scheduler is ________________ .
14. The program called PROGRAM1 is associated with the JOB1 job. A command to drop PROGRAM 1 is issued with the FORCE option. What is the effect of the FORCE option?
   a. The PROGRAM1 cannot be dropped.
   b. The PROGRAM1 is dropped by JOB1 is still active.
   c. The PROGRAM1 is dropped and JOB1 will be disabled.
   d. The PROGRAM 1 is dropped and JOB1 is dropped.

15. A window group is a method of logically grouping ________________ .
    a. Windows with similar names
    b. Windows
    c. Windows with similar requirements
    d. Windows that are overlapping
16. The ________________ clause of the ANALYZE command is used to obtain detailed and accurate statistics.
17. The DBA of a 10*g* database wishes to analyze all the objects of the database. What would you recommend?
    a. Creating a script that will analyze all tables one after another.
    b. Do nothing; a job exists in the Scheduler that automatically gathers statistics.
    c. Create a job that will gather statistics for all objects of the database.
    d. Create a script that will execute the DBMS_STATS.GATHER_SCHEMA_STATS package for all schemas in the database.
18. The ________________ job is a pre-defined job in the Scheduler that gathers object statistics for all objects that have null or stale statistics in the database.
19. The database administrator is creating a Job. Which of the following objects can be referenced?
    a. SCHEDULE
    b. JOB CLASS
    c. WINDOW
    d. RESOURCE CONSUMER GROUP
    e. RESOURCE PLAN
    f. PROGRAM
20. Write a calendaring expression that will run in the second to last day of the month of September, every year.

Hands-On Assignments

Please make sure you run the script **C9_SETUP.SQL** from the Chapter09 folder of the student datafiles once before you begin these assignments. The script should be executed under the MEDUSER schema. Refer to the instructions in the section-Setup for the Chapter.

Assignment 9-1 Creating a stored procedure

1. Start SQL*Plus and log in as the user MEDUSER.
2. Create a stored procedure called DISPATIENTS as shown below. This procedure inserts all rows of patients who have been discharged into the PATIENT_HISTORY table. Further the patient records of discharged patients are deleted from the original C9_PATIENT table.

```
CREATE OR REPLACE PROCEDURE DISPATIENTS
IS
BEGIN
INSERT INTO PATIENT_HISTORY
```

```
SELECT * FROM C9_PATIENT
WHERE STATUS='DISCHARGED';
DELETE FROM C9_PATIENT
WHERE STATUS='DISCHARGED';
END;
/
```

3. Remain connected to SQL*Plus.

Assignment 9-2 Creating a program

1. Connect as the user MEDUSER, if you are not already connected.
2. Create a program called PROG92. It should execute the stored procedure DISPATIENTS. Enable the program during creation.
3. Query the data dictionary to make sure the program has been created.
4. Remain connected to SQL*Plus.

Assignment 9-3 Creating a schedule

1. Connect as the user MEDUSER, if you are not already connected.
2. Create a schedule called SCH93. It should begin on the current date. Repeat every hour on the hour. For instance, 12 A.M., 1 A.M., 2 A.M., and so on. It should never expire.
3. Query the data dictionary to make sure the schedule has been created.
4. Remain connected to SQL*Plus.

Assignment 9-4 Creating a job

1. Connect as the user MEDUSER, if you are not already connected.
2. Create a job called JOB94. The job should execute the program PROG92 using the schedule SCH93. The job should be disabled during creation.
3. Query the data dictionary to make sure the job has been created.
4. Remain connected to SQL*Plus.

Assignment 9-5 Copying a job

1. Connect as the user MEDUSER, if you are not already connected.
2. Copy the job called JOB94 to a job called JOB94COPY.
3. Query the data dictionary to make sure the copied job has been created.
4. Remain connected to SQL*Plus.

Assignment 9-6 Enabling a job

1. Connect as the user MEDUSER, if you are not already connected.
2. Enable the job JOB94.
3. Remain connected to SQL*Plus.

Assignment 9-7 Running a job

1. Connect as the user MEDUSER, if you are not already connected.
2. Execute the job JOB94, using the appropriate packaged procedure.
3. Query the PATIENT_HISTORY table to see if the records of the 4 patients who have been discharged have been inserted.

4. Query the C9_PATIENT table to see if the records of the 4 patients who have been discharged have been deleted.
5. Remain connected to SQL*Plus.

Assignment 9-8 Querying details of the job

1. Connect as the user MEDUSER, if you are not already connected.
2. Query the appropriate data dictionary view that will display information about the job (JOB94) that was executed. Did it complete successfully? What was the Error#?
3. Launch Enterprise Manager, log in with SYSDBA privileges and view the details of the job from the Scheduler Jobs Page.
4. When is the job scheduled to run again? Is it on the hour?
5. Log out of Enterprise Manager, and remain connected to SQL*Plus.

Assignment 9-9 Disabling a job

1. Connect as the user MEDUSER, if you are not already connected.
2. Using the appropriate packaged procedure, disable the job called JOB94.
3. Remain connected to SQL*Plus.

Assignment 9-10 Creating a job class

1. Connect as a user with SYSDBA privileges.
2. Create a job class called JOB910. Assign the job class to the LOW_GROUP consumer group. Assign the level of logging to LOGGING_RUNS and ensure that all log information is purged every 10 days.
3. Remain connected to SQL*Plus.

Assignment 9-11 Modifying the job class attribute of the job

1. Connect as the user MEDUSER, if you are not already connected.
2. Using the appropriate packaged procedure, assign the job JOB94, to the job class JOB910. You will need to change an attribute of the job JOB94.
3. Remain connected to SQL*Plus.

Assignment 9-12 Creating a schedule and a window

1. Connect as a user with SYSDBA privileges, if you are not already connected.
2. Create a schedule called SCH912. The schedule must begin on the current date. It should repeat itself every day at 9 A.M.
3. Create a window called WIN912. The window should activate the SYSTEM_PLAN resource plan. The window must be associated with the SCH912 schedule and be active for a period of 3 hours.
4. Remain connected to SQL*Plus.

Assignment 9-13 Open a window

1. Connect as a user with SYSDBA privileges, if you are not already connected.
2. Open the window called WIN912. Let the window be open for a period of 2 hours. Make sure the window is opened even if a window with a higher priority is currently open.
3. Remain connected to SQL*Plus.

Assignment 9-14 Closing the Window and Dropping it

1. Connect as a user with SYSDBA privileges, if you are not already connected.
2. Use the appropriate packaged procedure to close the window called WIN912.
3. Use the appropriate packaged procedure to drop the window called WIN912.
4. Remain connected to SQL*Plus.

Assignment 9-15 Gathering objects statistics for the MEDUSER schema

1. Connect as the user MEDUSER.
2. Use the appropriate packaged procedure to gather statistics for all objects belonging to the MEDUSER schema.
3. Use a packaged procedure to gather statistics for the table called C9_PATIENT belonging to the user MEDUSER.
4. Exit SQL*Plus.

Case Study

1. Revisit the scenario presented in the beginning of the chapter and recommend a method that may be used to resolve the problem faced by Ryan.
2. Using a diagram, identify the relationships that exist between the objects of the Scheduler that have been discussed in this chapter.
3. A job called GRPJOB has been created based on the Schedule called DAYSCHEDULE. This job must be granted the same resources as the members of the consumer group called OLTP_CGP. How can this be achieved?

CHAPTER **10**

SPACE MANAGEMENT

LEARNING OBJECTIVES

After completing this lesson you should be able to understand:

- Tablespaces and the proactive tablespace monitoring
- Setting and modifying thresholds for space usage
- Different types of segments that optimize space usage
- Advisories in the Oracle database that monitor space usage
- Managing Resumable Space Allocation using the DBMS_RESUMABLE package

ORACLE CERTIFICATION EXAM OBJECTIVES COVERED IN THIS CHAPTER INCLUDE:

- Tune redo writing and archiving operations
- Issue statements that can be suspended upon encountering space condition errors
- Reduce space-related error conditions by proactively managing tablespace usage
- Reclaim wasted space from tables and indexes using the segment shrink functionality
- Estimate the size of new tables and indexes
- Use different storage options to improve the performance of queries

INTRODUCTION

As we already know, the Oracle Database 10*g* product has introduced various new features that help the DBA proactively manage the database. By proactive we mean that the DBA is able to configure the database such that warnings will be provided even before problems occur within the database.

This chapter introduces you to some more new features that are built in to the Oracle database that can simplify the job of the DBA when dealing with space-related issues. Space is utilized when objects are created in the database or new data is added to existing objects. The DBA must always ensure that users have the space they need for their objects. Space within an object must also be utilized efficiently. If many rows of a table are deleted, the table may no longer be space efficient. In earlier versions of Oracle, monitoring space usage could be performed by the administrator by writing custom scripts that queried data dictionary views. Based on recent surveys, such tasks consume nearly 20% of an administrator's time.

This chapter discusses how space can be managed in the Oracle 10*g* database using a number of new tools and features. We will discuss the methods available for efficient space management in tablespaces, in individual segments, in undo tablespaces, and in redo log files. The chapter also discusses the Resumable Space Allocation feature that describes how time may be saved when a long-running operation runs out of space.

THE CURRENT CHALLENGE AT KELLER MEDICAL CENTER

The database at Keller Medical Center runs a mixed workload. During the day, users of the database make changes to the database. Often many rows are deleted from the tables. During the night, queries and reports are generated. Ryan has observed that though many of the tables have very few rows in them, reports that query these tables take a long time. Further, these tables populate many blocks into the Database Buffer Cache when queries are performed. This should not be the case especially when the tables have few rows.

In addition to this problem, lately the alert log file has been displaying errors indicating the checkpoints have not completed.

SETUP FOR THE CHAPTER

In this chapter, you will be asked to execute certain scripts prior to performing a specific practice task or hands-on assignment. All scripts are available in the Chapter10 folder of the student datafiles.

TABLESPACES AND PROACTIVE MONITORING

The Oracle database has a logical and physical structure. The logical structure of the database consists of a series of storage structures that permit you to easily access, manage, organize, and manipulate the data in the database. The logical structure of the database is visible only within the Oracle database. The logical structure includes the Database, Tablespaces, Segments, Extents, and Oracle Blocks. The physical structure on the other hand is visible at the operating system and consists of datafiles and operating system blocks. The logical and physical structures are closely related to each other. A tablespace is made up of one more datafiles and an Oracle block consists of one or more operating system blocks.

Tablespaces are logical structures that help simplify administration in the database. The SYSTEM and SYSAUX tablespaces are created at database creation time. A DBA may choose to create additional tablespaces in the database to organize the different types of data stored in the Oracle database. For example, tablespaces may be created to store undo segments, temporary segments, segments belonging to specific applications, indexes, and so on (See Appendix A). Tablespaces may be locally managed or dictionary managed. In locally managed tablespaces, both extent allocation and segment space management may be managed automatically by the Oracle database. Locally managed tablespaces are more efficient than dictionary-managed tablespaces and are the default kind since Oracle *9i*. In a nutshell, administrators should create tablespaces to separate the different types of data that is stored and generated within the database.

When a tablespace is created, a datafile(s) is also created. Figure 10-1 describes the association between tablespaces and datafiles. Datafiles are files created on the operating system file system; they are given a name and have a size. A typical command to create a tablespace is:

```
CREATE TABLESPACE <tablespace_name>
DATAFILE '<path>\datafile_name' SIZE 500K;
```

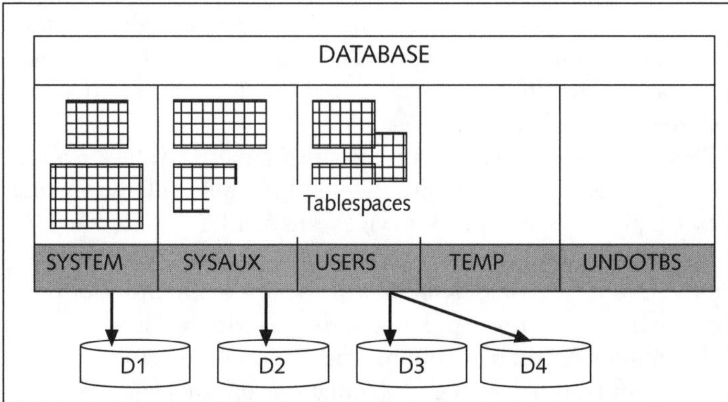

FIGURE 10-1 Associating tablespaces and datafiles

Users create objects in the tablespaces. The objects will be physically stored in the datafiles of the tablespace. Space from the datafile may be utilized as long as there is free space in the file. When there is no space left in the datafile, an administrator may choose to add another datafile to the tablespace, resize the datafile by increasing its size, or set it to extend automatically. The property by which a datafile can be made to extend automatically is known as the auto-extensible property of a datafile. Finally, a DBA may also choose to reorganize sparsely populated objects to generate unused free space.

An important function of a DBA is to look for tablespaces that are low on space and proactively add space so that applications do not generate out-of-space errors. This may involve monitoring the database by running scripts or querying the data dictionary views to identify such tablespaces. If such a tablespace is identified, the DBA must take suitable corrective action. This process can be time consuming. The Oracle 10g database has introduced a number of new features that allow the administrator to proactively manage space within the Oracle database. These features remove the burden of monitoring the database for space issues from the administrator.

The first topic that will be discussed is related to automatic monitoring of tablespace usage by the Oracle database. This is performed by a component of the Common Manageability Infrastructure (discussed in Chapter 7) known as Server-Generated Alerts. We will begin with an overview of Server-Generated Alerts and then see how this feature may be used to proactively manage tablespaces.

SERVER-GENERATED ALERTS

Server-Generated Alerts is a component of the Common Manageability Infrastructure (CMI). We already know that statistical data is continuously gathered and maintained in the Automatic Workload Repository (AWR). The Oracle database also calculates metrics using this statistical data. The metrics that are computed are associated with events in the database. Events may be predefined in the database or created by the administrator based on business requirements. An example of such a pre-defined event is a *Tablespace Space Usage* event. Events may be associated to the alerting mechanism in Oracle 10g by means of thresholds. A boundary value of a metric is a threshold. If the actual value of a metric violates the threshold value a pre-defined number of times during a certain time period, an alert is issued. Thresholds may be classified as **warnings** (less serious) and **critical** (more serious, requiring immediate action).

The **MMON background process** is responsible for computing metric values every minute. If it identifies events that repeatedly violate pre-defined threshold values, it generates alerts. Outstanding alerts are placed in a queue known as the ALERT_QUE owned by the SYS user. The alerts are visible from the Enterprise Manager and the DBA_OUTSTANDING_ALERTS data dictionary view. The alert will specify the identity of the object (such a tablespace) on which the alert was produced, the severity of the problem, a description, and recommendations for corrective action. The alerting mechanism may even be configured to notify the administrator of the problematic event by paging or sending an e-mail message.

The alerting mechanism of the Oracle 10g database can be managed using the Enterprise Manager or the DBMS_SERVER_ALERT package.

Server-Generated Alerts and Tablespace Usage

As mentioned earlier, database administrators spend a large portion of their time in managing space within the Oracle database. This is done to ensure that problems resulting from insufficient space do not arise when users or applications create or extend objects.

The server-generated alerts feature of the database makes space management easy for the administrator. The DBA no longer has to manually monitor the database to identify tablespaces that are running low on space. *Tablespace space usage* is an out-of-the-box, server-generated alert in the Oracle 10g database. This means that by default, all tablespaces are constantly monitored for space.

The default threshold values for tablespace usage are 85% and 97%. The 85% threshold indicates the warning threshold and the 97% indicates the critical threshold. The MMON background process computes metrics for space usage of all tablespaces and displays a warning alert when it identifies a tablespace that is 85% full and a critical alert when space usage exceeds 97%. Both warnings are displayed with information about the tablespace that is low on space and the actions that may be performed by DBA to eliminate the problem. After the DBA has taken corrective action on the tablespace the alert is automatically cleared.

Guidelines The following are a few guidelines that must be kept in mind in relation to proactive tablespace management using server-generated alerts:

- The feature is supported only by locally managed tablespaces.
- The STATISTICS_LEVEL parameter must be set to either TYPICAL or ALL.
- In temporary tablespaces, the objects created are temporary and hence any threshold values will correspond to the space currently used by sessions creating temporary segments.
- In undo tablespaces the threshold values correspond to the total space used by active and unexpired extents.
- For tablespaces that have auto-extensible datafiles, the thresholds are computed based on the maximum size the datafile can take or the operating system file size limitation, whichever is applicable.
- Thresholds that are set for read-only or offline tablespaces have no effect because the contents of these tablespaces do not change.

Even though the database comes with a default set of database thresholds, the DBA may override these values by using SET_THRESHOLD procedure of the DBMS_SERVER_ALERT package or the Enterprise Manager.

Practice 1: Managing space usage in tablespaces using Enterprise Manager

This example demonstrates space management in the tablespaces using EM. In the exercise you will create tablespace C101 and a table T101 that will reside in the tablespace. The table will then be populated with a large number of rows. As a result, the tablespace will become full and an alert will be generated. You will then view the critical alert displayed from EM and resolve the out-of-space error condition.

1. Connect to the database as a user with SYSDBA privileges.

```
SQL> CONNECT DB_ADMIN/DB_ADMIN AS SYSDBA
```

2. Create a tablespace called C101, with a datafile called C101.DBF having a size of 1 M. Create the datafile in the same location as the other files of the DB101 database.

```
SQL> CREATE TABLESPACE C101
     DATAFILE 'C:\<PATH>\C101.DBF' SIZE 1M;
```

3. Minimize the SQL*Plus session. Do not close it.
4. Launch a browser, enter the URL to start Enterprise Manager, and log in a SYSDBA.
5. From the **Database Control Home** page, select the **Administration** tab.
6. Go to the **Storage** section and select the **Tablespaces** link.
7. From the **Tablespaces** page view the details of tablespace C101.(See Figure 10-2.)

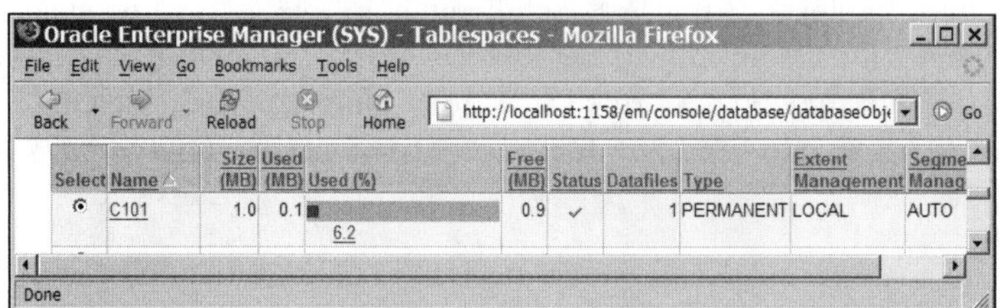

FIGURE 10-2 Details of the C101 database from the Tablespaces Page

8. Select the link on **C101**. The **View Tablespace: C101** page will be displayed. From the top-right corner select the **Edit** button.
9. The **Edit Tablespace: C101** page will be displayed. Select the **Thresholds** tab, and scroll to the **Tablespace Full Metric Thresholds** section.
10. From the **Space Used (%)** section, select the radio button for **Specify Thresholds,** and then for the Warning (%) type **50**, and for Critical (%) type **60**. (See Figure 10-3.) Select the **Apply** button at the bottom of the page. An update message will be displayed indicating the tablespace was successfully modified.

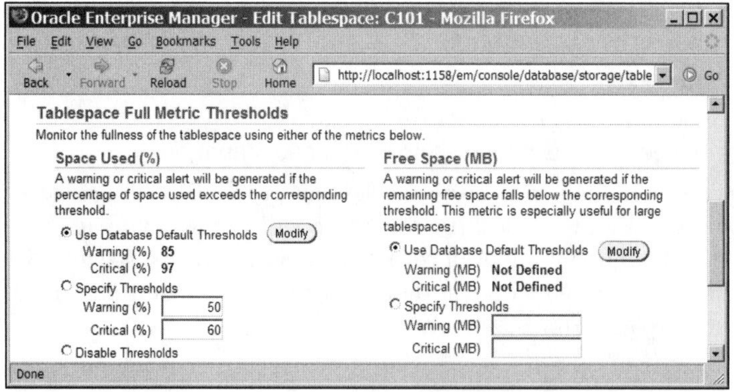

FIGURE 10-3 Overriding default thresholds for the C101 tablespace

11. Select the **Tablespaces** link at the top of the page to return to the **Tablespaces** page.
12. Minimize the browser—do not close it.
13. Return to the SQL*Plus window and create a table called T101 using the data dictionary view called DBA_TABLES.

```
SQL> CREATE TABLE T101
     TABLESPACE C101
     AS SELECT * FROM DBA_TABLES;
```

14. Return to the Enterprise Manager, and reload the page by selecting the Reload button on the browser.
15. You will notice the amount of used space in the tablespace C101 has increased.
16. Return to the SQL*Plus window and issue the following INSERT command to add more rows into the table T101. Commit the change.

```
SQL> INSERT INTO T101
     SELECT * FROM DBA_TABLES;

SQL> COMMIT;
```


17. Return to the Enterprise Manager, and reload the page by selecting the Reload button of the browser. You will notice the amount of space used in C101 will be quite high. In Figure 10-4 the tablespace is 87.5% full. If it has not exceeded 60% on your machine repeat the insert statement followed by the commit again (Step 16).

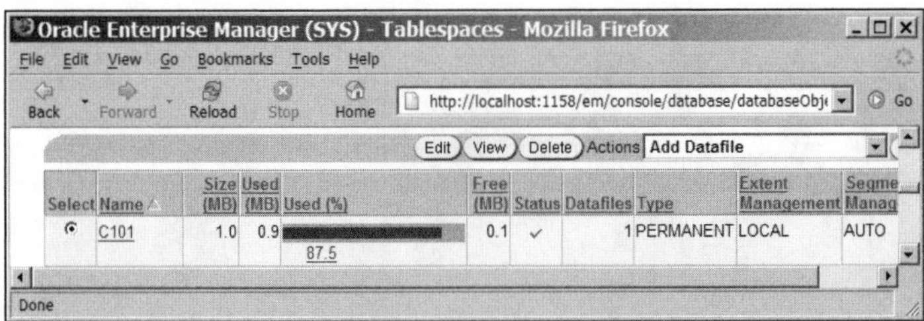

FIGURE 10-4 The space used in C101 has reached 81.25%

18. Select the **Database Instance: database_name** link at the top-left corner of the Tablespaces page. Then select the **Home** tab to view to the Database Control Home page. (See Figure 10-5.)

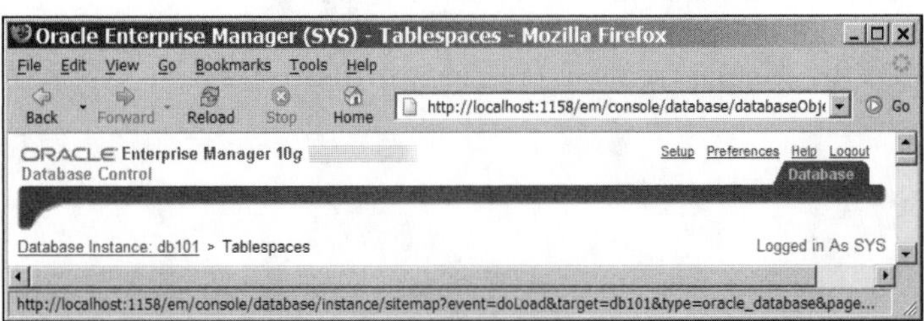

FIGURE 10-5 The Database Instance:<Database Name> breadcrumb

19. Scroll to the **Space Summary** section. The **Problem Tablespaces** will have a red colored **X** (indicating critical error) and the number 1 beside it. (See Figure 10-6.) From the Alert section you will also notice alerts about the tablespace. This might not happen immediately; you may have to wait and keep clicking the **Refresh** button on the top-right corner of the page a number of times.

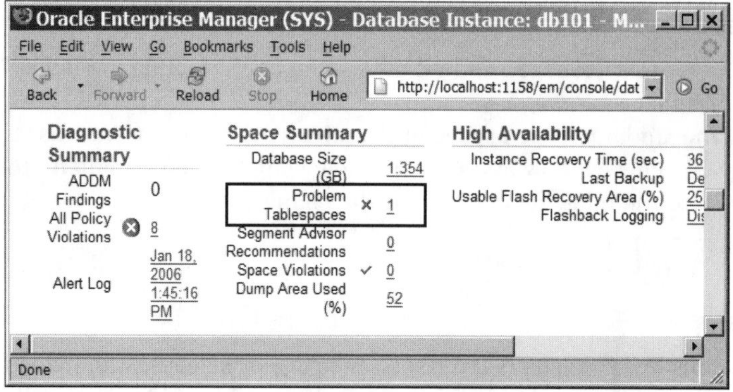

FIGURE 10-6 A problem tablespace has been identified

20. Click the link under the Number **1**. The **Problem Tablespaces** page will be displayed. (See Figure 10-7.)

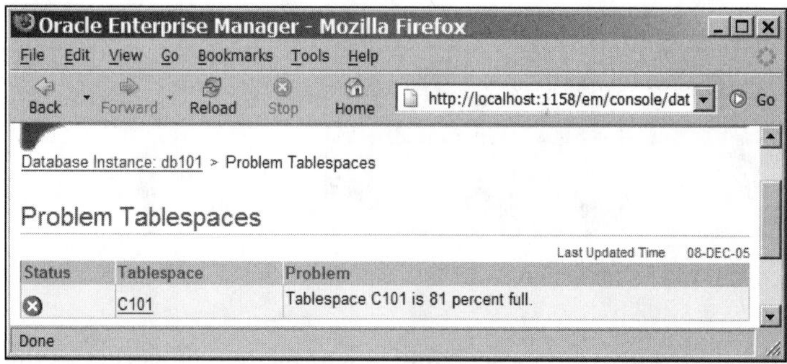

FIGURE 10-7 The Problem Tablespaces Page, providing additional information

21. To fix the problem, click on the link on the name **C101**.
22. The **Edit Tablespace: C101** page will be displayed. Scroll to the bottom of the page until you see the datafiles section. (See Figure 10-8.)

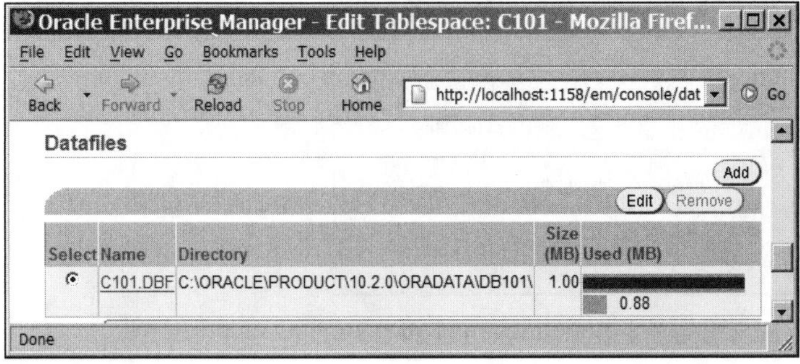

FIGURE 10-8 The Datafiles section of the Edit Tablespace page

23. Select the link on the file name **C101.DBF**. The **Edit Tablespace: C101: Edit Datafile** page will be displayed.
24. To resolve the tablespace space error, one of the options you have is to resize the datafile and make it larger. You do this by changing the **File Size** from 1 M to a larger value. Change it to **2 M**. (See Figure 10-9.)

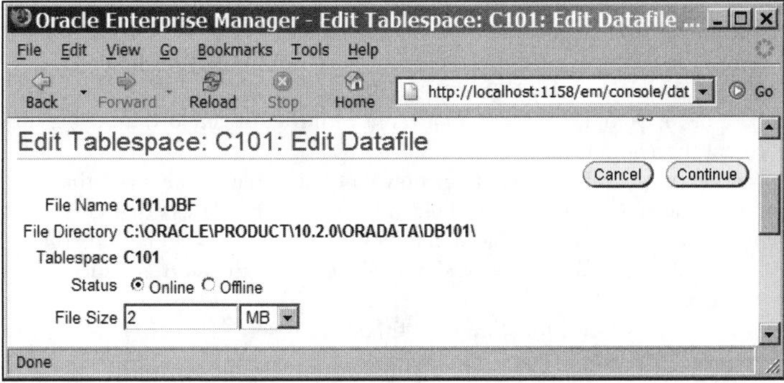

FIGURE 10-9 Increasing the size of the datafile to 2 M

25. Select the **Continue** button. The **Edit Tablespace: C101** page will be displayed.
26. Select the **Apply** button on the top-right corner. An update message will be displayed.
27. Return to the **Tablespaces** page by selecting the **Tablespaces** link on the top-left side of the page.
28. You will notice that the (%) of space used in the tablespace C101 would have dropped. In Figure 10-10 it has fallen to 43.8%.
29. Select the **Database Instance:<Database_name>** link on the top-left corner and then the **Home** tab to return to the **Database Control Home** page.
30. The alert about the tablespace will automatically disappear after some time. You may have to wait for a few minutes and keep clicking the **Refresh** button a number of times.
31. Exit SQL*Plus and Enterprise Manager.

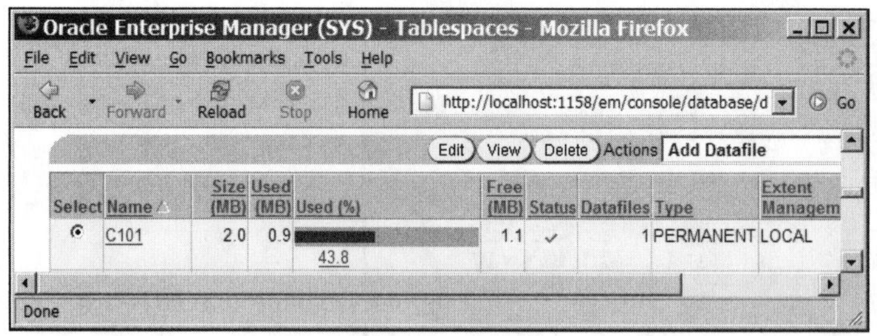

FIGURE 10-10 The space used in tablespace C101 has dropped to 43.8%

The Oracle-supplied DBMS_SERVER_ALERT package may also be used to manage thresholds for metrics. It contains two important procedures that can be used to set and view thresholds, as illustrated in Table 10-1.

TABLE 10-1 Subprograms of the DBMS_SERVER_ALERT package

Subprogram	Description
SET_THRESHOLD	Used to set thresholds that override defaults for a number of metrics. The parameters that can be set are: • The internal name of the metric (tablespace_pct_full) • The operator for comparing the actual value with the threshold value • The warning threshold value (80) • The operator for comparing the actual value with the threshold value • The critical threshold value (95) • The observation period which defines how long the actual behavior of the system must deviate from the threshold value before the alert is issued • The consecutive occurrences that define how many observation periods the metric value should violate the threshold values before the alert is issued (1 observation period) • The name of the instance for which the threshold is set • The type of metric (object_type_tablespace) • The name of the object for which the thresholds are set
GET_THRESHOLD	Used to view the value of thresholds that have been set

Practice 2: Setting tablespace thresholds using the DBMS_SERVER_ALERT package

In this practice example you will set the threshold limits for the Tablespace Percent Full metric on the C101 tablespace using the DBMS_SERVER_ALERT package.

1. Start SQL*Plus and connect as an administrator.

   ```
   SQL> CONNECT DB_ADMIN/DB_ADMIN
   ```

2. Type the following PL/SQL block to set the warning and critical threshold values to 75 and 80 respectively for the C101 tablespace using the SET_THRESHOLD procedure. The tablespace must deviate from these threshold values for at least 2 hours before an alert is issued. Further, at least three consecutive observation periods must be violated for the alert to be issued—6

hours must elapse after the violation is first noticed. The instance is the DB101 instance.

```
SQL> BEGIN
     DBMS_SERVER_ALERT.SET_THRESHOLD(
     DBMS_SERVER_ALERT.TABLESPACE_PCT_FULL,
     DBMS_SERVER_ALERT.OPERATOR_GE,75,
     DBMS_SERVER_ALERT.OPERATOR_GE,80,2,3,'DB101',
     DBMS_SERVER_ALERT.OBJECT_TYPE_TABLESPACE,'C101');
     END;
     /
```

3. To view the values of the threshold values you can use the GET_THRESHOLD procedure. In the following code, a number of variables are created by using the VARIABLE command of SQL*Plus to hold the values that are sent out by the procedure. The values of the variables are then displayed using the PRINT command.

```
SQL> -- Creating variables
SQL>VARIABLE WARN_OPER VARCHAR2(40)
SQL>VARIABLE WARN_VALUE NUMBER
SQL>VARIABLE CRIT_OPER VARCHAR2(40)
SQL>VARIABLE CRIT_VALUE NUMBER
SQL>VARIABLE OBS_PER NUMBER
SQL>VARIABLE CONS NUMBER

SQL> -- Invoking the GET_THRESHOLD procedure
SQL>BEGIN
    DBMS_SERVER_ALERT.GET_THRESHOLD(
    DBMS_SERVER_ALERT.TABLESPACE_PCT_FULL,:WARN_OPER,
    :WARN_VALUE,:CRIT_OPER,:CRIT_VALUE,:OBS_PER,:CONS,
    'DB101',DBMS_SERVER_ALERT.OBJECT_TYPE_TABLESPACE,'C101'
    );
    END;
    /

SQL> --Displaying the values of the variables
SQL>PRINT WARN_VALUE CRIT_VALUE OBS_PER CONS
```

4. Exit SQL*Plus.

Data dictionary views that provide information about server alerts are:

- DBA_OUTSTANDING_ALERTS—outstanding alerts
- DBA_ALERT_HISTORY—time-limited history of alerts that are no longer outstanding
- DBA_THRESHOLDS—threshold settings defined for the instance
- V$ALERT_TYPES—information of each alert

SEGMENTS IN THE ORACLE DATABASE

A segment is an object of the Oracle database. There are different types of segments that can be created such as tables, partitioned tables, index-organized tables, clusters, indexes, temporary segments, and undo segments. In this topic we will discuss Index Organized Tables (IOT) and Clusters that can help you to manage space more efficiently.

Indexed Organized Tables (IOTs)

Traditionally data is stored in regular tables known as heap-organized tables. These tables store row data. To improve data access you may create indexes on one or more frequently accessed columns. Indexes are internally created on columns on which primary or unique keys have been defined.

Indexes, by default, are created in a B-TREE format. These indexes are depicted as an inverted tree, with the root on the top and leaves at the bottom. Index entries are stored in the leaf nodes and contain the value of the column on which the index was created along with the ROWID of the actual row in the table.

Certain tables that are primarily accessed based on the value of a single column such as the primary key column may benefit by implementing them as index-organized tables. These tables are not stored in a heap-organized format but rather in the form of a B-TREE index. The leaf nodes of the IOT do not contain index values and ROWIDs. Instead they hold the entire row or part of the row of the table.

To help you understand the concept better, consider the table MEDICAL_CODES maintained at Keller Medical Center. The table has three columns namely CODE, DESCRIPTION, and SYMPTOMS. The column names are self-explanatory; the CODE is a number that represents a certain medical condition. The DESCRIPTION column is a short description of the condition and the SYMPTOMS column contains detailed information about the symptoms associated with the condition. The Table 10-2 displays the contents of the MEDICAL_CODES table.

TABLE 10-2 Contents of the MEDICAL_CODES table

CODE	DESCRIPTION	SYMPTOMS
461	Acute Sinusitis	Facial Pains, Headaches, Bad Breath, Sore-throat
462	Acute Pharyngitis	Respiratory Distress, Inability to Swallow Liquids, Vomiting, Abdominal Pain
463	Acute Tonsillitis	Dehydration, Enlarged tonsils
464	Acute Laryngitis	Fever, Weak and Hoarse Voice, Sore throat
465	Upper Respiratory Infections	Cough, Dry Cough, Persistent Cough, Flu-like Symptoms

Suppose queries on this table were primarily of the type:

```
SQL>SELECT CODE, DESCRIPTION
    FROM MEDICAL_CODES WHERE CODE=n;
```

where *n* is a code you are searching. Such a table will be more space and access efficient if created as an IOT rather than a heap-organized table, the primary key column being the CODE column. If this table is created as an IOT, the IOT itself will hold all the requested data rather than accessing the index to find out the ROWID and then accessing the table. This will save space as well as access time. An IOT may be created using the following syntax:

```
CREATE TABLE table_name
(COLUMN1   datatype [size],
```

```
COLUMN2   datatype[size] ...,
CONSTRAINT constraint_name PRIMARY KEY (column_name))
ORGANIZATION INDEX
[TABLESPACE tablespace_name]
[PCTTHRESHOLD n | INCLUDING (column_name)]
[OVERFLOW TABLESPACE tablespace_name]
```

There is another point that you must be aware of when creating IOTs that have columns that are infrequently accessed. Such columns can be kept separate from the IOT, in an area known as the **overflow tablespace**. The portion of the row that must be kept in the overflow tablespace can be specified in the form of a percentage of the row or a column name at which the split will occur. The portion of the IOT stored in the overflow tablespace is a segment by itself.

In the example presented above, it has been mentioned that the columns CODE and DESCRIPTION are frequently accessed. Let us assume the column SYMPTOMS is a long column that is infrequently accessed. Rather than storing the data in the SYMPTOMS column within the IOT you may store the column separately in an overflow tablespace. In this way the length of the row in the IOT is restricted.

Information about IOTs may be obtained by querying the USER_SEGMENTS and USER_TABLES data dictionary views.

Practice 3: Creating Index-Organized Tables

In this practice you will create the IOT called MEDICAL_CODES. The column SYMPTOMS will be stored as a separate segment in the overflow tablespace.

1. Start SQL*Plus and connect as the user MEDUSER.

   ```
   SQL> CONNECT MEDUSER/MEDUSER
   ```

2. Type the following CREATE TABLE command to create an index-organized table called MEDICAL_CODES consisting of the columns CODE, DESCRIPTION, and SYMPTOMS. CODE is the primary key column. The IOT is created in the USERS tablespace. The row is split at SYMPTOMS. In the example, the overflow data is also stored in the USERS tablespace. Please substitute an appropriate tablespace name if USERS does not exist on your machine.

   ```
   SQL> CREATE TABLE MEDICAL_CODES
        (CODE    NUMBER(3),
        DESCRIPTION     VARCHAR2(40),
        SYMPTOMS        VARCHAR2(100),
        CONSTRAINT CPK PRIMARY KEY (CODE))
        ORGANIZATION INDEX
        TABLESPACE USERS
        INCLUDING SYMPTOMS
        OVERFLOW TABLESPACE USERS
        /
   ```

3. Issue the following query to display information about the IOT and the data segment that is created in the overflow tablespace. Notice the IOT overflow segment has an Oracle-assigned name. (See Figure 10-11.)

   ```
   SQL> SELECT TABLE_NAME, IOT_NAME, IOT_TYPE, TABLESPACE_NAME
        FROM USER_TABLES
        WHERE TABLE_NAME='MEDICAL_CODES'
        OR IOT_NAME='MEDICAL_CODES';
   ```

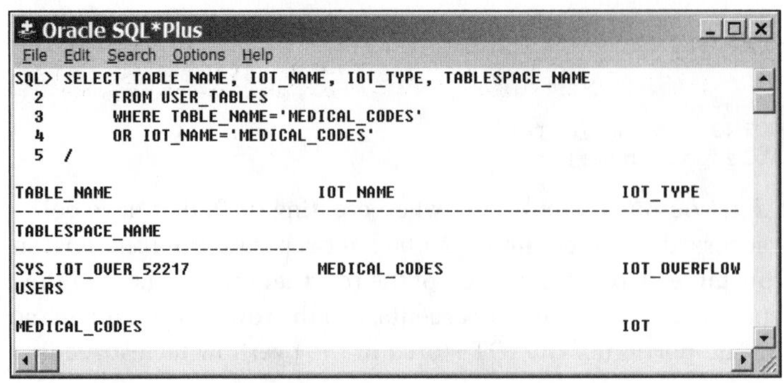

FIGURE 10-11 Querying DBA_TABLES for IOT information

4. Exit SQL*Plus.

Clusters

In heap-organized tables, a user cannot control where the rows are to be stored when they are inserted into a table. They are stored in the data blocks that have free space in them.

A cluster is another method of storing data. In a cluster, one or more tables may share the same data blocks. This method is used when tables share common columns and they are frequently accessed together in join queries. Storing them in a cluster provides faster access to the rows. Tables are clustered or stored together based on a common column(s) called the cluster key. An advantage of using a cluster is the space that is saved by storing the cluster key value *once* irrespective of the number of rows that contain that value. After the cluster has been created the tables that will be part of the cluster may be created. Clusters may also be created on tables with low insert, update, or delete activity. It is also important that the number of child records associated with the cluster key values be roughly similar.

Consider two tables, a PATIENT table, containing the details of patients being treated at Keller Medical Center, and a table called PHYSICIAN that contains the details of physicians. Because patients are treated by physicians, the PHY_ID column (representing the Physician ID) is common to both tables. Tables 10-3 and 10-4 display the contents of the PATIENT and PHYSICIAN tables, respectively. Based on the data, Physician 7001 treats patients 101, 102, and 104.

TABLE 10-3 Data in the PATIENT table

Table Name: PATIENT				
PAT_ID	PAT_NAME	PHY_ID	DATE_IN	WARD_NO
101	Michael	7001	10-AUG-05	1
102	John	7001	12-AUG-05	1
103	Ian	7002	12-AUG-05	2
104	Maria	7001	14-AUG-05	2

TABLE 10-4 Data in the PHYSICIAN table

Table Name: PHYSICIAN	
PHY_ID	PHY_NAME
7001	BOB HENRICKS
7002	DAVID SHOEMAKER

Let us assume that queries are frequently performed in such a way that the two tables are joined on the PHY_ID column. A typical query being:

```
SQL> SELECT PAT_NAME, PHY_NAME FROM PATIENT NATURAL JOIN PHYSICIAN;
```

In tables such as these, rather than creating separate heap-organized tables and then performing joins on them, Oracle recommends the use of Clusters.

The details of a physician with a specific ID, say 7001, will be stored along with all the patients treated by 7001 in the same data block. When a query joining the two tables is performed, data will be retrieved faster because all the requested data is available within the same data block. Because the cluster key value is stored only once for all rows with the same key value (in this case the PHY_ID column), space is saved. The clustered table for the example is displayed in Table 10-5.

TABLE 10-5 A cluster created using the PATIENT and PHYSICIAN table

PHY_ID		PHY_NAME		
7001		BOB HENRICKS		
	PAT_ID	PAT_NAME	DATE_IN	WARD_NO
	101	Michael	10-AUG-05	1
	102	John	12-AUG-05	1
	104	Maria	14-AUG-05	2
7002		DAVID SHOEMAKER		
	103	Ian	12-AUG-05	2

Clusters are of two kinds: index clusters and hash clusters.

Index Clusters

An index cluster uses a B-Tree index to maintain the data within the cluster. The index is called the Cluster Index. The index entries hold the cluster key value along with the address of the data block where the rows of the cluster key are stored. The index is used to determine the data block that holds the rows of a certain cluster key value. The steps for creating an index cluster are:

1. Create the cluster by giving it a name and specifying the column on which clustering will occur—the cluster key column.

2. Create the cluster index, which is used to store, maintain, and access the data in the cluster.
3. Create the tables that need to be clustered.

Practice 4 : Creating an Index Cluster

This practice demonstrates how to create a clustered table. Instead of creating C10PATIENT and C10PHYSICIAN tables as two separate heap-organized tables, we will create them as clustered tables—internally and completely transparent to the user—the rows of both tables will be stored in the same data block.

1. Start SQL*Plus and connect as the user MEDUSER.

```
SQL> CONNECT MEDUSER/MEDUSER
```

2. Create a cluster called PAT_PHY. The cluster key column is PHY_ID, which is a character column with a width of 4 characters.

```
SQL> CREATE CLUSTER PAT_PHY (PHY_ID  VARCHAR2(4));
```

3. Create a cluster index called PAT_PHY_CI on the PAT_PHY cluster.

```
SQL> CREATE INDEX PAT_PHY_CI ON CLUSTER PAT_PHY;
```

4. Create the tables called C10PATIENT and C10PHYSICIAN as displayed below. These tables should belong to the PAT_PHY cluster. The column of the table that is associated with the cluster key must be mentioned. In both tables it is the PHY_ID column.

```
SQL> -- Creating C10PATIENT
SQL> CREATE TABLE C10PATIENT
     (PAT_ID     NUMBER(4),
     PAT_NAME   VARCHAR2(40),
     PHY_ID     VARCHAR2(4),
     DATE_IN    DATE,
     WARD_NO    NUMBER(2))
     CLUSTER PAT_PHY(PHY_ID);

SQL> -- Creating C10PHYSICIAN
SQL> CREATE TABLE C10PHYSICIAN
    (PHY_ID    VARCHAR2(4),
     PHY_NAME   VARCHAR2(40))
     CLUSTER PAT_PHY(PHY_ID);
```

5. Exit SQL*Plus.

Hash Clusters

In an index cluster, the cluster index is used to determine the data block that contains the row. When a query is issued the index cluster is first accessed to determine the data block that may contain the row followed by a search on the actual data block to retrieve the requested row. Another type of cluster known as a hash cluster uses a hashing algorithm to determine the physical location of a row in a clustered table. In this method an index search is not performed. A hashing function is applied on the cluster key value and the data block determined. The advantage of the hash cluster is that data retrieval is faster whenever queries are issued on equality of the cluster key value.

Hash clusters must not be used if the tables are continuously growing and if there are many full table scans being performed on the clustered tables. The steps for creating a hash cluster are:

- Create the cluster by giving it a name and specifying the column on which clustering will occur and the maximum number of hash values (HASHKEYS) that can be generated by the hashing algorithm. The hash key values must be specified based on the number of unique cluster key values you are likely to have. The HASH IS clause is used to specify the cluster key column.
- Create the tables that need to be clustered.

Practice 5: Creating a Hash Cluster

In this practice a hash cluster called HASH_PAT_PHY will be created consisting of the tables PAT2 and PHY2.

1. Start SQL*Plus and connect as the user MEDUSER.

```
SQL> CONNECT MEDUSER/MEDUSER
```

2. Create a hash cluster called HASH_PAT_PHY. The cluster key column is PHY_ID, on which the hash algorithm will be applied. The range of numbers generated by the algorithm is 1 through 100.

```
SQL> CREATE CLUSTER HASH_PAT_PHY
     (PHY_ID     NUMBER(4))
     HASH IS PHY_ID
     HASHKEYS 100 ;
```

3. Create the tables PAT2 and PHY2 that will be stored together as part of the HASH_PAT_PHY cluster. The clustering column must be mentioned when creating the tables.

```
SQL> -- Creating the PAT2 table
SQL> CREATE TABLE PAT2
     (PAT_ID     NUMBER(4),
     PAT_NAME    VARCHAR2(40),
     PHY_ID      NUMBER(4),
     DATE_IN     DATE,
     WARD_NO     NUMBER(2))
     CLUSTER HASH_PAT_PHY(PHY_ID);

SQL> -- Creating the PHY2 table
SQL> CREATE TABLE PHY2
     (PHY_ID     NUMBER(4),
     PHY_NAME    VARCHAR2(40))
     CLUSTER HASH_PAT_PHY(PHY_ID);
```

4. Exit SQL*Plus.

Sorted Hash Clusters

The Sorted Hash Clusters functionality is new in Oracle 10*g*. It is an extended functionality of hash clusters. In hash clusters, when a row is inserted into a table, the appropriate data block into which the row will be placed is determined by the value obtained after applying the hash function on the cluster key value. The row is placed in the block in the order in which it was *inserted*. The sorted hash cluster functionality allows the row to be inserted into the block by maintaining a specific order. This is useful when queries are issued based on equality conditions of the cluster key value along with the ORDER BY clause to display the data in the sorted order of a column. In a sorted hash cluster, because the rows are stored in the sorted order of a certain column(s) during insertion, the need for the ORDER BY clause no longer exists. This eliminates the need for resources and space incurred during sorting operations performed by the ORDER BY clause.

Consider Table 10-6, which contains information about when medicines were administered to patients by nurses.

TABLE 10-6 Contents of the MED_ADMINISTRATION table

PATIENT_NO	NURSE	DATE_ADMINISTERED
101	Fred	10-May-2005 20:30:00
101	Mary	10-May-2005 3:00:00
101	Fred	10-May-2005 22:00:00
101	Fred	11-May-2005 6:30:00
102	John	10-May-2005 11:30:00
102	John	10-May-2005 16:00:00

When viewing patient information to see when medicines were administered to certain patients, you want to see the output in the sorted order of the DATE_ADMINISTERED column. This can be done by the following query :

```
SELECT * FROM PATIENT
WHERE PATIENT_NO=101
ORDER BY DATE_ADMINISTERED;
```

This ORDER BY clause will result in a sort operation being performed during query execution. Using sorted hash clusters, this sort can be eliminated.

Similar to hash clusters, one or more columns of the table can be identified as the cluster key columns. Consider the PATIENT_NO to be the cluster key column. The hashing function will be applied on the PATIENT_NO column to generate a hash key value that determines the data block into which the row will be placed. Using sorted hash clusters you can go one step further and tell Oracle to store the row in a sorted order of the DATE_ADMINISTERED column within the data block. When this is done a query to view the records of when a patient was administered medication will always appear in a sorted order of DATE_ADMINISTERED irrespective of how they were inserted into the table. This is done even without an ORDER BY clause, using a query like:

```
SELECT * FROM PATIENT WHERE PATIENT_NO=101;
```

Practice 6: Creating a Sorted Hash Cluster

This practice demonstrates the creation of a sorted hash cluster.

1. Start SQL*Plus and connect as the user MEDUSER.

```
SQL> CONNECT MEDUSER/MEDUSER
```

2. Create a cluster called MED_CLUSTER. The cluster key column is PATIENT_NO. The data must be stored in a sorted order of the DATE_ADMINISTERED column. The HASHKEYS clause is set to 100 specifying the number of unique values that can be generated by the hash function.

```
SQL> CREATE CLUSTER MED_CLUSTER
     (PATIENT_NO               NUMBER(3),
     DATE_ADMINISTERED         TIMESTAMP SORT)
     HASHKEYS 100
     SINGLE TABLE HASH IS PATIENT_NO;
```

3. Create a table called MED_ADMINISTRATION to store details of when patients are administered their medications. The PATIENT_NO is the cluster key column. The NURSE column represents the nurse who administered the medication. The DATE_ADMIN column will contain the date and time when the medication was given.

```
SQL> CREATE TABLE MED_ADMINISTRATION
     (PATIENT_NO     NUMBER(3),
     NURSE           VARCHAR2(20),
     DATE_ADMIN      TIMESTAMP)
     CLUSTER MED_CLUSTER(PATIENT_NO, DATE_ADMIN);
```

4. Insert the records displayed below into the MED_ADMINISTRATION table. The data is not in any specific order for a patient. However when they are inserted into the hash cluster, they will be stored in ascending order of the DATE_ADMIN column.

```
SQL> INSERT INTO MED_ADMINISTRATION
     VALUES(101,'FRED',TIMESTAMP '2005-05-10 20:30:00');

SQL> INSERT INTO MED_ADMINISTRATION
      VALUES(101,'MARY',TIMESTAMP '2005-05-10 3:00:00');

SQL> INSERT INTO MED_ADMINISTRATION
      VALUES(101,'FRED',TIMESTAMP '2005-05-10 22:00:00');

SQL>INSERT INTO MED_ADMINISTRATION
     VALUES(101,'FRED',TIMESTAMP '2005-05-11 06:30:00');

SQL> INSERT INTO MED_ADMINISTRATION
     VALUES(102,'JOHN',TIMESTAMP '2005-05-10 11:30:00');

SQL> INSERT INTO MED_ADMINISTRATION
      VALUES(102,'JOHN',TIMESTAMP '2005-05-10 16:00:00');

SQL> COMMIT;
```

5. Issue a query to display the records of the MED_ADMINISTRATION table. Notice the records are sorted on the DATE_ADMIN column even without the ORDER BY clause. (See Figure 10-12.)

```
SQL> SELECT * FROM MED_ADMINISTRATION WHERE PATIENT_NO=101;
```

```
SQL> SELECT * FROM MED_ADMINISTRATION WHERE PATIENT_NO=101;

PATIENT_NO NURSE                DATE_ADMIN
---------- -------------------- ------------------------------
       101 MARY                 10-MAY-05 03.00.00.000000 AM
       101 FRED                 10-MAY-05 08.30.00.000000 PM
       101 FRED                 10-MAY-05 10.00.00.000000 PM
       101 FRED                 11-MAY-05 06.30.00.000000 AM

SQL>
```


FIGURE 10-12 Querying the data of patient 101 retrieves the output in sorted order of DATE_ADMIN

6. Exit SQL*Plus.

SEGMENT SHRINK FUNCTIONALITY

A segment is an object of the database. When a table is created, Oracle identifies it as a data segment. Data segments (tables) store data and must be managed by proper sizing, as a result reducing space waste. Before we proceed to understand the segment shrink functionality let us understand how segments were normally managed by administrators in the database prior to Oracle 10*g*.

When the segment is initially created, space will be allocated to it in the form of one or more extents. An extent is a unit of space allocation when the segment is being created or requires additional space. A segment consists of one or more extents. Extents are, in turn, made up of Oracle blocks. An Oracle block is the smallest unit that Oracle can read or write to. The block size is determined during database creation time, and is set by the DB_BLOCK_SIZE initialization parameter.

NOTE

The term High water mark (HWM) is used to indicate the last block that contained data in a segment.

In Figure 10-13 the segment is made up of 5 extents numbered 0, 1, 2, 3, and 4. The HWM is the fifth block in the fourth extent. The data blocks of extents 0, 1, and 2 currently contain row data. The blocks of extent 3 and a part of 4 at some time contained rows that have been deleted. These blocks have been depicted as deleted blocks in the figure. The blocks with deleted rows are maintained by Oracle for new rows that will be inserted into the segment.

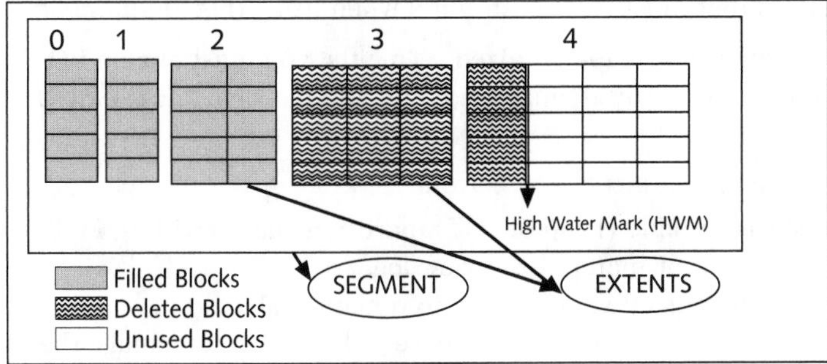

FIGURE 10-13 The structure of a segment

The main problem with the segment described is that when full table scans are done on the table, all blocks below the HWM will be retrieved. This is inefficient especially because many of the blocks contain deleted rows. These blocks will be populated in memory when they do not have any useful information in them. Such a segment is inefficient causing unnecessary I/O to be performed. Such a segment must be reorganized. In versions of Oracle prior to 10*g*, this could be done in a number of ways: The object could be dropped, recreated, and reloaded. It could be reorganized by moving it to another tablespace or an online table re-definition could be performed. All these methods have their own advantages and disadvantages.

In Oracle 10*g*, segment management has been greatly simplified. The new segment shrink functionality in Oracle 10*g* helps administrators reorganize or shrink and reclaim wasted space from segments easily by means of simple commands.

The segment shrink functionality is an online operation that can be performed when the segment is currently being used by the database. Segment shrinking involves two steps. The first step, **Compacting**, results in the data in the blocks being moved as far as possible toward the beginning of the segment, followed by a resetting of the HWM. This is performed by a series of DELETE and INSERT statements. The second step, **Shrinking,** causes all the space above the HWM to be released to the tablespace as free space. (See Figure 10-14.) This free space can be reused by objects requiring space in the future. The main advantage of this feature is that because blocks containing row data become fewer and denser, fewer blocks need to be read during queries involving full table scans.

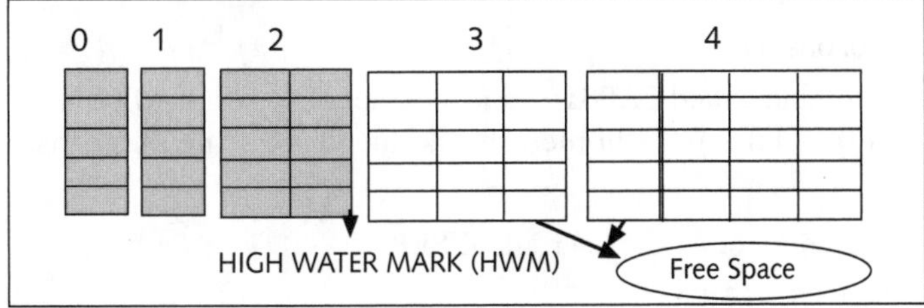

FIGURE 10-14 The extents 3 and 4 are released as free space

There are certain guidelines that must be kept in mind when using this functionality:

- When using this feature for heap-organized segments, you must enable ROW MOVEMENT. You can do so by issuing the command displayed at the SQL prompt:

  ```
  ALTER TABLE tablename ENABLE ROW MOVEMENT;
  ```

- It is possible to shrink a table (heap or IOT), partition, sub-partition, LOB, index, materialized view, or materialized view log.
- Indexes created on the object will continue to remain usable.
- In locally managed tablespaces you may choose to have Oracle manage the space within the Oracle blocks. Such tablespaces are known as Automatic Segment Space Managed (ASSM) tablespaces. The segment shrink functionality poses certain restrictions with respect to ASSM tablespaces. Segments cannot be shrunk if:
  - The table has function-based indexes or long columns.
  - The table is clustered.
  - The table has a LOB segment.
  - The table has on-commit materialized views or ROWID-based materialized views. Materialized views that are based on a primary key need not be refreshed or rebuilt after a shrink operation.
  - If it is an IOT overflow segment.

Segment shrink functionality can be performed by issuing SQL commands or from the Enterprise Manager.

The ALTER TABLE... SHRINK SPACE command is used to shrink a table. The syntax of the command is:

```
ALTER TABLE tablename
SHRINK SPACE [COMPACT] [CASCADE];
```

where:

`SHRINK SPACE`: Is used to compact and shrink space in a segment. Both steps explained above are performed.

`COMPACT`: Only the first step will be done, rows will be moved as far left in the segment as possible.

`CASCADE`: Results in the shrink operation being cascaded to all dependent segments that support a shrink operation.

Practice 7: Segment Shrink functionality

In this practice you will create a table called LABS10 using a script. The script will then insert and delete many rows of the table. You will then shrink the object using Enterprise Manager.

1. Start SQL*Plus, and connect as the user MEDUSER.

   ```
   SQL> CONNECT MEDUSER/MEDUSER
   ```

2. Run the script **c10shrink.sql** from the Chapter10 folder of the student datafiles. Please go through the contents of the script before executing it.

   ```
   SQL> @<PATH>\C10SHRINK.SQL
   ```

3. Issue the following ALTER table command, to enable row movement for the table LABS10.

```
SQL> ALTER TABLE LABS10 ENABLE ROW MOVEMENT;
```

4. Launch a browser, and enter the URL to access the Enterprise Manager. Log in as a SYSDBA.
5. From the **Database Control Home** page, select the **Administration** tab.
6. From the **Schema** section, select the **Tables** link. (See Figure 10-15.)

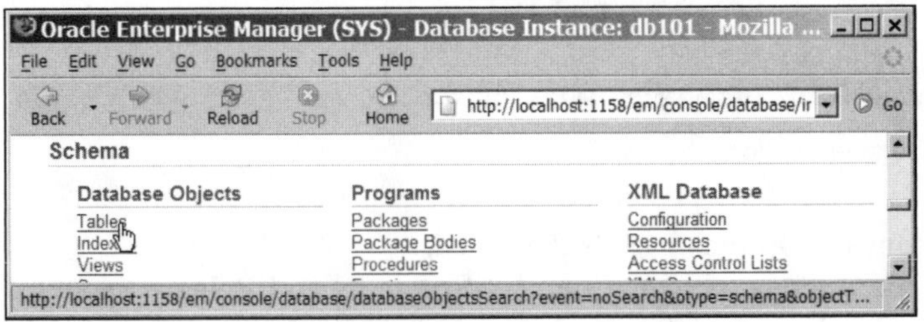

FIGURE 10-15 The Tables Link in the Schema Section

7. The **Tables** page will be displayed. From the top-right corner, select the **Object Type** as **Table**.
8. Type in **MEDUSER,** within the **Schema** text item.
9. Click on the **Go** button. A list of tables belonging to MEDUSER will be displayed.
10. Choose the table **LABS10** by selecting the radio button next to the name. (See Figure 10-16.)

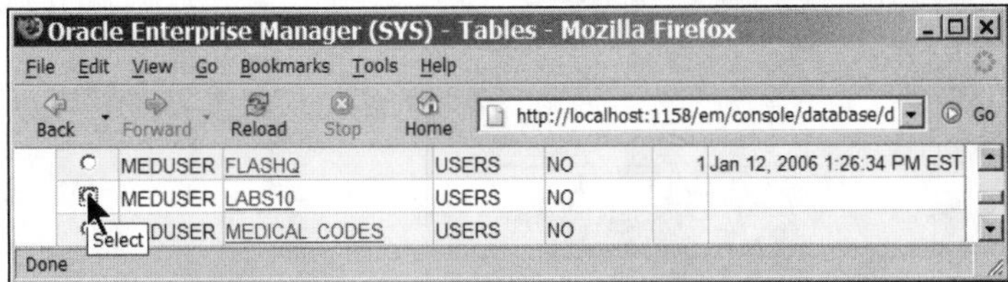

FIGURE 10-16 Selecting the LABS10 table

11. From the **Actions** list choose **Shrink Segment**, and click on the **Go** button. (See Figure 10-17.)

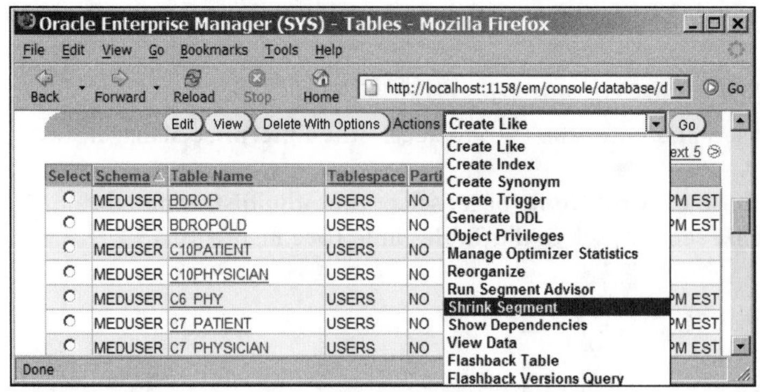

FIGURE 10-17 The Shrink Segment option

12. The **Shrink Segment: Options** page is displayed.
13. From the **Shrink Options,** choose **Compact Segments and Release Space.** Select the **Continue** button.
14. The **Shrink Segment: Schedule** page will be displayed. Specify the Job Name as **MYSHRINK**. Leave the Scheduling option as it is. Select the **Submit** button. A confirmation will be displayed.
15. The **Scheduler Jobs** page will be displayed.
16. Click the **Refresh** button until you see no jobs running.
17. Select the **History** tab. You will see the MYSHRINK job. The status must display SUCCEEDED. (See Figure 10-18.)

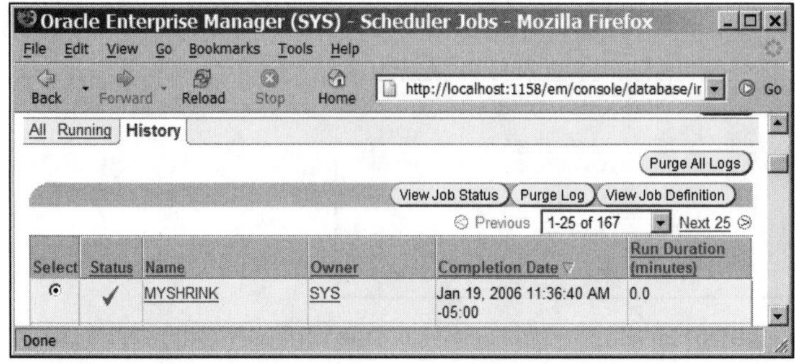

FIGURE 10-18 Viewing the Run History of the MYSHRINK job

18. Select the link under MYSHRINK to view the details of the job that was executed.
19. Log out of SQL*Plus and Enterprise Manager.

The Segment Advisor

The Segment Advisor is a new feature in Oracle 10g that can be used to help identify objects within schemas and tablespaces that are good candidates for a shrink operation. Because we are already aware that space management is an important function of an administrator, the Segment Advisor is a handy tool.

The Segment Advisor serves three important purposes:

- Identifies objects that have wasted space.
- Helps the administrator predict the future growth trends for selected segments.
- Used to estimate the amount of disk space that an object requires, even before its creation based on its columns, datatypes, sizes, and the PCTFREE parameter.

The segment advisor can be invoked using the Enterprise Manager and the Oracle-supplied DBMS_ADVISOR package.

The Segment Advisor may be invoked in a Comprehensive or Limited mode. The comprehensive mode takes longer and is more accurate with a more complete set of recommendations. You may specify the time duration for the analysis. A longer duration will result in more comprehensive results. A DBA can choose to ignore or implement the suggestions presented by the Segment Advisor.

NOTE

In Oracle Database 10.2, Oracle provides an Automatic Segment Advisor job which automatically detects segment issues.

Practice 8: The Segment Advisor

This practice example demonstrates how you can invoke and work with the Segment Advisor.

1. Start SQL*Plus and connect as the user MEDUSER.

   ```
   SQL> CONNECT MEDUSER/MEDUSER
   ```

2. Execute the **c10seqadv.sql** script from the Chapter10 folder of the student datafiles. The script creates a table called LABS10, populates it with rows, and deletes many of the rows. The execution of the script may take a few minutes.

   ```
   SQL> @<PATH>\C10SEGADV.SQL
   ```

3. Minimize SQL*Plus—do not close the window.
4. Launch a browser and enter the URL to access the Enterprise Manager. Connect as a user with SYSDBA privileges.
5. From the **Database Control Home** page, scroll down to the **Related Links** section and select the **Advisor Central** link.
6. The **Segment Advisor** link is visible in the Advisors section. Select it. (See Figure 10-19.)

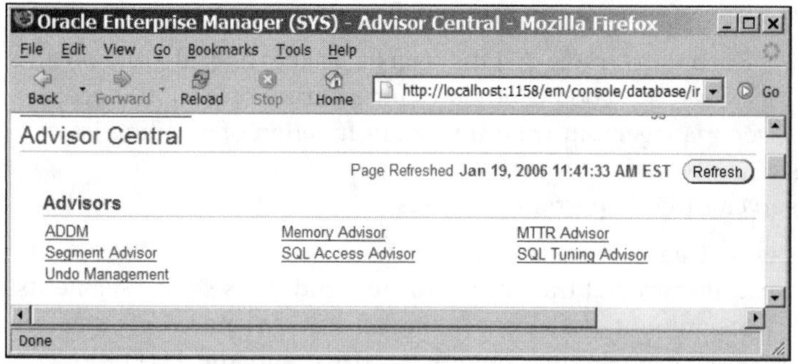

FIGURE 10-19 The Segment Advisor Link

7. The **Segment Advisor: Scope** page is displayed. The advisor gives you the ability to choose between getting advice on objects in tablespaces or schemas. Select **Schema Objects**. Select **Next**. (See Figure 10-20.)

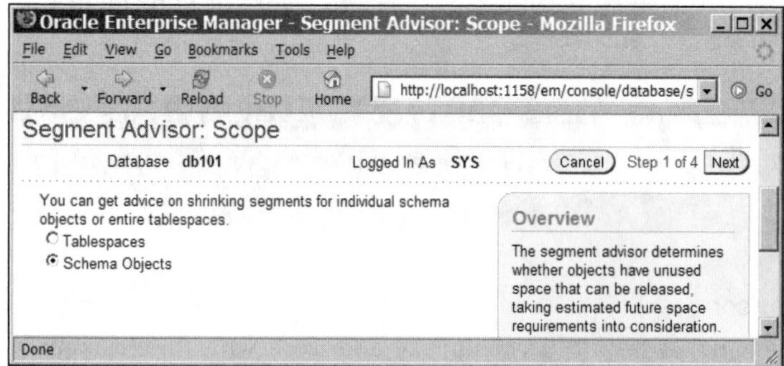

FIGURE 10-20 Selecting the Options for the Segment Advisor

8. The **Segment Advisor: Schema Objects** page will be displayed. You will be able to add the name of the object to be analyzed. Select the **Add** button. (See Figure 10-21.)

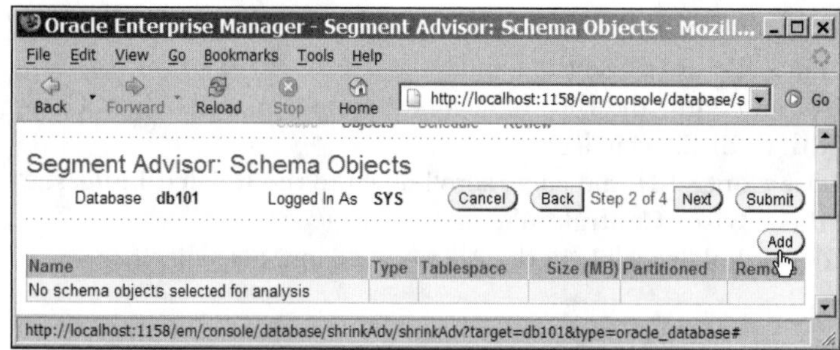

FIGURE 10-21 Adding the schema objects to be analyzed

9. The **Schema Objects: Add** page is displayed. From the Type list select **Table**. Type **MEDUSER** for Schema and for the Object type, **LABS10.** (See Figure 10-22.)

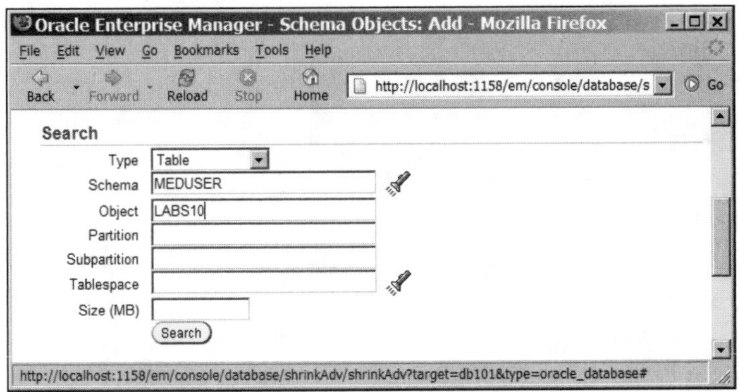

FIGURE 10-22 The Schema Objects: Add Page

10. Select the **Search** button. The **Results** pane on the same page will display the details of the MEDUSER.LABS10 table.
11. Select the **Checkbox** beside the name MEDUSER.LABS10. Select the **OK** button at the bottom of the page.(See Figure 10-23.)

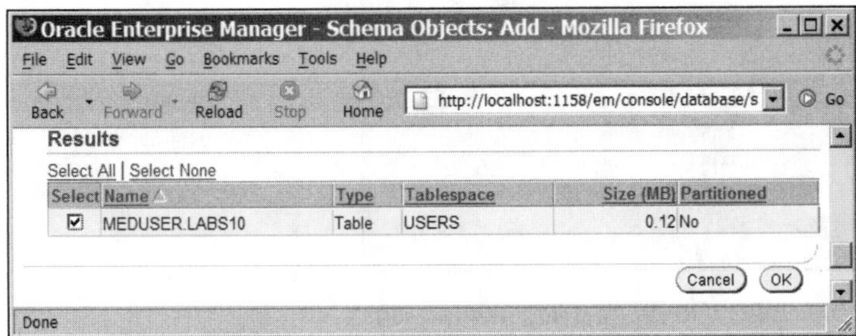

FIGURE 10-23 Selecting the MEDUSER.LABS10 table

12. You will be returned to the **Segment Advisor: Schema Objects** page. Select the **Next** button.
13. The **Segment Advisor: Schedule** page will be displayed.
14. In the text box for Task Name, remove the existing name and type **SHRINK1**.
15. Under Schedule, from the list for **Schedule Type**, select **Standard**.
16. Leave the Repeating option as **Do Not Repeat** and Start as **Immediately**. Select the **Next** button.
17. The **Segment Advisor: Review** page will be displayed. Go through the page and select the **Submit** button.

18. Information about the shrink operation will be displayed and you will be returned to the **Advisor Central** page. Scroll along this page until you see details of the SHRINK1 job that you just created. You may have to refresh this page for the job to display a COMPLETED status. (See Figure 10-24.)

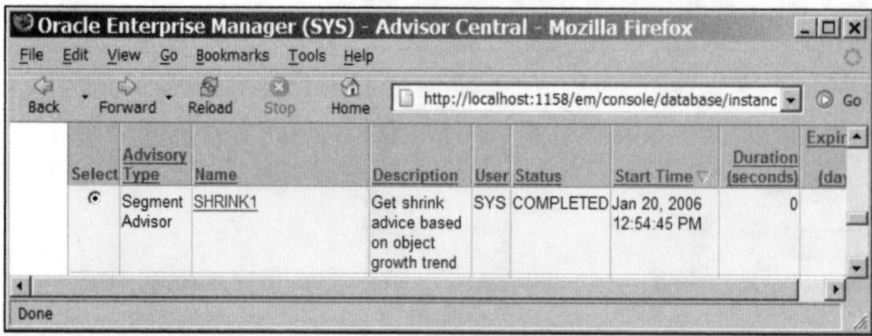

FIGURE 10-24 The status of the SHRINK1 Job

19. Select the link on the name **SHRINK1**.
20. The **Segment Advisor Task: SHRINK1** page will be displayed. Scroll along this page to see if any recommendations are generated. You will see one recommendation. (See Figure 10-25.) Select the link to view the recommendation.

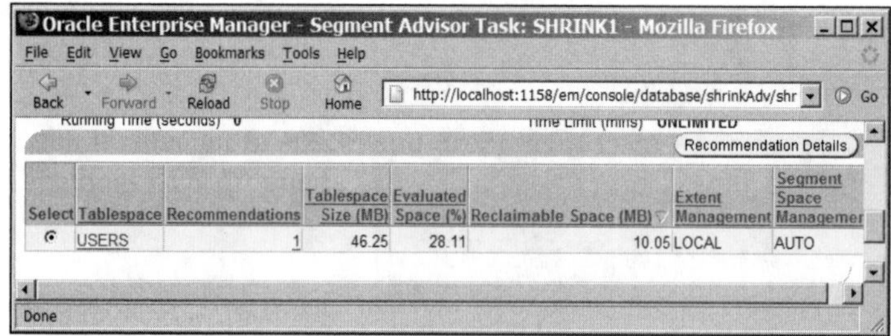

FIGURE 10-25 Viewing the recommendations of the segment advisor

21. The **Recommendation Details for Tablespace: USERS** page will be displayed. On this page you will see the recommendation to shrink the MEDUSER. LABS10 table. Figure 10-26 indicates 10.05 MB of space can be reclaimed by shrinking it.

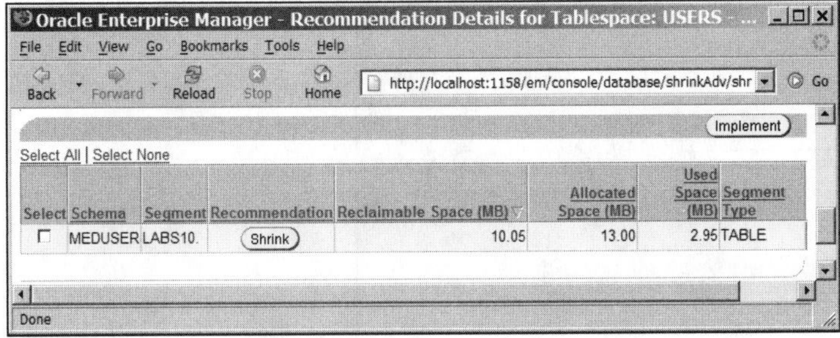

FIGURE 10-26 A recommendation to shrink the object is displayed

22. Select the **Shrink** button displayed. This will open the **Shrink Segment: Options** page. Select **Compact Segments and Release Space**. Select the **Implement** button.
23. The **Shrink Segment: Schedule** page will be displayed. Change the Job Name to **JOBSHRINK** and select the **Submit** button.
24. The **Scheduler Jobs** page will be displayed. Select the **All** tab. The details of the JOBSHRINK will be displayed. You may view more information about the job that was executed and the PL/SQL block that was executed by the job by selecting the link on the name JOBSHRINK.
25. At this point, you may select the link on the **Database Instance: <database name>** on the top-left corner of the page to return to the Database Control Home page. Select the **Administration** tab.
26. Scroll the **Schema** section and select the **Tables** link. The **Tables** page will be displayed.
27. In the search section, type **MEDUSER** in the schema text box, and **LABS10** in the object name text box. Select the **Go** button.
28. The page will be refreshed. Select the **Edit** button. (See Figure 10-27.)

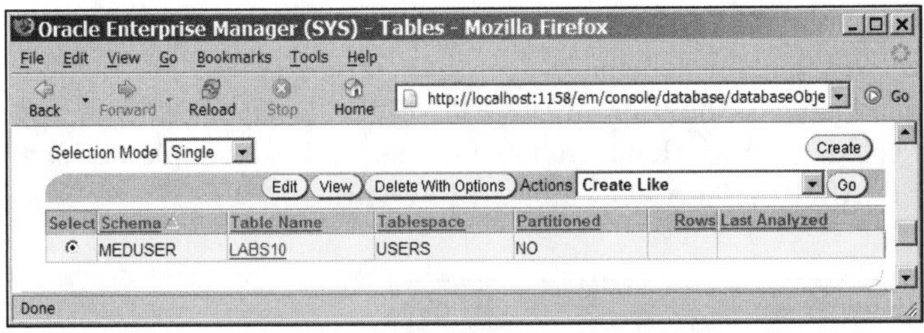

FIGURE 10-27 Edit the option of the MEDUSER.LABS10 table

29. The **Edit Table: MEDUSER.LABS10** page will be displayed. Select the **Segments** tab and view the percentage of Wasted Space in the object. Figure 10-28 indicates Wasted Space (%) as only 16.62%.

    At this point you have successfully used the Segment Advisor to identify a space-inefficient segment and implement the recommendation provided by it.

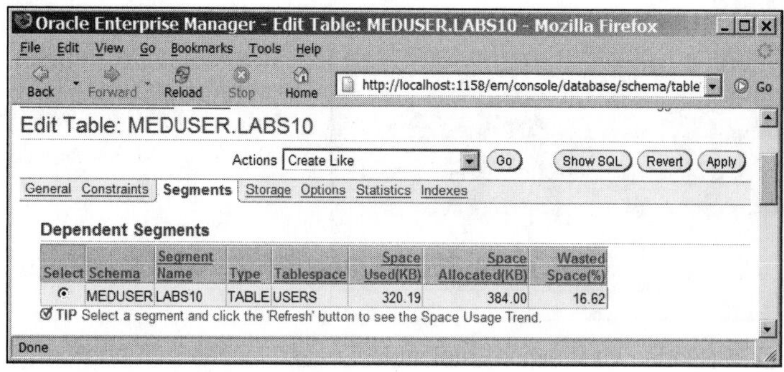

FIGURE 10-28 Viewing the Wasted space (%)

30. Log out of Enterprise Manager and SQL*Plus.

Growth Trend Reports

In addition to providing recommendations about segment shrinking, the Segment Advisor can also be used for generating growth trend reports. Growth trend data is collected in the Automatic Workload Repository (AWR) and can be used to predict the growth of certain selected segments. The growth trend can be viewed in the form of a graph from the Enterprise Manager.

Practice 9: Growth Trend Reports

In this practice example you will display the growth trend chart of a table belonging to the user MEDUSER using Enterprise Manager.

1. Launch the browser and enter the URL to access the Enterprise Manager. Log in with SYSDBA privileges.
2. From the **Database Control Home** page, select the **Administration** tab.
3. From the **Schema** section, select the **Tables** link.
4. The **Tables** page will be displayed. Select **Object Type** to be **Table**, and type **MEDUSER** in the textbox for Schema. Select the **Go** Button.
5. A list of tables belonging to the user MEDUSER will be displayed. Choose any one of them by selecting the link on the table name. In this example we have selected the MED_ADMINISTRATION table. (See Figure 10-29.)

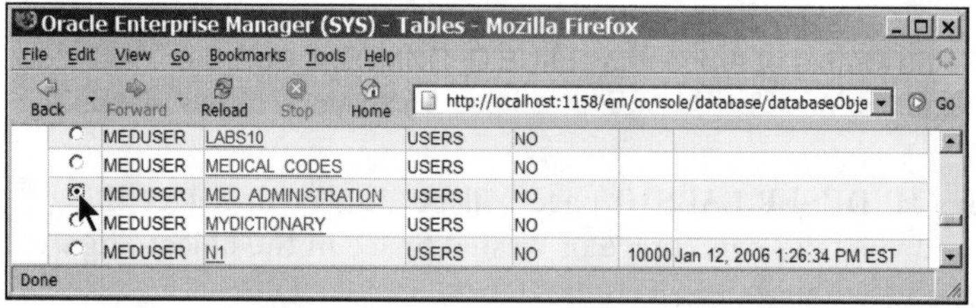

FIGURE 10-29 Selecting the MED_ADMINISTRATION Table

6. The **View Table: MEDUSER.<tablename>** page will be displayed. Select the **Edit** button.
7. The **Edit Table: MEDUSER.<tablename>** page will be displayed.
8. Select the **Segments** tab. View the **Space Usage Trend Graph** that is displayed. In Figure 10-30, because the MED_ADMINISTRATION table has not been used frequently, you do not notice a significant growth trend for the table.

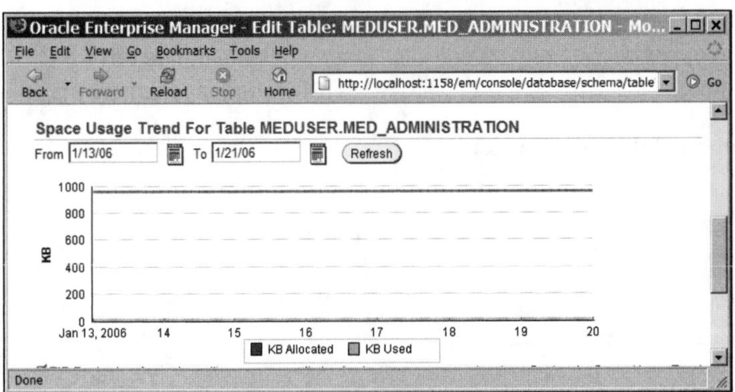

FIGURE 10-30 Viewing the Space usage trend

9. Log out of Enterprise Manager.

Estimating the Size of New Tables

In Oracle 10*g*, a tool called the Segment Resource Estimation Tool may be used to estimate the amount of space that will be required for a new table. The tool estimates the value based on the structure of the table, its column datatypes and sizes, and the PCTFREE value for the table.

Practice 10: Estimating the size of new tables

This practice example demonstrates the method to access and view the output of the segment resource estimation tool.

1. Launch your browser and enter the URL to access the Enterprise Manager. Log in with SYSDBA privileges.
2. From the **Database Control Home** page, select the **Administration** tab.
3. Select the **Tables** link from the **Schema** section.
4. The **Tables** page will be displayed. Let the **Object Type** be **Table**, and select the **Create** button displayed on the page.
5. The **Create Table: Table Organization** page will be displayed.
6. Select **Standard, Heap Organized**. Select the **Continue** button.
7. The **Create Table** page will be displayed.
8. Type in the following information for the inputs requested. (See Figure 10-31.)

```
Name : EMERGENCY_ASSTS
Schema : MEDUSER
Tablespace : <Default>
```

Column Name	Datatype	Size
EMER_ID	NUMBER	4
EMER_NAME	VARCHAR2	40
SHIFT	VARCHAR2	10

9. Select the **Estimate Table Size** button.

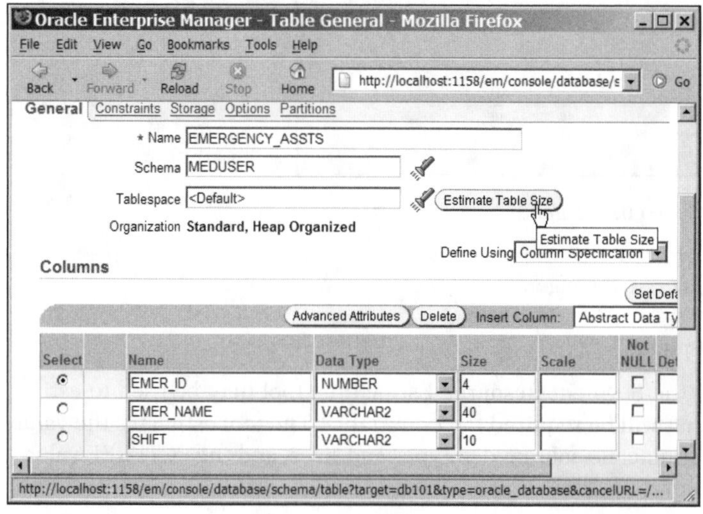

FIGURE 10-31 Creating a table and its columns

10. The **Estimate Table Size** page will be displayed.
11. Type **2000** for **Projected Row Count** and select the **Estimate Table Size** button. (See Figure 10-32.)

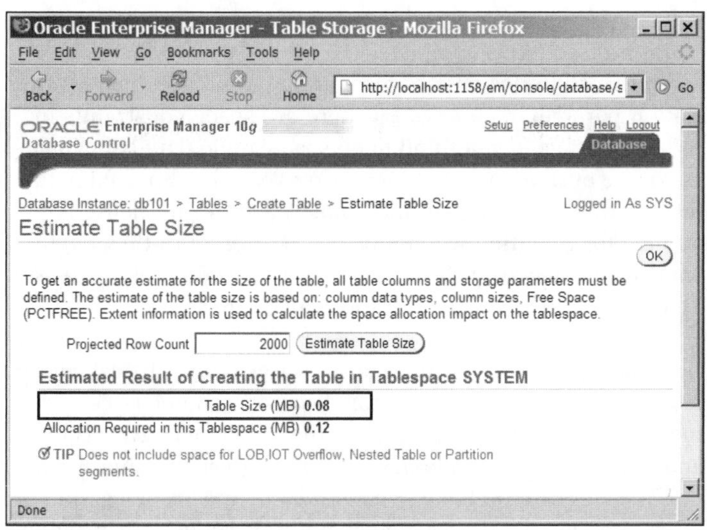

FIGURE 10-32 Setting the initial number of rows and estimating the size

12. The size of the table in megabytes will be displayed. Figure 10-32 indicates that the estimated size of the table as 0.08 M.
13. Select the **OK** button. You will return to the **Create Table** page. Select the **Cancel** button to cancel the creation of the table.
14. Log out of Enterprise Manager.

OTHER SPACE MANAGEMENT TOOLS

In addition to Segment Advisor, in this chapter we will also discuss the Undo Advisor and the Redo Logfile Advisor. Both these advisors are new in Oracle 10g and help the DBA size the undo tablespace and redo log files properly.

The Undo Advisor

Undo data is generated by transactions that are executed in the database.

NOTE

A transaction is a series of DML statements—inserts, updates, or deletes—that must either succeed or fail together.

Undo data is the previous consistent value that existed prior to a change. Undo data is maintained in the database for a number of reasons. It is used for transaction rollback, transaction recovery, flashback technology features and other features. In Chapter 5, we discussed undo tablespaces and how they are used for the flashback features. To store and maintain undo data, a DBA must create one or more undo tablespaces in the database. This may be done using the CREATE UNDO TABLESPACE command. The Oracle database creates undo segments in the tablespaces and stores undo data generated by ongoing transactions in them. After a transaction is completed, its undo data can be released unless it is being retained for ongoing queries based on the time period specified by the UNDO_RETENTION initialization parameter. However, if there are space constraints in the undo tablespace, and new transactions cannot find undo space, undo data being maintained for retention purposes will be overwritten. This can be prevented by specifying the GUARANTEE RETENTION clause when creating an undo tablespace. If this clause is specified the undo data being held for retention will not be overwritten until they expire. An important part of undo management is ensuring that the active undo tablespace is large enough to hold undo data for ongoing transactions as well as those being held for retention.

In Oracle 10g, the Undo Advisor may help in this regard. It uses the statistical data in the AWR to come up with recommendations about the optimal size of the undo tablespace. Based on a representative time period (probably a time when the database activity is the highest) and the required undo retention, the undo advisor can suggest the appropriate value for the undo tablespace. The suggested value can be viewed by means of a graph. It is important that the AWR has sufficient statistical data about undo generated during the representative time period.

Practice 11: The Undo Advisor

The following practice example demonstrates how to view the suggestions of the undo advisor for sizing the undo tablespace.

1. Launch a browser, enter the URL for the Enterprise Manager, and log in with SYSDBA privileges.
2. From the **Database Control Home** page, scroll to the **Related Links** section. Select the **Advisor Central** link.
3. From the **Advisors** section, select the **Undo Management** link.
4. The **Undo Management** page will be displayed.
5. Select the **Undo Advisor** button from the top-right corner.
6. The **Undo Advisor** page will be displayed. Set the value of the New Undo Retention to **10** minutes. Select the **OK** button. The **Undo Management** page will reappear. Once again select the **Undo Advisor** button. Based on a 10-minute Undo retention period, the required size of the Undo tablespace is 10 MB. (See Figure 10-33.)

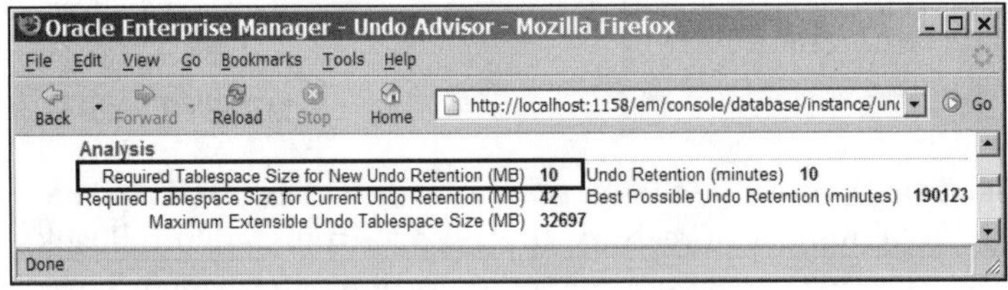

FIGURE 10-33 The default Undo Advisor Page

7. Now change the **New Undo Retention** value and set it to **10080 minutes** (1 week) and the Analysis Time Period to the **Last Seven Days**. Select the **OK** button. Select the **Undo Advisor** button and view the required size from the **Analysis** section. (See Figure 10-34.) Figure 10-35 indicates the size of the undo tablespace as 1596 MB.

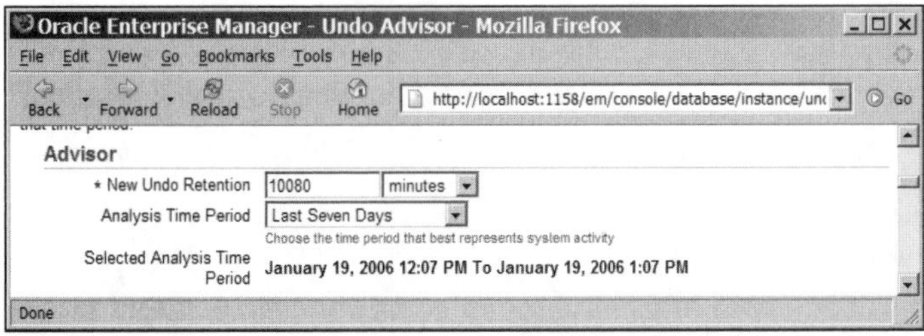

FIGURE 10-34 The Undo Advisor Page after specifying a new Undo Retention period

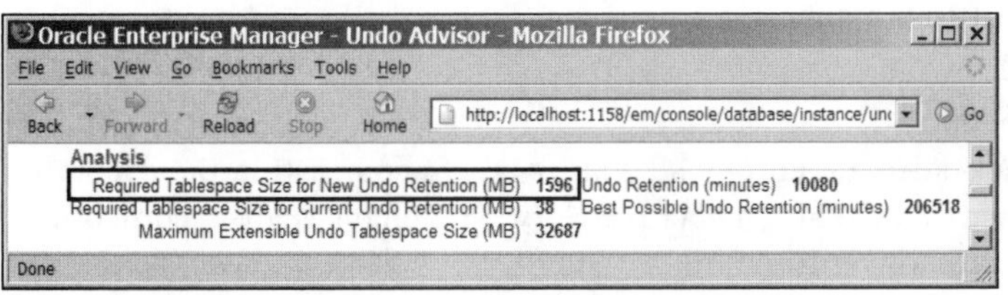

FIGURE 10-35 The required size of the undo tablespace

Identifying the required undo tablespace size can also be done by selecting an undo retention value from the graph displayed in the section **Required Tablespace Size by Undo Retention Length**. To change the Undo retention, click anywhere on the blue line running through the center. The first parameter will indicate the new retention value and the second is the recommended undo tablespace size in megabytes. Figure 10-36 indicates that for an undo retention value of 139,403 minutes, the tablespace size must be 7086 MB.

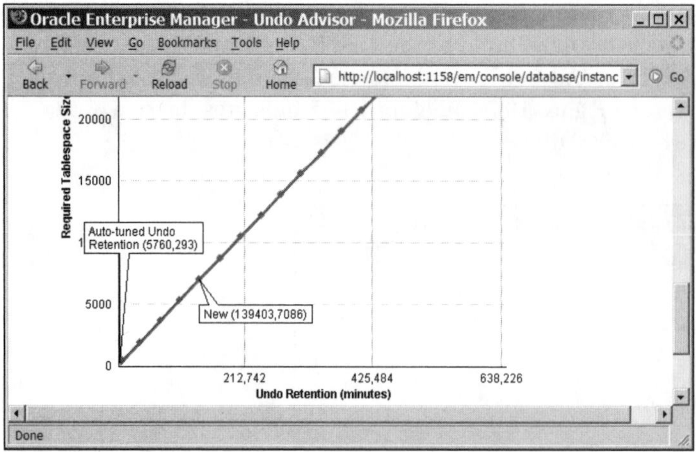

FIGURE 10-36 Viewing the size of the undo tablespace, graphically

8. Log out of Enterprise Manager.

Redo Log File Size Advisor

Redo log files in the database keep a record of all changes that occur within the database. They are primarily used for instance and media recovery. The changes are recorded in these files before they are actually written into the datafiles.

A minimum of two redo log groups must exist in the database. The Log Writer (LGWR) background process transfers the contents of the redo log buffer (in memory) to the online redo log files periodically. When it completes writing to the first log file it starts writing to the next redo log. This event is known as a *log switch*. A log switch initiates a checkpoint. During a checkpoint, a group of changes are written from the database buffer cache to the datafiles by the database writer (DBWR) background process. After the write is done, the checkpoint background process (CKPT) updates the headers of the datafiles and control files with information about the write that just occurred.

The size of the redo log file affects how often the checkpointing occurs. The smaller the redo log file, the quicker the log switches, resulting in more frequent checkpoints. When checkpoints are performed, input/output (I/O) operations are performed. Increased I/O affects the runtime performance of the database. The advantage of frequent checkpoints is that instance recovery will be faster because fewer changes need to be written to the datafiles. On the other hand, if the redo log files are larger, checkpointing will be less frequent, reducing I/O but increasing instance recovery time.

An initialization parameter that affects instance recovery time is FAST_START_MTTR_TARGET. Its value is specified in terms of time (seconds). It specifies the maximum amount of time instance recovery should take at all times. For example, if you set the parameter to 60 seconds, the DBWR will write modified blocks to the datafiles in such a way that if an instance failure occurs, the instance recovery process will take no longer than 60 seconds.

A tricky situation that administrators may find themselves in is determining the correct size for the redo log files so that checkpoints do not occur too frequently or infrequently. In Oracle 10g, an advisor known as the Redo Logfile Sizing Advisor has been introduced to recommend an optimal size for the redo logs so that excessive log switches are avoided, archiving occurs without issues, and incomplete as well unnecessary checkpoints do not occur.

Because the size of redo log files and checkpointing play an important role in Oracle's ability to recover within a certain time, the Redo Log Advisor uses the value of the FAST_START_MTTR_TARGET to suggest an optimal size for the redo logs. The value of the parameter must be set for the redo log file advisor to come up with suitable recommendations. If it is not set, the advisor will not provide recommendations.

The optimal size generated by the advisor can be viewed by querying the V$INSTANCE_RECOVERY view or from within Enterprise Manager.

Practice 12: The Redo Log File Advisor

This practice example demonstrates the ease with which the administrator can identify the ideal size for the redo log files by setting the FAST_START_MTTR_TARGET, which is the amount of time instance recovery must take.

1. Start SQL*Plus and connect as a user with SYSDBA privileges.

   ```
   SQL> CONNECT DB_ADMIN/DB_ADMIN AS SYSDBA
   ```

2. Issue the following SELECT statement to display the group number and the size of the redo log groups in megabytes. (See Figure 10-37.)

   ```
   SQL> SELECT GROUP#, BYTES/(1024*1024) FROM V$LOG;
   ```

```
Oracle SQL*Plus
File Edit Search Options Help
SQL> SELECT GROUP#, BYTES/(1024*1024) FROM V$LOG;

    GROUP# BYTES/(1024*1024)
---------- -----------------
         1                10
         2                50
         3                50

SQL>
```

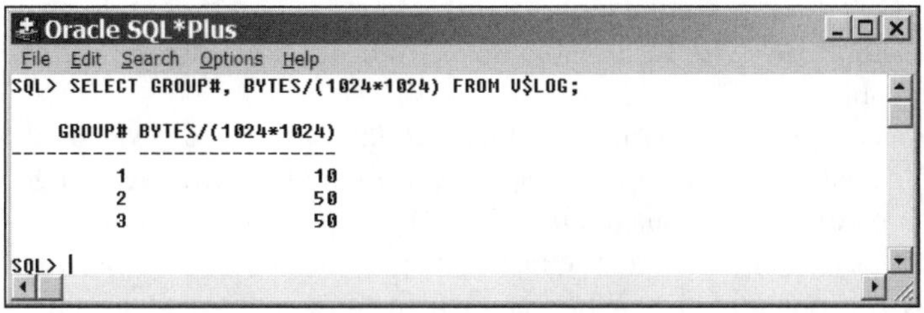

FIGURE 10-37 The size of the Redo logs groups in megabytes

3. Modify the FAST_START_MTTR_TARGET to take a value of 1 minute (60 seconds).

   ```
   SQL> ALTER SYSTEM SET FAST_START_MTTR_TARGET = 60;
   ```

4. Issue a query on the V$INSTANCE_RECOVERY view to display the optimal size of the redo log groups, based on the FAST_START_MTTR_TARGET value that you set. Figure 10-38 indicates the optimal size to be 49 MB.

   ```
   SQL> SELECT OPTIMAL_LOGFILE_SIZE FROM V$INSTANCE_RECOVERY;
   ```

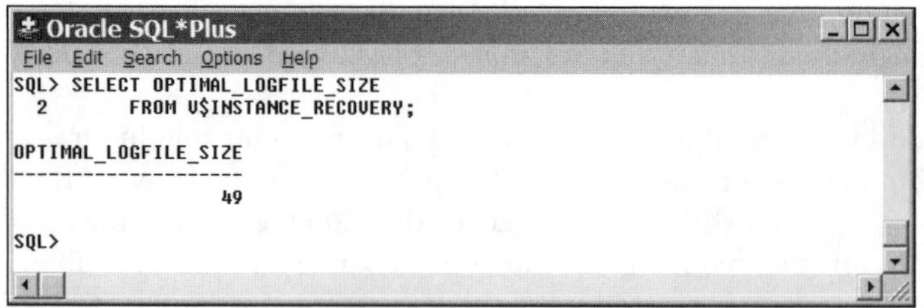

FIGURE 10-38 The optimal log file size based on the new FAST_START_MTTR_TARGET

5. Exit SQL*Plus.

In this section of the chapter we discussed how the undo advisor and redo log advisor can be used to help the administrator identify the appropriate sizes for undo tablespace and redo log groups.

MANAGING RESUMABLE SPACE ALLOCATION

Resumable Space Allocation was introduced in Oracle 9*i* to manage space-related issues that could arise during long-running tasks. Consider a large amount of data being populated into a table during an import operation. There is a possibility that some time during the import, the tablespace into which the data is being populated runs out of space. When this occurs, the import will be terminated and the entire import operation undone. This can result in a lot of wasted time. The Resumable Space Allocation feature was introduced as a solution to this problem.

Using the Resumable Space Allocation feature the long-running task to be performed is broken into a number of logical pieces. If an out-of-space error occurs when executing a certain logical piece, the job is temporarily suspended. The DBA can then take action by adding the additional space required and resume the task. The previously completed pieces need not be re-run. This saves time and effort. When configuring a resumable space allocation task, the DBA may choose to specify a timeout. This timeout is a value in terms of seconds specifying the amount of time within which corrective action must be taken. If the administrator does not resolve the out-of-space condition within the timeout period, the long running task will be aborted and all changes made will be rolled back.

To use the feature, the Resumable Space Allocation feature must be enabled. To set the timeout value at a system-wide level you can set the RESUMABLE_TIMEOUT initialization parameter in the parameter file or issue the ALTER SYSTEM SET RESUMABLE_TIMEOUT=<*n*> command. *n* is a value in seconds, indicating the timeout value. Sessions that are likely to run long transactions may individually enable the feature by issuing the ALTER SESSION ENABLE RESUMABLE command.

The syntax of the command is displayed:

```
ALTER SESSION ENABLE RESUMABLE [TIMEOUT timeout_value] [NAME name];
```

where:

`TIMEOUT timeout_value` : Is a timeout value that will override the value of the RESUMABLE_TIMEOUT initialization parameter.

NAME name: A user-defined name for the resumable session. If not specified, a system-generated name will be assigned.

A long-running task executing in the session may be suspended if any of the following situations occur:

- The tablespace used by the operation runs out of space.
- The value defined by the MAX_EXTENTS parameter for an object is reached.
- The quota on the tablespace for the user executing the long-running operation has been reached.

The different types of statements that can trigger a Resumable Space Allocation condition are:

- SQL statements that result in sorting being done. The sort may run out of temporary space.
- Inserts, Updates, and Deletes.
- Exports, Imports, and SQL*Loader operations.
- DDL commands such as CREATE TABLE, CREATE TABLE...AS SELECT, ALTER TABLE, CREATE INDEX, and ALTER INDEX commands.

Once a resumable task has been created, how is the administrator notified of the error condition? This can be configured by writing a trigger on the AFTER SUSPEND event. A trigger is a PL/SQL block that executes automatically when a certain condition occurs. Within the trigger, the administrator can write code to send an e-mail to the administrator, and even set a timeout value.

The DBMS_RESUMABLE Package

The Oracle-supplied DBMS_RESUMABLE package may be used to manage sessions that have enabled Resumable Space allocation.

Table 10-7 describes some of the useful subprograms of the DBMS_RESUMABLE package.

TABLE 10-7 Subprograms of the DBMS_RESUMABLE Package

Subprogram Name	Description
ABORT	To cancel a suspended task
SET_SESSION_TIMEOUT	Used to set a timeout value for a particular session
GET_SESSION_TIMEOUT	To view the timeout value for a particular session
SET_TIMEOUT	To set a timeout value for the current session
GET_TIMEOUT	To view the timeout value for the current session

Practice 13: Working with the DBMS_RESUMABLE package

This practice example demonstrates the use of some of the subprograms of the DBMS_RESUMABLE package and how resumable space allocation tasks can be created and managed in the Oracle 10g database. Examples of subprograms that have not been covered in the practice task are provided in the Syntax Guide at the end of the chapter.

1. Open a SQL*Plus session, and connect as a user with SYSDBA privileges.

```
SQL> CONNECT DB_ADMIN/DB_ADMIN AS SYSDBA
```

2. Issue the following CREATE TABLESPACE command to create a tablespace called C10TAB. Name its datafile C10TAB01.DBF with a size of 100 K. Create the datafile in the same location as other datafiles of the database.

```
SQL> CREATE TABLESPACE C10TAB
     DATAFILE 'C:\<PATH>\C10TAB01.DBF' SIZE 100K;
```

3. Issue the ALTER USER command to grant an unlimited quota on the C10TAB tablespace to the user MEDUSER.

```
SQL> ALTER USER MEDUSER QUOTA UNLIMITED ON C10TAB;
```

4. Grant the RESUMABLE system privilege to MEDUSER.

```
SQL> GRANT RESUMABLE TO MEDUSER;
```


5. Type the following code to create a trigger called TASK_SUSPENDED. This trigger executes automatically when a resumable task is suspended in the database. It would typically be used to send a message by a pager or e-mail to a DBA indicating that the task has suspended. In our example, we simply display a message on the screen.

```
SQL> CREATE OR REPLACE TRIGGER TASK_SUSPENDED
     AFTER SUSPEND ON DATABASE
     BEGIN
     DBMS_OUTPUT.PUT_LINE('YOUR TASK HAS TERMINATED
     WITH AN ERROR, PLEASE FIX');
     END;
     /
```

6. Open a second SQL*Plus session and connect as MEDUSER.

```
SQL> CONNECT MEDUSER/MEDUSER
```

7. Issue the following ALTER SESSION command to enable resumable space allocation, setting a timeout value of 600 seconds. Name the resumable session C10TASK.

```
SQL> ALTER SESSION ENABLE RESUMABLE TIMEOUT 600 NAME 'C10TASK';
```

8. Next, create a table called C10 consisting of a single numeric column called COLUMN1 with a size of 10. Create this table in the C10TAB tablespace. Then type the PL/SQL block displayed to insert rows into the table. Because this block executes a loop that runs 10,000 times, many rows are being inserted into the table. At some time the execution of the PL/SQL block will hang because the datafile holding these rows will run out of space.

```
SQL> CREATE TABLE C10
     (COLUMN1 NUMBER(10))
     TABLESPACE C10TAB ;

SQL> SET SERVEROUT ON

SQL> BEGIN
     FOR I IN 1..10000
     LOOP
```

```
    INSERT INTO C10 VALUES (I);
    END LOOP;
    END;
    /
[The cursor will wait, indicating a suspended task]
```

9. Return to the first session and issue a query on the DBA_RESUMABLE data dictionary view. Retrieve the user ID, session ID, time when the task was suspended, the time when the task will resume, the SQL text that caused the task to suspend, and the error message. Figure 10-39 indicates that the insert statement could not be completed because there was no space in the C10TAB tablespace.

```
SQL> SELECT USER_ID, SESSION_ID, SUSPEND_TIME,
     RESUME_TIME, SQL_TEXT, ERROR_MSG
     FROM DBA_RESUMABLE;
```


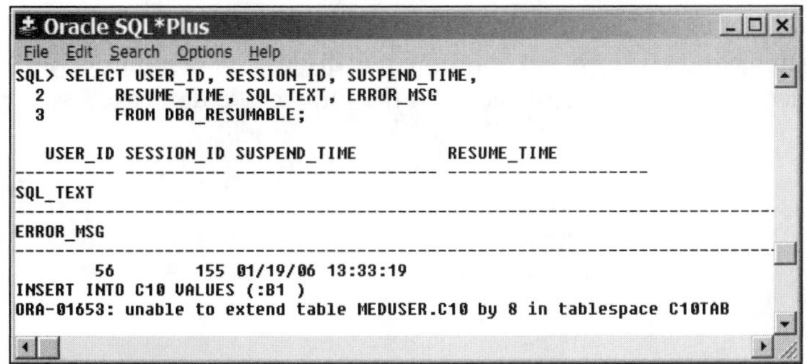

FIGURE 10-39 Querying the DBA_RESUMABLE data dictionary view

10. In the same session, issue the ALTER DATABASE DATAFILE... RESIZE command to increase the size of the C10TAB01.DBF to 500 K.

```
SQL> ALTER DATABASE DATAFILE
    'C:\<PATH>\C10TAB01.DBF' RESIZE 500K;
```

11. Return to the session in which you were connected as MEDUSER. Notice that the PL/SQL block completed successfully. You will also be able to see the message displayed by the trigger. In a production environment, the trigger notifies the DBA about the error using a method such as an e-mail message. The DBMS_OUTPUT statement has been written to give you a sense of how the trigger executes after the task is suspended. (See Figure 10-40.)

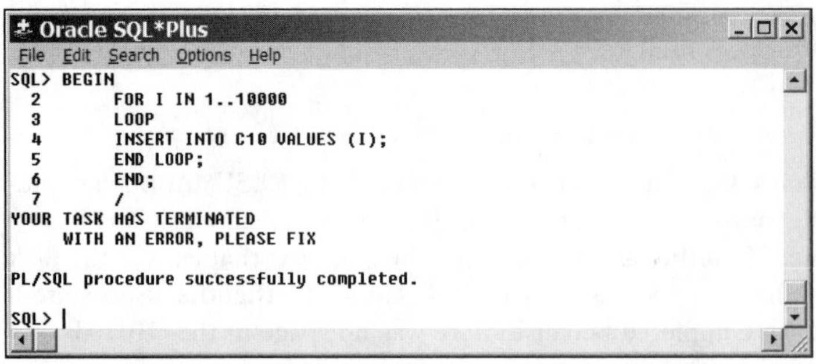

FIGURE 10-40 The suspended task automatically resumes after fixing the error

12. Log out of SQL*Plus.

In the chapter we discussed various topics associated with space management in an Oracle database. Many new features that have been introduced to simplify space management tasks were reviewed. In Chapter 11, we will continue our discussion of administrative and tuning issues and see how memory is managed in the Oracle 10*g* database.

Chapter Summary

- Events in an Oracle database are associated with metrics and metrics in turn with threshold values.
- When a metric exceeds the threshold value, a server-generated alert is activated.
- A pre-defined alert exists for tablespace usage, and warnings are generated by default at a warning threshold of 85% and critical threshold of 97%.
- Alerts may be viewed from Enterprise Manager or the DBA_OUTSTANDING_ALERTS data dictionary view.
- The DBMS_SERVER_ALERT package can be used to set or view threshold values for different metrics in the database.
- Index Organized Tables and Clusters can be used to manage space within segments more efficiently.
- The ORGANIZATION INDEX clause is used when creating index-organized tables.
- An IOT table stores table data in the form of a B-TREE index.
- Clusters are used to store data from one or more tables within the same data blocks. This feature is particularly useful for tables that are more often queried by means of joins rather than individually.
- Hash clusters must be created when queries are performed based on a condition of equality of the cluster key value.
- Sorted hash clusters are new in Oracle 10*g*. They can be used to store rows in the data block of a hash cluster in a sorted manner, thus eliminating the need for the ORDER BY clause when queries are issued based on the equality of the cluster key value.
- The Segment Shrink functionality that is new in Oracle 10*g* helps the administrator identify segments that have many deleted rows, and assists in reclaiming this wasted space.
- The Segment Advisor helps identify objects within individual schemas or tablespaces that may be good candidates for the shrink operation.
- The Redo Log Advisor helps determine the ideal size for the redo log files based on the workload of the database.
- The Undo Space Advisor helps to determine the ideal size of the undo tablespace based on the amount of undo generated in the database and the desired undo retention value.
- The Resumable Space Allocation feature helps the DBA have more control over out-of-space errors that may be generated when executing long-running tasks.

Syntax Guide

SYNTAX GUIDE		
Command	**Description**	**Example**

`CREATE TABLESPACE`	Used to create a tablespace.	`SQL> CREATE TABLESPACE TS`
		`DATAFILE 'C:\ts01.dbf'`
		`SIZE 400M;`

`CREATE TABLE...ORGANIZATION INDEX`	Used to create an index organized table.	`SQL> CREATE TABLE T1`
		`(C1 NUMBER PRIMARY KEY,`
		`C2 DATE)`
		`ORGANIZATION INDEX`
		`TABLESPACE TS`
		`PCTTHRESHOLD 30`
		`OVERFLOW TABLESPACE USERS;`

`CREATE CLUSTER`	Used to create an index cluster. You must mention the cluster key column.	`SQL> CREATE CLUSTER CL1` `(C1 NUMBER(2));`

`CREATE CLUSTER...`
`HASH IS...`
`HASHKEYS`
	Used to create a hash cluster.	`SQL> CREATE CLUSTER CL2`
		`(C2 NUMBER(2))`
		`HASH IS C2`
		`HASHKEYS 1000;`

`CREATE CLUSTER...`
`(COLUMN DATATYPE SORT)`
`HASKEYS`
	Used to create a sorted hash cluster.	`SQL> CREATE CLUSTER CL3`
		`(C3 NUMBER(2),`
		`C4 VARCHAR2(10) SORT)`
		`HASHKEYS 1000;`

`ALTER TABLE...SHRINK`	Used to reorganize the row data, reset the HWM, and release the free space.	`ALTER TABLE T1` `SHRINK SPACE;`
`ALTER TABLE...` `SHRINK SPACE COMPACT`	Used to reorganize the row data and reset the HWM.	`ALTER TABLE T1 SHRINK SPACE COMPACT;`
`ALTER SESSION ENABLE RESUMABLE;`	Used to enable resumable space allocation within a session.	`ALTER SESSION ENABLE RESUMABLE;`
Subprograms of the DBMS_SERVER_ALERT_Package		

`SET_THRESHOLD`	Used to set the values for warning and critical thresholds.	`DBMS_SERVER_ALERT.SET_`
		`THRESHOLD(`
		`DBMS_SERVER_ALERT.TABLESPACE_`
		`PCT_FULL,`
		`DBMS_SERVER_ALERT.OPERATOR.`
		`GE,60, DBMS_SERVER_ALERT.`
		`OPERATOR.GE,75,1,1,NULL,`
		`DBMS_SERVER_ALERT.OBJECT_`
		`TYPE_TABLESPACE,'TS');`

SYNTAX GUIDE		
Command	**Description**	**Example**
Subprograms of the DBMS_SERVER_ALERT_Package		
`GET_THRESHOLD`	Used to view values of warning and critical thresholds.	`DBMS_SERVER_ALERT.GET_ THRESHOLD( DBMS_SERVER_ALERT.TABLESPACE_ PCT_FULL,WARNOP, WARNVAL, CRITOP, CRITVAL, VOBS, CONS, NULL, DBMS_SERVER_ALERT.OBJECT_ TYPE_TABLESPACE, 'TS');` `Note: The variables defined in the example have to be created prior to running this procedure.`
Subprograms of the DBMS_RESUMABLE Package		
`ABORT`	Aborts the session running a suspended resumable task. The Session ID is passed as a parameter.	`EXEC DBMS_RESUMABLE. ABORT(124);`
`GET_SESSION_TIMEOUT`	To view the timeout value that has been set for suspended tasks of a session. The session ID is passed as a parameter.	`SELECT DBMS_RESUMABLE.GET_ SESSION_TIMEOUT(124) FROM DUAL;`
`GET_TIMEOUT`	Returns the timeout value set for resumable tasks in the current session.	`SELECT DBMS_RESUMABLE.GET_ TIMEOUT FROM DUAL;`
`SET_SESSION_TIMEOUT`	Used to set the timeout value for resumable tasks in a session. The Session ID and timeout value in seconds is passed as parameters.	`EXEC DBMS_RESUMABLE.SET_ SESSION_TIMEOUT(124,1800)`
`SET_TIMEOUT`	Used to set the timeout value for resumable tasks in the current session.	`EXEC DBMS_RESUMABLE.SET_ TIMEOUT(1800)`

Review Questions

1. The USERS tablespace was created using the following command:

```
CREATE TABLESPACE USERS
DATAFILE '/disk1/users01.dbf'
SIZE 1M AUTOEXTEND ON MAXSIZE 100M;
```

   When will the warning threshold be displayed?

   a. When 850 KB is used.

   b. When 970 KB is used.

   c. When 85 MB is used.

   d. When 97 MB is used.

   e. When 100 MB is used

2. Identify the name of the package that is used to set threshold values that will override the defaults set in the Oracle database.

   a. DBMS_SERVER_THRESHOLDS

   b. DBMS_METRIC_THRESHOLDS

   c. DBMS_SERVER_ALERTS

   d. DBA_SERVER_ALERTS

3. Tim is a DBA in a large retail company. He sets the warning threshold for the flash_recovery_area to 80%. Where within the Oracle 10*g* database can he look for information when space usage exceeds this threshold value? [Choose 2.]

   a. DBA_ALERTS

   b. DBA_SERVER_ALERTS

   c. DBA_OUTSTANDING_ALERTS

   d. DBA_ALERT_AREA

   e. EM console

4. The USERS tablespace is a dictionary-managed tablespace. Which of the following statements are true of this tablespace?

   a. Thresholds are by default 0 for the USERS tablespace.

   b. Thresholds are by default 100 for the USERS tablespace.

   c. Proactive tablespace management is not enabled for the USERS tablespace.

   d. The DBA has to manually issue the ALTER TABLE ENABLE ROW MOVEMENT for server alerts to be generated for the USERS tablespace.

5. Jamie is the senior DBA for an Oracle 10*g* database called PROD. She wishes to ensure resumable space allocation at an instance level. Which parameter would she need to set?

   a. RESUMABLE_SPACE=TRUE

   b. RESUMABLE_TIMEOUT=n (where n represents a value in seconds)

   c. DBMS_RESUMABLE

   d. This can be done only at a session level using the ALTER SESSION command.

   e. Set STATISTICS_LEVEL=TYPICAL

6. If the RESUMABLE_TIMEOUT parameter is set to 0, what does it indicate?
   a. Resumable space allocation is enabled only for the SYS user sessions.
   b. Resumable space allocation is initially disabled for all sessions.
   c. A suspended statement resumes immediately.
   d. The above parameter cannot be set to zero because an error will be generated.
7. A DBA wishes to ensure the success of queries at all times to ensure that long-running queries do not receive the Snapshot Too Old error. Which clause can he specify when creating the undo tablespace to do so?
   a. GUARANTEE UNDO
   b. RETENTION GUARANTEE
   c. It cannot be done in Oracle 10*g*.
   d. SERIALIZABLE

8. Server-generated alerts are displayed for ________________. [Choose 3.]
   a. Locally Managed Tablespaces
   b. Read-Only Tablespaces
   c. Dictionary-Managed Tablespaces
   d. Online Tablespaces
   e. Read-Write Tablespaces
9. The background process that is responsible for detecting tablespace threshold violations is:
   a. RBAL
   b. MMON
   c. MMAN
   d. MMNL
   e. PMON
   f. SMON
10. Tom is the DBA who wishes to perform a shrink operation on the table called SUPPLIERS belonging to the PROD database. Which step would he have to perform before he issues the ALTER TABLE SUPPLIER SHRINK SPACE command?
    a. Set the SKIP_UNUSABLE_INDEXES to a value of FALSE.
    b. Disable all triggers.
    c. Issue the command ALTER TABLE ENABLE ROW MOVEMENT.
    d. Check if any constraint violations may occur.
    e. Drop all existing indexes on the table.
11. A DBA issues the following command: ALTER TABLE SUPPLIERS SHRINK SPACE COMPACT CASCADE;

    What will be the effect of this statement on objects that are dependent on the SUPPLIERS table?

a. An error will be generated because the CASCADE option is not allowed.

b. The dependent objects will be invalidated and recompilation is needed.

c. All dependent segments that support shrink operations will also be shrunk.

d. Shrinking is not permitted on segments.

12. A PROD database contains many segments that contain a large number of deleted rows. The DBA wishes to determine the segments that are good candidates for shrinking. Which advisor could he use?

 a. Segment Advisor

 b. Objects Advisor

 c. SGA Advisor

 d. Undo Advisor

13. As a DBA you set thresholds for the USERS tablespace in the following manner.

```
DBMS_SERVER_ALERT.SET_THRESHOLD(
DBMS_SERVER_ALERT.tablespace_pct_full,
DBMS_SERVER_ALERT.operator_ge, 80,
DBMS_SERVER_ALERT.operator_ge, 95, 2, 3, PROD,
DBMS_SERVER_ALERT.object_type_tablespace, 'USERS');
END;
```

 The USERS tablespace becomes 80% full. After what period of time will the alert be displayed?

 a. 2 minutes and again after 3 minutes

 b. 6 minutes

 c. 6 hours

 d. 3 hours

 e. 6 seconds

14. Name the privilege that must be granted to a user who wishes to enable resumable space allocation within a session.

15. Identify two ways in which a portion of the rows of an IOT can be stored in an overflow tablespace.

16. Identify the kinds of clusters that can be created in the Oracle database.

 a. B-TREE clusters

 b. Index Clusters

 c. Sorted Hash Clusters

 d. Hash Clusters

 e. Sorted Index Clusters

17. Name the Oracle-supplied package that can be used to invoke the Segment Advisor.

18. The output of the Redo Log File Advisor can be obtained from ________________ and ________________.

 a. Enterprise Manager

 b. DBMS_ADVISOR Package

 c. V$INSTANCE_RECOVERY view

d. DBA_OUTSTANDING_ADVICE

e. V$FAST_START_MTTR_TARGET

19. Which initialization parameter must be set for the Redo Log Advisor to provide an optimal redo log size?
20. Name the Oracle-supplied package that can be used to set a timeout value for a resumable task within a session.

Hands-On Assignments

Assignment 10-1 Viewing Metrics from Enterprise Manager

1. Launch a browser, start Enterprise Manager, and log in with SYSDBA privileges.
2. From the Related Links section select the All Metrics link.
3. Expand the Tablespaces Full Metric. What Metric is displayed below it?
4. Select the link on the Tablespace Space Used (%) metric.
5. Select the Manage Metrics link.
6. From the Manage Metrics page, scroll on the Thresholds tab until you can see Threshold values set for the various tablespaces of the database.
7. Return to the Database Control Home page.
8. Log out of Enterprise Manager.

Assignment 10-2 Viewing the extent management of tablespaces

1. Start SQL*Plus and connect as a user with SYSDBA privileges.
2. Describe the DBA_TABLESPACES data dictionary view. Identify the column names that can be used to display the tablespace names and the extent management.
3. Write a query to display the tablespace name and the extent management for all tablespaces of the database.
4. What are the different values displayed under the EXTENT_MANAGEMENT column?
5. Remain connected to SQL*Plus.

Assignment 10-3 Creating a tablespace

1. From SQL*Plus, connected as an administrator, create a tablespace called CAS103 with a datafile called CAS103.DBF that is 500 K in size.
2. Remain connected to SQL*Plus.

Assignment 10-4 Setting and Viewing threshold values using the DBMS_SERVER_ALERTS package

1. For the tablespace CAS103 created in Assignment 10-3, use the appropriate packaged procedure to set the warning and critical threshold values to 70% and 85%, respectively. One hour must elapse after the violation is noticed and the alert is displayed. The alert must be displayed on the first violation of the threshold.
2. Write a PL/SQL block that will display the threshold values that were set in step 1 for the tablespace CAS103. Make sure you create the required variables.
3. Remain connected to SQL*Plus.

Assignment 10-5 Querying the data dictionary for alerts

1. From SQL*Plus, query the DBA_OUTSTANDING_ALERTS view to display any alerts.
2. Query the DBA_ALERT_HISTORY view to display all the alerts that have been generated in the database.
3. Remain connected to SQL*Plus.

Assignment 10-6 Creating an index-organized table

1. From SQL*Plus, connect as the user MEDUSER.
2. Create an IOT called MYDICTIONARY based on the structure displayed.

Column Name	Data type	Size
Word	Varchar2	50
Meaning	Varchar2	50
Pronunciation	Varchar2	50

   The IOT must consist of the columns Word and Meaning. The Pronunciation column must be stored in the overflow area. The primary key column is WORD. The overflow tablespace is USERS. If this tablespace does not exist in your database, choose an appropriate overflow tablespace.

3. Query the USER_TABLES data dictionary view and display details of the IOT and overflow segment that were created for MYDICTIONARY.
4. Remain connected to SQL*Plus.

Assignment 10-7 Creating a cluster

1. From SQL*Plus, connect as the user MEDUSER.
2. Create the cluster and tables of the cluster based on their descriptions shown below:

Table Name: C107PHY

Column Name	Datatype	Size	Comment
PHY_ID	NUMBER	4	
PHY_NAME	VARCHAR2	50	
PHY_SPEC	VARCHAR2	50	Clustering column

Table Name: C107SPEC

Column Name	Datatype	Size	Comment
SPECIALITY	VARCHAR2	50	Clustering column

Cluster Name: C107_PHY_SPEC

Column Name	Datatype	Size	Comment
Column Name	Datatype	Size	Comment
SPECIALITY	VARCHAR2	50	Cluster key column
Cluster Index Name: PHY_SPEC_INDX			

3. Describe the USER_CLUSTERS data dictionary view. Identify the columns that will display the cluster name and cluster type.
4. Write a query on the USER_CLUSTERS view to display the cluster name and cluster type of all clusters created by MEDUSER.
5. What is the cluster type of the cluster you created in this assignment?
6. Remain connected to SQL*Plus.

Assignment 10-8 Segment shrinking

1. From SQL*Plus, connect as the user MEDUSER.
2. Run the script **c108shrink.sql** from the Chapter10 folder of the student datafiles. A table called TABLE108 will be created. A number of rows will be added and then some deleted.
3. Issue the command to enable row movement for the table TABLE108.
4. Issue the SQL command to shrink the table TABLE108, reset the HWM, and release free space generated.
5. Remain connected to SQL*Plus.

Assignment 10-9 Estimating the optimal size of the redo log files

1. From SQL*Plus, connect as a user with SYSDBA privileges.
2. Issue a query on the V$LOG view to display the group# and size of the groups in megabytes.
3. Set the FAST_START_MTTR_TARGET value to 180 seconds.
4. Query the V$INSTANCE_RECOVERY view to display the optimal size of the redo log groups.
5. Remain connected to SQL*Plus.

Assignment 10-10 Enabling resumable space allocation timeout

1. From SQL*Plus, connect as a user with SYSDBA privileges.
2. Issue the appropriate ALTER SYSTEM command to set the value of the RESUMABLE_TIMEOUT initialization parameter to 15 minutes (900 seconds).
3. Remain connected to SQL*Plus.

Assignment 10-11 Resuming a suspended task

1. From SQL*Plus, connect as a user with SYSDBA privileges.
2. Create a tablespace called c1011, name the datafile c1011.dbf, and create it with a size 100 K.
3. Grant the user MEDUSER, an unlimited quota of the C1011.
4. Grant the user MEDUSER, the RESUMABLE system privilege.

5. Create a trigger called BEF_SUSPEND, which will execute after a resumable task is suspended. Display the string TASK HAS SUSPENDED as part of the trigger code.
6. Open another SQL*Plus session, and connect as the user MEDUSER.
7. Create a table called T1011 with a single numeric column N1. Make sure you create it in the C1011 tablespace.
8. Write a PL/SQL block that will run a LOOP 10000 times. Insert the value 40 into the table T1011, within the LOOP.
9. Does it get suspended at some time?
10. Return to the first SQL*Plus session in which you are connected as a user with SYSDBA privileges. Issue the command to resize the C1011.DBF datafile to 600 K.
11. Does the suspended task resume? Do you see the string displayed by the trigger?
12. From the first SQL*Plus session, drop the tablespace C1011 and CAS103.
13. Exit the SQL*Plus sessions.

Case Study

1. Revisit the challenge presented at the beginning of this chapter. What steps can Ryan perform to resolve the problem? What could he do to proactively identify all objects in various tablespaces that need to be reorganized?
2. List the various advisors in the Oracle 10*g* database that you are aware of and identify their main functions.
3. You are a user of the database responsible for populating large quantities of data into various tables. Write down the steps you would perform to ensure that when an out-of-space error occurs during a data load you are immediately notified.

CHAPTER **11**

AUTOMATIC MEMORY MANAGEMENT

LEARNING OBJECTIVES

After completing this lesson you should be able to understand:

- The memory structures in the Oracle Instance and their function
- Manual configuration of the memory structures of the System Global Area
- Automatic configuration of the memory structures of the System Global Area
- The Program Global Area, its structure, and functions
- Automatic management of PGA memory in Oracle

ORACLE CERTIFICATION EXAM OBJECTIVES COVERED IN THIS CHAPTER INCLUDE:

- Implement Automatic Shared Memory Management
- Manually configure SGA parameters for various memory components in the SGA
- Use Automatic PGA memory management

INTRODUCTION

Memory is an important component of the Oracle database because that is where all the action takes place. Memory is the scratchpad of the Oracle database. It is where caching of user and dictionary data, and sorting and sharing of statements and data is done. Data is temporarily stored in memory to make sharing of objects possible and retrieval of data faster, and to increase the speed of processing. It is from memory that the data to be stored permanently is written back to disk. Movement of information to and from memory is made possible by the background processes. Managing the various memory structures created and maintained by the Oracle database is an important function of the DBA. This is not an easy task because memory requirements are dependent on the type of processing that occurs in the database and the nature of processing is not constant. Under-allocation of memory may result in performance issues, out-of-memory errors and excessive paging and swapping. Over-allocation may result in wastage of memory that can be utilized by other applications.

Methods to allow easier memory management were introduced in Oracle 9*i*, with Automatic PGA Memory Management. This effort has been continued in Oracle 10*g* with the introduction of the Automatic Shared Memory Management (ASMM) feature.

This chapter discusses some of the problems that administrators face when configuring memory manually. It also presents the interesting new ASMM feature, which eliminates many of the problems. We will discuss two major memory structures—the System Global Area (SGA) and the Program Global Area (PGA). In addition to understanding the structural components of the SGA and PGA, we will discuss how they can be configured manually and automatically.

THE CURRENT CHALLENGE AT KELLER MEDICAL CENTER

The database at Keller Medical Center has been configured to execute as an OLTP database during the day. To this end, the Oracle instance has been configured by editing the initialization parameter file and setting sizes for various memory structures. On Wednesday afternoon, Ryan the administrator issued a parallel query to retrieve information from a large table called OLD_RECORDS_2002. The parallel query (see the note below) he issued was:

```
SQL> SELECT /*+PARALLEL*/ * FROM OLD_RECORDS_2002;
```

After partial execution of the query the following error was displayed:

```
ORA -04031: unable to allocate NNNNN bytes of shared memory ("large
pool","unknown object","large pool hea","PX msg pool")
```

After further examination, Ryan concluded that the error was a result of a lack of space in the large pool. There wasn't sufficient memory to complete the parallel query. This chapter discusses a new and exciting solution to Ryan's problem.

NOTE

The query issued by Ryan includes the hint /*+PARALLEL*/. Hints are a means by which users can influence the optimizer to execute a query in a certain way. The hint will force the optimizer to use only the method specified by the hint during query execution. Hints are specified by the /*+ hint */ syntax. In the query written by Ryan, the query initiates simultaneous parallel query processes for faster data retrieval.

MEMORY STRUCTURES OF THE DATABASE

The Oracle Server consists of the Oracle Database and the Oracle Instance.

The Oracle database consists of a number of operating system files that store the data on the hard disk(s).

The Oracle Instance is created in the real memory or RAM of the computer. As you may be aware, the contents of RAM are temporary and are used by the operating system to temporarily store information about currently running applications. The Oracle database also runs on the operating system as an application. The Oracle instance has a predefined structure. When the Oracle database is started, it creates specific structures in memory that have names, are sized individually, and maintain specific pieces of information. For example, SQL statements issued by the different users of the database are maintained for reuse in a memory structure known as the Library Cache.

The data held within the memory structures is erased when the machine is powered off or the database is shutdown. The contents of memory are periodically transferred to Oracle files on disk by the background processes.

The memory components can be broadly divided into two areas—the System Global Area (SGA) and the Program Global Area (PGA).

The SYSTEM GLOBAL AREA (SGA)

The SGA forms a large part of the Oracle instance. A lot of important activity goes on in the SGA. For example, all changes made in the database are recorded and executed in the SGA. Data requested by queries is populated into the SGA before being displayed to the user, and data dictionary information is temporarily cached in the SGA. Figure 11-1 describes the elements of the SGA consisting of various pools and caches.

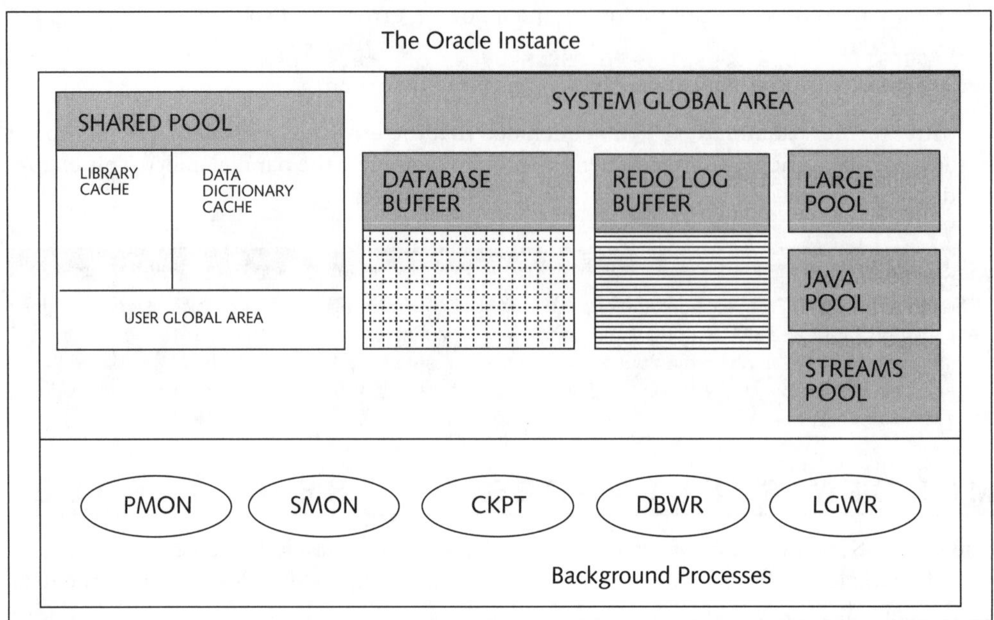

FIGURE 11-1 The Oracle Instance

Various individual components of the SGA are described in the following section.

The Shared Pool

The shared pool as its name indicates stores information that is to be shared among the users of the database. It consists of three caches—the Library Cache, the Data Dictionary Cache (Row Cache), and the User Global Area.

The library cache contains the SQL and PL/SQL statements that are executed in the database, along with their parsed code and execution plans. These are stored, so that when users issue similar statements, the parsed representations and execution plans can be reused. Space in the library cache is managed by the *least recently used (LRU)* algorithm. When additional space is required in the cache for new statements and execution plans, the least recently used statement will be removed from the cache.

The data dictionary cache holds data dictionary information. When the database is created, the data dictionary is created in the SYSTEM tablespace. Because data dictionary information is continuously accessed, data dictionary information is populated into memory for faster access. Ideally, the entire data dictionary must be populated into memory so that disk reads (known as physical reads) are minimized.

The User Global Area (UGA) is a third component of the shared pool. This structure may exist in the shared pool if the large pool has not been configured and the database has been configured as an Oracle Shared Server (OSS) environment (See Appendix A). The

UGA memory maintains information about shared server connections, including user session data, cursor state, sort areas, and private SQL areas. In an OSS environment, user session data must be made available to all shared server processes, and must be stored in sharable memory.

The size of the shared pool may be manually set by the SHARED_POOL_SIZE initialization parameter. It is not possible to specify sizes for the individual caches of the shared pool. Their sizes are dynamically maintained by Oracle based on the overall size of the shared pool and the current workload on the system.

The Database Buffer Cache

The Database Buffer Cache (DBC) is a memory structure that consists of a series of buffers. This cache is also known as the *default* database buffer cache. Each buffer can hold one Oracle data block. When users issue statements, such as queries, the blocks containing the requested data are retrieved from the datafiles and populated into the buffer cache. Such reads are known as physical reads. Queries that are issued, requesting the data blocks that already exist in the cache, read directly from the cache. Such reads are known as logical reads. When a logical read occurs, it is known as a *Cache Hit*. When a physical read occurs it is known as a *Cache Miss*. Logical reads are faster than physical reads.

The database buffer cache also holds modified blocks. For example, when a user issues an update statement, the block(s) containing the row(s) to be changed are first read into the cache. The changes are made in memory and then written back to disk by the database writer (DBWR) background process at periodic intervals. These modified blocks are known as dirty blocks. The buffers in the DBC may be in one of the following states:

- Free—a buffer is in this state when the instance has just started and the block has not yet been used.
- Pinned—a buffer is in this state when it is currently being accessed (read/modified) by an ongoing transaction. Other transactions may be waiting to access this block's contents.
- Clean—a buffer is in this state when its contents are not required (unpinned) and may be aged out if necessary.
- Dirty—a buffer is in this state when it is not pinned but its contents have not been written back to disk by the database writer background process.

The database buffer cache is sized by the DB_CACHE_SIZE initialization parameter. It must be sized to ensure that free space is always available for new blocks that are being read into the cache. Space usage in the buffer cache is also managed by the *least recently used* (LRU) algorithm. When additional space is required, the blocks that were least frequently referenced will be the first to leave the cache.

In addition to the default buffer cache, an administrator may choose to configure additional (optional) caches—the Keep Cache and the Recycle cache. The keep cache may be configured to hold blocks that must be retained in memory for longer periods of time, such as frequently accessed objects. The keep cache is configured by the DB_KEEP_CACHE_SIZE initialization parameter. The recycle cache may be configured to hold blocks that need not be retained for a long time because they are infrequently used. The recycle cache is configured by the DB_RECYCLE_CACHE_SIZE initialization parameter.

The Redo Log Buffer

The Redo Log Buffer is a small circular buffer in the SGA. It contains a record of all the changes made in the database. Whenever users issue statements—DML (Inserts, Updates, or Deletes) and DDL (Create, Alter, Drop, etc.) statements—the statements are recorded in the redo log buffer. The statements are written sequentially as they occur in the database. The contents of the redo log buffer are transferred to disk (online redo log files) periodically by the Log Writer (LGWR) background process. The events that cause the LGWR to write the changes from the redo log buffer to the online redo log files include:

- When a COMMIT statement is issued, indicating the completion of a transaction.
- When the redo log buffer is one-third full.
- When the DBWR background process writes dirty buffers from the database buffer cache to the datafiles.
- Every three seconds.

The redo log buffer is sized by the LOG_BUFFER initialization parameter. The size of the redo log buffer must be set properly so that contention by processes wanting to simultaneously write into the buffer does not occur. A record of the changes is maintained for recovery.

The Large Pool

The large pool is an optional memory structure. It may be configured to enhance the performance of an Oracle Shared Server (OSS) environment, manage input/output requirements of the Recovery Manager during backup and restore operations or handle the requirements of parallel query operations. It is especially useful when user sessions require large memory allocations. In the absence of the large pool, these components use the shared pool for their functioning. If you configure the large pool and use shared servers, the UGA will be stored in the large pool instead of the shared pool. The large pool is configured by the LARGE_POOL_SIZE initialization parameter.

The Java Pool

The Java pool is another optional pool. It can be configured for environments that run Java programs and Java code. If configured, the Java pool is used by the JVM for session-specific Java code and data. The Java pool is configured by the JAVA_POOL_SIZE initialization parameter.

Streams Pool

In Oracle 10g, a new feature known as Oracle Streams has been introduced. To facilitate the smooth functioning of this feature, a memory structure called the Streams Pool may optionally be configured. This streams pool is configured by the STREAMS_POOL_SIZE initialization parameter.

Fixed Area Size

The fixed area size is a portion of the SGA that holds certain fixed views such as the dynamic performance views (V$) and other information pertinent to the database.

The maximum size of the SGA is determined by the SGA_MAX_SIZE initialization parameter. By default, the SGA_MAX_SIZE is set to the sum of the sizes of all the memory structures of the SGA. You may set it to any value depending on the requirements of the system. Changes to the sizes of individual memory components are permitted as long as the total size of all memory structures remains lower than the SGA_MAX_SIZE defined for the database.

Prior to Oracle 10*g*, the memory structures of the SGA had to be individually sized by means of initialization parameters. A challenging situation that administrators may find themselves in, is determining an appropriate size for the memory structures. Memory is expensive, making it important that the values set for the parameters can optimally meet the demands of the environment without waste.

Sizing the structures too small may result in performance problems such as poor hit ratios, contention, and out-of-memory errors. Sizing them too large may result in unnecessarily wasting memory.

Automatic Shared Memory Management (ASMM)

ASMM is a new feature in Oracle10*g* that simplifies administration and management of memory structures. In Oracle 10*g*, the DBA only needs to specify the total memory that may be used by all the SGA components. The **SGA_TARGET** initialization parameter can be specified to do so. The value that the parameter takes indicates the total amount of memory that may be consumed by both manually and automatically sized memory structures. Oracle will use this value to distribute memory among the various components dynamically based on the workload of the database. When SGA_TARGET is set to zero (0), the ASMM feature is disabled. The SGA_TARGET value must be less than or equal to the SGA_MAX_SIZE initialization parameter. It can be modified dynamically using the ALTER SYSTEM command and any changes you make to it will only affect the *auto-tuned parameters*.

Auto-Tuned Parameters

If the SGA_TARGET is set to a non-zero value, the database buffer cache, shared pool, large pool, and Java pool are automatically sized. The streams pool is also automatically sized in Oracle 10*g* Release 2. The initialization parameters DB_CACHE_SIZE, SHARED_POOL_SIZE, LARGE_POOL_SIZE, and JAVA_POOL_SIZE are the auto-tuned parameters. The sizes of the dynamically sized auto-tuned parameters can be viewed from the V$SGA_DYNAMIC_COMPONENTS view.

NOTE

In Oracle 10*g* Release 2 the STREAMS_POOL_SIZE initialization parameter is also an auto-tuned parameter.

When ASMM is configured, Oracle automatically and dynamically sets values for the auto-tuned parameters based on current usage and need. The DB_KEEP_CACHE_SIZE, DB_RECYCLE_CACHE_SIZE and individual caches for tablespaces with nonstandard block sizes (DB_*n*K_CACHE_SIZE) are manually configured parameters. They need to be explicitly set in the initialization parameter file.

The sizes of the auto-tuned memory structures will be determined based on the target value specified by SGA_TARGET. It must be noted that when SGA_TARGET is set, the amount of memory to be allocated to the auto-tuned parameters will be obtained after subtracting the total sizes of the manually set parameters. For example, consider the case where the SGA_TARGET is set to 500 M. The DB_RECYCLE_CACHE_SIZE is 1.5 M, DB_KEEP_CACHE_SIZE is 1.5 M, LOG_BUFFER is 2 M, and FIXED SIZE is 1 M. These memory structures together consume 6 M of memory. Subtracting this from 500 M (SGA_TARGET), we get 494 M. This 494 M will be allocated to the auto-tuned parameters. (See Figure 11-2.) The individual sizes of the structures will vary depending on the workload on the database at that time.

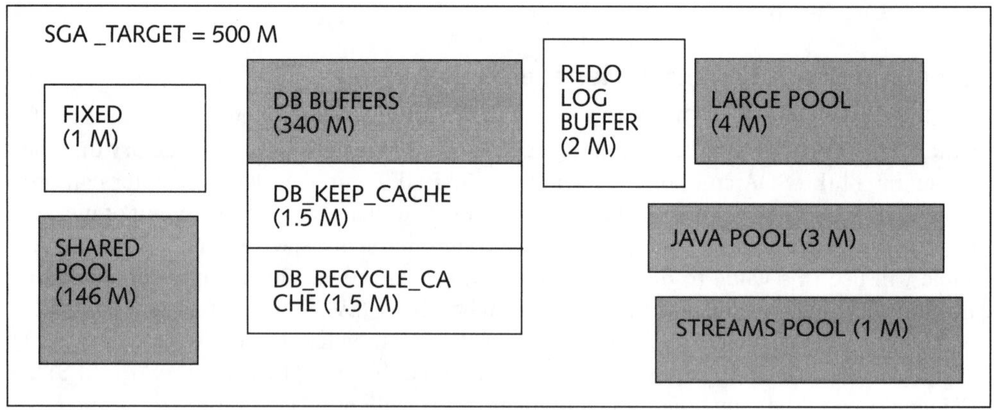

FIGURE 11-2 An example of the setting the SGA_TARGET value

A new background process called the **Memory Manager (MMAN)** is responsible for coordinating the sizes of the auto-tuned memory structures dynamically based on the database workload. It may add or remove memory from individual structures based on usage and need. It uses statistics that are gathered in the database to arrive at appropriate sizes for the memory structures.

The STATISTICS_LEVEL initialization parameter must be set to TYPICAL or ALL for this functionality.

NOTE

Memory is allocated and de-allocated in units called granules. A granule can be either 4 M or 16 M. The granule size is 4 M when the total SGA size, specified by SGA_MAX_SIZE is less than or equal to 1 G (gigabyte). The granule size is 16 M, when the overall SGA size is greater than 1 G.

When the SGA_TARGET initialization parameter is specified, it is recommended that you set the values of the individual auto-tuned parameters to zero. You may, however, set values for them to act as a lower limit, establishing the smallest size the memory structure can take. For example, if you set DB_CACHE_SIZE to 2 G, then the ASSM feature may increase the size of the database buffer cache over 2 G, but the size will never fall below 2 G.

The size of an auto-tuned memory may be changed dynamically; however the change may not take place right away if the change results in lowering the size of the cache. For example, if the database buffer cache is currently sized at 2 G and you alter it to 1.5 G, this change may not take place immediately because the actual usage may exceed 1.5 G at the time the command was issued. When the memory usage falls below 1.5 G, the new change will be made effective. If the change results in increasing the size of the memory structure, the change will be made effective immediately and memory will be allocated from another auto-tuned memory structure. As a result, increasing the size of the buffer cache to 2.5 G may result in the shared pool, large pool, or Java pool decreasing in size. This occurs even when automatic sizing is done. Dynamic resizing of memory structures occur at the expense of other auto-tuned structures.

The problem faced by Ryan, at Keller Medical Center can be resolved using ASSM. The error was generated when Ryan executed the large parallel query. Even though the large pool had been configured for the instance, it was not large enough to meet the demands of the parallel query. If Ryan enables ASSM in the database, then this error will not be generated because the demands of the statement would be automatically taken care of by using memory not being utilized by the other auto-tuned memory structures. Figure 11-3 describes how memory is de-allocated from the shared pool and re-allocated to the large pool, for the completion of the large parallel query.

If you dynamically change SGA_TARGET and set it to 0, then the ASMM feature will be disabled and the size of the auto-tuned memory structures will freeze to their current sizes. They will not take default values or values set by the initialization parameters.

You can view the values of the auto-tuned parameters as set in the initialization parameter file querying the V$PARAMETER dynamic performance view. If you set a value for the SGA_TARGET and do not specify sizes for the auto-tuned size parameters, the value that is displayed by the V$PARAMETER view for these parameters is 0. The current values of the auto-tuned parameters as established by the ASMM feature can be viewed using the V$SGA_DYNAMIC_COMPONENTS view.

Practice 1: Configuring ASSM

This practice example demonstrates the effect of ASSM on the various memory structures of the Oracle database.

1. Start SQL*Plus and connect as a user with SYSDBA privileges.

   ```
   SQL> CONNECT DB_ADMIN/DB_ADMIN AS SYSDBA
   ```

2. Query the V$SGA performance view to display the components of the SGA and their sizes. The output values may vary on your machine. (See Figure 11-4.)

   ```
   SQL> SELECT * FROM V$SGA;
   ```

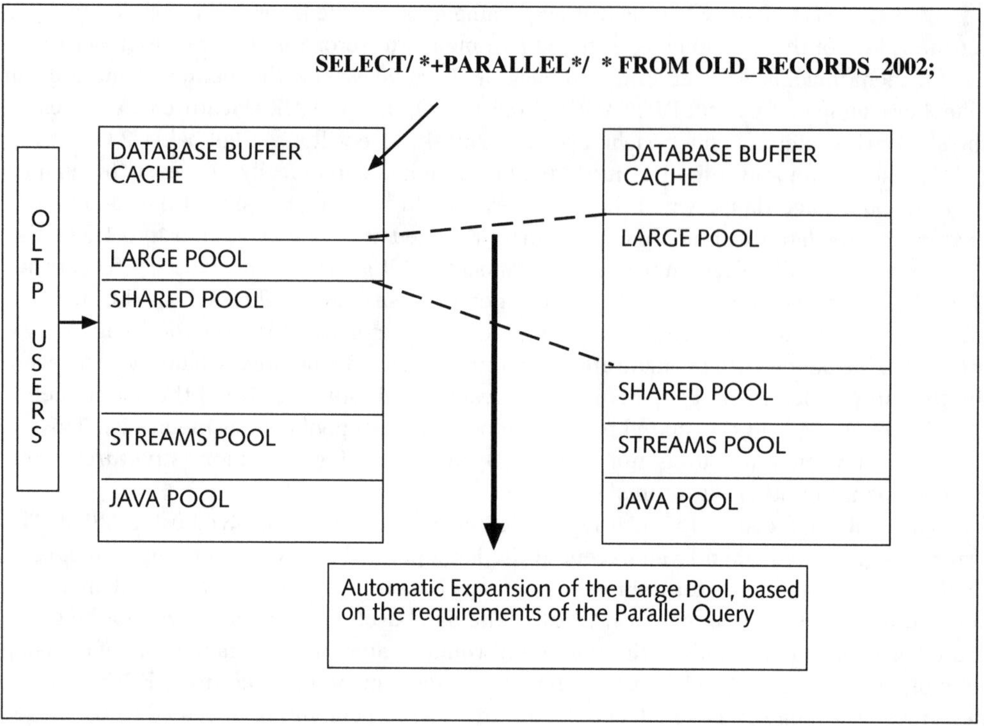

FIGURE 11-3 Automatic Shared Memory Management

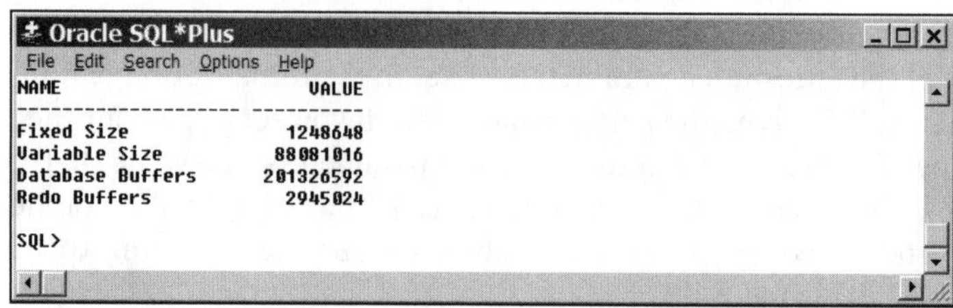

FIGURE 11-4 The output of querying the V$SGA dynamic view

3. Issue the SHOW PARAMETER command to view the current value of the SGA_MAX_SIZE initialization parameter. In Figure 11-5, the value is 280 M. The value may vary on your machine.

   ```
   SQL> SHOW PARAMETER SGA_MAX_SIZE
   ```

4. Issue a SHOW PARAMETER command to display the current value of the SGA_TARGET initialization parameter. A non-zero value for this parameter indicates that ASMM is enabled. Figure 11-6 displays a value of 280 M. The value may vary on your machine.

   ```
   SQL> SHOW PARAMETER SGA_TARGET
   ```

```
Oracle SQL*Plus
File Edit Search Options Help
SQL> SHOW PARAMETER SGA_MAX_SIZE

NAME                                 TYPE        VALUE
------------------------------------ ----------- ------------------------------
sga_max_size                         big integer 280M
SQL> |
```

FIGURE 11-5 The current value of the SGA_MAX_SIZE initialization parameter

```
Oracle SQL*Plus
File Edit Search Options Help
SQL> SHOW PARAMETER SGA_TARGET

NAME                                 TYPE        VALUE
------------------------------------ ----------- ------------------------------
sga_target                           big integer 280M
SQL>
```

FIGURE 11-6 The current value of the SGA_TARGET parameter

5. Issue a command to display the value of the STATISTICS_LEVEL initialization parameter.

   ```
   SQL> SHOW PARAMETER STATISTICS_LEVEL
   ```

6. If the value of STATISTICS_LEVEL was not TYPICAL or ALL, issue this ALTER SYSTEM command to set it to TYPICAL, otherwise proceed to step 7.

   ```
   SQL> ALTER SYSTEM SET STATISTICS_LEVEL=TYPICAL;
   ```

7. Issue an ALTER SYSTEM command to set the value of the SGA_TARGET parameter to a value greater than the SGA_MAX_SIZE parameter. In this example, an attempt is made to set it to 320 M when the SGA_MAX_SIZE was 280 M. Figure 11-7 displays the error that is displayed when SGA_TARGET is assigned a value greater than the SGA_MAX_SIZE parameter.

   ```
   SQL> ALTER SYSTEM SET SGA_TARGET=320M;
   ```

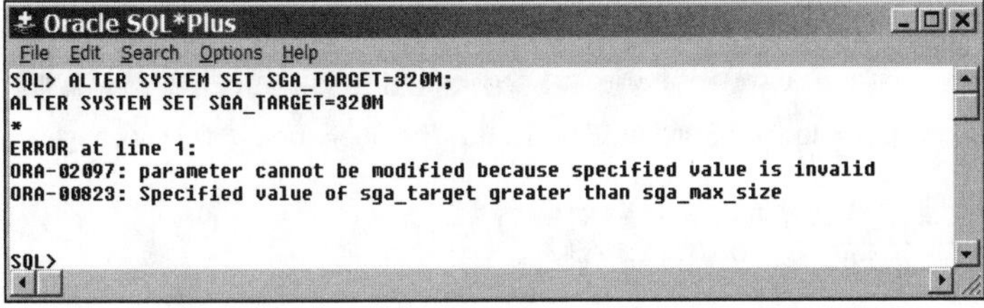

Oracle SQL*Plus
File Edit Search Options Help
SQL> ALTER SYSTEM SET SGA_TARGET=320M;
ALTER SYSTEM SET SGA_TARGET=320M
*
ERROR at line 1:
ORA-02097: parameter cannot be modified because specified value is invalid
ORA-00823: Specified value of sga_target greater than sga_max_size
SQL>

FIGURE 11-7 The error displayed when SGA_TARGET is greater than SGA_MAX_SIZE

8. Issue an ALTER SYTEM command to increase the size of the SGA_MAX_SIZE parameter to a value 25 M greater than its existing value. In the example it is set to 305 M.

```
SQL> ALTER SYSTEM SET SGA_MAX_SIZE=305M SCOPE=SPFILE;
```

9. For the change to take effect you must bounce the database.

```
SQL> SHUTDOWN IMMEDIATE;
SQL> STARTUP
```

10. Issue the SHOW PARAMETER commands displayed below to view the current values of the auto-tuned initialization parameters. In Figure 11-8, notice all the values are zero except for the DB_CACHE_SIZE that has a low-threshold value of 4 M.

```
SQL> SHOW PARAMETER SHARED_POOL_SIZE
SQL> SHOW PARAMETER JAVA_POOL_SIZE
SQL> SHOW PARAMETER LARGE_POOL_SIZE
SQL> SHOW PARAMETER DB_CACHE_SIZE
SQL> SHOW PARAMETER STREAMS_POOL_SIZE
```


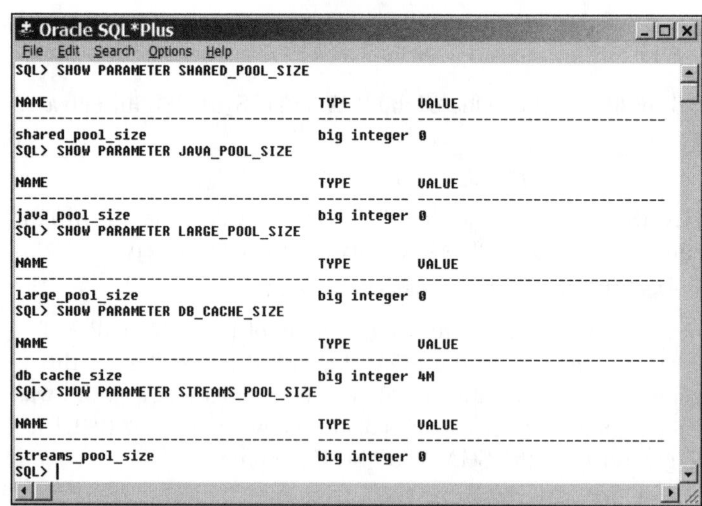

FIGURE 11-8 The sizes of the auto-tuned pools as set in the initialization parameter file.

NOTE

A similar output may be obtained by querying the V$PARAMETER view. The query below displays a typical query and its output.

```
SQL> SELECT NAME, VALUE FROM V$PARAMETER
     WHERE NAME LIKE '%_pool_size%';
```

11. Retrieve the COMPONENT, CURRENT_SIZE, USER_SPECIFIED_SIZE, GRANULE_SIZE columns of the V$SGA_DYNAMIC_COMPONENTS view to display the sizes of the auto-tuned parameters that were dynamically assigned by ASMM. Figure 11-9 displays the values that were set dynamically by Oracle (CURRENT_SIZE) along with what is specified in the initialization parameter file (USER_SPECIFIED_SIZE).

```
SQL> COLUMN COMPONENT FORMAT A25
SQL> SELECT COMPONENT, CURRENT_SIZE,
     USER_SPECIFIED_SIZE, GRANULE_SIZE
     FROM V$SGA_DYNAMIC_COMPONENTS;
```

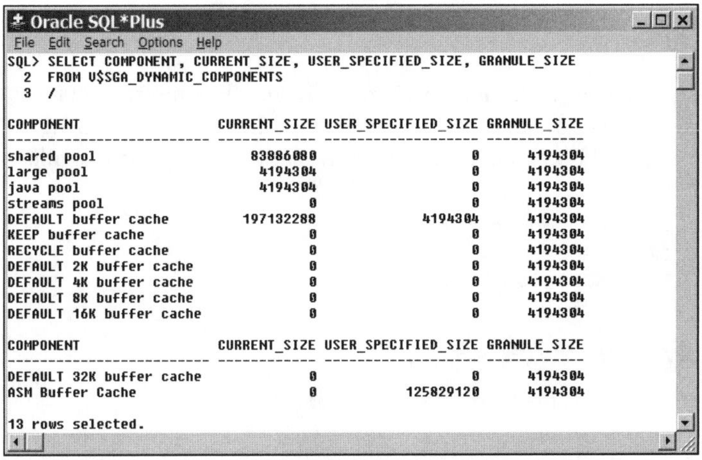

```
Oracle SQL*Plus
File Edit Search Options Help
SQL> SELECT COMPONENT, CURRENT_SIZE, USER_SPECIFIED_SIZE, GRANULE_SIZE
  2  FROM V$SGA_DYNAMIC_COMPONENTS
  3  /

COMPONENT                 CURRENT_SIZE USER_SPECIFIED_SIZE GRANULE_SIZE
------------------------- ------------ ------------------- ------------
shared pool                   83886080                   0      4194304
large pool                     4194304                   0      4194304
java pool                      4194304                   0      4194304
streams pool                         0                   0      4194304
DEFAULT buffer cache         197132288             4194304      4194304
KEEP buffer cache                    0                   0      4194304
RECYCLE buffer cache                 0                   0      4194304
DEFAULT 2K buffer cache              0                   0      4194304
DEFAULT 4K buffer cache              0                   0      4194304
DEFAULT 8K buffer cache              0                   0      4194304
DEFAULT 16K buffer cache             0                   0      4194304

COMPONENT                 CURRENT_SIZE USER_SPECIFIED_SIZE GRANULE_SIZE
------------------------- ------------ ------------------- ------------
DEFAULT 32K buffer cache             0                   0      4194304
ASM Buffer Cache                     0           125829120      4194304

13 rows selected.
```

FIGURE 11-9 The output of V$SGA_DYNAMIC_COMPONENTS

12. Next, display the values of initialization parameters that must be set manually. Figure 11-10 indicates that the Keep and Recycle pool have not been configured.

```
SQL> SHOW PARAMETER LOG_BUFFER
SQL> SHOW PARAMETER DB_KEEP_CACHE_SIZE
SQL> SHOW PARAMETER DB_RECYCLE_CACHE_SIZE
```

13. Increase the size of the SGA_TARGET by 25 M. In our example, the current value of SGA_TARGET is 280 M. It is being modified by 305 M. Though a value of 305 M is used, Oracle will set SGA_TARGET to 308 M, rounding it to the size of a granule (4 M).

```
SQL> ALTER SYSTEM SET SGA_TARGET=305M;
```

```
SQL> SHOW PARAMETER LOG_BUFFER

NAME                                 TYPE        VALUE
------------------------------------ ----------- ------------------------------
log_buffer                           integer     2899456
SQL> SHOW PARAMETER DB_KEEP_CACHE_SIZE

NAME                                 TYPE        VALUE
------------------------------------ ----------- ------------------------------
db_keep_cache_size                   big integer 0
SQL> SHOW PARAMETER DB_RECYCLE_CACHE_SIZE

NAME                                 TYPE        VALUE
------------------------------------ ----------- ------------------------------
db_recycle_cache_size                big integer 0
SQL> |
```

FIGURE 11-10 The sizes of the individual structures that can be manually set

14. Re-execute the query you wrote in step 11, to view the dynamic size changes made to the auto-tuned parameters as a result of increasing the SGA_TARGET value. Figure 11-11 indicates the additional memory that was allocated to the database buffer cache.

```
SQL> SELECT COMPONENT, CURRENT_SIZE,
     USER_SPECIFIED_SIZE, GRANULE_SIZE
     FROM V$SGA_DYNAMIC_COMPONENTS;
```

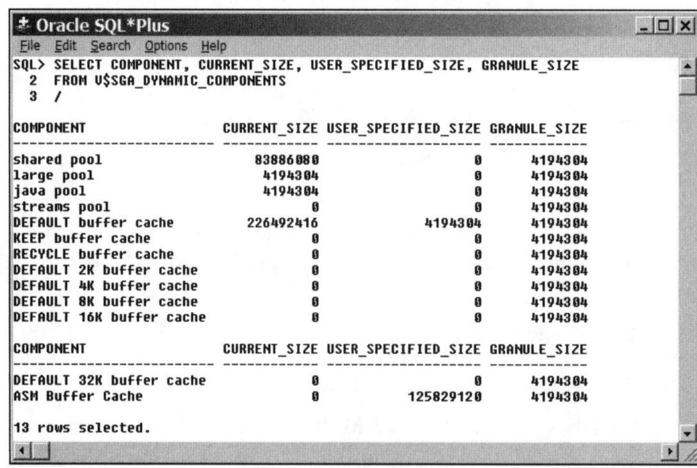

```
SQL> SELECT COMPONENT, CURRENT_SIZE, USER_SPECIFIED_SIZE, GRANULE_SIZE
  2  FROM V$SGA_DYNAMIC_COMPONENTS
  3  /

COMPONENT                 CURRENT_SIZE USER_SPECIFIED_SIZE GRANULE_SIZE
------------------------- ------------ ------------------- ------------
shared pool                   83886080                   0      4194304
large pool                     4194304                   0      4194304
java pool                      4194304                   0      4194304
streams pool                         0                   0      4194304
DEFAULT buffer cache         226492416             4194304      4194304
KEEP buffer cache                    0                   0      4194304
RECYCLE buffer cache                 0                   0      4194304
DEFAULT 2K buffer cache              0                   0      4194304
DEFAULT 4K buffer cache              0                   0      4194304
DEFAULT 8K buffer cache              0                   0      4194304
DEFAULT 16K buffer cache             0                   0      4194304

COMPONENT                 CURRENT_SIZE USER_SPECIFIED_SIZE GRANULE_SIZE
------------------------- ------------ ------------------- ------------
DEFAULT 32K buffer cache             0                   0      4194304
ASM Buffer Cache                     0           125829120      4194304

13 rows selected.
```

FIGURE 11-11 The output of V$SGA_DYNAMIC_COMPONENTS.

15. Exit SQL*Plus.

The Memory Advisor

The Memory Advisor may be accessed using the Enterprise Manager. It can be used to help you identify an appropriate value for SGA_TARGET based on statistical data collected within the system.

Practice 2: The Memory Advisor

This practice example demonstrates how the Memory Advisor can be accessed and ASMM configured using Enterprise Manager.

1. Launch a browser, enter the URL to access the Enterprise Manager, and log in as a user with SYSDBA privileges.
2. From the **Database Control Home** page, scroll to the **Related Links** section.
3. Select the **Advisor Central** link.
4. Select the **Memory Advisor** from the **Advisors** section. (See Figure 11-12.)

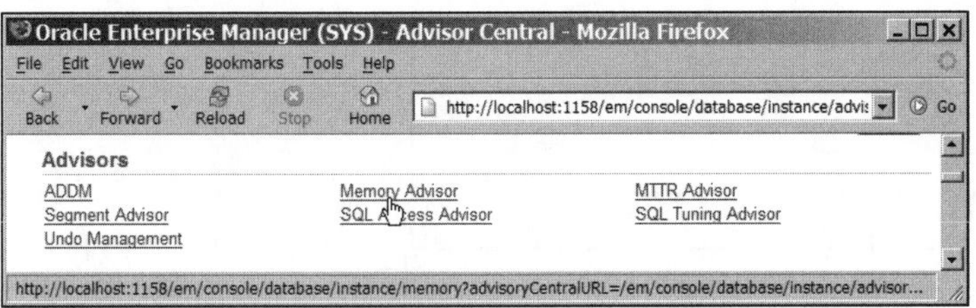

FIGURE 11-12 The Memory Advisor

5. The **Memory Parameters** page will be displayed.
6. On this page, you can see that **Automatic Shared Memory Management** has been **Enabled**. To disable it you would select the Disable button. In the **Current Allocation** section, notice, the Total SGA Size (M) has been set to 308 M. (The last change done to the SGA_TARGET parameter in the Practice 1.) The individual SGA components and their sizes are also displayed graphically. The Maximum SGA Size section displays the value of the SGA_MAX_SIZE initialization parameter. It may be modified by entering a new value in the text box provided. (See Figure 11-13.)
7. Select the **Disable** button.
8. The **Disable Automatic Shared Memory Management** page is displayed. Notice, that if you disable ASSM the new values of the auto-tuned parameters will freeze to their current values. (See Figure 11-14.) Select the **Cancel** button, to return to the **Memory Parameters** page.
9. Next, modify the **Total SGA Size** value to **280**, by typing it into the text box provided. Scroll to the bottom of the page, and select the **Apply** button.

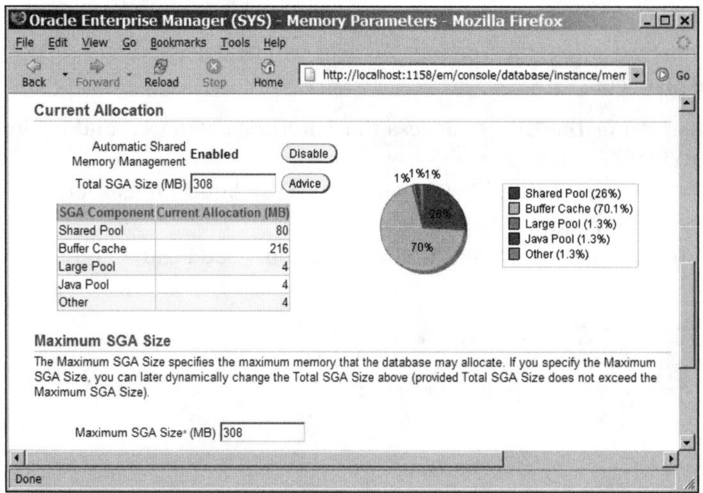

FIGURE 11-13 The SGA Tab

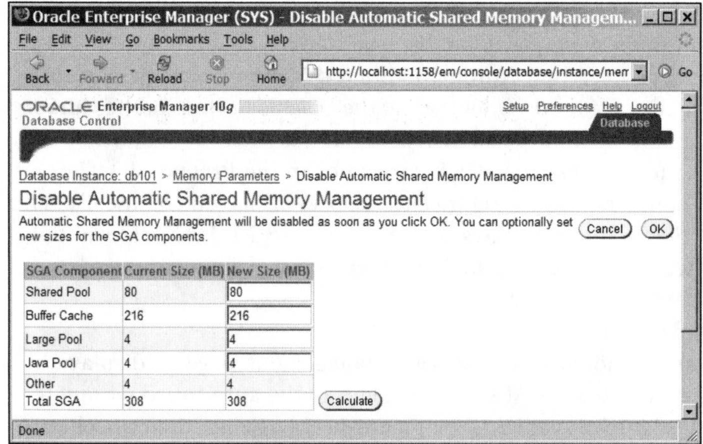

FIGURE 11-14 The values set to the Auto-tuned parameters if ASMM is disabled.

10. Select the **Refresh** button on the top-right corner of the page. Observe the values of the SGA components. In Figure 11-15 notice the size of the buffer cache decreased to 188 M, as a result of the change to the SGA target value.
11. Exit Enterprise Manager.

In this section we reviewed the SGA, its components, configuration, and the Automatic Shared Memory Management feature. The next topic discusses another memory structure known as the Program Global Area.

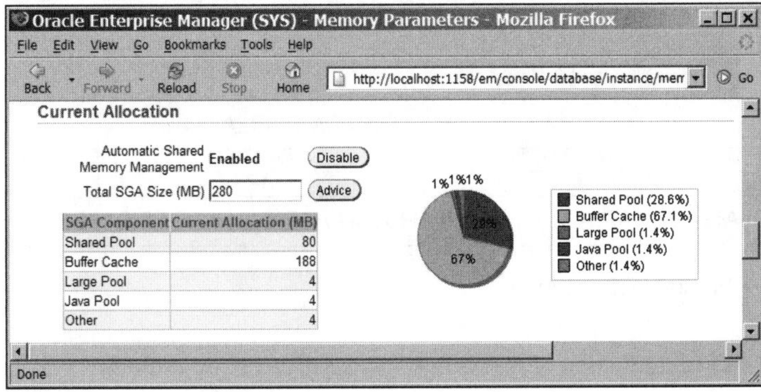

FIGURE 11-15 The result of modifying the SGA_TARGET parameter

THE PROGRAM GLOBAL AREA (PGA)

Another important memory area that is maintained within the Oracle database is the Program Global Area (PGA). PGA memory is allocated when a user connects to the database. Table 11-1 describes the processes created when a user connects to the database.

TABLE 11-1 Processes of the Oracle database and their functions

Processes	Description/Function
User Process	When a client tool such as SQL*Plus is launched and a user connects to the Oracle database, a process called the user process is created on the client side. This process is responsible for sending requests to the database. The communication pathway created between the client and the database is known as a session. The session ends when the client disconnects from the database.
Server Process	The server process is the process created on the server side to handle the requests made by a user process. A server process may be a dedicated process or a shared server process. A dedicated server process remains attached to a single user process for the life of the user process. A shared server process can handle the requests of several user processes.

Server processes are created to service the requests made by user processes. Server processes maintain data and control information about the user process. The memory space that is allocated and maintained by the server process to store this information is the PGA.

Broadly, the PGA maintains the following internal components: Session Data, Private SQL area, and SQL work area. Figure 11-16 displays a typical PGA.

The Session Data component stores information about the user, such as the username, password, machine name, user's terminal name, and other session-related data.

The Private SQL area consists of two areas—Persistent Area and Runtime Area.

- The Persistent Area stores information about the bind variables and status of the cursors of the most recently executed commands.
- The Runtime Area stores information about the currently executing SQL statement that has been submitted by the user process.

SESSION DATA			
PRIVATE SQL AREA			
PERSISTENT AREA		RUNTIME AREA	
SQL WORK AREA			
BITMAP MERGE AREA	CREATE BITMAP AREA	HASH JOIN AREA	SORT AREA

FIGURE 11-16 Structure of the Program Global Area

The SQL work area of the PGA consists of four major structures. They include:

- **Bitmap Merge Area**: This area is used when a statement accessing two or more bitmap indexes, whose contents must be merged, is executed. The merge operation will be done in this memory space. The bitmap merge area may be manually sized by means of the BITMAP_MERGE_AREA_SIZE initialization parameter.
- **Create Bitmap Area**: This area is used when bitmap indexes are created by the CREATE BITMAP INDEX command. This part of the PGA may be manually sized by means of the CREATE_BITMAP_AREA_SIZE initialization parameter.
- **Hash Join Area**: When queries are executed on multiple tables, a common technique used by the optimizer to retrieve the data is known as a hash join. Hash join operations requiring memory space can use this area in the PGA. The hash join area may be manually sized by means of the HASH_AREA_SIZE initialization parameter.
- **Sort Area**: This is one of the most important and frequently accessed portions of the SQL Work area. Whenever a user issues a command that may require a sort to be performed, such as a SQL statement with an ORDER BY, GROUP BY, or DISTINCT clause(s), a temporary work area is required where the sorting can be done. The sort area space in the PGA is used for such sort operations. The sort area may be manually sized by the SORT_AREA_SIZE initialization parameter.

The structure of the program global area varies depending on whether it is maintained by a dedicated or shared server process. In a dedicated server environment, the PGA memory holds session information including the entire UGA (user session data, cursor state, and stack space). In an Oracle Shared Server environment, part of the UGA is removed from the PGA (user session data and cursor state) and stored in the Shared Pool or Large Pool (if it is configured). In the OSS environment only the stack space of the UGA is held in the PGA. This is necessary because the user session information needs to be shared between the shared server processes.

Prior to Oracle 9*i*, it was part of an administrator's job to configure the sizes of the internal structures of the SQL work area by setting values for the CREATE_BITMAP_AREA_SIZE, BITMAP_MERGE_AREA_SIZE, HASH_AREA_SIZE, and SORT_AREA_SIZE initialization parameters.

The following example illustrates the difficulty faced by a DBA in identifying an appropriate value for the SORT_AREA_SIZE parameter. This is a parameter that administrators tend to pay closer attention to because users of the database are likely to issue statements that will involve sorting. Sorting is done when statements that contain ORDER BY, GROUP BY, DISTINCT, ROLLUP, or other clause(s) are issued in the database. A DBA decides to set the value of the SORT_AREA_SIZE parameter to 200 K. This value would be suitable if all the users issued statements that needed 200 K or less of sort space to complete the entire sort operation. If a certain user issues statements that performed a sort operation requiring more than 200 K of sort space, the entire sort would be unable to complete in memory and disk space will be utilized. If, on the other hand, the DBA sets the sort area size to a large value like 1 M and most users do not perform large sorts, memory will be unnecessarily wasted. The example, gives you a sense of how difficult it might be for the DBA to obtain a suitable value for the SORT_AREA_SIZE initialization parameter.

Since Oracle 9*i*, the DBA can choose between **Automatic PGA Memory Management** (APMM) and manual PGA memory management. In APMM, Oracle automatically configures the sizes of the internal components of the PGA memory without DBA intervention. In manual PGA memory management, the DBA must manually set the sizes of various initialization parameters associated with PGA memory. The values that are configured will determine how PGA memory will be utilized and managed.

NOTE

Since Oracle 9*i*, Automatic PGA Memory Management is enabled by default.

APMM can be enabled by setting the value of the **WORKAREA_SIZE_POLICY** initialization parameter to **AUTO**. The parameter may alternatively take the value MANUAL, in which case manual PGA memory management is requested. If WORKAREA_SIZE_POLICY is set to AUTO (the default), then Oracle will manage the different work areas automatically and dynamically based on the requirements of the user and the workload on the database. If it is set to MANUAL, then it would be the responsibility of the DBA to set the values of the SORT_AREA_SIZE, CREATE_BITMAP_AREA_SIZE, BITMAP_MERGE_AREA_SIZE, and HASH_AREA_SIZE initialization parameters. These parameters will be collectively referred to as the *_AREA_SIZE parameters.

If WORKAREA_SIZE_POLICY is set to AUTO, then the DBA would need to configure only one additional parameter—the **PGA_AGGREGATE_TARGET** initialization parameter. This parameter takes a value in terms of bytes of space—kilobytes, megabytes, or gigabytes; and specifies the total amount of PGA memory that can be utilized by *all* user sessions. Oracle uses this value as an upper limit and allocates space for PGA memory from it. For large sorts, more memory will be allocated; for smaller sorts, less memory will be allocated. When APMM is enabled, any values set for the *_AREA_SIZE parameters will be ignored. The PGA_AGGREGATE_TARGET parameter, defaults to a value of 10 M or 20 percent of the SGA size, whichever is larger. However, if you wish to modify it to take a value other than its default, you must make sure to set it correctly, ensuring that sufficient PGA memory is available for all user processes.

The performance of PGA memory may be measured by means of its *cache hit* percentage. A hit percentage of 100% indicates that all sorts being performed in the database are able to complete in memory. This percentage can fall below 100 percent if sorts are partly done using the temporary tablespace on disk. It is important to configure the PGA_AGGREGATE_TARGET to a value that will result in a cache hit percentage of 100 percent.

Another measure of the performance of PGA memory is the count of the number of optimal pass executions, one-pass executions, and multi-pass executions that occur in the database. When sorts cannot complete in memory, one-pass or multi-pass executions are performed. Table 11-2 describes these types of executions.

TABLE 11-2 Types of execution that may be performed in the PGA

Execution	Description
Optimal Execution	Occurs when the work area in the PGA is large enough for the current operation being performed.
One-pass Execution	Occurs when the work area in the PGA is not large enough to complete the current operation and one additional step has to be performed.
Multi-pass execution	Occurs when the work area is not sized properly and the current operation requires multiple steps to complete the current operation.

An appropriate value for the PGA_AGGREGATE_TARGET results in all sorts being optimal executions.

The database provides many data dictionary views that may be queried to obtain information about the PGA memory. Table 11-3 describes some of these views.

TABLE 11-3 Data dictionary views associated with PGA.

View Name	Description
V$PGASTAT	Provides information about current utilization of PGA memory.
V$SYSSTAT	In addition to statistics about the entire system, this view provides information about the type of executions (optimal, one-pass, or multi-pass executions) occurring in the database.
V$PGA_TARGET_ADVICE	The view acts as an advisory, predicting how the cache hit percentage will be impacted if the value of the PGA_AGGREGATE_TARGET is changed. The prediction is based on the past and current workload.

Practice 3: Automatic PGA Memory Management

This practice example demonstrates how APMM may be configured in the Oracle database using SQL*Plus.

1. Start SQL*Plus, and log in as a user with SYSDBA privileges.

2. Issue the SHOW PARAMETER command to view the value of the WORKAREA_SIZE_POLICY initialization parameter. The value, by default, is AUTO therefore enabling automatic PGA memory management. (See Figure 11-17.)

```
SQL> SHOW PARAMETER WORKAREA_SIZE_POLICY;
```

```
Oracle SQL*Plus
File Edit Search Options Help
SQL> SHOW PARAMETER WORKAREA_SIZE_POLICY;

NAME                                 TYPE        VALUE
------------------------------------ ----------- ------------------------------
workarea_size_policy                 string      AUTO
SQL>
```

FIGURE 11-17 The default value of WORKAREA_SIZE_POLICY

3. Display the value of the PGA_AGGREGATE_TARGET initialization parameter. Figure 11-18 displays a value of 92 M. The value may vary on your machine.

```
SQL> SHOW PARAMETER PGA_AGGREGATE_TARGET
```

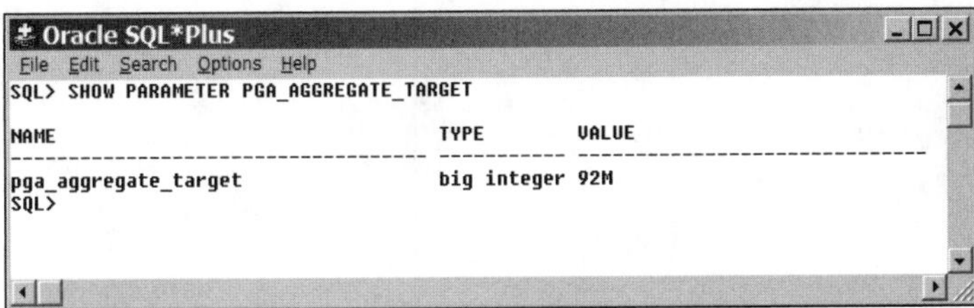

```
Oracle SQL*Plus
File Edit Search Options Help
SQL> SHOW PARAMETER PGA_AGGREGATE_TARGET

NAME                                 TYPE        VALUE
------------------------------------ ----------- ------------------------------
pga_aggregate_target                 big integer 92M
SQL>
```

FIGURE 11-18 The current value of the PGA_AGGREGATE_TARGET

4. The PGA_AGGREGATE_TARGET value can range from 10 M to (4096 G -1). Using an ALTER SYSTEM command set it to 5 M. View the error that is displayed. (See Figure 11-19.)

```
SQL> ALTER SYSTEM SET PGA_AGGREGATE_TARGET=5M;
```

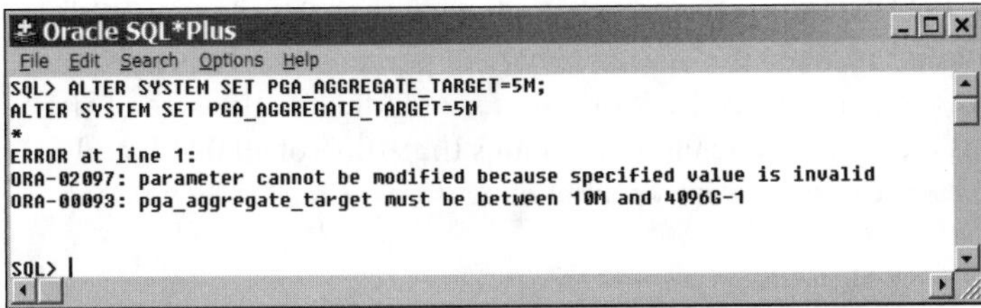

```
Oracle SQL*Plus
File Edit Search Options Help
SQL> ALTER SYSTEM SET PGA_AGGREGATE_TARGET=5M;
ALTER SYSTEM SET PGA_AGGREGATE_TARGET=5M
*
ERROR at line 1:
ORA-02097: parameter cannot be modified because specified value is invalid
ORA-00093: pga_aggregate_target must be between 10M and 4096G-1

SQL>
```

FIGURE 11-19 Modifying the PGA_AGGREGATE_TARGET to 5 M

5. Change the value of PGA_AGGREGATE_TARGET to 15 M.

```
SQL> ALTER SYSTEM SET PGA_AGGREGATE_TARGET=15M;
```

6. Exit SQL*Plus.

Practice 4: The Memory Advisor

This practice example demonstrates how APMM can be configured using the Enterprise Manager. You will also see how the Memory Advisor provides recommendations on an ideal value for the PGA_AGGREGATE_TARGET based on the database workload.

1. Launch a browser, enter the URL for Enterprise Manager, and connect as a user with SYSDBA privileges.
2. From the **Database Control Home** page, scroll to the **Related Links** section.
3. Select the **Advisor Central** link.
4. Select the **Memory Advisor** link. The **Memory Parameters** page will be displayed.
5. Select the **PGA** tab. Notice in Figure 11-20 the PGA Aggregate value is set to 15 M. This value was set in the Practice 3.

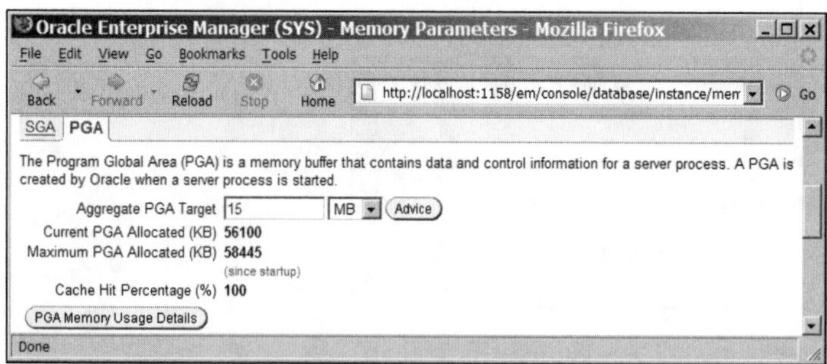

FIGURE 11-20 The Memory Parameters Page

6. Select the **Advice** button. View the graph that is displayed. Figure 11-21 indicates that, based on the current activity in the database, a value of 15 M is achieving a cache hit percentage of 100 percent. This indicates that all sorts are occurring in memory. Close the page by selecting the **OK** button.
7. Next, select the **PGA Memory Usage Details** button. Another graph will be displayed. The graph in Figure 11-22 displays the percentage of optimal, one-pass, or multi-pass executions. The Work area size indicates the size of the memory that was requested. The figure indicates that 100% of all 0–4 K and 512 K–1 M memory requirements were optimal executions. Close this window.

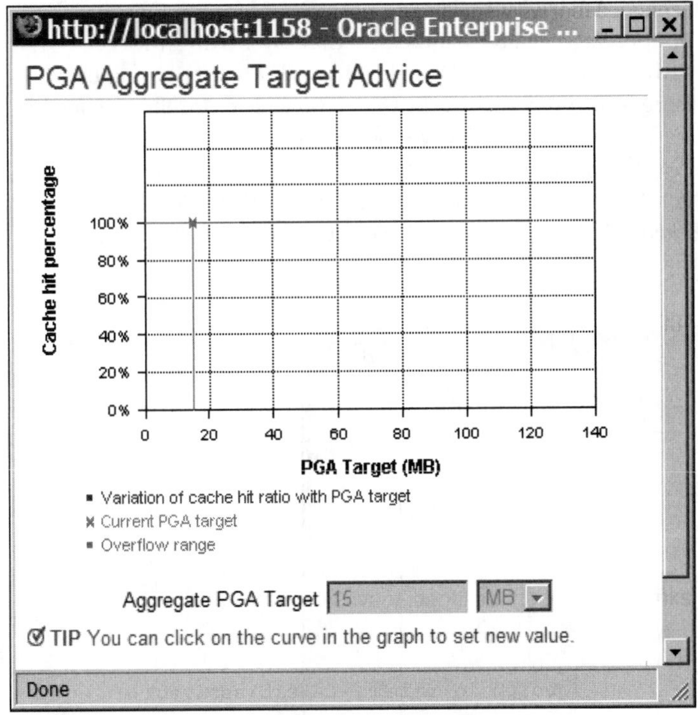

FIGURE 11-21 The PGA Aggregate Target Advice Page

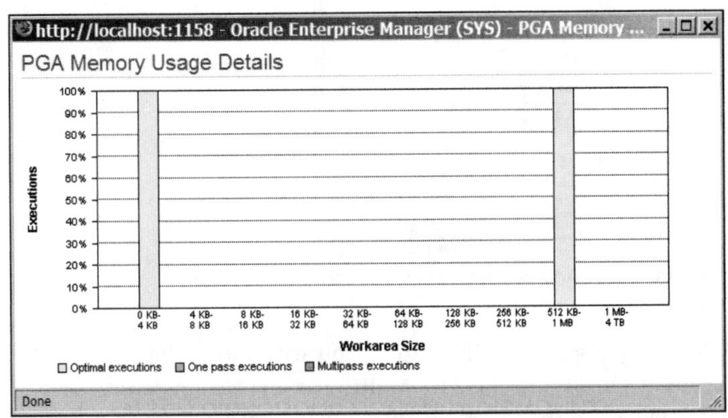

FIGURE 11-22 The PGA Memory Usage Details Page

8. From SQL*Plus, log on as a user with SYSDBA privileges and issue a command that will result in a huge sort being performed, such as the one displayed below. Wait for the statement to complete. It may take several minutes.

```
SQL> SELECT * FROM DBA_OBJECTS ORDER BY TIMESTAMP;
```

9. Once again select the **Advice** button from Enterprise Manager. Observe the change in the graph. Figure 11-23 indicates that by setting the PGA_AGGREGATE_TARGET value to 15 M, you achieved a hit ratio of approximately 90%. Setting it to about 45 M results in a 100% hit ratio. This advice has been provided based on the workload you generated on the system. If you click on the curve, you will see the Aggregate PGA target value change, and the graph accordingly. It will give you an idea of what the hit ratio will be, if you change the aggregate PGA target value. Close the window by selecting the **OK** button.

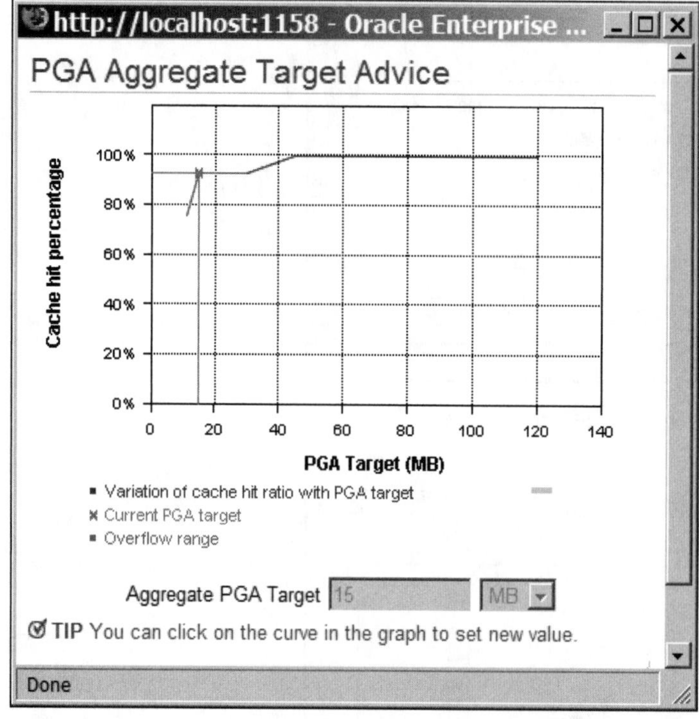

FIGURE 11-23 The PGA Aggregate Target Advice Page after running the workload

10. Select the **PGA Memory Usage Details** button. You will notice that the graph now looks different. (See Figure 11-24.) Multi-pass executions were performed in the database when the query on DBA_OBJECTS was performed. The amount of memory requested for this sort was between 4 M and 8 M, and only 50% of the execution was optimal.
11. From the list for **Show memory usage details for PGA Target**, select a value of 21 M. Select the **Go** button. Notice the way in which the graph changes. The graph in Figure 11-25 indicates that changing the PGA_AGGREGATE_TARGET value to 21 M results in 50% of the executions being one-pass executions.

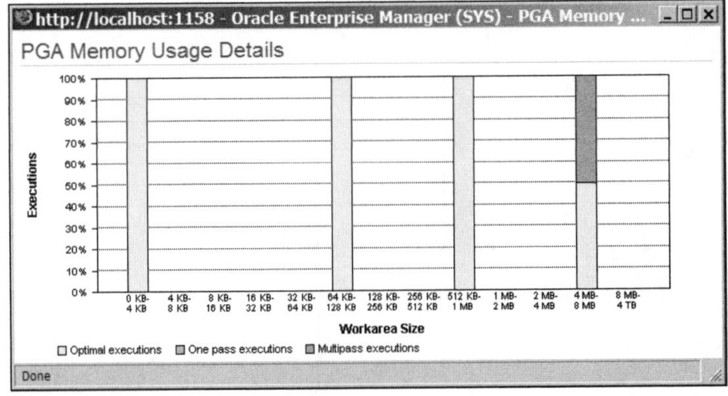

FIGURE 11-24 The PGA Memory Usage Details Page after the workload

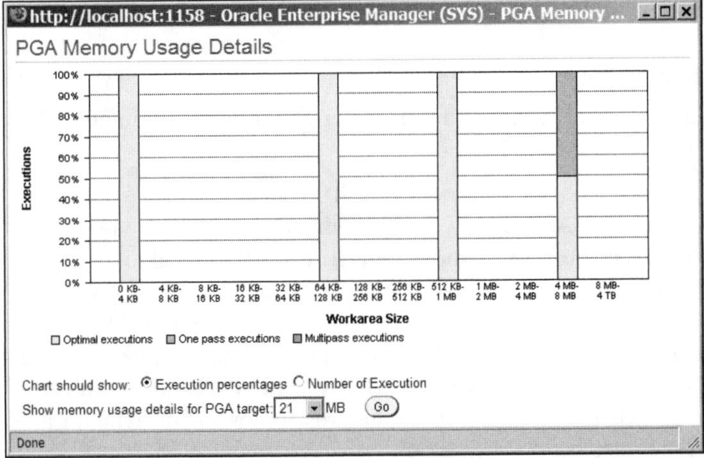

FIGURE 11-25 The graph after changing the PGA aggregate value to 60 M

12. Next, change it to 45 M. Select the **Go** button. Notice the change in the graph. The graph indicates that changing the PGA_AGGREGATE_TARGET value to 45 M will result in optimal sorts only. (See Figure 11-26.)
13. Log out of Enterprise Manager.

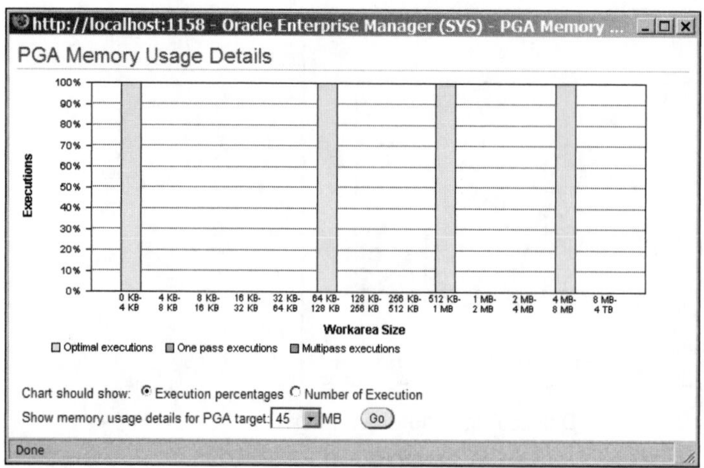

FIGURE 11-26 The graph after changing the PGA aggregate value to 45 M

Practice 5: Querying the data dictionary

In this practice example you will perform some queries to retrieve information about the PGA memory.

1. Start SQL*Plus and connect as a user with SYSDBA privileges.
2. Issue a query on the V$PGASTAT view to display its contents. This view provides information about the PGA memory. In Figure 11-27 the value *aggregate PGA target parameter* refers to the value of the PGA_AGGREGATE_TARGET parameter. The *aggregate PGA auto target* refers to the amount of PGA memory the Oracle database can use for work areas running in automatic mode. Notice that the *total PGA inuse* is greater than the PGA_AGGREGATE value, indicating that the PGA_AGGREGATE_TARGET value was set low. The cache hit percentage for PGA memory is 94.79%.

```
SQL> SELECT * FROM V$PGASTAT;
```

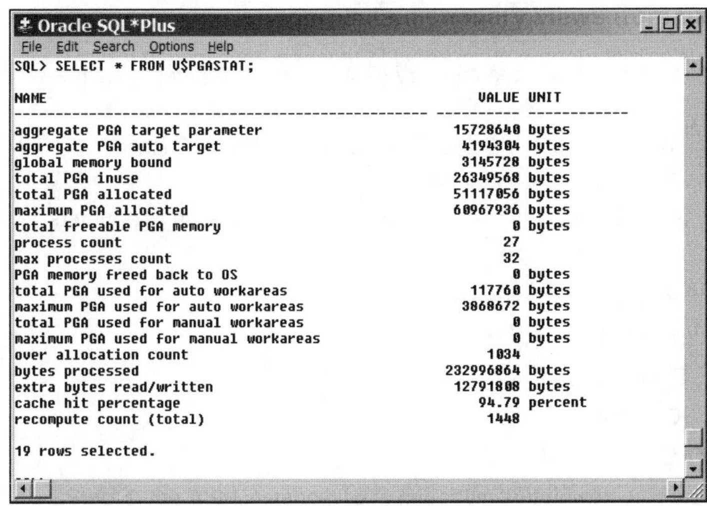
```
SQL> SELECT * FROM V$PGASTAT;

NAME                                                  VALUE UNIT
-------------------------------------------------- ---------- ------------
aggregate PGA target parameter                       15728640 bytes
aggregate PGA auto target                             4194304 bytes
global memory bound                                   3145728 bytes
total PGA inuse                                      26349568 bytes
total PGA allocated                                  51117056 bytes
maximum PGA allocated                                60967936 bytes
total freeable PGA memory                                   0 bytes
process count                                              27
max processes count                                        32
PGA memory freed back to OS                                 0 bytes
total PGA used for auto workareas                      117760 bytes
maximum PGA used for auto workareas                   3860672 bytes
total PGA used for manual workareas                         0 bytes
maximum PGA used for manual workareas                       0 bytes
over allocation count                                    1034
bytes processed                                     232996864 bytes
extra bytes read/written                             12791808 bytes
cache hit percentage                                    94.79 percent
recompute count (total)                                  1448

19 rows selected.
```

FIGURE 11-27 The output of V$PGASTAT

3. Type the following query on the V$SYSSTAT view to display the number of optimal, one-pass, and multi-pass executions occurring in the database. From Figure 11-28 you can see that 9,207 executions were optimal and 2 were one-pass.

```
SQL> SELECT NAME, VALUE FROM V$SYSSTAT
     WHERE NAME LIKE 'workarea executions%';
```

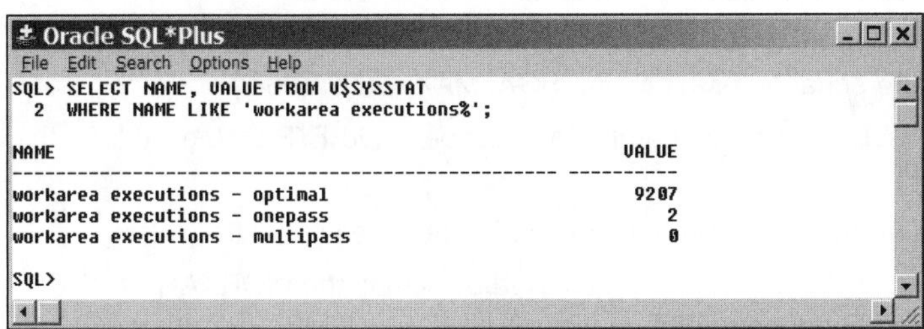
```
SQL> SELECT NAME, VALUE FROM V$SYSSTAT
  2  WHERE NAME LIKE 'workarea executions%';

NAME                                                    VALUE
-------------------------------------------------- ----------
workarea executions - optimal                            9207
workarea executions - onepass                               2
workarea executions - multipass                             0

SQL>
```

FIGURE 11-28 The output of V$SYSSTAT.

4. Exit SQL*Plus.

In this chapter we discussed the various memory structures in Oracle 10g and how they could be configured both manually and using the automatic features of Oracle 10g. Chapter 12 discusses a new feature of Oracle 10g known as Automatic Storage Management (ASM).

Chapter Summary

- The System Global Area is created in the memory (RAM) of the computer system when the database is started.
- The System Global Area consists of the Shared Pool, Database Buffer Cache, Redo Log Buffer, Large Pool, Java Pool, and Streams Pool.
- The memory structures can be manually sized by means of initialization parameters.
  - Shared Pool: SHARED_POOL_SIZE
  - Database Buffer Cache: DB_CACHE_SIZE
  - Redo Log Buffer: LOG_BUFFER
  - Large Pool: LARGE_POOL_SIZE
  - Java Pool: JAVA_POOL_SIZE
  - Streams Pool: STREAMS_POOL_SIZE
- ASMM is new in Oracle10*g*. It facilitates managing memory easily compared to earlier versions of Oracle.
- In Oracle 10*g* Release 1, the auto-tuned parameters are SHARED_POOL_SIZE, DB_CACHE_SIZE, LARGE_POOL_SIZE, and JAVA_POOL_SIZE.
- In Oracle 10*g* Release 2, the STREAMS_POOL_SIZE is also an auto-tuned parameter.
- The manual parameters include LOG_BUFFER, STREAMS_POOL_SIZE, DB_*n*K_CACHE_SIZE, DB_KEEP_CACHE_SIZE, and DB_RECYCLE_CACHE_SIZE.
- The SGA_TARGET initialization parameter must be set for ASMM. It specifies the total amount of memory that can be allocated for the SGA components. Oracle will use this value to dynamically size the values of the auto-tuned parameters.
- The SGA_MAX_SIZE parameter determines the maximum size of SGA. The SGA_TARGET value must be equal or less than the SGA_MAX_SIZE value.
- The STATISTICS_LEVEL initialization parameter must be set to TYPICAL or ALL for the ASMM functionality.
- PGA memory is created by server sessions for storing user session data.
- APMM was introduced in Oracle 9*i*. This is achieved by setting the WORKAREA_SIZE_POLICY initialization parameter to AUTO.
- The PGA_AGGREGATE_TARGET initialization parameter can be specified to indicate the total amount of memory allocated for the PGA memory for all connected user sessions.
- The individual sizes of PGA memory will vary depending on the needs of the user session and the workload on the database.
- ASSM and APMM can both be configured using SQL*Plus and Enterprise Manager.

Syntax Guide

SYNTAX GUIDE		
Command	Description	Example
`SHOW PARAMETER`	To display the value of an initialization parameter	`SQL> SHOW PARAMETER JAVA_POOL_SIZE`
`ALTER SYSTEM SET`	To set the value of an initialization parameter dynamically.	`SQL> ALTER SYSTEM SET SGA_TARGET=100M;`

Review Questions

1. The new initialization parameters that need to be configured for ensuring that memory components are automatically sized based on current workload is:
   a. SGA_MAX_SIZE
   b. SHARED_POOL_TARGET
   c. SGA_TARGET
   d. COMPATIBLE

2. The auto-tuned memory parameters in Oracle 10*g* are: [Choose 4.]
   a. LOG_BUFFER
   b. SHARED_POOL_SIZE
   c. DB_KEEP_CACHE_SIZE
   d. DB_RECYCLE_CACHE_SIZE
   e. DB_CACHE_SIZE
   f. LARGE_POOL_SIZE
   g. JAVA_POOL_SIZE
3. The parameters that must be configured manually in Oracle 10*g* are: [Choose 4.]
   a. LOG_BUFFER
   b. SHARED_POOL_SIZE
   c. DB_KEEP_CACHE_SIZE
   d. DB_RECYCLE_CACHE_SIZE
   e. DB_CACHE_SIZE
   f. LARGE_POOL_SIZE
   g. JAVA_POOL_SIZE
   h. DB_2K_CACHE_SIZE [where DB_BLOCK_SIZE=4K]
4. Identify the functions of the Shared Pool. [Choose 2.]
   a. Store modified blocks that need to be written to the datafiles.
   b. Store the SQL text and executions plans of recently executed statements.
   c. Store data dictionary information for logical reads.
   d. Store a sequential record of all statements executed in the database.

5. Identify the function of the Redo Log Buffer.
   a. Store modified blocks that need to be written to the datafiles.
   b. Store the SQL text and executions plans of recently executed statements.
   c. Store data dictionary information for logical reads.
   d. Store a sequential record of all statements executed in the database.
6. Identify the function of the Database Buffer Cache.
   a. Store modified blocks that need to be written to the datafiles.
   b. Used by the Recovery Manager while performing I/O operations.
   c. Store data dictionary information for logical reads.
   d. Store a sequential record of all statements executed in the database.
7. Identify a function of the Large Pool.
   a. Store modified blocks that need to be written to the datafiles.
   b. Used by the Recovery Manager while performing I/O operations.
   c. Store data dictionary information for logical reads.
   d. Store a sequential record of all statements executed in the database.
8. Identify the function of the Streams Pool.
   a. Store modified blocks that need to be written to the datafiles.
   b. Used by the Recovery Manager while performing I/O operations.
   c. Store data dictionary information for logical reads.
   d. Stores the dynamic performance views of the database and other important database information.
   e. Used by the Streams feature that is new in Oracle 10*g*.
9. The ASSM feature can be disabled by setting the SGA_TARGET parameter to 0 (zero). True/False.
10. With regards to Automatic Shared Memory Management, choose the statements that are true. [Choose 3.]
    a. The SGA_TARGET parameter should be set to a non-zero value.
    b. STATISTICS_LEVEL should be set to TYPICAL or ALL.
    c. SGA_TARGET can be greater than SGA_MAX_SIZE.
    d. ASSM can be disabled by setting it to a value of -1.
    e. SGA_TARGET can be set dynamically using the ALTER SYSTEM command.
11. Name the data dictionary view that can be used to display the structure of the SGA.
12. Name the advisor that gives you advice on how to configure the ASSM.

13. Name the processes that are created on the client side and server side when a user connects to the database. [Choose 2.]
    a. Listener process
    b. User Process
    c. Server Process
    d. PGA memory
    e. Background Processes
14. The DBA wishes to enable automatic PGA memory management in the database. Which of the following parameters would need to be set to AUTO?
    a. PGA_MEMORY_MANAGEMENT
    b. PGA_AGGREGATE_TARGET
    c. SGA_TARGET
    d. WORKAREA_SIZE_POLICY
    e. SGA_MAX_SIZE

15. The DBA issues the following command. What is the outcome?

```
ALTER SYSTEM SET PGA_AGGREGATE_TARGET=6M;
```

    a. The total amount of PGA memory consumed by all sessions will be equal to or less than 6 M, at any moment in time.
    b. The command will fail with an error.
    c. The SORT_AREA_SIZE parameter still must be set so that sufficient memory is available for sorting operations.
    d. The SGA_MAX_SIZE must be at least as large as the SGA_TARGET value.
16. John is the database administrator. He issues the following commands:

```
SQL> ALTER SYSTEM SET WORKAREA_SIZE_POLICY=AUTO;
SQL> ALTER SYSTEM SET PGA_AGGREGATE_TARGET = 100M;
```

    Based on the commands he issued, which of the following statements are false?
    a. The value of SORT_AREA_SIZE will be automatically adjusted.
    b. The value of HASH_AREA_SIZE will be automatically adjusted.
    c. The value of BITMAP_MERGE_AREA_SIZE will be automatically adjusted.
    d. The value of SORT_AREA_SIZE must be explicitly set because it is an important parameter.
    e. The value of CREATE_BITMAP_AREA_SIZE will be automatically adjusted.
17. An ideal value for PGA_AGGREGATE_TARGET should result in __________.
    a. One-pass executions most of the time.
    b. Optimal executions most of the time.
    c. Multi-pass executions most of the time.
    d. All the above.
    e. None of the above.

18. You have configured SGA_TARGET to 800 M. The SHARED_POOL_SIZE initialization parameter currently takes a value of 300 M. Which of the following statements is true?
    a. The value of the SHARED_POOL_SIZE will be reset to 0, because ASMM has been enabled.
    b. The value of SHARED_POOL_SIZE will dynamically increase or decrease below 300 M, based on the workload on the database.
    c. The amount of memory allocated to the shared pool will never deviate from 300 M.
    d. The memory allocated to the shared pool may increase above 300 M, but will never shrink below 300 M.
19. John, the administrator wishes to create a tablespace with a non-standard blocksize (8 K). The default oracle block size in the database is 4 K. Which of the following statements are true about the creation of the tablespace?
    a. The DB_4K_CACHE_SIZE initialization parameter must be set.
    b. The DB_KEEP_CACHE_SIZE initialization parameter must be set.
    c. The DB_RECYCLE_CACHE_SIZE initialization parameter must be set.
    d. The DB_8K_CACHE_SIZE initialization parameter must be set.
    e. He need not set any initialization parameters because ASMM has been enabled in the database.
20. Name the area of PGA memory that would be used when performing a sort or a bitmap merge operation.

Hands-On Assignments

Assignment 11-1 Displaying the value of the STATISTICS_LEVEL parameter

1. Start SQL*Plus, and connect as a user with SYSDBA privileges.
2. Display the current value of the STATISTICS_LEVEL initialization parameter.
3. If it is not TYPICAL or ALL, set the value of STATISTICS_LEVEL to TYPICAL.
4. Exit SQL*Plus.

Assignment 11-2 Displaying the values of the auto-tuned initialization parameters

1. Start SQL*Plus, and connect as a user with SYSDBA privileges.
2. View the value of the following initialization parameters.
```
SHARED_POOL_SIZE
LARGE_POOL_SIZE
JAVA_POOL_SIZE
DB_CACHE_SIZE
STREAMS_POOL_SIZE
```
3. Issue the command to set the DB_CACHE_SIZE initialization parameter to 21 M.
4. Display the value of the DB_CACHE_SIZE initialization parameter. What is the size of the granule on your machine?
5. Issue the command to set the SHARED_POOL_SIZE initialization parameter to 40 M.

6. Verify the change. What did ASMM set as the value for the size of the shared pool?
7. Exit SQL*Plus.

Assignment 11-3 Displaying the contents of V$SGA_DYNAMIC COMPONENTS

1. Start SQL*Plus and connect as a user with SYSDBA privileges.
2. Query the COMPONENT, CURRENT_SIZE, USER_SPECIFIED_SIZE columns from the V$SGA_DYNAMIC_COMPONENTS view to see the sizes automatically assigned to the auto-tuned parameters and their values in the initialization parameter file.
3. Exit SQL*Plus.

Assignment 11-4 Displaying and modifying the SGA_MAX_SIZE parameter

1. Start SQL*Plus and connect as a user with SYSDBA privileges.
2. Display the value of the SGA_MAX_SIZE initialization parameter.
3. Modify its value to be 30 M larger than its current size.
4. What do you need to do for the change to come into effect?
5. When the database is restarted, where can you see the new SGA_MAX_SIZE value being displayed?
6. Exit SQL*Plus.

Assignment 11-5 Setting the SGA_TARGET for ASMM

1. Start SQL*Plus and connect as a user with SYSDBA privileges.
2. Issue the command to set the SGA_TARGET to take a value 100 M less than the SGA_MAX_SIZE parameter.
3. Verify the change you made.
4. Exit SQL*Plus.

Assignment 11-6 Viewing the change you made from Enterprise Manager

1. Launch a browser and enter the URL to access the Enterprise Manager. Connect as a user with SYSDBA privileges.
2. Navigate the pages of enterprise manager to access the Memory Advisor.
3. Disable ASMM using the Enterprise Manager.
4. Start SQL*Plus and log in with SYSDBA privileges. Issue the command to see if the ASMM has been disabled.
5. Log out of Enterprise Manager and SQL*Plus.

Assignment 11-7 Displaying information about APMM

1. Start SQL*Plus and connect as a user with SYSDBA privileges.
2. Issue the command to display whether automatic PGA memory management has been enabled.
3. Exit SQL*Plus.

Assignment 11-8 Modifying the PGA_AGGREGATE_TARGET value

1. Start SQL*Plus and connect as a user with SYSDBA privileges.
2. Display the current value of the PGA_AGGREGATE_TARGET parameter.
3. Modify its value to 10 M lower than its current value. If the value you set it to was lower than 10 M, what happened.
4. Set the value of the PGA_AGGREGATE_TARGET to 10 M.
5. Exit SQL*Plus.

Assignment 11-9 Displaying information about executions in the database

1. Start SQL*Plus and connect as a user with SYSDBA privileges.
2. Query an appropriate data dictionary view to display the number of optimal, one-pass, and multi-pass executions that occurred in the database.
3. Issue a query to retrieve the entire DBA_SEGMENTS data dictionary view, and order the output on the OWNER column. Let it complete execution.
4. Query an appropriate data dictionary view to display the number of optimal, one-pass, and multi-pass executions that occurred in the database.
5. Exit SQL*Plus.

Case Study

1. You are the administrator in a mid-sized organization that uses Oracle 10*g*. You notice applications frequently terminate with ORA-4031: out-of-memory errors. Clearly define what steps you would implement to reduce the occurrence of such errors in the database, based on the existing hardware available.
2. Create a chart listing the different memory structures of the Oracle database, their main functions, and the parameters that can be used to configure them. You may also draw a diagram describing the Oracle instance. Clearly label the different structures.

CHAPTER 12

AUTOMATIC STORAGE MANAGEMENT

LEARNING OBJECTIVES

After completing this lesson you should be able to understand:

- The main purpose of using Automatic Storage Management (ASM)
- The architectural components of ASM
- The ASM instance and its commands
- Various commands associated with ASM components
- ASM Filenames
- Redundancy and Rebalancing
- Obtaining information from the data dictionary about ASM
- Using RMAN to migrate your database to ASM

ORACLE CERTIFICATION EXAM OBJECTIVES COVERED IN THIS CHAPTER INCLUDE:

- Set up initialization parameter files for ASM and database instances
- Execute SQL commands with ASM filenames
- Start up and shut down ASM instances
- Administer ASM disk groups
- Use RMAN to migrate your database to ASM

INTRODUCTION

An important function of a DBA is managing the physical storage structures of the Oracle database. The physical storage structures consist of the physical files of the Oracle database. It is important to ensure not just their availability but also their optimal performance. It is not uncommon for administrators to manage databases that have thousands of database files. Another common issue administrators face is that these datafiles are not uniformly utilized, some datafiles may be over utilized and others underutilized, resulting in an uneven use of I/O. Database administrators often find themselves trying to identify the datafiles that are over utilized (commonly known as hot spots) and performing maintenance tasks involving relocating or eliminating such I/O intensive files. This can be a laborious task requiring the database to be taken offline.

As modern databases grow larger in size and user requirements more demanding, it is necessary for DBAs to be equipped with better tools that can help increase their productivity and help automate many menial tasks.

This new feature in Oracle 10*g*, known as Automatic Storage Management (ASM) is another powerful tool made available to help administrators better manage storage than in previous versions of Oracle. It not only simplifies database administration but also reduces the cost of managing storage.

In this chapter you will be introduced to ASM and will appreciate how it helps administrators face many of the challenges associated with storage administration. The ASM architecture and its implementation are discussed in length. The chapter ends with a description of how to migrate an existing database to ASM using Recovery Manager.

THE CURRENT CHALLENGE AT KELLER MEDICAL CENTER

The database administrators at Keller Medical Center have been increasingly concerned about the number of datafiles that have been added to the production databases. Ryan, the administrator has been spending a couple of hours everyday tuning datafiles and monitoring them for I/O problems. Identifying datafiles that perform excessive read and write operations and relocating them has become a frequent task. During the weekly meeting, he expresses his concerns to the senior administrator Anita. Anita has been actively trying to implement all the new features of Oracle 10g, that would make life simpler for her team members. She tells Ryan to look into the Oracle 10g feature called Automatic Storage Management.

SETUP FOR THE CHAPTER

To complete the hands-on exercises in this chapter, you must have at least 4 GB of free disk space available on the machine you are working on.

AN OVERVIEW OF ASM

The introduction of this chapter discussed many of the problems faced by database administrators who directly manage thousands of database files. Before we proceed any further, let us review some of the physical files of the Oracle database. The main files of the Oracle database include:

Datafiles—These files store data. Data can either by system data or user data. Datafiles are created when tablespaces are created in the Oracle database.

Online Redo Log Files—These files contain a record of all changes made to the database. The contents of redo log files may be stored in the form of offline files called Archive log files. Redo log files are used for recovery.

Control Files—These files contain information about the database, such as the database identifier, database name, timestamp of database creation, physical structure of the database, and synchronization information etc. The control file is required to mount a database. It is not possible to access a database without a control file.

Parameter Files—These files contain values necessary to configure various parameters associated with the database. Parameters could be associated with memory structures, archiving, and file locations. Parameter files may be of two kinds, the Initialization Parameter File (*pfile*) or the Server Parameter File (*spfile*). (Refer Appendix A.) Parameter files are required to start the Oracle instance.

Password File—A file containing details of privileged users of the database—users who possess the SYSDBA or SYSOPER roles.

In this chapter we will focus on the datafiles of the Oracle database, which store data. In a typical database, datafiles are added whenever additional space is required by objects and there is no free space left in existing datafiles. A common problem that administrators may face is excessive I/O operations being performed on datafiles that contain frequently accessed objects. Creating and laying out databases in such a way that I/O is spread evenly across all available disks to prevent hot spots, and at the same time maximizing performance is not an easy task. Further, administrators must ensure high availability at a low cost.

The Automatic Storage Management (ASM) feature is a solution to many of the problems faced by administrators when managing storage. It is a vertically integrated file system and volume manager for Oracle database files.

NOTE

Only Oracle files can be managed using ASM.

ASM preserves all existing database functionality and existing file systems, database, and storage can operate as they always have. Some of the features and benefits provided by ASM:

- It simplifies database administration and reduces the cost of managing storage.
- It helps maximize storage utilization, reduces cost and complexity without compromising performance or availability.
- It enables the online reorganization of storage, evenly spreading data across all available storage resources, thereby increasing disk utilization and performance while ensuring high availability.
- It eliminates the need for manually tuning storage devices and moving them around to reduce I/O and contention.
- ASM provides a simple storage management interface that is consistent across all server and storage platforms.
- It eliminates the need for third-party file systems and volume managers to manage Oracle files.
- It provides mirroring options for protection against failure.
- It is accessible by means of SQL*Plus and Enterprise Manager.

The next topic discusses the architectural elements of ASM.

ASM ARCHITECTURE

As already mentioned, ASM is an integrated file system and volume manager for Oracle database files. It is an option or method of managing the files of an Oracle database. The DBA can choose to store data in files managed by ASM. If you wish to use ASM to store data you must understand the different elements that comprise the ASM architecture. In this part of the chapter, you will be introduced to the different elements. In subsequent sections of the chapter, some of the components will be discussed in detail. Before proceeding to understand the ASM components a few basic terms should be explained.

Basic Terminology

- **Striping**—Is a technique for spreading data across multiple disk drives. Striping can be done at an operating system or hardware level to speed up read/write operations on disks. The data to be stored is divided into smaller units and spread across all available disks. Striping can be performed using a number of different methods; a popularly used technique is RAID 0.
- **Mirroring**—Is a technique in which data is written to two or more disks simultaneously. Mirroring results in data redundancy thereby increasing fault tolerance. An example is RAID 1.

NOTE

RAID is an acronym for Redundant Array of Inexpensive Devices. It is a technology commonly used in computing environments to reduce I/O contention and increase fault tolerance.

ASM Components

Diskgroups—Data is stored in physical files that are stored on physical disks. A number of physical disks can be logically grouped together to create a diskgroup. By creating diskgroups ASM needs to manage only a few diskgroups rather than many individual disks. A diskgroup is a pool of disks within which Oracle manages the placement of database files. It is recommended that all disks that are part of a diskgroup have the same capacity and have similar performance characteristics. When data is stored in diskgroups, it is automatically striped across the underlying pool of storage. When a physical file, such as a datafile is created, the file is striped across all the physical disks that are part of the diskgroup. By default, the datafile is written to the disks in 1 M units, known as extents.

In Figure 12-1, the physical disks called DISK1, DISK2, and DISK3 are collectively treated by ASM as a single DISKGROUP called DATA. Disks can be added and removed from diskgroups by means of simple commands. Oracle recommends the creation of two diskgroups only, one to store data and the other to store backup and recovery data (the destination of the flash recovery area). Traditionally, a datafile such as the one displayed in Figure 12-1 as F1 of size 3 M in DISK1 would reside entirely on a single physical disk. However if it were created using ASM, the datafile would be striped across all the available physical disks in as such a way that the 1st 1 M would be stored on the first disk, the 2nd 1 M on the second disk, and the 3rd 1 M on the third disk. Every 1 M of data stored is referred to as an extent.

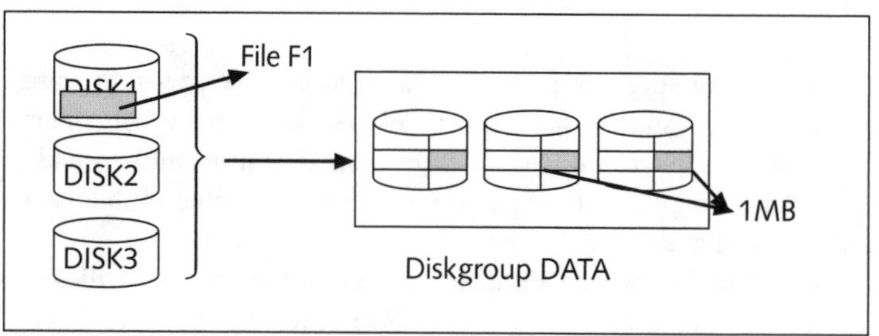

FIGURE 12-1 A diskgroup is a logical collection of disks.

Diskgroups may be mirrored for higher availability of data. With diskgroup mirroring, data is duplicated in two or three locations. The mirroring options can be NONE (mirroring is not done), NORMAL (two way in which case every file extent is stored in two locations of the diskgroup), or HIGH (three way in which case every file extent is stored in three locations of the diskgroup).

NOTE

Multiple databases may store their datafiles within a single diskgroup.

Disks—Disks are the physical devices on which data can be stored. Disk devices can be hard disks, storage arrays, or network storage devices such as SAN or NAS devices. Before a device can be added to a diskgroup, it must be recognized by the operating system. However, it is not necessary to create logical volumes on these devices using a volume manager or to create a filesystem on them. Every disk of a diskgroup is assigned a unique number. Data is evenly distributed across all disks and administrators will never face a situation of identifying and tuning hot spots. Disks may be added to an existing diskgroup by means of a simple command. A disk can only belong to a single diskgroup. However, a disk that is already a member of a diskgroup may be forced to belong to another diskgroup by using the FORCE option. When a new disk is added, the extents of the diskgroup are automatically redistributed. This action is known as **rebalancing**.

ASM Files—ASM files are physical files of the database, namely datafiles, redo log files, archive log files, or control files. When these files are created, their location is specified in terms of a diskgroup rather than a hierarchical directory path. Oracle provides two methods of managing physical files. They are User-Managed File Management (UMF) and Oracle Managed File Management (OMF). When using the UMF method it is necessary to specify the name of the ASM diskgroup and the location of the file, during file creation. The ASM file will have a name that begins with a (+) symbol. However, Oracle recommends the use of OMF, because files are better managed that way. When using OMF, the DB_CREATE_FILE_DEST parameter should be set to the diskgroup name.

Table 12-1 demonstrates the difference between creating a datafile using the UMF and OMF methods. The tablespace called MYTAB is being created. You should be aware that when a tablespace is created, a datafile is associated with it.

TABLE 12-1 File Management types available in Oracle

Method	Description	Example
User Managed File	The location of the datafile and its size are specified. The file will be created in the DATAGRP diskgroup, with a size 300 M.	`CREATE TABLESPACE MYTAB DATAFILE '+DATAGRP' SIZE 300M;`
Oracle Managed File	The location of the datafile need not be specified. The file will be created in the location specified by the DB_CREATE_FILE_DEST initialization parameters. The size of the file will default to 100 M.	`CREATE TABLESPACE MYTAB;`

A detailed description of ASM filenames is provided later in this chapter.

An ASM file by default is striped across all the disks of a diskgroup, in the form of an allocation unit (AU) known as an extent.

ASM Instance—Is an instance that is similar to the Oracle database instance, but performs a specialized function of mounting and managing diskgroups. If you wish to implement ASM for managing data storage, it is necessary to create the ASM instance independent of the Oracle database instance. The ASM instance is called **+ASM** and is responsible for keeping track of what disks are in the diskgroups. It also contains metadata about the files that resides in the diskgroup and is dedicated to managing disk/diskgroup activity. A database instance is a client of the ASM instance. On a single node, multiple databases may access a single ASM instance. For a database that manages storage using ASM, the ASM instance must be started. Upon starting the ASM instance any diskgroups recognized by it are mounted. The ASM instance is referenced only when certain actions, such as startup/shutdown, addition or removal or disks, and rebalance operations are performed. An ASM instance is started using an initialization parameter file called "**init+ASM.ora**." Table 12-2 lists some of the important initialization parameters associated with the ASM instance.

TABLE 12-2 Initialization Parameters of the ASM instance

Initialization Parameter	Description
`INSTANCE_TYPE`	Refers to the type of instance. In an ASM instance the value is ASM, in a database instance the value is RDBMS.
`DB_UNIQUE_NAME`	Specifies the name of the ASM instance. The ASM instance name is +ASM.
`ASM_DISKGROUPS`	A comma-separated list of diskgroups that must be mounted when the ASM instance is started.
`ASM_DISKSTRING`	Specifies the location where ASM can find all the physical disks that are part of the diskgroup.
`LARGE_POOL_SIZE`	The memory structure that stores extent-related information in memory.

TABLE 12-2 Initialization Parameters of the ASM instance (continued)

Initialization Parameter	Description
ASM_POWER_LIMIT	A parameter that determines the speed at which rebalancing operations will be performed. The parameter can take a value 0 through 11. A value of 11 indicates the rebalance must be performed at the fastest speed, making use of all system resources required for completion. A speed of 1 indicates the rebalance has a lower priority and a value 0 disables rebalancing.

In addition to the usual background processes such as PMON, SMON, DBW0, LGWR, and CKPT, the ASM instance has some specialized background processes. They include:

RBAL—A background process that is responsible for coordinating rebalance activity for diskgroups.

ARBn—A background process that is responsible for performing data extent movements, where n = 0, 1, 2, etc.

Figure 12-2 displays how the components of the ASM interact with one another. The ASM instance mounts the diskgroup that contains the datafiles of the database. The database instance is used to mount and open the database for users. The database instance is a client of the ASM instance on a given node. The diskgroup consists of three disks, called D1, D2, and D3. These disks are striped with extents that are 1 M in size.

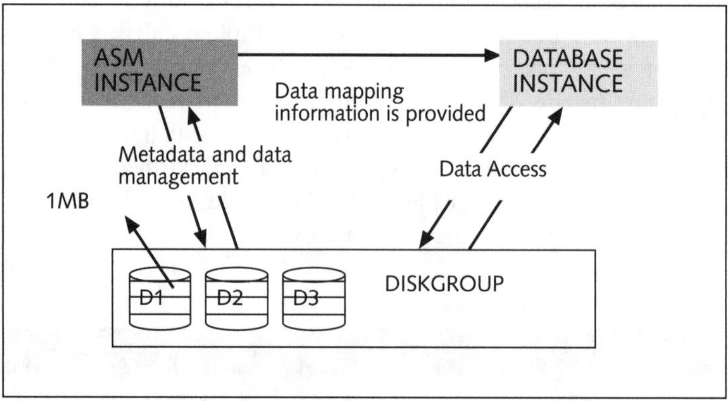

FIGURE 12-2 Interaction between the database instance, ASM instance, and diskgroups.

Practice 1: Creating an ASM Instance and ASM database

This practice example demonstrates the creation of a database that uses ASM for its data storage. You must have at least a minimum of 3 GB of disk space on you machine, for the successful completion of this task.

In the first part of the practice, you will create files that simulate disks. You will not need additional hard disks or unpartitioned space on the hard disk to understand how ASM works. An Oracle-supplied tool known as the **asmtool** is used to initialize drive headers and mark drives for use by ASM. In this task we use asmtool to create files that will represent disks. The files will be initialized for ASM, but will not contain any data in them. You will then learn how to create an ASM instance followed by the creation of the database.

Part 1: Creating files that simulate ASM disks.

1. From the operating system, open a command prompt window.

```
Start -> All Programs -> Accessories -> Command Prompt
```

2. From the command prompt, issue a command to create a directory called AD. The code below displays the MD command to create a directory called AD.

```
C:\>MD C:\AD
```

3. Next, invoke the ASMTOOL tool to create two files called DISK1 and DISK2 in the directory AD, each with a size of 1250 M. Space from them will be utilized in 1 M allocation units when the physical files of the database are created. The creation of each file may take several minutes.

NOTE

This method of creating files/disks has been displayed only as a means to help you understand how to work with ASM and familiarize you with the ASM feature. This is not a substitute method of allocating and configuring physical disks for use with ASM.


```
C:\>ASMTOOL -CREATE C:\AD\DISK1 1250
C:\>ASMTOOL -CREATE C:\AD\DISK2 1250
```

4. From the operating system, navigate to the C:\AD folder to verify if the two files were created.

Part 2: Creating the ASM instance

5. Open a text editor like NOTEPAD, and create a file called **init+ASM.ora**. The file should be saved in the %ORACLE_HOME%\DATABASE directory. The _ASM_ALLOW_ONLY_RAW_DISKS parameter is necessary in this initialization parameter file, so that a diskgroup can be created using the files that we have created in step 3. Remember, we are using files instead of physical disks. If you do not specify this, an error will be generated, indicating an invalid file type was specified. Type the following lines into the file.

```
INSTANCE_TYPE=ASM
DB_UNIQUE_NAME= +ASM
_ASM_ALLOW_ONLY_RAW_DISKS=FALSE
ASM_DISKSTRING='C:\AD\*'
LARGE_POOL_SIZE=8M
```

6. Because this example is being presented on a Windows platform, the instance creation requires the creation of a new Oracle service. This can be done using the **ORADIM** tool. Open a command prompt window, and type in the following ORADIM command to create a new ASM instance called +ASM that will automatically be started when the operating system is started.

```
Start -> All Programs -> Accessories -> Command Prompt
C:\>ORADIM -NEW -ASMSID +ASM -STARTMODE AUTO
```

7. Next, set the ORACLE_SID to +ASM. This is done so that you will be able to connect to the ASM instance.

```
C:\> SET ORACLE_SID=+ASM
```

8. Execute the ORAPWD utility to create the password file for the +ASM database. (Refer to Appendix A for more information about the password file.) In this example, the password of the SYS user is being set to "ORACLE" and 10 users of the database may be assigned the SYSDBA role.

```
C:\> ORAPWD FILE=C:\ORACLE\PRODUCT\10.2.0\DB_1\DATABASE\PWD+asm.
ora PASSWORD=ORACLE ENTRIES=10
```

9. Invoke SQL*Plus, from the command prompt and log in as a user with SYSDBA privileges. Note the password of the SYS user is ORACLE.

```
C:\>SQLPLUS SYS/ORACLE AS SYSDBA
```

10. Issue a STARTUP command. Notice that after the instance has started a message is displayed indicating that no diskgroups were mounted. That is because diskgroups have not yet been created. (See Figure 12-3.) When executing the STARTUP command if you see the error displayed in Figure 12-4 then, perform the steps displayed in the following note.


```
SQL> STARTUP
```

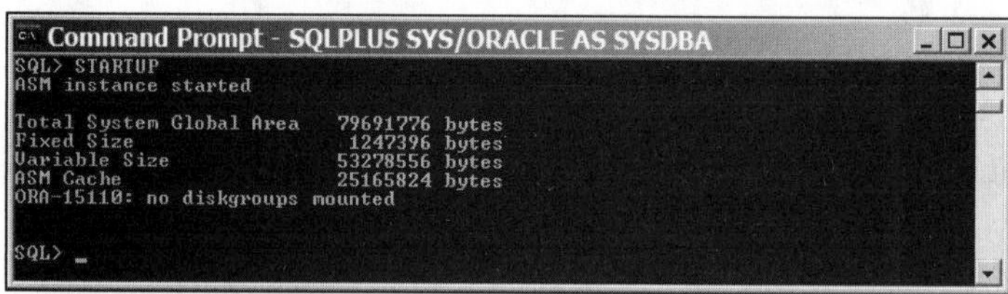

FIGURE 12-3 Starting up the ASM instance

FIGURE 12-4 Error that may be displayed when trying to start up the ASM instance

NOTE

If you received the error displayed in Figure 12-4, then the Oracle Cluster Synchronization Service has not been configured and started. To do so, open a command prompt window and type in the following line. In the command, the portion of the command formatted *bold* is the ORACLE_HOME directory. (See Figure 12-5.)

C:\> **C:\ORACLE\PRODUCT\10.2.0\db_1**\bin\localconfig add

At this point, repeat step 10 from the SQL prompt. You must see an output similar to Figure 12-3.

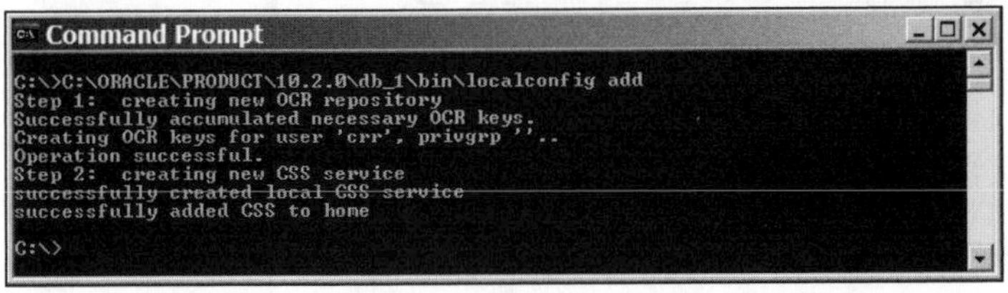

```
Command Prompt
C:\>C:\ORACLE\PRODUCT\10.2.0\db_1\bin\localconfig add
Step 1:  creating new OCR repository
Successfully accumulated necessary OCR keys.
Creating OCR keys for user 'crr', privgrp ''..
Operation successful.
Step 2:  creating new CSS service
successfully created local CSS service
successfully added CSS to home

C:\>
```

FIGURE 12-5 Configuring the Oracle Cluster Synchronization service

11. In the next step, you will issue the CREATE DISKGROUP command to create a diskgroup. The name of the diskgroup is DATAGRP. The diskgroup will consist of the 2 disks (in this example they are files) that you created in step 3 of this practice. Note: The complete syntax of the diskgroup commands will be discussed in the section "Managing diskgroups" of this chapter. After executing the command a message 'Diskgroup Created' will be displayed.

    ```
    SQL> CREATE DISKGROUP DATAGRP DISK 'C:\AD\DISK1','C:\AD\DISK2';
    ```

12. Next, create a server parameter file (*spfile*) using the existing parameter file. This step creates a spfile using the init+ASM.ora file created in step 5.

    ```
    SQL> CREATE SPFILE FROM PFILE;
    ```

13. Bounce the database, so that the SPFILE is used during startup.

    ```
    SQL> SHUTDOWN
    SQL> STARTUP
    ```

14. In the next step, you will set the ASM_DISKGROUPS initialization parameter to DATAGRP. The parameter will be written to the spfile so that the ASM instance will automatically mount the DATAGRP diskgroup when it is started.

    ```
    SQL> ALTER SYSTEM SET ASM_DISKGROUPS=DATAGRP SCOPE=SPFILE;
    ```

15. Shut down and restart the ASM instance. Notice, when it is started, the DATAGRP will be automatically mounted. (See Figure 12-6.)

```
SQL> SHUTDOWN
SQL> STARTUP
```

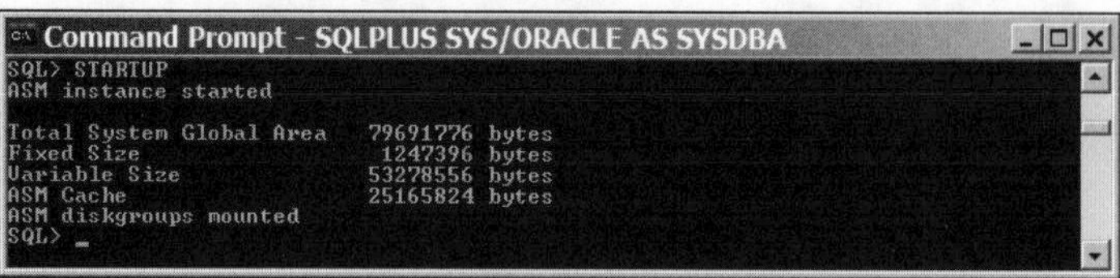

FIGURE 12-6 Starting up the ASM instance, the diskgroups are mounted.

16. Exit SQL*Plus.

Part 3: Creating an ASM database that will use the DATAGRP diskgroup to store its files.

In this part of the practice example you will create a new database called ASMDB. This database will use ASM for its storage. The database will be created using the Database Configuration Assistant utility. This utility is a graphical interactive interface that can be used to create, delete, or reconfigure databases.

17. Open a command prompt, if one isn't already open and type DBCA.

```
C:\> DBCA
```

18. The **Database Configuration Assistant: Welcome** screen is displayed. Select **Next**.
19. The next page displays a list of operations you can perform. Select **Create a Database**. Select **Next**.
20. This screen displays a number of template options to choose from. Select **General Purpose**. Select **Next**.
21. This screen prompts you for the Global Database Name and System Identifier (SID). Type **ASMDB** for both prompts. Select **Next**. (See Figure 12-7.)

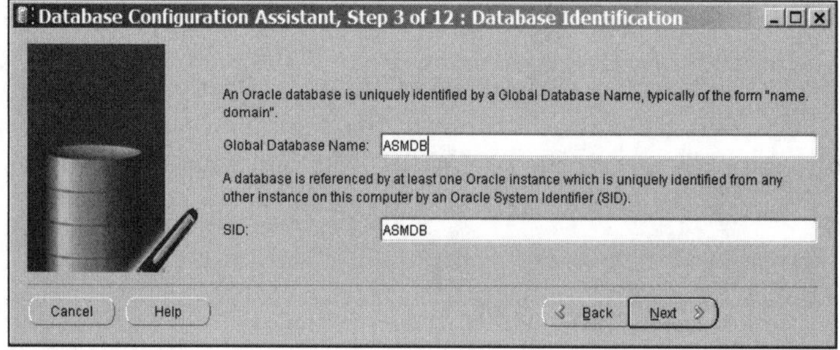

FIGURE 12-7 Specifying the database and SID name

22. This next screen displays options regarding how the database would need to be managed. Check the option **Configure the Database with Enterprise Manager** and select the option **Use Database Control for Database Management**. All other options may be unchecked. Select **Next**.
23. This screen prompts you for passwords. Select the option **Use the Same Password for All Accounts.** Type in a password and confirm it. Make sure you remember the password. Select **Next**.
24. This screen displays options for storage. This is where the ASM option becomes available. Select the second option on the screen **Automatic Storage Management (ASM)**. Select **Next**.
25. A dialog box prompting you for the SYS password specific to ASM will be displayed. Enter a password. In the example the word *ORACLE* was typed because that was the password assigned to the SYS user in the password file in Step 8. (See Figure 12-8.) Select the **OK** button.

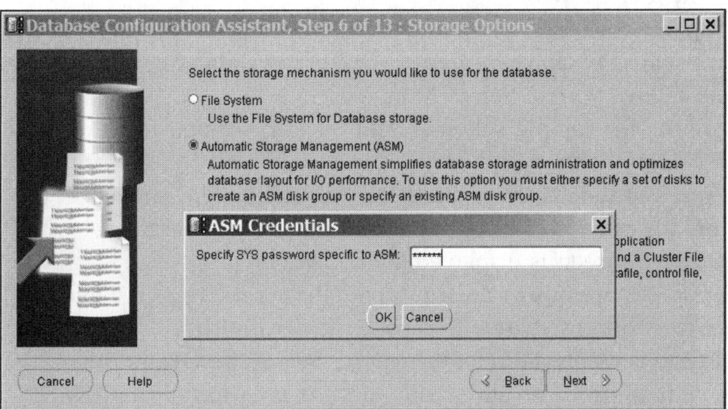

FIGURE 12-8 Selecting the ASM option

26. The ASM diskgroups page will be displayed. This screen prompts you for one or more diskgroups that can be used as storage for the database. Because we have already created the diskgroup DATAGRP and it has been mounted by the ASM instance, you will see the name DATAGRP displayed as one of your choices. Select the **Checkbox** against the DATAGRP diskgroup. (See Figure 12-9.) Select **Next**.

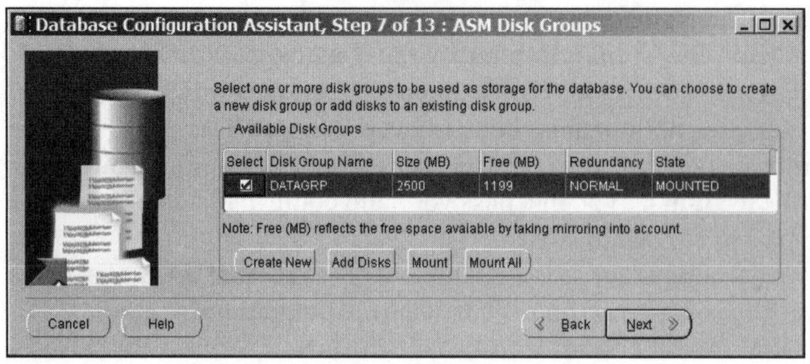

FIGURE 12-9 Selecting the diskgroup DATAGRP

27. This screen, prompts you for the locations that the database files will be created in. Select the option, **Use Oracle-Managed Files**, and the data area should display +DATAGRP. Select **Next**.
28. This screen, displays recovery options. Deselect the option **Specify Flash Recovery Area.** Because we have limited space for this database, it is best not to specify a flash recovery area. Select **Next**.
29. This screen prompts for sample schemas and custom scripts. Don't select anything. Click **Next**.
30. This screen displays initialization parameters. Select **Custom**, and select the option **Automatic for Shared Memory Management**. Select **Next**.
31. The Database Storage screen is displayed. Select **Next**.
32. The next page displays options to create the database or save as a database template. Select the option **Create a Database**. Select **Finish**.
33. A confirmation page is displayed. Read the page. Select the **OK** button.
34. The Database Configuration Assistant will start the creation of the ASMDB database. Wait for it to complete successfully.
35. A completion page will be displayed, presenting some important information about the newly created database. Note the information for future reference. Select the **Exit** Button.
36. At this point you have successfully created a database that will use ASM for data storage. Exit all open windows.

In this section of the chapter, we discussed the purpose, benefits, and architectural elements of ASM. You also learned how to create diskgroups and create a database that will use ASM as the method for storing data. The next section discusses concepts and administrative operations associated with the architectural components of ASM.

ADMINISTERING ASM

Starting and Shutting Down the ASM Instance

For a database that uses ASM for managing data storage, the database instance must be a client of the ASM instance (+ASM) on that node. The ASM instance should be started independent of the database instance on the node. During startup, the ASM instance is created in memory with its memory structures and background processes. Any diskgroups known to the ASM instance are mounted during startup. As already mentioned, diskgroups contain the files of one or more databases. The database instance can then be started using a usual startup command. The database instance will be created, the database mounted and opened. During the open stage of the database the ASM instance will be referenced to make all physical files of the database available.

The STARTUP command is used to open an ASM instance. The syntax of the command is displayed:

```
STARTUP [NOMOUNT|MOUNT|RESTRICT]
```


where:

`NOMOUNT`: only the ASM instance is started. The diskgroups need to be mounted explicitly.

`MOUNT`: the instance is started and diskgroups mounted.

`RESTRICT`: the instance is started; the diskgroups will be mounted; however, databases that are ASM enabled will not be permitted to connect to the ASM instance.

The SHUTDOWN command is used to shut down an ASM instance. The options for SHUTDOWN are similar to those issued on a database. You can shut down the ASM instance using the NORMAL, IMMEDIATE, TRANSACTIONAL, and ABORT options.

In Oracle 10*g* Release 2, if the first three options are used and any client databases are still open, an error will be generated (See Figure 12-10) and the ASM instance will continue running. You will first have to shut down the database and then shut down the ASM instance.

In Oracle 10*g* Release 1, when a shut down using the options NORMAL, IMMEDIATE, or TRANSACTIONAL is used, the command is first automatically propagated to the databases and then the ASM instance is shut down. For example, if you issue a SHUTDOWN IMMEDIATE command for the ASM instance, an immediate shut down will be first performed on all connected databases and then the ASM instance will be shut down.

If you issue a SHUTDOWN ABORT, the ASM will be aborted, causing all database instances connected to it to abort. Instance recovery will be performed on the database instances during the next startup.

Practice 2: Starting and shutting down an ASM instance

This practice example demonstrates starting and shutting down of the ASM instance.

1. Open a command prompt. We shall refer to this window in the example as *CP1*.

   ```
   Start -> All Programs -> Accessories -> Command Prompt
   ```

2. Set the ORACLE_SID to +ASM. This ensures that the command that you issue from SQL*Plus will be performed on the ASM instance.

```
C:\> SET ORACLE_SID=+ASM
```

3. From the command prompt, start SQL*Plus and connect as the SYS user with SYSDBA privileges. If you are continuing from the previous practice example it is likely that the ASM instance is already started. Issue the command to shut down the ASM instance in the IMMEDIATE mode. (See Figure 12-10.) If you receive an error similar to the one displayed by Figure 12-11, see the note below.

```
C:\> SQLPLUS SYS/ORACLE AS SYSDBA
SQL> SHUTDOWN IMMEDIATE;
```

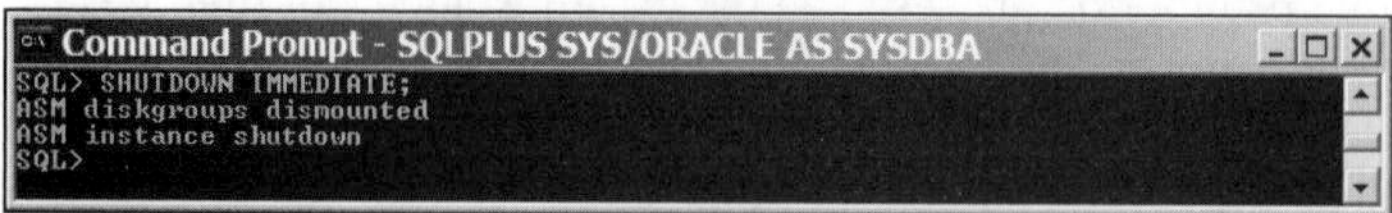

FIGURE 12-10 Shutting down the ASM instance

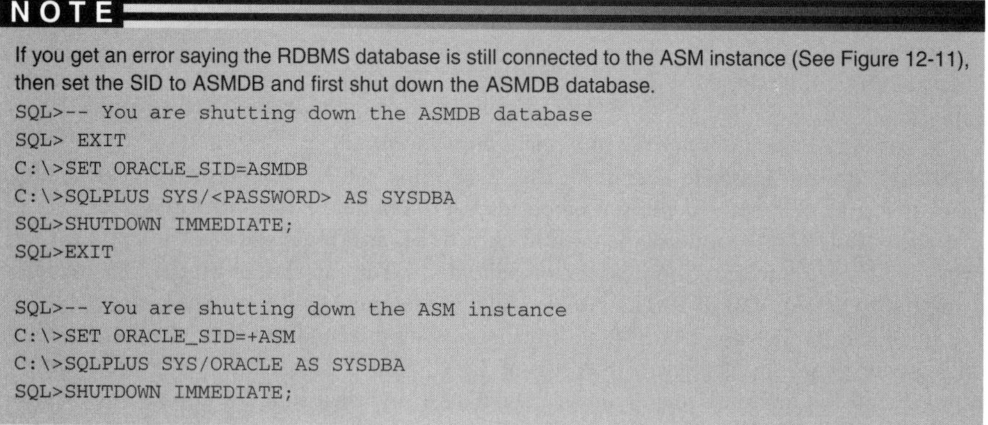

NOTE

If you get an error saying the RDBMS database is still connected to the ASM instance (See Figure 12-11), then set the SID to ASMDB and first shut down the ASMDB database.

```
SQL>-- You are shutting down the ASMDB database
SQL> EXIT
C:\>SET ORACLE_SID=ASMDB
C:\>SQLPLUS SYS/<PASSWORD> AS SYSDBA
SQL>SHUTDOWN IMMEDIATE;
SQL>EXIT

SQL>-- You are shutting down the ASM instance
C:\>SET ORACLE_SID=+ASM
C:\>SQLPLUS SYS/ORACLE AS SYSDBA
SQL>SHUTDOWN IMMEDIATE;
```

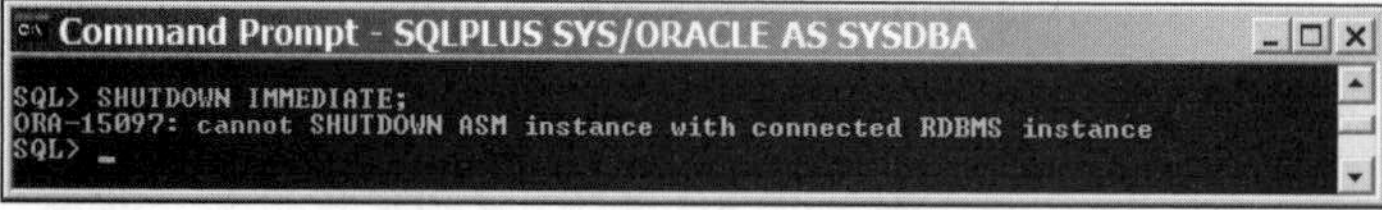

FIGURE 12-11 Shutting down the ASM instance

4. Next, start the ASM instance in the NOMOUNT mode. Notice that the diskgroups will not be mounted.

```
SQL> STARTUP NOMOUNT
```

5. Issue the ALTER DISKGROUP... MOUNT command to mount the diskgroup called DATAGRP.

```
SQL> ALTER DISKGROUP DATAGRP MOUNT;
```

6. Open another command prompt, and set the ORACLE_SID to be ASMDB. We refer to this window as *CP2*.

```
Start -> All Programs -> Accessories -> Command Prompt
C:\>SET ORACLE_SID=ASMDB
```

7. Invoke SQL*Plus connect as a SYSDBA and issue the STARTUP command to start the ASMDB database. Notice that in this startup, the database instance is created, the database mounted and then opened.

```
C:\> SQLPLUS SYS/<password> AS SYSDBA
SQL> STARTUP
```

8. Return to *CP1*. The V$ASM_CLIENT dynamic view can be queried to display the names of all databases that are clients to the ASM instance. Type the following SELECT statement on the view to see all the client database instances. (See Figure 12-12.)

```
SQL> SELECT * FROM V$ASM_CLIENT;
```

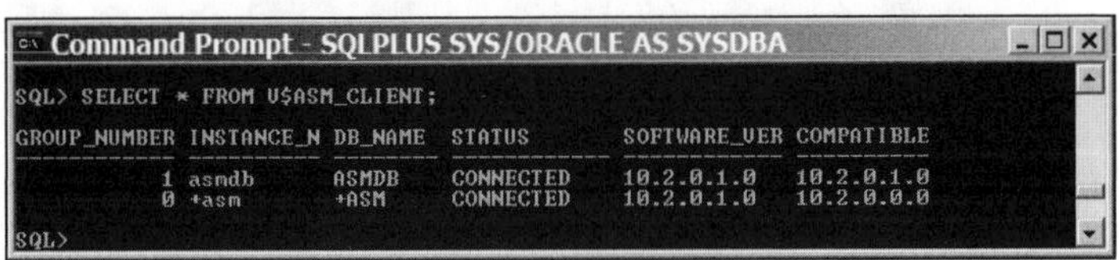

```
SQL> SELECT * FROM V$ASM_CLIENT;

GROUP_NUMBER INSTANCE_N DB_NAME  STATUS       SOFTWARE_VER COMPATIBLE
------------ ---------- -------- ------------ ------------ ------------
           1 asmdb      ASMDB    CONNECTED    10.2.0.1.0   10.2.0.1.0
           0 +asm       +ASM     CONNECTED    10.2.0.1.0   10.2.0.0.0

SQL>
```


FIGURE 12-12 The output of V$ASM_CLIENT

9. From *CP1*, issue a command to shut down the ASM instance using the IMMEDIATE option. Notice you get an error that the ASM instance is connected to an RDBMS instance. (See Figure 12-13.)

```
SQL> SHUTDOWN IMMEDIATE;
```

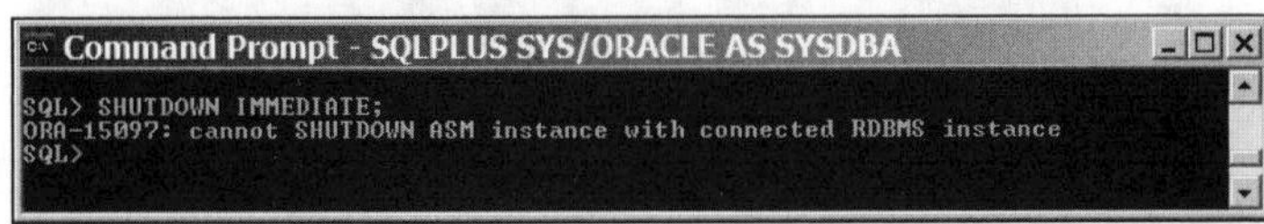

```
SQL> SHUTDOWN IMMEDIATE;
ORA-15097: cannot SHUTDOWN ASM instance with connected RDBMS instance
SQL>
```


FIGURE 12-13 The error displayed if the ASM instance is connected to the RDBMS instance

10. Exit all open windows.

ASM Filenames

When a physical file such as a datafile, control file, or redo log file is created in an Oracle 10g database using ASM, the file is automatically assigned a name. ASM filenames can take several forms that include:

- Fully Qualified
- Numeric
- Alias
- Alias with Template
- Incomplete
- Incomplete with template

The appropriate format depends on the context with which the filename is used. (See Table 12-3.) The contexts include: Referencing an existing file, a single file creation, and multiple file creation.

TABLE 12-3 File Naming methods and their usage

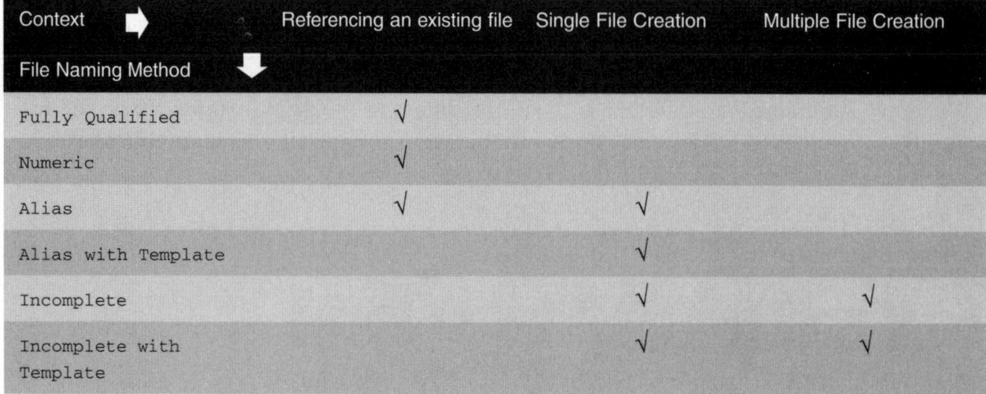

Context ➡ / File Naming Method ⬇	Referencing an existing file	Single File Creation	Multiple File Creation
`Fully Qualified`	√		
`Numeric`	√		
`Alias`	√	√	
`Alias with Template`		√	
`Incomplete`		√	√
`Incomplete with Template`		√	√

Before going any further it is important to understand the different file types that are available in the Oracle 10*g* database. Table 12-4 displays a partial listing of some Oracle file types and other relevant information about these file types. We will discuss the columns of this table as we learn more about file naming.

TABLE 12-4 The different Oracle file type recognized by the ASM database

Oracle File Type	File Type specification in filename	Tag	Default Template
Control file	controlfile	cf (control file)bcf (backup control file)	CONTROLFILE
Data files	datafile	tablespace name.file#	DATAFILE
Online redo logs	online_log	log_thread#	ONLINELOG
Archive logs	archive_log	Parameter	ARCHIVELOG
Temp files	temp	tablespace name.file#	TEMPFILE
Initialization parameters	init	spfile	PARAMETERFILE
RMAN datafile/incremental/archive log backup piece	backupset	Client-specified	BACKUPSET
Flashback logs	rlog	thread#_log#	FLASHBACK
Change tracking bitmap	ctb	bitmap	CHANGETRACKING

Fully qualified

This method of file naming is used when referencing existing ASM files. A fully qualified name is automatically assigned for every ASM file when it is created. Because these names are automatically assigned, the method should not be used when creating the file. A fully qualified name takes the following form:

```
+<diskgroup>/<dbname>/<filetype>/<tag>.<file#>.<incarnation#>
```

where:

+<diskgroup>: is the diskgroup name

<dbname>: is the database name

<filetype>: is the type of file. Valid values include those specified in the second column of Table 12-4.

<tag>: a name providing specific information about the file, such as the tablespace name for a datafile.

<file#>.<incarnation#>: a pair of numbers separated by a dot (.) that is unique to every file.

An example of a fully qualified filename of a datafile created in the INDX tablespace may be:

```
+DATAGRP/ASMDB/datafile/indx.262.581086909
```

Numeric ASM Filenames

This method is used when referencing existing ASM files. This file-naming method is derived from the fully qualified name and consists of the diskgroup name, the file number, and incarnation number. Because the file# and incarnation# are automatically assigned, the method should not be used when creating the file. A numeric ASM filename takes the form:

```
+<diskgroup>.<file#>.<incarnation#>
```

An example of a numeric ASM filename is:

```
+DATAGRP.262.581086909
```

Alias ASM Filename

This method may be used when creating a new ASM file or referencing an existing file. An alias filename uses a hierarchical directory structure format similar to a path you would specify for a file on a file system. An alias name consists of a disk group name and a user-defined string. An alias filename differs from the fully qualified and numeric naming methods in that the name does not end with the dotted pair of numbers.

An alias ASM filename takes the form:

```
+<diskgroup>/directory/filename
```

Rather than reference a file by its full or numeric name, which can be difficult to remember, you can provide an alias name for the file during or after creation.

Consider a file whose fully qualified name is: +DATAGRP/ASMDB/datafile/indx.262.581086909. To create an alias ASM filename for this file, you must first create a hierarchical directory path for the diskgroup DATAGRP in the following manner:

```
ALTER DISKGROUP DATAGRP ADD DIRECTORY '+datagrp/dbfiles/'
```

Once the directory path for the diskgroup has been created, an alias for the filename can be created as:

```
ALTER DISKGROUP DATAGRP
ADD ALIAS '+datagrp/dbfiles/indx01.dbf'
FOR '+DATAGRP/ASMDB/datafile/indx.262.581086909';
```

The file can be referenced using the name +datagrp/dbfiles/indx01.dbf rather than its fully qualified name. This is the kind of filename that most users are accustomed to.

It should be noted that files that have been given alias names will not be treated as OMF files, and will not be dropped automatically when the tablespace is dropped. The file can be manually dropped after the tablespace is dropped using a command like:

```
ALTER DISKGROUP DATAGRP DROP FILE '+datagrp/dbfiles/indx01.dbf';
```


Alias ASM Filenames with Templates

This method is used only when new ASM files are being created. A template is a named collection of attributes that can be automatically applied to files during their creation. The Oracle 10*g* database comes with pre-defined templates for different file types. These templates determine some of the attributes of the file. For example, the pre-defined template for redo log files, results in striping log files in 128 K chunks rather than in 1 M pieces that is normally done for files such as datafiles or archivelog files (See Table 12-5). When creating a new file you may specify what template may be applied to that file and also provide an alias name. A list of the different default templates available are displayed in the last column of the Table 12-5. Filenames created using this format take the form:

```
+<diskgroup>(template)/aliasfilename
```

If you are creating a datafile that must possess attributes of the default template DATAFILE, with an alias of indx02.dbf, you would specify the name as:

```
+DATAGRP(datafile)/indx02.dbf
```

Table 12-5 describes some of the mirroring attributes in the default templates of common file types of the Oracle 10*g* database.

TABLE 12-5 Some default templates available in an Oracle 10*g* database

Template Name	Number of mirrors for External Redundancy	Number of mirrors for Normal Redundancy	Number of mirrors for High Redundancy	Granularity
controlfile	0	2	3	Fine (128K)
datafile	0	2	3	Coarse (1M)
onlinelog	0	2	3	Fine (128K)
archivelog	0	2	3	Coarse (1M)

Incomplete ASM Filenames

This method is used when one or more files are being created. The filename takes the form:

```
<+diskgroup>
```

An example of an incomplete ASM filename is: `+DATAGRP`

The file will be created with a fully qualified name that can be viewed using the V$DATAFILE dynamic view.

Incomplete ASM Filenames with Templates

This method is used when one or more files are being created. The name of the template whose attributes must be taken by the file is specified along with the diskgroup name. The filename takes the form:

```
<+diskgroup>(template)
```

An example of an incomplete ASM filename with a *datafile* template is: `+DATAGRP(datafile)`

Practice 3: ASM File naming

This practice example demonstrates how filenames can be specified using some of the above-mentioned methods. Please complete Practice 1 before attempting this task.

1. Open a command prompt, set the ORACLE_SID for the ASM instance and start up the ASM instance, in case it is shut down. This command prompt window will be referred to as *CP1*.

   ```
   Start -> All Programs -> Accessories -> Command Prompt
   C:\> SET ORACLE_SID=+ASM
   C:\> SQLPLUS SYS/ORACLE AS SYSDBA
   SQL> STARTUP
   ```

2. Open a second command prompt window and start up the ASMDB database, in case it is shut down. This command prompt window will be referred to as *CP2*.

   ```
   Start -> All Programs -> Accessories -> Command Prompt
   C:\> SET ORACLE_SID=ASMDB
   C:\> SQLPLUS SYS/<PASSWORD> AS SYSDBA
   SQL> STARTUP
   ```

3. From the *CP2* window, create a new datafile belonging to the USERS tablespace using the incomplete filename method in the diskgroup DATAGRP. If the USERS tablespace does not exist on your machine please choose an alternate tablespace or ask your instructor.

   ```
   SQL> ALTER TABLESPACE USERS ADD DATAFILE '+DATAGRP';
   ```

4. From the *CP2* window, issue a query on NAME column of the V$DATAFILE view to display the names of the datafiles of the database. Notice the filenames are displayed with fully qualified names. In Figure 12-14, notice there are two datafiles belonging to the USERS tablespace.

   ```
   SQL> SELECT NAME FROM V$DATAFILE;
   ```

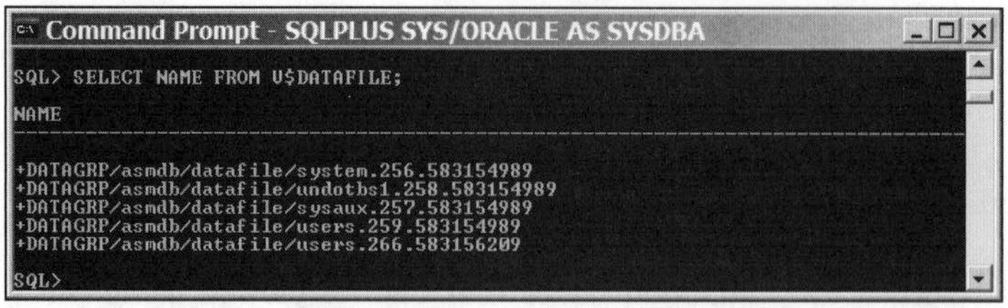

```
Command Prompt - SQLPLUS SYS/ORACLE AS SYSDBA
SQL> SELECT NAME FROM V$DATAFILE;

NAME
--------------------------------------------------------------------------------
+DATAGRP/asmdb/datafile/system.256.583154989
+DATAGRP/asmdb/datafile/undotbs1.258.583154989
+DATAGRP/asmdb/datafile/sysaux.257.583154989
+DATAGRP/asmdb/datafile/users.259.583154989
+DATAGRP/asmdb/datafile/users.266.583156209

SQL>
```

FIGURE 12-14 All datafiles have been created in the +DATAGRP diskgroup

5. Note the fully qualified name generated for the new datafile. In this example it is `+DATAGRP/asmdb/datafile/users.266.583156209`
6. Open the *CP1* window, where the ASM instance was started, and issue an ALTER DISKGROUP command to create a hierarchical directory path for the DATAGRP diskgroup as '+DATAGRP/ASMDBFILES'.

```
SQL> ALTER DISKGROUP DATAGRP
     ADD DIRECTORY '+DATAGRP/ASMDBFILES/';
```


7. From the *CP1* window, issue the command to generate an alias filename for the file called +DATAGRP/asmdb/datafile/users.266.583156209 as +DATAGRP/ASMDBFILES/users02.dbf.

```
SQL> ALTER DISKGROUP DATAGRP
     ADD ALIAS '+DATAGRP/ASMDBFILES/users02.dbf'
     FOR '+DATAGRP/asmdb/datafile/users.266.583156209';
```

8. Exit all SQL*Plus windows.

Managing ASM Diskgroups

The concept of a diskgroup was introduced earlier in this chapter. Before you learn how to create and manage ASM diskgroups, it is important that you understand the following terms:

Failure Groups—A failure group is a subset of a diskgroup or a collection of disks that can become unavailable due to the failure of one of its associated components. On a computer, very often you may have only one single I/O controller managing I/O operations for multiple disks. In case of failure of the I/O controller, all its associated disks become inaccessible. The physical disks connected to the I/O controller together form a failure group.

Rebalancing—Rebalancing is an interesting feature of the ASM feature. It is done automatically when new disks are added or existing disks are removed from a disk group. One of the main advantages of using ASM is the fact that administrators no longer have to identify disks that have too many read/write operations being performed on them. As a result of striping, every single disk of the diskgroup contains an equal number of extents. When a new disk is added or an existing disk is removed, rebalancing is automatically done, resulting in some of the extents being moved around so that all disks of the diskgroup once again have an even distribution of extents. Rebalancing is an I/O intensive operation and should be done during off-peak hours. When rebalancing you may specify a numeric value for the ASM_POWER_LIMIT initialization parameter to establish the speed at which rebalancing should be done. The values range from 0 through 11. A value of zero disables rebalancing. A value of 11 indicates rebalancing should be done at the fastest speed possible, whereas a value of 1 indicates a much lower speed. When done at a higher speed, more system resources will be utilized for the operation to complete at the desired rate. The power limit can also be specified when adding or removing a disk from a diskgroup, to override the value specified in the initialization parameter file.

A diskgroup is a logical grouping of disks that are treated as a single storage unit for files belonging to one or more databases. If you choose to store data using ASM, the first step involves the creation of the diskgroup and then specifying the physical disks that will belong to the diskgroup.

The physical files of the database(s) may then be created in the disks of the diskgroup. ASM diskgroups always perform striping. Striping results in every file being split into 1 M units when being written to physical disks of the diskgroups. Mirroring however can be set when creating the diskgroup. The different mirroring or redundancy options available are **external redundancy** (no mirroring), **normal redundancy** (every extent in the diskgroup is written two different disks), and **high redundancy** (every extent in the diskgroup is written to three different disks). In external redundancy, mirroring or duplication of data is not performed. In normal redundancy, the first extent written is called the primary extent and its duplicate is called the secondary extent. In high redundancy, there is a single primary extent and two secondary extents.

Creating a Diskgroup

To use ASM for storing data, one of the first things to do is create a diskgroup. You will need to specify the name of the diskgroup, optionally specify the level of mirroring (default is normal) and list the disks that will be part of the diskgroup. When mentioning the disks you can specify them in terms of failure groups. If normal or two-way mirroring is required and failure groups are specified, then when creating the diskgroup at least two separate failure groups must be specified. In this case, the primary extent will be placed in one failure group and the secondary extent in the other failure group. If you have requested high redundancy or three-way mirroring, then at least three failure groups must be specified and the primary and secondary extents will be written to separate failure groups.

A diskgroup is created using the CREATE DISKGROUP command. You will specify the name of the diskgroup followed by a comma-separated list of disk devices. When disks are mentioned, you can also assign a user-defined name to the disk using the NAME keyword.

The example below displays the creation of a diskgroup called DISKGROUP1. The diskgroup consists of two physical disks (D:\> and E:\>). The syntax of the command has been displayed for Windows platforms. The dot represents the local node, so \\.\ gets you to the server on which ASM runs. The redundancy on this diskgroup will be normal so every extent written to D:\ will also duplicated on disk E:\. The disk represented by D:\ is being assigned a name DISKD and the disk E:\ the name DISKE.

```
CREATE DISKGROUP DISKGROUP1
DISK '\\.\D:' NAME DISKD,
'\\.\E:' NAME DISKE;
```

This next example displays the creation of a diskgroup DISKGROUP2, using failure groups. The disks D:\ and E:\ are part of a failure group called FG1, and F:\ and G:\ are part of a failure group called FG2. If a primary extent is written to a disk on the FG1 failure group, its secondary extent will be written to a disk on failure group FG2.

```
CREATE DISKGROUP DISKGROUP2 NORMAL REDUNDANCY
FAILGROUP FG1 DISK '\\.\D:','\\.\E:'
FAILGROUP FG2 DISK '\\.\F:','\\.\G:';
```

If a certain disk already belongs to a diskgroup, and you want it to belong to a new diskgroup, by default, you will not be allowed to do so. However, you can use the FORCE option to force the disk to be part of a new disk group.

Dropping a Diskgroup

A diskgroup may be dropped, if you do not want to use it for storing data, by executing the DROP DISKGROUP command. If the diskgroup already has data you must specify the INCLUDING CONTENTS clause after the diskgroup name.

To drop a disk called DISKGROUP1 that does not contain data you would issue:


```
DROP DISKGROUP DISKGROUP1;
```

To drop a diskgroup DISKGROUP2 that contains data you would issue:

```
DROP DISKGROUP DISKGROUP2 INCLUDING CONTENTS;
```

Adding Disks to a Diskgroup

After the creation of a diskgroup, new disks may be added to it. When new disk(s) are added, automatic rebalancing will be performed so that all disks (including the new disk) contain an equal number of extents. Additional failure groups can be added using the FAILGROUP keyword.

A disk is added using an ALTER DISKGROUP command. In the next example, a new disk represented by drive letter H:\ is being added to the diskgroup DISKGROUP1. The disk is assigned a name by Oracle.

```
ALTER DISKGROUP DISKGROUP1 ADD DISK '\\.\H:';
```

The next example displays the addition of a failure group to diskgroup DISKGROUP2. The failure group consists of two disks represented by H:\ and I:\.

```
ALTER DISKGROUP DISKGROUP2 ADD FAILGROUP FG1 DISK '\\.\H:','\\.\I:';
```

Dropping Disks from a Diskgroup

A disk may be dropped from a diskgroup. When a disk is dropped, automatic rebalancing will be done to redistribute the extents that existed on the disk being dropped to other disks of the diskgroup. When dropping the disk you may specify its name. When a disk is dropped it goes through a WAIT state followed by a RUN state.

The ALTER DISKGROUP command is used to perform this action.

In the example, the disk DISKD is being dropped from the diskgroup DISKGROUP1.

```
ALTER DISKGROUP DISKGROUP1 DROP DISK DISKD;
```

Undropping Disks from a Diskgroup

An UNDROP DISK command issued on a disk that is currently in a wait (pending) state can result in "undropping" the disk—the drop operation will be cancelled. The command will not work successfully on disks that have already been dropped, or on disks that were dropped by the execution of the DROP DISKGROUP command.

In the example, the disks that were dropped in diskgroup DISKGROUP1 are being undropped.

```
ALTER DISKGROUP DISKGROUP1 UNDROP DISKS;
```

Manually Rebalancing a Diskgroup

As mentioned earlier, the rate at which rebalancing occurs is dependent on the ASM_POWER_LIMIT parameter set in the initialization parameter file of the ASM instance. This limit or value set will be automatically inherited by all diskgroups managed by the instance. However, you can specify the power of rebalancing for diskgroups individually. It is done using the REBALANCE POWER clause of the ALTER DISKGROUP command.

In this example, the power with which rebalancing is performed for diskgroup DISKGROUP2 is set to 5.


```
ALTER DISKGROUP DISKGROUP2 REBALANCE POWER 5;
```

Mounting Diskgroups

Diskgroups are automatically mounted by the ASM instance, during startup. A diskgroup must be mounted for the information in it to be accessed and stored. A diskgroup may be manually mounted using the MOUNT clause of the ALTER DISKGROUP command.

The example mounts the diskgroup called DISKGROUP1.

```
ALTER DISKGROUP DISKGROUP1 MOUNT;
```

Dismounting a Diskgroup

A diskgroup may be dismounted to make it unavailable. This is done by using the DISMOUNT clause of the ALTER DISKGROUP command.

In the example, the diskgroup called DISKGROUP1 is being dismounted.

```
ALTER DISKGROUP DISKGROUP1 DISMOUNT;
```

OBTAINING DATA DICTIONARY INFORMATION

A number of ASM components and commands have been discussed in this chapter. Information about these components can be obtained from a number of data dictionary views. Table 12-6 describes some of the useful data dictionary views associated with ASM.

TABLE 12-6 Data dictionary views associated with ASM elements

View	Description
`V$ASM_DISKGROUP`	In an ASM instance, the view displays information about the known diskgroups. Information includes the number, name, size, state, and redundancy type. In a DB instance, it contains one row for every ASM disk group mounted by the local ASM instance.
`V$ASM_CLIENT`	In an ASM instance, it identifies databases using disk groups managed by the ASM instance. In a DB instance, it contains one row for the ASM instance if the database has any open ASM files.
`V$ASM_DISK`	In an ASM instance, it contains one row for every disk discovered by the ASM instance, including disks that are not part of any disk group. In a DB instance, it contains rows only for disks in the disk groups in use by that DB instance.
`V$ASM_FILE`	In an ASM instance, it contains one row for every ASM file in every disk group mounted by the ASM instance. In a DB instance, it contains no rows.
`V$ASM_TEMPLATE`	In an ASM instance, it contains one row for every template present in every disk group mounted by the ASM instance. In a DB instance, it contains no rows.
`V$ASM_ALIAS`	In an ASM instance, it contains one row for every alias present in every disk group mounted by the ASM instance. In a DB instance, it contains no rows.
`V$ASM_OPERATION`	In an ASM instance, it contains one row for every active ASM long running operation executing in the ASM instance. In a DB instance, it contains no rows.

Practice 4: ASM commands and Data Dictionary views

This practice example demonstrates the use of some ASM commands and queries on data dictionary views.

1. Open a command prompt window. We shall refer to the window as *CP1*. Using the **asmtool** we will create a file that will simulate the presence of a disk. The new disk is called DISK3, and will be created in the C:\AD folder.

```
Start -> All Programs -> Accessories -> Command Prompt
C:\> ASMTOOL -CREATE C:\AD\DISK3 250
```

2. At the command prompt, set the ORACLE_SID to the +ASM instance.

```
C:\> SET ORACLE_SID=+ASM
```

3. Start SQL*Plus and connect as a SYSDBA.

```
C:\> SQLPLUS SYS/ORACLE AS SYSDBA
```

4. Start the ASM instance if it is not yet started.

```
SQL> STARTUP
```

5. Issue the ALTER DISKGROUP...ADD DISK command to add DISK3 to the existing diskgroup called DATAGRP. Name the disk D3 when adding it.

```
SQL> ALTER DISKGROUP DATAGRP ADD DISK 'C:\AD\DISK3' NAME D3;
```

6. The addition of this disk causes a rebalance to begin. The V$ASM_OPERATION view may be queried to display information about the rebalance operation. The query displayed below can be used to view information about the rebalance operation. The GROUP_NUMBER is the diskgroup number, the OPERATION column represents the kind of operation to be performed, a value 'REBAL' may be displayed to indicate rebalancing. The STATE column is the status of the operation, a value 'RUN' may be displayed during rebalancing. The POWER column is the rate of rebalancing. The SOFAR column represents the number of allocation units that have been completed by the operation. The EST_WORK column represents the estimated number of allocation units that have to be moved. The EST_RATE column represents the number of allocation units that are being moved per minute by the operation. The EST_MINUTES indicates the estimated amount of time in minutes that the remainder of the operation is expected to take. In Figure 12-15, 5 allocation units have been moved and the operation will be completed in about 4 minutes.

```
SQL> SELECT * FROM V$ASM_OPERATION;
```


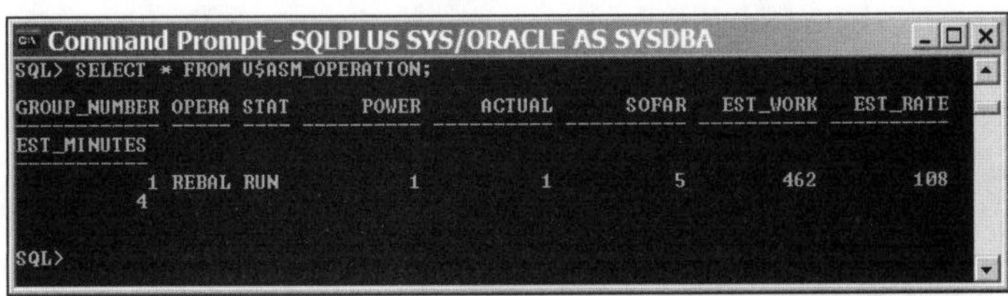

FIGURE 12-15 Displaying the details of the rebalancing after adding the disk

7. The V$ASM_DISK may be queried to obtain information about the amount of data currently stored in all the disks. The query below displays the name of the file, its size, and free space in megabytes. (See Figure 12-16.)

```
SQL> SELECT NAME, FREE_MB, TOTAL_MB FROM V$ASM_DISK;
```

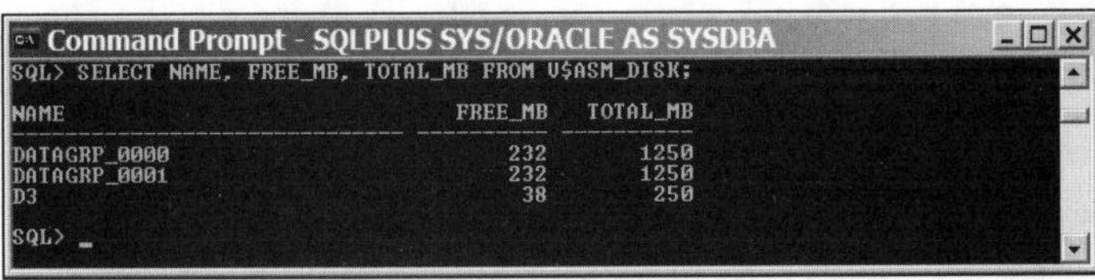

FIGURE 12-16 Querying the V$ASM_DISK view to display the details of the disks

8. Open another command prompt window. We shall refer to this window as *CP2*. Set the ORACLE_SID to ASMDB. Connect to SQL*Plus and shut down the ASMDB database in an IMMEDIATE mode, if it is started.

```
Start -> All Programs -> Accessories -> Command Prompt
C:\> SET ORACLE_SID=ASMDB
C:\> SQLPLUS SYS/< PASSWORD> AS SYSDBA
SQL> SHUTDOWN IMMEDIATE;
```

9. Return to *CP1*, and issue the command to dismount the DATAGRP diskgroup.

```
SQL> ALTER DISKGROUP DATAGRP DISMOUNT;
```

10. Issue the command to mount the DATAGRP diskgroup.

```
SQL> ALTER DISKGROUP DATAGRP MOUNT;
```

11. Issue the command to drop the disk called D3, created earlier in this exercise.

```
SQL> ALTER DISKGROUP DATAGRP DROP DISK D3;
```

12. Re-issue the query you issued in step 5. Because a disk was dropped, a rebalance will be performed. The V$ASM_OPERATION will give you information about the rebalance. If you receive an output 'no rows selected', it indicates that the rebalance has already completed. In Figure 12-17, the rebalance operation is expected to complete in less than one minute.

```
SQL> SELECT * FROM V$ASM_OPERATION;
```

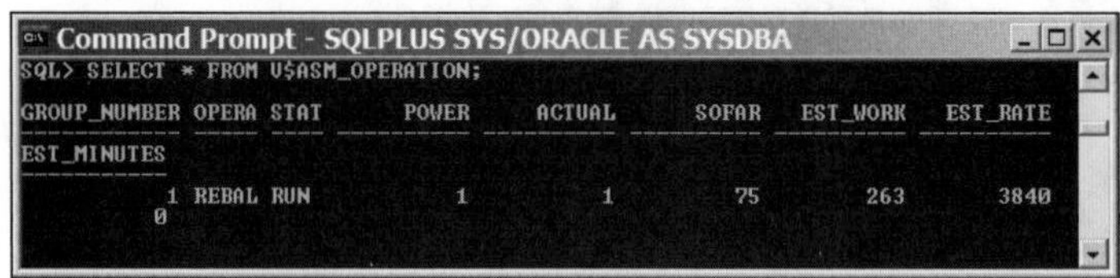

FIGURE 12-17 The rebalance operation after dropping a disk

13. Exit all open windows.

MIGRATING A DATABASE TO ASM USING RMAN

Migrating a database to ASM involves moving all the physical files that exist on the filesystem into diskgroups. The files will be subsequently managed by ASM. The following steps describe how a database may be migrated to diskgroups using the Recovery Manager. The Recovery Manager was discussed in Chapter 1 and is a recommended method for performing backup and recovery operations. During the migration process, RMAN is used to create a backup of the original files onto the ASM diskgroup. The backup will then become the ASM files of the database.

- As a pre-requisite for the process, disable change tracking if it has been enabled.

```
ALTER DATABASE DISABLE BLOCK CHANGE TRACKING;
```

- Shut down the database whose files need to be migrated.

```
SHUTDOWN IMMEDIATE
```

- As mentioned earlier, OMF files are recommended when using ASM. To use OMF you must modify the initialization parameter file of the target database and set the `DB_CREATE_FILE_DEST`, `CONTROL_FILES`, and `DB_CREATE_ONLINE_LOG_DEST_n` initialization parameters to point to the ASM diskgroups.
- Start the database in a nomount mode.

```
STARTUP NOMOUNT
```

- Using RMAN, issue the RESTORE command so that controlfile is created in the ASM diskgroup using the original control file.

```
RMAN> RESTORE CONTROLFILE FROM 'old_control_file_name';
```

- Mount the target database.

```
RMAN> ALTER DATABASE MOUNT;
```


- The BACKUP AS COPY DATABASE command is used to backup the entire database. The backup you are performing in this step will backup all the files database onto the ASM diskgroup.

```
RMAN> BACKUP AS COPY DATABASE FORMAT '+disk_group';
```

- The SWITCH DATABASE command will result in updating the control file. The control file will now be aware of the new location of the physical files of the database.

```
RMAN> SWITCH DATABASE TO COPY;
```

- Open the database.

```
RMAN> ALTER DATABASE OPEN;
```

- Enable change tracking if you wish to do so.

```
ALTER DATABASE ENABLE BLOCK CHANGE TRACKING;
```

- After the migration, you can delete the old physical files of the database to free up the space used by them.

Practice 5: Migrating a non-ASM database to ASM

This practice example demonstrates migration of a non-ASM database to use ASM storage.

This practice exercise requires that you have:

- Ample disk space in the diskgroup DATAGRP so that the files of the non-ASM database can be migrated successfully. You may need to create a large file at least 2 G in size using the ASMTOOL utility and add it to the diskgroup DATAGRP. Please refer to step 3 of Practice 1 on how to use the ASMTOOL and step 5 of Practice 4 on how to add it to the DATAGRP diskgroup.

- Create a general-purpose database called ASMIG using Database Configuration Assistant. The ASMIG database must store its files on the operating file system. Do not choose options such as Flash Recovery area or sample schemas because these options will require additional space.

1. Open a command prompt and set the ORACLE_SID to ASMIG.

```
C:\> SET ORACLE_SID=ASMIG
```

2. Start SQL*Plus and connect as a user with SYSDBA privileges. Query the NAME column of the V$DATABASE view to display the name of the database. It should be ASMIG.

```
SQL> CONNECT SYS/<PASSWORD> AS SYSDBA
SQL> SELECT NAME FROM V$DATABASE;
```

3. Issue a query to display the locations of the datafiles of the database, by querying the NAME column of the V$DATAFILE view. These files should exist in the <ORACLE_BASE>\oradata\<SID>\ folder by default. (See Figure 12-18.)

```
SQL> SELECT NAME FROM V$DATAFILE;
```


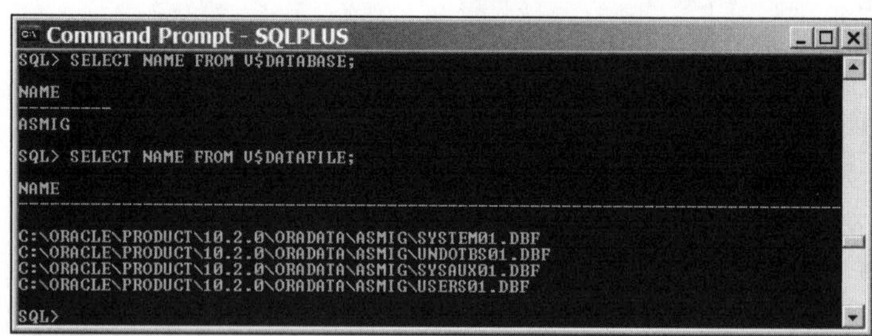

FIGURE 12-18 The names of the database and the location of its datafiles.

4. Query the V$CONTROLFILE view to display the names and locations of the control files. Note this location because you will need it in step 10 of this practice.

```
SQL> SELECT NAME FROM V$CONTROLFILE;
```

5. Issue the command to disable block change tracking.

```
SQL> ALTER DATABASE DISABLE BLOCK CHANGE TRACKING;
```

6. Issue the following commands to modify the spfile of the ASMIG database. You are setting the locations of the datafiles and control files of the database to the diskgroup DATAGRP. (See Figure 12-19.)

```
SQL> ALTER SYSTEM SET DB_CREATE_FILE_DEST='+DATAGRP'
     SCOPE=SPFILE;
SQL> ALTER SYSTEM SET CONTROL_FILES='+DATAGRP' SCOPE=SPFILE;
```

7. Shut down the database using the IMMEDIATE option.

```
SQL> SHUTDOWN IMMEDIATE;
```

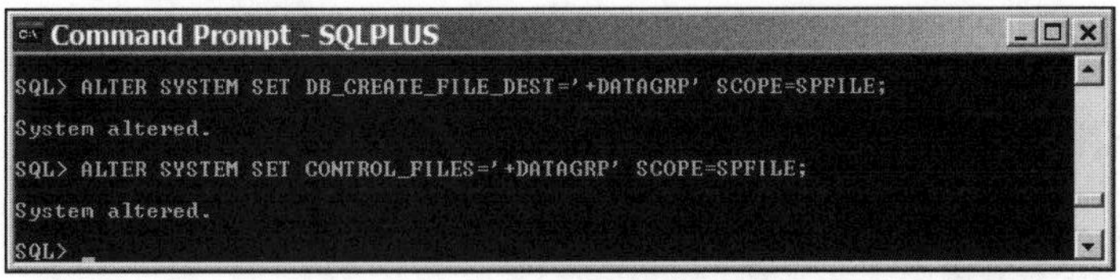

```
Command Prompt - SQLPLUS
SQL> ALTER SYSTEM SET DB_CREATE_FILE_DEST='+DATAGRP' SCOPE=SPFILE;

System altered.

SQL> ALTER SYSTEM SET CONTROL_FILES='+DATAGRP' SCOPE=SPFILE;

System altered.

SQL> _
```

FIGURE 12-19 Setting the destination for datafiles and control files to DATAGRP

8. Open a command prompt window and set the ORACLE_SID to ASMIG. Launch RMAN. Connect to the target database ASMIG.

```
C:\>SET ORACLE_SID=ASMIG
C:\>RMAN
RMAN>CONNECT TARGET
```

9. From the RMAN prompt, issue a command to only start the ASMIG instance. Use the NOMOUNT option of STARTUP.

```
RMAN> STARTUP NOMOUNT
```

10. From the RMAN prompt, issue the following RESTORE command. Please make sure you use the correct location of the one of the control file as you have noted in step 4 of this practice. (See Figure 12-20.)

```
RMAN> RESTORE CONTROLFILE FROM 'C:\<PATH>\CONTROLFILENAME.CTL';
```

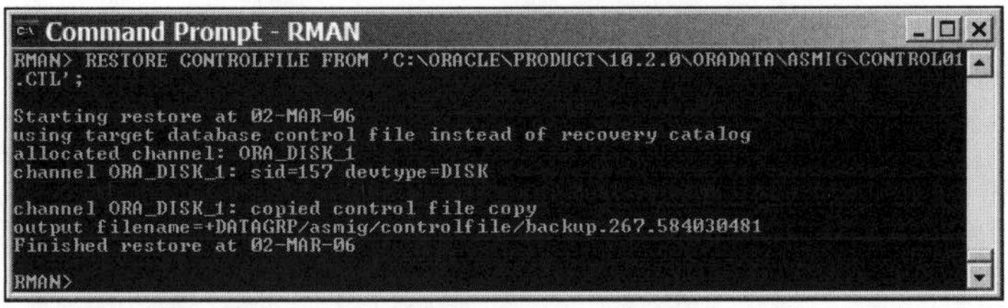

```
Command Prompt - RMAN
RMAN> RESTORE CONTROLFILE FROM 'C:\ORACLE\PRODUCT\10.2.0\ORADATA\ASMIG\CONTROL01
.CTL';

Starting restore at 02-MAR-06
using target database control file instead of recovery catalog
allocated channel: ORA_DISK_1
channel ORA_DISK_1: sid=157 devtype=DISK

channel ORA_DISK_1: copied control file copy
output filename=+DATAGRP/asmig/controlfile/backup.267.584030481
Finished restore at 02-MAR-06

RMAN>
```

FIGURE 12-20 Restoring the controlfile

11. Next, issue the ALTER DATABASE MOUNT command to mount the ASMIG database.

```
RMAN> ALTER DATABASE MOUNT;
```

12. Issue the BACKUP AS COPY DATABASE command to create a backup of all files in the DATAGRP diskgroup. A partial output of the command is displayed in Figure 12-21.

```
RMAN> BACKUP AS COPY DATABASE FORMAT '+DATAGRP';
```

13. After the backup has completed, issue the SWITCH DATABASE TO COPY command. (See Figure 12-22.)

```
RMAN> SWITCH DATABASE TO COPY;
```

14. Issue the command to open the database. Exit RMAN.

```
RMAN> ALTER DATABASE OPEN;
RMAN> EXIT
```

```
Command Prompt - RMAN
RMAN> BACKUP AS COPY DATABASE FORMAT '+DATAGRP';

Starting backup at 02-MAR-06
allocated channel: ORA_DISK_1
channel ORA_DISK_1: sid=153 devtype=DISK
channel ORA_DISK_1: starting datafile copy
input datafile fno=00001 name=C:\ORACLE\PRODUCT\10.2.0\ORADATA\ASMIG\SYSTEM01.DB
F
output filename=+DATAGRP/asmig/datafile/system.268.584030605 tag=TAG20060302T144
324 recid=1 stamp=584030649
channel ORA_DISK_1: datafile copy complete, elapsed time: 00:00:45
channel ORA_DISK_1: starting datafile copy
input datafile fno=00003 name=C:\ORACLE\PRODUCT\10.2.0\ORADATA\ASMIG\SYSAUX01.DB
F
output filename=+DATAGRP/asmig/datafile/sysaux.269.584030651 tag=TAG20060302T144
324 recid=2 stamp=584030671
channel ORA_DISK_1: datafile copy complete, elapsed time: 00:00:25
channel ORA_DISK_1: starting datafile copy
input datafile fno=00002 name=C:\ORACLE\PRODUCT\10.2.0\ORADATA\ASMIG\UNDOTBS01.D
BF
```

FIGURE 12-21 Backing up the datafiles

```
Command Prompt - RMAN
RMAN> SWITCH DATABASE TO COPY;

datafile 1 switched to datafile copy "+DATAGRP/asmig/datafile/system.268.5840306
05"
datafile 2 switched to datafile copy "+DATAGRP/asmig/datafile/undotbs1.270.58403
0675"
datafile 3 switched to datafile copy "+DATAGRP/asmig/datafile/sysaux.269.5840306
51"
datafile 4 switched to datafile copy "+DATAGRP/asmig/datafile/users.271.58403067
9"

RMAN> _
```

FIGURE 12-22 Switching the database to the copy

15. This step is optional. If block change tracking had been disabled, you may re-enable it using SQL*Plus.

    ```
    SQL> ALTER DATABASE ENABLE BLOCK CHANGE TRACKING;
    ```

16. To confirm that the datafiles have been moved to the DATAGRP diskgroup, open a command prompt set the ORACLE_SID to ASMIG. Start SQL*Plus and log in as a user with SYSDBA privileges.

    ```
    C:\>SET ORACLE_SID=ASMIG
    C:\>SQLPLUS SYS/<PASSWORD> AS SYSDBA
    ```

17. From the SQL prompt issue a command to display the NAME column from the V$DATAFILE and V$CONTROLFILE views. Figure 12-23 displays the new locations of the datafiles and controlfiles of the ASMIG database, which is now, diskgroup DATAGRP.

    ```
    SQL> SELECT NAME FROM V$DATAFILE;
    SQL> SELECT NAME FROM V$CONTROLFILE;
    ```

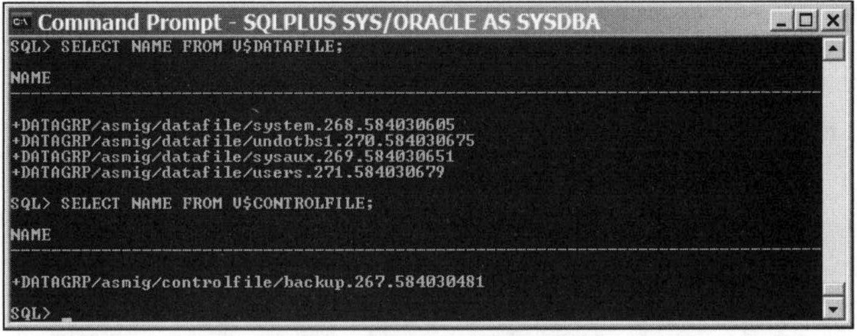

FIGURE 12-23 The datafiles have been migrated

18. You have successfully migrated an Oracle non-ASM database to an ASM database. Exit all open windows.

In this chapter, we discussed a new and interesting method of storing and managing database files known as Automatic Storage Management. The method eliminates many of the problems faced by database administrators during file management and tuning. Chapter 13 discusses globalization support in an Oracle database.

Chapter Summary

- ASM is a new feature in Oracle 10*g* that is used to simplify disk and storage management.
- ASM is optional and may be a method chosen to store and manage the physical files of the Oracle 10*g* database.
- ASM behaves as an integrated file system and volume manager for Oracle files.
- ASM eliminates many of the problems associated with storage management such as identification and resolution of hot spots as well as performing performance tuning actions to ensure an even distribution of I/O.
- ASM provides built-in striping and mirroring functionalities.
- ASM components include diskgroups, disks, ASM files, and the ASM instance.
- Diskgroups are a logical grouping of disks on which data may be stored.
- All files are striped in 1 M extents across all disks of a diskgroup.
- Disks are physical storage devices that store data.
- ASM files consist of Oracle physical files that are stored on the disks of the diskgroup.
- ASM files may be referenced and created using a number of methods. Their filenames may be fully qualified, numeric, alias, alias with template, incomplete, and incomplete with template.
- The ASM instance, called +ASM, is a specialized instance that is responsible for mounting, storing metadata about diskgroups, and making them available to the database.
- The ASM instance is configured by its own initialization parameter file and must be opened before the client database is opened.
- When the ASM instance is shut down, all client databases must also be shut down.
- The ASM instance is accessed during specific tasks such as adding or removing a disk from a diskgroup.
- Various clauses of the ALTER DISKGROUP command are available for managing and administering diskgroups.
- Striping is done automatically by ASM across all disks of a diskgroup (in the form of extents), ensuring an even distribution of files, thereby reducing hot spots.
- Mirroring is an option available with ASM, where duplication of extents is done automatically.
- Rebalancing is a process of re-distributing the extents across all the physical disks when a new disk is added or an existing disk removed.
- Migration of an existing disk to ASM may be achieved using Recovery Manager.

Syntax Guide

SYNTAX GUIDE		
Element	**Description**	**Example**
SET ORACLE_ SID	To set the SID of the Oracle instance.	C:\>SET ORACLE_SID=ASMDB
ASMTOOL	A command line tool that can be used to initialize drive headers and marks drives for use by ASM.	C:\>ASMTOOL -CREATE '\\.\E:\'
CREATE DISKGROUP	Used to create a new diskgroup. The name of the diskgroup and the disks that are part of the diskgroup need to be specified.	CREATE DISKGROUP DG1 DISK '\\.\E:','\\.\F:\';
		CREATE DISKGROUP DG2 FAILGROUP FG1 DISK '\\.\D:','\\.\E:' FAILGROUP FG2 DISK '\\.\F:','\\.\G:';
DROP DISKGROUP	Used to drop a diskgroup. The INCLUDING CONTENTS option is used when the disks have data stored in them.	DROP DISKGROUP DG1;
		DROP DISKGROUP DG1 INCLUDING CONTENTS;
ALTER DISKGROUP ... ADD DISK	Used to add one or more disks to a diskgroup.	ALTER DISKGROUP DG1 ADD DISK '\\.\H:','\\.\G:';
		ALTER DISKGROUP DG1 ADD FAILGROUP FGNAME DISK '\\.\I:';
ALTER DISKGROUP ... DROP DISK	Used to drop one or more disks from a diskgroup. The REBALANCE POWER clause may be used to determine the rate of rebalancing.	ALTER DISKGROUP DG1 DROP DISK '\\.\H:\;
		ALTER DISKGROUP DG1 DROP DISK '\\.\H:\ REBALANCE POWER 6;
ALTER DISKGROUP ... REBALANCE POWER	Used to manually set the rebalance power for a diskgroup.	ALTER DISKGROUP DG1 REBALANCE POWER 4;

SYNTAX GUIDE		
Element	**Description**	**Example**
`ALTER DISKGROUP ... MOUNT`	Used to mount a diskgroup	`ALTER DIKSGROUP DG1 MOUNT;`
`ALTER DISKGROUP ... DISMOUNT`	Used to dismount a diskgroup	`ALTER DISKGROUP DG1 DISMOUNT;`

Review Questions

1. Identify the parameter that is defined in the ASM instance responsible for controlling the speed of a rebalance operation.
   a. INSTANCE_TYPE
   b. ASM_DISKSTRING
   c. ASM_POWER
   d. ASM_POWER_LIMIT
   e. ASM_DISK_SPEEDS
2. When working with Automatic Storage Management, identify the two background processes that are created in the ASM instance.
   a. RBAL
   b. MMON
   c. MMAN
   d. MMNL
   e. ARB
   f. ASMN
3. Tom is the DBA in a large enterprise that has just migrated to Oracle 10*g*. He has been experimenting with the ASM feature. He has successfully configured the ASM instance that mounts the diskgroups that belong to two databases DB01 and DB02. During a certain maintenance operation, the ASM instance fails. Identify the appropriate response with respect to DB01 and DB02 from the list of options given below.
   a. The instances of DB01 and DB02 continue to function normally.
   b. The instances of DB01 and DB02 also fail.
   c. The instance of DB01 fails but DB02 continues to operate normally.
   d. The instance of DB02 fails but DB01 continues to operate normally.
   e. An alert is raised and the DBA is sent a message.

4. From the list of views displayed, identify the view that contains one row for every active ASM long-running operation executing in the ASM instance.
   a. V$ASM_DISKGROUP
   b. V$ASM_FILE
   c. V$ASM_OPS
   d. V$ASM_LONGOPS
   e. V$ASM_OPERATION
   f. V$ASM_TEMPLATE
5. An ASM filename has been defined as: +dgroupA.256.4509345. Identify the correct naming format.
   a. Fully qualified
   b. Numeric ASM filename
   c. Alias ASM filename
   d. Alias ASM filename with Templates
   e. Incomplete ASM filename

6. Assume that ASM disk discovery identified the following disks in the /devices directory.

```
/devices/diskA1--member of dgroup1
/devices/diskA2--member of dgroup1
/devices/diskA3--member of dgroup1
/devices/diskA4--candidate disk
```

   You wish to add a disk /devices/diskA4 and you issue the command.

```
ALTER DISKGROUP dgroup1
ADD DISK '/devices/diskA*';
```

   What would be the response to the command you issued:
   a. An error is displayed.
   b. An existing disk will the detached and diskA4 will be added.
   c. The diskA4 will be added without an error.
   d. None of the above.
7. To improve load balancing of disks, which of the following statements should a DBA issue:
   a. ALTER DISKGROUP DGROUPA DROP DISK DISKA1;
   b. ALTER DISKGROUP DGROUPA REBALANCE POWER 5;
   c. ALTER SYSTEM SET ASM_POWER_LIMIT=5;
   d. ALTER DISKGROUP DGROUPA DISMOUNT;
8. From the list of files displayed below, which file type cannot be stored on an ASM diskgroup. [Choose 3.]
   a. Control file
   b. Data file
   c. Redo log files
   d. Trace files

e. Archive log files

f. Temporary files

g. Alert logs

h. Export files

9. The DBA issued the following command against an ASM instance:

```
STARTUP OPEN;
```

Choose the correct result.

a. An error is generated, because OPEN is invalid for an ASM instance

b. The ASM instance will be opened.

c. The ASM instance will be aborted and restarted.

d. The ASM instance will be started without mounting any disk groups.

10. The DBA issues the following command to create a DISKGROUP. The disk /dev/disk3 currently belongs to another diskgroup called DATAGRP. What is the outcome of this CREATE command?


```
CREATE DISKGROUP diskgroup1 NORMAL REDUNDANCY
FAILGROUP failure_group_1 DISK
'/dev/disk1', '/dev/disk2',
FAILGROUP failure_group_2 DISK
'/dev/disk3', '/dev/disk4';
```

a. The diskgroup will be created successfully.

b. An error will be generated, because normal redundancy provides two-way mirroring, and failure groups are unnecessary.

c. An error will be generated because a disk cannot belong to more than one diskgroup.

d. The ASM instance will automatically mount the diskgroup.

e. The diskgroup will be added to the DISKGROUP1 and will be removed from DATAGRP.

11. You have configured a database to use ASM as its primary storage method. When a tablespace is created it must be stored in the diskgroup called DATAGRP. Which of the following parameters will specify the destination of OMF datafiles?

a. DB_DATAFILES=+DATAGRP

b. DB_CREATE_FILE_DEST=DATAGRP

c. DB_CREATE_FILE_DEST=+DATAGRP

d. DB_DATAFILES=DATAGRP

e. COMPATIBLE=10.0.1

12. You have configured the DB101 database as a client of the ASM instance. What is the outcome of issuing the following shutdown command against the ASM instance?

```
SQL>SHUTDOWN ABORT;
```

a. The ASM instance will be shut down normally after aborting the DB101 instance.

b. The ASM and DB101 instance will be aborted.

c. The ASM instance will be shut down in an immediate mode, the DB101 instance will also be aborted.

d. Shutdown options are available only for database instances.

13. Identify three features of ASM.
    a. Providing suggestions regarding size of datafiles
    b. Automatic row movement
    c. Automatic Rebalancing
    d. Striping
    e. Mirroring
    f. Automatic Undo management
14. Identify the type of file naming used for a file `+DGROUP1.263.581076909`
15. Which portion of a fully qualified filename makes the filename unique?
    a. Diskgroup
    b. Database name
    c. Tag
    d. File#.Incarnation#
16. Shaun is the DBA of an Oracle10*g* database called PROJDB, using ASM for data storage. He creates a diskgroup in the following manner:

    ```
    CREATE DISKGROUP DG1 DISK '\\.\D:','\\.\E:';
    ```

    Which of the following statement are true based on the action he just performed?
    a. The diskgroup will consist of two diskgroups represented by drive letters D and E.
    b. D:\ and E:\ may be disks that are not recognized by the operating system.
    c. External mirroring will be enabled for the diskgroup.
    d. Normal Mirroring will be enabled for the diskgroup.
17. For every database that uses a diskgroup currently mounted by ASM instance, for data storage, information about that database may be obtained from the ________________ view.
    a. V$ASM_DISKGROUP
    b. V$ASM_CLIENT
    c. V$ASM_DISK
    d. V$DATAFILE
18. When migrating a non-ASM database to ASM, target database must be in a ________________ state.
    a. OPEN
    b. NOMOUNT
    c. MOUNT
    d. It does not matter.
19. When mounting a diskgroup, what state should the ASM instance be in?
20. The ________________ clause of the DROP DISKGROUP must be used when dropping diskgroups that currently store data.

Hands-On Assignments

Assignment 12-1 Starting and Shutting down the ASM instance

Note: For the successful completion of the hands-on assignments you must complete the Practice 1 of this chapter.

1. Open a command prompt window and set the ORACLE_SID to +ASM.
2. Start SQL*Plus and connect as a user with SYSDBA.
3. Issue a command to shut down the ASM instance in IMMEDIATE mode. If the ASM instance is connected to the RDBMS instance, shut down the RDBMS instance.
4. Start the ASM instance, without mounting the diskgroups.
5. Mount the DATAGRP diskgroup.
6. Keep this command prompt window open. We shall refer to it as CP1.

Assignment 12-2 Starting the RDBMS instance (ASMDB database)

1. Open a second command prompt window and set the ORACLE_SID to ASMDB.
2. Start SQL*Plus and connect to the ASMDB database as a user with SYSDBA privileges.
3. Issue a STARTUP command. The database should go through the three stages of startup—instance creation, mounting, and opening of the database.
4. Issue a query to display the contents of the V$ASM_CLIENT dynamic view.
5. Keep this command prompt window open. It will be referred to as CP2 for future assignments.

Assignment 12-3 Querying data dictionary views from the ASM instance

1. Return to command prompt CP1 and issue a query to display the contents of the V$ASM_DISKGROUP view. Do you see the details of diskgroup DATAGRP? How much of free space (in megabytes) exists in this diskgroup?
2. Query the V$ASM_DISK view to display the following columns: `GROUP_NUMBER, DISK_NUMBER, NAME, PATH, HEADER_STATUS, TOTAL_MB` and `FREE_MB`.

   What is the status of the disk that was dropped in Practice 4?

   Notice the sizes of the various disks in the diskgroup and the amount of free space remaining in each disk.
3. Query the V$ASM_FILE to display the following columns: `GROUP_NUMBER, FILE_NUMBER, TYPE, REDUNDANCY,` and `STRIPED`.

   What type of striping is done for datafiles? Online log files?
4. Query the V$ASM_TEMPLATE view to display information about existing templates. Retrieve the following columns: `GROUP_NUMBER`, `NAME`, `STRIPE`, and `REDUNDANCY`.
5. Query the V$ASM_ALIAS view to display information about the aliases that exist in the database. Retrieve the following columns: `GROUP_NUMBER, FILE_NUMBER, FILE_INCARNATION, NAME,` and `ALIAS_DIRECTORY`
6. Keep the CP1 window open.

Assignment 12-4 Querying data dictionary views from the ASMDB instance

1. Return to command prompt CP2, and issue a query to display the contents of the V$ASM_DISKGROUP view.
2. Query the V$ASM_DISK view to display the following columns: `GROUP_NUMBER, DISK_NUMBER, NAME, PATH, HEADER_STATUS, TOTAL_MB,` and `FREE_MB.`

   On which disks does this database have its data stored?
3. Exit all open windows.

Assignment 12-5 Adding a Disk using the ASMTOOL command

1. Open a new command prompt window and issue a command using the ASMTOOL to create a file with a size of 250 M. Create the file in the AD directory that was created in Practice 1. Name the file DISKA126.

   ```
   C:\> ASMTOOL -CREATE C:\AD\DISKA126 250
   ```
2. Set the ORACLE_SID to +ASM. Start SQL*Plus and connect with SYSDBA privileges.
3. Startup the ASM instance if it is currently shut down.
4. Issue an ALTER DISKGROUP ADD DISK command to add the new disk that you created in step 1. Give the disk being added the name A126.
5. Display the contents of the V$ASM_OPERATION view.
6. Display the contents of the V$ASM_DISK view. Retrieve the columns: `PATH, NAME, MOUNT_STATUS, HEADER_STATUS, TOTAL_MB,` and `FREE_MB.`
7. Exit SQL*Plus and the command prompt window.

Assignment 12-6 Performing administrative operations on the Diskgroup

1. Open a new command prompt window and set the ORACLE_SID to +ASM. Start SQL*Plus and connect with SYSDBA privileges.
2. Shut down the ASM instance if it is currently active, using an IMMEDIATE option. If the ASM instance is connected to an RDBMS database, shut down the database.
3. Issue a command to start only the ASM instance. Do not mount any diskgroups.
4. Issue the command to mount the DATAGRP diskgroup.
5. Issue the command to dismount the DATAGRP diskgroup.
6. Query the V$ASM_DISKGROUP view to determine the STATE of the diskgroup.
7. Mount the diskgroup again.
8. Issue the command to drop the disk that you created in Assignment 12-5 called A126.
9. Perform this next step quickly before the drop completes. Issue the command to "undrop" the disk.
10. Exit the SQL*Plus and the command prompt window.

Case Study

1. Imagine that you were the database administrator of a medium to large organization. Prepare a short proposal describing why your organization should choose to implement Automatic Storage Management instead of file management using the filesystem provided by the operating system.
2. Compile a written series of steps to implement ASM.

CHAPTER 13

GLOBALIZATION SUPPORT

LEARNING OBJECTIVES

After completing this lesson you should be able to understand:

- The need for globalization support
- Character encoding and database character sets
- The Unicode database
- National language support
- Date-time datatypes
- Sorting linguistic data
- Retrieving information from the data dictionary

ORACLE CERTIFICATION EXAM OBJECTIVES COVERED IN THIS CHAPTER INCLUDE:

- Customize language-dependent behavior for the database and individual sessions
- Specify different linguistic sorts for queries
- Use date-time datatypes
- Query data using case-insensitive and accent-insensitive searches
- Obtain Globalization support configuration information

INTRODUCTION

In today's global and connected marketplace, designing applications that adapt to different cultures is a necessity. Data needs to be exchanged seamlessly across countries with differing currency symbols, date formats, and time zones. Consider an international airline with a central database containing reservation and flight details. Travel agents around the globe querying the database would need to see the data in a format that matches the local conventions of their language and country.

The Internet has in part driven globalization by giving companies an opportunity to make their goods and services available to a worldwide audience. Globalization with reference to software development is the process of designing and deploying applications that can adapt to different cultures.

The database is a key component in an application that needs to be deployed globally. The Oracle database product provides a number of features that meet this challenge. Some of the important features include multi-language support, NLS parameters, date-time datatypes, and linguistic sorting.

This chapter discusses some of the components required by a global application. We will first discuss character encoding, character sets, and the database character sets. Emphasis will be placed on the Unicode character set and Oracle's support of Unicode.

The chapter also covers National-Language Support (NLS) and date-time datatypes. These datatypes are especially useful for handling transactions that involve different time zones. The chapter concludes with a discussion on sorting and the sorting techniques available when dealing with multilingual data.

THE CURRENT CHALLENGE AT KELLER MEDICAL CENTER

A division of Keller Medical Center sells books and videos on health, nutrition, and fitness online. Initially targeted at a national audience the web site now draws visitors from across the globe. The existing applications were designed without international customers in mind and now need to be modified by the IT department.

Ryan has been instructed to assist the developers in converting the applications to include globalization support.

SETUP FOR THE CHAPTER

1. To complete the hands-on and practice examples you must install additional languages during the installation of Oracle on the machine. During installation, choose the **Advanced Installation** option to be able to access the contents displayed by Figure 13-1.
2. Select the **Product Languages** button to display and choose additional languages that the Oracle software will support. (See Figure 13-1.)

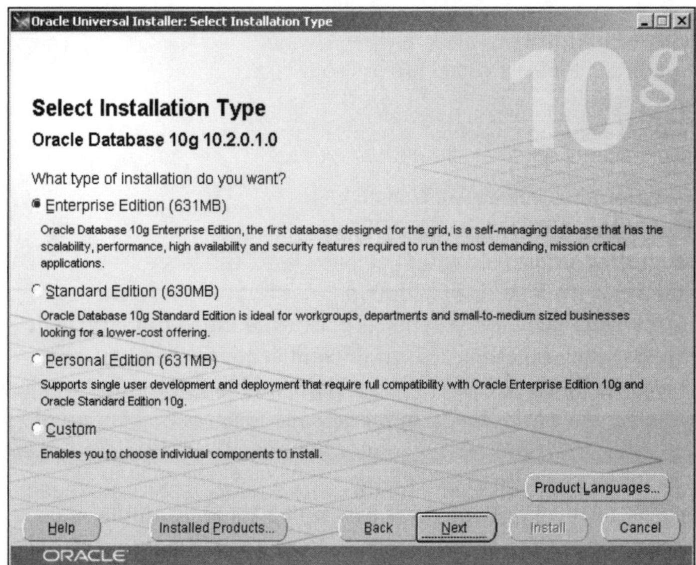

FIGURE 13-1 Selecting additional Product Languages for Globalization support

3. Execute the script **c13_setup.sql** located the Chapter13 folder of the student datafiles before performing the practice examples or hands-on exercises for this chapter. The script creates a table called MEDPROD that contains four columns and three rows.

```
SQL> CONNECT MEDUSER/MEDUSER
SQL> @<PATH>\C13_SETUP.SQL
SQL> EXIT
```

WHY GLOBALIZATION?

Globalization support gives you the ability to create applications and web sites that can enable users to access information easily crossing barriers of culture, language, and platform. It enhances the ability of companies to do business worldwide by reaching a larger audience. A potential customer is more likely to purchase a product, if product information is available in the native language. Consider a web-based application that displays the cost of books. A cost of 12.45 would need to be displayed as "$12.45" for a customer in the United States and "€12,45" for a customer in Germany. This is because the currency symbol in Germany is the Euro (€) and the radix symbol is a comma (,).

Oracle's efforts toward globalization began in the database version 7.x. The initial collection of features was known as National Language Support (NLS). Since then, NLS has become a subset of globalization support and is one feature that facilitates the creation of "globalized" applications and software. Globalization as a whole includes the process of developing multilingual applications and software products that can be accessed and executed from around the world simultaneously without modification, while rendering content to users in their native language and locale preferences.

In this chapter we will cover various aspects of globalization support. We will not be covering the actual process of creating global applications. We will discuss some of the features available in the database that facilitate globalization. The features covered in the chapter include:

- Character Sets
- National Language Support
- Date-time Datatypes
- Linguistic Sorting

CHARACTER ENCODING AND CHARACTER SETS

Every character that is visible on a keyboard when typed is converted into a numeric code or binary sequence. This sequence may be either a 7-bit or 8-bit sequence, known as a byte. For example the numeric code for the letter A is 65 which can be represented by the binary sequence 1000001. How did we arrive at the numeric code for A as 65? Different types of encoding schemes have been created by the computing industry. Common names include the ASCII and EBCDIC encoding schemes.

In the ASCII-7 encoding scheme, every character is assigned a standard numeric code or value. For example, A is assigned a value 65, B is assigned 66, the number 3 is assigned 51, and so on. Every numeric code can be represented by a sequence of 7 bits consisting of zeros and ones. In ASCII-7 a total of 128 (2^7) distinct characters are encoded. In ASCII-8, every numeric code is represented by 8 bits, resulting in 256 (2^8) distinct characters being encoded.

Encoding schemes can be either single-byte or multi-byte encoding schemes. When a character can be represented by a single byte it is known as a single-byte encoding scheme. When a character is represented by multiple bytes it is known as a multi-byte encoding scheme. In the initial days of computing, the characters of the English alphabet, numbers, punctuation marks, and a few special characters were sufficient for most applications. However, this is no longer true. A truly "globalized" application is one that can be accessed the world over and can handle data from any language. This resulted in a need to encode characters outside the English alphabet. Multi-byte encoding schemes serve this purpose.

A single-byte encoding scheme is one in which a single character corresponds to exactly one byte. However, single-byte encoding schemes do not allow more than a few characters to be represented. For example in a 7-bit byte only 128 characters can be represented. An example of a single byte encoding scheme is ASCII.

In a multi-byte encoding scheme, a character may be represented by 1, 2, 3, or 4 bytes. Multi-byte encoding schemes can represent many more characters. Multi-byte encoding schemes are needed to support characters used in Asian languages such as Chinese or Japanese or special characters.

In a multi-byte encoding scheme:

A Japanese character :	強	would occupy 3 bytes
A musical notation :	𝄞	would occupy 4 bytes
The character :	𝔹	would occupy 1 byte
The Latin character :	Ö	would occupy 2 bytes

Multi-byte encoding schemes are not as efficient as single-byte encoding schemes. Multi-byte encoding schemes may be fixed-width or variable-width. In a fixed-width multi-byte encoding scheme, a character is represented by a fixed number of bytes. The number of bytes is at least two in a fixed-width, multi-byte encoding scheme. Examples of a fixed-width multi-byte encoding scheme are UTF-16 and UCS-2. In variable-width, multi-byte encoding schemes, characters may be represented by one or more bytes. An example of a variable-width multi-byte encoding scheme is UTF-8.

The UTF-8, UTF-16, and UCS-2 encoding schemes will be discussed in detail under the topic Unicode.

Character Sets

A group of characters (alphabetic characters, numeric characters, punctuation marks, symbols, ideographs, and control characters) may be encoded as a character set. An encoded character set assigns unique numeric codes to each character in the character repertoire. Character sets differ in the number of characters available, the numeric code value assigned to each character, the encoding scheme and the languages they represent. Different character sets support different character repertoires. Most character sets are based on a particular writing script, and can therefore support more than one language. For example, a character set supporting Latin will support many of the Western European languages such as English, French, German, Spanish, and Dutch. Character sets are assigned a standard name and an Oracle defined name.

Oracle assigns the following naming convention for Oracle character set names.

<region><number of bits for a character><standard character set name>[S|C]

The character S stands of Server and C for client, indicating whether the character set can be used on the Server (S) or Client (C).

Table 13-1 provides some examples of Oracle character set names and their corresponding standard names.

TABLE 13-1 Some Oracle character sets

Oracle Character Set Name	Description	Region	Number of bits used to represent a character	Standard character set name
US7ASCII	U.S. 7-bit ASCII	United States (US)	7	ASCII
WE8ISO8859P1	Western European 8-bit ISO 8859 Part 1	Western European (WE)	8	ISO8859 Part 1
JA16SJIS	Japanese 16-bit Shifted Japanese Industrial Standard	Japan (JA)	16	SJIS

Length Semantics

When implementing single-byte character sets, the number of characters in a string and the number of bytes allocated toward its storage are always the same. For instance, a character string HELLO will utilize 5 bytes of storage space. However, in multi-byte character sets, a character may be internally represented by 1, 2, 3, or 4 bytes. Calculating the amount of storage to be allocated for such characters can be difficult in variable-width multi-byte character sets.

By default, the length of column names and variable names are defined in the Oracle database in terms of bytes. This is known as *byte semantics*. For example, if you define a column of a table as CHAR(10), then internally 10 bytes will be allocated for a value of that column.

Oracle 9*i* introduced the concept of *character semantics*. Character semantics allows you to measure column lengths in terms of characters rather than bytes. Character semantics is extremely useful for defining the storage requirements of variable-width multi-byte strings.

Consider a character column that is defined to be of VARCHAR2 type in a database that utilizes the AL32UTF8 character set which is a variable-width, multi-byte character set. Assume you wish to store 5 Japanese characters along with 5 English characters in the column. If each Japanese character was represented by 3 bytes, then 15 bytes will be totally used by the Japanese characters. Each English character would occupy a single byte. The total bytes used by the column would be (15+5=20 bytes). This would be the case if byte semantics was defined for the column. If you were using character semantics then the total number of characters stored in the column would be 5 Japanese+5 English = 10 characters.

It is possible to indicate whether to use byte or char semantics when defining the column. A column definition which would normally be written as:

```
column_name     datatype(size)
```

can be written as

```
column_name  datatype(size BYTE|CHAR) where BYTE is the default.
```

The NLS_LENGTH_SEMANTICS initialization parameter can be defined to specify the default semantics for a character column. The default value of the parameter is BYTE. It can take the values BYTE or CHAR.

In addition to columns of character datatype defined by CHAR, VARCHAR2 of CLOB, you can also create columns that have a datatype of NCHAR, NVARCHAR2, and NCLOB. Internally a NCHAR column is treated in the same manner as CHAR, NVARCHAR2 the same as VARCHAR2 and NCLOB the same as CLOB. The difference lies in the fact that when data is stored in say a CHAR column, the database character set will be used and when data is stored in an NCHAR column, the national database character set will be used. It is possible to define two separate character sets within a database that supports multilingual data. The datatypes beginning with the letter N can store multilingual data. A detailed discussion about the database character set and national character set will be done later in this chapter.

For columns of CHAR, VARCHAR2, and CLOB datatypes, BYTE semantics are implemented by default. For columns defined to be of NCHAR, NVARCHAR2, NCLOB type the default is CHAR semantics.

Practice 1: Byte and Character semantics

In this practice example you will create a table called TCB. The table will contain two character columns COLA and COLB where the first will store data using BYTE semantics and the second will use CHAR semantics.

1. Start SQL*Plus and connect as the user MEDUSER.

   ```
   SQL> CONNECT MEDUSER/MEDUSER
   ```

2. Create the table TCB in the following manner. Note the deliberate usage of the word BYTE and CHAR to identify byte and character semantics respectively.

   ```
   SQL> CREATE TABLE TCB
        ( COLA    CHAR(10 BYTE),
          COLB    CHAR(5  CHAR));
   ```

3. Exit SQL*Plus.

The Unicode Character Set

In the late 1980s, the creation of global applications drove a need for a more global character set. This requirement became even greater with the development of the Internet. The need for a character set that could represent characters from all languages became apparent. A global character set would be one that contains all major living scripts, support legacy data and implementations as well as be simple enough so that a single implementation of an application would be sufficient for worldwide use, along with the ability to support multilingual users and conform to international standards. These requirements lead to the creation of the *universal character set* that is popularly known as **Unicode**. The Oracle 10g database supports Unicode 3.2. In addition to characters from all major languages including ideographic languages such as Japanese, Chinese, and Korean, it also has numeric codes for nearly 45,960 supplementary characters. The Unicode 3.2 enables 1,048,576 characters to be defined.

Unicode 3.2 encodes characters in a number of different ways. They include: UTF-8, UCS-2, and UTF-16. Table 13-2 describes each of these encodings.

TABLE 13-2 Unicode Encoding schemes

Encoding	Description	Oracle's name for the Character set
UTF-8	This is an 8-bit encoding of Unicode. Every character in the ASCII character set is available in UTF-8 encoding. A character can be 1, 2, 3, or 4 bytes. Characters from European scripts are represented by 1 or 2 bytes. Asian characters by 3 bytes and supplementary characters by 4 bytes.	UTF8 AL32UTF8 AL24UTFFSS
UCS-2	This is a fixed-width, 16-bit encoding. Each character is 2 bytes. This encoding scheme does not support any supplementary characters. It supports all characters defined for Unicode 3.0.	
UTF-16	This is a fixed-width 16 bit encoding. It is an extension of UCS-2 with an added support for supplementary characters that were defined in Unicode 3.2. A character is either 2 bytes or 4 bytes. Characters from European and Asian scripts are represented in 2 bytes and supplementary characters in 4 bytes.	AL16UTF16
UTF-EBCDIC	This is an 8-bit encoding of Unicode similar to UTF-8 created specifically for EBCDIC platforms. It encodes characters in 1, 2, 3, or 4 bytes.	UTFE

Character Sets and the Oracle Database

The Oracle database allows you to define two character sets during its creation. They are the Database Character Set and the National Character Set.

The database character set is defined during database creation as part of the CREATE DATABASE command. Once a database character set has been defined, it cannot be modified without recreating the database with only one exception. The database character set is used for the following purposes:

- To store data defined in SQL character columns defined as CHAR, VARCHAR2, CLOB, and LONG datatypes.
- To identify the characters that can be used to name tables, columns, and PL/SQL variables.
- To code in SQL and PL/SQL.
- To store data in the columns of the data dictionary.

The choice for the database character set would largely depend on which languages would need to be supported by the database at present and in the future. Other considerations include the character set available on the operating system, on client machines as well as performance implications of the character set. If your database has to provide support for multilingual applications a Unicode character set would be a good choice. However, there is a significant overhead in terms of performance when utilizing a Unicode solution. It should be noted that from the list of character sets displayed in the third column of Table 13-2 the AL16UTF16 Unicode character set *cannot* be used as a database character set. A database that utilizes a Unicode character set as its database character set is known as a **Unicode Database**.

When defining a database character set, it is important to consider the character set used by client machines. If the character set on the client machine is different from the database character set, character set conversion will be done automatically by Oracle. However, if the character set used by the database is not a complete superset of the client machines, data may not be interpreted properly resulting in data loss or corruption. If all client machines use the same character set, then that character set is usually the best choice for the database character set. Finally, the database character set can only be modified if the new character set is a strict *superset* of the current character set.

The national character set is also defined during database creation as part of the CREATE DATABASE command. It acts as an alternate character set that enables you to store Unicode character data (all possible characters supported by Unicode) in a database that is not a Unicode database. If only a few columns in the database need to hold multilingual characters, then you can define these columns to be of NCHAR, NVARCHAR2, or NCLOB datatypes. The SQL NCHAR, NVARCHAR2, NCLOB columns can only support Unicode data. The national character set of a database can either be UTF8 or AL16UTF16. The default is **AL16UTF16**. Defining a national character set is particularly useful in situations where only certain columns store multilingual data. For example, a single table in the database containing customer names and addresses in the Hindi language.

NATIONAL LANGUAGE SUPPORT

National Language Support is a subset of globalization support. It gives you the ability to specify certain initialization parameters at a system or session level to specify locale-dependent behavior. A locale refers to a linguistic or cultural environment in which a system or application is running. When trying to understand National Language Support it is important to understand what is meant by Language and Territory. By language we refer to a spoken/written language in a region. For example, in Germany, German would be the language. In Canada, both English and French are spoken. Language determines the conventions for Oracle messages, sorting, day names, and month names. Territory refers to a geographic region, such as Germany, Canada, India, Japan, and so on. Territory specifies conventions for default date, monetary, and numeric formats.

A number of initialization parameters exist within the Oracle Database to specify language-dependent and territory-dependent behavior.

There are three ways to specify NLS parameters:

- As initialization parameters on the server side. When set at this level the parameters will determine the NLS values for the server environment. These parameters have no effect on the client.
- As environment variables on the client to specify locale-dependent behavior for the client. Values set will override those set for the server. This can be done

by using the SET command (on Windows) and the Export command (on Unix-based platforms) at the operating system prompt. On Windows-based systems you may also set environment variables by setting the value in the registry.
- At a session level, by issuing an ALTER SESSION command. They override values set for the client and server.

Character sets often support different character repertoires. Most character sets are based on a particular writing script, and can therefore support more than one language. For example, a character set supporting Latin will support many of the Western European languages such as English, French, German, Spanish, and Dutch.

The NLS_LANG Parameter

The first parameter we will discuss is the NLS_LANG parameter. This parameter can be set on the client and the server side and is the easiest method of specifying locale behavior for the Oracle software. Using the parameter you can specify the language, the territory, and the character set to be used on the client side.

It is set as an environment variable, from a command prompt window on UNIX and Windows platforms. The NLS_LANG parameter is specified as:


```
NLS_LANG=language_territory.charset
```

Table 13-3 gives you an idea of what language and territory definitions determine.

TABLE 13-3 Language and Territory definitions

Locale-Specific Data	Initialization Parameter
Language: Can be specified by the NLS_LANGUAGE initialization parameter	
It specifies the language for:	
• Oracle Messages	
• Day and Month Names and their abbreviations	NLS_DATE_LANGUAGE
• Symbols used for language-equivalents of A.M., P.M., A.D., and B.C.	NLS_DATE_LANGUAGE
• Default sorting sequence of character data	NLS_SORT
Territory: Can be specified by the NLS_TERRITORY initialization parameter	
It specifies the language for:	
• Default Date Format	NLS_DATE_FORMAT
• Decimal Character and Group Separator	NLS_NUMERIC_CHARACTERS
• Local Currency Symbol	NLS_CURRENCY
• ISO Currency Symbol	NLS_ISO_CURRENCY

The default value of NLS_LANG is AMERICAN_AMERICA.US7ASCII.

Consider that NLS_LANG is set to FRENCH_CANADA.WE8ISO8859P1 on a client machine for someone accessing the database from Canada. On querying a table from the database, all error messages, day and month names, sorting sequence will be done in French because the language is FRENCH. The date format, decimal character, thousands separator, local currency symbol, and so on, will be displayed based on conventions used in Canada, because the territory is CANADA.

Practice 2: The NLS_LANG environment variable

This practice example demonstrates how the NLS_LANG environment variable can be set on a Windows platform and its effect on queries.

1. Open a command prompt window.

   ```
   Start -> All Programs -> Accessories -> Command Prompt
   ```

2. At the command prompt, type

   ```
   C:\> SET NLS_LANG=FRENCH_CANADA.WE8ISO8859P1
   ```

3. Start SQL*Plus. Notice the language that is used to prompt for the username is no longer English. It is French! (See Figure 13-2.)

   ```
   C:\> SQLPLUS
   ```

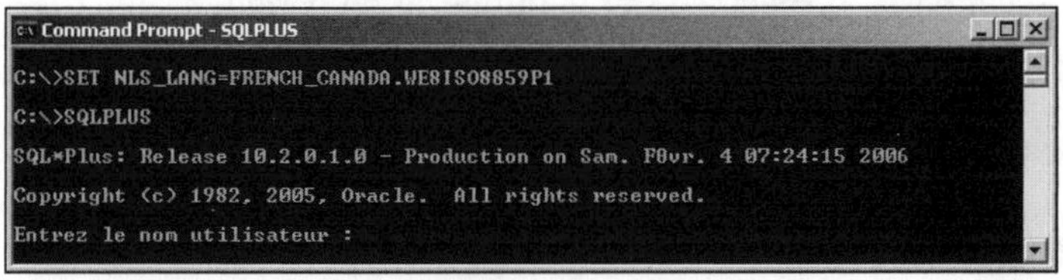

```
Command Prompt - SQLPLUS
C:\>SET NLS_LANG=FRENCH_CANADA.WE8ISO8859P1
C:\>SQLPLUS
SQL*Plus: Release 10.2.0.1.0 - Production on Sam. F0vr. 4 07:24:15 2006
Copyright (c) 1982, 2005, Oracle.  All rights reserved.
Entrez le nom utilisateur :
```

FIGURE 13-2 Setting the NLS_LANG as an environment variable

4. Enter the username and password of the user MEDUSER. At the SQL prompt, query a table called NOEXIST, which does not exist in the MEDUSER schema. Notice the language the error is displayed in. (See Figure 13-3.)

   ```
   SQL> SELECT * FROM NOEXIST;
   ```

```
Command Prompt - SQLPLUS
SQL> SELECT * FROM NOEXIST;
SELECT * FROM NOEXIST
              *
ERREUR α la ligne 1 :
ORA-00942: Table ou vue inexistante

SQL>
```

FIGURE 13-3 Messages are displayed in French

5. Query the entire MEDPROD table. Notice the format of the numeric column PRICE_PER_100, as well as the format of the date values. (See Figure 13-4.)

   ```
   SQL> SELECT * FROM MEDPROD;
   ```

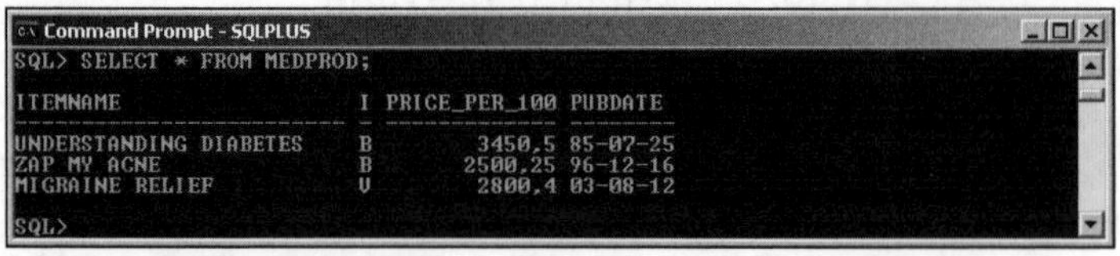

```
SQL> SELECT * FROM MEDPROD;

ITEMNAME                       I PRICE_PER_100 PUBDATE
------------------------------ - ------------- --------
UNDERSTANDING DIABETES         B        3450,5 85-07-25
ZAP MY ACNE                    B       2500,25 96-12-16
MIGRAINE RELIEF                V        2800,4 03-08-12

SQL>
```

FIGURE 13-4 The result of setting the territory to CANADA

6. Exit SQL*Plus and the command prompt.

The NLS_LANGUAGE Parameter

The NLS_LANGUAGE initialization parameter is a derived from NLS_LANG and can be used to define the value for language-dependent conventions only. It determines the language used for:

- Oracle Messages.
- Language for day and month name and their abbreviations.
- Symbols used for language equivalents of A.M., P.M., A.D., and B.C.
- The default sorting order of character data.
- The writing direction.

This parameter can be set either as an initialization parameter or using an ALTER SESSION command on a per-session basis. If specified in the initialization parameter file the language specified will become the default for all sessions in that instance. If the NLS_LANG parameter has been specified in the client environment, then the value of NLS_LANGUAGE initialization parameter is overridden at connection time.

Practice 3: The NLS_LANGUAGE parameter

In this practice we will set the NLS_LANGUAGE at a session level to GERMAN, and retrieve data from the MEDPROD table. You will notice how month names are displayed in German.

1. Start SQL*Plus and connect as the user MEDUSER.

   ```
   SQL> CONNECT MEDUSER/MEDUSER
   ```

2. Issue the following ALTER SESSION command to set the NLS_LANGUAGE to German. Notice the message indicating the "session was altered" is displayed in German.

   ```
   SQL> ALTER SESSION SET NLS_LANGUAGE=GERMAN;
   ```

3. Query the entire MEDPROD table. Notice the month names are displayed in German. (See Figure 13-5.)

   ```
   SQL> SELECT * FROM MEDPROD;
   ```

4. Exit SQL*Plus.

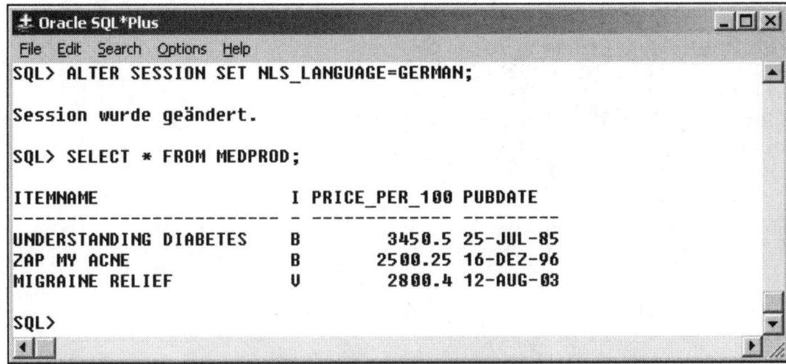

```
SQL> ALTER SESSION SET NLS_LANGUAGE=GERMAN;

Session wurde geändert.

SQL> SELECT * FROM MEDPROD;

ITEMNAME                  I PRICE_PER_100 PUBDATE
------------------------- - ------------- ---------
UNDERSTANDING DIABETES    B        3450.5 25-JUL-85
ZAP MY ACNE               B       2500.25 16-DEZ-96
MIGRAINE RELIEF           V        2800.4 12-AUG-03

SQL>
```

FIGURE 13-5 The month names are displayed in German

The NLS_TERRITORY Parameter

The NLS_TERRITORY initialization parameter is a derived from NLS_LANG and can be used to define the value for territory-dependent conventions only. It determines the language used for:

- Default date format.
- Decimal character and group separator.
- Local currency symbol.
- ISO currency symbol.
- Dual currency symbol.
- First day of the week.
- Credit and debit symbols.

This parameter can be set either as an initialization parameter or using an ALTER SESSION command on a per-session basis. If specified in the initialization parameter file the language specified will become the default for all sessions in that instance. If the NLS_LANG parameter has been specified in the client environment then the value of NLS_TERRITORY initialization parameter is overridden at connection time.

Practice 4: The NLS_TERRITORY parameter

In this practice we will set the NLS_TERRITORY at a session level to SWITZERLAND, and retrieve data from the MEDPROD table. You will notice how the currency symbol and default date format is automatically modified. (See Figure 13-6.)

1. Start SQL*Plus and connect as the user MEDUSER.

   ```
   SQL> CONNECT MEDUSER/MEDUSER
   ```

2. Issue the following ALTER SESSION command to set the NLS_TERRITORY to Switzerland.

   ```
   SQL> ALTER SESSION SET NLS_TERRITORY=SWITZERLAND;
   ```

3. Query the entire MEDPROD table. Type the query as shown below to ensure that the PRICE_PER_100 column is displayed with a currency symbol along with a decimal point (D) and thousands separator (G). The format used is L9G999D99. In Figure 13-7, notice the default date format was changed to

DD.MM.YY. The currency symbol is SFr. The thousands separator is an apostrophe (') and the decimal point is a dot (.).

```
SQL> SELECT ITEMNAME,
     TO_CHAR(PRICE_PER_100,'L9G999D99'), PUBDATE
     FROM MEDPROD;
```

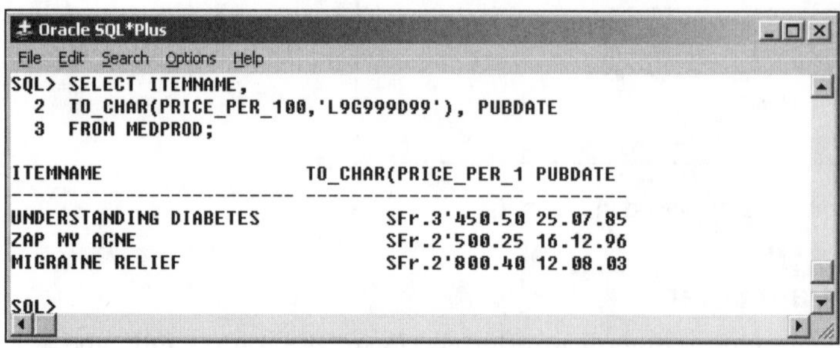

FIGURE 13-6 The territory parameters are automatically modified

4. Exit SQL*Plus.

Other Initialization parameters

In addition to the above-mentioned parameters it is possible to modify individual language and territory settings at an instance, environment, and session level. This is done by a number of initialization parameters. Table 13-4 describes some additional parameters, their description and the parameters from where they are derived.

TABLE 13-4 Other initialization parameters and their description

Initialization Parameter	Description	Derived From
NLS_DATE_LANGUAGE	Used to set day and month names and their abbreviations	NLS_LANGUAGE
NLS_SORT	Used to set default sorting sequence of character data	NLS_LANGUAGE
NLS_DATE_FORMAT	Used to set default date format	NLS_TERRITORY
NLS_NUMERIC_CHARACTERS	Used to set decimal character and group separator	NLS_TERRITORY
NLS_CURRENCY	Used to set local currency symbol	NLS_TERRITORY
NLS_CALENDAR	Used to set calendar system	NLS_TERRITORY
NLS_ISO_CURRENCY	Used to set ISO currency symbol	NLS_TERRITORY

A value assigned to the parameters will override a value for the parameter from which it has been derived. For instance, if you explicitly set the NLS_DATE_FORMAT parameter for a specific session it will override the value that is set for the NLS_TERRITORY parameter.

Practice 5: Other initialization parameters

In this practice you will set the values of some of the parameters mentioned in Table 13-4 at a session level and retrieve data from the MEDPROD table. You will notice how the output changes based on the initialization parameter being set.

1. Start SQL*Plus and connect as the user MEDUSER.

```
SQL> CONNECT MEDUSER/MEDUSER
```

2. Query the MEDPROD table using the query displayed below. Notice in Figure 13-7 that the default language is AMERICAN (English), the default data format is DD-MON-YY, the PRICE_PER_100 column is formatted with the currency symbol as ($), the thousands separator is a comma (,) and the decimal point is a dot (.).

```
SQL> SELECT ITEMNAME,
     TO_CHAR(PRICE_PER_100,'L9G999D99'), PUBDATE
     FROM MEDPROD;
```


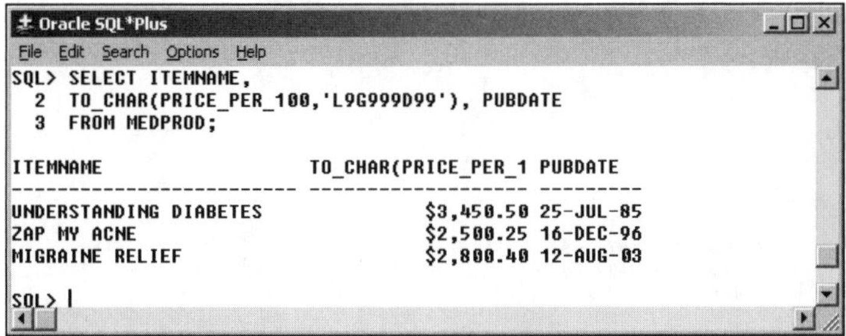

FIGURE 13-7 The output based on the defaults

3. Issue the following ALTER SESSION command to set the NLS_DATE_FORMAT to 'DD/MM/YYYY'. Here you want to display the date with a 2-digit day of month, a 2-digit month of year, and a 4-digit year, separating the date format elements with a forward slash.

```
SQL> ALTER SESSION SET NLS_DATE_FORMAT='DD/MM/YYYY';
```

4. Next, query the MEDPROD table and write a query similar to the one in step 2. In Figure 13-8, notice the difference in the output from step 2. The PUBDATE column uses the format specified by the NLS_DATE_FORMAT parameter.

```
SQL> SELECT ITEMNAME,
     TO_CHAR(PRICE_PER_100,'L9G999D99'), PUBDATE
     FROM MEDPROD;
```

```
Oracle SQL*Plus
File Edit Search Options Help
SQL> SELECT ITEMNAME,
  2  TO_CHAR(PRICE_PER_100,'L9G999D99'), PUBDATE
  3  FROM MEDPROD;

ITEMNAME                     TO_CHAR(PRICE_PER_1 PUBDATE
---------------------------- ------------------- ----------
UNDERSTANDING DIABETES                 $3,450.50 25/07/1985
ZAP MY ACNE                            $2,500.25 16/12/1996
MIGRAINE RELIEF                        $2,800.40 12/08/2003

SQL>
```

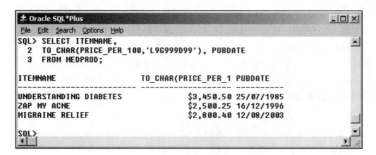

FIGURE 13-8 The result of changing the NLS_DATE_FORMAT parameter

5. Issue the following ALTER SESSION command to set the NLS_CURRENCY to 'Rs.'. Here you want to display the currency symbol as Rs.

```
SQL> ALTER SESSION SET NLS_CURRENCY='Rs.';
```

6. Next, query the MEDPROD table and write a query similar to the one in step 2. In Figure 13-9 notice the change made to the currency symbol. The new format set by NLS_CURRENCY has been applied.


```
SQL> SELECT ITEMNAME,
     TO_CHAR(PRICE_PER_100,'L9G999D99'), PUBDATE
     FROM MEDPROD;
```

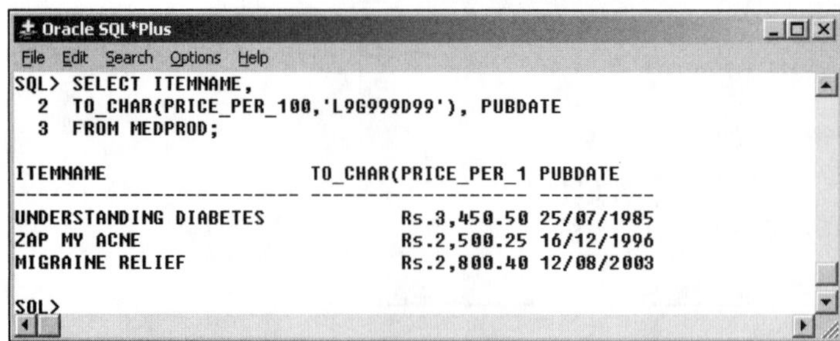

FIGURE 13-9 The result of changing the NLS_CURRENCY parameter

7. Issue the following ALTER SESSION command to set the NLS_NUMERIC_CHARACTERS to ',.'. Here you want to display the decimal point to display as comma(,) and the thousands separator as dot(.).

```
SQL> ALTER SESSION SET NLS_NUMERIC_CHARACTERS=',.';
```

8. Next, query the MEDPROD table and write a query similar to the one in step 2. In Figure 13-10 notice the way in which the radix symbol and thousands separator are displayed. The new format set by NLS_NUMERIC_CHARACTERS has been applied.

```
SQL> SELECT ITEMNAME,
     TO_CHAR(PRICE_PER_100,'L9G999D99'), PUBDATE
     FROM MEDPROD;
```

9. Exit SQL*Plus.

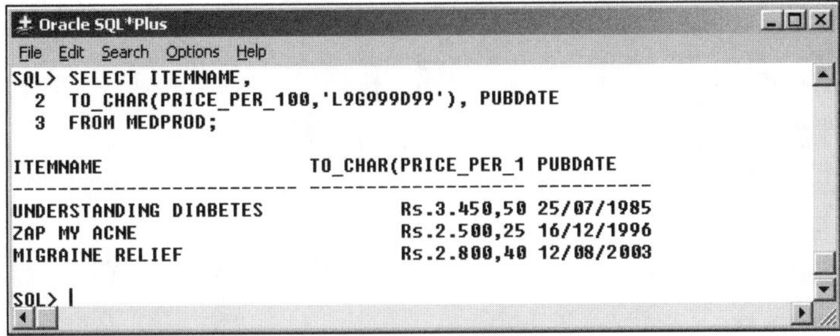

FIGURE 13-10 The result of changing the NLS_NUMERIC_CHARACTERS parameter

NLS Views

A number of data dictionary views are available that provide information relevant to National Language Support. Some important views are listed in Table 13-5.

TABLE 13-5 Some important NLS views

NLS View	Description
V$NLS_VALID_VALUES	Lists the valid values for the initialization parameters: NLS_LANGUAGE, NLS_TERRITORY, NLS_SORT, and NLS_CHARACTERSET etc.
NLS_SESSION_PARAMETERS	Displays the values for NLS parameters within the current session.
V$NLS_PARAMETERS	The view displays the current values of the NLS parameters.
NLS_INSTANCE_PARAMETERS	Displays the values of the NLS parameters set at an instance level. The parameter values were either set in the initialization parameter file or using an ALTER SYSTEM command.
NLS_DATABASE_PARAMETERS	Displays the default values set for the database during its creation. These values may be overridden by redefining the parameter at an instance, environment, or session level.

Practice 6: Querying the Data Dictionary

In this practice you will query some of the NLS views.

1. Start SQL*Plus and connect as a user with SYSDBA privileges.

   ```
   SQL> CONNECT DB_ADMIN/DB_ADMIN AS SYSDBA
   ```

2. Issue a query to display the contents of the NLS_DATABASE_PARAMETERS. Figure 13-11 displays all the default values set for the database during its creation.

   ```
   SQL> SELECT * FROM NLS_DATABASE_PARAMETERS;
   ```

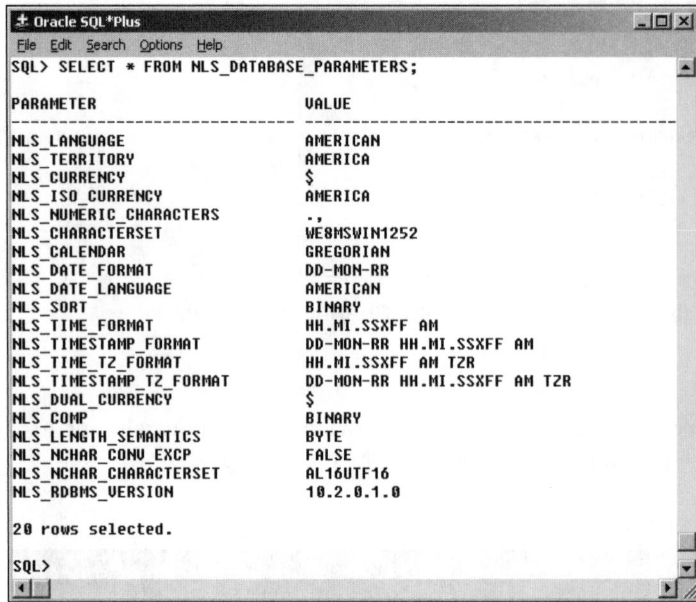
```
SQL> SELECT * FROM NLS_DATABASE_PARAMETERS;

PARAMETER                      VALUE
------------------------------ ----------------------------------------
NLS_LANGUAGE                   AMERICAN
NLS_TERRITORY                  AMERICA
NLS_CURRENCY                   $
NLS_ISO_CURRENCY               AMERICA
NLS_NUMERIC_CHARACTERS         .,
NLS_CHARACTERSET               WE8MSWIN1252
NLS_CALENDAR                   GREGORIAN
NLS_DATE_FORMAT                DD-MON-RR
NLS_DATE_LANGUAGE              AMERICAN
NLS_SORT                       BINARY
NLS_TIME_FORMAT                HH.MI.SSXFF AM
NLS_TIMESTAMP_FORMAT           DD-MON-RR HH.MI.SSXFF AM
NLS_TIME_TZ_FORMAT             HH.MI.SSXFF AM TZR
NLS_TIMESTAMP_TZ_FORMAT        DD-MON-RR HH.MI.SSXFF AM TZR
NLS_DUAL_CURRENCY              $
NLS_COMP                       BINARY
NLS_LENGTH_SEMANTICS           BYTE
NLS_NCHAR_CONV_EXCP            FALSE
NLS_NCHAR_CHARACTERSET         AL16UTF16
NLS_RDBMS_VERSION              10.2.0.1.0

20 rows selected.

SQL>
```


FIGURE 13-11 The output of NLS_DATABASE_PARAMETERS

3. Issue a command to display the contents of the NLS_INSTANCE_PARAMETERS. Notice that many of the values do not display. These parameters have not been explicitly set and derive their values from the higher-level parameters. For example, NLS_DATE_FORMAT derives its value from NLS_TERRITORY. (See Figure 13-12.)

   ```
   SQL> SELECT * FROM NLS_INSTANCE_PARAMETERS;
   ```

4. From the SQL prompt, connect as the user MEDUSER.

   ```
   SQL> CONNECT MEDUSER/MEDUSER
   ```

5. Issue the command to modify the NLS_TERRITORY to JAPAN.

   ```
   SQL> ALTER SESSION SET NLS_TERRITORY=JAPAN;
   ```

6. Next issue the command to display the contents of the NLS_SESSION_PARAMETERS view. In Figure 13-13 notice how the parameters that were dependent on the territory being Japan were also altered, such as NLS_CURRENCY. It now displays as ¥.

   ```
   SQL> SELECT * FROM NLS_SESSION_PARAMETERS;
   ```

7. Finally, issue a query on V$NLS_VALID_VALUES. This is a useful view, in case you do not remember what values are acceptable for the NLS parameters.

   ```
   SQL> SELECT * FROM V$NLS_VALID_VALUES;
   ```

8. Exit SQL*Plus.

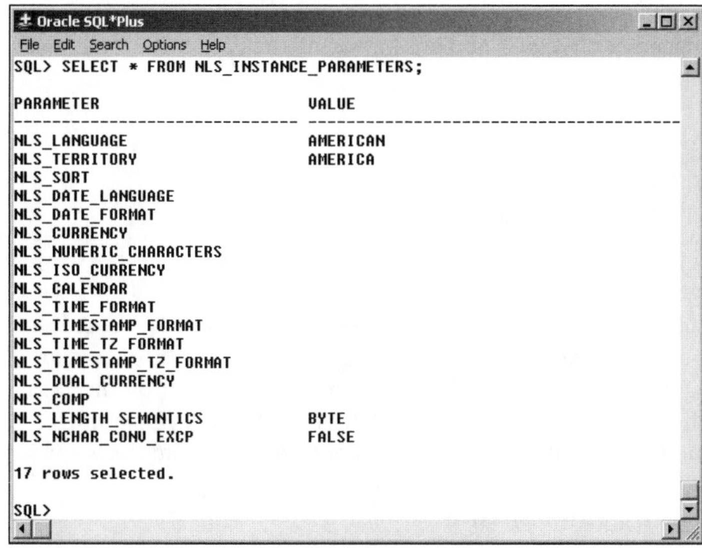

```
SQL> SELECT * FROM NLS_INSTANCE_PARAMETERS;

PARAMETER                      VALUE
------------------------------ ----------------------------------------
NLS_LANGUAGE                   AMERICAN
NLS_TERRITORY                  AMERICA
NLS_SORT
NLS_DATE_LANGUAGE
NLS_DATE_FORMAT
NLS_CURRENCY
NLS_NUMERIC_CHARACTERS
NLS_ISO_CURRENCY
NLS_CALENDAR
NLS_TIME_FORMAT
NLS_TIMESTAMP_FORMAT
NLS_TIME_TZ_FORMAT
NLS_TIMESTAMP_TZ_FORMAT
NLS_DUAL_CURRENCY
NLS_COMP
NLS_LENGTH_SEMANTICS           BYTE
NLS_NCHAR_CONV_EXCP            FALSE

17 rows selected.

SQL>
```

FIGURE 13-12 The NLS parameters set for the instance

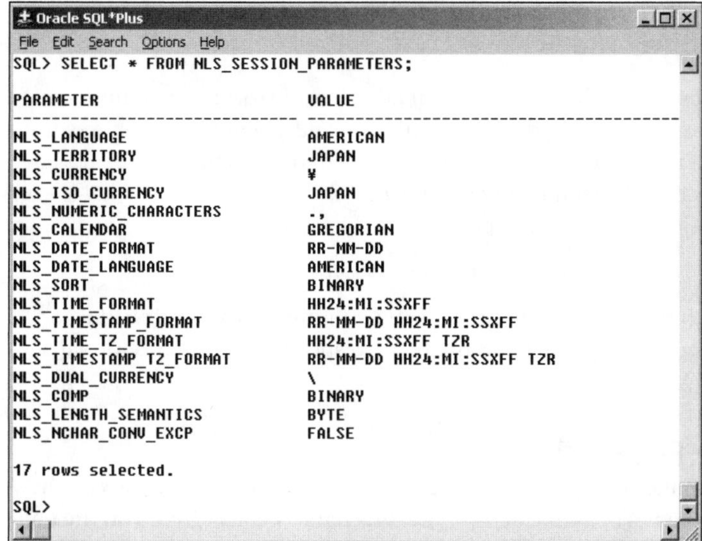

```
SQL> SELECT * FROM NLS_SESSION_PARAMETERS;

PARAMETER                      VALUE
------------------------------ ----------------------------------------
NLS_LANGUAGE                   AMERICAN
NLS_TERRITORY                  JAPAN
NLS_CURRENCY                   ¥
NLS_ISO_CURRENCY               JAPAN
NLS_NUMERIC_CHARACTERS         .,
NLS_CALENDAR                   GREGORIAN
NLS_DATE_FORMAT                RR-MM-DD
NLS_DATE_LANGUAGE              AMERICAN
NLS_SORT                       BINARY
NLS_TIME_FORMAT                HH24:MI:SSXFF
NLS_TIMESTAMP_FORMAT           RR-MM-DD HH24:MI:SSXFF
NLS_TIME_TZ_FORMAT             HH24:MI:SSXFF TZR
NLS_TIMESTAMP_TZ_FORMAT        RR-MM-DD HH24:MI:SSXFF TZR
NLS_DUAL_CURRENCY              \
NLS_COMP                       BINARY
NLS_LENGTH_SEMANTICS           BYTE
NLS_NCHAR_CONV_EXCP            FALSE

17 rows selected.

SQL>
```

FIGURE 13-13 The NLS parameters set for the current session

DATE-TIME DATATYPES

We began this chapter by discussing some of the issues faced by companies who conduct their business globally. For such companies an important factor is to consider the different times and time zones. The time when transactions occur must be stored in a consistent manner.

The Oracle database provides a number of datatypes that can be used for this purpose. These datatypes were introduced in Oracle 9*i* and are known as the date-time datatypes. The date-time datatypes include:

- DATE
- TIMESTAMP
- TIMESTAMP WITH TIME ZONE
- TIMESTAMP WITH LOCAL TIME ZONE

The Date Datatype

This datatype stores date and time information. When a column or variable is created that is defined to be of date type, then internally the following information is stored: year, month, day, hour, minute, and second. The default date format is dependent on the NLS_DATE_FORMAT parameter if one has been set or the NLS_DATE_LANGUAGE parameter. When specifying a date value if you omit the time component then by default it is set to midnight.

A column or variable of date type is defined as:

```
column_name | variable          DATE
```


A typical date value that can be stored in the column or variable would be `'12-MAR-07 11:30:33'`.

The Timestamp Datatype

This datatype is an extension of the date datatype. In addition to storing all components stored in the date datatype—year, month, day, hour, minute, and second, it also stores fractional seconds. Fractional seconds are specified after the seconds component, separated by a dot (.). The default fractional seconds precision is 6.

A column or variable of timestamp datatype is defined as:

```
column_name | variable  TIMESTAMP(seconds_precision)
```

A typical timestamp value that can be stored in the column or variable would be `'12-MAR-07 11:30:33.456'`. In this example, 3 digits were specified for the fractional seconds precision.

Timestamp with Time Zone Datatype

The Timestamp with Time Zone datatype is an extension of the timestamp datatype. In addition to storing all components of a timestamp type, this datatype also gives you the ability to store a time zone offset. A time zone offset is the difference between local time and UTC (Universal Time Coordinates). The offset is specified in hours and minutes. An example of a numeric offset could be -4:00. Instead of an offset, you may specify a time region if you wish. An equivalent time zone region for -4:00 is US/Eastern. A column or variable of timestamp with time zone datatype is defined as:

```
column_name|variable   TIMESTAMP(seconds_precision) WITH TIME ZONE
```

A typical timestamp value that can be stored in the column or variable would be `'12-MAR-07 11:30:33.456 US/Eastern'` or `'12-MAR-05 11:30:33.456 -4:00'`. In this example 3 digits were specified for the fractional seconds precision.

Timestamp with Local Time Zone Datatype

The timestamp with local time zone is a variant of the timestamp datatype. In this datatype the time zone information is not stored. The value being stored in the column or variable is always stored in the database time zone. When a client retrieves this data, the value is adjusted to the client's session time zone before displaying the value. A column or variable of timestamp with time zone datatype is defined as:

```
column_name|variable   TIMESTAMP(seconds_precision) WITH LOCAL TIME ZONE
```

Consider this example that demonstrates the behavior of timestamp with local time zone datatype.

Suppose a database in Chicago contains a table called TLTZ. The table contains a single column whose datatype is timestamp with local time zone. The table is accessed by clients across the United States. Chicago has a time zone of -6:00. A client in Washington, D.C. (time zone -5:00) inserts the following timestamp value '15-MAR-05 11:30:33.456' into the table. The row will be added into the database table as 15-MAR-05 10:30:33.456. This is because Chicago is one hour behind Washington, D.C.

However, when the same value is queried by the client in Washington, D.C. it will be displayed as 15-MAR-05 11:30:33.456.

The date-time datatypes are particularly useful during the creation of applications that need to be accessed by users all across the world.

Practice 7: Date-time datatypes

The following practice example demonstrates the usage of the date-time datatypes.

1. Start SQL*Plus and connect as the user MEDUSER.

   ```
   SQL> CONNECT MEDUSER/MEDUSER
   ```

2. Issue the following ALTER SESSION command to set the correct date format.

   ```
   SQL> ALTER SESSION SET NLS_DATE_FORMAT='DD-MON-YYYY HH24:MI:SS';
   ```

3. Query the entire MEDPROD table. In Figure 13-14 notice the time-related information is displayed with Zeroes.

   ```
   SQL> SELECT * FROM MEDPROD;
   ```

4. Create a table called TIME1 with a single column A of DATE datatype.

   ```
   SQL> CREATE TABLE TIME1 (A DATE);
   ```

5. Insert a row into the table TIME1 as shown below.

   ```
   SQL> INSERT INTO TIME1 VALUES('10-MAY-90 14:30:30');
   ```

6. Query the table TIME1 to see the row that was inserted. (See Figure 13-15.)

   ```
   SQL> SELECT * FROM TIME1;
   ```

7. Create a table called TIME2 with a single column A of TIMESTAMP datatype.

   ```
   SQL> CREATE TABLE TIME2(A TIMESTAMP);
   ```

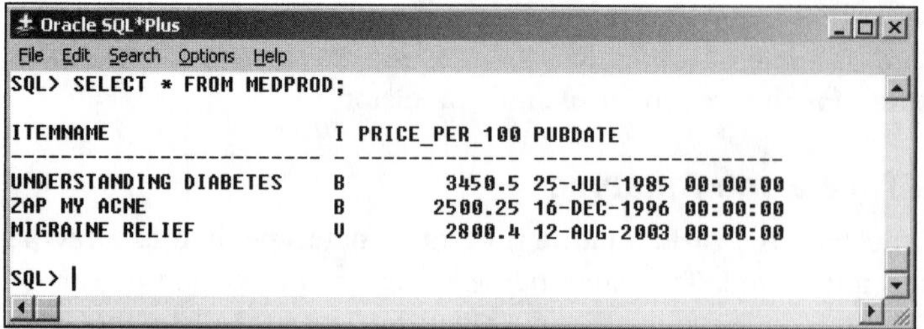

FIGURE 13-14 When the time is not specified, a default midnight is stored

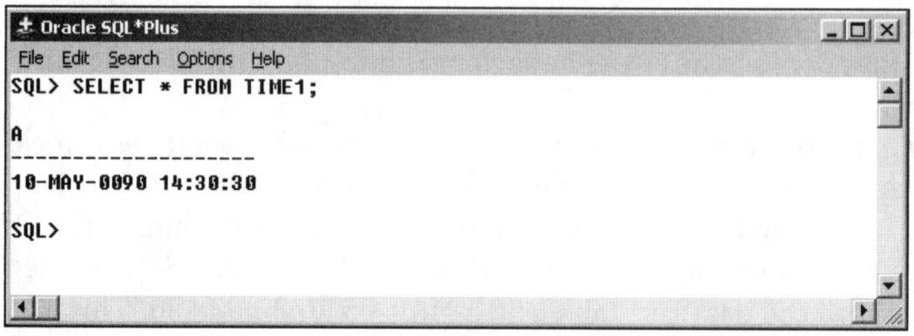

```
SQL> SELECT * FROM TIME1;

A
--------------------
10-MAY-0090 14:30:30

SQL>
```

FIGURE 13-15 The contents of table TIME1

8. Insert a row into the table TIME2 as shown below.

   ```
   SQL> INSERT INTO TIME2 VALUES('10-JUN-90 6:30:40.30 AM');
   ```

9. Query the table TIME2 to see the row that was inserted. (See Figure 13-16.)

   ```
   SQL> SELECT * FROM TIME2;
   ```

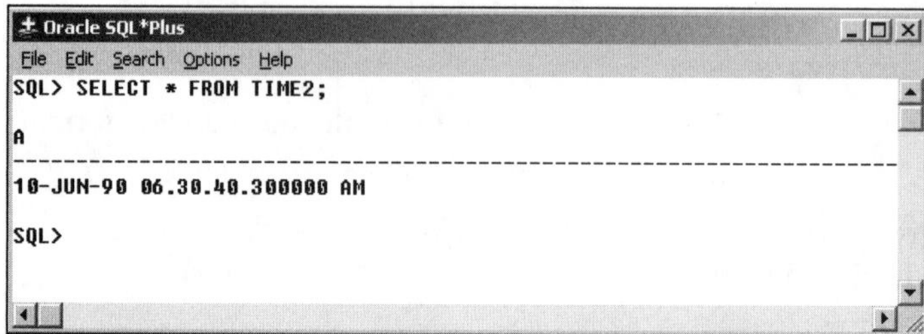

FIGURE 13-16 The contents of table TIME2

10. Create a table called TIME3 with a single column A of TIMESTAMP WITH TIME ZONE datatype.

    ```
    SQL> CREATE TABLE TIME3(A TIMESTAMP WITH TIME ZONE);
    ```

11. Insert a row into the table TIME3 as shown below.

    ```
    SQL> INSERT INTO TIME3 VALUES('13-APR-95 5:45:35.4567 AM -4:
    00');
    ```

12. Query the table TIME3 to see the row that was inserted. (See Figure 13-17.)

```
SQL> SELECT * FROM TIME3;
```

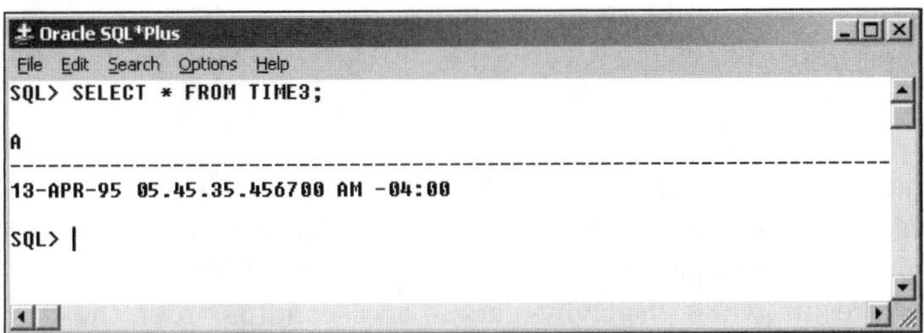

FIGURE 13-17 The contents of table TIME3

13. Create a table called TIME4 with a single column A of TIMESTAMP WITH LOCAL TIME ZONE datatype.

```
SQL> CREATE TABLE TIME4 (A TIMESTAMP WITH LOCAL TIME ZONE);
```

14. Insert a row into the table TIME4 as shown below.

```
SQL> INSERT INTO TIME4 VALUES('13-JUL-05 10:10:30.45 AM');
```

15. Query the table TIME4 to see the row that was inserted. (See Figure 13-18.)

```
SQL> SELECT * FROM TIME4;
```

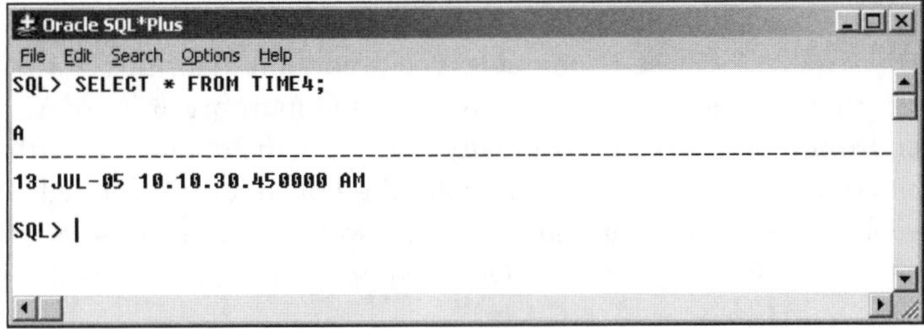

FIGURE 13-18 The contents of table TIME4

16. Exit SQL*Plus.

SORTING CAPABILITIES AND LINGUISTIC SORTING

Sorting is performed to display data in a certain order. When numeric values are sorted they appear in ascending or descending order. When characters are sorted they appear in alphabetic order. When date values are sorted they appear in a chronological order. In the English alphabet, the letter 'A' appears before 'C', and 'C' before 'G', and so on. Sort order can also be case sensitive. In an ASCII-based platform, 'A' will be sorted before 'a'. It should also be noted that often languages are derived from other languages. For example, the alphabets used in English, Norwegian, Polish, German, French, and Zulu are derived from the Latin alphabet.

The modern Latin alphabet consists of 52 letters. Many languages add a variety of accents to the basic letters. This is done to modify the pronunciation of a letter, or indicate pitch or emphasis. Examples of accented letters are Á, Ä, and Ð. The marks that accompany the characters are known as *diacritics*.

The Oracle 10g database provides two methods of sorting: Binary Sort and Linguistic Sort.

Binary Sort

The binary sorting technique uses the numeric values or codes assigned to characters during the process of sorting. Earlier in the chapter, it was mentioned that every character is assigned a numeric value. For example, the character 'A' is assigned 65, and the character 'a' assigned 97. As a result, when displaying data in an ascending order, the 'A' will always appear before 'a' because 65 comes before 97.

Binary sort is performed using the following table:

```
! " # $ % & ' ( ) * + , . / 0 1 2 3 4 5 6 7 8 9 : ; < = > ? @ A B C D E F G H I J K L M N
O Q R S T U V W X Y Z [ \ ] ^ _ ` a b c d e f g h i j k l m n o p q r s t u v w x y z { | } ~
¤ , ƒ „ … † ‡ ˆ ‰ Š ‹ Œ Ž ‘ ’ “ ” • – — ˜ ™ š › œ ž Ÿ   ¡ ¢ £ ¤ ¥ ¦ § ¨ © ª « ¬ ® ¯ ° ± ² ³
´ µ ¶ · ¸ ¹ º » ¼ ½ ¾ ¿ À Á Â Ã Ä Å Æ Ç È É Ê Ë Ì Í Î Ï Ð Ñ Ò Ó Ô Õ Ö × Ø Ù Ú Û Ü Ý
Þ ß à á â ã ä å æ ç è é ê ë ì í î ï ð ñ ò ó ô õ ö ÷ ø ù ú û ü ý þ ÿ
```


Binary sort is the fastest type of sorting technique. However, it does not always produce accurate results. When there are many characters involved that do not fall into the standard ASCII or EBCDIC character sets, the technique may produce erroneous sorting results. This is particularly true in the case of characters that contain diacritics. If the letters A, Ä, and Z had to be sorted, a binary sort would have resulted in a sort order of A, Z, Ä. This can be clearly seen from the table above. In many languages the characters with diacritics are actually variants of the base letter. For example, the Polish letters derived from the Latin alphabet are collated after their originals—A, Ä, Z would be the correct sort order in Polish. As a solution to such sort-related issues, Oracle supports Linguistic sorting.

Linguistic Sorting

Linguistic sorting handles the complex sorting requirements of different languages. In this method characters from any encoding scheme are sorted according to specific linguistic conventions, and not based on the numeric codes assigned to the characters.

Linguistic sorting may be divided into two categories:

- Monolingual Linguistic Sort
- Multilingual Linguistic Sort

Monolingual Linguistic Sort

In monolingual linguistic sorts Oracle compares character strings in two steps making use of a sort key. The sort key consists of two components, a major value and a minor value. Characters that have a similar base letter such as A, Ă, Ą, Ä hold the same major value. They are differentiated by their minor value. Table 13-6 describes a typical sort key for the base letter A.

TABLE 13-6 Major and Minor values in Monolingual linguistic sorting

Character	Major Value	Minor Value
a	15	5
A	15	10
ä	15	15
Ä	15	20
b	20	5

Therefore using monolingual sorting the characters A, Z, and Ä will be sorted as A, Ä, Z in the Polish language. Monolingual linguistic sorting is only available on Unicode multibyte character sets.

Multilingual Linguistic Sort

Monolingual linguistic sorting works quite well when sorting data in a single language. However, it cannot be used when multiple languages and writing systems come into play. Using multilingual linguistic sorting data from more than one language can be sorted in a single sort operation. This is useful in multilingual applications where a need to accurately search and organize data in any language may arise. Multilingual sorts are performed using three levels of precision: Primary Level Sorts, Secondary Level Sorts, and Tertiary Level Sorts.

To understand how this works, consider the following words that need to be sorted:

attaché, attache, Attaches, attaches, attachés, exposé, expose

At a primary sort level, the words will be distinguished between the Base letters. Individual locales define how base letters are sorted. In this example, A comes before E. Therefore at a primary level sorting will result in:

attache
attaché
Attaches
attaches
attachés
exposé
expose

At a secondary sort level, sorting based on the appearance of diacritics for a given base letter will be done. All strings without diacritics will come before strings with diacritics.

attache
attaché
Attaches
attaches
attachés
expose
exposé

At a tertiary sort level, sorting will be done based on case. Lowercase will appear before upper case.

attache
attaché
attaches
Attaches
attachés
expose
exposé

The NLS_SORT parameter, which is derived from the NLS_TERRITORY parameter, can be used to determine the type of linguistic sorting that must be performed. For example, if you set NLS_SORT=POLISH then sorting will be done considering the cultural conventions of the Polish language.

Another parameter worth mentioning is the NLS_COMP parameter. It controls the way in which comparison operators such as =, >, and < in the WHERE clause handle linguistic sorting. It can take values BINARY (the default) or ANSI. When set to BINARY the comparison is based on the binary value of the string. When set to ANSI, the comparison will be done linguistically based on the value of the NLS_SORT parameter.

Case-Insensitive and Accent-Insensitive Sorting

By default, sorting will always consider the accent and case of characters during the sorting operation. Sometimes you may want to perform case-insensitive and/or accent-insensitive sorting operations. Oracle has introduced this as a new feature in Oracle 10*g*. The characters _CI (case-insensitive) or _AI (accent-insensitive and case-insensitive) can be appended to name of the territory if a case-insensitive or accent-insensitive sort must be performed. The following series of examples help demonstrate this point.

- To perform a case-sensitive and accent-sensitive sort in Chinese, you would set: `NLS_SORT=CHINESE`
- To perform a case-insensitive and accent-insensitive sort in Japanese, you would set: `NLS_SORT=JAPANESE_AI`
- To perform an case-insensitive and accent-sensitive sort in French, you would set: `NLS_SORT=FRENCH_CI`
- To perform a case-insensitive and accent-insensitive sort in Binary, you would set: `NLS_SORT=BINARY_AI`

NOTE

The NLS_SORT initialization parameter may be set to GENERIC_BASELETTER. In Oracle, base letters are defined in a base letter table that maps each letter to its base letter. For example a, A, ä, and Ä all map to *a*, which is the base letter. By setting NLS_SORT=GENERIC_BASELETTER, you can simulate the behavior of a case-insensitive and accent-insensitive sort. However, the GENERIC_BASELETTER search is not a linguistically sensitive search because it is not based on any specific language.

Practice 8: Linguistic sorting

The following practice demonstrates the different outputs displayed as a result of performing binary sorting, monolingual linguistic sorting, and multilingual linguistic sorting. It is preferable that you use *i*SQL*Plus to perform this practice because SQL*Plus may not display the accented characters.

1. Launch a browser and start *i*SQL*Plus. You may have to supply a URL of the form:

   ```
   http://machine_name:5560/isqlplus
   ```

2. Connect as the user MEDUSER and supply the host string to the database. If you are unsure about the host string, ask your instructor.
3. From the input panel, enter the following CREATE TABLE command and click on the Execute button.

   ```
   CREATE TABLE TS (A  VARCHAR2(30));
   ```

4. Clear the contents of the input panel and type in the following code. Then click the Execute button. The statements will be executed one by one. Figure 13-19 displays the output of the SELECT statement issued at the end. It displays the rows of the table as they were entered.

   ```
   DELETE FROM TS;
   COMMIT;
   INSERT INTO TS VALUES('attache');
   INSERT INTO TS VALUES('attaché');
   INSERT INTO TS VALUES('Attaches');
   INSERT INTO TS VALUES('attaches');
   INSERT INTO TS VALUES('attachés');
   INSERT INTO TS VALUES('exposé');
   INSERT INTO TS VALUES('expose');
   COMMIT;
   SELECT * FROM TS;
   ```

5. Clear the contents of the input area, and issue the following SELECT statement with an ORDER BY clause. The ORDER BY clause will result in a sort operation being performed which by default is Binary sort. Figure 13-20 displays the results of a Binary sort. Notice, uppercase appears before lowercase.

   ```
   SELECT * FROM TS ORDER BY A;
   ```

6. Next, issue an ALTER SESSION command to set the NLS_SORT to FRENCH.

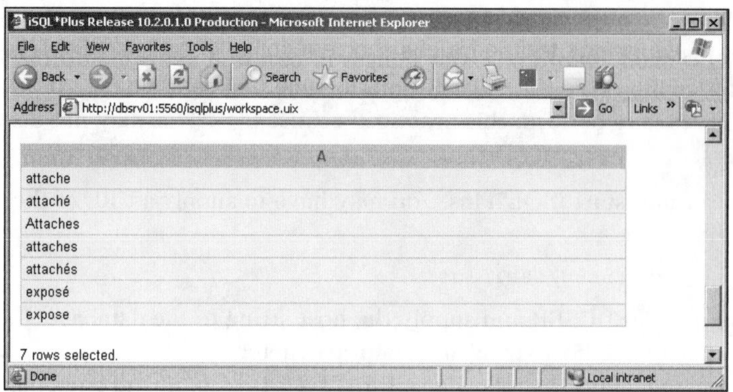

FIGURE 13-19 The contents of the table TS

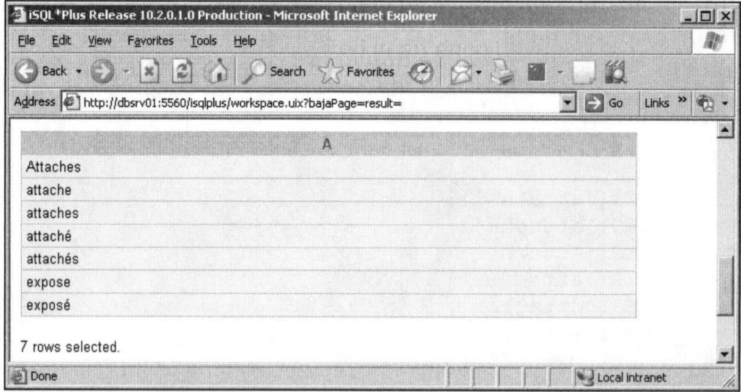

FIGURE 13-20 The contents of TS after a binary sort operation

Then click the Execute button. You are now requesting a monolingual linguistic sort to be performed using the French alphabet.

```
ALTER SESSION SET NLS_SORT='FRENCH';
```

7. Query the TS table, with an ORDER BY clause on the column A. Figure 13-21 displays a monolingual linguistic sort done in French.

```
SELECT * FROM TS ORDER BY A;
```

8. Next, issue an ALTER SESSION command to set the NLS_SORT to FRENCH_M. Then click the Execute button. You are now requesting a multilingual linguistic sort to be performed using the French alphabet.

```
ALTER SESSION SET NLS_SORT='FRENCH_M';
```

9. Query the TS table, with an ORDER BY clause on the column A. Select the Execute button. Figure 13-22 displays a multilingual linguistic sort done in French.

```
SELECT * FROM TS ORDER BY A;
```

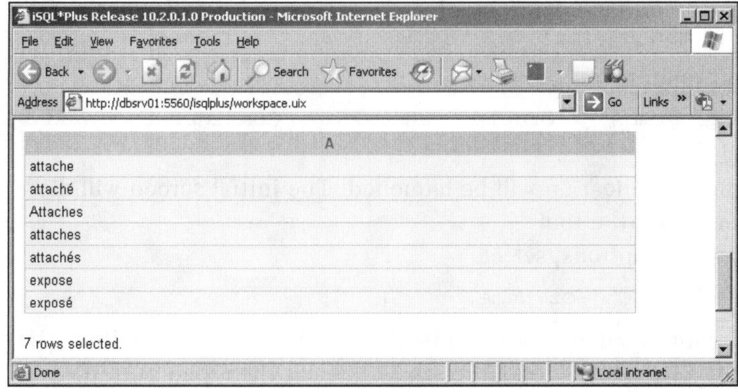

FIGURE 13-21 The contents of table TS after a monolingual linguistic sort

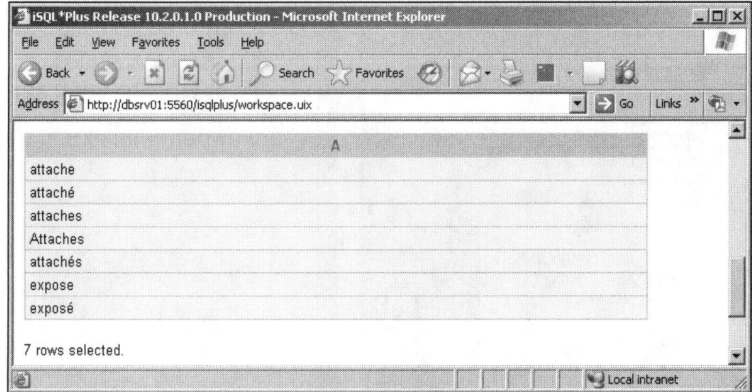

FIGURE 13-22 The contents of table TS after a multilingual linguistic sort

10. Logout of *i*SQL*Plus and close the browser.

THE ORACLE LOCALE BUILDER

The Oracle Locale Builder is a graphical user interface that can be used to easily configure and customize locale data. You can manage four types of locale definitions using Locale Builder. They include language, territory, character sets, and linguistic sorting. This interface allows you to create your own formats for these four locale definitions. Locale definitions that are shipped with the Oracle Database server are available in binary files that have the .NLB extension. You can create your own user-defined .NLB file with locale builder. Also available are .NLT files that define locale-specific data and their contents can be viewed and read because they are in text.

Practice 9: Oracle Locale Builder

In this practice example you will create a new territory using Locale Builder. You will then enable the new territory within a SQL*Plus.

1. Using an operating system command, create a directory called LB in the C:\ drive.
2. From the Windows Start button, select

```
Start -> All Programs -> Oracle-OraHome10 -> Configuration and
Migration Tools -> Locale Builder.
```

3. The Locale Builder application will be launched. The initial screen will display information about the tool.
4. From the main menu options, select

```
File -> Open -> By Object Name.
```

5. The Existing Definitions dialog box will be displayed. From the **Territory (ID)** pane, select **AMERICA(1).** (See Figure 13-23.) Select the **Open** button.

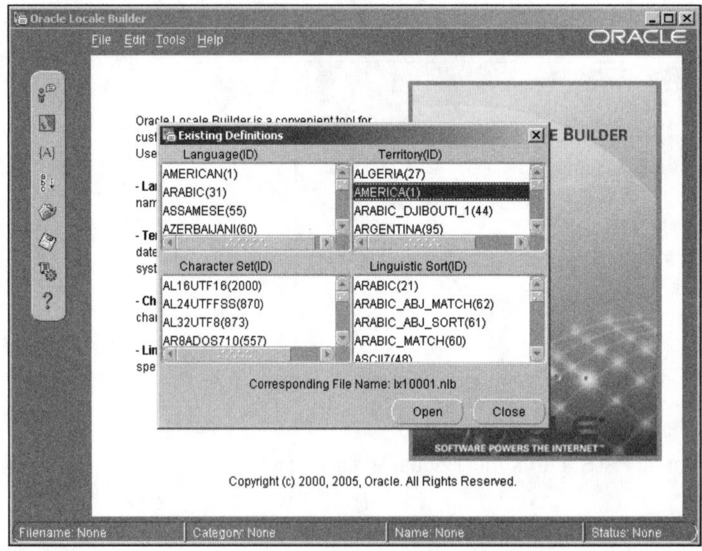

FIGURE 13-23 The Existing Definitions dialog window

6. The appearance of the window will be changed and a number of tabs will be displayed. In the **General** tab enter the following information. (See Figure 13-24.)

```
Territory Name: NEWTERR
Territory ID: 1001
Territory Abbreviation: NT
```

7. Select the **Date&Time** tab and make the following changes (See Figure 13-25.):

```
Short Date Format : fmMONTH/DD/RRRR
Oracle Date Format: MONTH/DD/RRRR
```

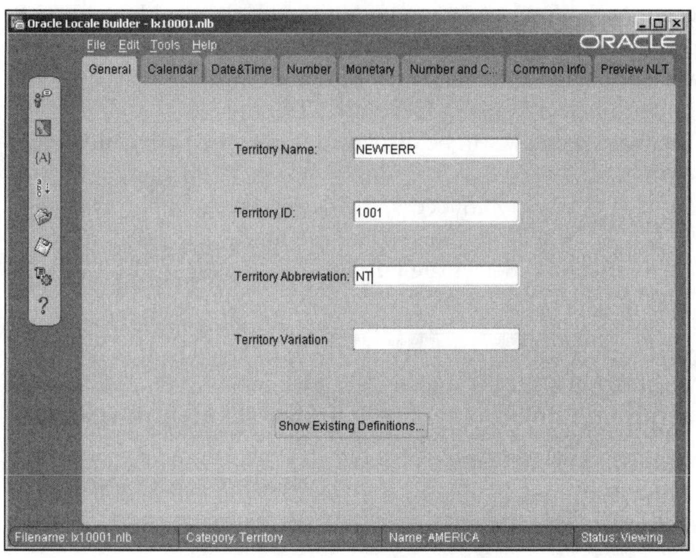

FIGURE 13-24 Specifying details of the new territory being created

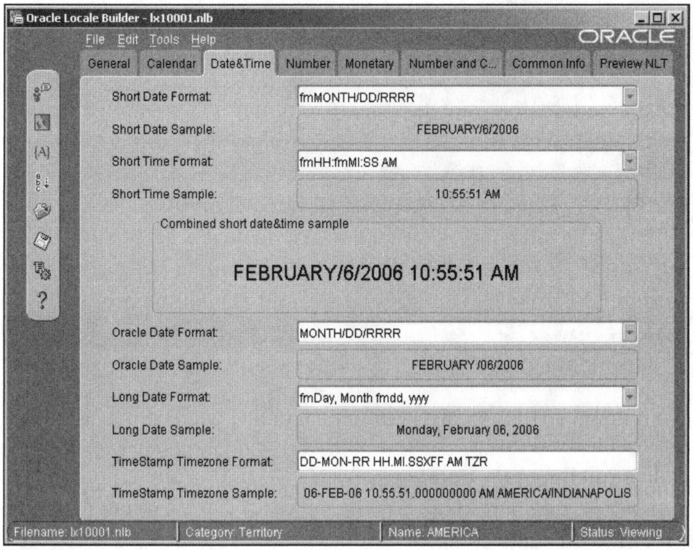

FIGURE 13-25 Setting the Date&Time format for the new territory

8. Select **File -> Save As** from the main menu. Set the location to the folder **LB** created in step 1. The file type will be .nlt. A file name will be displayed. Accept the filename without changing it. Select the **Save** button.
9. From the main menu, select **Tools -> Generate NLB**.
10. A Generate NLB dialog window will be displayed. Enter the path **C:\LB** and select the **OK** button.
11. A dialog window NLB Generation Success, indicating successful creation will be displayed. This window tells you to copy all the newly generated .nlb files to the ORA_NLS10 directory. Select the **OK** button. (See Figure 13-26.)

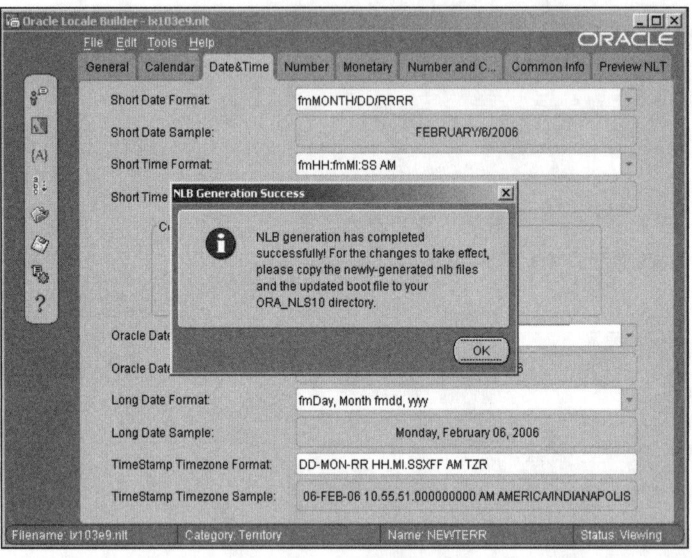

FIGURE 13-26 The NLB Generation Success dialog window.

NOTE

The ORA_NLS10 directory in Windows is %ORACLE_HOME%\nls\data

12. Select **File -> Exit**, to exit Locale Builder.
13. Using Windows explorer, navigate to C:\LB and copy all the files generated, to the %ORACLE_HOME%\nls\data directory. You will be prompted about overwriting some files. Select **Yes to All**.
14. Start SQL*Plus, and connect as a user with SYSDBA privileges.

```
SQL> CONNECT DB_ADMIN/DB_ADMIN AS SYSDBA
```

15. Shut down and start up the database.

```
SQL> SHUTDOWN IMMEDIATE;
SQL> STARTUP
```

16. Connect as the user MEDUSER whose password is MEDUSER.

```
SQL> CONNECT MEDUSER/MEDUSER
```

17. Issue the command to set the NLS_TERRITORY to NEWTERR.

```
SQL> ALTER SESSION SET NLS_TERRITORY=NEWTERR;
```

18. Issue a command to query the entire MEDPROD table.

```
SQL> SELECT * FROM MEDPROD;
```

19. Notice the format of the PUBDATE column. It displays with the format that was specified in the NEWTERR territory (Step 7). (See Figure 13-27.)

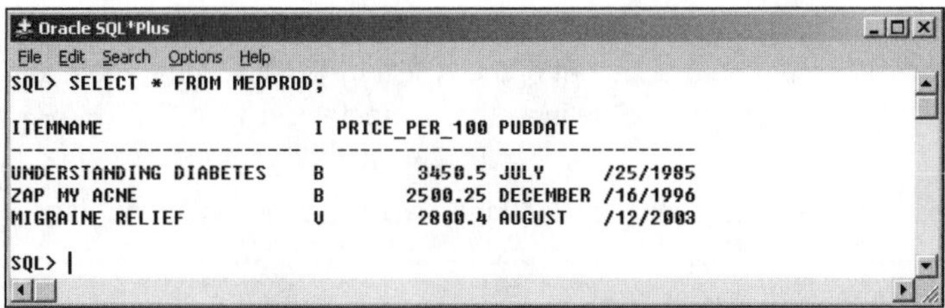

FIGURE 13-27 The format of the PUBDATE column is based on the new territory

20. Exit SQL*Plus.

In this chapter you learned many features of globalization support. These features facilitate the creation and management of global applications and web sites. Chapter 14 discusses a number of issues related to networking.

Chapter Summary

- Globalization support in Oracle encompasses a range of features that give users the ability to create multi-lingual applications.
- National Language support is a subset of globalization support.
- Encoding schemes may be single-byte, fixed-length multi-byte, or variable-length multi-byte.
- Character sets are created based on encoding schemes and may support multiple languages. Character sets have a standard name and an Oracle-defined name.
- When a database is created, its database character set and national character set is defined.
- The database character set must be a superset of the ASCII or EBCDIC character, for data storage in the data dictionary. It also defined the character set for SQL CHAR characters.
- The national database character set must be defined based on the additional languages that must be supported by the database and stored in SQL NCHAR columns. The default national database character is AL16UF16.
- The Unicode character set contains all available and known characters from all languages across the world.
- A Unicode character set, such as UTF8 or AL32UTF8, is a good option if any character column has to store variable-length multi-byte character data.
- National language support gives you the ability to display data based on the cultural conventions of a language and region (territory).
- National Language support can be enabled by setting the values of a number of parameters either in the initialization parameter file, as an environment variable for a specific client, or using the ALTER SESSION command within a specific session.
- A collection of datatypes known as the date-time datatypes are available to facilitate the creation of applications that are accessed from around the world and store time-related data across different time zones.
- Sorting is the ability to display data in a certain order. Oracle provides three types of sorting: binary, monolingual linguistic, and multilingual linguistic sorting.
- Binary sorting is suitable for ASCII-based systems.
- Linguistic sorting must be done when data is stored in languages other than English and specific language based sorting must be applied.

Syntax Guide

SYNTAX GUIDE		
Element	**Description**	**Example**
`SET variable`	A method of specifying the value of an environment variable on the Windows platform.	`C:\> SET NLS_LANG=FRENCH_FRANCE.UTF8`
`ALTER SYSTEM`	Specifying an initialization parameter at an instance level.	`SQL>ALTER SYSTEM SET NLS_DATE_ FORMAT='DD/MM/YYYY';`
`ALTER SESSION`	Specifying an initialization an a session level.	`SQL>ALTER SESSION SET NLS_DATE_ FORMAT='DD/MM/YYYY';`
Launching *i*SQL*Plus • Launch a browser • Enter the URL to access iSQL*Plus: `http://<hostname>:5560/isqlplus`		

Review Questions

1. From the list of character sets displayed, identify the Unicode character sets.
   a. AL16UTF16
   b. UTF16
   c. UTF8
   d. AL32UTF8
   e. All the above.
2. Identify the characteristics of National Language Support. [Identify 2.]
   a. Provides a clearer description of single byte and multi-byte character sets.
   b. Describes length semantics.
   c. Considers the cultural conventions of various languages.
   d. It is a superset of globalization support.
   e. It is a subset of globalization support.
3. The database character set is used for which of the following purposes? [Identify 3.]
   a. To store data in CHAR, VARCHAR2 columns
   b. To store in NCHAR, NVARCHAR2 columns
   c. To code in SQL and PL/SQL
   d. To store data in the columns of the data dictionary tables.
4. The ________________ character set cannot be defined to be a database character set.
5. The default national database character set is ________________ .

6. An NLS parameter can be set at a session level using a ________________ command.
   a. Environment Variable.
   b. ALTER DATABASE
   c. ALTER SESSION
   d. ALTER SYSTEM
7. The components of the NLS_LANG parameter are ________________. [Choose 3.]
   a. Language
   b. Date Formats
   c. Territory
   d. National Character Set
   e. Database character Set
8. Identify the parameters that are defined from the NLS_LANGUAGE initialization parameter.
   a. NLS_DATE_LANGUAGE
   b. NLS_DATE_FORMAT
   c. NLS_CURRENCY
   d. NLS_SORT
9. Identify the parameters that are defined from the NLS_TERRITORY initialization parameter.
   a. NLS_DATE_FORMAT
   b. NLS_NUMERIC_CHARACTERS
   c. NLS_SORT
   d. NLS_CALENDAR
10. Tom, a user of the database, wants to be able to display all dates on a certain report using the format 15:20:35 JUL-17-2005. What could he possibly do?
    a. Issue an ALTER SESSION SET NLS_DATE_LANGUAGE=Japan because the default date format for Japan differs from DD-MON-YY.
    b. Issue an ALTER SESSION SET NLS_DATE_FORMAT='HH24:MI:SS MON-DD-YYYY';
    c. Issue an ALTER SESSION SET NLS_DATE_TERRITORY=Japan because the default date format for Japan differs from DD-MON-YY.
    d. Issue an ALTER SESSION SET NLS_DATE_LANGUAGE='HH24:MI:SS MON-DD-YYYY';
11. Tanya is an application developer. She wishes to display a listing of all the valid values that can be used for the NLS_TERRITORY initialization parameter. Identify the data dictionary view that she can use for this purpose.
    a. NLS_DATABASE_PARAMETERS
    b. V$DATABASE_VALID_VALUES
    c. NLS_VALID_VALUES
    d. V$NLS_VALID_VALUES

12. Which of the following data dictionary views would you query to display the name of the database character set?
    a. V$DATABASE
    b. V$DATABASE_PARAMETERS
    c. V$INSTANCE_PARAMETERS
    d. It is available as an initialization parameter.
13. Identify the names of the date-time datatypes.
    a. DATE
    b. DATETIME
    c. TIMESTAMP
    d. TIMESTAMP WITH LOCAL TIME ZONE
    e. TIMESTAMP WITH TIME ZONE
    f. CURRENT_TIMESTAMP
14. Name the default method of sorting.
15. Your database is currently using WE8ISO8859P1 as the database character set and AL16UTF16 as the national character set. A number of new applications need to be created that will store Chinese, Japanese, and Korean names. What would you recommend as an ideal solution to this requirement?
    a. Change the database character set to UTF8, and use SQL CHAR data types.
    b. Change the database character set to AF16UTF16 and use SQL CHAR data types.
    c. Keep the national character set as it is and use SQL NCHAR data types.
    d. Change the database character set to AL32UTF8 and use SQL CHAR data types.
16. A Unicode database is one in which:
    a. The database character set is a Unicode character set.
    b. The national character set is a Unicode character set.
    c. Both the database character set and the national character sets are Unicode character sets.
    d. The operating system uses a Unicode character set.
17. You wish to create a column that stores time-specific data. You are not concerned about time zone information. You wish to specify a 4-digit fractional second. Which of the following data type definitions would you use?
    a. TIMESTAMP
    b. TIMESTAMP(4)
    c. TIMESTAMP(4) WITH LOCAL TIME ZONE
    d. DATE

18. While performing multilingual linguistic sorting, identify the correct action performed during the secondary level sort.
    a. Words will be distinguished between base letters.
    b. Sorting based on the appearance of diacritics for a given base letter will be done.
    c. Sorting based on the case of the letter will be done.
19. The NLS_SORT parameter has been specified with the following value:

    ```
    NLS_SORT=FRENCH_CI
    ```

    Which of the following statements is true regarding the setting of the parameter?
    a. Accent-insensitive and case-insensitive French sort
    b. Accent-sensitive and case-sensitive French sort
    c. Accent-insensitive and case-sensitive French sort
    d. Accent-sensitive an case-insensitive French sort
20. To enable linguistic sorting for a certain session, which parameter would need to be set?

Hands-On Assignments

Note: Please run the script c13_asetup.sql from the Chapter13 folder of the Student Datafiles before performing the Hands-On assignments. The script creates a table called MEDICINES with three rows and three columns.

Assignment 13-1 Create a table using Length Semantics

1. Start SQL*Plus and connect as the user with SYSDBA privileges.
2. Display the value of the initialization parameter NLS_LENGTH_SEMANTICS.
3. Create a table called AS131, having two character columns. Define the first column as A1 with a width of 5 bytes using character semantics, and the second A2 with a width of 15 bytes using byte semantics.
4. Exit SQL*Plus.

Assignment 13-2 Displaying the NLS parameters defined for the database

1. Start SQL*Plus and connect as a user with SYSDBA privileges.
2. Query the NLS_DATABASE_PARAMETERS data dictionary view.
3. Identify the name of the database character set and national character set from the output.
4. Exit SQL*Plus.

Assignment 13-3 Modifying the Language for a session

1. Start SQL*Plus and connect as the user MEDUSER.
2. Query the NLS_SESSION_PARAMETERS data dictionary view to display the default NLS parameters defined for the session.
3. Identify the default language and default territory for the session.
4. Issue an ALTER SESSION command to set the NLS_LANGUAGE to CZECH.
5. Query the NLS_SESSION_PARAMETERS view to see the change in the NLS_DATE_LANGUAGE and NLS_SORT parameters. They are automatically modified to CZECH.

6. Query the MEDICINES table and view the output of the DATE_INTRO column. The month names will be displayed in CZECH.
7. Exit SQL*Plus.

Assignment 13-4 Modifying the Territory for a session

1. Start SQL*Plus and connect as the user MEDUSER.
2. Query the NLS_SESSION_PARAMETERS data dictionary view to display the default NLS parameters defined for the session.
3. Identify the default territory for the session.
4. Issue an ALTER SESSION command to set the NLS_LANGUAGE to SINGAPORE.
5. Query the NLS_SESSION_PARAMETERS view to see the change in the NLS_TERRITORY, NLS_CURRENCY, NLS_ISO_CURRENCY, NLS_DATE_FORMAT. They are automatically modified based on the change in territory.
6. Query the MEDICINES table using the query displayed and view the output of the PRICE and DATE_INTRO column. The currency symbol and date format have been set based on the territory being set to SINGAPORE.

```
SQL> SELECT MNAME,
     TO_CHAR(PRICE,'L99G999D99') PRICE, DATE_INTRO
     FROM MEDICINES;
```

7. Exit SQL*Plus.

Assignment 13-5 Setting individual parameters of NLS_LANGUAGE

1. Start SQL*Plus and connect as the user MEDUSER.
2. Display the value of the NLS_DATE_LANGUAGE initialization parameter from the NLS_SESSION_PARAMETERS view.
3. Issue an ALTER SESSION command to change the value of the NLS_DATE_LANGUAGE parameter to Romanian.
4. Query the MEDICINES table and notice the month names.
5. Exit SQL*Plus.

Assignment 13-6 Setting value for individual parameters of NLS_TERRITORY

1. Start SQL*Plus and connect as the user MEDUSER.
2. Issue the following query to display data from the MEDICINES table. The format symbol C represents ISO currency.

```
SQL> SELECT MNAME, TO_CHAR(PRICE,'C9G999D99') PRICE,
     DATE_INTRO FROM MEDICINES;
```

3. Issue an ALTER SESSION command to set the NLS_ISO_CURRENCY to CANADA.
4. Repeat the query in step 2, and view the output in the ISO currency of Canada.
5. Issue an ALTER SESSION command to set the NLS_NUMERIC_CHARACTERS. Set the radix symbol to ! and the thousands separator *.
6. Repeat the query in step 2, to see how the output was altered.
7. Exit SQL*Plus.

Assignment 13-7 Working with Date-time datatypes

1. Start SQL*Plus and connect as the user MEDUSER.
2. Create a table called T137. Create the table with the following column definitions.

Column Name	Datatype
COLD	DATE
COLT	TIMESTAMP
COLTZ	TIMESTAMP WITH TIME ZONE
COLTLZ	TIMESTAMP WITH LOCAL TIME ZONE

3. Insert the following values into the table T137 to create a new row.
```
'16-APR-05','15-OCT-05 8:45:25.45 AM',
'22-NOV-05 3.30.00.45 AM -6:00',
'31-DEC-05 11.59.59.01 PM'
```
4. Query the T137 table.
5. Issue an ALTER SESSION command to set the TIME_ZONE to 2:00. (If the default time zone for your session is 2:00, then set it to -4:00).
6. Requery the T137 table and notice that all the values remain the same except for the timestamp with local time zone value that was automatically adjusted based on the time zone of the client session.
7. Exit SQL*Plus.

Assignment 13-8 Sorting Options in Oracle

It is recommended that the following assignment be done using *i*SQL*Plus, since accented characters do not display in SQL*Plus.

1. Launch a browser and enter the URL to start *i*SQL*Plus. Log in as the user MEDUSER.
2. Create a table called T138, with a single character column called COLA, 20 characters in width.
3. Issue the ALTER SESSION command to set the NLS_SORT parameter to BINARY;
4. Type in the following sequence of commands. You are first deleting all the rows in the table T138 and then inserting a number of rows.
```
DELETE FROM T138;
INSERT INTO T138 VALUES('Resume');
INSERT INTO T138 VALUES('Résumés');
INSERT INTO T138 VALUES('resume');
INSERT INTO T138 VALUES('Resumes');
INSERT INTO T138 VALUES('resumes');
INSERT INTO T138 VALUES('résumé');
INSERT INTO T138 VALUES('Résumé');
INSERT INTO T138 VALUES('résumés');
COMMIT;
```
5. Issue a query to display the data in the T138 table.

6. Issue a query to retrieve the data in the T138 table, ordering on the column COLA. What type of sorting do you think will be performed?
7. Next, issue an ALTER SESSION command to set the NLS_SORT to monolingual linguistic sort in French.
8. Issue a query to retrieve the data in the T138 table, ordering on the column COLA. Notice the difference in the output. (The accented characters appear after their base letter because they have a higher minor value.)
9. Next, issue an ALTER SESSION command to set the NLS_SORT to multilingual linguistic sort in French.
10. Issue a query to retrieve the data in the T138 table, ordering on the column COLA. Notice the difference in the output. (This output is derived by applying the three levels of sorting: primary, secondary, and tertiary levels).
11. Issue an ALTER SESSION command to set the NLS_SORT to a French Case Insensitive sort.
12. Issue a command to query the T138 table, ordering on the COLA column. Notice the change in the output.
13. Issue an ALTER SESSION command to set the NLS_SORT to a French Case Insensitive sort and Accent Insensitive sort.
14. Issue a command to query the T138 table, ordering on the COLA column. Notice the change in the output.
15. Log out of *i*SQL*Plus.

Case Study

A retailer in the United States wants to create a web-based application. The company wishes to cater to customers all over the world and ensure that the application supports as many languages as possible. Customers should be able to view data in their native locale. Identify some of the important aspects that the company should keep in mind during the development of the application.

CHAPTER 14

DIAGNOSTIC TOOLS AND THE ORACLE LISTENER

LEARNING OBJECTIVES

After completing this lesson you should be able to understand:

- Diagnostic tools—log and trace files
- The function of the listener process
- The vulnerabilities of the listener process
- Securing the listener process

ORACLE CERTIFICATION EXAM OBJECTIVES COVERED IN THIS CHAPTER INCLUDE:

- Secure the listener
- Remove default EXTPROC entry and add a separate listener to handle external procedure calls
- Use the alert log and database trace files for diagnostic purposes

INTRODUCTION

The need to access the database from a wide variety of applications presents a number of security challenges. Databases are accessed by various applications such as client-server, web-based and e-commerce applications. Consequently, security of the database is a major concern for database administrators. Security breaches frequently occur because security features are not enabled or misconfigured. Perhaps the most common mistake made by a DBA is using the default installation with default passwords. Other reasons for security breaches include bugs in the product that create security holes.

In this chapter we will discuss two distinct topics. The first topic deals with diagnostic tools that are available within the database. These tools provide administrators information about the database and problems within the database. The diagnostic tools that will be discussed are log and trace files, which assist in troubleshooting and problem resolution. The second topic is the listener process and security issues associated with it. We will discuss the vulnerabilities of the listener and the different methods of securing it. We will also review the external procedure support provided by the listener process and protection from security threats arising as a result of this functionality.

SETUP FOR THE CHAPTER

Please run the script **ch14_setup.sql** as the user MEDUSER, before performing the practice examples and hands-on exercises presented in this chapter. The script creates a table called PRESCRIPTIONS with four rows in it.

1. Start SQL*Plus and connect as the user MEDUSER.

   ```
   SQL>CONNECT MEDUSER/MEDUSER
   ```

2. From the SQL prompt run the ch14_setup.sql script.

   ```
   SQL>@<PATH>\CH14_SETUP.SQL
   ```

3. Exit SQL*Plus.

THE CURRENT CHALLENGE AT KELLER MEDICAL CENTER

Ryan goes through the various log files in the Oracle database at least once a day. When going through the listener log file on Monday morning he notices the "TNS-01169: The listener has not recognized the password" error appearing repeatedly.

```
25-FEB-2006 11:30:39 * services * 1169169
1 TNS-01169: The listener has not recognized the password
25-FEB-2006 11:31:39 * services * 1169169
2 TNS-01169: The listener has not recognized the password
25-FEB-2006 11:32:39 * services * 1169169
```

Discussing the error with other administrators he realizes that the error indicates *invalid password attempts* leading him to conclude that someone has been trying to gain unauthorized access to the listener process over the weekend.

DIAGNOSTIC TOOLS

A database administrator's primary function is to ensure the smooth running of the Oracle database. This involves not only setting up the database initially but maintaining it on a daily basis. The Oracle server provides a number of simple tools in the form of log files that may be used to help the administrator in his job. A log file is a chronological record of all changes, errors, and messages that may occur within the database. There are two types of files that hold information generated within the database—Log Files and Trace Files. In this chapter we will discuss the following files:

- The Alert Log File
- Trace Files
- User Trace Files

The Alert Log File

Log files contain a record of changes, errors, and messages arising from database activity. An important log file in the Oracle database is the Alert Log file. It contains information about all important events that occur in the database. These include a time-stamped record of startups, shutdowns, instance recovery operations, media recovery operations, changes to the structure of the database, such as the addition of a tablespace, block corruption errors, ORA-600 or critical errors, non-default values of initialization parameters, ALTER SYSTEM commands, checkpoint information, waits incurred by various processes, and so on.

A DBA must go through the latest entries in the log file on a regular basis, preferably at least once a day, to identify potential problems and rectify them in a timely manner. An alert log file is available in the location specified by the BACKGROUND_DUMP_DEST initialization parameter. If this parameter is not set, Oracle will automatically create the alert log file in the `%ORACLE_HOME%\RDBMS\TRACE` directory. The alert log file has a naming convention of `ALERT_<SID>.log` on Windows machines. If the alert log file already exists, new entries are appended to the end of the file. Over a period of time, the size of the alert log file may reach the maximum file size limitations imposed by Oracle or the operating system.

When this occurs, new entries will not be added and valuable information may be lost. To avoid this situation, administrators must back up, rename, or delete the contents of the file to make room for new entries. If an alert log file is not found, the Oracle server will automatically create it the next time it needs to write an entry into the log file, without generating an error.

The contents of the alert log file may be viewed using an editor or from Enterprise Manager.

Practice 1: Viewing the contents of the Alert Log file.

In this practice you will locate the alert log file and open it to view its contents. The contents of the alert log file may be different on your machine. A partial listing of an alert log file has been displayed in the practice to describe some of its contents. The practice also demonstrates how to view the contents of the alert file using Enterprise Manager.

1. Start SQL*Plus, and connect as a user with SYSDBA privileges.

   ```
   SQL> CONNECT DB_ADMIN/DB_ADMIN AS SYSDBA
   ```

2. Issue the command to display the contents of the BACKGROUND_DUMP_DEST initialization parameter. Note the value; it will be required in step 4 of this practice.

   ```
   SQL> SHOW PARAMETER BACKGROUND_DUMP_DEST
   ```

3. Exit SQL*Plus.
4. Using Windows Explorer, navigate to the location specified by the BACKGROUND_DUMP_DEST initialization parameter. Locate the file called `ALERT_<sid>.log`. The `<SID>` value is related to the System Identifier of your database. For example, the name of the alert log file for the DB101 database is ALERT_db101.log.
5. Open the alert log file and go through the contents. Shown below is a part of the file. Certain portions of the file have been highlighted to give you an idea of the kind of information stored in the file.

The contents of the ALERT log file

```
SYS auditing is disabled
Starting up ORACLE RDBMS Version: 10.2.0.2.0.
System parameters with non-default values:
processes                = 150
shared_pool_size         = 83886080
large_pool_size          = 8388608
java_pool_size           = 50331648
control_files            =
C:\ORACLE\PRODUCT\10.2.0\ORADATA\DB101\CONTROL01.CTL,
C:\ORACLE\PRODUCT\10.2.0\ORADATA\DB101\CONTROL02.CTL,
C:\ORACLE\PRODUCT\10.2.0\ORADATA\DB101\CONTROL03.CTL
```

```
db_block_size                 = 8192
db_cache_size                 = 25165824
compatible                    = 10.2.0.2.0
db_file_multiblock_read_count= 16
db_recovery_file_dest         = C:\oracle\product\10.2.0\
flash_recovery_area
db_recovery_file_dest_size= 2147483648
undo_management               = AUTO
undo_tablespace               = UNDOTBS1
remote_login_passwordfile= EXCLUSIVE
db_domain                     =
dispatchers                   = (PROTOCOL=TCP) (SERVICE=db101XDB)
job_queue_processes           = 10
background_dump_dest          = C:\ORACLE\PRODUCT\10.2.0\ADMIN\DB101\BDUMP
user_dump_dest                = C:\ORACLE\PRODUCT\10.2.0\ADMIN\DB101\UDUMP
core_dump_dest                = C:\ORACLE\PRODUCT\10.2.0\ADMIN\DB101\CDUMP
sort_area_size                = 65536
db_name                       = db101
open_cursors                  = 300
pga_aggregate_target          = 25165824
Wed Nov 09 09:58:00 2005
starting up 1 dispatcher(s) for network address
'(ADDRESS=(PARTIAL=YES)(PROTOCOL=TCP))'...
starting up 1 shared server(s) ...
CKPT started with pid=6, OS id=1692
SMON started with pid=7, OS id=1696
MMAN started with pid=3, OS id=1680
RECO started with pid=8, OS id=1700
DBW0 started with pid=4, OS id=1684
PMON started with pid=2, OS id=1672
CJQ0 started with pid=9, OS id=1704
LGWR started with pid=5, OS id=1688
Wed Nov 09 09:58:02 2005
alter database mount exclusive
Wed Nov 09 09:58:02 2005
Controlfile identified with block size 16384
Wed Nov 09 09:58:07 2005
Setting recovery target incarnation to 2
Wed Nov 09 09:58:07 2005
Successful mount of redo thread 1, with mount id 1043773418
Wed Nov 09 09:58:07 2005
Database mounted in Exclusive Mode.
Completed: alter database mount exclusive
Wed Nov 09 09:58:07 2005
alter database open
Wed Nov 09 09:58:07 2005
Beginning crash recovery of 1 threads
Wed Nov 09 09:58:07 2005
Started first pass scan
Wed Nov 09 09:58:08 2005
Completed first pass scan
3626 redo blocks read, 321 data blocks need recovery
```

Non-default values of the initialization parameters when the instance is started

```
Wed Nov 09 09:58:08 2005
Started redo application at
Thread 1: logseq 28, block 3, scn 0.0
Recovery of Online Redo Log: Thread 1 Group 3 Seq 28 Reading mem 0
Mem# 0 errs 0: F:\ORACLE\PRODUCT\10.1.0\ORADATA\DB101\REDO03.LOG
Wed Nov 09 09:58:12 2005
Completed redo application
Wed Nov 09 09:58:12 2005
Completed crash recovery at
Thread 1: logseq 28, block 3629, scn 0.566214
 321 data blocks read, 321 data blocks written, 3626 redo blocks read
Wed Nov 09 09:58:13 2005
Thread 1 advanced to log sequence 29
Maximum redo generation record size = 120832 bytes
Maximum redo generation change vector size = 116476 bytes
Private_strands 7 at log switch
Thread 1 opened at log sequence 29
Current log# 1 seq# 29 mem# 0:
C:\ORACLE\PRODUCT\10.2.0\ORADATA\DB101\REDO01.LOG
Successful open of redo thread 1
Wed Nov 09 09:58:13 2005
MTTR advisory is disabled because FAST_START_MTTR_TARGET is not set
Wed Nov 09 09:58:13 2005
SMON: enabling cache recovery
Wed Nov 09 09:58:15 2005
Successfully onlined Undo Tablespace 1.
Wed Nov 09 09:58:15 2005
SMON: enabling tx recovery
Wed Nov 09 09:58:15 2005
Database Characterset is AL32UTF8
Wed Nov 09 09:58:15 2005
Published database character set on system events channel
Wed Nov 09 09:58:15 2005
All processes have switched to database character set
Wed Nov 09 09:58:18 2005
Starting background process QMNC
QMNC started with pid=13, OS id=1756
Wed Nov 09 09:58:22 2005
replication_dependency_tracking turned off (no async multimaster replication
found)
Wed Nov 09 09:58:23 2005
Starting background process MMON
MMON started with pid=14, OS id=1764
Wed Nov 09 09:58:23 2005
Starting background process MMNL
MMNL started with pid=15, OS id=1768
Wed Nov 09 09:58:25 2005
Completed: alter database open
```

Instance recovery being performed

Startup of the database

6. Close the alert log file.
7. Launch a browser and enter the URL to access the Enterprise Manager. Log in with SYSDBA privileges.
8. From the **Database Control Home** page, navigate to the **Related Links** section. Select the **Alert Log Content** link. (See Figure 14-1.)

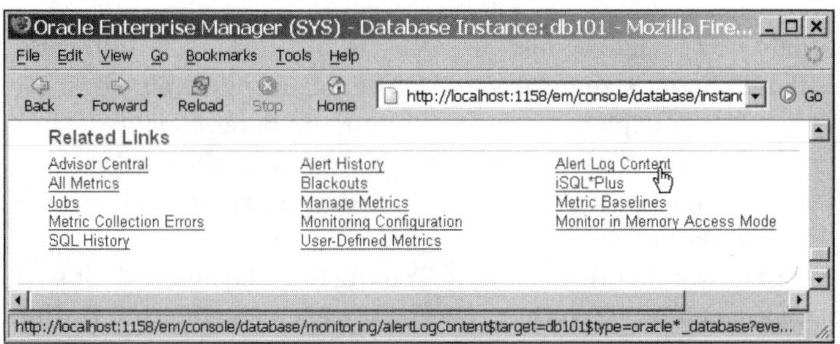

FIGURE 14-1 The Alert Log Content Link

9. The **Most Recent Alert Log Entries** page will be opened displaying the last 100,000 bytes of the alert log. Read the contents of this page. (See Figure 14-2.)

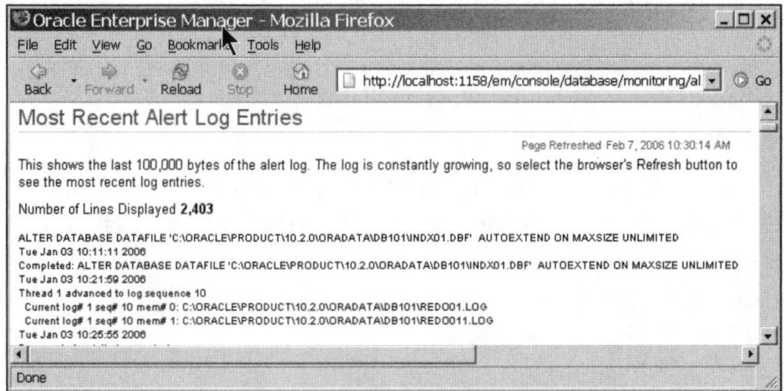

FIGURE 14-2 Viewing the Alert Log entries from the Enterprise Manager

10. Log out and exit the browser.

Trace Files

Trace files can be of two kinds—background trace files or user trace files. A background trace file is created by a background process when it encounters an error or exception. Trace files contain diagnostic data. If the DBA identifies a problem by reading the alert log file, then the trace files may be viewed to get a complete picture of how, when, and where the error might have occurred. Trace files are usually large, with a lot of information, and are created whenever a dump event occurs. A dump event occurs when the "systemstate" or "errorstack" is dumped to a file. Trace files created by background processes are also created in the location specified by BACKGROUND_DUMP_DEST initialization parameter. These trace files have a naming convention of `<SID>_<background_process>_pid.trc`; where <background_process> can be substituted by the name of the process that generated the file and <pid> is an operating system process ID. A trace file generated by the Log Writer (LGWR) background process that encountered an exception may have name like ORA_LGWR_1011.trc.

Another parameter that may be of relevance is the MAX_DUMP_FILE_SIZE initialization parameter. It specifies the maximum size for trace files. By default, the value of this parameter is set to UNLIMITED. If you explicitly set a value for the parameter to 1 M (1 Megabyte), and the size of the file reaches 1 M, then new trace information will no longer be added to the file. A DBA must periodically either backup or delete existing information in the trace and log files to make room for new entries.

Trace files may also be created by network processes. Tracing must be enabled for such processes only when you notice a specific error; otherwise you may be overwhelmed by the amount of information generated. As data passes from one network layer to another, within the network stack of the database, each layer writes information into the trace file. Going through the trace file helps you identify which internal network layer encountered a problem.

Practice 2: Viewing the contents of background process trace files

In this practice you will locate a trace file generated by a background process and view its contents.

1. Start SQL*Plus, and connect as a user with SYSDBA privileges.

   ```
   SQL> CONNECT DB_ADMIN/DB_ADMIN AS SYSDBA
   ```

2. Issue the command to display the contents of the BACKGROUND_DUMP_DEST AND MAX_DUMP_FILE_SIZE parameters. Note the values specified by these parameters.

   ```
   SQL> SHOW PARAMETER BACKGROUND_DUMP_DEST
   SQL> SHOW PARAMETER MAX_DUMP_FILE_SIZE
   ```

3. Exit SQL*Plus.
4. Using Windows Explorer, navigate to the location you noted in step 2. Locate any file that has a naming convention like <SID>_<background_process>_PID.trc. If none exists, then none of the background trace file encountered an exception. Figure 14-3 displays a number of background trace files, created by the ARCH(arc*n*) and Log Writer(LGWR).
5. Open any trace file and view it contents.
6. Close the trace file.

User Trace Files

In addition to background trace files, the Oracle database allows users to create trace files to help them tune SQL statements. This feature is often used by developers, during application development, to view the execution plan and performance impact of their SQL

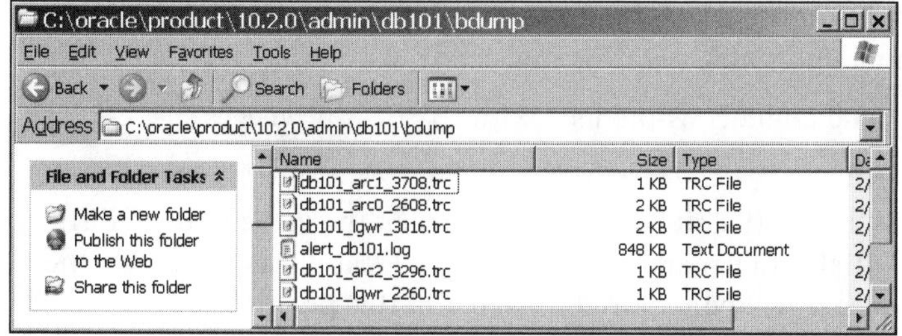

FIGURE 14-3 A list of trace files in the BACKGROUND_DUMP_DEST location

statements. SQL tuning is not always an easy task and user trace files can help developers fine tune their SQL statements. A user trace file will contain the execution plan generated by Oracle along with statistical information about the number of logical reads/ physical reads incurred by the SQL statement.

To enable SQL tracing, a user must first set the SQL_TRACE initialization parameter to TRUE within the session. If timing information is required the TIMED_STATISTICS parameter may also be set to TRUE. To be able to identify the trace files easily from among all the trace files generated by various users, a user may specify a tag or identifier that can be appended to the trace file name. This is done by the TRACEFILE_IDENTIFIER parameter. The value can be any user-defined string that will act as a suffix to the name of the trace file. User trace files are not easily readable, and must be formatted. This can be done by using the TKPROF utility.

User trace files are created in the location specified by the USER_DUMP_DEST initialization parameter.

The Oracle-supplied DBMS_MONITOR package contains a number of subprograms that may be used to enable/disable SQL tracing within individual user sessions. Database administrators can remotely enable or disable tracing within user sessions by specifying the SID and SERIAL# of the session. Table 14-1 displays some important procedures of the DBMS_MONITOR package.

TABLE 14-1 Subprograms of the DBMS_MONITOR package

Subprogram Name	Description	Example
SESSION_TRACE_ENABLE	To enable SQL tracing within a session.	SQL> EXEC DBMS_MONITOR. SESSION_TRACE_ENABLE(SESSION_ID => 145, SERIAL_NUM => 25);
SESSION_TRACE_DISABLE	To disable SQL tracing for a user session.	SQL> EXEC DBMS_MONITOR. SESSION_TRACE_DISABLE(SESSION_ID => 145, SERIAL_NUM => 25);

Practice 3: Generating user trace files

This practice example demonstrates how to create and read a user trace file.

1. Start SQL*Plus and connect as the user with SYSBDA privileges.

```
SQL> CONNECT DB_ADMIN/DB_ADMIN AS SYSDBA
```

2. Issue the SHOW PARAMETER command to display the value of the USER_DUMP_DEST initialization parameter. Note the location specified by the parameter because it will be required in step 7 of this practice.

```
SQL> SHOW PARAMETER USER_DUMP_DEST
```

3. Connect as the user MEDUSER.

```
SQL> CONNECT MEDUSER/MEDUSER
```

4. Issue the ALTER SESSION commands displayed below. The first command enables SQL tracing within the current session. The second ALTER SESSION command enables the generation of timing-related information in the trace file and the third ALTER SESSION command is used to generate trace files that have the suffix MEDUSER at the end of the trace file name.

NOTE

If you receive an "Insufficient privileges" error when issuing the ALTER SESSION command, then connect as a user with SYSDBA privileges and grant the ALTER SESSION privilege to MEDUSER.

```
SQL> CONNECT DB_ADMIN/DB_ADMIN AS SYSDBA
SQL> GRANT ALTER SESSION TO MEDUSER;
```



```
SQL> CONNECT MEDUSER/MEDUSER
SQL> ALTER SESSION SET SQL_TRACE=TRUE;
SQL> ALTER SESSION SET TIMED_STATISTICS=TRUE;
SQL> ALTER SESSION SET TRACEFILE_IDENTIFIER='MEDUSER';
```

5. Issue a command to query the entire PRESCRIPTIONS table.

```
SQL> SELECT * FROM PRESCRIPTIONS;
```

6. Exit SQL*Plus.
7. Using the Windows Explorer, navigate to the location you noted in step 2.
8. Locate the file name that has a suffix of MEDUSER, and name similar to `<SID>_<ORA>_PID_MEDUSER.trc`. Note the name of the file created on your machine. This name will be required for the completion of Step 10. Figure 14-4 displays a user trace file with the name db101_ora_680_meduser.trc.
9. Open the user trace file and view its contents. It is not very readable and it would be difficult to make any sense from it.
10. The TKPROF is a utility provided by Oracle to format the output of user trace files and make them readable. The utility is invoked from the command prompt as TKPROF. It receives as an input the name and location of the user trace and generates an output file. Using the command prompt, invoke the TKPROF utility as shown below. The output file generated by TKPROF is OUTTK.TRC.

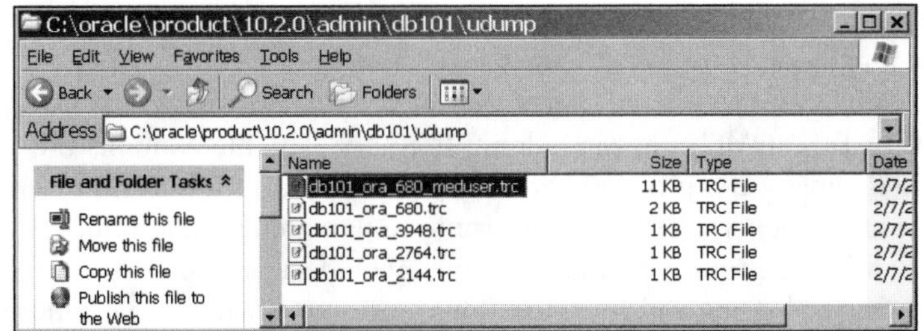

FIGURE 14-4 Locating the user trace file on the operating system

When issuing the command, substitute the name of the user trace file as displayed on your machine in Step 8, in place of db101_ora_680_meduser.trc.

```
Start -> All Programs -> Accessories -> Command Prompt
C:\> TKPROF  <PATH>\db101_ora_680_meduser.trc  OUTTK.TRC
```

11. The OUTTK.TRC file will be created in the current directory. Open the file using the TYPE command on Windows and view its contents. The trace file will contain the execution plan used to execute the SQL statement that was issued in step 5 along with statistical and tuning data.

```
C:\> TYPE OUTTK.TRC
```

12. Close the file and exit the command prompt window.

THE LISTENER PROCESS

The listener process (`tnslsnr`) is a critical Oracle process. In a networked environment it listens for incoming client requests and hands over the client requests to the database server. The listener process is the first point of communication between a client and a server. By default, the listener listens on port 1521 for clients requiring database access. The name of the default listener is LISTENER. It is configured to listen for TCP requests and listens at port 1521.

On receiving the request the listener may start an Oracle server process (in a dedicated server configuration) which in turn informs the listener about the port it is waiting on. The listener then informs the client of this port and the client directly connects to the database server process. In a shared server environment the listener process establishes communication between the client and a dispatcher process.

A listener process is configured to listen for incoming requests at a specific protocol address. The protocol address defines the type of requests the listener listens for which could be TCP, IPC, and so on.

A database presents itself as a service on a machine. A database may be configured as a dedicated server or shared server configuration. When a database is started, the database server may automatically register itself with the listener, by a procedure known as service registration. Service registration is done automatically by the PMON background process of the database. After service registration, the listener becomes aware of the name of the database, the name of the instance, the type of service handlers (dedicated or dispatcher), and other important information about the database. Alternatively, the listener may be configured to use static registration. This was used in databases prior to Oracle 8*i* where information about the database service was written into a configuration file known as listener.ora.

The listener process is configured using a file known as the *Listener.ora* file which by default is located in the %ORACLE_HOME%\network\admin directory. The file contains the name of the listener(s) in the database, the protocol address including the port, information about database services and other services along with runtime parameters that influence the behavior of the listener process. The runtime parameters may include a password for controlling the listener, time-out values, logging and trace locations, and so on. When the listener process is started, the listener.ora file will be read to configure the listener. The database services will then register themselves with the listener or static registration may occur.

When a client wishes to connect to a remote database via the network, it supplies authentication information such as the username and password and a host string that is resolved into the network address of the database server. This network address consists of the database service name, the port on which the listener process is listening and the protocol being used. When the request is received on the database server side, the listener that is listening at the port validates the request, either accepting it (if the requested database service is known to it) or rejecting it (if the requested database service is unknown to it).

In addition to providing database services, the listener process also provides a method by which PL/SQL program units may access operating system executables and programs.

Figure 14-5 displays a typical listener.ora file. The name of the listener process is LISTENER and it listens for TCP requests at port 1521 on the machine called localhost. It also listens for inter-process communication (IPC) requests that support external procedure functionality. The listener LISTENER accepts requests made by clients requesting access to the DB101 database as well as requests by PL/SQL program units requesting the execution of external procedures in shared libraries or Dynamic Link Libraries (DLLs).

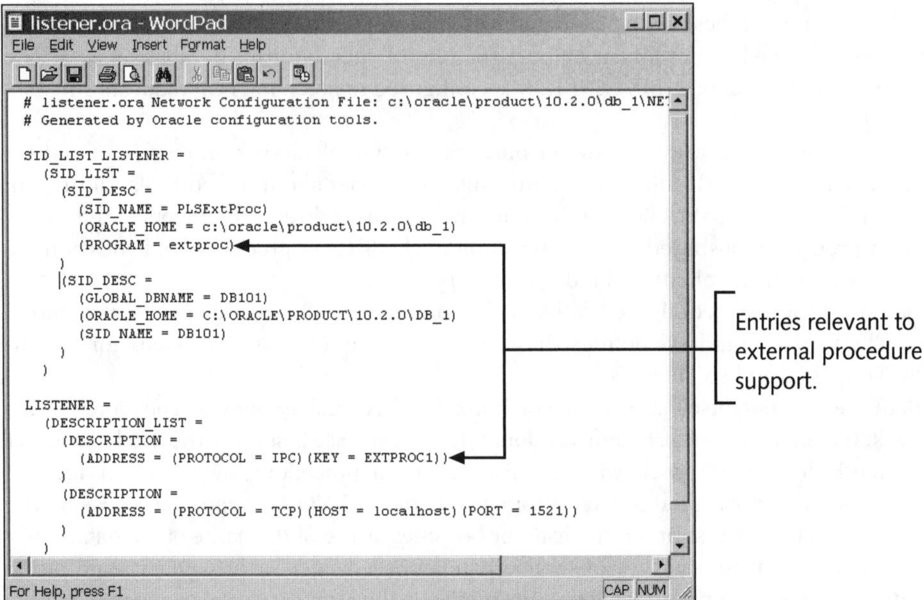

FIGURE 14-5 The contents of a typical listener.ora file

The listener process may be controlled by the Listener Control utility and the Enterprise Manager.

The Listener Control Utility (LSNRCTL.EXE)

The listener process may be managed by the Listener Control Utility. This utility is invoked from an operating system prompt, by the LSNRCTL command. The utility may be used to issue commands to the listener and set runtime parameter values. Some important commands issued to the listener are listed in the Table 14-2. You may specify the name of the listener beside the command, if the command is to be performed on the non-default listener. The third column in the table indicates whether a password (if one has been specified) needs to be supplied when issuing the command.

TABLE 14-2 Some basic commands to control the listener

Command	Description	Password Protected Command
`HELP`	To display a list of all valid commands that may be issued to the listener.	
`START`	To start the listener.	
`STOP`	To stop the listener.	√
`STATUS`	To display the status of the listener.	
`SERVICES`	To display a list of all the database services the listener listens on behalf of.	√
`RELOAD`	To restart the listener. Used to activate some changes made using the SET commands.	√
`SAVE_CONFIG`	To make changes made to the listener permanent.	√
`CHANGE_PASSWORD`	To change the password of the listener.	√
`SET commands`	To set the runtime parameters of the listener, before issuing password protected commands.	Some SET commands
`SHOW command`	To display the runtime parameters of the listener.	Some SHOW commands

Practice 4: The listener control utility

This practice demonstrates invoking the Listener Control utility and executing a few basic commands.

1. Start a command prompt window and type LSNRCTL. You would have to type **lsnrctl** in lower case on Unix-based platforms.

```
Start -> All Programs -> Accessories -> Command Prompt
C:\> LSNRCTL
```

2. At the prompt, type HELP. This will display a help screen describing the different commands that can be issued to the listener. (See Figure 14-6.)

```
LSNRCTL> HELP
```

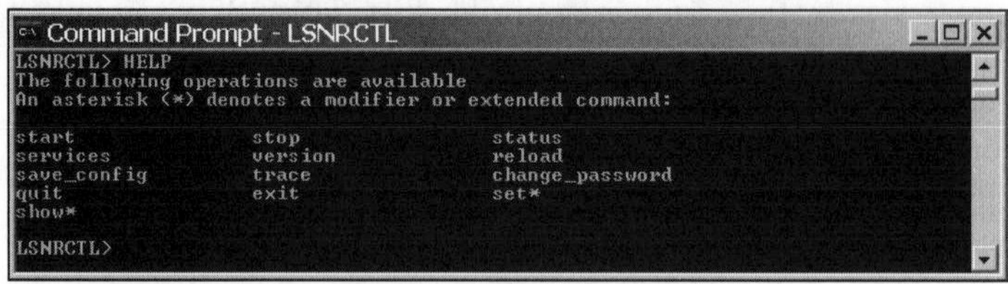

FIGURE 14-6 The output of the HELP command

3. Exit the listener control utility by typing EXIT.

```
LSNRCTL> EXIT
```

4. Exit the command prompt window.

The LSNRCTL.EXE executable is owned by the *oracle* account on UNIX and the *Administrator* on Windows machines. These are privileged accounts. When the listener process is started, it runs within this privileged shell, which permits the listener process to acquire the rights of the privileged account, making it a target for hackers and malicious users.

Managing the Listener using Enterprise Manager

The listener process may be administered using the Enterprise Manager.

Practice 5: Controlling the listener process from Enterprise Manager

This practice example describes how to access and manage the listener process using Enterprise Manager.

1. Launch a browser and enter the URL to start the Enterprise Manager. Log in as a user with SYSDBA privileges.
2. From the **Database Control Home** page, go to the **General** section.
3. Click the **link on listener name** next to the label Listener. In Figure 14-7 it is displayed as LISTENER_localhost.

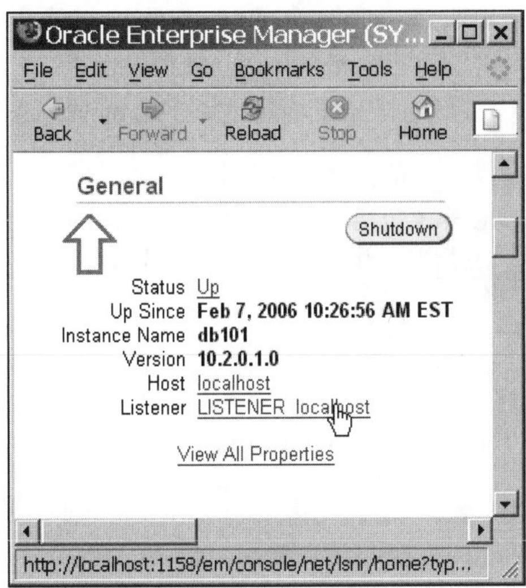

FIGURE 14-7 The Listener_<hostname> link

4. The **Listener:LISTENER_<hostname>** page will be displayed. This page gives you information about the listener; including the network address of the listener, the location the listener.ora file, and the status of the listener. The **Serviced Databases** tab displays the information about the database services the listener listens for. Please select the different links/tabs on this page to get an idea about the current listener.
5. Log out of Enterprise Manager and exit the browser.

At this point you should have a fair understanding about the listener process and its functions. The rest of the chapter will focus on the security risks presented by the listener and the methods available for securing it.

Vulnerabilities of the Listener

As mentioned earlier, the listener process is managed by the LSNRCTL program and is configured using the listener.ora file. Most database administrators are not aware that it is very easy to gain control of the listener remotely. Once this is done, many commands may be successfully issued on the listener to gain control over it and gather information about the database services.

The following steps will give you an idea of how simple it is to remotely administer a listener.

1. On a remote client machine, install the Oracle software for client-side connectivity. Choose the client-side option that will install Oracle Net components which are required for network connectivity. Then copy the lsnrctl.exe executable from the server as it is not installed as part of the client-side software.

2. On the client, configure the listener.ora file to include the lines displayed below, to access the remote listener. The entry is similar to a tnsnames.ora entry.

```
<listener_alias> =
    (ADDRESS_LIST =
            (ADDRESS =
            (PROTOCOL=TCP) (HOST=<hostname>) (PORT=<port>)))
```

In the example shown below, the name of the remote listener is LISNAME. It is located on the machine called DBSERVER. It is listening for TCP connections at port 1521.

```
LISNAME =
          (ADDRESS_LIST =
                   (ADDRESS=
                         (PROTOCOL=TCP)(HOST=DBSERVER)(PORT=1521)))
```

3. From the client you can now control the remote listener using the listener control utility.

```
Prompt>lsnrctl
```

Example:

```
C:\>lsnrctl
```

4. Now all commands on the remote listener are valid except the START command.

Securing the Listener

The listener is the first process involved in a successful client-server connection and it is important to secure it. Some methods that may be used to secure the listener have been described in this chapter.

Set the Listener Password

This action is mandatory when attempting to secure the listener. By setting a password for the listener you will be expected to supply it when executing commands that control the listener. For example, to stop the listener, you will have to provide its password.

The password information is written to the listener.ora file. The listener.ora file may be manually edited to include the PASSWORD_<listener name> entry, however, this is not recommended because the password will be stored in plain text when using this method. It is recommended that you execute the CHANGE_PASSWORD command using the Listener Control Utility. By issuing the command you will be prompted twice to confirm the password and an encrypted password will be stored in the listener.ora file. After a password has been set, many commands executed on the listener will require you to supply the password using the SET PASSWORD command.

The listener password may be set using the graphical Net Manager application or the command-line Listener Control utility.

Practice 6: Setting the listener password using Net Manager

This practice demonstrates setting the listener password using Net Manager.

1. Invoke the Net Manager application by selecting from the Windows taskbar:

   ```
   Start -> All Programs -> Oracle - OraDb10g_home1
   -> Configuration and Migration Tools -> Net Manager
   ```

2. From the left panel displayed, expand **Local**.
3. Expand **Listeners**.
4. Select the listener called **LISTENER**.
5. From the right panel, from the drop-down list select **General Parameters**.
6. Select the **Authentication** tab.
7. On this page are displayed options to set or remove the listener password.
8. Select the option **Require a password for Listener Operations**.
9. A dialog window will be displayed, prompting you for the old password and the new password with confirmation.

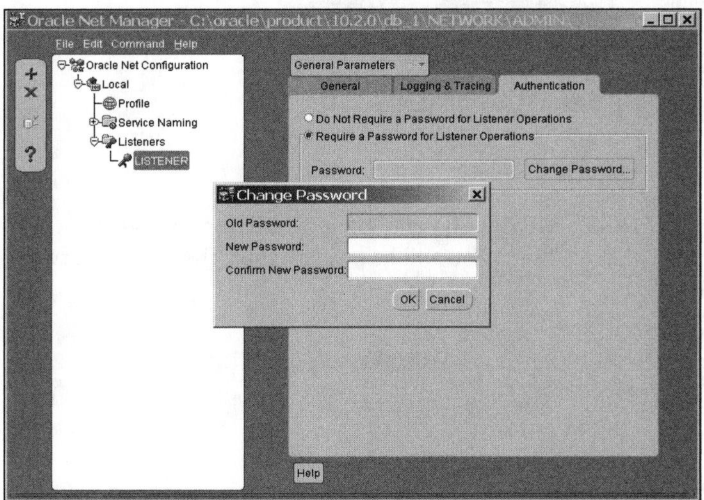

FIGURE 14-8 Setting the password using Net Manager

10. Cancel the operation at this time because you will set the listener password using SQL*Plus, by selecting the **Cancel** button.
11. Select **File -> Exit** to exit the Net Manager utility. Select the **Discard** button.

Practice 7: Setting the listener password using the Listener Control Utility (LSNRCTL)

This practice demonstrates setting the listener password.

1. Open a command prompt and issue the LSNRCTL command to start the listener control utility.

   ```
   Start -> All Programs -> Accessories -> Command Prompt
   C:\> LSNRCTL
   ```

2. From the LSNRCTL prompt, issue the STOP command to stop the listener, followed by a START command to start the listener. When you start the listener, notice all the services that are started. Figure 14-9 indicates the current listener (LISTENER) listens on behalf of the DB101, RCDB, and PLSExtProc instances.

```
LSNRCTL>STOP
LSNRCTL>START
```

```
Command Prompt - lsnrctl
STATUS of the LISTENER
------------------------
Alias                     LISTENER
Version                   TNSLSNR for 32-bit Windows: Version 10.2.0.1.0 - Produ
ction
Start Date                07-FEB-2006 10:56:34
Uptime                    0 days 0 hr. 0 min. 4 sec
Trace Level               off
Security                  ON: Local OS Authentication
SNMP                      OFF
Listener Parameter File   c:\oracle\product\10.2.0\db_1\network\admin\listener.o
ra
Listener Log File         c:\oracle\product\10.2.0\db_1\network\log\listener.log

Listening Endpoints Summary...
  (DESCRIPTION=(ADDRESS=(PROTOCOL=ipc)(PIPENAME=\\.\pipe\EXTPROC1ipc)))
  (DESCRIPTION=(ADDRESS=(PROTOCOL=tcp)(HOST=dbsrv01)(PORT=1521)))
Services Summary...
Service "DB101" has 1 instance(s).
  Instance "DB101", status UNKNOWN, has 1 handler(s) for this service...
Service "PLSExtProc" has 1 instance(s).
  Instance "PLSExtProc", status UNKNOWN, has 1 handler(s) for this service...
Service "RCDB" has 1 instance(s).
  Instance "RCDB", status UNKNOWN, has 1 handler(s) for this service...
The command completed successfully
LSNRCTL> _
```


FIGURE 14-9 Starting the listener

3. Next, issue the CHANGE_PASSWORD command to set a password for the default listener called LISTENER. You will be prompted for the password twice. (See Figure 14-10.)

```
LSNRCTL> CHANGE_PASSWORD
Old Password: <hit enter if no password was set>
New Password: <type in a password>
Reenter New Password:  <re-type the password>
```

FIGURE 14-10 Issuing the CHANGE_PASSWORD command

4. To save the changes made, type the `SAVE_CONFIG` command.

```
LSNRCTL> SAVE_CONFIG
```

5. Next, issue the command STATUS. The output of this command will indicate that the listener is now password protected. (See Figure 14-11.)

```
LSNRCTL> STATUS
```

6. Exit the listener control utility and the command prompt.

```
Command Prompt - lsnrctl
LSNRCTL> STATUS
Connecting to (DESCRIPTION=(ADDRESS=(PROTOCOL=IPC)(KEY=EXTPROC1)))
STATUS of the LISTENER
------------------------
Alias                     LISTENER
Version                   TNSLSNR for 32-bit Windows: Version 10.2.0.1.0 -
ction
Start Date                07-FEB-2006 10:56:34
Uptime                    0 days 0 hr. 2 min. 24 sec
Trace Level               off
Security                  ON: Password or Local OS Authentication
SNMP                      OFF
Listener Parameter File   c:\oracle\product\10.2.0\db_1\network\admin\liste
```

FIGURE 14-11 The output of the STATUS command

7. Open the listener.ora file. By default it is located in the %ORACLE_HOME%\network\admin directory. Look for an entry that reads as PASSWORD_LISTENER=<encrypted password>. Figure 14-12 displays an encrypted password set for the current listener.

NOTE

If the TNS_ADMIN environment variable has been set, the listener.ora file would be located in the location specified by the environment variable.

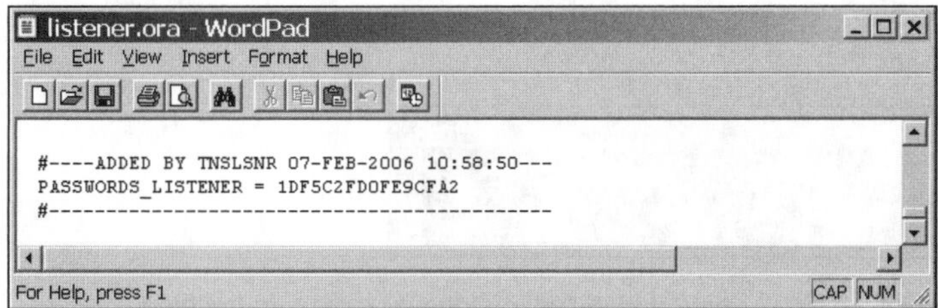

FIGURE 14-12 The PASSWORD_LISTENER entry in the listener.ora file

8. Close the Listener.ora file

After a password has been set for the listener, malicious users trying to gain access to the listener from *a remote client*, without knowing the password, will display an error message similar to the one displayed below:

```
LSNRCTL> status listener
Connecting to (ADDRESS=(PROTOCOL=TCP)(HOST=DBSRV01)(PORT=1521))
TNS-01179:The listener has not recognized the password
TNS-01189: The listener could not authenticate the user
```

Because the listener password is stored in the listener.ora file, it is easy for anyone who has access to it to open the file and edit it to remove the password entry. For this reason, it is also important to ensure that the file permissions on the listener.ora file are set properly so that read/write/execute permissions are available only for the primary oracle account.

Activate Listener Logging

Another security measure that may be taken is to activate listener logging. Listener logging may be enabled to capture all important commands, errors, and messages that are generated on/by the listener. This is useful if you wish to capture password break-in attempts. Listener logging is enabled by default and the default location of the log files is the %ORACLE_HOME%\network\log directory.

Logging may be enabled by setting the LOG_STATUS parameter to TRUE. The location and log file name may be explicitly specified by setting values for the LOG_DIRECTORY and LOG_FILE parameters respectively in the listener.ora file. It can be done using the LSNRCTL utility.

Practice 8: Enabling listener logging

In this practice you will display the status of listener logging for the default listener called LISTENER. If logging is not enabled, the practice demonstrates how to enable it.

1. Open a command prompt and issue the LSNRCTL command to start the listener control utility.

   ```
   Start -> All Programs -> Accessories -> Command Prompt
   C:\> LSNRCTL
   ```


2. Issue the SHOW LOG_STATUS command to display the status of listener logging. Figure 14-13 indicates that logging has been enabled.

   ```
   LSNRCTL> SHOW LOG_STATUS
   ```

```
Command Prompt - LSNRCTL
LSNRCTL> SHOW LOG_STATUS
Connecting to (DESCRIPTION=(ADDRESS=(PROTOCOL=IPC)(KEY=EXTPROC1)))
LISTENER parameter "log_status" set to ON
The command completed successfully
LSNRCTL> _
```

FIGURE 14-13 The SHOW LOG_STATUS command indicating logging has been enabled

3. Issue the SHOW commands displayed below to display the location and name of the listener log file.

   ```
   LSNRCTL> SHOW LOG_DIRECTORY
   LSNRCTL> SHOW LOG_FILE
   ```

4. The remaining part of this practice is applicable if listener logging was not enabled. It demonstrates how listener logging can be turned on, and how to specify the location and file name of the listener log file.

   ```
   LSNRCTL> SET LOG_STATUS ON
   ```

5. Using an operating system command create a directory called LISTENER_LOCATION in the C:\>drive. Issue the command to set the directory for the location of the log file.

   ```
   LSNRCTL> SET LOG_DIRECTORY <location of log file>
   ```

   For example, to create the log file in C:\LISTENER_LOCATION,type:

   ```
   LSNRCTL> SET LOG_DIRECTORY C:\LISTENER_LOCATION
   ```

6. Next, issue the command SET LOG_FILE and then indicate the name of the log file.

   ```
   LSNRCTL> SET LOG_FILE <Name of log file>
   ```

   For example, if you want to name the log file, LLOG.LOG you would type:

   ```
   LSNRCTL> SET LOG_FILE LLOG.LOG
   ```

7. Exit the listener control utility and the command prompt.

Valid Node Checking

In a typical client server or *n*-tier environment, many client machines may access a central database. The listener process, residing on the server side, listens for incoming client requests and either accepts or rejects requests, based on the database service requested by the client.

It is possible to restrict traffic from certain clients nodes based on their host name or IP address. This is a powerful feature that can be configured easily on the server side. Let's say, you don't want the client machine with an IP address of 10.10.10.134 to connect to a particular database. You can configure node checking to automatically reject connectivity requests from that client.

To set up valid node checking you must edit the SQLNET.ora file located in the %ORACLE_HOME%\network\admin directory on the server side. The parameter TCP.VALIDNODE_CHECKING must be set to TRUE. You can then specify the names/IP addresses of acceptable clients against the TCP.INVITED_NODES parameter or the names/IP addresses of unacceptable clients against the TCP.EXCLUDED_NODES parameter. These two parameters are mutually exclusive and must not be specified together. However, if both have been specified and a conflict occurs, TCP.INVITED_NODES has precedence. After setting the parameters, you must restart the listener for the changes to take effect. The syntax for the TCP.INVITED_NODES parameter does not permit wildcard characters, and every name/IP address must be listed explicitly. Valid node checking is only applicable to TCP connections.

Shown below is a SQLNET.ORA file that contains entries to enforce valid node checking. The listener will only accept connection requests made by the client whose machine name is CL1 and the client whose IP address is 10.10.10.134.

```
TCP.VALIDNODE_CHECKING = YES
TCP.INVITED_NODES = CL1, 10.10.10.134
```

NOTE

For hostnames to be accepted, an IP address to Hostname translation mechanism must be available (for example, a host's file or DNS).

If the number of clients to be managed is large and the network environment is volatile, Oracle Connection Manager is a better alternative to valid node checking.

External Procedures

Oracle's proprietary programming language is PL/SQL. In the recent years, Java programming is also widely supported by the Oracle database. Though PL/SQL is adequate for most programming requirements, developers may want to choose programming languages such as C or C++ for low-level programming requirements, faster speed, or better performance. It is possible to write C or C++ programs and link them to PL/SQL programs. When a PL/SQL program is invoked it can call the C/C++ program, execute it, and continue with its own code until completion. Program units that are written in other programming languages are known as External Procedures.

In addition to listening for database requests, the listener process is also responsible for external procedure support if required. Normally, external procedures are part of shared libraries (on Unix) or Dynamic Link Libraries (on Windows). Dynamic link libraries are often referred to as DLLs.

As already mentioned, PL/SQL packages may be extended to call external functions. When a PL/SQL program unit executing in the database is required to run an external procedure it first connects to the listener and requests the listener to load the required library. The listener does not load the library on its own but in turn launches another process, the external procedure agent known as EXTPROC or (EXTPROC.EXE). The agent resides on the server side. Using the network connection established by the listener, the application passes the name of the DLL and the name of the external procedure and any relevant parameters to the external procedure agent. The external procedure agent then loads the required DLL and runs the external procedure, passing any values returned by the external procedure back to the application.

When support for external procedures is required, the listener process must be configured to accept calls and launch the external procedure agent. An external procedure agent is launched in a manner similar to dedicated server processes—one agent for a session. It remains alive for the duration of the session.

In default installations, the listener process is automatically configured to handle external procedures. However, in a majority of environments this service is never used. Figure 14-14 displays a number of entries relevant to external procedure support.

The external procedure functionality of the listener process also poses some security threats. The external procedure agent (EXTPROC) runs within the privileges of the database listener, which we already know runs within the rights of the Oracle process owner. Therefore if the external procedure is compromised, the hacker might find themselves in a privileged shell.

The external procedure service is not always used and in most environments may be removed completely. This will entirely eliminate any attempts to exploit the EXTPROC agent. If it cannot be removed, you could create a separate listener that strictly handles external procedure requests or even restrict the libraries from which procedures can be executed. This new listener can then be configured to run with minimum operating system privileges.

Removing the External Procedure Functionality One of the measures taken to reduce security threats presented by the external procedure functionality is to completely remove support for this service. This can be done in environments that do not run external procedures.

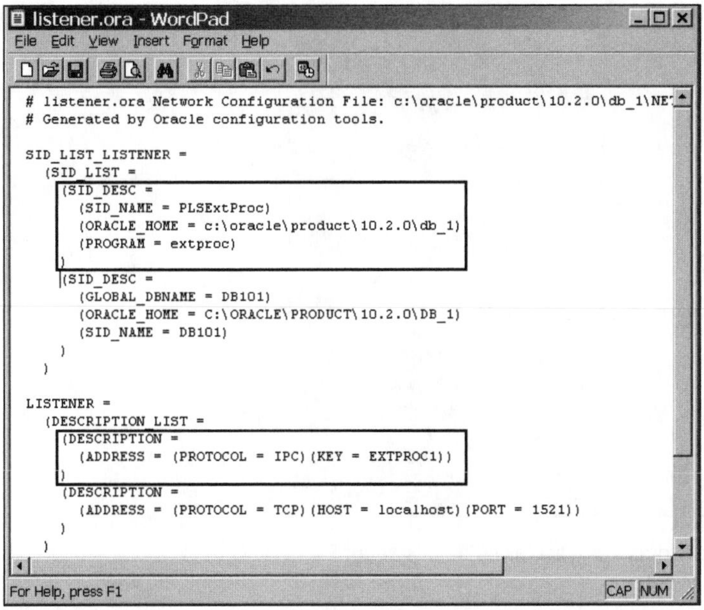

listener.ora - WordPad

File Edit View Insert Format Help

```
# listener.ora Network Configuration File: c:\oracle\product\10.2.0\db_1\NE
# Generated by Oracle configuration tools.

SID_LIST_LISTENER =
  (SID_LIST =
    (SID_DESC =
      (SID_NAME = PLSExtProc)
      (ORACLE_HOME = c:\oracle\product\10.2.0\db_1)
      (PROGRAM = extproc)
    )
    (SID_DESC =
      (GLOBAL_DBNAME = DB101)
      (ORACLE_HOME = C:\ORACLE\PRODUCT\10.2.0\DB_1)
      (SID_NAME = DB101)
    )
  )

LISTENER =
  (DESCRIPTION_LIST =
    (DESCRIPTION =
      (ADDRESS = (PROTOCOL = IPC)(KEY = EXTPROC1))
    )
    (DESCRIPTION =
      (ADDRESS = (PROTOCOL = TCP)(HOST = localhost)(PORT = 1521))
    )
  )
```

For Help, press F1 CAP NUM

FIGURE 14-14 Entries related to external procedures in the Listener.ora file

To remove any external procedure functionality you would remove all references to the external procedures. This can be done by opening the Listener.ora file and removing the entries associated with external procedures or by using the Oracle Net Manager utility.

Practice 9: Removing external procedure functionality

This practice describes how external procedure functionality can be removed using the Net Manager and displays the contents of the Listener.ora file after the removal.

1. From the Windows task bar, select:

   ```
   Start -> All Programs -> Oracle - OraDB10g-home1 -
   > Configuration and Migration Tools -> Net Manager.
   ```

2. From the left panel, expand **Local** and expand the **Listeners** option. A listener by the name LISTENER will be displayed.
3. Select **LISTENER**.
4. From the right panel, **select the drop down list** and select the option **Listening Locations**.
5. One or more Network Address Tabs will be displayed. Select the first tab, **Address1**. The network address will be displayed for EXTPROC1 key. Figure 14-15 below displays this information.
6. Select the button, **Remove Address**.
7. Select **File**, then **Save Network Configuration**.
8. From the drop-down list, select **Other Services**. (See Figure 14-16.) From the bottom of the screen, select the button **Remove Service**. Select **File**, then **Save Network Configuration**.

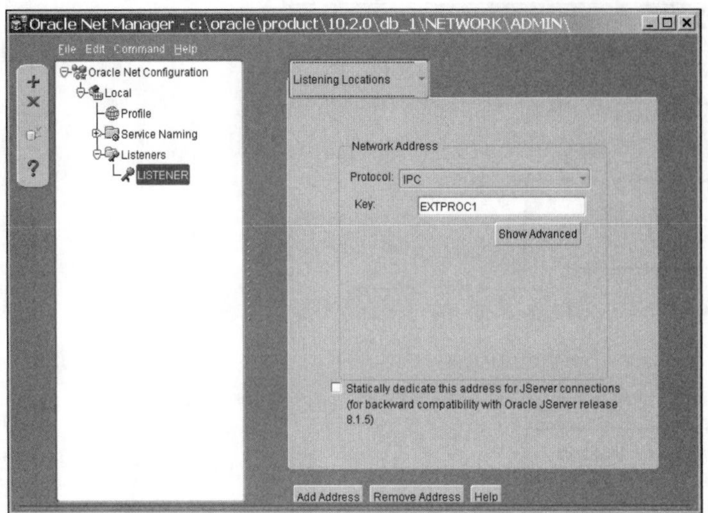

FIGURE 14-15 The network address tab displaying details about EXTPROC

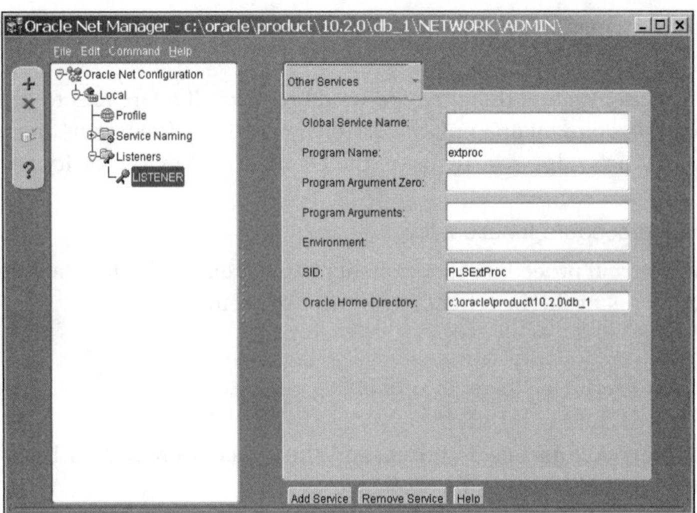

FIGURE 14-16 The Other Services Tab

9. Exit the Net Manager Utility, by selecting **File**, then **Exit**.
10. Next, go to the %ORACLE_HOME%\network\admin directory and open the Listener.ora file, you will notice that the contents of the file have changed and all directives relevant to external procedure functionality are removed. Figure 14-17 displays the contents of the Listener.ora file after removing the external procedure functionality.

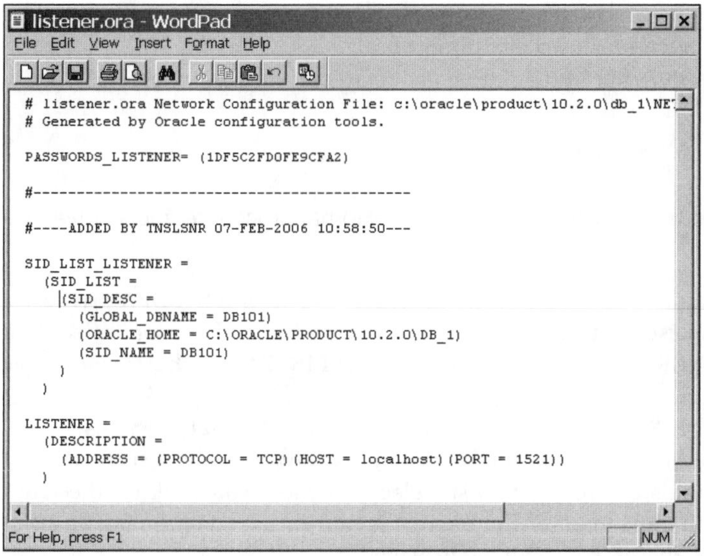

```
listener.ora - WordPad
File Edit View Insert Format Help

# listener.ora Network Configuration File: c:\oracle\product\10.2.0\db_1\NE
# Generated by Oracle configuration tools.

PASSWORDS_LISTENER= (1DF5C2FD0FE9CFA2)

#-------------------------------------------

#----ADDED BY TNSLSNR 07-FEB-2006 10:58:50---

SID_LIST_LISTENER =
  (SID_LIST =
    (SID_DESC =
      (GLOBAL_DBNAME = DB101)
      (ORACLE_HOME = C:\ORACLE\PRODUCT\10.2.0\DB_1)
      (SID_NAME = DB101)
    )
  )

LISTENER =
  (DESCRIPTION =
    (ADDRESS = (PROTOCOL = TCP)(HOST = localhost)(PORT = 1521))
  )

For Help, press F1                                    NUM
```

FIGURE 14-17 The listener.ora file after External procedure support has been removed

11. Close the listener.ora file.
12. To confirm that the listener no longer listens for external procedure requests, you may invoke the listener control utility and stop and start the listener. You will notice the listener has only handlers for the database(s).

Creating a Separate Listener for External Procedure Functionality A separate listener can be used if external procedure functionality is required in your environment. You can create and configure a new listener process that strictly handles only external procedure functionality. Further, the listener must be executed by a user who possesses the minimum operating system privileges. To do so, create a user on the operating system with minimal privileges. Then ensure that the new listener runs under the ownership of this user. This ensures that when the external procedure agent is started it inherits minimal operating system privileges. The user who owns this new listener process must not have access to files owned by the Oracle user. The user must not have read/write/execute permission on database files, but only read access to the listener.ora file.

In addition to creating a separate listener you may also restrict this listener to specific shared libraries only. In default installations, the external procedure agent (EXTPROC) can execute procedures from any shared library stored in the %ORACLE_HOME%\bin directory. In the listener.ora file you can specify parameters for extproc. One such parameter is ENVS that defines the environment variables required by the agent. The behavior of extproc is determined by the values of the ENVS parameter. A specific variable of relevance is EXTPROC_DLLS. The variable can either be used to restrict extproc to only specific DLLs and shared libraries. If the ENVS setting is not specified, the agent can access any procedure in the shared libraries and DLLs of the %ORACLE_HOME%\bin directory. When specifying the EXTPROC_DLLS variable you may also specify the ONLY or ANY directives. The ONLY directive is used to specify the DLLs that the agent has access to. A list of DLL names may be specified as a colon-separated list. The ANY directive is less restrictive, permitting the agent to access any library file.

A typical entry in the listener.ora file limiting access to only the executables, D1.DLL and D2.DLL would be:

```
(ENVS="EXTPROC_DLLS=ONLY: F:\DLL_LIB\d1.dll: F:\DLL_LIB\d2.dll")
```

Practice 10: Creating an additional listener process for external procedure support using Enterprise Manager

1. Launch browser and start Enterprise Manager. Log in with SYSDBA privileges.
2. From the **Database Control Home** page, go to the **General** section, select link on the **LISTENER_<Hostname>**. The **Listener: LISTENER_<hostname>** page will be displayed.
3. Navigate to the **Related Links** section and click the **Net Services Administration** link. The **Net Services Administration** page is displayed.
4. From the **Administer** drop-down list, select **Listeners** and click on the **Go** button. You will need to enter the Username and Password of the host user.
5. The **Listeners: <path>** page will be displayed.
6. Select the **Create** button. The **Create Listener** page will be displayed.
7. In the text item corresponding to Listener Name **type** in a unique listener name. The name given in the example is EXTLIST. (See Figure 14-18.)

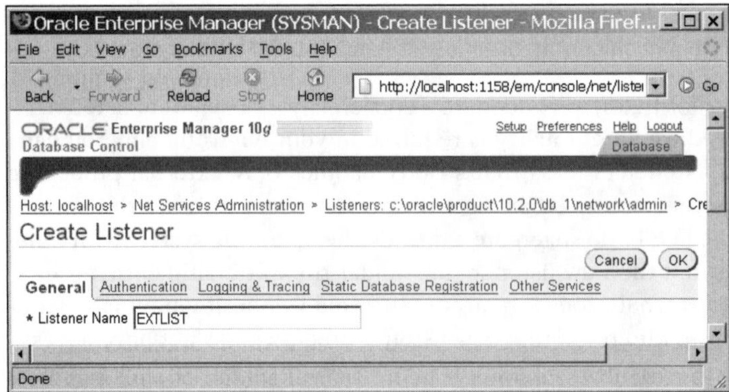

FIGURE 14-18 Specifying the name of the new listener process

8. From the **Addresses** section, select the **Add** button.
9. The **Add Addresses** page will be displayed. Select **IPC** from the Protocol drop-down list.
10. In the Key text item, type in a unique key value, **EXTPROC**. Click the **OK** button. The **Create Listeners** page will be displayed again.
11. Click the **Other Services** tab and select the **Add** button. The **Create Other Service** page will be displayed.
12. For Program Name, type, **extproc**.
13. For the Oracle Home Directory text item, type in the location of the home

directory. In the example it has been typed as C:\oracle\product\10.2.0\db_1. It may be different on your machine.

14. Against Oracle System Identifier type, **PLSExtProc**.
15. From the **Environment Variables** section, select the **Add Another Row** button.
16. Enter the value **EXTPROC_DLLS** in the Name text item.
17. For values, type the list of DLLs that the EXTPROC can access. (See Figure 14-19.) Examples are displayed below: C:\oracle\product\10.2.0\db_1\bin\corejava.dll: C:\oracle\product\10.2.0\db_1\bin\oci.dll were typed. (Note: these DLLS were chosen just for the sake of the example).

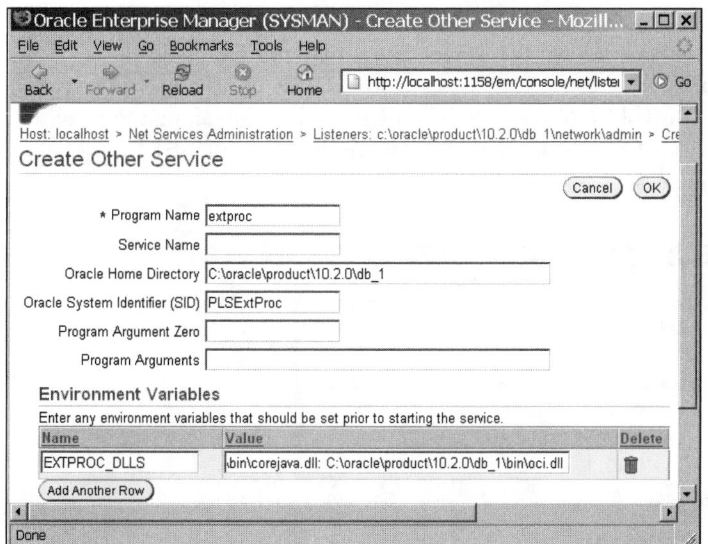

FIGURE 14-19 The service entries related to external procedures being added

18. Select the **OK** button.
19. You will be returned to the **Create Listener** page. Select the **OK** button.
20. The **Listeners:<path>** page will be displayed. The names of all listeners will be displayed including the EXTLIST listener. The current status will be displayed as Stopped. Select the radio button next to the listener called EXTLIST. From the **Actions** drop-down list, select **Start/Stop** and then the **Go** button. Select the **OK** button to start it. (See Figure 14-20.)

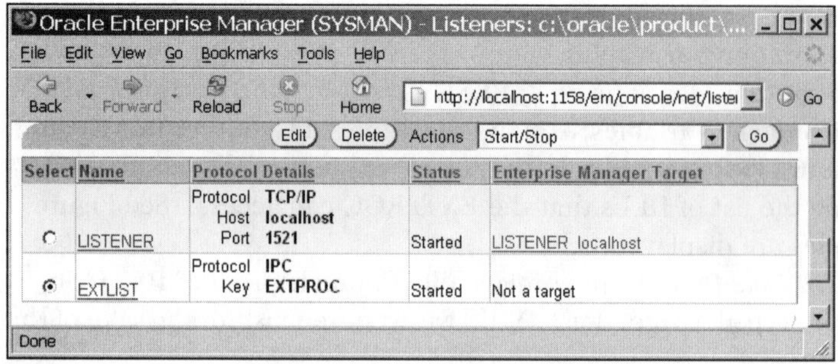

FIGURE 14-20 The EXTLIST listener has been successfully created and started

21. From the **Actions** drop-down list, select **Show Listener Control Status**. Select the **Go** button.
22. The **Listener Control Status** page will be displayed. Scroll along the page to view the services (PLSExtProc) that were started for the EXTLIST listener. (See Figure 14-21.)

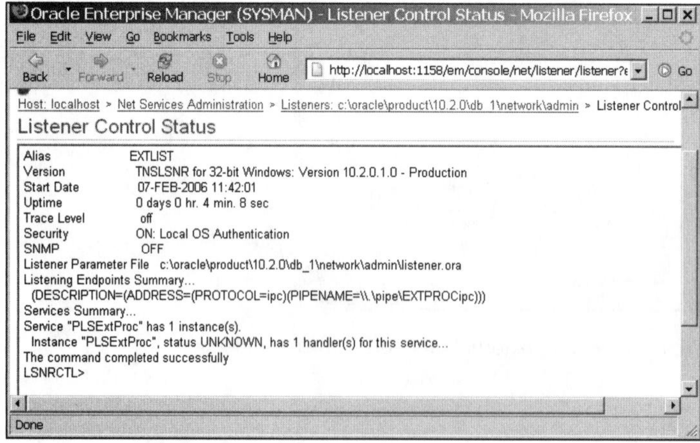

FIGURE 14-21 The listener.ora file with entries pertaining to the EXTLIST listener

23. To verify that the changes you made through Enterprise Manager were successfully written to the listener.ora file, open the listener.ora file from the %ORACLE_HOME%\network\admin directory. Notice the new entries included for the EXTLIST listener. Figure 14-22 displays a partial listing of the listener.ora file.

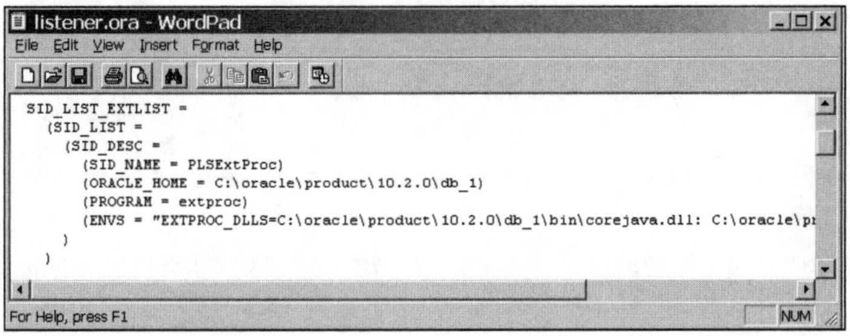
listener.ora - WordPad
File Edit View Insert Format Help
SID_LIST_EXTLIST =
(SID_LIST =
(SID_DESC =
(SID_NAME = PLSExtProc)
(ORACLE_HOME = C:\oracle\product\10.2.0\db_1)
(PROGRAM = extproc)
(ENVS = "EXTPROC_DLLS=C:\oracle\product\10.2.0\db_1\bin\corejava.dll: C:\oracle\pr
)
)
For Help, press F1
NUM

FIGURE 14-22 The listener.ora file with entries pertaining to the EXTLIST listener

24. Close all the open windows.

In this chapter we learned about the log and trace files that are available in the database as diagnostic sources. They are very useful for troubleshooting errors in the database. We also discussed the listener process and its function in setting up client-server connectivity. A number of different methods to secure the listener were also presented.

Chapter Summary

- Diagnostic tools are available in the Oracle database in the form of log files and trace files.
- Log files contain events, changes, errors, and messages in them. The most important log file is the Alert Log file.
- Trace files contain diagnostic information. They are created by background processes, network processes, and as a result of user tracing.
- Trace files contain details of the errors.
- Background trace file and the Alert Log file may be found in the location specified by the BACKGROUND_DUMP_DEST initialization parameter.
- The listener process acts as a proxy, setting up the connection between the client and the server.
- The listener listens on a specific protocol address on behalf of database services and external procedures.
- The listener is prone to security threats and can be hacked.
- Some methods available to secure the listener include setting a listener password, enforcing valid node checking, activating listener logging, and managing external procedure support.
- The external procedure agent (EXTPROC) by default runs with privileged user rights and hence must either be removed if not required or assigned to a separate listener.

Syntax Guide

SYNTAX GUIDE		
Element	Description	Example
ALTER SESSION	Used to set the value of a parameter within a session.	SQL>ALTER SESSION SET TIMED_STATISTICS=TRUE;
TKPROF	Used to format the output of SQL tracing. It receives the name of the SQL trace file and the output file as its inputs.	C:\> TKPROF C:\db101_ora_324_meduser.trc OUTFILE.TRC
LSNRCTL	Command to invoke/launch the listener control utility.	C:\>LSNRCTL
SET	To set a listener parameter.	LSNRCTL>SET LOG_STATUS OFF
SHOW	To display the value of a listener parameter.	LSNRCTL>SHOW LOG_STATUS

Review Questions

1. You are the database administrator at a medium-sized company. You wish to locate the alert log file. Which of the following commands would you issue to find it?
   a. SHOW PARAMETER USER_DUMP_DEST
   b. SHOW PARAMETER BACKGROUND_DUMP_DEST
   c. SHOW PARAMETER ALERT_DUMP_DEST
   d. It is not possible to find it from within the database; you would need to search for the file using an Operating System command.
2. A database administrator wishes to turn SQL tracing on remotely for a user. Which of the following commands would the DBA use to successfully turn tracing on?
   a. DBMS_MONITOR.SESSION_ENABLE_TRACING
   b. DBMS_MONITOR.SESSION_TRACING
   c. DBMS_MONITOR.SESSION_TRACE_ENABLE
   d. DBMS_MONITOR.SESSION_TRACE_DISABLE
3. You have been hired as a database administrator in a large company. You have been asked to identify whether the listener called LIST1 is password protected. Which command would you issue to find out this information?
   a. SERVICES LIST1
   b. PASSWORD LIST1
   c. SET PASSWORD LIST1
   d. STATUS LIST1
4. From the list below, identify the types of information you would find in the alert log file. [Choose 4.]
   a. Non-default values of initialization parameters
   b. Startup and Shutdowns
   c. Crash Recovery
   d. Table creation
   e. Structural changes to tables and views
   f. Structural changes to the database
5. You wish to set the password for the listener, what steps would you perform to accomplish this?
   a. Open the listener.ora file and type in the password on the upper-left corner, and save the file.
   b. Using the listener control utility, issue the CHANGE_PASSWORD command.
   c. Using the listener control utility, issue the CHANGE_PASSWORD command followed by the SAVE_CONFIG command.
   d. Issue the SET PASSWORD command.

6. The contents of the Alert log file can be viewed using _______________ and _______________.
   a. The Net Manager and Enterprise Manager.
   b. The operating system and Enterprise Manager.
   c. The Network configuration assistant and Enterprise Manager.
   d. The Listener Control utility and the Operating system.
   e. The operating system and SQL*Plus.
7. The _______________ initialization parameter sets the maximum size of a log or trace file.
8. The SQL_TRACE parameter has been set to TRUE using the ALTER SYSTEM command. Which initialization parameter would you set at a session level to help you identify your trace files easily among all the trace files being generated?
   a. USER_DUMP_DEST
   b. SQL_TRACE = FALSE
   c. TRACEFILE_IDENTIFIER
   d. TRACEFILE_SUFFIX
9. Name the utility that can be used to format the output file generated as a result of user tracing.

10. You wish to enable logging for the listener process. Which of the following parameter would you set?
   a. LOG_STATE, LOG_DIRECTORY, LOG_FILE
   b. LISTENER_LOGGING, LOG_DIRECTORY, LOG_FILE
   c. LOG_STATUS, LOG_DIRECTORY, LOG_FILE
   d. LOG_STATUS, LOG_TRACING, LOG_FILE
11. The database administrator has modified the default location of the network-related files. Which environment variable can be viewed to identify the location?
   a. TNS_NETWORK
   b. TNS_FILES
   c. ORACLE_HOME
   d. TNS_ADMIN
12. You are the database administrator in a small production company. The database is accessed by the following clients, C1, C2, C3, C4, and B2. You wish to configure valid node checking to allow clients C1, C2, C3, and C4 to access the database. B2 must be denied access to the database. You set the following parameters in the SQLNET.ORA file.

```
TCP.VALIDNODE_CHECKING = YES
TCP.INVITED_NODES   = C*
```

   What is the outcome of setting the parameters?
   a. An error will be generated because C* is not a valid client machine.
   b. None of the clients will be allowed to access the database because wildcard characters such as * as not allowed.

c. An error will be generated because B2 must be listed in the TCP.EXCLUDED_NODES parameter.

d. No error will be generated.

13. You are the database administrator in a small production company. The database is accessed by the following clients, C1, C2, C3, C4, and B2. You set the following parameters in the SQLNET.ORA file.

```
TCP.VALIDNODE_CHECKING    = YES
TCP.INVITED_NODES  = C1,C2,C3
TCP.EXCLUDED_NODES = B2
```

What is the outcome of setting the parameters?

a. An error will be generated because C4 was omitted in the list of invited nodes.

b. An error is generated because B2 must be an invited node.

c. An error is generated because both TCP.INVITED_NODES and TCP.EXCLUDED_NODES cannot be specified together.

d. No error will be generated; however, it is not recommended that both parameters be specified.

14. Identify the functions of the listener process. [Choose 2.]

a. Listens for incoming client requests.

b. Listens for incoming server process requests.

c. Listens on behalf of network protocols.

d. Supports external procedure functionality.

e. All of the above.

15. Name the command you would use to specify the password before issuing a password-protected command.

16. When an application makes a call to run an external procedure, it first calls the ________________.

a. Extproc agent

b. Server process

c. Listener Process

d. A privileged user on the operating system

17. The DBW0 background process encounters an exception. Identify the correct trace file that is generated by this process. The SID of the database is DB101.

a. db101_DBW0_1211.TRC

b. DBW0_DB101.1211.TRC

c. DBW0_DB101_1211.TRC

d. 1211_DBWO_DB101.TRC

18. A DBA wishes to secure the listener against attacks on its external procedure functionality. Which of the following methods would be most appropriate?
    a. Send an e-mail to all developers that it is best to stick to PL/SQL programming because there are too many risks presented by external procedure support.
    b. Delete all entries referencing external procedure functionality from the listener.ora file, even if the functionality is required.
    c. Drop the existing listener and create a new one.
    d. Create a separate listener and configure it so that it only listens for external procedure requests.
19. Name the variable that can be used to specify only a select list of accessible DLLs or shared libraries.
20. Why is it better to use the Listener Control Utility when setting the password of the Listener process in comparison to manually editing the Listener.ora?
    a. The password is stored in plaintext and is easier to read and remember.
    b. The password is stored in an encrypted format.
    c. It is easier to make errors in the listener.ora file, because there are so many parentheses to deal with.
    d. None of the above.

Hands-On Assignments

Note: Please execute the script **c14_setup.sql** before performing the hands-on assignments.

Assignment 14-1 Identifying the locations of the log and trace files

1. Start SQL*Plus and connect as a user with SYSDBA privileges.
2. Using an appropriate command display the location of the Alert log file. Note this value.
3. Using an appropriate command, display the location of the background trace files.
4. Using an appropriate command, display the location of the user trace files.
5. Exit SQL*Plus.

Assignment 14-2 Identifying the status of logging and tracing of the default listener

1. Launch an operating system command prompt and invoke the listener control utility.
2. Using the HELP SHOW command display all the options that are available with the SHOW command. From the list, identify the options that will display the status of logging and tracing.
3. Using appropriate SHOW commands, display the status of logging, the log directory, and the log file name.
4. Using appropriate SHOW commands, display the level of tracing, the trace directory, and the trace file name.
5. Exit the listener control utility.

Assignment 14-3 Displaying the contents of the alert log file from Enterprise Manager

1. Launch a browser and enter the URL to start the Enterprise Manager. Log in as a user with SYSDBA privileges.
2. From the Database Control Home page, navigate to the Related Links section.
3. Select the Alert Log Content link.
4. Where do you find the most recent entries, at the top or the end of the page? Don't close the browser.
5. Using Windows Explorer, navigate to the location of the Alert Log file.
6. Delete the file using an operating system command.
7. Start SQL*Plus, connect with SYSDBA privileges and shut down the database in immediate mode. You also may perform the operation using Enterprise Manager.
8. Start up the database once again.
9. Using Windows Explorer, return to the location of the alert log file, you will notice that is has been automatically recreated. It will contain entries pertaining to the most recent shutdown and startup.
10. Exit all windows that you have opened.

Assignment 14-5 Identifying trace files

1. Using Windows Explorer, navigate to the location specified by the BACKGROUND_DUMP_DEST initialization parameter.
2. Look for trace files generated by the LGWR, SMON, or PMON background processes. Open them and view their contents.
3. Exit the file and Windows Explorer.

Assignment 14-6 Generating User Trace Files

1. Start SQL*Plus and connect as a user with SYSDBA privileges. We will refer to this session as S1.
2. Open a second session and connect as the user MEDUSER, we shall refer to this session as S2.
3. Return to session S1, and issue the following query on the V$SESSION view to display the SID, SERIAL# and USERNAME of all users currently connected to the database.

```
SQL> SELECT SID, SERIAL#, USERNAME FROM V$SESSION;
```

4. Identify the row in the output, displaying the SID and SERIAL# of the user MEDUSER. Note the SID and SERIAL#.
5. From session S1, issue the command displayed to enable tracing in the session created by MEDUSER (i.e. S2). In place of m and n, substitute the SID and SERIAL# values that you noted in step 4.

```
SQL> EXECUTE DBMS_MONITOR.SESSION_TRACE_ENABLE(SESSION_ID=>m,
SERIAL_NUM=>n);
```

6. From session S2, issue the command to set the TRACEFILE_IDENTIFIER for the current session to MUSER.
7. From session S2, retrieve all the data in the PRESCRIPTIONS table.

8. Return to session S1, and issue the following command to disable tracing. Substitute the Session ID in place of m, and the serial number in place of n.

```
SQL> EXEC DBMS_MONITOR.SESSION_TRACE_DISABLE(SESSION_ID =>m, -
   > SERIAL_NUM => n);
```

9. Using Windows Explorer, navigate to the location specified by the USER_DUMP_DEST parameter and locate the file with a suffix _MU.
10. Open a command prompt and using the TKPROF utility format the output of the SQL Trace file generated.
11. Exit all open windows.

Assignment 14-7 Creating a new Listener from Enterprise Manager

1. Launch a browser, enter the URL to access the Enterprise Manager and log in as a user with SYSDBA privileges.
2. From the Database Control home page, go to the General section and select the link next to the Host label. (i.e., select the hostname).
3. From the Host:<hostname> page, scroll to the Related Links section.
4. Select the Net Services Administration link.
5. From the Net Services Administration page, select Listeners from the Administer drop-down list.

6. Select the Go button. If you are prompted for the Username and Password of the Host User, enter it appropriately.
7. From the Listener:<path> page, Select all Listener names other than LISTENER and delete them.
8. After you have deleted all the listeners, with the exception of LISTENER, select the Create button to create a new listener.
9. From the Create Listener page, type the name of the listener as NEWLIST.
10. From the Addresses section, select the Add button.
11. From the Add Address page, don't modify the Protocol and Host. Type in the Port as 1522. Then select the OK button.
12. From the Create Listener page, select the OK button.
13. A Creation Message indicating the Listener was successfully created should be displayed.
14. Log out of Enterprise Manager and close the browser.

Assignment 14-8 Controlling the New Listener

Please complete assignment 14-7 before this assignment.

1. Start an operating system command prompt window. Then launch the listener control utility.
2. Issue a command to start the listener called NEWLIST.
3. Issue the command to display the status of the listener called NEWLIST.
4. What kind of Security is enabled on the listener by default?
5. Display the services that listener NEWLIST supports.
6. Issue the command to set the password for the NEWLIST listener.
7. Issue the command to save the configuration of the NEWLIST listener.

8. Stop the listener called NEWLIST.
9. Exit the listener control utility and exit the command prompt window.

Assignment 14-9 Viewing the Listener.ora file

1. Using Windows Explorer, navigate to the %ORACLE_HOME%\network\admin directory.
2. Locate the file called listener.ora and open it.
3. Locate entries about the NEWLIST listener. Look for the encrypted password associated with the NEWLIST listener.
4. Look for the protocol address of the listener NEWLIST. Which is the port it is currently listening on?
5. Close the Listener.ora file.

Assignment 14-10 Managing the listener using Enterprise Manager

1. Launch a browser and enter the URL to access the Enterprise Manager. Login with SYSDBA privileges.
2. From the Database Control Home page, the Home tab, navigate to the General section.
3. Information about the listener will be displayed. Select the link next to Listener.
4. The Listener: LISTENER_<machine_name> will be displayed. Read the information displayed on the page.
5. Select the Edit button on the page. The Net Services Administration: Host Login page will be displayed. Enter the operating system user credentials.
6. The Edit Listener:LISTENER page is displayed.
7. Notice the addresses the Listener listens for, there will be one or more protocols listed. If you needed to remove external procedure support you can also remove it from this page, by selecting the IPC protocol whose key is EXTPROC1 and click the Remove button. It is not displayed in this output because it was deleted in an earlier practice.
8. Select the Authentication tab. Notice you have options to set or remove the listener password.
9. Select the Logging & Tracing tab, you may enable/disable logging and tracing and set the level of tracing on this page.
10. Select the Static Database Registration page. This page may display one or more database names depending on the databases that the listener listens for.
11. Select the Other Services tab. If external procedure functionality is supported by the listener, the name of the program (EXTPROC) will be displayed.
12. Return to the General tab, and select the OK button on the right side of the page.
13. An Edit Confirmation:LISTENER page will be displayed. Select the Don't Restart option followed by the OK button.
14. You will be returned to the Listener: LISTENER_localhost page. Select the Stop button. This is to stop the listener.
15. The Start/Stop: LISTENER page will be displayed. Select the OK button to restart the listener.
16. You will be returned to the LISTENER_localhost page. Log out of Enterprise Manager and exit the browser.

Case Study

1. Revisit the scenario presented at the beginning of this chapter and identify the reason for the error and provide an appropriate solution to the problem faced by Ryan.
2. You have been given the job of a database administrator in a startup company that uses Oracle 10*g*. List the different things you would do on a daily basis to get information about the status of the database. Also, list the different methods you would employ to secure the listener from security threats.

APPENDIX A

ORACLE ARCHITECTURE

In this appendix we discuss the primary architectural elements of the Oracle Database 10*g*. An understanding of this architecture is fundamental to being able to administer the Oracle database.

Database — Is a collection of related and relevant data. Data is maintained within a database in a centralized manner with minimum redundancy and maximum consistency.

Oracle Server — Consists of the Database Management System (DBMS) that allows users to store and manage data. The Oracle Server also comprises of the Oracle Instance and the Oracle Database. (See Figure A-1.)

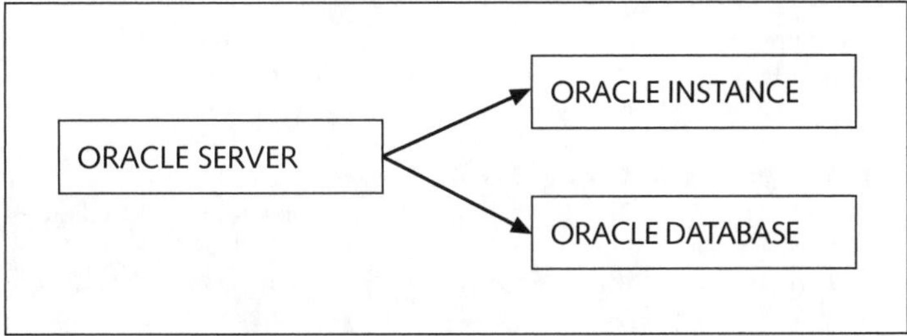

FIGURE A-1 The components of the Oracle server

ORACLE INSTANCE

The Oracle Instance is made up of memory structures and background processes that are created by the Oracle Server when the database is started. These memory structures are created in the real memory of the computer. The background processes of the instance perform various input-output (I/O) functions of behalf of the database. A user is able to access the data within the database using the Oracle instance. The Oracle instance speeds up database operations and performance by storing data and program code in memory. The memory components of the instance are collectively known as the System Global Area (SGA). The

SGA is made up of a number of individual memory structures. Figure A-2 displays the memory structures of the SGA.

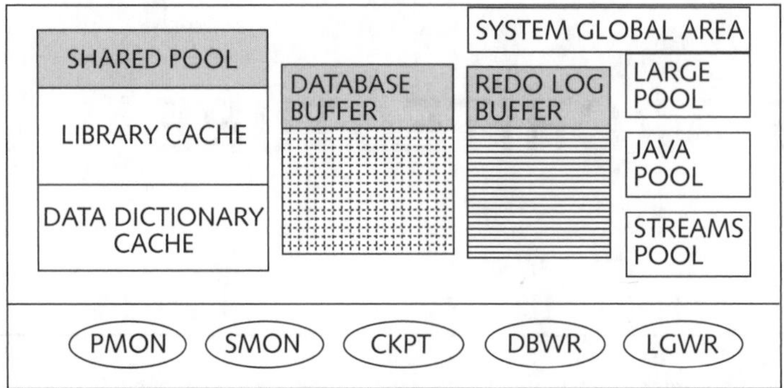

FIGURE A-2 The components of the System Global Area (SGA)

TABLE A-1 The memory structures of the SGA

Memory Structure	Description/Function
`System Global Area (SGA)`	The SGA is a shared memory region that contains data and control information for an Oracle instance. The SGA is created during database start up and is released when the database is shut down. The SGA is made up of a number of different structures, including pools and caches.
`Shared Pool`	The shared pool is the area in the SGA that holds data and control information that can be shared among different users of the database. The shared pool is sized using the SHARED_POOL_SIZE initialization parameter. It consists of two parts—the Library Cache and the Data Dictionary Cache. Library Cache—The library cache contains the most recently executed SQL statements and their parsed representations and execution plans. The function of the library cache is to allow sharing or reusability of parsed code and execution plans during SQL statement processing. Sharing this information speeds up query processing of identical statements in the database. Data Dictionary Cache—This cache is also known as Rowcache. The data dictionary cache holds data dictionary information in memory. The data dictionary is physically stored in the datafiles of the SYSTEM tablespace. To minimize expensive physical reads from disk, the contents of the data dictionary are stored in memory. This improves performance because reads from memory are faster than reads from disk. Because data dictionary information is constantly referenced in the database, ideally, the entire data dictionary should be stored in memory in this cache.

TABLE A-1 The memory structures of the SGA (continued)

Memory Structure	Description/Function
`Database Buffer Cache`	The database buffer cache, also called the *default* database buffer cache, holds data blocks that have been read into memory during the execution of SELECT and Data Manipulation Language (DML) statements. For example, when a user issues a SELECT statement and reads an entire table, all the blocks that hold the rows of the table are retrieved from the datafiles and populated in the database buffer cache. Similarly, if a user issues an UPDATE statement that modifies a row(s) in a table, the block containing the row(s) are read into the database buffer cache. The row is modified in the database buffer cache. This modified block is referred to as a dirty block. A dirty block is then written back to the datafiles. The database buffer cache has a limited size and as blocks fill the cache, room must be made for new blocks that may need to be brought in. For this reason, the cache is managed using the Least Recently Used algorithm (LRU algorithm) indicating that the oldest blocks are the first to leave the cache. The database buffer cache is sized by the DB_CACHE_SIZE initialization parameter. In addition to the default cache, other caches may be optionally created, including the keep cache and the recycle cache. The keep cache can be created to store the blocks of objects that must be stored in memory for a longer period of time. This cache is also managed using the LRU algorithm; however, the rate at which the blocks leave the cache is much slower compared to the default cache. The keep cache is sized using the DB_KEEP_CACHE_SIZE initialization parameter. The recycle cache can be created to store the blocks of objects that must leave memory faster because it is unlikely that they will be referenced again. The recycle cache is sized using the DB_RECYCLE_CACHE_SIZE initialization parameter. For a database that uses tablespaces with non-standard block sizes, additional caches will have to be created for the blocks of these tablespaces. These caches will be sized using the parameters DB_*n*K_CACHE_sIZE, where *n* can be a value 2 K, 4 K, 8 K, 16 K, 32 K, or 64 K.
`Redo Log Buffer`	The redo log buffer contains a record or log of all the changes made in the database. The changes written to the redo log buffer are called redo entries. Redo entries are generated when INSERT, UPDATE, DELETE, CREATE, ALTER, and DROP statements are issued in the database. Every statement issued in the database is logged (unless the NOLOGGING option has been set for the object). The contents of the redo log buffer are transferred to online redo log files on disk by the LGWR background process. Redo entries are used for database recovery. In the event of a failure the changes, or redo entries, can be used to recreate the changes that may have been lost. The redo log buffer is sized by the LOG_BUFFER initialization parameter.
`Large Pool`	The large pool is an optional memory structure that may be configured to enhance I/O functions and satisfy memory requirements of an Oracle Shared Server configuration, Recovery Manager (RMAN), and for parallel query processing. The size of the large pool is configured by the LARGE_POOL_SIZE initialization parameter.

TABLE A-1 The memory structures of the SGA (continued)

Memory Structure	Description/Function
`Java Pool`	This optional pool may be configured when installing and using Java code. The pool is used for servicing the parsing requirements of Java-based applications. The size of the pool can be configured using the JAVA_POOL_SIZE parameter.
`Streams Pool`	This is an optional pool that may be configured to support the functionality of the new Oracle Streams feature. The streams pool is sized by the STREAMS_POOL_SIZE parameter.

The instance also contains a number of mandatory and optional background processes. The five mandatory background processes are the Database Writer (DBWn), Log Writer (LGWR), Checkpoint (CKPT), System Monitor (SMON), and Process Monitor (PMON). Optional background processes are started when a specific database option or functionality is required. For example, if you wish to enable archiving in the database, the ARCH background process is started by default. Table A-2 displays a list of the background processes started in the Oracle instance and their primary functions.

TABLE A-2 The background processes

Background Process	Function
`Database Writer (DBWn)`	Performs input/output (I/O) functions. Is responsible for transferring all modified blocks, called dirty buffers, from the database buffer cache to the datafiles on disk.
`Log Writer (LGWR)`	Performs input/output (I/O) functions. Is responsible for transferring the contents of the redo log buffer to the online redo log files on disk.
`System Monitor (SMON)`	Performs instance recovery in the event of an instance failure. Instance failure may occur as a result of a power outage or an improper shutdown of the database. During instance recovery, the SMON background process applies all the committed changes and rolls back uncommitted changes that were executing at the time of failure. A record of all the committed and uncommitted changes is available in the online redo log files. Other functions of the SMON background process include the coalescing of free space in dictionary-managed files for reuse by other segments. It is also responsible for cleaning up temporary segments that are no longer in use.
`Process Monitor (PMON)`	PMON is responsible for cleaning up failed user processes. When a user process disconnects from the database abnormally, certain system resources may remain attached to the user process. The PMON process periodically checks for such failed user processes and releases resources and locks that might have been held by them when they terminated.
`Checkpoint (CKPT)`	The checkpoint process is responsible for database synchronization. It instructs the Database Writer to write a group of changes to the datafiles. After the write has completed, it updates the headers of the datafiles and control files. More frequent checkpointing would result in less recovery time, which, however, would result in more I/O being performed.

TABLE A-2 The background processes (continued)

Background Process	Function
`Archiver (ARCH)`	This optional process is responsible for automatically archiving the contents of the online redo log files to archive log files. This is done when the database is running in *archivelog* mode. Running the database in this mode ensures complete recovery of the database in the event of media failure, such as the loss of a disk. The ARCH process automatically creates an archived log file when a log switch occurs. A log switch is the term used to indicate the event when the Log Writer completes writing to a redo log file and starts writing to the next log file.

Table A-3 describes some more memory structures and processes found in the Oracle database.

TABLE A-3 Additional processes and memory structures

Other Memory Structures and Processes	Description/Function
`User Processes`	When a client tool such as SQL*Plus is launched, Oracle creates a process called the user process on the client-side. This process is responsible for sending requests to the database. The communication pathway created between the client and the database is known as a session. The session begins when the client successfully connects to the database and ends when the clients disconnects from the database.
`Server Processes`	The server process is the process that is created on the server side to handle the requests made by a user process. The server process may be a dedicated server process or a shared server process. A dedicated server process is one that remains attached to a specific user process until the user process is terminated. It is started when a user session begins and handles all requests on behalf of that user process. Shared server processes are available in an Oracle shared server environment, and may handle the requests of several user processes. The server process can perform one or more of the following : • Parse and run SQL statements. • Read data blocks from datafiles into the database buffer cache. • Return the requested results back to the application.
`Dispatcher Processes`	Dispatcher processes are created when running the database in a shared server mode. The dispatcher process allows user processes to share a limited number of server processes. Multiple dispatcher processes may be created for a single database instance. At least one dispatcher must be created for each network protocol used with Oracle.
`Program Global Area`	When user process/server process connectivity is established, the server process maintains some data and control information about the user process. The memory area used to hold this information is known as the Program Global Area (PGA) (see Figure A-3). The contents of the PGA include session/user information, runtime and bind variables created in the user's session, and space for operations such as sorting, creating, and merging bitmap indexes.

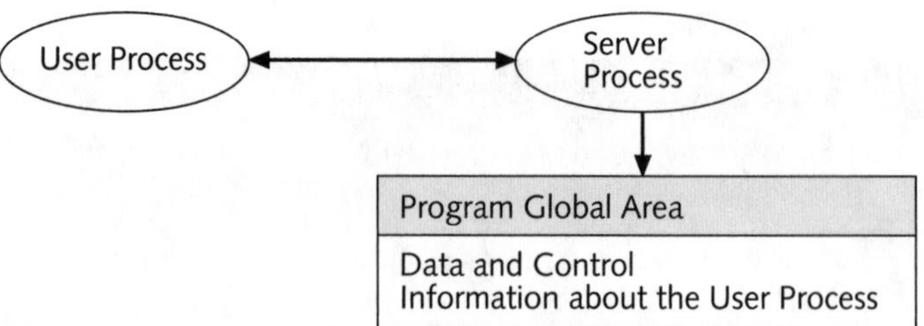

FIGURE A-3 The Program Global Area

ORACLE DATABASE

Data is stored in an Oracle database. An Oracle database may be created manually by the CREATE DATABASE command or by using the graphical tool known as the Database Configuration Assistant. A database is given a name and is created with a collection of system tables known as its data dictionary.

The Oracle database has a logical and physical structure. The physical structure consists of operating system files known as the physical files of the database. These files are visible at an operating system level. The logical structure of a database consists of various structures that are created and maintained within Oracle. They are created primarily to simplify database administration.

The Physical Structure of the Database

Figure A-4 displays the different physical files of the database. Table A-4 describes the physical files of the database.

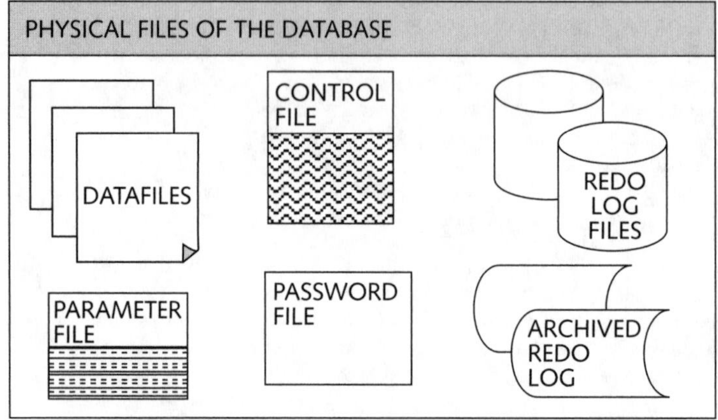

FIGURE A-4 The physical files of the database

TABLE A-4 The physical files of the database and their description

Physical Files	Description/Function
`DataFiles`	These files store the data dictionary and the user data. The data dictionary is a collection of system tables that store metadata, which is data about the data that is stored in the database. Every time Data Definition Language (DDL) statements are issued in the database the data dictionary is updated. Database administrators and users of the database can reference the contents of the data dictionary, but can never modify it. The user data is a logical collection of all the objects created by the users of the database such as tables, indexes, sequences, etc. A datafile is associated with a tablespace.
`Control Files`	Control files are the most important files in the database. A control file contains information about the database such as its name, date of creation, names of the other physical files of the database, synchronization, log sequence numbers, backup and recovery, archiving information, and so on. It is a binary file that is updated by Oracle and is required for normal database operations. If Oracle is unable to write to a control file, the database will be automatically shut down. It is important to maintain multiple copies of the control file.
`Redo Log Files`	The redo log files contain a record of all the changes that are made in the database. A minimum of two redo log groups are required in the database, and Oracle recommends multiplexing redo log files. Multiplexing is the process of creating additional members for the redo log groups. Redo log files are used for database recovery. The contents of redo log files are continuously overwritten and if complete recovery is required, the contents of the redo log files must be archived. Archiving a redo log file creates an offline backup of the redo log contents before it is overwritten.

TABLE A-4 The physical files of the database and their description (continued)

Physical Files	Description/Function
`Initialization Parameter Files`	Parameter files contain parameter names and values. These parameters are used to configure the Oracle instance and data structures, specify values for various processes, and identify the name of the database and instance. The parameter file is the first file that is read during database startup. There are two kinds of parameter files, namely the Initialization Parameter file (*pfile*) and the Persistent Server Parameter file (*spfile*). An entry in a parameter file takes the form: parameter_name = parameter_value A typical entry in the parameter file would be SHARED_POOL_SIZE = 350 MB that sets the size of the Shared Pool to 350 MB. Some of the parameter values may be dynamically modified during normal database operation using an ALTER SYSTEM command. The difference between the parameter file and server parameter file lies in the fact that when a dynamic change is made using the spfile, the change may be set to affect not only the current instance but also future instances of the database. This is not possible when using a pfile where a dynamic change made to a parameter will only affect the current instance. When using the spfile, the keyword SCOPE can be specified to indicate whether the change should affect future instances. When SCOPE is set to BOTH, the change will affect the current and future instances of the database. When set to MEMORY it will only affect the current instance of the database, when set to SPFILE the change will be written to the server parameter file and will only affect future instances of the database. If the spfile exists for a database, it will be the one used by default during database startup. If it does not exist then the parameter file would be used. Changes made to any one parameter file are not automatically synchronized. For example, a dynamic change using a SCOPE=SPFILE option will update the spfile only. There would sometimes be a need to synchonize the two types of parameter files. A pfile can be created using an spfile by issuing the SQL command `CREATE PFILE FROM SPFILE;`. An spfile can be created using a pfile by using the SQL command `CREATE SPFILE FROM PFILE;`.

TABLE A-4 The physical files of the database and their description (continued)

Physical Files	Description/Function
`Password File`	The password file is a file that is used to authenticate privileged users of the database. It contains the usernames and passwords of database users who have been granted the SYSDBA or SYSOPER role. These roles are predefined roles of the database that contain administrative privileges that permit users to start up or shut down the database, create a database, or alter a database. It should also be noted that if the password file is to be used to valid authenticated users, the REMOTE_LOGIN_PASSWORDFILE initialization parameter must be set to a value EXCLUSIVE. The password file can be created from the operating system, using the ORAPWD command. An example of the creation of a password file is: C:\> ORAPWD FILE=%ORACLE_HOME%\database\<passwordfile_name> PASSWORD=<SYS_password> ENTRIES=n where: FILE: is the name of the password file. On Windows machine the name of the password file will take the form PWD<sid>.ora. PASSWORD: is the password of the SYS user. ENTRIES: is the number of users who may be granted the SYSDBA or SYSOPER roles.
`Archive Files`	Archive files are optional files that are created when the database is running in ARCHIVELOG mode. Archive files are offline copies of the redo log files. They contain a sequential record of all the changes that occur in the database. They are used for media recovery.

The Logical Structure of the Database

The Oracle database also presents a logical structure. (See Figure A-5.) The logical structure of the database is associated with its physical structure. The logical structure of a database is recognized only within Oracle. Table A-5 describes the components of the logical structure of the database.

TABLE A-5 Components of the logical structure of the database

Logical Structure	Description/Function
`Database`	The database is a collection of all the data stored in the database. It is a centralized repository of related data.
`Tablespaces`	A database is made up of one or more tablespaces. Tablespaces are logical structures that may be created to separate and organize the data in the database. Tablespaces can be used to logically separate different types of data based on storage and fragmentation characteristics. Different kinds of data are stored within the database in addition to the data dictionary. These include user data, undo data, index data, temporary data, and so on. In the Oracle 10*g* database, a database is automatically created with two mandatory tablespaces—the SYSTEM and SYSAUX tablespaces. The SYSTEM tablespace contains the data dictionary and all the objects owned by the SYS user. The SYSAUX tablespace is the default tablespace of a number of schemas such as the intelligent agent user DBSNMP, the data mining user, and ODM. These users are created when certain options such as Ultra search, Data Mining, XDP, Oracle Spatial, Oracle interMedia, and OLAP are selected during database creation. To effectively manage a database, a DBA may choose to create additional tablespaces. To ensure that objects are stored in the appropriate tablespace during their creation, a default and temporary tablespace may be specified for a user. Once you have defined a default tablespace for a user, all objects created by the user will automatically be created in this default tablespace. Similarly, when a temporary tablespace is defined, all temporary segments created by the user will be created in the temporary tablespace. New in Oracle 10*g* is a *bigfile* tablespace. Oracle lets you create tablespaces up to 8 exabytes (8 million terabytes) in size. The creation of such tablespaces eliminates the need for administering many smaller datafiles. All operations that can be performed on datafiles can be directly performed on bigfile tablespaces.
`Segment`	A segment corresponds to an object of the database. When a table is created Oracle refers to it as a data segment. Some other segments that are recognized within the Oracle database are index segments for indexes, undo segments that hold undo data, and temporary segments that hold temporary data. Segments are created in tablespaces and are made up of one or more extents.
`Extents`	An extent is a unit of space allocation. When a data segment is created, Oracle initially allocates a certain amount of space for the object's data (rows). This initial allocation of space is known as the initial extent. When additional space is required by the object, a second extent will be allocated. Extents that are allocated for an object need not be contiguous. A collection of the extents belonging to an object form a segment. The total size of all extents will determine the total size of the segment.

TABLE A-5 Components of the logical structure of the database (continued)

Logical Structure	Description/Function
`Oracle Block`	An Oracle block is the smallest unit of input/output (I/O) for Oracle. It defines the unit that Oracle can read or write at a time. The size of the default Oracle block is determined by the DB_BLOCK_SIZE initialization parameter. Since Oracle 9*i*, tablespaces with non-standard block sizes may be created within a database. The Oracle block size should be a multiple of the operating system block size. For example, if the OS block size is 2 K, the Oracle block size can be 2 K, 4 K, 8 K, 16 K, 32 K, or 64 K. A number of Oracle blocks form an extent and all the blocks of an extent are contiguous.

The association between the Logical and Physical Structure of the Database

The logical and physical structures of the Oracle database are associated with one another. Figure A-5 describes the relationship between the logical and physical structure of the Oracle database.

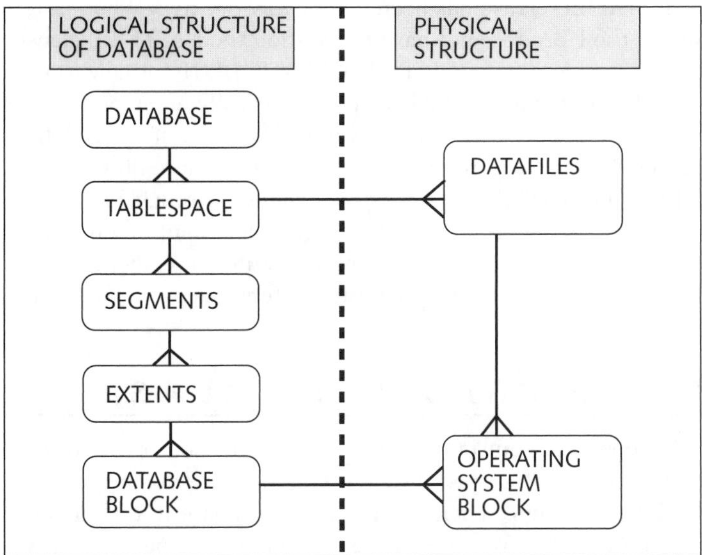

FIGURE A-5 The association between the logical and physical structure of the database

The datafiles of the database hold user and system data. When a tablespace is created, it is associated with one or more datafiles. A datafile can be viewed from the operating system and is made up of operating system blocks.

A typical command to create a tablespace is:

```
CREATE TABLESPACE tablespace_name
DATAFILE '<PATH>\datafile_name' SIZE n;
```

Where: `tablespace_name`: is the name of the tablespace
`datafile_name`: is the name of the datafile belonging to the tablespace
`n`: is the size of the datafile in bytes, kilobytes, megabytes, etc.

User-Managed and Oracle-Managed Files

Files of a database may be User-Managed Files (UMF) or Oracle-Managed Files (OMF). OMF files were introduced in Oracle 9*i* to simplify file management. In the command shown above for the creation of the tablespace, notice the name and location of the datafile have been specified in the DATAFILE clause. The example presents the creation of a user-managed datafile. In the UMF method of file creation, the location, the name of the file, and the size of the datafile have to be specified during creation. If the same tablespace was to be created using OMF, the create command would have been:

```
CREATE TABLESPACE tablespace_name;
```

Notice in this syntax the DATAFILE clause has been completely omitted. When issuing the command in this manner the DBA does not have to mention the DATAFILE clause. However, the DBA must specify a value for the DB_FILE_CREATE_DEST initialization parameter. The value must be a location where Oracle can automatically create a file with a default size of 100 MB. The file that is created will be given a unique name. The OMF method can be used to create log files and control files. The location of these files is specified by the DB_CREATE_ONLINE_LOG_DEST_*n*, (*n* may be a value 1 through 5), initialization parameter. Oracle recommends the use of OMF files. An Oracle-managed file is easier to administer and Oracle takes care of uniquely naming it, automatically sizing it when it runs out of space, and dropping it from the operating system when the tablespace it belongs to is dropped.

ARCHIVING IN THE ORACLE DATABASE

A database may be configured to operate in one of two modes—Noarchivelog or Archivelog mode. In noarchivelog mode the contents of the online redo log files are overwritten without creating a backup of those contents. When operating the database in this mode, complete database recovery is not possible. When a failure in the database occurs, recovery is possible only until the last complete backup taken. Further, complete backups are the only option available and may be performed only when the database is shut down.

When operating the database in archivelog mode, every time a log switch occurs and Oracle needs to write to a redo log file, it will proceed with the write only after the contents of that redo log file have been archived or backed up to an offline file. The offline file created using the contents of an online redo log file is known as an archive log file. Archiving can be performed either automatically or manually. In automatic archiving, the ARCH background process performs the archiving automatically when a log switch occurs. In manual archiving, it is the responsibility of the database administrator to issue the command to perform archiving. In Oracle 10*g*, when archiving is enabled, automatic archiving is also enabled. A number of initialization parameters are available that are used to configure archiving. Table A-6 describes some of the parameters and their purpose, including some examples.

TABLE A-6 Parameters associated with archiving

Parameter	Description	Example
LOG_ARCHIVE_DEST_*n*	Establishes the destination of the archive log files. The value *n* can range from 1 through 10.	`LOG_ARCHIVE_DEST_n = C:\ARCHIVES`

LOG_ARCHIVE_FORMAT	Establishes the naming convention used for the archive log files. Valid symbols that can be used in the filenames include:
	
	%s — log sequence number
	
	%t — thread number
		`LOG_ARCHIVE_FORMAT = arch_%s.arc`
		
		`A typical filename generated using this format would be : arch_1.arc, where 1 is the log sequence number of the redo log file.`

LOG_ARCHIVE_START	Enables or disables automatic archiving. When set to TRUE, it enables automatic archiving. When set to FALSE, it enables manual archiving.	`LOG_ARCHIVE_START=TRUE`

AUTOMATIC UNDO MANAGEMENT

Undo data is continuously generated in the database when changes are made to database objects. Previous values held by an object, such as a table being modified by an UPDATE, is known as undo data. Undo data is required for three main purposes: transaction rollback, instance recovery, and read consistency. If a user making changes in a transaction decides to roll back the changes, the undo data can be used to restore the original values. During instance recovery, all the changes that were uncommitted at the time of the instance failure must be undone; the undo data is once again used for this purpose. Finally, when a user is making a change to a certain row and another user tries to read the same row, Oracle does not allow the user to read the data in the state of change because the user making the change may choose to undo the transaction. A user who reads data currently in the state of change will read the undo data because it is consistent data.

To manage undo data more efficiently, a new feature called Automatic Undo Management was introduced in Oracle 9*i*. Oracle stores undo data in segments known as undo segments. The undo data must remain in the undo segments until the transaction that generated it is completed. Using automatic undo management, the DBA has to configure only a few options to identify the location where undo segments must be created and the duration of time undo data must remain in the undo segments. To enable automatic undo management, the UNDO_MANAGEMENT initialization parameter must be set to AUTO. The location or tablespace where undo segments must be created is identified by the UNDO_TABLESPACE parameter. The duration of time (in seconds) that undo data must remain in the undo segments even after the transaction that generated them has completed is determined by the UNDO_RETENTION parameter. Setting an appropriate value for UNDO_RETENTION facilitates many of the Flashback Technology features. Typical values that can be set for the undo parameters are:

UNDO_MANAGEMENT=AUTO
UNDO_TABLESPACE=undotbs1
UNDO_RETENTION=900

THE ORACLE DATA DICTIONARY

The Oracle data dictionary is a set of tables and views created during database creation. Data dictionary tables store metadata about the data that is stored in the database. The data dictionary is constantly updated and maintained by the Oracle server when Data definition Language (DDL) statements such as CREATE, ALTER, DROP, and Data Control Language (DCL) statements such as GRANT and REVOKE are executed in the database. The data dictionary may be referenced by database administrators and users, for read purposes to obtain information about currently stored objects. For example, an administrator can determine the names of all tables created by a particular user by querying the data dictionary.

The data dictionary is stored in the datafiles belonging to the SYSTEM tablespace. Every Oracle database must have a data dictionary that is accessible at all times after the database has been opened.

ACCESSING THE DATABASE

In most production environments, networked access to the database is required. Clients access the database using front-end tools and applications across the network. Oracle provides a number of network services that facilitate distributed processing and distributed databases. An important component of the network services is Oracle Net, which enables network connectivity between a client application and the Oracle database server. The Oracle Net component acts as a data courier on behalf of the client and server. (See Figure A-6.)

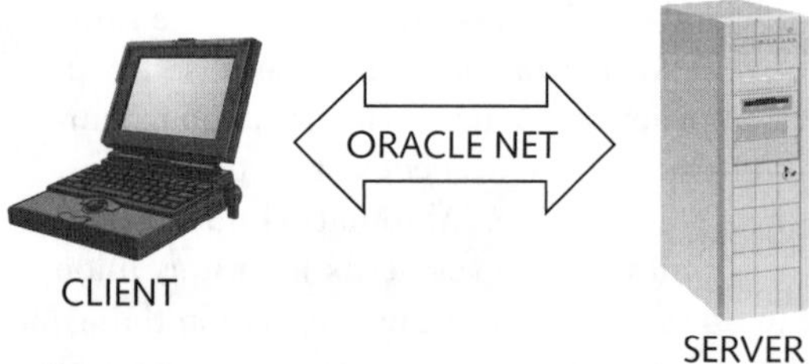

FIGURE A-6 The Oracle Net component

ENTERPRISE MANAGER

OVERVIEW OF ENTERPRISE MANAGER

The Enterprise Manager in Oracle Database 10g is a web-based application that provides a single, integrated interface for administering and monitoring applications and systems. Using the Enterprise Manager, the DBA can get a complete overview of the health and status of the database. Its graphical interface makes it easy to understand and administer the database.

If you create a database using the Database Configuration Assistant tool, you can choose to administer your database using Enterprise Manager. You can also choose additional options such as Database Control or Database Grid Control. Database Control gives you the ability to administer a single database whereas Grid Control can be used to administer more complex database environments with multiple databases on a network. If you choose the Grid Control option, the Oracle Management server must be installed on the system.

Appendix B focuses on the Database Control option which is also the default option. If you wish to administer your database using Enterprise Manager you must know how to launch it. The next topic describes how the Enterprise Manager may be launched on a Windows platform.

LAUNCHING ENTERPRISE MANAGER

The Enterprise Manager may be launched by using any browser, such as Internet Explorer, Mozilla Firefox, the Netscape browser, and so on. In the address bar, the URL to launch the Enterprise Manager must be specified.

> **NOTE**
>
> After creating a database using Database Configuration Assistant, a screen is displayed providing important details about the database. The screen also displays the URL that can be used to launch Enterprise Manager. Figure B-1 displays an example of the window that provides this information.

In general, the URL is of the form:

```
http://<hostname>:<port_number>/em
```

Based on Figure B-1, the URL to access the Enterprise Manager and administer the DB101 database is:

```
http://dbsrv01.mydomain.com:1158/em
```

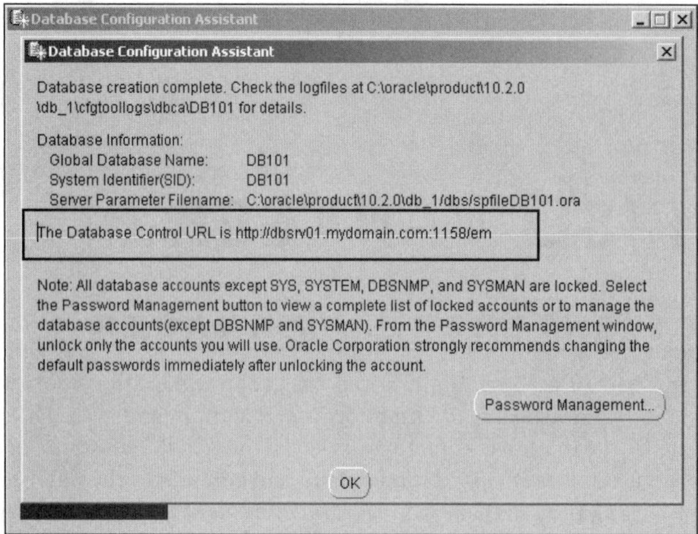

FIGURE B-1 The URL for Enterprise Manager

When Enterprise Manager is launched, a login screen is displayed, prompting you for a valid username and password of a NORMAL user or one with SYSDBA or SYSOPER privileges. You may enter the username and password of the SYS user. From Connect As, select SYSDBA. You can then click the Login button. (See Figure B-2.)

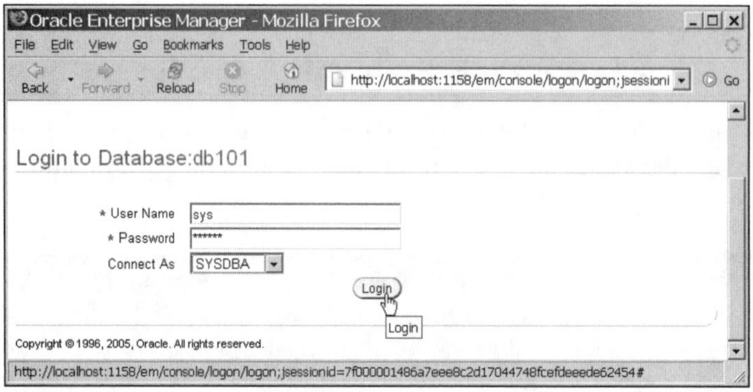

FIGURE B-2 The login screen

The Database Control Home Page

After you have successfully logged on, the **Database Control Home** page is displayed. (See Figures B-3 through B-7.) On the top-right corner are options to modify the **Setup, Preferences, Help,** and to **Logout** from Enterprise Manager. The Setup option allows you to manage administrators, create notification methods, and configure patch management.

The Preferences link allows you to specify preferred credentials, notification schedules, and other preferences.

On the top-left corner of the Database Control Home page, below the database name, are various tabs (Home, Performance, Administration, and Maintenance) that provide quick access to pages associated with performance monitoring, administration, and maintenance of the Oracle 10g database.

On the top-right corner is a **View Data** drop-down list that gives you the ability to refresh the page, either manually or automatically, every 60 seconds. The **Refresh** button can be used to refresh the page to display the most current status of the database.

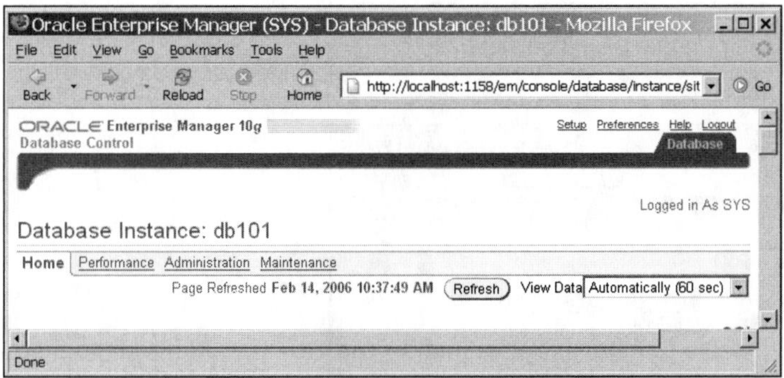

FIGURE B-3 The tabs and options available in the Database Control Home page

The Database Control Home page has various sections. The sections include: **General, Host CPU, Active Sessions, SQL Response Time, Diagnostic Summary, Space Summary, Advice, High Availability, Alerts, Related Alerts, Job Activity,** and **Related Links.**

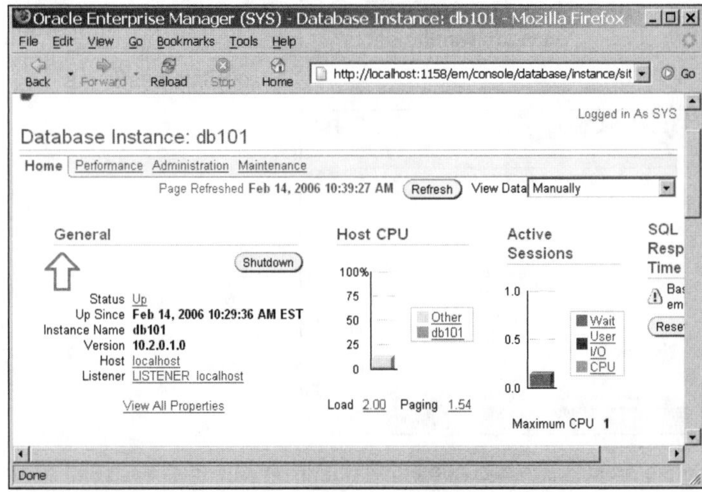

FIGURE B-4 The Database Control Home page continued

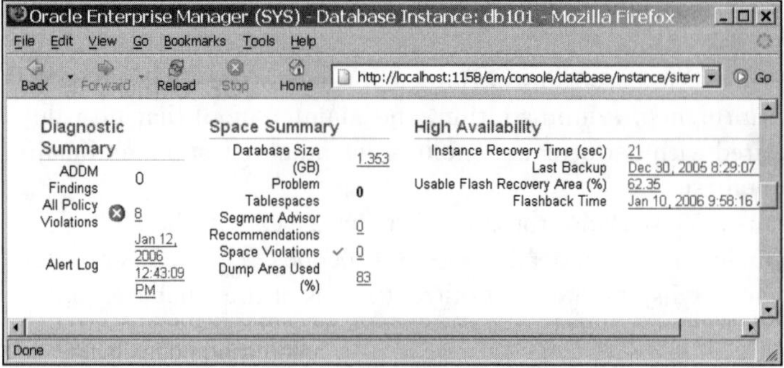

FIGURE B-5 The Database Control Home page continued

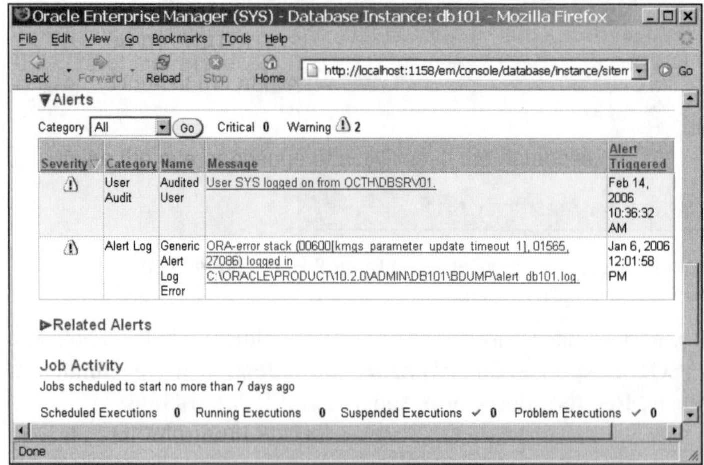

FIGURE B-6 The Database Control Home page continued

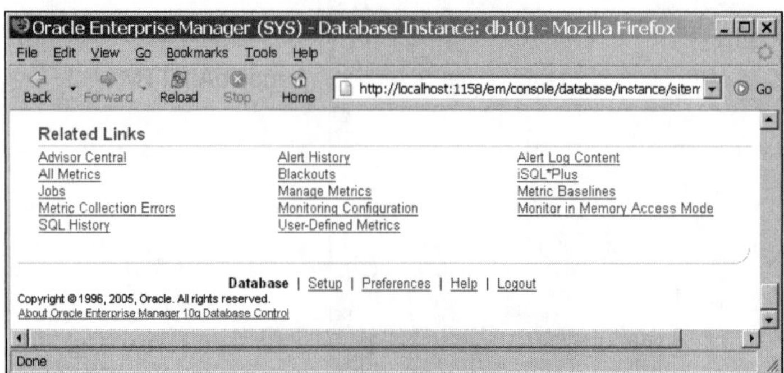

FIGURE B-7 The Database Control Home page continued

The General section displays information about the status of the database, the date and time since the database has been running, the name of the instance, the read status of the database, the path of the ORACLE_HOME, the name of the listener, and the host machine on which the database is running. A button is available to STARTUP or SHUTDOWN the database depending on the current status of the database.

The Host CPU, Active Sessions, and High Availability sections describe the activity on the database in terms of paging, I/O and database waits, instance recovery time, and so on. The Oracle 10*g* database provides a new functionality known as Server-Generated Alerts. This is an alerting mechanism that signals a database administrator about error situations in the database. Errors could be informative, warning, or critical in nature. The Alerts, Related Alerts, and Diagnostic Summary sections warn of performance problems and errors that affect the operation of the database. These sections may contain links that can be selected to obtain additional information about a problem, such as its severity level, its impact on the database, timing information, and recommendations that may be optionally implemented by the DBA. (See Figure B-8.)

The Space Summary section displays the size of the database in Gigabytes. It also displays information about tablespaces that have encountered problems such as out-of-space errors. It also gives you an idea about misconfigured segments and fragmentation issues that may exist.

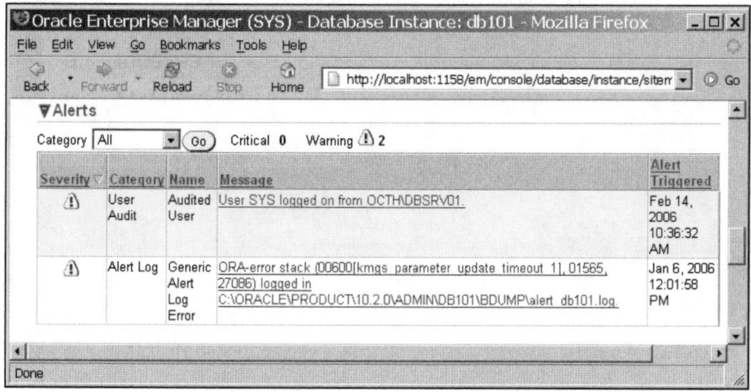

FIGURE B-8 The Alerts section

The Job Activity section provides information about the status of jobs that have been started or scheduled to start in the database within the last seven days.

The Related Links section gives the database administrator quick links to various administrative functions, such as viewing the contents of the alert log or managing metrics within the database.

The other tabs in the Enterprise Manager will be discussed during the course of this textbook.

NOTE

Frequently within Enterprise Manager you may be prompted to specify a valid username and password of a Host User (Operating System user). For example, you would need to specify a host username and password when you select the Maintenance tab and try to schedule backups or perform recoveries. In order to successfully specify a username and password of a host user on a Windows machine, please make sure you perform the following steps.

- Create an operating system user
- Click **Start** on the Windows Taskbar
- Select **Programs**
- Select **Administrative Tools**
- Select **Local Security Policy**
- Under Security Settings select **Local Policies** and **User Rights Assignment**
- Double-click the entry for **"Log on as batch job"**
- Click **Add User or Group**
- Add your **Windows Username** under **"Enter the object names to select"**
- Click **OK** to close both dialog boxes and close local security settings
- Log out and back into Windows for the changes to take effect

GLOSSARY

advisory framework a collection of advisors that identify bottlenecks in the database, analyze the problem, and provide expert recommendations that may be optionally implemented by the database administrator.

alert log the log file containing errors, messages, and a record of structural changes that occur in the database.

archiving the process of creating offline copies of the redo log files. The files are used for media recovery of the database.

ASM File a file of the database such as a datafile, redo log file, archive log file, or control file that is stored on an ASM diskgroup.

ASM Instance an instance that performs the specialized function of mounting and managing diskgroups.

automatic archiving the process of archiving the redo logs automatically by the ARCH process when a log switch occurs.

automatic database diagnostic monitor (ADDM) a central component of the advisory framework that analyzes the information contained in the AWR for the duration of time pertaining to the last two snapshots.

automatic shared memory management a feature that helps an administrator to simplify management of memory structures.

automatic storage management a feature that helps administrators better utilize storage by evenly distributing data across all available storage resources.

automatic workload repository (AWR) a collection of tables that hold performance related statistical data that is gathered based on the current workload and activity of the database.

backup the process of creating copies of the database files. The files can be used in the event of recovery.

backup piece an output file created by RMAN that belongs to a backupset.

backupsets a logical object that stores files backed up by recovery manager in a specific format.

block change tracking a procedure that can be enabled in the database to maintain a record of all changes along with the physical location in a file called the block change tracking file.

block corruption a condition that may result in an Oracle block becoming unreadable.

block media recovery a procedure performed by RMAN that can be used to restore and recover corrupt blocks. It is performed by the BLOCKRECOVER command.

byte semantics a method of defining the size of columns and variables in terms of bytes.

change tracking file the file containing a record of the changed blocks. The file is used during incremental backups.

character semantics a method of defining column and variable lengths in terms of characters. The method is most often used for variable multi-byte columns.

character set a grouping of characters that can be used to represent various languages and scripts.

closed database recovery the process of recovering the database when it is in a mounted state.

cluster a method of storing data from one or more segments in the same Oracle block. The segments chosen to be part of a cluster are usually those that are joined frequently.

common manageability infrastructure a complete manageability architecture that is used to self-tune the Oracle database. It comprises of the automatic workload repository (AWR), Server-Generated Alerts, the Advisory Framework, and the Automated Routine Administrative tasks.

compacting a segment a process by which the data in the Oracle blocks are moved as far left as possible to the beginning of the segment followed by a resetting of the high water mark.

consumer group a logical grouping of users with similar resource requirements.

cumulative incremental backup an *'n'* level differential backup is a backup of all blocks that have been modified since the most recent *'n-1'* backup.

database resource manager a utility provided in the database that helps the DBA better manage resources such as CPU usage, degree of parallelism, active session pool, undo space limits, maximum execution time, etc.

differential incremental backup an *'n'* level differential backup is a backup of all blocks that have been modified since the most recent *'n'* or *'n-1'* backup.

diskgroups a logical grouping of physical disks that are treated as a single storage entity.

failure groups a subset of a diskgroup that may become unavailable due to the failure of one of its associated components.

flash recovery area a centralized location for the management of backup and recovery related files.

full backup a backup of all the used blocks of the datafiles only.

globalization support a collection of features that can be used when creating applications that enable users to access data easily crossing barriers of culture, language, and platform.

grid computing a new architecture that harnesses low-cost computing resources to be more efficiently utilized to create more resilient and powerful computing environments.

hash cluster a cluster that uses a hashing algorithm to determine the physical location of a row in a clustered table.

image copies an identical copy of a physical file of the database.

incremental backup a backup of all blocks that have been modified since the previous incremental backup.

index cluster an index that is used to maintain the data in a cluster. The index entries hold the cluster key value along with the address of the data block where the rows of the cluster key are stored.

index organized tables are objects that may be created in the database to store table data in an index-like format. It provides the advantages of an index that is faster access to data during query operations.

job a scheduler object that refers to a user-defined task that needs to be executed.

job classes a method of grouping jobs into logical entities based on characteristics and system requirements.

linguistic sorting a technique that handles sorting operations based on linguistic conventions and not numeric codes assigned to the characters of a character set.

listener process a process that is started on the server side, and that listens for incoming client requests. User requests may be redirected to a server process or a dispatcher process.

memory advisor provides recommendations about how system memory and memory components of the Oracle database can be optimized.

metrics values that are derived from base statistics determining the rate of change of activities in the database.

mirroring the technique of storing data in multiple disks to increase fault tolerance.

multiplexing the act of maintaining multiple copies of a file.

national language support a subset of globalization support that gives you the ability to define initialization parameters at a system or session level to specify locale-dependent behavior.

noarchivelog mode the mode of the database in which offline copies of the redo log files are not created.

open database recovery the process of recovering the database when it is open.

program a scheduler object that refers to a collection of metadata about a particular executable that can be run by the scheduler.

rebalancing an operation that is performed automatically when disks are added or removed from a diskgroup to evenly re-distribute the data.

recovery the process during which archive log file contents are applied to restored files.

recovery catalog a separate database that may be created to hold the Recovery Manager repository.

recovery manager a tool that can be used specifically for backup and recovery purposes.

resource plan a method of allocating system resources. A plan is given a name and may comprise of directives for subplans or consumer groups.

resource plan directives a method of associating subplans and consumer groups with the resource plan with directives for system resources.

restoration the process of replacing missing files using a backup during media recovery. Restoration may be to the original location or to an alternate location if the original location is not intact. Restoration is followed by recovery.

rman backups backups performed by the Recovery Manager.

rman repository a collection of tables holding information about backups and recoveries performed by Recovery Manager.

schedule a scheduler object that determines when and how often a job is executed.

scheduler a feature of the Oracle database that is used to manage the execution of repetitive tasks without manual intervention.

segment advisor an advisor that provides information regarding space issues within a database object.

self-tuning database the ability of the database to monitor its own health and provide the database administrator with information about impending or current problems along with recommendations for resolution.

server-generated alerts a component of the common manageability infrastructure that signals the database administrator about warnings and critical errors that may occur in the database.

shrinking a segment a process following compacting of a segment where the free space generated is released as space that can be reused by other objects.

sorted hash clusters an extension of the hash cluster functionality. It allows the cluster keys values to be stored in a sorted order during insertion into the table.

striping the technique of spreading data across multiple disk drives.

SQL Tuning advisor provides tuning recommendations for poorly executing SQL statements of the database.

SQL Access advisor provides recommendations about schema objects and identifies the need/removal of indexes and materialized views.

system global area a collection of memory structures that are part of the Oracle instance.

target database the database being backed up by Recovery Manager.

trace file files created by background processes when they encounter certain problems.

unicode character set a global character set that contains characters from all major languages across the world.

undo advisor provides recommendations on the proper sizing of the undo tablespace based on current and previous workload history.

undo retention the feature that permits undo data to remain in undo segments even after the transaction that generated the undo has ended.

user managed backups backups performed by the database administrator by copying the files using operating system commands.

window a scheduler object that defines a time interval with a well-defined beginning and end time.

window group a scheduler object that is a logical collection of windows.

INDEX

A

B

C

D

E

F

G

H

M

N

O

P

R

S

T

U

V

W